CISTERCIAN FATHERS SERIES: NUMBER FIFTY-FOUR

Bernard of Clairvaux

SERMONS FOR THE AUTUMN SEASON

CISTERCIAN FATHERS SERIES: NUMBER FIFTY-FOUR

Bernard of Clairvaux

Sermons for the Autumn Season

Translated by
Irene Edmonds, OCSO

Revised by
Mark Scott, OCSO

Introduction by
Wim Verbaal

Cistercian Publications
www.cistercianpublications.org

LITURGICAL PRESS
Collegeville, Minnesota
www.litpress.org

A Cistercian Publications title published by Liturgical Press

Cistercian Publications
Editorial Offices
161 Grosvenor Street
Athens, Ohio 54701
www.cistercianpublications.org

Based on the critical edition in Bernard of Clairvaux, *Sermones II*, Sancti Bernardi Opera, 8 vols., edited by Jean Leclercq and H. M. Rochais (Rome: Editiones Cistercienses, 1957–77), 5:288–447.

Scripture texts in this work are translated by the translator of the sermons.

© 2016 by Order of Saint Benedict, Collegeville, Minnesota. All rights reserved. No part of this book may be reproduced in any form, by print, microfilm, microfiche, mechanical recording, photocopying, translation, or any other means, known or yet unknown, for any purpose except brief quotations in reviews, without the previous written permission of Liturgical Press, Saint John's Abbey, PO Box 7500, Collegeville, Minnesota 56321-7500. Printed in the United States of America.

Library of Congress Cataloging-in-Publication Data

Names: Bernard, of Clairvaux, Saint, 1090 or 1091–1153, author.
Title: Sermons for the autumn season / Bernard of Clairvaux ; translated by Irene Edmonds, OCSO ; revised by Mark Scott, OCSO ; introduction by Wim Verbaal.
Description: Collegeville, Minnesota : Cistercian Publications, 2016. | Series: Cistercian Fathers series ; Number fifty-four | Includes bibliographical references and index.
Identifiers: LCCN 2015034631| ISBN 9780879074548 | ISBN 9780879071547 (ebook)
Subjects: LCSH: Catholic Church—Sermons—Early works to 1800. | Sermons, Medieval.
Classification: LCC BX891.3 .B4513 2016 | DDC 252/.02—dc23
LC record available at http://lccn.loc.gov/2015034631

Contents

General Introduction	ix
Editor's Note and Acknowledgments	lxvii
Table of Abbreviations	lxix

The Sermons

On the Time of Harvest (In lab mess)	1
Sermon One: How a Twofold Evil Works for Good	1
Sermon Two: Of the Two Tables	4
Sermon Three: *This is the generation of those who seek the Lord, of those who seek the face of the God of Jacob* (Ps 23:6)	7
On the Solemnity of the Assumption of the Blessed Virgin Mary (Asspt)	14
Sermon One: Of the Double Assumption	14
Sermon Two: Of Cleaning, Adorning, and Furnishing the House	18
Sermon Three: Of Mary, Martha, and Lazarus	26
Sermon Four: Of the Four Days of Lazarus and the Celebration of the Virgin	33
Sermon Five: On the Same as Before	41
Sermon Six: To Establish "full of grace" in Mary in Three Ways	53
Sunday within the Octave of the Assumption (OAsspt)	55
Of the words of the Apocalypse: *A great wonder appeared in heaven, a woman clothed with the sun, and the moon under her feet, and on her head a crown of twelve stars* (Rev 12:1)	55
On the Nativity of Blessed Mary (NatBVM)	70
Of the Bringing of Water	70

v

A Sermon to the Abbots (Abb)   85
    How Noah, Daniel, and Job Crossed the Sea,
       Each in His own Way: on a Ship, by a Bridge, by the Shallows   85

On the Feast of Saint Michael (Mich)   91
    Sermon One: Of the Threefold Reasons that the Angels
       Care for Us   91
    Sermon Two: Of the Words of the Lord, *If anyone offends
       one of these little ones* (Matt 18:6)   97

Sunday of the First Week of November (1 Nov)   101
    Sermon One: Of the Vision of Isaiah   101
    Sermon Two   104
    Sermon Three   109
    Sermon Four   114
    Sermon Five   118

On the Feast of All Saints (OS)   130
    Sermon One: Of the Gospel Reading: Jesus Seeing the Crowds   130
    Sermon Two: Of the State of the Saints before their
       Resurrection   146
    Sermon Three: *In What Way Shall They Be without Blemish
       or Wrinkle?* (Eph 5:27)   154
    Sermon Four: Of Abraham's bosom, and of the altar beneath
       which Blessed John heard the voices of such souls of the saints,
       and of the seven loaves from which we read that the same
       number of baskets remained   159
    Sermon Five: Of the Advantage of Their Memory   167

For the Dedication of a Church (Ded)   178
    Sermon One: Of the Five Sacraments of the Dedication   178
       Sermon Two: How We Should Cling to Ourselves and Others   184
       Sermon Three: Of Three Sorts of Equipment We Possess for
          Godly Vigilance   188
    Sermon Four: Of the Threefold Dwelling-Place   193
       Sermon Five: Of the Twofold Consideration of Oneself   200
    Sermon Six: Concerning the word of Jacob: *Truly the Lord
       is in this place* (Gen 28:16)   210

On the Feast of Saint Martin, Bishop (Mart)   213
    Of Examples of Obedience   213

On the Feast of Saint Clement (Clem)	229
Of the Three Waters	229
Sermon on the Passing of Saint Malachy the Bishop (Mal)	235
On the Vigil of Saint Andrew the Apostle (VAnd)	244
How We Should Prepare for the Solemnities of the Saints with Fasting	244
On the Feast of Saint Andrew (And)	249
Sermon One: Concerning Clean Fish	249
Sermon Two: Of the Four Arms of the Cross	258
On the Death of Master Humbert (Humb)	266
Index of Scriptural References in Bernard's Liturgical Sermons (CF 51–54)	275
Index of Subjects in Bernard's Liturgical Sermons (CF 51–54)	334

General Introduction

AS HAS BEEN AMPLY elaborated in the introduction to the translations of both Bernard's *Sermons for Advent and the Christmas Season* (CF 51) and his *Sermons for Lent and the Easter Season* (CF 52), the growth and development of the series of liturgical sermons was the result of a long and painstaking process of selection, rewriting, and ordering. Dom Jean Leclercq distinguished three preliminary series (B, M, and L) that he interpreted as the successive steps in the construction of the final collection Pf, which he edited in Sancti Bernardi Opera, volumes 4 and 5.[1] In my previous introductions, I have demonstrated that the relationship among the four redactions is much more complicated than suggested by the supposition of a simple chronological sequence, going from the most simple (B) to the final and most complicated version (Pf) that Leclercq published in his edition.

While M and Pf are clearly structured along the lines of the liturgical year, it is not at all clear what the structure is for the first redaction, B, in which the dominant argument seems rather to be found in the captivation and liberation of the human soul, the phases of which Bernard loosely projects onto some solemnities of the ecclesiastical year.[2] L, on the contrary, is structured in a liturgical way only in its

---

[1] See the introduction to the edition (*Sermones II*, ed. Jean Leclercq and Henri Rochais, SBOp 4 [Rome: Editiones Cistercienses, 1968], ix–xvii), and Leclercq's preliminary study, "La tradition des sermons liturgiques de s. Bernard," *Scriptorium* 15 (1961): 240–84, reprinted in *Recueil d'études sur saint Bernard et ses écrits* 2 (Rome: Edizioni di storia e letteratura, 1966), 203–60.

[2] See my elaboration in the introduction to Bernard of Clairvaux, *Sermons for Lent and the Easter Season*, trans. Irene Edmonds, CF 52 (Collegeville, MN: Cistercian Publications, 2013), vii–lxiii, here xxxvii–xli.

last part (L^B). Its largest part, the first ninety-six texts (L^A), is in some manuscripts distinguished as a first book; it is of an exegetical nature and offers an interesting insight into the way Bernard seems to have organized his personal archives.[3] Moreover, the two truly liturgical redactions, M and Pf, present a remarkable difference in approach. Whereas M is organized according to the traditional bipartition of sermons *De tempore* and *De sanctis*, Pf shows no such division but offers a continuous reading of the liturgical year.[4]

These fluctuations in the arrangement of the series indicate Bernard's shifting organizational principles. Apparently he hesitated among several options for how to express the message he wanted to convey. It is not even originally clear whether the Christian year did offer an answer to his quest, as the liturgical strand is only latently present in the first redaction, B, and might even be the result of the modern editor's retrospective shaping of the later collections in accord with this earlier one. More important for Bernard than the liturgical movement seems to have been the moral strand of how the human soul in its threefold capacities of reason, will, and memory can be delivered and freed from its captivity in sin.

The moral plot of B falls apart roughly in two movements, treating fall and conversion on the one hand, and growth to spiritual fecundity on the other; this bipartition is echoed and reinforced in M, the collection almost contemporaneous with B. M also offers a moral interpretation, like that of B, but now dependent on the traditional division inside the liturgical year, with the sermons grouped in two portions, *De tempore* and *De sanctis*. Bernard seems simultaneously to have tried out two distinct narrative structures: one more linear and moral on an abstract level, the other circular or repetitive, according to the two successions of liturgical solemnities.

---

[3] See my introduction to Bernard of Clairvaux, *Sermons for Advent and the Christmas Season*, trans. Irene Edmonds, Wendy Mary Beckett, and Conrad Greenia, ed. John Leinenweber, CF 51 (Kalamazoo, MI: Cistercian Publications, 2007), vi–lix, here xxxviii–xl.

[4] See my introductions to CF 51 and to CF 52.

None of these solutions appears to have fully satisfied him, but it took him some ten years more to complete the final redaction, Pf,[5] in which both of the themes that can be distinguished in B and M were integrated and even enriched by supplementary strands. In the intervening years his literary attention must have turned to continuing and completing his sermons on the Canticle, which in many aspects exhibit a related compositional scheme.[6]

In their ultimate form of Pf the liturgical sermons give the clearest evidence of Bernard's literary genius. Not only do they develop both the circular-time perspective of the liturgical year with its returning festivities and the linear perspective of historical and human experience of time, but they also manage to achieve in the reader a sense of a-temporality because of both the sense of the simultaneity of distinct liturgical solemnities, created by continuous liturgical cross-references, and a consciously anti-chronological use of events in time, thus offering a perfect meditative reading for the monk's *lectio divina*, for which Bernard finally intended the collection as a whole.

The final redaction, Pf, now consists of 128 sermons that Bernard organized in four blocks. Each opens with a group of sermons that can be connected to the Virgin Mary and closes with a sermon in which the central theme of the block is translated to human reality. Thus the first block of Sermons for the Christmas Season opens with the seven sermons for Advent, in which many of the themes and motives also found in the four Homilies for the Virgin Mother recur. This block, containing twenty-nine sermons, closes with the one on Paul's Conversion, confirming the central position of Conversion in this block. Indeed Bernard elaborates successively on the conversion of memory, will, and reason, concluding with the blinding of Paul as the embodiment of the point where reason has turned away from its earlier worldly occupations and discovered the truth of God in its

---

[5] L^B can be considered an intermediate collection, like the collection contained in Luxembourg 32 (*Ar*) from Orval, to which we will return.

[6] For the arguments that make me consider the Sermons on the Canticle a finished work, see my article "Les Sermons sur le Cantique de S. Bernard: Un chef-d'oeuvre achevé?" *Collectanea Cisterciensia* 61 (1999): 167–85.

earthly appearance, making reason even more conscious of its lack of the insight that is wisdom.

Bernard shows reason as slowly arriving at insight during the period of Lent. This second block, again containing twenty-nine sermons, opens with the sermons on the Purification and ends with a sermon on Saint Benedict. It also contains the long exegesis of Psalm 90 in seventeen sermons. Movement and progression dominate the entire block, from the procession of the candles at the solemnity of Purification to Bernard's allusions to the procession of Palm Sunday in the sermon for Saint Benedict. In the sermon on Saint Benedict, however, the movement changes from a horizontal to a vertical progression, from the linear movement of the donkey trotting forward to the verticular up and down movement of trees bearing fruit and seeds beginning to germinate. The Lenten block thus concentrates on the theme of progress, of purification as a process that moves forward until one achieves the maturity that may itself become fruitful. The sermons for Lent thus show the inner maturation of a spiritual person.

The third block consists of thirty-six sermons. It opens with the three sermons for the Annunciation and closes with the three Harvest sermons. Once again movement is a central topic in all the sermons, but in these it has yet another significance. It becomes more internalized, evoking first of all the resurrection of the Word in the human soul or, better, of the soul in the Word, which is the true sense of Easter. Yet, according to Bernard, one must not keep the living Word enclosed in one's own life. To do so is in fact impossible, for the Word will escape and retreat in order to make the soul long for its return. To make it return, the soul will recognize, she must reach out to it with her love. She has to rise in order to make the Word descend: that is the experience of Pentecost.

This tension between ascending and descending, between the love going up and the Word coming down, is next concretized in the bringing out of the Word. The soul realizes that being pregnant with the Word implies working for the Word. In her own words, she must follow the footsteps of those who announced the coming of the Word, and in her own life she must bear witness to her own experience of the presence of the Word, as did the apostles. No longer do the sermons treat the soul's own spiritual process as an isolated task. Instead, they link the soul's progression to her fruitfulness, to the way she manages to cultivate the Word and to be fruitful in the harvest she gathers for the Word.

The theme of this third block in the liturgical series is the labor of sowing and harvest, the labor of the preacher of the Word. In a first movement, therefore, the Easter sermons, the preacher must unite with the Word: he has to die with it in order to be resurrected in it. The second movement—the sermons for Ascension and Pentecost—contains the slow process of learning to live without the presence of the Word while recognizing how in longing for it one experiences its strength. In the last movement the virtue of the Word is working in the spiritual person, causing him to preach in both words and deeds. This theme appears in the sermons for the feasts of John the Baptist and of Peter and Paul, and also in those that, by their succession, give a rhythm to the summer season and its labor.

This series concludes with the Harvest sermons, which link the toil on the land both to the moral suffering of the monks (In lab mess 2) and to the saintliness of monastic life (In lab mess 1) as the simultaneous actualization of the angelic, the prophetic, and the apostolic existence (In lab mess 3). This image of the monk as at once angel, prophet, and apostle, carrying out the Word in the deeds of his own body and in the intentions of his own heart, prepares for the last block in the series, the sermons for the Autumn Season, which are central to this introductory essay.

BUILDING UP THE AUTUMN SEASON

As the introductions to the former volumes of Bernard's liturgical sermons in translation have demonstrated, it is revealing to see how the single blocks of the liturgical series came into being.[7] The different organization within each block, with the elimination and addition of specific texts, sheds light on the messages Bernard seeks to convey. The outcome is never entirely new as compared to the

---

[7] CF 51:vi–lxii; CF 52:xxxv–xlviii.

former editions but indicates his goal of arranging the sermons in such a way that their message is as clear and comprehensive as possible, even if not immediately obvious. As a result, each step in the development of the series creates another aspect, which in its turn Bernard incorporates into the final narrative.

When we try to approach the sermons for the Autumn Season in a similar way, however, the attempt leaves us a bit perplexed. Within the history of the series, the Autumn Season has left hardly any traces. Fifteen of the thirty-four sermons do not appear in any of the earlier collections, a much higher percentage of new texts than in any of the other blocks.[8] Many of these new elements (six in all) appear in the last part of Pf. They form the group of the sermons on saints: Saint Martin, Saint Clement, Saint Malachy, two sermons for the celebration of Saint Andrew the apostle, and a sermon for the Vigil of Saint Andrew.

This concentration of new texts at the end of the collection becomes even more conspicuous when considering the manuscript Luxembourg 32 (*Ar*), from the abbey of Orval.[9] This manuscript is an important source for many of Bernard's smaller works, which are now included among the *Sententiae* and the sermons on different subjects (*de Diversis*). It is clearly divided into two parts, both of which contain several texts that ended up as part of the liturgical series. In its bipartition and its collection of mixed texts and some liturgical sermons, it recalls the structure of that other miscellaneous collection, L, which Dom Jean Leclercq considered to be one of the preliminary versions of the final liturgical edition Pf.

---

[8] In Bernard's sermons for Advent and Christmastide (translated in CF 51), one sermon of the twenty-nine (The Feast of the Conversion of Paul) was only introduced in the final series. In the sermons for Lent and Eastertide (translated in CF 52), seven of the twenty-nine sermons were new in Pf (QH 10–17). The Easter and Summer Season (thirty-six sermons in Pf) was enlarged with the addition of ten sermons (Ann 3, Palm 3, Asc 6, Pent 3, JB, VPP, PP 1, VI Pent 1 and 2, Lab 3).

[9] Dom Jean Leclercq traced two other manuscripts deriving from *Ar*: Brussels 10559-61 (*Ld¹*), from Saint Lawrence in Liège, and Trier 101-1067 (*Tv*). See his "Inédits bernardins dans un manuscrit d'Orval," *Analecta monastica* 1 (1948): 142–66.

Indeed, a closer look at the content and structure of *Ar* suggests that the function of the underlying collection is similar to the one at the base of L.[10] Both give an idea of the way Bernard organized his textual archives. Yet they also offer more, showing Bernard in the different blocks reflecting on how to construct his liturgical series. Both *Ar* and the manuscripts of L contain texts absent from the earlier versions, B and M. But L shows no overlap at all with the other collections. For the final edition of Pf, Bernard drew heavily on the liturgical part of both collections, as contained in *Ar* and in the manuscripts of L, including all of the liturgical sermons in *Ar*, albeit with some of his usual adaptations in the way of rewriting and reorganization.

When *Ar* is taken into consideration, the number of new elements in the Autumn Season of Pf diminishes to eight, all found in the portion devoted to the saints, showing even more clearly Bernard's desire to expand this element in the final edition of the work.

The Autumn Season thus seems to consist of three groups of sermons, each of which has a history of its own. The first is the large group of Marian sermons, which contains texts that also appear in the liturgical collections M and L^B. In Pf, these texts (eight in total) are reorganized around the solemnity of the Assumption, the Octave of the Assumption (the only new one in this group), and the Nativity of the Virgin. The second group of nineteen sermons extends from the sermon for Abbots to the Dedication of a Church. All but two of these—1 Nov 5 and Ded 6—can be found in the other collections. The last group consists of the sermons for the saints (seven) and contains no texts that appear elsewhere, except the last one, on the death of Humbert. Let us have a closer look then at each of these groups, how they developed, and what we can learn from the way Bernard reorganized them.

DILECTUS MEUS MIHI ET EGO ILLI: ESPOUSING THE WORD

The opening group of Marian sermons is the largest unit within the Autumn Season. As we now have it, it contains six sermons for

---

[10] Leclercq's category of L is based upon 15 manuscripts. See SBOp 4:135–38.

the Assumption (Asspt 1–6) and one each for the Octave of the Assumption (OAsspt) and for the Nativity of the Virgin (NatBVM). This last text, however, with its eighteen paragraphs, is one of the longest in the entire collection.[11] It is also one of the most famous Marian texts by Bernard, equating Mary with an aqueduct.

As a group, this unit was developed in three steps. With the exception of the fifth sermon (Asspt 5), the entire group for Assumption was already in the first liturgical collection, M. Together with other Marian texts it opens the section *De sanctis* after the *De tempore*, which ends with two sermons for Pentecost. Asspt 1 to 4 can be found in their final order at the end of the Marian sequence in M. As they are followed by the sermons for the archangel Michael and three sermons for the Dedication, it is clear that in M they already refer to the solemnity of the Assumption.

As regards Asspt 6 the situation is different in M. It follows four texts that finally end up as the first sermon for the Annunciation (Ann 1) and the three sermons for Purification (Pur 1–3), while it is itself succeeded by the text that has been inserted in Pf as the second sermon for the Annunciation (Ann 2). Neither Ann 1 nor Ann 2 is a purely Marian text. Rather, Ann 1 treats the heavenly and allegorical preliminaries to the Redemption, while Ann 2 describes the descent of the Spirit.[12] In a liturgical sense, both thus seem to adhere more closely to the Easter and Pentecost solemnities. Yet in between comes the sequence for the Purification, which leads to the text Asspt 6, which contains a true yet very short praise of Mary.

The liturgical intent in this part of M is thus fluid. Even when taking seriously the bipartition between *De tempore* and *De sanctis*, the opening of the second part seems to concentrate less on Mary herself than on linking her to the mysteries of Easter and Pentecost. The most important theme in the entire series seems to be the converging of heavenly descent and human elevation. Where the Word has decided to come down for the redemption of humankind, a human answer is expected, an answer that is offered by the Purification pro-

---

[11] Only the first sermon for Easter and the sermon for Saint Martin are equal to it in length.

[12] See for these two sermons CF 52:l–liii.

cession, which itself constitutes a progression toward the sacrifice of humility.[13] Mary not only leads the procession and offers her firstborn to the temple but is actually the temple itself. For in M, the procession of Purification leads to the praise of Mary in Asspt 6, to the praise of her virginity, her humility, and her fertility. Only then will the Spirit descend to accomplish the Incarnation (Ann 2).

But the Word's incarnation in the Virgin means also the assumption of Mary into the Word (Asspt 1). Only by way of her assumption will the Word deign to descend into the pure body that is ready to receive him. He will continue to descend into human bodies as long as they are purified (Asspt 2–3) and even go down into the grave where they rest in order to resuscitate humans from their sins (Asspt 4). In the resurrection of Lazarus, the descent changes again into the ascending movement, thanks to the intervention of the living and vivifying Word. There, exactly at this turning point, the Virgin rises once more, and the entire movement of descending and ascending closes on a new praise of Mary, her virtues, her fertile virginity, her purity, her humility, and her mercifulness (Asspt 4.5–8).

The entire block in M thus contains two movements, both ending with the praise of Mary. The first can be labeled the preparatory movement of humankind, by which humans have to purify themselves in order to respond to the heavenly condescension to redeem them. Mary offers the way but also the goal of this purification. The second movement concentrates on the descent of the Word from the coming down of the Spirit through the mediation of Mary to the liberation of humankind, captured in the grave of sin. Here Mary is the way to human redemption, and for that reason she is also its coronation.

M clearly does not take the liturgical strand as the leading one. More important to Bernard are the purification of the body and the liberation from sin that are necessary to make the Word descend to each person. For that reason he engages freely with chronological sequence, as he continues to do in the final collection, Pf.[14] Mary offers the child to the temple before the Spirit has descended and the

---

[13] See for the sermons on Purification CF 52:xxiii–xxv.

[14] See the commentary on the sermons for the Annunciation in CF 52:l–liii.

Word has come down. The sense may be clear, though: the historical Incarnation Mary made possible by her own purity will have to repeat itself in a spiritual descent of the Word to each sinful and laboring person thanks to her mediation. Christmas, Easter, and Pentecost imply one another. They coincide.

Two sermons of the final series did not appear in M: the fifth sermon for Assumption (Asspt 5) and the sermon for the Nativity of the Virgin (NatBVM). They occur for the first time in the liturgical part of L (L^B). There they belong to a sequence of texts that for the most part have no immediate link to any Marian solemnity.[15] Practically all of them were omitted in the final liturgical collection but ended up in the *Sententiae* or in the sermons *De Diversis*. As in M, the focus lies on the upward and downward movements but with a stronger emphasis on the descending motion.

The entire group in L^B is preceded by three texts that deal with the opening of the tomb and are thus closely linked to the Easter solemnity.[16] The first and third (Pasc 2, Div 58) show the women at the tomb (Matt 16:1-3), while the second one (Div 57) is a short exegesis on a verse from the Apocalypse about the breaking of the seals (Rev 5:5). As a whole, however, they all refer to the Incarnation. Easter, Christmas, and the End of Time coincide, and time becomes fleeting.

Next starts a block of sermons to which belong the two future Marian texts Asspt 5 and NatBVM. First come some sermons that develop variations on the descent of the Spirit. The first one treats the Ascension, but in its significance for humans (Div 60). Just as the Ascension of Christ is the complement to his Descent, humankind must descend in humility in order to be able to ascend in grace. After the sermon on the Ascension, four texts use various numerical explanations to elaborate on the work of the Spirit in humans: the way it becomes visible when a person is touched by the Spirit (Div 88), the parallel between the seven gifts of the Spirit and the seven Beatitudes (Sent III.126), the opposition between the seven gifts of the Spirit

---

[15] In L, both texts appear in the following context: Div 60, Div 88, Sent III.126, Sent III.19, Sent I.2, Div 47, Asspt 5, Div 48, Div 52, and NatBVM.

[16] The sermons are preceded by Pasc 2, Div 57, and Div 58 and followed by Ded 4 and Ded 5.

and the seven vices (Sent III.19), and the fivefold operations of the Spirit (Sent I.2). Those two last texts are true *sententiae*, concise expressions of an idea that Bernard possibly intended to develop more fully later.

While this group can be considered a draft for sermons on the Ascension and Pentecost, in the next texts Mary becomes more central. The first uses Mary's humility at the Annunciation as a beginning for a very short treatise on four forms of human arrogance and five remedies (Div 47). Then follows the text that will become Asspt 5 and that, based on Luke 10:38-42, treats the way the entry of the Word will transform the carnal fortress of the human body and life into a spiritual one, characterized by the unity of body and spirit, of action and contemplation. It is followed by a text that offers a variant exegesis of the same pericope, focusing on the difference between Martha and Mary (Div 48). There follows an exegesis of Proverbs 9:1 on the building of the house of wisdom, applied to Mary as the seat for Christ and linked to the Annunciation (Div 52). The group closes with what later becomes the NatBVM on Mary as both the aqueduct and the stairs that connect heaven and earth, God and humankind.

The most remarkable aspect of this group of sermons is that Asspt 5 has no explicit connection to Mary except in the pericope from the reading for the feast of the Assumption. A more important link, however, exists in its belonging to a group framed by texts closely linked to Mary. Yet none of these clearly Marian texts refers unambiguously to the solemnities to which they will ultimately be linked. Rather, they seem to develop themes connected with the Annunciation and the Incarnation. Mary appears as the mediator between heaven and earth, being elevated by her own humility and thus making possible the descent of the Word. NatBVM develops this topic in a marvelous way, presenting Mary's plenitude and mediation in terms of the Canticle. Yet here too the sermon alludes more to the Annunciation than to the solemnity of her nativity.

In the last texts of the group, however, an additional theme emerges, as all contain some kind of architectural element. Both Asspt 5 and Div 48 talk about the *castellum*, the fortress that Christ enters. In Asspt 5 Bernard equates the *castellum* with the human body and spirit, and in Div 48 he explains it as the voluntary poverty that he normally equates with the monastic life. Then follow successively the comparison of Mary with the House of Wisdom, the Aqueduct, and the Stairs.

This architectural element seems to become the central theme in these texts. It results from the descent of the Spirit that leads first of all to the Edifice of Mary, into which the Word enters and is received. The succession of events becomes somewhat immobile because of the simultaneity of the different movements. The Edifice of Mary can only be built where the Word has entered, because only after having already entered can the Word be received. The Word will only enter, however, where one has prepared oneself to receive the Word by the working of the Spirit. Once entered into the corporeal fortress of a person, Bernard's sermons say, the Word will change that fortress into a spiritual stronghold, granting it a unity of body and spirit, of action and contemplation that it did not know before. In this new stronghold the Word today erects the House of Wisdom as he did once in Mary when his coming was announced. Thus only after having entered will the Word make known that he comes.

The true Annunciation is not a single movement: it is a movement within a movement, a building within a building. It is movement ending in the stability of the construction, but it implies that the construction starts to move. For the House of Wisdom mutates in the flowing course of water that the aqueduct pours over the soul before transforming itself into the ladder that parallels the descending movement from heaven with the ascending movement of humankind. Then and only then can the divine union take place, when the double movement has become entirely silent and the Word is heard in silence. Then the lovers will meet where the Beloved feeds his flocks in the middle of the lilies.

In the end of this series Bernard exhorts his reader to become a lily with Mary by fighting the angel, by breaking the silence of the Word, so that he may descend to feed his flocks among men and women. So he did with Mary, and she will never refuse to mediate between the offering of humans' pure lilies and the divine grace that has been poured out in her. In the tumultuous rest at the end of NatBVM, in the floating stability of its architectural movements, in the loving struggle with the angel beloved, Mary remains humanity's sole point of repair. If humans cannot be a lily by themselves, they will be more than a lily when sustained by her hands.

While L^B as a whole clearly remains a rather sketchy project, its general line is much more fluently and strongly developed than the one in M. In M, the downward and upward movements appear as successive stages in the spiritual liberation of humankind. They lead to a collapse of the liturgical events, giving rise to the simultaneity of the Christmas, Easter, and Pentecost mysteries as one single event during the life of humanity. In L^B, however, Bernard focuses more exclusively on the Annunciation as the moment when the irreconcilable is reconciled. This focus leads him to create an almost incredibly paradoxical unity, a converging of movement and stability, a collapse of ascent and descent, of silence and its rupture, of rest in flight, and of the impurity in the purity of lilies. The Annunciation as both the underlying theme and the initial act of the Incarnation embodies the concord of discordances to the highest degree.

Given the way he reorganized the other liturgical blocks, Bernard might now be expected in his final series, Pf, to strive to harmonize both the movements and the themes from the earlier collections. This time, however, he seems to have opted for another approach. He actually maintains the construction laid out in M while fusing it with the two texts from L^B. Of course this combination results in a new unity, in which the second movement of M dominates. The central idea in this series of manuscripts thus remains the descent of the Word. Bernard has even largely kept the order of the texts as transmitted in M, only developing the series of four Assumption texts by adding Asspt 5 and 6, the first coming from L^B and the other transposed from the end of the first movement in M to the end of its second movement. NatBVM remains the conclusion of this group, as it does in L^B.

Yet the new order implies some smaller shifts of accent. In M, the descent of the Word started with the coming down of the Spirit, as described in Ann 2. In Pf this immediate link between the descent of the Spirit and that of the Word is interrupted. Now the entire movement starts with Mary's elevation to be the intermediary between heaven and earth. Mary's Assumption equals Christ's descent. Both are to be understood as a kiss of the kiss of his mouth (Asspt 1.4). By means of this arrangement, Bernard already anticipates the ultimate climax of the entire movement in NatBVM 14–18 at the end of the first sermon. By ending the four Assumption sermons from M with NatBVM, Bernard achieves a beautifully closed ring composition.

Moreover, both texts, Asspt 1 and NatBVM, emphasize the coincidence of upward and downward movement, stressing the unity of the events of Christmas and Assumption. The reader of the liturgical sermons, having already been obliged to accept the simultaneity of Christmas, Easter, and Ascension—that is, of the most important Christ-centred solemnities—now recognizes that a similar process takes place with the Mary-centred solemnities of the year. Christmas, celebrating the Birth of the Word from the Virgin, not only overlaps with Christ's death, Easter, and ascent into heaven, Ascension, but it also coincides with the Assumption of the Virgin. The downward movement of the Word into the flesh by way of Mary not only responds to its upward movement by way of death to heaven, but it also evokes the upward movement of the Virgin. Just as is true for the Word, for Mary too death is the hinge that connects descent and ascent, Incarnation, Glorification, humility and elevation.

The final text in this group of Marian sermons, NatBVM, celebrates the nativity of the Virgin. Yet more than half of it contains an expanded exegesis of the Annunciation scene according to Luke (NatBVM 4–13). The solemnity thus becomes linked to the Incarnation and Advent, leading up to Christmas. Mary's nativity is overshadowed by the descent of the Word, the Incarnation, which, according to Bernard's arrangement of the sermons, can only take place after her Assumption, after she has been elevated and glorified because of being open to the Word.

By according this much attention to the Annunciation, Bernard has taken up the story line he broke off at the solemnity of the Annunciation itself. In that series of sermons, Gabriel is sent to Nazareth only in the end, after three sermons and after Bernard's conscious playing with biblical chronology. Indeed the sermons for the Annunciation give almost no attention to the event itself, as if it did not belong there. Only, now, at the Nativity, does Bernard explain the sense of the Annunciation, in words that often recall his earlier Homilies in Praise of the Virgin Mother. At the solemnity of the Annunciation, it seems, it was still too early to confront the reader with the Incarnation. Now, after the Virgin has been celebrated in her elevation, which leads to her plenitude in grace as extolled in the text that originally concluded the series of Purification sermons (Asspt 6), can her Nativity be celebrated, while only now does the Annunciation of the Word take on her flesh for his incarnation.

In his final liturgical collection, Bernard opts for the idea as he has embedded it in M, completely confusing readers about the exact solemnity he is discussing in these texts. Not unlike the way he interprets the liturgical apogees around Christ, making them all coincide, he treats the solemnities of the Virgin as similarly all-inclusive. Yet where Christ's death and ascent are already enclosed in Christ's descent at Christmas, for Mary this co-incidence happens only at the end, in the solemnities of her Assumption and Nativity. For the divine Word, there can be no beginning or end, no before or after. All happens simultaneously, or, better, everything takes place in one and the same event. Humans, however, have to elevate themselves as did the Virgin. She offers them the way to prepare for their glorification, that is, to their reception of the Word. They must purify their humanity in order to be the Spouse and to receive the kiss of the Word's kiss, to be glorified and born again in the announcement that the Word will become flesh in them. Then they will experience in themselves how accurately are the words, "And the name of the Virgin was Mary."[17]

In his final revision of this group of Marian sermons, Bernard added one entirely new one, a sermon for the Sunday within the Octave of the Assumption (OAsspt), inserted as a bridge between Asspt 6 and NatBVM. A more remarkable change, however, is that now, as in L^B, two texts separate Asspt 5 and NatBVM. And the message has become a different one. In L^B the architectural element prevailed in Asspt 5, Div 48, Div 52, and NatBVM. Bernard abandoned this building element in his final collection—not entirely, of course, as he kept two of the sermons—but he reduced its dominant position. Asspt 6 and OAsspt do not contain any clearly architectural allusions.

---

[17] See Miss 2.17.

More important than the architecture now has become the preparation for the descent of the Word. Asspt 5 emphasizes the importance of unity between spirit and deed, Asspt 6 lauds Mary in her plenitude of grace, and NatBVM returns to all the former elements so as to end in the union of Groom and Spouse in Christ and Mary. But Bernard must have found the transition from Asspt 6 and its beautiful praise of the Virgin to her elaboration as aqueduct and ladder in NatBVM too abrupt or insufficient. He inserted this one text, OAsspt, built on a long exegesis of a pericope from the Apocalypse: "and there appeared a great wonder in heaven, a woman clothed with the sun, and the moon under her feet, and on her head a crown of twelve stars" (Rev 12:1).

Once again, it is a long text.[18] It opens with a short introduction on the necessity for humans to have both Christ and Mary as mediators, Christ as the *mediator Dei et hominis* (1 Tim 2:5) and Mary as the mediator between humans and her Son, who incorporates not only divine mercy but also divine judgment. Bernard presents Mary as the most secure retreat for humans against divine wrath. The introduction closes with a short hymn on her: "In short, she became all things to all, and of her great charity she made herself debtor to all, both wise and foolish.[19] She opened her bosom of mercy to all, so that of her fullness all might receive:[20] the captive redemption, the sick healing, the sad consolation, the sinner pardon, the just grace, the angel joy, the whole Trinity glory, and the Son the substance of human flesh, so that no one should be hidden from her warmth" (OAsspt 1–2).

Bernard introduces his main topic with a question: "Don't you think that this is the woman clothed with the sun?" Without quoting the pericope, as he is accustomed to do, he counters it in this indirect manner. Now he develops the image of Mary, clothed with the sun and with the moon under her feet (OAsspt 3–6). He immediately answers his question with a clear reference to the ecclesiological interpretation of the image, but he seems to prefer to give it a Marian

---

[18] It has fifteen paragraphs, like Asc 6 and OS 1. The only longer sermons are Pasc 1, NatBVM, and Mart (all with eighteen paragraphs) and QH 7 (sixteen paragraphs).
[19] 1 Cor 9:22, Rom 1:14.
[20] John 1:16.

sense: "Let us suppose that the rest of the prophetic vision shows the image to refer to the present-day church—but surely it is not unsuitable to attribute it to Mary" (OAsspt 3). In the interpretation that follows, the boundaries between Mary and the church somehow become very fluid. When talking about Mary, Bernard refers to her as to the church, and when clearly referring to the church, he treats her as Mary. Only in his exegesis of the moon does he make it clear that it is Mary who has the church beneath her feet, because she is set between Christ and the church.

A quotation of the Canticle that is used as the Introit at the Mass for the crown of thorns closes this part. A short phrase provides the transition to the crown of stars: "But this is elsewhere. Go in rather in the meantime and see the queen in the diadem with which her Son crowned her" (OAsspt 6).[21] A literal quotation follows, opening the second part: "On her head, it says, is a crown of twelve stars." Now Bernard gives a numerical exegesis of the twelve stars. He distinguishes them into three groups of Mary's singular graces: the graces of heaven, of the flesh, and of the heart. Each group contains four stars. Mary's heavenly graces are her birth, the greeting of the angel, the overshadowing of the Spirit, and the indescribable conception of the Son of God. Her graces of the flesh are her unprecedented choice to remain a virgin, her untainted fecundity, her easy pregnancy, and her painless childbearing. Her graces of the heart are her gentle diffidence, her devout humility, her magnanimous belief, and the martyrdom of the heart (OAsspt 7).

Bernard treats each of these graces separately, but he rather quickly passes over the first eight (OAsspt 8–9). They are singularly hers. As human believers, we can only admire them, adore them, devote ourselves to them, and find comfort in them. The last four, however, ask to be imitated, and so Bernard grants them more attention (OAsspt 10–15). He specifically elaborates the link between and unity of

---

[21] The sentence is missing in some of the (less accurate) manuscripts, a fact that seems to imply that Bernard inserted it to join the preceding paragraphs to the following ones and that the sermon is constructed from different originally independent sermons. This inference is also supported by his two different approaches to the same pericope in this sermon.

Mary's gentleness, her humility, and her magnanimity (OAsspt 10–13). In short, he enters upon Mary's martyrdom to conclude finally that thanks to all these things, Mary is the only and best mediator between humankind and Christ.

In the entire Marian cycle of the final liturgical collection, OAsspt is the first truly Marian sermon, taking up the most central Marian themes.[22] Indeed the preceding sermons for the Assumption pay almost more attention to Martha and Mary Magdalene than to Mary herself. Only Asspt 6 contains a true eulogy on the Virgin. It can thus be supposed that Bernard wanted to reinforce the Marian character of the entire group and for that reason inserted this new text.

Its insertion had some further consequences. The entire sermon is one large exegesis of Revelation 12:1, of the image of the woman clothed with the sun, the moon under her feet, and on her head a crown of twelve stars. As such OAsspt forms a logical sequel to the eulogy in Asspt 6 that praised Mary's plenitude. What can illustrate the plenitude of her grace better than the image in which she appears in the vision of the End of Time? But that is not all. The sermon takes up practically all Marian images as they appear in the prophets and the Old Testament: the woman promised long ago by God, who was to bruise the head of the ancient serpent with righteous foot (OAsspt 4), Gideon's fleece between the dew and the threshing-floor (OAsspt 5 and 8), the bush burning without being consumed (OAsspt 5), the woman who encompasses a man (OAsspt 6), the rod of the priest that flowered without a root (OAsspt 8), the gate facing the sunrise in Ezekiel's vision, open to no one (OAsspt 8), and Isaiah's rod, which should arise from the root of Jesse (OAsspt 8). In no earlier sermon did that many images follow one another at such speed, making this sermon not only a true Marian sermon but also a sermon heavily packed with symbolic significance. As such it prepares for the more elaborate images of the aqueduct and the ladder in the following sermon.

More important to Bernard than these prophetic images for the Virgin are the images the Virgin offers in connection to the final four stars, the moral stars that are to be imitated by humans. Bernard

---

[22] As Gerhard B. Winkler noted in his annotation of the text in *Bernhard von Clairvaux. Sämtliche Werke* VIII (Innsbruck, Austria: Tyrolia, 1997), 1010n44.

presents Mary in her silence, pointing out that she only speaks four times in the gospels. He shows her in her humility, receiving the highest promise of an angel and presenting herself only as a servant, and, when Elizabeth lauds her, answering by praising God. Finally, he shows her in her martyrdom at the foot of the cross, being pierced by the lance as it penetrates the side of her Son—or even worse:

> Did not these words wound you more than a sword, truly piercing your soul, reaching even to the division of soul and spirit: *Woman, behold your son?* What a substitution! John will be to you as Jesus, the son of Zebedee in place of the Son of Man, a man pure and simple instead of the true God! When you heard this, how could it not pierce your most affectionate soul when ours, although of stone, although of iron, are torn by its very description? (OAsspt 15)

Mary has become very close to the reader. Her suffering is a human suffering, different from that of Christ. He suffered for humankind, but Mary suffered in her Son. His pains brought human redemption, but her pains were the pains of humankind: "Marvel not, brothers, that Mary is called a martyr in soul. Let the one wonder who does not remember hearing that Paul mentioned among the crimes of the heathen that they were without affection" (OAsspt 15). Who could ever mediate between humans and their Judge, who never knew the sentiments of humans? Mary is the mediator because in her heart she died with her Son at the cross. She did not herself suffer in her body, but she suffered in her love. That suffering made her the aqueduct, bringing down the Word and simultaneously offering to humans the ladder that leads them to her Son.

REAEDIFICANDI MURI: RESTORING HEAVEN

In the collection L^B, the liturgical simultaneity combined with the overlap of ascending and descending movements is even more complicated by the spiritual architecture accomplished in and by Mary, but this element declines somewhat in the final series. Apparently Bernard did not think it the most important contribution to his image of the Virgin. And indeed the building metaphor in L^B serves there to prepare for his ultimate comparisons of Mary with the aqueduct and the ladder. So here too the movement was fundamental to his way of interpreting Mary's mediation.

Bernard did not forget his original idea, however. On the contrary, the spiritual architecture was part of the project from the outset, as can be seen in the evolution of the following group of sermons, all of which appear to be linked in one way or another to the ideas of building, of restoring, of erecting a construction. Yet his plans developed, and perhaps no other group of sermons demonstrates so clearly as these the criteria he used to select, to eliminate, and to build his ideal liturgical year.

The group of architectural sermons contains nineteen texts, divided into four smaller groups with the sermon to the Abbots (Abb) as an introductory sermon: two sermons in honor of Saint Michael (Mich 1 and 2), five sermons for the Sunday of the First Week of November (1 Nov 1–5), five sermons for All Saints (OS 1–5), and six sermons for the Dedication of a Church (Ded 1–6). Of these, only two, 1 Nov 5 and Ded 6, are not found in a preliminary state in the other collections.

Six texts, however, only appear in the separate tradition formed by the manuscript *Ar* (OS 3 and 4, 1 Nov 1–4). This manuscript seems to be an important intermediary between M and L^B on the one side and Pf on the other, as can be seen immediately when comparing the blocks in which these sermons appear in each of the different collections:

M	Mich 1–2 / Ded 1–3 / OS 1 – Conv – OS 2			
L^B	Ded 4–5 /	OS 5		
Ar	Mich 1–2 / . . . / OS 2–4 ||	1 Nov 1–4	/	Ded 3, 1, 2
Pf	Abb / Mich 1–2 / 1 Nov 1–5 /	OS 1–5	/	Ded 1–6

When looking at the different collections, one immediately notices that Bernard did not only strive to develop each of the subthemes in order to fit into his final liturgical scheme. Apparently he felt some hesitation about how to organize the entire group. His first hesitation concerned the position of the sermons for the Dedication of a Church in relation to those for All Saints. He started by putting the sermons for the Dedication first, but somewhere in the editorial process he changed his mind and exchanged the two groups.

At the same time he introduced an entirely new group, the sermons for the First Sunday of November, and inserted them between the two other groups, immediately preceding those for the Dedication. Yet this arrangement also clearly did not suit him. So in the end he brought the sermons for the First Sunday forward, to end up between the sermons for Saint Michael and those for All Saints.

This repeated shifting of sermons of course has implications for the interpretation of the narrative line, as I have shown in my treatment of all the groups of sermons during the entire liturgical year.[23] This time, however, an extra element is involved. All sermons are dedicated to feast days linked to specific moments in the liturgical year. All Saints falls on November 1. Changing the Dedication sermons from before to after this date implies the transposition of the dedication date of the church in question. But of course in that case, Bernard cannot be thinking of the same specific church, as each church has its fixed dedication day.

Originally Bernard must have connected this group to the dedication of the church of Clairvaux, which was commemorated on October 13 and thus clearly situated between the Feast of Saint Michael on September 29 and November 1. Locating the group after All Saints, however, implied a shift of focus. It is clearly not that suddenly the dedication day for Clairvaux was changed but rather that Bernard decided to link it to another commemoration, that of the dedication of Saint John in the Lateran, considered the *mater ecclesiarum*, the Mother of all churches. That feast was celebrated on November 9, between All Saints and the Feast of Saint Martin on November 11, which in the final edition opens the next subgroup of autumn sermons.

The changed position of these sermons does not only imply that they referred to another church; above all, it meant a complete and radical change of perspective. At first, Bernard had envisaged the

---

[23] See the introductions to CF 53 and CF 52, *passim*, as well as the preceding part on the Marian sermons.

sermons to refer to the dedication of the abbey church of Clairvaux and thus addressed his words to the monks there, identifying them with the living stones needed to complete the building. After the sermons' transposition, however, they came to address the readers in general, those who were children of the mother of all churches, i.e., of the church itself. This change widened the perspective enormously. The texts aim not to spur on a smaller monastic community but Christianity as a whole. With this change Bernard has transformed the liturgical series of sermons into a meditative reading for all Christians, whom he invites to become part of the celestial Jerusalem by way of the text he is addressing to them.

The other uncertainty demonstrated by these liturgical sermon collections concerns the group of sermons for the First Sunday of November. They appear for the first time in *Ar*, where they open the second part of the collection, immediately preceding the sermons for the Dedication. Chronologically, they thus indicate that they refer to the Sunday between November 1 and 9. Finally, however, they ended up before All Saints. Now it would not be a liturgical problem if they are used for a Sunday before or after All Saints. These sermons refer to the Sunday closest to November 1, which could comfortably fall before that date, although Bernard's hesitation may indicate that his natural reflex was to put them afterward. The change could thus indicate his wish to disorient the reader.

Yet the more important aspect of this displacement may have been the narrative line Bernard wanted to construct. Thus it becomes important once more to deduce the evolution of his thought from the arrangement of the sermons in the different collections.

Building Heaven in Oneself: M

In its oldest form, in M, this group, which consists of Mich 1 and 2, Ded 1–3, OS 1, Conv, and OS 2, followed the first four sermons for Mary's Assumption. These concluded with the ascending movement of the Virgin after Christ's descent into the grave to call Lazarus back to life. The entire preceding block of Marian sermons builds on the theme of coinciding upward and downward movements.

This theme continues in the sermons for Saint Michael. The downward movement of the angels in order to minister to humankind mirrors the descent of Christ, who humbled himself below the angels to redeem humankind (Mich 1.1–4). Humans must show themselves worthy of this grace by imitating the angels—that is, they should assimilate themselves to the angels' way of being, preserving unity and harmony in the community and thus elevating themselves to the angelic life (Mich 1.5–6 and 2.1–2). Therefore they ought to discard all that hinders them in bringing their conduct into union with that of the angels (Mich 2.3–4). They must rise in order to meet those descending to humankind. Heaven and earth meet where the angels find their own Jerusalem on earth (Mich 1.5).

In these sermons, indeed, a new element appears that Bernard more or less discarded from the preceding Marian sermons: the building of heaven. One of the reasons for the angels to come to the help of humans is their longing to restore the celestial city and to fill in the breaches in the heavenly walls caused by the fall of Lucifer. Only humankind offers the living stones that are capable of repairing the ruins of the celestial Jerusalem, and the building of heaven can only be achieved on earth: "If you love the beauty of God's house [Ps 25:8], or rather because you truly love it, let the living and thinking stones [1 Pet 2:5] experience your zeal, since for the restoration of God's house they can be built up only together with you" (Mich 1.4).

Making oneself fit for restoring the gaps in the celestial walls means installing on earth the mirror of heavenly Jerusalem, when the community of humans living together becomes the image of angelic union. To build up the House of God means to live an angelic life and thus to create a unity between God, angels, and humans. While it belongs to angels to embody God's will spontaneously, humans need to be disciplined before being able to live the harmonious life of heaven, for only in a disciplined life are they able to amputate the spiritual limbs that impede their angelic state of life.

This idea of building God's house is continued in the following sermons for the Dedication of a Church (Ded 1, 2, 3). The community becomes the house itself. It becomes the temple of the Lord because of the sanctity of its life. Having abolished all that obstructs the rise of the celestial Jerusalem, the community may celebrate its own sanctification in building up and dedicating the house of God in the proper church, the proper body, and the proper soul. Church, body, and soul merge into one saintly edifice. The material church is saintly because of the saintly bodies visiting it. The bodies are saintly because of the saintly souls that vivify them, and the souls are saintly because of the Holy Spirit inhabiting them (Ded 1.1–2).

As soon as Bernard starts talking about the consecration of the building, he is focusing on the consecration of the monks themselves, of their lives dedicated to God. And the sacraments of the dedication only have meaning when depicting the community life of the monks (Ded 1.3–6). Thus Bernard creates an indissoluble union of the spiritual house, which leaves no place for the least suspicion to cause cracks in the living walls (Ded 1.7).

But to arrive at that point, God's house must first be built in the soul (Ded 2), because only the soul is capable of embracing his magnitude, "for she is created in his image" (Ded 2.2). That is why the temple must be erected in each single soul by cleaning reason of all errors, will of all iniquity, and memory of all stain (Ded 2.3). Only then will the Word come to inhabit each soul as well as the community of all, thanks to the mutual love each bears for the other. Yet this erection of God's dwelling in the soul demands continuous striving because, unlike God's house in heaven, which is a house of joy, God's house on earth remains a house of war (Ded 2.4).

War continues in the last sermon of this first group (Ded 3), in which the house of God reappears as a fortified town besieged by its enemies. Bernard incrementally analyzes all the elements needed to sustain the blockade and the attack: the spiritual bulwarks, the spiritual weapons, and the spiritual provisions (Ded 3.1–2). Yet those will not suffice once the defenders show themselves to be unreliable, once they include traitors, cowards, and indolent combatants among themselves (Ded 3.3–5).

On this negative image of the besieged the Dedication sermons end. Those who in the first sermon were addressed as saints giving the building its saintliness end up here alarmed by the presence among them of those who will either betray the House of God or do nothing to defend it. A downward movement results from this sequence, from the meeting of human and angel to the pact between human and devil, from the unified and disciplined community as the earthly image of heavenly Jerusalem to a besieged and internally divided town where everyone must suspect everyone else. As in the preceding sermons on the Assumption (Asspt 1–4), the reader tumbles down toward the grave, now not that of the individual person, but of the entire community. Will there be a contrary movement to stop and reorient the community to its spiritual vocation?

There is. M continues with three sermons for All Saints (OS 1, Conv, and OS 2), which conclude the entire collection. Two of these texts remain in the liturgical collection (OS 1 and 2). The third (Conv) had another destination: it was or became the written version of the sermon Bernard preached to the students of Paris during the winter of 1140–41. Twice Bernard preached to the students: on All Saints 1140 and once again on Epiphany 1141. He started twice from the same premises that are found in the different versions of Conv. The final text is a more or less open attack on Abelard, which is completely lacking in the early version as it was inserted in M.[24]

This new significance that the central sermon took on in the confrontation with Abelard may explain its disappearance from the liturgical collection. In M, however, it still formed part of the narrative line on which this first collection closed. And it certainly served the purpose of redirecting the narrative line. OS 1 starts by inviting the reader to the spiritual nutrition offered by the living Word and needed by the besieged in the preceding sermon. The alimentation offered here consists of the Beatitudes as they were offered in the Sermon on the Mount and as they have been the sustenance of all the saints ever since.

This theme reappears in the short version of Conv. Now, however, the Beatitudes are not presented as food necessary to endure the attacks of the enemy. This time Reason offers them to Will as medicaments to raise her from her sickbed, to which her attachment to her body has brought her. Only by way of the Beatitudes can she find the peace she longs for.

---

[24] I have analyzed the development of the sermon in my book, *Een middeleeuws drama. Het conflict tussen scholing en vorming bij Bernardus en Abaelardus* [*A Medieval Drama. The Conflict between Schooling and Formation in Bernard and Abelard*] (Kampen/Kalmthout: Clement/Pelckmans, 2002), 278–83.

This inner peace is attained in the last sermon, OS 2, in which memory becomes purified in the remembrance of the saints. Participation in their rest nestles itself in the conscience and spirit of those who remember their deeds and rejoice in the spiritual peace they enjoy. The memory of the saints thus changes into desire to join them in the eternal peace and rest of beatitude.

The narrative line as contained in M is very clear and develops in an almost unilinear way. The spiritual House of Wisdom as erected in Mary must be rebuilt on earth in the monastic community, where earthly life becomes angelic and mirrors the heavenly city. In the perfect community humans and angels meet, but this meeting implies each one's erecting the spiritual house in the self, both in the communal life lived with brothers and in the soul. There, in the soul, the person must sustain the attacks of the besiegers and thus arm the self with the spiritual weapons needed to repel enemies. These arms are found in the memory of the saints, in their deeds, and in the peace they now enjoy. This memory may give the person the strongest resistance, the desire to be worthy to join them. Thus open-endedly the M collection finishes.[25]

Building Heaven on Earth: L

In L^B only three texts make up this part of the autumn sermons, Ded 4 and 5 and OS 5. They immediately follow NatBVM, the famous sermon on Mary as the aqueduct and the ladder between heaven and mankind. This strong use of architectural images in L^B is confirmed in the next sermons. In this collection Ded 4 is titled *On the Threefold Dwelling-Place*, though this title fits only the second part of the sermon, which Bernard introduces by a statement similar to that with which he introduces Ded 1: "a house is holy because of the bodies within it, and the bodies because of the souls, and the souls because of the Spirit dwelling within them" (Ded 4.4). Whereas in

---

[25] Three texts follow that might be attributed to Bernard's secretary, Nicolas of Montiéramey. See SBOp 4:130, 133–35; Leclercq, "La tradition," 214–17. We will return to the first of these.

Ded 1 this beginning led Bernard to transpose the consecration of the building with the consecration of the monks, in this sermon he sticks more closely to the architectural image. On the basis of two quotations from Psalm 83, he makes a clear distinction between the house of God and God's tents and courts. The human's road to God has to pass by each of them. In the tents, humans must camp during their battle for sanctification (Ded 4.4), and in the courts, they may enjoy their rest after the battle has passed and they can be secure in the peace they gained (Ded 4.5). In God's house, however, glorification will be their part. It invites people from afar with its promises of power, splendor, and glory (Ded 4.6).

The first part of the sermon enters the moral level of interpretation as an introduction to the allegorical one as it will be applied in the last paragraphs. The walls of the church have been sanctified by the mystery of consecration, by readings from Scripture, by prayers, by relics, and by angelic vigilance (Ded 4.1). It is not the celestial Jerusalem that needs to be watched over, Bernard emphasizes. Rather, it is the human walls, over which the angels keep diligent watch: "You are kind, O Lord; you cannot be content with this fragile protection of our walls, but over those who are themselves over others you have set an angelic guard so that they may defend both the walls and those who are contained within the circuit of the walls" (Ded 4.2). In a hardly remarkable move, Bernard has identified the church walls with the superiors, who need the guidance and vigilance of angels to perform their task. But it is not solely the walls that are sanctified by prayers, lectures, and relics. Instead, the superiors are; Bernard is. The vigilance of the angels contains his ministry, just as his ministry contains his monks. Humans' failure to see their spiritual guards with their physical eye is unimportant so long as they are aware of the angels' help, so long as their conviction remains unshaken that within these walls, within this guardianship, they are sanctified (Ded 4.3). For the life in the community is a life of strife, of battle. It is life in God's tents, preparing the way to God's house.

But what exactly is meant by God's house? The next sermon, Ded 5, opens with this question, and Bernard answers it at once. Using as its point of departure the Responsorial verse used at the consecration of a church (Rev 21:2), he identifies the house with the heavenly

Jerusalem coming down as a bride. Yet Bernard suggests that his audience wants to know more, that they wish to know "who in the world it is who should merit to be called and to be the house of this *Paterfamilias*, the temple of God, the city of this King, and indeed the bride of this glorious Bridegroom" (Ded 5.2).

And here Bernard introduces his actual theme for the sermon. He hesitates to express his opinion, he writes, because he is not "a man of deep experience." But anyway, he continues,

> I will say what I sometimes experience being acted out in me so that if others should judge it useful for themselves they can imitate me. For I am convinced that if I should but once have mercy on my own soul it would please my God! I frequently think about my soul; if only I might do so more extensively and always! For there was a time when it was acted upon, but just a little, or even less, of course because I loved it just a little or really hardly at all. For how can it be said that someone loves that whose death he loves? Because if—this is true and beyond dispute—wickedness is the death of the soul, then the truth in the saying *the one who loves iniquity hates his own soul* is proved absolutely. I used to hate my soul and would still if he who first loved my soul had not bestowed on me this, the beginnings of his love. (Ded 5.2)

Bernard now begins a meditation on the soul, on its being nothing in and by itself: "Surely, man is made as an emptiness, man is brought to nothing, man is nothing" (Ded 5.3). Is it not an incredible contradiction then, Bernard cries out, that humans have been so dignified by God: "How is one nothing upon whom God has set his heart?" (Ded 5.3).

From now on the entire sermon builds up the consistent pattern of contradictions that constitute human beings. In the judgment of truth, humans are nothing, but in the testimony of God's love they are magnified. At one and the same moment, they see themselves in the light of truth as humiliated and tumbling down and, in the light of love, as exalted and elevated (Ded 5.5). The reality about themselves tears them down, but hope may lift them up. Their own judgment shows them to be nothing, but their belief in God's love knows them to be predestined to the glory (Ded 5.6–7). Human beings are a coherent mass of contradictions.

Departing from this image of humankind as a unity of paradoxes, Bernard suddenly returns to his initial question: "Now either by moving on from what we find in those imitations to something superior or else devoting a bit more attention to them, let us ask what is the house of God, let us ask what is the temple, let us ask what is the city, let us ask what is the bride" (Ded 5.8). So Bernard returns to the question he left open at the beginning of the sermon. What is the house of God? "I have not forgotten, but I say it with fear and reverence: 'We are.' 'We are,' I say, 'but in the heart of God'" (Ded 5.8). Humans are the house of God! In all their inconsistencies, being both nothing and magnified by God, they are the house of God, God's temple, and God's bride. The more people descend in humility, in the confession of sins, in praying, Bernard says, the more they rise in continence, in peace, in belief (Ded 5.8–9). Humankind is heavenly Jerusalem, because humans have the potential of ascending while descending, because in their prayers they are the house of God, in their continence they are God's temple, in their community life they are the heavenly city, and in their love they are the bride (Ded 5.10). Building heaven is earthly business.

This is where the saints enter. L^B continues with a sermon for All Saints that in the end will be the fifth in the series, OS 5. In this sermon Bernard insists that sanctity does not equal uniformity: "For there are saints of heaven, and there are saints of earth, and among those of earth some are still on earth, while some are already in heaven!" (OS 5.1). Holiness comprises the angels, who are triumphant without enduring any battle, and it comprises both those humans "who have washed their robes white in the blood of the Lamb" and those who are still hidden, "who still strive, still fight, still run, but have not yet received the prize."

He goes on, however, with his audience and with himself, suggesting that they may already reckon themselves members of this last group: "As for us, we are forbidden to sing the praises of human beings in their lifetime" (OS 5.2). But at the same time, for what reason are the saints in heaven praised on earth? They do not need it. They are fulfilled:

> We venerate their memory to our advantage, not to theirs. Do you wish to know how greatly that is to our advantage? I confess that a great longing flares up in me when I think of them, a threefold longing. People say, "What the eye does not see, the heart does not grieve for." My memory is my eye! To reflect on the saints is in some way to see them. This is our portion in the land of the living, and it is no mean portion if affection accompanies memory, as it should. Thus, I say, our citizenship is in heaven, but ours is not like theirs. They are there in fact, but we in desire. They are there in reality; we are there through memory. (OS 5.5)

Remembering the deeds and words of the saints means sharing their life in heaven, becoming among the citizens of the heavenly city, being among the living stones that build up the New Jerusalem. They are already there in substantiality. We may join them in desire when we praise their memory.

Once again Bernard imposes the contradictions of human existence on his audience. Humans are not to become saintly in heaven; they must do so on earth. Saints are those who have finished the battle and brought home the victory. They enjoy the presence of God and comprise part of the heavenly city immediately. Those on earth can only long to join them. Thus they must remember the saints and by their memory nourish the desire that can bridge the abyss separating humans from what makes up the truthfulness of their memory.

The house of God is built with stones of desire. It is memory's architecture, not of the past but of the future. Longing for the saints means longing to enter their unity with Christ and to be reformed in one's humble body and configured to the glory of the head as they are (OS 5.9). For the time being, however, the heavenly building comprises those on earth as well as those in heaven, joining them in the oneness of opposing poles. For "we rejoice together with them, and they suffer along with us; through devout meditation, we reign with them, while they by devoutly intervening fight with us and in us" (OS 5.11). While enjoying the undisturbed rest and peace of the heavenly homeland, the saints fight and suffer with humans on earth. And whereas living men and women are in the middle of the battle, they may with the saints enjoy the glory and the triumph. Humans on earth still have to make temporary camp in the tents of military campaign, but not without tasting the peace of the court or without dwelling in the glory of the house. All movements coincide in memory's longing for what lies ahead.

Building the Vision: Ar

The interest of the manuscript *Ar*, from the abbey of Orval, lies primarily in the introduction of the new group of sermons for the First Sunday of November. They appear in close connection to the oldest group of sermons for the Dedication of a Church, but, probably because of the new combination, these last sermons have a new arrangement that indicates a narrative line diverging from the former collection.

Yet the manuscript has still other interesting points. In addition to the disjunction of the sermons for All Saints from those for the Dedication, some groups of sermons must clearly be considered as already fixed unities. This is true for the two sermons in honor of the Archangel Michael that appear again in this collection in the same order as in M. It is also true for the first three sermons for Dedication, which were taken over from M but rearranged to fit the connection with the newly introduced group for the First Sunday of November.

On the other hand, *Ar* shows that the connection between the first two sermons for All Saints, both of which belonged to M, did not comprise a similarly fixed group. OS 2 is now joined with two new texts that in the final edition, Pf, will end up as OS 3 and 4. These three texts now form a new unity. As to the link between the different groups, the sermons for the First Sunday of November and those for the Dedication of a Church must be taken together. This seems the logical way to explain the rearrangement of these sermons in *Ar*.[26]

---

[26] As to the texts that separate Mich 1 and 2 from OS 2–4, it is hard to say whether they continue any line of liturgical thinking. The manuscript requires more careful study of the principles of its organization.

Bernard takes care to provide a close thematic unity in this new grouping of three sermons for All Saints. The focus in OS 2 on the peace and rest enjoyed by the saints recurs in both of the new texts (OS 3 and 4), which so closely follow OS 2 that they seem the result of one continuous succession of sermons. Both of these sermons open with a reference to the preceding sermon at the point at which it broke off. OS 2 and 3 even end by announcing a follow-up of the subject in a succeeding sermon. Given the appearance of OS 2 alone in the earlier collection M, it seems plausible that Bernard is evoking the connection here for literary and stylistic reasons. In any case it seems clear that he considered OS 2–4 to be a unity, developing the central theme of saintly rest in the Lord in accord with the way he originally treated it in OS 2 alone.

OS 2 considers the saintly rest first of all from the perspective of living humans. As life on earth is a battle and a continuous warfare, the saints' rest may be considered remuneration for the victory they brought home from their strife. For this reason, it is worth remembering them in reading and writing so that living men and women may realize the state these holy souls enjoy.

OS 3 continues on this theme, developing the saints' three states of being, linked to three states of the church. In the last state, the church will consist of souls without the slightest wrinkle, so as to be able to follow the Lamb wherever he goes. The Lamb, indeed, goes to the rest of the Lord, but only in the future, at the end of time. Until that moment the saints enjoy another rest, under the altar of the Apocalypse.

Bernard postpones his discussion of the meaning of the altar and the saints' resting underneath to OS 4. Here he distinguishes three states of death. Before the birth of Christ, all, just and unjust alike, were condemned to darkness and pain. The just experienced this death as the pain of desire and longing, figured by Abraham's bosom. Since Christ died for mankind, the just rest beneath the altar, that is, they repose in joy under the human nature of Christ. As soon as he returns, they will be exalted above the altar, where they may contemplate his glory.

Bernard then jumps to the three visions of God that humans may enjoy even now: seeing him in all creatures, possessing him in oneself, and knowing him in himself. From this threefold vision he deduces a sevenfold beatitude, consisting of three beatitudes of the soul that result from holding God in oneself and the four of the body, which result from the vision of the outside world.

The three sermons for All Saints thus show a clear and ongoing reflection, leading from the saints' rest by way of the church's rest to the rest in death that one achieves in a threefold vision of God. From here the sermon returns to the sevenfold beatitude of living humans. The rest that the saints enjoy "under the altar" is attainable for all persons who consider God in themselves and in the world around. Not unlike the way Bernard treats of the saints in the other two collections, he here portrays holiness as a coherence of contradictions. Humans will come to know the saints' rest in the middle of their life struggles. Even while in the place of unrest, people's vision of the world around and inside themselves opens to them the delight that the holy souls enjoy in their vision of God.

The following sermon, OS 4, closes with one of those numerical explications that constitute one of Bernard's strengths in composing sermons. This time it leads to an enumeration of the seven Beatitudes of body and soul. These sermons thus develop the subject differently from the treatment in M. There the point of departure was the eight Beatitudes that were the subject of both OS 1 and the older version of Conv. OS 2, as a description of the rest of the saints, functioned somehow as the conclusion to both, and the Sermon on the Mount laid the foundations for the rest that the holy souls come to enjoy.

This time, the saintly rest has itself become the starting point for an evolution that ends with seven other Beatitudes. Bernard has shifted his focus. Instead of a linear development from Christ's teaching to the reward after death for those able to follow him, now he installs a much more complicated movement, in which the rest itself is less central than the audience's remembering and considering this rest of holy souls. The church becomes an important mediator between the recollection of the saintly rest and the preparation of the resting place under the altar. The sermon reintroduces the architectural image with the altar as the place from where the vision of God can take a new start to send living humanity out into the world again.

The two movements do not exclude each other. Rather, they are complementary. And it can be expected that in the final version of his liturgical collection Bernard will bring them together in one continuous flow.

Before moving on to the final liturgical series, we still have to learn from manuscript *Ar* something about Bernard's rearrangement of the sermons for the Dedication of a Church. The second, originally independent part of the manuscript, opens with two groups of texts. First come four sermons for the First Sunday of November (1 Nov 1–4). They are immediately followed by the first three sermons for the Dedication in a new order (Ded 3, 1, 2).

The four sermons for the First Sunday of November contain an ongoing but not continuous meditation on the Vision of Isaiah (Isa 6:1-3). The starting point is the Responsory of the day, composed of Isaiah 6:1 and 3: "I saw the Lord seated upon a throne, high and lifted up, and the whole earth was full of his majesty." The last two sermons discuss the intermediate verse, on the two seraphim and their six wings. Sermons 1 Nov 1 and 2 clearly constitute a compositional unity, the first ending with an allusion to the second. Similarly 1 Nov 3 and 4 can be considered a unity, although Bernard does not explicitly draw the link.

Simultaneously, each of the sermons treats an independent topic derived from the biblical text. The first, 1 Nov 1, focuses on the vision itself. First contrasting the vision as described in Isaiah 6 with the one in Isaiah 53, Bernard points out the difference between the shared vision of 53—"We saw him"—and the personal, individual vision of 6: "I saw the Lord." The common vision of Christ is the one of the humble and suffering man on the cross. It is the vision of wintertime, when humans stay below in the winter quarters. It evokes compassion in the just or disdain in the unjust.

But it is granted only to the individual to contemplate the Lord seated upon his throne, to see him in his glory, and to mount up to the summer quarters in his mansion. There that individual may see the Lord upon his throne and wonder from what material it is built: "No material substance seems fit for such a throne, such an occupier. The spiritual structure, which the true and eternal life has chosen for his dwelling place, must be built of living stones" (1 Nov 1.4). Since Lucifer and his followers were expelled from heaven, the number of angels no longer suffices, so humans have to supply the material.

That is why Bernard describes the throne as both *high*, because of the angels, and *lifted up*, because of humankind.

In the second sermon, the topic is the last part of the verse: "the whole earth is full of his majesty" (Isa 6:3). The actual situation where earth and heaven will be filled with his majesty is postponed to the future, when God's will shall reign everywhere. In order for this state to become true, there must be a reformation of the flesh and its configuration to the spiritual body that is Christ's body without sins. Now, however, the temple is filled with those who live in humility, while the proud have been thrown out of it, for only the humble, angels and humans, will help to build the throne.

The third sermon takes up this last point and opposes the seraphim standing above the throne (Isa 6:2) to Lucifer and the fallen angels. Bernard takes up the name of Lucifer to demonstrate the failing of the devil: "O unhappy one, you had light, but you had no warmth" (1 Nov 3.1). There is one thing that, like the sun, gives both light and warmth, because the two are substantially united, but there is another, like the moon, that gives light without warmth. The first is the symbol for wisdom and is manifested in John the Baptist, who may be considered the true Lucifer, the true Light-Bearer. The other is the symbol for foolishness, as became manifest in the fall of Lucifer. But unlike Lucifer, the seraphim are stable, not because they are stable in themselves, as is only true for the Trinity, but because they have their stability from God. For that reason they stand instead of sitting, which is the prerogative of the Trinity alone.

1 Nov 4, which is the final sermon of the group in *Ar*, continues the former line of thought. It follows the second verse of Isaiah's vision in Isaiah 6, speculating about the stability of the seraphim despite their six wings. How can one be stable while flying? Or why should one have wings while remaining in stability? Bernard immediately gives the answer: "For where should the seraphim fly but to him for whom they burn with love? See how a flame flies and stands still at the same time, and you will not find it strange that the seraphim fly while they stand and stand while they fly" (1 Nov 4.1).

Two wings they have with which they fly: the one is the wing of perception, which makes them know, and the other is the wing of devotion, which makes them love. Knowledge without love makes one fall because of failing in devotion. So too love without knowledge causes one to fall because of the lack of perception.

With two wings the Seraphim cover the head; with two they cover the feet. Humans cannot see to what they were predestined; neither can they see to what they will be called. Beginning and end are hidden. Therefore, they are dependent on the grace bestowed on them. Only in the middle, between beginning and end, do humans notice what is expected of them, so justifying themselves through works of charity and knowledge so that they may through free will collaborate with grace.

This meditation on Isaiah 6:1-3 fits in well with aspects of Bernard's earlier projects. Several elements return: the architectural element in the construction of the throne, the tension between movement and stability, and the connection of angels and humankind. Additionally, the image of Lucifer falling often recurs in Bernard's works, almost always at the opening of a new sequence of thought. All these elements point to the possibility that Bernard has been composing these sermons deliberately to fit into the narrative line he wants to develop in the liturgical series.

In manuscript *Ar* these sermons are followed by the first three sermons for the Dedication of a Church but starting with Ded 3 rather than Ded 1. This sermon is the most military of these texts, setting out all that is needed to protect the House of God against the enemy. As such, it well follows the previous sermon, 1 Nov 4, which ended with the duty of humans to conform themselves to God's grace in order to be justified. As life is a battle, God's house can only be erected (Ded 1 and 2) after one has done everything possible to keep the enemy out, exactly as has been done in the first sermon, Ded 3. Reforming one's life to the life of the saints cannot have another sense.

Crossing the Bridge: Pf

All these different strands finally come to perfection in the final form of the liturgical series, Pf. In comparison to the placement of the entire subgroup in the earlier collections, Pf includes three previously untreated sermons, only two of which are truly new. The series opens with the Sermon to the Abbots (Abb), a text that appears for the first time in the exegetical part of L. There it belongs to a large group of texts that treat the ascent of the soul. Four of its preceding texts handle the relation between the soul and reason in different ways. Abb itself fits into the following part, which focuses on humility and obedience.

From that position, where it had no liturgical significance, it is now transposed to Pf, where it is incorporated as part of the liturgical year. Several manuscripts mention that this sermon was preached during one of the yearly general chapters at Cîteaux. These normally took place after the Solemnity of the Elevation of the Cross, on September 14, as fits perfectly with this sermon's current position in the collection, between the Nativity of the Virgin (September 9) and the Feast of Saint Michael (September 29).

Yet more interesting than this chronological insertion is the question of why Bernard thought it at all necessary to introduce this sermon into his project. Apparently placing the sermons for Saint Michael immediately after the sermon block for the Virgin, as in M, no longer satisfied him. He wanted something in between, a kind of intermediate text that would break the all too immediate transition from Mary's mediation to that of the angels, putting them somehow on one line.

By inserting the sermons to the abbots into this sequence, Bernard breaks this almost instinctive link. Now the abbots intervene. Their role has to be defined in terms of the celestial mediators between whom they now appear.

Another rupture can be discovered when reading the sermon. While in NatBVM and Mich 1 and 2 the dominating movements are vertical, going up and down between heaven and earth, in Abb the principal movement is horizontal. The text treats the crossing of the "great and wide sea" from Psalm 103, accessible to three groups of humans, equated with Job, Daniel, and Noah.[27] Thus Bernard makes a connection to Asspt 3.5, where he mentioned these three in a similar context, alluding to the ark and the crossing of the sea.

[27] After Ezek 14:14.

Bernard follows the traditional treatments of these men, equating Job with the laity (here specifying him as a married man), Daniel (referred to as a man of longing) with monks, and Noah with superiors. In this sermon Bernard focuses on the needs of the monks who cross the narrow bridge while he simultaneously preaches to their superiors about how to build the ark that will help them to pass over the sea and to guide the monks entrusted to their care. For each of the three groups must pass "this great and wide sea" in its own way. Married people are bound to take the shallows, "troubled and dangerous though they are, and the path they take is long, for they take no shortcut. Since the way is dangerous, we grieve that many perish on it, and consequently we see very few who complete the journey" (Abb 1). The monks take the "easier and shorter way" of the bridge, which is also the safer way (Abb 2). The superiors in their turn "are not confined to clearly marked bridges or footpaths" (Abb 6). They go down in ships and are free to go wherever they wish in order to meet those in trouble and assist them.

The sermon seems to offer a clear-cut image of horizontal movement, opposing itself to both the verticality of the ladder, with which NatBVM closed, and to the verticality resulting from the meeting of angels and humankind in Mich 1 and 2. But of course reading Bernard is not that easy; a more careful consideration of his sermon offers a rather different insight.

Bernard states that he will not linger on the third category of human life, those living a married life in the world, "as they have little to do with us" (Abb 1). This remark seems obvious, as he was originally preaching the sermon at a general chapter. Yet taking it in merely that sense would obscure the broader implications of these words. Indeed, in spite of being strongly involved in the worldly affairs, Bernard did not leave any works addressed to an audience consisting of "married men." All his works, his entire pedagogical activity, focus on the groups in society that had not taken or had not yet chosen married life, had not taken the road through the shallows: students (Conv, Gra, Dil), secular clergy (Dil, Csi, VMal), and monks or semimonastic groups (Apo, Hum, Miss, Pre, Tpl). The same is true for his Commentary on the Song of Songs. The only possible exception is his epistolary collection, the final edition of which came into being during the same period as the last redaction of the liturgical series Pf. Apparently in his letters Bernard wanted to address a lay public. Yet even that wish is not entirely evident.[28]

Bernard's remark about married men thus seems to have a broader application than just the suggested evocation of the Cistercian chapter. Does he want to exclude the non-celibate reader from his teaching in the liturgical series? But why is he doing so at this point, almost at the end of the liturgical year? Why did he not give a similar warning earlier in the collection? Or is the exclusion only valid for the last part of the year, for the architectural and saintly sermons?

To answer these questions requires returning to the starting point. Abb was only introduced into the liturgical series in Pf, originally not having appeared in any liturgical context. One of the reasons for inserting this text into the collection thus had to do with the final composition, in which the sermons on the saints constituted an entirely new element. Apparently the message of these sermons was not aimed at "the rank of married men," as is obvious, as they focus on bishops, an apostle, and a monk.

But the position of Abb even seems to exclude married men from the architectural sermons that immediately follow. The reason can be found in the placement of this sermon both after the last Marian sermons and before the sermons on the angels. Mary, though Virgin, though Mother of God, was married. The angels are not. In the homilies on the Annunciation, Bernard dwells at length on the historical and moral necessity of Mary's being married (Miss 2.12–16). Bernard's exclusion of married men causes a reconsideration of Mary's role in the entire collection. Her Assumption and Nativity conclude the Marian part. By her elevation Mary is born as the universal and unique mediator between mankind and her Godly Son.

---

[28] As I demonstrated in my forthcoming book chapter, "Voicing your Voice: the Fiction of a Life. Early 12th-Century Letter Collections and the Case of Bernard of Clairvaux," Bernard's purpose in collecting and editing his letters was first of all to give insight to the way a monk could become involved in secular affairs. The corpus shows both the attitude such a monk ought to have vis-à-vis worldly exigencies and the ultimate tragedy of his inevitable failure. Of all Bernard's works, his epistolary corpus most strongly displays a tragic tone that, remarkably, comes close to the one in Abelard's *Historia calamitatum*.

Mary's mediation englobes all humanity, and in this sense she forms the true image of what the church on earth must be: the house for all, for celibate and non-celibate, for clergy and seculars, for sinners and saints. The church must bring the divine water down for each to drink and hold the ladder for each to climb. Mary's Virgin Motherhood encompasses the entire universe.

The angels too have a universal task. But as opposed to the Virgin, their task is not so much to plead for humankind as to offer humans' spiritual sacrifice in praying to God and to bring down again divine grace upon humans. Their vocation is to minister to humans in their relation to God. Theirs is also a celibate existence. Now, inside the church, their task can thus only be fulfilled by the celibate ranks in society, that is, the superiors in the world and in the monastery. They alone are able to restore the heavenly Jerusalem on earth.

Bernard does not really occupy himself with life hereafter. He writes for the living and thus focuses on the needs of men and women on earth. After having by way of his sermons given life to the universal community of true Christians, culminating in Mary's Assumption and Nativity, now he undertakes the arduous task of using his words in order to create God's spiritual ministers on earth, his earthly angels. And so, from now on, the rank of married men has "little to do with us." "We must speak" of those who are destined to offer universal humankind their spiritual service and of those who must guide and form spiritual ministers on earth. "We must speak" of those who take the bridge and the ship and are confined to both the shorter and the freer ways of crossing "this great and wide sea."

The monks have taken the straight way, the bridge of abstinence and continence. It is the shortest and safest road but also the narrow way that leads to life. Bernard's evocation becomes very concrete in painting the bridge over a wild and rough sea, a bridge built of only three planks, with no mention of a rail. One need not have a weak head for heights to start getting dizzy with the idea, especially at the sight of the waves' swelling and washing against the bridge. Lust of the flesh, lust of the eyes, and pride of life assail those walking upon it (Abb 4). Then they have to cling to the planks that make up the bridge: starvation of the body, poverty, and humble obedience (Abb 3). Yet they must continue. They cannot sit down, retreat, or try to outstrip the one in front. The bridge is too narrow, and they would fall (Abb 2). So the only way to pass safely over is by rushing headlong over the sagging planks above the surging waves, driven only by the desire to reach the other side. Was Daniel not called a *vir desideriorum*, a man of longing? A monk's life is a life of dreaming: while traveling in the world he lives by his longing in the place he desires. This journey makes the monk the ideal minister between humanity and its dream, between each man or woman and God.

Of course, the monk needs guidance to be able to pass lightly over the bridge, and he needs assistance in case he stumbles or hesitates. Those who are to guide and assist him must be free to arrive at the places where their help is needed. They are abroad on the ship that must bring them safe over the sea. "But what ship can be found that can withstand such mighty waves and remain safe in so great a danger?" (Abb 6). And indeed the sea is rough, the waves are surging to frightening heights: "So *they mount up to the heavens, and they descend to the depths*" (Ps 106:26; Abb 6). The ship is tossed between heaven and earth. It is thrown even deeper into the depths of hell (*ad inferos*), because at one moment those abroad treat heavenly themes, and at the next they pass judgment on infernal and horrible deeds (Abb 6). So in order to survive, they need to be driven by pure love. For only love is strong as death, as long as it is made up *of a pure heart and of a good conscience and of faith unfeigned* (1 Tim 1:5).

The horizontal movement of passing over the sea has become floating once again. While the monks still run over the bridge, even if on bouncing planks, the superiors, both the monastic and the secular, see themselves as going up and down more than forward. Though bound to the earth, their task comes close to that of the angels, ministering to the monks by reminding them of both heaven and hell. Thus they invigorate their dream and their longing and make them hasten more securely toward the goal that they desire. Their moving forward depends on the love that reaches from heaven to hell. They will be able to pass over the bridge only thanks to the waves of love.

As a matter of course, the new way in which Bernard ultimately opened the architectural series gives the subsequent sermons an entirely different direction. The ascending and descending movements of angels and humanity in Mich 1–2 are now posed in contrast to the tossing up and down of the superiors in order to show the correspondence inside the church between the superiors and the angelic rank. The emphasis on discipline as elaborated in Mich 1 and 2 now finds its true and obvious sense within the ecclesiastical or even monastic context.

These sermons are now followed by the sermons for the First Sunday of November, so the theme of the angels continues, both in the treatment of the Throne of God (1 Nov 1–2) and in the meditation on the seraphim (1 Nov 3–4). A new sermon, 1 Nov 5, concludes the entire development. It contains another long meditation on the verses of Isaiah 6:1-3, in which many of the themes of the preceding sermons return while being diversified. This sermon places most of the emphasis on the seraphim, who occupy more than half of the sermon (1 Nov 5.6–12). Once again Bernard describes them in opposition to Lucifer, and now he interprets their wings' concealing of head and feet as a demonstration of the right attitude toward God: veneration and admiration to God's head, voluntary ministry to God's feet. The wrong attitude, exemplified by Lucifer, expresses admiration linked to envy and involuntary ministry.

The reading of the biblical passage is preceded, however, by an introduction meditating on Christ's unity with the Father. Bernard develops this theme by way of the prepositions that can be applied to both persons in the Trinity: Christ's divinity as a union out of (*ex*), with (*cum*), and in (*in*) the Father (1 Nov 5.1); Christ's humanity as a movement from (*a*), for (*pro*), and under (*sub*) the Father (1 Nov 5.3). An unexpected culmination, however, is Bernard's conclusion of this short meditation: "Shall we dare to say that he was ever without the Father? No one would presume to say this if he himself had not first said, *My God, My God, why have you forsaken me?* There was some kind of dereliction there, and there was no show of courage in such tribulation, no demonstration of majesty" (1 Nov 5.3). Even Christ could be without (*sine*) the Father! At the moment of his death, in the utter abandonment of a man having to die, Christ felt the supreme and ultimate loneliness of man deserted by God.

This miserable state becomes the starting point for the new meditation on Isaiah's visions. But even then, as the sermon proceeds with the majesty of God's enthronement, the naked cry of the abandoned man at the cross shivers through the heavenly vision and brings about a bizarre and somehow shocking assimilation of the images of Christ and of Lucifer. Both are presented as deserted by God. Both remain alone and cut off from the vision of God's splendor.

Yet an abyss separates them. Christ is abandoned out of love and because of his own voluntary choice to submit himself to divine justice. Lucifer's abandonment is due to his envy and arrogance, to his eternal revolt against divine order. The Son of God restored the universal harmony, creating the community of Christians in their loving ministry to God. He opened the way to elevate humans into the angelic ranks. The first angel, however, refused to serve the original unity and thereafter put all his efforts into destroying the universal community of God, angels and humankind.

While Mich 1 and 2 conclude with the inner unity of humankind, the sermons for the First Sunday of November end in the fearful tensions that threaten to disrupt all coherence inside the community of humans, of angels, of the monks who have to cross the bridge. These tensions toss them up and down between the humility and the humiliation of the suffering and lonely but divine Christ and the arrogant complacency of the rebelling Lucifer, banished to Hell. The monastery becomes in a small way the mirror of universal success and failure.

But Bernard's pedagogy is directed toward success, and that is attainable only when his teaching is based on Christ. Those who come closest to the angelic state are the saints. Thus the ultimate goal of spiritual doctrine must be the community of saints. For this reason the meditation on Isaiah's vision of God must be followed by the sermons for All Saints instead of being preceded by them. All five of them are now united for the first time, leading to a marvelous circular movement.

Thanks to the teaching of the Word, humans know how to attain the state of holiness by way of the Beatitudes (OS 1). The rest that the saints enjoy can only be the result of strife and struggle to conquer the truth of the Word (OS 2–3). Yet only in this quiet will humans enjoy the vision of God, by remembering the saints and what awaits (OS 4). This vision leads the mind back to the seven Beatitudes, which kindle desire as the motor of memory. And only in memory can the unity of Christ's Body be enjoyed on earth (OS 5).

The Dedication sermons incorporate the unity of Christ's Body into the community of the church. The celestial edifice is built and consecrated (Ded 1), built as the inner temple (Ded 2), fortified and defended (Ded 3), sanctified (Ded 4), and unified in spite of all contradictions (Ded 5). As such, the community becomes the House of God, his temple, celestial city, and bride. Bernard concludes the Dedication series and thus the entire block of architectural sermons with one short sermon on the vision of Jacob (Gen 28:12), recalling that the patriarch saw the angels ascending and descending the ladder, at the top of which he saw the Lord bending forward. This sight provoked in him the terrified cry, *Truly the Lord is in this place, and I knew it not*: "*How frightful is this place*, how evident and certain that the Lord is in this place, where not only two or three but a great multitude is gathered together and perseveres in his name! Let no one be unaware; let none of you be ignorant" (Ded 6.1). Bernard is not speaking of Jacob's Bethel. Rather, God is present where a multitude is gathered in a common will, with a common purpose, in a spirit of unity. God is present in the monastic community but as well in the community that is created by his sermons, created in his words.

But how can one ignore that God is present? Is he not everywhere, "in every place, embracing all things and disposing all things" (Ded 6.2)? He is, Bernard declares, but in that place he truly is and truly as the Lord "where in his name angels and humans gather together" (Ded 6.2). In that place he is, and for that reason we say, "Our father who art in heaven." For "he may show himself as present there in some other way that is particularly his own—though not because he himself is different, but because each one distinguishes different things" (Ded 6.2).

The place where angels and humans gather is the place of the heavens, where God shows himself as he is. That place, however, is situated in the longing of the monk. It lies in the desire that makes him join the saints who already see God present. God is in the dream of the monk, absent to his bodily eyes but present to the eyes of memory, to the eyes of loving desire. There God manifests himself in hiding to the impious, in truth to the righteous, in happiness to the angels, in brutality to those below. God is all—not to all, but he is what human longing calls him to be: "For where he makes it rain on the just and on the unjust, he is our father and the father of mercies, hoping for people to repent. When he condemns the stiff-necked, he is judge, and *It is dreadful to fall into the hands of the living God*. Where he takes his rest, he is spouse, and happy is the soul whom he takes into his chamber" (Ded 6.2).

God can thus only be true in that place where he is served "*in spirit and in truth*" (Ded 6.3). For only there can he be truly what he is, Spirit and Truth. How can he be with those who do not fulfill what he says? There he must by necessity be absent as he is and manifest himself only in hiding himself, until the day when this terrifying Truth manifests itself in the eternal abandonment of humans buried in darkness.

Truly, the Lord is in this place, and we know it not. Yet present he is, even when absent to our eyes or to the heart. He is where he has built the house and where he mounts the guard. And how else could humans support and persevere when they do not dwell in the house that God has built and that he guards? "What, then? In what way ought we to be here, in such great reverence standing in the very place where God is, working and serving, and where the angels are, ascending and descending? Clearly, it behoves us to be penitent and expectant" (Ded 6.3).

Penitence and expectance! On the one side, forgetting what lies behind, ignoring, condemning, and thinking over those years past with bitterness—not looking backward, but feeling pushed by the desire to leave it all behind. On the other side, in our thoughts and yearning stretching forward to what lies ahead, fleeing forward in desire, and being stimulated by the urge to depart from where we come, "we have come to this place; here we stand fast" (Ded 6.3). We are on the bridge, hovering over "the great and wide sea," pushed along and carried only by three shaky planks and by our desire to reach the place of our longing. And our only guarantee of that place is the love of him whose words mount and descend, whose images paint heaven and hell, who places us where he is himself: in between all, lost and safe over "the great and wide sea" that is in the House of the Lord.

SIMILIS NOBIS PASSIBILIS: DEATH, WHERE IS YOUR VICTORY?

A final group of seven sermons remains to close the liturgical year. Three of them treat saintly bishops: Saint Martin (Mart), Saint Clement

(Clem), and Saint Malachy (Mal). Three of them deal with the Apostle Andrew (VAnd, And 1–2), and the last one is a sermon to the memory of Humbert, former abbot of Igny (Humb). None of these is linked to any of the greater solemnities during which the abbot was expected to preach according to the Cistercian statutes.[29] Worse, twice they concern the memory of the defunct (Mal, Humb), and the statutes even forbade preaching in annual commemoration of the dead.[30]

Bernard thus once again takes all the liberty he needs as a writer to construct the series according to his personal aims. That this time his decision to incorporate these sermons is less evident than in the preceding parts of the corpus may be indicated by the fact that only one of these seven sermons appears in an earlier collection: the sermon to the memory of Humbert is already present in L^B. All the others appear for the first time in the final liturgical series Pf. Only this final collection can thus give the necessary cues for correctly interpreting these sermons.

As has been noted above, Pf is divided into four groups. Each opens with some sermons that are directly or indirectly connected to the Virgin, and each closes with a human concretization of the central theme. Thus the first group of the Christmas season opens with the sermons for Advent (Adv 1–7), which are internally closely related to the four Homilies to the Praise of the Mother-Virgin, and closes with the sermon on the Conversion of Saint Paul. The central theme of this group is insight and conversion. The second group, the sermons for Lent, starts with the sermons for the Purification, closes with the sermon on Saint Benedict, and treats the inner labor required to purify one's conscience. Both groups contain exactly twenty-

---

[29] See Danièle Choisselet and Placide Vernet, eds., *Les* Ecclesiastica officia *cisterciens du xiième siècle*, La documentation cistercienne 22 (Reiningue: Abbey d'Oelenberg, 1989), 190, chap. 67; Marielle Lamy, "Introduction," in *Bernard de Clairvaux: Sermons pour l'année I.1: Avent et Vigile de Noël*, SCh 480 (Paris: Éditions du Cerf, 2004), 27. See also my remarks in the introduction to *Sermons for Advent and the Christmas Season*, CS 51:xv–xvii.

[30] *Ecclesiastica Officia Cisterciensis Ordinis according to Cod. 1711 Trente*, ed. Bruno Griesser, ASOC 12 (1956): 253–88: chap. (XC) LXVII: *In his etiam diebus, excepto commemoratione defunctorum, et in dominica prima adventus domini et in dominica palmarum habeantur sermones in capitulo.*

nine sermons. The third unit, containing the Easter and Summer sermons, contains thirty-six sermons, opening with the sermons for the Annunciation and closing with the Harvest Sermons. It focuses on preaching the Word as the spiritual equivalent of agricultural labor, of sowing and harvesting.

The final unit of thirty-four sermons is no exception to this general structure. The sermons on the Virgin's Assumption and Nativity open it, and the sermon on Humbert forms its conclusion. Both show that the central theme here is death and its defeat. Just as Mary's Assumption implies her Nativity, which makes possible the Annunciation, so Humbert's death is actually a victory over death, because Humbert died to gain eternal life. In the sermon, Bernard addresses death and cries out,

> It is only the flesh you have taken; you have no power over the soul. It flies to its Creator, whom it had desired so ardently and followed so faithfully all the days of its life. That very body that you think you possess will be taken from you, but when you, the last enemy, have been destroyed, then you too will be swallowed up in victory. You will give it back, without a doubt; one day you will give back that body that yesterday, greatly rejoicing and applauding, you entangled in your nets, that as the sign of your arrival you filled with spittle and curses, with squalor and dirt. The Only-begotten of the Father will come with great power and glory to seek Humbert and to configure this cadaver to the body of his brilliance. But what of you? Assuredly, as it is written in Jeremiah, at the end of days you will still be foolish; while Humbert goes on living eternally, you will go on dying. (Humb 1)

Yet the sequence of seven sermons focusing on saints and humans also gives a human conclusion to the entire collection. As such it echoes the seven sermons for Advent. As these elaborated the desire for the Word to be born, now once again desire is central in the movement of the sermons, notably in those on Saint Andrew, but it is the human desire for eternal rebirth in death. Waiting and longing for the life of the New Man has become in the end a waiting and longing for the New Life of humankind.

The seven sermons on the saints thus constitute the final concretization of Bernard's message within his liturgical sermons as a whole.

Humans can only enjoy eternal life and glory thanks to the Word as it was born in Christmas, as it lived its life of patience and endurance, as it died at Easter in order to be sown by the Spirit in those who must labor in the soil, that is, who are preaching the Word. And this preaching must be like the sowing of the Word, so that the harvest will come when humankind is elevated and fertilized by the Word, becoming part of the House of God, worthy to replace the fallen angels and thus by death entering into the Glory of God.

These final sermons complete one of the three elementary readings as we distinguished them from the outset. The liturgical year stands for the life of humankind, for its linear evolution from the time of conception and expectation to the moment of death and transition. It contains the one-way narrative of earthly human life with no possibility of return. It starts with the state of happy expectancy, where all is waiting for the future newborn. It concludes where humankind's terrestrial journey must by necessity find its end, in the decaying corpse, the *cadaverosum corpus* (Humb 1).

But one's earthly and material life incorporates a second story, the spiritual narrative of the Word that wants to be born and live in humankind. As such, it starts with the desire to see the spiritual birth in men and women when they have conceived the Word. As soon as it is born in them, they will turn away from worldly occupation. As they see the futility of the world, a desire will be born in them for more lasting goods of a less material substance. In the end this desire leads to their conversion, when they place themselves under the guidance of a spiritual guide.

First, their new life will leave them blinded, as reason almost revolts against the idea that God could be found in a similar life of misery. But reason wins insight by a long process of purification until the old man dies and a new life in the Spirit can take its start. Reason now directs will into preaching to others, into the spiritual fertility of sowing the Word in the souls of others. The former disciple has become a teacher and a guide. The Bride did become a Virgin Mother.

By way of learning and teaching, thanks to word and deed, spiritual people can be elevated in order to conceive and be fruitful, giving birth to the Word in others. Then they become active builders, co-architects of the House of God that is constituted by the community of those united in the Word. This is Jerusalem, the true one, the heavenly one.[31] Here a place is constructed where heaven is built on earth, "where God is, working and serving, and where the angels are, ascending and descending" (Ded 6.3). This place of community united in the Word is a place of shared and purified memory. The House of God is a house of desire and is built in memory. Its stones are the living stones of the saints. Commemoration of the saints, of the apostles, of the dead who have been close to us helps us to build the House of Memory and to enkindle in us the desire for God.

The seven concluding sermons thus form a kind of recapitulation of the entire development of the liturgical collection. They round off humans' spiritual growth by offering them the stones they need in order to finish their divine architecture and to receive God in the house of their memory. As such, these sermons also form the natural continuation within the architectural unit that began with the sermons on the Assumption and continued through the sermons for the Angels, for All Saints, and for the Dedication of a Church. Memory is erected in the saints who offer men and women the living stones to build their house of desire. A purified memory will arouse their desire to join the saints who already enjoy the divine vision. It will give them the wings to cross the bridge in security and speed.

But a purified memory will also help to construct the union of community. In Bernard's sermons the saints offer the fundamental moral building stones to assure the coherence of a spiritual body. Bernard presents Saint Martin as a shining example of obedience and Saint Clement as an image of endurance, patience, and perseverance. Saint Andrew is a living flame of desire, longing to embrace the cross: "Brothers, this is flashing fire! It is not a talking tongue, or if it is a tongue, it is certainly fiery—coals of that fire that Christ sent down from heaven to the martyr's bones" (VAnd 3).

But most important, the saints are human, like us:

---

[31] See Bernard's famous Letter 64 to the bishop of Lincoln about his canon Philip, who made the choice to stay in Clairvaux instead of finishing the pilgrimage to Jerusalem, as he had promised his superior to do. For a fine interpretation of this passage, see Marinus Burcht Pranger, *Bernard of Clairvaux and the Shape of Monastic Thought* (Leiden: Brill, 1994), 32–35.

> I ask you, my brothers, is it a man who speaks thus? Or is it an angel or some other creature? He is a man like us, subject to suffering. Truly his passion proves that he is subject to suffering, yet when it is near he exults with great joy. When was there such unheard-of exultation, such strange joy, in a human? When was there such constancy in such weakness? When was there such a spiritual mind in a human, such burning charity, such strength of mind? Let us never imagine that such valor had its origin in him alone. It was a gift, the work of God, coming down from the Father of lights, from him *who alone does great marvels*. (And 2.3)

For a human being may protest that angels have it easy being obedient to God. They enjoy "perfect beatitude, eternal glory, and the highest pleasure" (Mart 7). As to the patriarchs or apostles, either they enjoyed different visions of God or they even enjoyed his physical presence: "What would I not have done if an opportunity like that had been presented to *me*! But *he has not dealt so with all the nations*, either before or since" (Mart 8). For that reason Bernard brings in Saint Martin and Saint Clement. Both were men, like each of us who is listening or reading: *a man like us, subject to suffering* (Mart 9, Clem 3, VAnd 3, And 1.3):

> For today he is seen like us in all things, endowed with feeling and subject to suffering. He lived long after the times of the visions of patriarchs and prophets. He was pure human being, having nothing of the divine nature but believing in one whom he had not seen, full of the fruit of obedience, and rich in virtues. He forsook earth and strove after heaven, entrusting to earth what he had from earth and directing his spirit to the Father of spirits, whom he served faithfully in the spirit of adoption. He was not a heavenly body, nor was he a heavenly spirit. He was a rational animal, a mortal, an earth-dweller, a son of man. He was born on earth, brought up on earth, on earth trained and tested, on earth, too, accomplished. He was not a patriarch or one of the prophets, of whom Truth in the gospel said *the law and the prophets were until John*. He was not by any means Christ, though without a doubt Christ was in him by faith and faith alone. (Mart 9)

For that same reason, the sermons on saints and apostles from ancient times are followed by sermons on contemporaries, on people even more human than those ancient heroes. Malachy was human, Humbert even all too human. But even they help to construe memory, help to arouse in us the flame of desire, the flame of longing for the other side of the bridge that we have to cross, moving forward with no return.

Linear reading, however, is only one of the elementary ways in which one can approach Bernard's liturgical collection, and not the most essential one. Indeed the concluding sermons also offer a key for the other two readings. As far as the circular reading is concerned, these sermons must be considered, strangely enough, in the linear succession of the liturgical year.

In fact, the beginning and end of the collection overlap. Originally, the time of Advent numbered forty days of fasting. In the eleventh and twelfth centuries, the time was reduced to four weeks. Thus originally both the solemnity for Saint Andrew (November 30) and the commemoration of Humbert (December 7) fell within Advent, and the chance was great that the solemnity of Saint Clement (November 23) would also occur during Advent. At least four of these seven sermons thus had to be read during Advent and in a certain sense as though parallel to the sermons for Advent.

In both the sermons for Advent and those for Saint Andrew, desire is the central element. In the Advent sermons the longing goes out to the Word, which desires to be born again in the world. Saint Andrew's desire embraces death as the long-aspired-for union with Andrew's Lord and Master. Longing for death thus overlaps with the longing for life. Moreover, after the death of both Saint Andrew and Humbert, the Word is born, and the cycle of life takes another turn. Spiritual life is only possible thanks to the desire to die for the world. Inversely, death can only result in new birth.

In that sense, the entire cycle repeats what was demonstrated in the group of sermons dedicated to the Virgin, in her Assumption and her Nativity. Mary was only born after her Assumption, i.e., after she died. For the same reason, the true Christmas can only be the result of Easter. Death, as long as it is an elevation of life, can only give new life to the Word. The deaths of both Saint Andrew and of Humbert cannot be the end of life. On the contrary, they overlap with the period of happy expectancy, looking forward to the newborn Word in another soul. The cycle restarts, life leading to death but only when in death new life arises. The resurrection of Humbert's decaying body is not the only topic here but also the birth of the Word, the birth of spiritual life in a newborn soul. Linearity is turned into a curve. Human life starts to become cyclical and spiral, continuing both in heaven with the saints and on earth with the living.

Bernard strengthens this experience of a cyclical reading, of the intersection of different moments in time, with his technique of mixing liturgical references. The most obvious example occurs in the sermon for Saint Clement as he focuses on the three types of water with which the jars are filled at the Wedding of Cana. Bernard already treated these three jars in the first sermon for the first Sunday after Epiphany, focusing there on the number and measure of the jars. Now he draws attention to the water with which they have to be filled.

Between then and now lies almost the entire liturgical year, or ninety-nine sermons that had to prepare the jars, Bernard's readers, for the water that must fill them. Once filled with water, they are ready to undergo the miracle that changes the water into wine. But that is possible only after Christmas, as it contains the first sign the Word will fulfill when he has become alive. The solemnity of Saint Clement by necessity must at great distance follow the preparation of the jars at Epiphany. But the miracle of Epiphany is only possible after the fulfilment of the sermon on Saint Clement: "No one reaches the top in an instant; the top of the ladder is reached by climbing, not by flying. Let us climb, therefore, as it were with two feet: meditation and prayer. Meditation teaches us what is lacking; prayer takes care that it is not lacking. The one shows the way; the other takes you along it. By meditation we learn the dangers that threaten us; by prayer we avoid them, by the help of our Lord Jesus Christ" (And 1.10).

Humankind cannot fly over the years, cannot reach heaven in one step. Desire may give wings, but the body is heavy and trails behind.[32]

---

[32] See Bernard's evocation of his own progress in his treatise on humility: flying in words and spirit through the superior heavens while actually limping behind with lazy feet (*Liber de gradibus humilitatis et superbiæ*, SBOp 3:24–26).

The jars must be prepared before they can be filled with water. And they must be filled with water before the miracle can take place. Year after year the water has to be renewed, the jars restored and refilled, waiting for the miracle to take place. Patience and endurance are the building stones offered to the soul in the sermon on Saint Clement. Meditation and prayer will help one to persevere, to sustain the martyrdom of every day: "But what is your struggle, my brothers? Every day suggestions enter your heart: Break your rule! Murmur! Malign people! Slack off! Pretend to be sick! To satisfy your feelings, answer back to someone who might have spoken harshly! But no one is told, 'If you don't do it, you will die!' Yet only with difficulty and labor will you make a firm stand against them in your soul" (Clem 4). Humans die every day, and the Word must be born in them every day. The entire liturgical cycle never comes to an end. It takes its start right here and now when it comes to its end. And its only purpose is to make men and women conscious that the cycle is no closed circle, but it moves them in a spiral, forward along the bridge.

Both the temporal reading in its linearity and the reading according to nature and liturgy with their returning seasons and festivities are confirmed by the final sermons in the collection. The truly divine reading, however, was the punctual one, because for God there is no time past, present, or future. Time is one, and in God's traces Bernard as the supreme organizer of his liturgical year has the right and the power to mix temporal succession according to his own spiritual insights. For God, the liturgical year has no extension. Easter overlaps with Christmas, because only he who descends can ascend again. Christ's Death is his Birth, just as Mary's Assumption is her Nativity, as well as being the moment of the Annunciation. But to have a good grip on this aspect of reading in the final sermons, it is illuminating to have a closer look at the one sermon with a clear temporal history.

Humb, "On the Death of Master Humbert," appears for the first time in the final, liturgical part of L, where it is the penultimate text. It follows Ded 4, Ded 5, OS 5, and a text that ended up among the sermons *De diversis* (Div 16). And following it comes Div 90. The movement thus goes from the sanctification of the House of God, bringing into harmony the contradictions in humans as the recipients of the House of God, to the unity between the saints and the living, thanks to the desire of those who are still on their way. Div 16 is dedicated to Saint Andrew but focuses on spiritual progress from the natural good, by way of the spiritual good, to the eternal good. Humb appears as a sequel to and exemplum of this route of spiritual elevation.

Div 90 treats the three ointments of Scripture. The first was intended for Christ's feet—pity and justice—and the second for Christ's head. Mary the sinner used both to obtain justification.[33] The third ointment was prepared for Christ's body and was made through the love for the living Christ; for that reason, it could not be wasted on the dead. The text ends with Christ's Resurrection.

So originally Humb was not meant to conclude the liturgical development. The death of Humbert ought to be read against the background of Christ's resurrection as an image for the general resurrection into eternal life, but Bernard did not maintain this plan. Instead, he chose Humb to conclude the sermons, so ending the liturgical year with one man's death. Even when the sermon evokes the ultimate defeat of death, the last image is that of a dying man, of humankind in the claws of death.

Some other elements, however, urge adaptation of this interpretation. First, there is a double Cistercian tradition as to Humbert's day of death. Almost consistently it is given in later sources as December 7, as conforms well to Bernard's liturgical chronology.[34] An independent tradition also exists, however, of September 7 as the day of his death.[35] Now a scribal error taking XII for IX (or *decembris* for *septembris*) is always possible. But one could imagine that a scribe who knew where the sermon was located in the collection was astonished to read that Humbert had died three months before and so

---

[33] See Luke 7:37-38.

[34] See Elphège Vacandard, *Vie de saint Bernard abbé de Clairvaux*, 2 vols. (Paris: Librairie Victor Lecoffre, 1895), 2:392n1 (404n1 in the 1927 ed.), for the reference, notably the twelfth-/thirteenth-century MS 401 from the municipal library of Troyes.

[35] See Vacandard, *Vie de saint Bernard*, 2:392n1 (404n1 in the 1927 ed.); Gerhard Winkler, *Bernhard von Clairvaux*, 8:26. Vacandard quotes the edition of the *Fasciculus Sanctorum Ordinis Cistercienis* (Brussels, 1623) by Henriquez, fragments of which are published in PL 185:1559–60, and the *Menologium Cisterciense* (1630).

took the date of September to be an error. This disagreement about dates provides another indication of Bernard's adapting historical reality to his narrative purposes.

This conjecture is strengthened by another adaptation Bernard irrefutably made. Malachy died during the night of All Souls (November 2). His commemoration date was first set for November 3, then later for November 5.[36] Within the collection, however, the sermon for his commemoration appears after the solemnity of Saint Clement (November 23) and before the Vigil of Saint Andrew (November 29). Bernard consciously transposed the sermon (and thus the date of Malachy's commemoration) to a place that fit better in his overall plan. Malachy could not precede Saint Martin or Saint Clement; he had to follow them to show that while the heroic time of the first martyrs was not complete, saintliness was still possible.

For the same reason Humbert could not precede Saint Andrew in the collection but had to follow him. His commemoration had to be the coronation of the sermons on desire that characterized those of Saint Andrew. Bernard shows Humbert's death too as a death of desire:

> Look, most sweet father: he is before your eyes, that fount of purity for whom you thirsted with such intensity of spirit. See, you are plunged into that depth of godly goodness, the memory of whose abundant sweetness you were accustomed so devotedly to bring forth! When did you ever speak words that did not resonate with true purity, or in which the holy goodness of God was not heard? Therefore I do not grieve for you, Humbert, for God gave you your heart's desire. Rather, I grieve for myself that your sweet counsel has been taken away, your great help, a man of sympathetic mind, one after my own heart. (Humb 6)

Humbert was a man of desire—perhaps not at the same height as Saint Andrew, but on a more human level, a level closer to those who

---

[36] David Hugh Farmer, "Malachy," in *The Oxford Dictionary of Saints* (Oxford: Clarendon Press, 1980), 257–59, esp. 258. Also Jean Leclercq, "Documents on the Cult of St. Malachy," *Seanchas Ardmhacha (Journal of the Armagh Diocesan Historical Society)* 3 (1959): 318–32; reprinted in *Recueil* 2:131–48, esp. 131 and 142–43.

read and listen. Saint Andrew may have been *a man like us, subject to suffering*; the joy he felt when approaching his martyrdom makes Bernard rightly ask, "I ask you, my brothers, is it a man who speaks thus? Or is it an angel or some other creature?" (And 2.3).

Humbert, however, is truly human, all too human. He died as humans die, not in a heroic way. Apparently he had suffered during his whole life from epilepsy, and death awakened the illness of his body: "That very body . . . that as a sign of your arrival you filled with spittle and curses, with squalor and dirt" (Humb 1). Humbert lived a human life, obedient but also recalcitrant:

> He would have made it a rule always to drink water if I had not strenuously dissuaded him. If ever he was forced to drink wine, he diluted it so much that it was wine more in color than in taste. He scarcely ever entered the infirmary, and then only when compelled by obedience, and when he did enter it, he could scarcely be kept there. I confess that the insufficient obedience in this respect was because his great authority overwhelmed me. Am I to praise him? I do not praise him in this, because, as you know, he persisted too obstinately in this kind of thing. (Humb 4)

In spite of all this, Bernard chose to make his sermon for Humbert overlap with the period of longing for the newborn Word of eternal Life. Humbert's all-too-human life and death becomes the cradle for the Word Incarnate, exactly because of its all-too-human humanity. Did death make Humbert spit and curse? Did it fill his body with squalor and dirt? Now just that is the humanity to which the Word has lowered itself. God lies in a cradle. He cries and weeps in the squalor of a trough. His diapers become dirty, and his mother must give him her breast. For that is humanity. Who would ever recognize God in the babe "wrapped in swaddling clothes" (Epi 2.4)? And who would ever recognize him pierced by nails, hanging on the cross? But he can be recognized in the dying Humbert, in his "spittle and curses," in his decaying corpse. For out of this death the Word is born again, new and eternal: "Death, where is your victory?" As was true with Malachy, "Death struck against life, but life came to grips with death and was swallowed up in life" (Mal 3).

The cyclical reading of the liturgical year obliges us to see the overlap of Humbert's death with the newborn Word. It forces us to identify Humbert's decaying corpse with the crying child in its dirty diapers, to see the spittle of death on the lips of the baby, to understand the unity of death and life. Not that a human is born to die: each is born as he dies. Death is swallowed up in life. In the Word of God, there is no longer any place for death. For in the Spirit of God, there is also no place for time.

Bernard began many of his sermons with the exhortation to celebrate today (*celebrare hodie*). The little word *hodie* often also indicates the start of a new subunit, a new movement within the overall progress. In these last seven sermons, however, it appears in almost each one, alternating with the concept of every day (*quotidie*). Moreover, for the first time, Bernard takes the opportunity to explain his concept of today:

> And now in the same way *the word is near you, in your heart and in your ear*, if only you seek him with an upright heart. Indeed this is the apostle's interpretation of what Moses said: this is the *word of faith*. And the same apostle says in another place, *Jesus Christ is the same yesterday, today, and forever. Yesterday* refers to the time from the beginning to the Ascension of the Lord, *today* from now to the end of the world, and again *tomorrow* is eternity, after the common resurrection. Christ is not absent from any of these; from none is Jesus absent, from none is anointing absent, from none salvation. (Mart 10)

Today is the historical time from Christ's Ascension to the end of time. It is the liturgical time from the solemnity of his Ascension to the end of the liturgical year, Humbert's death. It is the present, taken from a divine perspective: the *quotidie hodiernum*, that is, today's every day. It is the present, also taken from the reader's perspective: the *celebrare hodie*, the today of every day's celebration. And to celebrate every day's today signifies the call to strive every day for Christ's presence, for being anointed in every day's today, and for enjoying salvation in every day's today.

"Today, brothers, we celebrate the beginning of Advent" (Adv 1.1). For "Today you are seated at the rich man's table; *consider carefully what is put before you*" (Mart 12). At the end of the liturgical reading, Bernard's words have attempted to fill our memory with images of the Word. Now our reading can begin again, now not with words but in deeds:

> I myself know that it is hard for someone who is negligent to embrace discipline, for a talkative person, silence, for one who is used to going here and there, stability; but it will be harder, much harder, to bear those future troubles. And as I myself have always known, that person who is buried here endured many temptations of this kind at first, but he fought bravely and was victorious. Then it was hard for him to maintain the fight in the midst of temptations; afterward, though, it would have been harder for him to return to those frivolities, because good habits had become natural to him. (Humb 8)

Bernard's liturgical sermons in the end have little to do with pure liturgy. They constitute a school of discipline, a school of meditation and perseverance, an effort to offer support in every day's struggle to make a school of every day's today, a day of the Word, a day of the entire liturgical year. In short, Bernard offers his readers a way to make every day's today a day of living Liturgy.

Editor's Note and Acknowledgments

This final volume of Bernard's Liturgical Sermons has been a long time coming. The task of digitizing Sr. Irene Edmonds's original translation of the sermons, updating her text, and preparing two indices of all four volumes has required the efforts of a number of people, not all of whom I can name here. I would like to express my special gratitude, though, to David Smith, who entered a great many of Sr. Irene's faded typescripts for this volume into the computer; Fr. Mark Scott, OCSO, who did most of the necessary revising and correcting of the thirty-seven sermons in this volume; and Br. Lawrence Jenny, OCSO, and Br. Placid Mokris, OCSO, who indexed the sermons in the four books. Compiling indices of 111 sermons published over twenty-four years in four volumes by two translators and three editors was an enormous job; I am deeply indebted to both Br. Lawrence and Br. Placid. I also received valuable assistance from Elana Harnish, Brian McGuire, Zander Meyers, Megan Milano, Emily Stuckey, and especially Barbara Grueser. I cannot say how grateful I am to all of them.

Finally, I want to thank Prof. Beverly Mayne Kienzle, of Harvard University, and Prof. Wim Verbaal, of the University of Ghent, for their brilliant introductions to the four Cistercian Publications volumes of Bernard's Liturgical Sermons (CF 51, 52, 53, 54). Having translated the nineteen sermons in *Sermons for the Summer Season* in 1991, Prof. Kienzle used her introduction to discuss the sermons' manuscript tradition and Bernard's method of composition; Professor Verbaal expanded both discussions in his introductions to the other three volumes. Between the two of them, they have greatly contributed to all of us through their illuminating discussions of Bernard's meticulous and thoughtful shaping of these sermons, revealing the attention Bernard gave to creating a whole thing out of a year's round of sermons.

Abbreviations

Biblical Books and Apocrypha

In the sermons, direct scriptural quotations, even with minor variations from the Vulgate text, are italicized. Scriptural phrases and allusions that are not quoted verbatim are noted but not italicized. Psalms are cited according to the Vulgate numbering.

Gen	Genesis	Song	Song of Songs
Exod	Exodus	Wis	Wisdom
Lev	Leviticus	Sir	Sirac (Ecclesiasticus)
Num	Numbers	Isa	Isaiah
Deut	Deuteronomy	Jer	Jeremiah
Josh	Joshua	Lam	Lamentations
Judg	Judges	Bar	Baruch
1 Sam	1st Samuel	Ezek	Ezekiel
2 Sam	2d Samuel	Dan	Daniel
1 Kgs	1st Kings	Hos	Hosea
2 Kgs	2d Kings	Joel	Joel
1 Chr	1st Chronicles	Amos	Amos
2 Chr	2d Chronicles	Jonah	Jonah
Ezra	Ezra	Mic	Micah
Neh	Nehemiah (2 Esdras)	Nah	Nahum
Tob	Tobit	Hab	Habbakuk
Jdt	Judith	Zeph	Zephaniah
Esth	Esther	Hag	Haggai
Job	Job	Zech	Zechariah
Ps(s)	Psalm(s)	Mal	Malachi
Prov	Proverbs	Sus	Susanna
Eccl	Ecclesiastes	1 Macc	1st Maccabees

Matt	Matthew	1 Tim	1st Timothy
Mark	Mark	Titus	Titus
Luke	Luke	Phlm	Philemon
John	John	Heb	Hebrews
Acts	Acts	Jas	James
Rom	Romans	1 Pet	1st Peter
1 Cor	1st Corinthians	2 Pet	2d Peter
2 Cor	2d Corinthians	1 John	1st John
Gal	Galatians	2 John	2d John
Eph	Ephesians	3 John	3d John
Phil	Philippians	Jude	Jude
Col	Colossians	Rev	Revelation
1 Thess	1st Thessalonians	LXX	Septuagint
2 Thess	2nd Thessalonians	VL	*Vetus Latina*

Series and Works

CCSL	Corpus Christianorum Series Latina
CF	Cistercian Fathers series
CS	Cistercian Studies series
CSEL	Corpus Scriptorum Ecclesiasticorum Latinorum
Dialogus	Sulpicius Severus. "Dialogvs Secundus (Tertius)." In *Opera*, edited by C. Halm. CSEL 1:180–216. Salzburg, 1866.
Ep(p)	Epistula(e)
Ep M	Sulpicius Severus. "Epistula 3." In *Opera*, edited by C. Halm. CSEL 1:146–51. Salzburg, 1866.
Hom in Ev	*Homiliae in Evangelia*, by Gregory the Great. Edited by Raymond Étaix. CCSL 141. Turnhout: Brepols Publishers, 1999.
Int Heb Nom	*Liber Interpretationis Hebraicorvm Nominum*, by Jerome. In S. *Hieronymi Presbyteri Opera*, Pars 1, 1. Edited by P. de Lagarde, G. Morin, M. Adriaen. CCSL 72. Turnholt: Brepols Publishers, 1959.
PG	Patrologia Graeca. Edited by J.-P. Migne.
PL	Patrologia Latina. Edited by J.-P. Migne.
Pro	Prologue
RB	Regula Benedicti; Rule of Saint Benedict
S(s)	Sermon(s), Sermo(nes)

SBOp	Sancti Bernardi Opera. Ed. Jean Leclercq, C. H. Talbot, and H. M. Rochais. Rome: Editiones Cistercienses, 1957–63.
SC	*Sermons on the Song of Songs*, by Bernard of Clairvaux. SBOp 1–2.
SSOC	Series Scriptorum Sacri Ordinis Cisterciensis
V Mart	Sulpicius Severus. *Vita Sancti Martini, Episcopi et Confessoris.* In *Opera*. Edited by C. Halm. CSEL 1:108–37. Salzburg, 1866.

Bernard's Sermons

Abb	Sermo ad abbates: SBOp 5:288–93; CF 54:85–90
Adv	Sermo in adventu Domini: SBOp 4:161–96; CF 51:3–42
And	Sermo in natali sancti Andreæ: SBOp 5:427–40; CF 54:249–65
Ann	Sermo in annuntiatione Domini: SBOp 5:13–42; CF 52:63–98
Asc	Sermo in ascensione Domini: SBOp 5:123–60; CF 53:29–68
Asspt	Sermo in assumptione BVM: SBOp 5:228–61; CF 54:14–54
Ben	Sermo in natali sancti Benedicti: SBOp 5:1–12; CF 52:53–62
Circ	Sermo in circumcisione Domini: SBOp 4:273–91; CF 51:133–53
Clem	Sermo in natali sancti Clementis: SBOp 5:412–17; CF 54:229–34
Conv	Sermo de conversione ad clericos: SBOp 4:69–116; CF 25:1–79
Ded	Sermo in dedicatione ecclesiæ: SBOp 5:370–98; CF 54:178–212
Div	Sermo de diversis: SBOp 6; CF 68
Epi	Sermo in epiphania Domini: SBOp 4:291–309; CF 51:154–75
4 HM	Sermo in feria iv hebdomadæ sanctæ: SBOp 5:56–67; CF 52:114–26
5 HM	Sermo in cena Domini: SBOp 5:67–72; CF 52:127–31
Humb	Sermo in obitu domni Humberti: SBOp 5:440–47; CF 54:266–73

In lab mess	Sermo in labore messis: SBOp 5:217–28; CF 54:1–13
Innoc	Sermo in festivitatibus sancti Stephani, sancti Ioannis, et sanctorum innocentium: SBOp 4:270–73; CF 51:129–32
JB	Sermo in nativitate sancti Ioannis Baptistæ: SBOp 5:176–84; CF 53:88–96
Mal	Sermo in transitu sancti Malachiæ episcopi: SBOp 5:417–23; CF 54:235–43
Mart	Sermo in festivitate sancti Martini episcopi: SBOp 5:399–412; CF 54:213–28
Mich	Sermo in festo sancti Michaëlis: SBOp 5:294–303; CF 54:91–100
Nat	Sermo in nativitate Domini: SBOp 4:244–70; CF 51:99–128
NatBVM	Sermo in nativitate BVM: SBOp 5:275–88; CF 54:70–84
1 Nov	Sermo in dominica I novembris: SBOp 5:304–26; CF 54:101–29
OAsspt	Sermo in dominica infra octavam assumptionis: SBOp 5:262–74; CF 54:55–69
OEpi	Sermo in octava epiphania Domini: SBOp 4:310–13; CF 51:176–79
OPasc	Sermo in octava paschæ: SBOp 5:112–21; CF 52:177–87
OS	Sermo in festivitate omnium sanctorum: SBOp 5:327–70; CF 54:130–77
Palm	Sermo in ramis palmarum: SBOp 5:42–55; CF 52:99–113
Pasc	Sermo in die paschæ: SBOp 5:73–111; CF 52:132–76
Pent	Sermo in die sancto pentecostes: SBOp 5:160–76; CF 53:69–87
P Epi	Sermo in dominica I post octavam epiphaniæ: SBOp 4:314–26; CF 51:180–93
4 p P	Sermo in dominica quarta post pentecosten: SBOp 5:202–5; CF 53:115–18
6 p P	Sermo in dominica sexta post pentecosten: SBOp 5:206–16; CF 53:119–30
PP	Sermo in festo ss. apostolorum Petri et Pauli: SBOp 5:188–201; CF 53:100–14
Pur	Sermo in purificatione BVM: SBOp 4:334–44; CF 52:3–13
Quad	Sermo in quadragesima: SBOp 4:353–80; CF 52:24–52
Rog	Sermo in rogationibus: SBOp 5:121–23; CF 53:27–28
SC	Sermo super Cantica canticorum: SBOp 1–2; CF 4, 7, 31, 40
Sept	Sermo in septuagesima: SBOp 4:344–52; CF 52:14–23
SP	Sermo in conversione sancti Pauli: SBOp 4:327–34; CF 51:194–202

VAnd	Sermo in vigilia sancti Andreæ: SBOp 5:423–26; CF 54:244–48
VNat	Sermo in vigilia nativitatis domini: SBOp 4:197–244; CF 51:43–98
VPP	Sermo in vigilia apostolorum Petri et Pauli: SBOp 5:185–87; CF 53:97–99

Bernard's Treatises

Apo	*Apologia ad Guillelmum abbatem.* SBOp 3:61–108; "St Bernard's Apologia to Abbot William." Translated by Michael Casey. In *The Works of Bernard of Clairvaux*, vol. 1, *Treatises I*. CF 1. Spencer, MA, and Shannon, Ireland: Cistercian Publications, 1970.
Conv	*Ad clericos ad conversione.* SBOp 4:69–116. "On Conversion, a Sermon to Clerics." Translated by Marie-Bernard Saïd. In Bernard of Clairvaux, *Sermons on Conversion*. CF 25. Kalamazoo, MI: Cistercian Publications, 1981. 1–79.
Csi	*De consideratione.* SBOp 3:379–493; *Five Books on Consideration: Advice to a Pope.* Translated by John D. Anderson and Elizabeth T. Kennan. *Bernard of Clairvaux*, vol. 13. CF 37. Kalamazoo, MI: Cistercian Publications, 1976.
Dil	*Liber de diligendo Deo.* SBOp 3:109–54; *On Loving God.* Translated by Robert Walton. CF 13B. Kalamazoo, MI: Cistercian Publications, 1995.
Gra	*De gratia et libero arbitrio.* SBOp 3:155–203; *On Grace and Free Choice.* Translated by Daniel O'Donovan. In *Bernard of Clairvaux, Treatises III.* CF 19. Kalamazoo, MI: Cistercian Publications, 1977. 3–111.
Miss	*Homiliae super "Missus est" in Laudibus Virginis Matris.* SBOp 4:3–58; *Magnificat: Homilies in Praise of the Blessed Virgin Mary.* Translated by Marie-Bernard Saïd. CF 18. Kalamazoo, MI: Cistercian Publications, 1979. 1–58.
Mor	*Ep de moribus et officiis episcoporum.* SBOp 7:100–31; *On Baptism and the Office of Bishops.* Translated by Pauline Matarasso. CF 67. Kalamazoo, MI: Cistercian Publications, 2004.
Pre	*De praecepto et dispensatione.* SBOp 3:241–94; "St Bernard's Book on Precept and Dispensation." Translated by Conrad Greenia. In *The Works of Bernard of Clairvaux*, vol. 1, *Treatises I*. CF 1. Kalamazoo, MI: Cistercian Publications, 1970. 71–150.

Tpl   *Liber ad milites templi (De laude novæ militiæ)*. SBOp 3:205–39. "In Praise of the New Knighthood." Translated by Daniel O'Donovan. In *The Works of Bernard of Clairvaux,* vol. 7, *Treatises III*. CF 19. Kalamazoo, MI: Cistercian Publications, 1977. 113–67.

V Mal   *Vita S. Malachiæ,* by Bernard of Clairvaux. SBOp 3:293–378; *The Life and Death of Saint Malachy the Irishman*. Translated by Robert T. Meyer. CS 10. Kalamazoo, MI: Cistercian Publications, 1978.

Bernard of Clairvaux

Sermons for the
Autumn Season

On the Time of Harvest[1]

Sermon One

How a Twofold Evil Works for Good

1. We seem to be poor, and indeed we are, but if we have received *the spirit that is of God, so that we may know the things that have been given to us by God,** great glory and great power accrue to us. *As many as received him, to them he gave power to become children of God.** Is not this the power of the children of God, that all things are subservient to us? For the apostle himself knew that *all things work together for good to them that love God.** But perhaps one of you will say "What has that to do with me?" and in the cowardice of his heart will reflect in this way: "God's children, in whom filial love toward him burns and affection* flourishes, certainly glory in their power, and they presume that all things work together for good to them, for they love God in truth. *But I am poor and needy,** lacking filial affection, without the devotion I should have."

But notice what follows. The one who speaks elsewhere leaves no room for despair in his Scriptures: *That through patience and consolation of the Scriptures we may have hope.** But the feeling you are looking for is

*1 Cor 2:12

*John 1:12

*Rom 8:28

*affectus

*Ps 39:18

*Rom 15:4

---

[1] *Sermo in labore messis* (In lab mess 1).

peace, not patience, and peace is found at home, not on the way; there is no need for those who are already there to be consoled by Scripture.

2. Let us therefore have hope through the patience and consolation of Scripture, although we cannot yet claim peace. For when the apostle said that all things worked together for good to those who love God, he added shrewdly, *to those who are called saints according to his purpose.** Do not let the mention of sanctity in this saying scare you, for he calls them saints not because of any merit of theirs but for his own purpose, nor through any feeling,* but for his own design, as the prophet says, *Preserve my soul, for I am holy.** Not even Paul himself, weighed down as he was by a corruptible body, thought he had taken hold of the sanctity you are considering. *This one thing I do,* he said, *forgetting the things which are behind and reaching out to the things which are before: I press on toward the mark of the prize of the heavenly calling.** You see that although he had not yet won the victory, he was already called to sanctity.

Therefore if you have decided in your heart to turn from evil and do good,* to hold to what you have begun and go forward always to what is better, and to repent and make amends as far as you can, if you sometimes do what is less righteous (such is human frailty) and are determined not to persist in it, you will without doubt be a saint, but in the meantime you must still cry, *Preserve my soul, for I am holy.**

3. Do you wish to know how all things work together for good* for saints such as this? I shall not mention them all separately, for the hour does not permit a long sermon to be put forth. Time is passing us by, and the time for Vespers has arrived. Hear therefore a short explanation of how everything is to our advantage and all things work together for good. *Enemies are our judges,** so if they are for us, who can be

*Rom 8:28

*affectionem
*Ps 85:2

*Phil 3:13-14

*Ps 36:27

*Ps 85:2

*Rom 8:28

*Deut 32:31

against us?* If our enemies act in our interest, how can it be that all things do not act with them? *Rom 8:31

4. Now clearly there are two kinds of enemy who oppose us, an obvious twofold evil: what we do and what we suffer. They are, to put it more plainly, the guilt and the penalty. So although both are against us, both can be for us if we wish, for the first will free us from the second, and likewise the second will aid us considerably against the first. I mean, look, we are pierced in the heart as well as in the bed of our consciences* over past sins, but our penitence, with the penalty that we voluntarily undergo, soothes our conscience and grinds down the gnawing teeth of sins, giving us the hope of pardon. Moreover, it drives away not only the things that are past but also the things that are to come, for it wards off the faults that assail us and annihilates some of them so that they can rarely or never rear their poisonous heads. *see Ps 4:5

Thus the penalty acts for us against the guilt, so that it exists no longer, or at least is less. But the guilt, too, acts in such a way that the penalty either exists no more or is less. Not that it is entirely nonexistent, even if it is considerably less, because that would not be in our interests, but that it is no punishment, or less of a punishment, so that it is not burdensome at all, or at least less burdensome. For whoever feels the burden of sin to the full and the damage to the soul will either feel the bodily punishment less or will not feel it at all; nor will such a one find it difficult in the future to avoid sins known to have been destroyed in the past. For holy David did not think about the wrongs done by the servant who taunted him, because he was mindful of the son who was pursuing him.* *2 Sam 16:5-13

On the Time of Harvest[1]

Sermon Two

Of the Two Tables

1. This labor, my brothers, reminds us of our exile, of our poverty, and, no less, of our roughness.* Why are we killed every day, in lengthy vigils, labor, and troubles?* We were not created for this, were we? Far from it. Granted, humans were born by labor,* but they were hardly created for labor. Their birth is in crime, and therefore also in punishment. We must all cry out with the prophet, *I was conceived in wickedness, and in sin did my mother conceive me.** The first creation was far different from this, for God did not create crime or punishment. And Scripture says plainly about that which is more powerful than all things, namely death, *Through the wickedness of the devil death came into the world*, and elsewhere, *God did not create death*,* and so on.

Therefore, just as the eye does not close while the hands are at work nor the ear cease to listen, so all the more while the body labors the mind is intent on its work and takes no rest. Therefore while people work they ponder why they work, so that the very punishment they suffer reminds them of the crime

*iniquitatis
*see Ps 43:22;
2 Cor 11:27

*Job 5:7

*Ps 50:7

*Wis 2:24;
1:13

[1] *Sermo in labore messis* (In lab mess 2).

they committed to deserve it; when they see the binding covering the wounds, they consider the wounds themselves under the bandages. So, thinking like this, we are humbled under the mighty hand of God,* and our minds are also full of sweetness and goodness, showing them to be pitiful in his eyes. So Scripture warns us, *Have pity on your soul, pleasing God.** For there is no doubt that the wretchedness that is pleasing to God can easily get God's pity. We are not going to say why we should have pity on our souls; unless we foolishly deceive ourselves, much can be found in them that needs pity.

*see 1 Pet 5:6

*Sir 30:24

2. Yet one thing I do say, as an example of how you might similarly approach the other things yourselves. Are we not like people placed between two tables, feasting from the one while considering the other? We are; we are exactly like that. From where come laughter, jokes, levity, arrogance, pride?* Or perhaps we do not notice the tables, we do not think of the feast, we do not see the delicacies? I see some living a pampered life amid all the good things of this world, but then I notice others to whom Christ has appointed a kingdom where they eat and drink at his table in his Father's Kingdom.* In both cases I see human beings like myself, I see brothers, but—what a damnable thing!—I cannot extend my hand to either! I am kept away from each table, from the one by the bonds of my profession, from the other by the bonds of my body, so that I dare not go to the lower one and I cannot reach the higher. What else can I do but eat the bread of sorrow,* so that my tears may be my meat day and night,* and hope that one of those who eat in heaven may be moved to pity and throw some crumbs of those delicacies into the mouths of barking puppies under the table!*

*Sir 23:5

*Luke 22:29

*Ps 126:2
*Ps 41:4

*Matt 15:27

And there is a lesser thing we can look at, about which we can pity ourselves: the regard we give to those whom we know to be living a pampered life in this world is a sign of a sick mind, and such a disposition* in a spiritual soul in no way pleases me. For the one is far removed from true judgment* who considers those happy whom he ought to mourn as wretched, those who sin and do not repent—the one who thinks himself unhappy not by consent of judgment but by consent of feeling* that he is not like them, when he ought rather to hope that all should be as he is.†

3. Only such a way of thinking as this is praiseworthy, that people, either for the love or the fear of God, should resolve to bear patiently the very thing they esteem a misery and say to God with devotion, *Because of the words of your lips I have kept to the hard ways.** This way of thinking is proper for beginners, like milk for babes. But when the soul begins to grow to maturity and with feeling to follow reasonable judgment,* it will doubtless consider all things but loss and count them as dung,* grieving with the prophet over people who embrace dung!*

Such souls, though, will despise all these things with a holy and humble pride and, established in utter noble-mindedness, will call the people who have all these things not blessed but miserable; but blessed is the one whose God is the Lord.* And truly while they pity some in comparison with themselves, if they look to the riches of heaven and the eternal pleasures at the right hand of God, they will see that in comparison with others they must pity themselves!* So it happens that the one who previously poured out tears over the things that are below and kept lamenting* *for your sake I die every day** now weeps even more copiously for the things that are above, saying, *alas; how long will this damnable exile last!**

*affectio
*a iudicio veritatis

*non sane consensu iudicii, sed affectionis sensu
†1 Cor 7:7

*Ps 16:4

*affectione sequi iudicium rationis
*Phil 3:8
*Lam 4:5

*Ps 143:15

*Ps 15:11

*Judg 1:15
*Ps 43:22

*Ps 119:5

On the Time of Harvest[1]

Sermon Three

This is the generation of those who seek the Lord, of those who seek the face of the God of Jacob.*   *Ps 23:6

1. Worn out by all sorts of crowds seeking* all kinds of things, how gladly do I come today to this little corner* to refresh my spirit! Thanks be to God, I have not been disappointed in my desire or deceived in my hope. I have desired to see, I have seen, and my soul has been melted!* *I am filled with comfort; I abound with joy.*† My whole being blesses the name of the Lord,# *and all my bones say, Lord, who is like you?*‡ To tell you the truth, those I saw with my bodily eyes when I was on my way here, still at a distance, are those whom the prophet foresaw in the spirit, and immediately there came to mind what he had uttered with his mouth, so that I sang this psalm with him: *This is the generation of those who seek** *the Lord!*†

    *quaerentibus
    *cuneus

    **liquefacta est anima mea;* Song 5:6
    †2 Cor 7:4
    #Ps 102:1
    ‡Ps 34:10

    *quaerentium
    †Ps 23:6

2. Many are the human generations, and if I am not mistaken, this is the third generation that now appears and flourishes among you. For the first generation did not seek the Lord, nor was it sought by

---

[1] *Sermo in labore messis* (In lab mess 3).

the Lord; indeed mothers bore each of their children in forgetfulness and the accusation of sin. The second generation followed immediately, showing us the necessary remedy by water and the spirit.* That was the generation not of those who sought the Lord but of those who were nevertheless sought, because they did not yet know how to seek the Lord, nor were they strong enough to seek him. Therefore he has sought us and possessed us in the second generation, that we should be the people of his possession.* And if the older brother should murmur and be eaten up by envy, he is told that *it was right to make merry and be glad, for this your brother had perished and has been found.**

3. Now the Lord has sought us without delay, so that he might be sought at a seasonable time, when he could be not only sought but found. Woe to us who have for so long hidden ourselves and neglected to seek life, to seek him who alone *is good to those who seek him,** *to the soul who hopes in him!*† And woe to you, *evil and uncouth generation, wicked and adulterous generation,** still seeking a lie and loving vanity and not keeping faith, to which you were betrothed in truth. Does this generation have no need to be born again, to be created afresh?* Indeed it has great need. A people who have become the offspring of vipers* have all the more need to enter again into their mothers' wombs and be born,* in that their latter deeds are known to be worse than their former!*

Thank God for the grace and, if I can put it this way, the mercy that is more than gratuitous,* which overwhelms with its kindnesses without measure not only the undeserving but also, beyond measure, those who are wicked and ungrateful. Thanks to him who has begotten you again to the hope of life so that you might receive the adoption of sons.* For *of his own will he has begotten us with the word of truth.*† If he begot you before by the sacrament of godliness,# still, although

---

*John 3:5

*1 Pet 2:9

*Luke 15:32

*Lam 3:25
†Ps 77:8

*Matt 16:4

*John 3:7
*Matt 23:33

*John 3:4
*2 Pet 2:20

*gratias ipsi gratiae et . . . plus quam gratuitae miserationi

*1 Pet 1:3;
Gal 4:5
†Jas 1:18
#1Tim 3:16

the begetter was willing, yet the begotten could not be willing, in whom there was no exercise of the will, no use of reason, and no recognition of the begetting or knowledge of the begetter. But now finally a willing generation produces the willing sacrifice, according to the saying, *I will joyfully offer you sacrifice and will praise your name, O Lord, for it is good.**   *Ps 53:8

4. *This is the generation of those who seek the Lord.**   *Ps 23:6
Do I mean those who seek, or those who have? Both those who have and those who seek: those who don't have can't seek. But what do they have, or, rather, what do they seek? Or, more important, how do they have, how do they seek? Being begotten by the Word, they possess the Word.* Is not the Word the Lord? Hear   *Jas 1:18
what John says: *and the word was God.** What more can   *John 1:1
they seek, the generation of those who have the Lord? Consider what follows in the psalm: *This is the generation of those who seek, who seek the face of the God of Jacob.** What they have and what they seek is the same,   *Ps 23:6
because the Word of the Father is one and the same with the splendor of the Father's glory.* One who has   *Heb 1:3
not been sought can be possessed, but in no way can such a one be sought without being possessed.

This is what Wisdom says: *Whoever eats me will hunger still.** Furthermore, the Father is even able to give   *Sir 24:29
himself to the one who has not sought, he who, as we saw above, through his abundant grace and sweet blessing seeks and goes to meet those who have not yet the strength to seek!* For no one is able to seek   *Ps 20:4
except the one who already possesses, because *no one comes to me unless the Father draws him.** The one who   *John 6:44
draws is present and yet in some way not present, for he draws nowhere else but to himself. For at no time and no place is the Father present by faith without the Son, so that he may attract by beauty.*   **ut ad speciem trahat*

How shall my spirit then not rejoice?† How shall   †Luke 1:47
it be other than utterly joyful among this generation

of those who seek the Lord? Is violent hunger not the sure proof that Wisdom has been tasted? That he draws you so strongly to himself is to me the strongest argument, without any shadow of doubt, that you already have him whom you thus seek, and that he dwells in you. This impetuosity is not within human possibility; it is his right hand that gives strength,* and it is to him that you must always cry, *Draw us after you; we will run in the fragrance of your ointments.** I do not say that this is a normal way of speaking, nor do we seek any other proof that you have Christ in you,* save that you seek Christ.

<small>*Ps 117:16</small>

<small>*Song 1:3</small>

<small>*2 Cor 13:3</small>

5. You see, brothers, what sort of spirit you have received, the spirit that is of God, so that you may know what gifts have been given to you by God.* We have heard of the position held by the apostles, the prophets, and the angels, and I do not think we can aspire to anything higher than them. I think, though, that I find something of each of them in you, and something great. For who would hesitate to say that the celibate life is the heavenly life, the angelic life? What will all the elect be in the resurrection if not what you yourselves are now, like the angels of God in heaven, utterly abstinent with regard to marriage?*

<small>*see 1 Cor 2:12</small>

<small>*Matt 22:30</small>

My brothers, what you embrace is the pearl of great price!* You embrace purity as a way of life, a way of life that makes you like saints and members of the household of God!* As the Scripture says, *Incorruptibility brings one near to God.** So it is not by your own merit but by the grace of God that you are what you are:* as regards chastity and purity, angels on earth, or rather citizens of heaven, but pilgrims on earth in the meantime. For *while we are in this body we are away from the Lord.**

<small>*Matt 13:46</small>

<small>*Eph 2:19</small>
<small>*Wis 6:20</small>

<small>*1 Cor 15:10</small>

<small>*2 Cor 5:6</small>

6. What shall we say about prophecy? Truth says, *the law and the prophets until John.** But after John it was a disciple of Truth, not an adversary, who said, *Now*

<small>*Luke 16:16</small>

we know in part, and we prophesy in part.* Prophecy has become inactive because now we know, yet it is not entirely inactive; it still exists in some measure. *When what is perfect comes, then that which is in part shall be done away.** Those who were prophets before John prophesied both comings of the Lord, and neither moment of salvation came from knowledge, but both in prophecy.

    Great indeed is the kind of prophecy I see you are dedicated to! Great is the pursuit of prophesying I see you have surrendered yourselves to! What kind? Not to observe the things that are seen but those that are unseen is, according to the apostle, without a doubt to prophesy.* *To walk in the spirit*, to live by faith, to seek those things that are above, not those that are upon earth, forgetting those things that are behind and stretching forward to those things that are before,*—these are for the most part prophecy. Otherwise, how is our conversation in heaven, except by the spirit of prophecy?† For the ancient prophets did not live among the people of their time, but transcending those days in the strength and vehemence of a certain spirit,* they rejoiced to see the day of the Lord; and they saw and rejoiced in it.*

    7. But let us hear what the apostles declare: *Look, we have abandoned all and followed you.** If it is all right to boast, let us boast; but if we are wise, we will take care to do it before God.* For this is the true boasting: *let the one who boasts boast in the Lord.** For it is not that we have excelled by our own power, but it is the Lord who has done this thing.* He that is mighty has done great things for us so that our soul may truly show how great the Lord is!* It is by his great gift that we may follow with great pride the great plan that the great apostles boasted in! If I too want to boast in this, I am not a fool for doing so, and to tell the truth, there are some right here who have left more than a ship and some nets!* What does this mean? That the apostles

*1 Cor 13:9

*1 Cor 13:10

*2 Cor 4:18

*see Gal 5:16; Rom 1:17; Col 3:1-2; Phil 3:13
†Phil 3:20

*Ezek 1:12
*John 8:56

*Matt 19:27

*Rom 4:2
*1 Cor 1:31

*Deut 32:27

*Luke 1:49, 46

*Matt 4:21-22

left all, but to follow the Lord present in the flesh. Do not take our word for it; we are on solid ground if we hear the Lord himself: *Because you saw me, Thomas, you believed; blessed are those who have not seen yet have believed.** Perhaps this will be seen to be a more excellent prophecy because it looks not toward temporal things, which will pass sooner or later, but toward things that are spiritual and eternal?* Just the same, the treasure of chastity is brighter in earthen vessels,* and virtue is in any case more laudable in weak flesh!

8. When therefore we live in this flesh like angels, with prophetic hope in the heart and apostolic perfection in both, what a mighty heap of grace it is! What will you give back to the Lord for all he has given back to you?* It is an exalted position, but then the fall is all the more dangerous! Are there not three heavens to which we ascend? *So let the one who stands take care lest he fall. I saw,* he says, *Satan falling as lightning from heaven.** He fell from on high; he was broken and crushed; *his wound is incurable,** he has become *a breath that passes and does not return.**

Will you also go away?* Satan has fallen; will you also fall? How much better it is for you to walk in the ways of the Lord and to stand firm in the grace you are already standing in.* For the person who walks in the way of sinners is not blessed.* *Blessed* rather *is the one whose help comes from you,* Lord.* For *they go from strength to strength, to see the God of gods in Sion,** to see the prosperity of your chosen ones, so that they may glory with your descendents.* Truly, they are heirs, they are gods, and sons of the Most High, all of them!†

9. And so, my brothers, since truly and beyond all doubt *this is the generation of those who seek the Lord, of those who seek the face of the God of Jacob,** what more am I to say to you than what the prophet himself said—*Let the heart of those who seek the Lord rejoice. Seek the Lord and his strength, seek his face always,**—and what

another said, *if you will seek, seek.** What is the meaning of this, *if you will seek, seek*? *Seek him in simplicity of heart.** Nothing as much as him, nothing except him, nothing after him. *Seek him in simplicity of heart*. Simplicity of nature asks simplicity of heart. Finally *his conversation is with the simple.** *A double-minded man is unstable in all his ways.** He whom you seek cannot be found by those who *believe for a while and in time of temptation fall away.** He is eternity! Without diligent seeking, he will not be found.

Woe, then, *to the sinner who lives a double life*, for *no one can serve two lords.** For true integrity, true perfection, true plenitude has no love for duplicity. You are unworthy of him who offers himself to be found unless you seek him with a perfect heart. Now if *a dog that returns to its vomit and a sow that once washed returns to rolling in the mire* are loathsome,* and if God spews the tepid from his mouth,* where will the hypocrite be, and the betrayer? If he is accursed who negligently does the Lord's work,* what shall the one merit who does it deceitfully?* Let us flee this duplicity, beloved, and let us beware at all times of the leaven of the Pharisees.*

God is truth and requires that those who seek him do so in spirit and in truth.* If we do not wish to seek the Lord in vain,* let us seek him with truth, frequency, and perseverance and seek nothing in place of him nor along with him, nor let us exchange him for any other thing! *For it is easier for heaven and earth to pass away** than that one who seeks like this should not find,* that one who asks like this should not obtain, and that to one who knocks like this it should not be opened.

*Isa 21:12

*Wis 1:1

*Prov 3:32
*Jas 1:8

*Luke 8:13

*Sir 2:14;
Matt 6:24

*2 Pet 2:22
*Rev 3:16

*1 Pet 4:18
*Jer 48:10

*Matt 16:6

*John 4:24
*Isa 45:19

*Luke 16:17
*Matt 7:8

On the Solemnity of the Assumption
of the Blessed Virgin Mary[1]

Sermon One

Of the Double Assumption

1. The glorious Virgin who mounts to the heavens today has without a doubt heaped joy upon joy for the citizens of the world above. For it is she whose voice of greeting makes those whom the maternal womb still encloses leap with joy!* And if the soul of an unborn child melted† when Mary spoke, how great do you think was the joy of the citizens of heaven when they succeeded in hearing her voice, seeing her face, and enjoying her blessed presence?

*Luke 1:41
†*liquefacta est*

But what, dearly beloved, does this solemnity of her assumption hold for us? What is there for us to be happy about? What is the reason for our displays of joy? The whole world has been made bright by the presence of Mary, so that the heavenly country itself shines more brightly by the radiant light of the virginal torch. *Thanksgiving and the voice of praise** rightly resound in the heavens. Doesn't it seem better for us, though, to beat our breasts rather than clap our hands? For as much as heaven exults at her presence, does it not follow that our world below should mourn her absence just as much?

*Isa 51:3

[1] *Sermo in assumptione Beatae Virginis Mariae* (Asspt 1).

But enough of this sad contrariness! Truly, here we have no abiding city!* Instead, we seek that to which blessed Mary has come today. If we are true citizens of that city, it is fitting that we should remember it even by the rivers of Babylon,* that we should join in its pleasures and share its joy, especially that which so fully makes glad the city of God,* and should feel the showers that water the earth.* Our queen has gone before us; she has gone before and has been caught up in glory, so that we may follow her as servants follow their mistress, crying, *draw us after you: we shall run in the odor of your ointments!** Someone to plead our cause† has been sent before us in our journey, she who is the mother of the judge, the mother of pity! She will transact the business of our salvation effectively and with prayer.

*Heb 13:14

*see Ps 136:1

*Ps 45:5
*Ps 71:6

*Song 1:3
†*advocatam*

2. Our earth has today sent to heaven a precious gift, that by giving and receiving a happy bond of friendship human affairs should be joined to the divine; the earthly should be joined to the heavenly and the highest to the lowest. For the exalted fruit of the earth has gone up to the place* from where all good and perfect gifts* come down. Therefore the Blessed Virgin, when she goes up on high, will give gifts to humans.* Why should she not? At least she will not lack the opportunity, nor the will. She is the Queen of Heaven, she is merciful; she is the Mother of the only-begotten Son of God. Nothing can so commend the greatness of her power and holiness, and unless you think that the Son of God does not honor his mother, do you doubt entirely that the womb of Mary, in which God is Love rested bodily for nine months, has passed over into the attachment of love?*

*Isa 4:2
*Jas 1:17
*Eph 4:8

**in affectum caritatis transisse*

3. I say this for our sakes, brothers, knowing that it is difficult, weak as we are, to find that perfect charity that does not seek its own.* I will not speak of the blessings that we receive on account of her glorification;

*1 Cor 13:5

if we love her we will instead rejoice because she goes to the Son.* I put it plainly: we will congratulate her—unless, God forbid, we are found to be total ingrates to the one who has found* grace. He whom she first received when he entered the village* of this world† today receives# her as she enters the holy city.‡ Can you imagine with what honor, what exultation, what glory? There is no place in the world more worthy than the temple of the virginal womb in which Mary received the Son of God, nor is there any place in the heavens better than the royal throne where Mary's Son set Mary on high today. How happy is each of these receptions,* how defying description, how surpassing thought!

Why do you think it is we read in church today the gospel about the woman—blessed is she among women!—who welcomed the Savior?* I think so that what we are celebrating might to some extent be rightly assessed* in the light of that reception or, better, so that next to the inestimable glory of that one, the woman who received Jesus, this one, the woman whom Jesus received, should also be considered of inestimable glory. For who, even if speaking with the tongues of men and of angels,* can explain how, by the operation of the Holy Spirit* and by the overshadowing of the power of the Most High, the Word of God, by whom all things were made,* was made flesh, how the God of Majesty, who the created world cannot contain,[2]* was made a man and was enclosed within a virgin's womb?

4. Who can imagine how glorious appears the queen of the world today and the devout affection of the multitude of heaven's hosts that goes forth to meet her; with what songs she is led to the throne of glory, and with what a gentle expression, with what a cheerful

---

[2] Gradual *Benedicta et venerabilis*, in Mass BVM.

*John 14:28

*inventrici
*castellum
†Luke 10:38
#susceperat . . . suscipitur
‡Matt 27:53

*susceptio

*Luke 10:38-42

*aestimetur

*1 Cor 13:1
*John 1:14

*John 1:3

*1 Kgs 8:27

face, with what holy embraces she is received* by her Son and exalted above all creatures with the honor that such a mother deserves and with the glory that befits such a Son? As a nursing infant he would plant happy kisses on her lips,[3] as she, a virgin mother, played patty-cake with him, holding him in her lap! But can we think of anything happier than what she heard from the mouth of him who sits at the Father's right hand, who today received her with a blessing when she ascended to the throne of glory, singing the nuptial song, *Let Him kiss me with the kiss of his mouth?** The generation of the Christ, the assumption of Mary: who can describe them?* As much grace is gained for others on earth as the unique glory she has obtained in heaven. For if *eye hath not seen nor ear heard, and the things that God has prepared for those who love him have not entered into the heart of humans,** who shall say what he has prepared for her who bore him and who loves him more than any, as is clear to all? Happy indeed is Mary, and many times happy, both when she received the Savior and when she is received by the Savior. On the one hand, the wonderful dignity of the maidenhood of the Mother of God; on the other, the adorable honor of her majesty.

*suscepta

**Song 1:1*

**Isa 53:8*

**1 Cor 2:9*

He entered, Scripture says, *into a certain village,* and a certain woman received him into her house.** But this day should be kept free for praises, a day for celebrating a festival. The words of this reading give us plentiful material, and tomorrow also, when we come together, we shall share what will be generously given us from above, so that not only is the affection of devotion awakened by the memory of such a virgin, but our characters are built up to advance in the monastic life,* to the praise and glory of her Son, our Lord, *who is God above all, blessed for all ages.**

*castellum
**Luke 10:38*

*conversationis
**Rom 9:5*

---

[3] Ambrosius Autpertus, *Sermo* (PL 39:2131, PL 101:1303).

On the Solemnity of the Assumption of
the Blessed Virgin Mary[1]

Sermon Two

Of Cleaning, Adorning, and Furnishing the House

*Luke 10:18

1. **J**esus *entered into a certain village.** It seems to me that the exclamation of the prophet should be quoted at this point: O Israel, how great is the house of the Lord and how vast the place of his pos-

*Bar 3:24

session!* Is it not vast when the whole wide earth is only a village compared to it? Is it not a vast country and a region immeasurable when it is said that the Savior coming from there into earth's sphere is en-

*castellum

tering a village!* (Unless perhaps someone wants to understand the village as the house of the strong man fully armed, the prince of this world, whose goods

*Luke 11:21;
John 12:31;
Matt 12:29
†Heb 4:11

a stronger man comes to plunder.)* Let us hasten to enter into the fullness of that blessedness,† my brothers, where no one crowds out another, so that we can comprehend with all saints what is its breadth and

*Eph 3:18

length and depth and height.* And let us not give up hope about this, seeing that he himself who dwells in the heavenly country, even the Creator, does not shun the narrow confines of this earthly village.

---

[1] *Sermo in assumptione Beatæ Virginis Mariæ* (Asspt 2).

2. But why do we say that he entered into a village? He entered into the narrowest inn of a virgin's womb. Indeed *a certain woman received him into her house.** Happy the woman who was worthy to receive not the spies of Jericho* but the strong man, the despoiler of the foolish one who is as changeable as the moon,* not the messengers of Jesus son of Nun, but truly Jesus the Son of God.

*Luke 10:38

*Josh 2:1
*Sir 27:12

Happy the woman, I say, whose house when the Savior has entered is found clean* but clearly not empty—unless someone can say she is empty whom the angel greets as full of grace.* Nor is this all, but he also says that the Holy Spirit will overshadow her.* Why do you think this should be, unless he is to fill her even more? Why unless so that she who was already full in herself when the Spirit came should, when he overshadows her, be overly filled and overflowing for us? May the fragrance of her graces flow upon us!* May we all receive of such fullness!† For surely she is our mediator, she it is through whom we have received your mercy, O God,* and she it is through whom we have received the Lord Jesus into our homes. We each have our own fortress, our own house, and Wisdom knocks at everyone's door. If anyone opens, he will enter and dine with him.* There is a well-known proverb being spread around generally by word of mouth but even more from heart to heart: "He keeps a sound fortress who cares for his body."* The wise one does not put it exactly that way, but rather, *Keep your heart with all diligence, because from it comes life.** †

*Matt 12:44

*Luke 1:28
*Luke 1:35

*Song 4:16
†John 1:16

*Ps 47:10

*Rev 3:20

*Bonum servat castellum qui custodierit corpus suum
*Prov 4:23
†omni custodia serva cor tuum, quia ex ipso vita procedit

3. But let us agree with popular opinion: the one who cares for the body keeps a sound fortress. We must ask what in the world is meant by keeping a sound fortress. Do you think that the soul has done a good job keeping the fortress of her body sound when she relinquishes her power over its members

to the enemy, as though taking part in a conspiracy? For there are those who make a pact with death, who enter into an agreement with the lower regions.* It is said that *the beloved has grown fat and recalcitrant: fat, thick, and bloated.** Clearly, this is the safekeeping praised by people who *sin in the desires of their flesh.**

What do you think, my brothers? Should we agree with popular opinion in this matter? God forbid. Let us rather ask Paul, since he is the mighty commander of a spiritual army! Tell us, apostle, who keeps your fortress safe? He answers, *This is how I run—not in fits and starts—this is how I fight—not as if punching the air! I punish my body and drive it back into subjection; otherwise, I am afraid it should turn out that after having preached to others I myself should end up rejected!** And in another place, *Let not sin reign in your mortal body, obedient to its desires.** Truly safekeeping is expedient, and happy the soul who keeps her body safe so that the enemy shall never claim it.

For there was a time when the enemy held my fortress captive to his impious tyranny, commanding my powers or, if you will, all my members. My present desolation and poverty shows how much damage he did to them then. Alas! He left neither the wall of self-control nor the bulwark of patience. He destroyed the vineyards, he reaped the crops, he uprooted the trees;* yes, even my own eye plundered my soul! In short, *unless the Lord had helped me, my soul would soon be living in the lower regions!** And I mean the lowest of the lower regions,* where there is no praise† or exit!#

4. Then, to go on, neither prison nor hell was lacking to my members. Seized from the very beginning by conspiracy and foul betrayal, my soul was handed over as a prisoner in her own home, and her torturers were none other than those of her own household. For conscience was the prison, and reason and memory the torturers, and they are cruel, stern, and

*Isa 28:15

*Deut 32:5
*Ps 10:3

*1 Cor 9:26-27

*Rom 6:12

*Ps 79:14; Lev 19:9
*Ps 93:17
*Ps 85:13
†*confessio*
#Ps 6:6

pitiless—but not as much as those who roar, ready to devour,* to whom she was about to be handed over!   *see 1 Pet 5:8

But *blessed is the Lord, who has not given* me *as a prey to their teeth!* Blessed,* I repeat, *is the Lord, who has visited and redeemed.** For when the evil one made haste to throw my soul into the deepest dungeon and to burn my fortress with everlasting fire so that there should be a fitting revenge for my faithless limbs, a stronger one than he came upon him.* Jesus came into the village* and bound the strong man, despoiling his goods,* so that the one who was previously held in dishonor should be held in honor.* He broke down the gates of brass and crushed the iron bars,* leading the shackled one from the prison house and from the shadow of death.²* Having come out, that one admits his guilt: this is the broom by which the prison is cleansed and adorned.* Then, with the monastic practices, as with beautiful verdant rushes, he changes the prison into a home again.*

*Ps 123:6
*Luke 1:68

*Luke 11:22
*Luke 10:38
*Matt 12:29
*Rom 9:21
*Ps 106:16

*Isa 42:7; Ps 106:14

*Ps 99:4; Matt 12:44
*Luke 10:38

Now a woman keeps her house so she can have a place to receive the one to whom she stands indebted for the many favors shown her. So I hate to think what will happen to her if she refuses to receive him and, if she does entertain him, if she does not compel him to remain with her, for evening is at hand.* For the one who was sent out returns and finds the house clean and adorned, but empty!*

*Luke 24:29

*Matt 12:44

5. But if the woman neglects to make her house fit for entertaining the Savior, she will be left with an empty house. How can that be? you ask. Can the house, cleansed of its former deeds by confession and adorned by the observation of the monastic practices, be judged an unworthy vessel of grace, unworthy of the Savior's coming? Certainly, if on the surface it is

---

² Antiphon O *clavis*, for Dec. 20.

cleaned and spread with green rushes, as I have said, but inside it is covered in mud! For who would think of receiving the Lord in the whitewashed sepulcher of the dead,* which looks beautiful from the outside but inside is all full of filth and corruption?* Supposing that, pleased by its appearance, he began to enter, granting the first favor of his visitation to such a one; will he not draw back from it in distaste? Will he not hasten away, calling out, *I sink in the deep mire, and there is no place to stand?**

    *Matt 23:25, 27
    *Matt 23:27

    *Ps 68:3

It has the appearance of goodness but not the reality, the likeness but not the substance. Indeed the mere entry from outside of the one who penetrates all things and whose dwelling is in the human heart cannot give any support to a tenuous, superficial, manner of life.* And if the spirit of discipline† does not dwell in the body subject to sin, he not only turns aside but hastens away from the false one and keeps himself aloof. Or is it only a detestable lie that if you scratch at the surface of a fault you will not root it out completely? You may be sure that it will flourish the more, and the evil enemy, who was thrown out, will enter the empty house with seven others worse than himself!* *The dog returns to his vomit;*† he will be an object of hatred and will become many times over the child of hell.* He has fallen into the same filth as before, just as *the sow that has been washed returns to her wallowing in the mire.**

    conversatio
    †Wis 1:5

    *Matt 12:44–45
    †2 Pet 2:22

    *Matt 23:15

    *2 Pet 2:22

6. Do you wish to see a house clean, adorned, and empty? Look at the people who have confessed and abandoned the sins that brought them to judgment* and now apply their hands only to the work they are commanded to do; led by habit while their hearts are completely dry, they are just like *Ephraim, a heifer trained to enjoy threshing.** For they do not pass over one jot or tittle of external things, which have little value, but they strain at a gnat and swallow a camel.*

    *1 Tim 5:24

    *Hos 10:11

    *Matt 23:24

For in their hearts they are slaves to their own will; they foster avarice, are greedy for glory, and love ambition, cherishing within all these vices, or even just one of them.

Falsehood deceives itself,* but *God is not mocked.*† You may sometimes see a person so wrapped up in the self as to become deceived, taking no notice of the worm that feeds within. What is superficial survives, and such a person thinks that all his affairs are secure. *Strangers have devoured his strength, and he did not know it,* said the prophet.* He says, *Because I am rich and want for nothing,* when he is *poor, wretched, and miserable.** But sooner or later pus that lay hidden in the ulcer will ooze out, and you will see the tree, cut down but not rooted out, sprouting into thicker growth. If we want to avoid this danger we must put the axe to the root of the tree, not to its branches.* Let us not be content only with corporeal practice, which in any case is of little value,* but with goodness and spiritual practice, which are useful in all cases.

*Ps 26:12
†Gal 6:7

*Hos 7:9
*Rev 3:17

*Luke 3:9

*1 Tim 4:8

7. *A certain woman named Martha received him into her house, and she had a sister named Mary.** They are sisters, and they must be collaborators in the same enterprise. The one is occupied with much serving, the other intent upon the words of the Lord.* The adorning falls to Martha, but fulfillment* to Mary. She is empty for the Lord, so that her house be not empty. But to whom can we ascribe the cleaning, so that we may find the house in which the Savior is received clean, adorned, and not empty?* Let us give that job to Lazarus, if you think it good, for since he is their brother, by right he shares ownership of the house in common with his sisters. I speak of Lazarus, whom the voice of power wakes up from the dead after four days, when he was already stinking,* so that he suitably enough bears the pattern of a penitent. Let the Savior enter the house, then, and let him visit it frequently, and let the penitent

*Luke 10:38

*Luke 10:40
*impletio

*Matt 12:44

*John 11:39-43

Lazarus clean it, Martha adorn it, and Mary, given to internal contemplation, fill it.

8. But maybe some attentive person will ask why there is no further mention of Lazarus in the gospel reading prescribed for today. I don't think this is in any way at odds with the suggested comparison. For the Spirit, wanting us to understand that the home was virginal, was accordingly silent about penitence, which is always connected with evil. So let it never be said that this house has any inherent impurity for Lazarus's broom to go after! Even if Mary inherited original sin from her parents, nevertheless Christian piety forbids us to believe that she was less sanctified in the womb than Jeremiah was*—or, rather, not filled to a greater extent than John with the Holy Spirit*— or that her birth should not be celebrated with festive praises. Finally, it is well known by all sorts of folks that Mary was cleansed from original sin only by grace and that now only grace in baptism washes away that stain, just as formerly only the stone knife of circumcision would cut it away.

If, as is absolutely right to believe, Mary had no personal sin, then penitence was also far from an innocent heart. So let Lazarus be among those whose consciences need to be cleansed from dead works;* let him withdraw to be among the wounded who sleep in their tombs,* so that Martha and Mary may be found in a virgin's bridal chamber. For it is Mary who for three months humbly served Elizabeth, who was heavy with child and heavy with years,* she who *kept, pondering in her heart* all the words which were spoken by her Son.†

9. Let no one be surprised that the woman who received the Lord was called not Mary but Martha, since in this unique and most high Mary we find both the activity of Martha and the engaged leisure of Mary.* Yes, *all the glory of the king's daughter is from within*, but nevertheless *wrapped in golden borders, richly embroidered*.†

*Jer 1:5
*Luke 1:15

*Heb 9:14

*Ps 87:6

**gravidae et grandaevae;* Luke 1:56
†Luke 2:19

**Marthae negotium, et Mariae non otiosum otium invenitur*
†Ps 44:14–15

She is not of the company of foolish virgins: she is a wise virgin; she has a lamp, and she carries oil in a vessel.* You haven't forgotten that parable, have you, that tells how the foolish virgins were forbidden to go into the marriage feast? Their house was clean, for they were virgins; it was adorned, for all of them, the foolish as well as the wise, had trimmed their lamps, but it was empty, because they took no oil in their vessels. This is why the heavenly bridegroom was not received into their house* and why he did not think them worthy to be allowed into the marriage feast.* *Matt 25:1-13 *Luke 10:38 *Matt 25:11-12

Not so was the mighty woman* who crushed the serpent's head!* For when all her other many praises are sung, you still have this: that *her light will not be extinguished at night.** This is said to censure the foolish virgins who when the bridegroom comes at midnight complain and say, *because our lamps are extinguished.** The glorious Virgin went forth, and her most brilliant lamp was a miracle of light even to the angels,* so that they said, *Who is this, who comes forth like dawn, fair as the moon, bright as the sun?** Indeed she shone more brightly than all the others, for Christ Jesus her Son, our Lord, had filled her with the oil of grace above her companions.* *Prov 31:10 *Gen 3:15 *Prov 31:18 *Matt 25:8 *2 Cor 11:14 *Song 6:9 *Ps 44:8; Heb 1:9

On the Solemnity of the Assumption of
the Blessed Virgin Mary[1]

Sermon Three

Of Mary, Martha, and Lazarus

1. *Jesus entered into a certain village, and a certain woman named Martha received him into her house.** Why is it, my brethren, that we read that only one of the two sisters welcomed him, and she was the one who seems to have been less important? After all, the one whom Martha received affirms that Mary *chose the better part.** Martha appears to have been the elder, and action has a greater claim on the beginnings of salvation than contemplation does. Christ praises Mary, but he is received by Martha. Jacob loves Rachel, but Leah is substituted unawares. When he complains about the trickery, he is told that it is not the custom for the younger to be given in marriage first.*

*Luke 10:38

*Luke 10:42

*Gen 29:18-26

*luteam; Job 4:19

If you picture this house as made of clay,* it will be easy to acknowledge that Martha should receive him in it rather than Mary. When the apostle says *glorify and bear God in your body,** it is said to Martha, not to Mary. The first uses her body as an instrument, whereas to the other it is a hindrance. *A perishable body*, it is said, *weighs down the soul, and its frame of clay burdens the soul, which is full of thoughts.** It is not the same for the one

*1 Cor 6:20

*Wis 9:15

---

[1] *Sermo in assumptione Beatæ Virginis Mariæ* (Asspt 3).

who works, is it? Martha, then, receives the Lord into her home on earth, but Mary thinks rather how she may be received by him in a house not made with hands but an eternal one in heaven.* Yet perhaps even she seems to have received the Lord, but in spirit: *Our Lord is a spirit.**

2. She had *a sister named Mary, who sat at the Lord's feet and listened to his word.** You notice that each received the Word, the one in the flesh, the other in the voice. *But Martha was busy about much serving, and she stood and said, "Lord, do you not care that my sister has left me alone to serve?"** Is it possible, do you think, for murmuring to be heard in the house where Christ is received? Happy the house, and blessed the community where Martha complains about Mary! On the contrary, it is altogether both shameful and out of bounds for Mary to be jealous of Martha. Where do you read of Mary lodging the accusation, "My sister has left me alone to be still"? God forbid, and I repeat, God forbid that the person who is empty for God should aspire to the turbulent life of the brothers holding responsibilities in the monastery.* Let Martha always seem to herself insufficient and hardly qualified, and let her wish that the work she is entrusted with be confided to others instead!

But Jesus replies to her, *"Martha, Martha, you are troubled and anxious about many things."** See Mary's privilege, that in every conflict she has an advocate. The Pharisee is indignant,* the sister complains,† and even the disciples murmur,# but Mary remains silent, and Christ speaks for her. *Mary*, he says, *has chosen for herself the better part, which shall not be taken away from her.** For that is the one thing necessary,* that one thing that the prophet so constantly asked for: *one thing have I asked for from the Lord; this I seek.**

3. But what does it mean, brothers, when it is said that she chose the better part? Will we continue saying

*2 Cor 5:1

*2 Cor 3:17

*Luke 10:39

*Luke 10:40

**fratrum officialium*

*Luke 10:41

*Luke 7:39
†Luke 10:40
#Matt 26:8

*Luke 10:42
*Luke 10:42

*Ps 26:4

*a man's wickedness is better than a woman's goodness,** accustomed as we are to finding fault with Martha and assuming that her work of service is judged inferior? What are we to make of this saying, *If anyone serves me, my father will honor him,** and of this, *He who is greatest among you will be your servant?** Finally, is it any consolation to the one who works to extol her sister's part? Is that not more like an insult?

I think one of two things is happening here. Either Mary's part is praised because it is the part that we should all choose, as far as possible, or, if not, then because she is capable of both and does not choose her part impulsively but is ready to assume either part at the command of a superior. *For who is as faithful as David, who goes in and out and advances at the command* of *the king?** Then *my heart is ready, my heart is ready,*† not once only, but a second time also—both to be empty for you* and to serve my neighbors. Truly this is the better part that shall not be taken away; this is the best intention that will not change, whatever you call her to.

For the one who has been a good servant shall be of good standing. The one who is rightly empty for God probably does better, but the one who is perfect in both does best. This one thing I say, even if it means being critical of Martha. Doesn't it seem that Martha thought Mary was lazy when she asked that Mary be assigned as her helper? But that person is carnal and totally blind to the things of the Spirit of God who denies* her own empty soul because of its emptiness! Let her accept, therefore, that the best part is the one that lasts forever.* Doesn't it seem awkward† that a soul entirely inexperienced in divine contemplation should enter an environment where everyone has this one occupation, this one pursuit, and this same way of life?

4. But let us consider, brothers, how in our own house the law of charity distributes these three things:

---

*Sir 42:14

*John 12:26
*Matt 23:11, 21

*1 Sam 22:14
†Ps 56:8

*vacare tibi

*redarguit

*Heb 7:24
†rudis

On the Solemnity of the Assumption: Sermon Three

the household management of Martha, the contemplation of Mary, and the penitence of Lazarus. Any soul that is perfect has all three elements, yet different elements seem to belong to different people, so that some give their time to the contemplation of God while some are occupied in the administration of the affairs of the brothers, and others again in the bitterness of their soul* mull over their past as though wounded and dead in their graves.* So it is clear that Mary experiences her God with sublime and tender feelings, Martha her neighbor with kind and merciful ones, and Lazarus himself with wretched and humble ones. Let each of us consider where he is.

*Isa 38:15
*Ps 87:6

*If Noah, Daniel, and Job were to be found in this city, they would save themselves by their own righteousness, says the Lord,** but they would not save either son or daughter.† Let us not flatter ourselves; let no one of your companions lead himself astray!* Those to whom no stewardship is given, no task of administration entrusted,* ought either to stay seated with Mary at the feet of Jesus or at least wrapped up with Lazarus inside the grave. Why not let many things throw Martha into confusion, her who is concerned about many things?* But for you whom no necessity compels, one of two things is necessary: you should either be thoroughly undisturbed and find your delight in the Lord* or, if you cannot do this, be disturbed not about many things but, like the prophet, about yourself.*

*Ezek 14:14
†Ezek 14:20

*1 Cor 3:18
*1 Cor 9:17

*Luke 10:41

*Ps 36:4

*see Ps 41:7

5. I tell you again, so that no one may have any excuse for ignorance:* you, my brother, who have no inclination to build an ark or steer it through the waters,* must be a man of longing, like Daniel,* or, like blessed Job, *a man of sorrows and acquainted with grief.** Otherwise I fear that he who is eager to find you either hot in contemplating him and burning with the fire of charity or cold in your thought of him but quenching the fiery darts of the devil with the water of compunction*

*see RB 66.8
*Gen 6:8
*Dan 9:23
*Isa 53:3

*see Eph 6:16

will spew you out of his mouth for being lukewarm and repugnant to him.* But it is also necessary that every Martha must herself be kept on her toes; this is especially looked for in stewards, that one be found faithful.* Now that person will be faithful who seeks not his own but the things that are of Christ, so that his intention is pure; he does not do his own will, but that of the Lord,* so that his actions may be ordered. For there are some whose eye is not simple, and they receive their reward.* There are some who are carried away by their own emotions and feelings and manage to turn everything into their own will so that whatever they offer is defiled.*

    Come with me to the marriage song, and let us consider how the bridegroom, when he calls his bride, omits none of these three things, nor does he add anything further: *Arise up, hasten*, he says, *my beloved, my fair one, my dove, and come.** Is she not a friend who is occupied with the Lord's affairs and sets aside the interests of her own soul for his sake? As often as one of these little ones interrupts her spiritual occupation, she lays down her life for him spiritually!* Is she not beautiful who, with unveiled face reflecting as in a mirror the glory of the Lord, is transformed from glory to glory in its likeness, as if by the Spirit of God?* Is she not a dove who moans and cries in the clefts of the rock, in the crevices of the wall, as though buried under a stone?*

    6. *A woman*, it is said, *named Martha received him into her house.** Clearly they take her place, those brothers who hold offices, whom concern for fraternal charity assigns to various administrative positions. May I deserve to be found among those faithful stewards!* For to whom do the words that the Lord speaks, *Martha, Martha, you are anxious,** seem more applicable than to leaders, if they are truly worthy to take the lead in matters of concern?* Or, rather, who is thrown into

Margin notes:
- *see Rev 3:15-16
- *see 1 Cor 4:2
- *see Phil 2:21; Luke 22:42
- *see Matt 6:22; 6:2
- *see Hag 2:15; Isa 58:3
- *Song 2:10
- *John 13:37
- *2 Cor 3:18
- *John 11:38
- *Luke 10:38
- *see 1 Cor 4:2
- *Luke 10:41; *sollicita es*
- *in sollicitudine*

confusion about many things if not the one on whom presses the concern for all: for Mary in her emptiness, for Lazarus in his penitence, and for those with whom he shares his burdens?* *RB 21.3

Look at Martha, who is anxious,* Martha, thrown into confusion about many things. I speak of the apostle who, while warning the leaders about concern,* himself bears the concern of all the churches.* *Who is weak and I am not weak?* he says, *who is offended and I do not burn?* Let Martha then receive the Lord into her house, for without doubt the management of the house is entrusted to her. She is the mediator, who may obtain salvation for those under her and may receive grace herself; as it is written, *May the mountains receive peace for the people, and the hills justice.* Let all others who minister be rewarded according to the quality of their ministry; let them welcome Christ, let them serve Christ, let them minister to him in his members, for he is in the weak brothers, in the poor, and in strangers and pilgrims.*

*sollicitam

*sollicitudinis
*2 Cor 11:28

*2 Cor 11:29

*Ps 71:3

*see Matt 25:31-46; RB 36.1, 4; 53.15

7. While these are concerned† about much serving, see how empty# Mary is, and see *how sweet the Lord is.*‡ See how she sits at Jesus' feet with a devout mind and tranquil soul, keeping him always before her eyes and drinking in all the words of his mouth, for his appearance is delightful, and his words are sweet. His lips pour out gracious words; he is fairer than the sons of men* and even surpasses all the glory of the angels.† Rejoice and give thanks, Mary, because you have chosen the best part. Blessed are the eyes that see what you see, and the ears that are worthy to hear what you hear.*

†*quibus ita sollicitis*
vacet
‡Ps 33:9

*Ps 44:3
†Heb 1:4

*Matt 13:16-17

Blessed indeed are you who feel the pulsations of the divine sigh in the silence, in which it is surely good for one to wait for the Lord.* Be simple: not only without guile and pretense, but also without a multitude of distractions, so that your conversation

*see Job 4:12; Lam 3:16

may be with him whose voice is sweet and whose face is beautiful.* But beware of one thing, that you do not begin to abound in your own esteem and wish to seem wiser than you should, lest perchance while you follow the light you be plunged into darkness, and the midday devil—of which this is not the time to talk—trick you.*

But what has become of Lazarus? *Where have you put him?*† I address his sisters, who buried their brother with sermons, services, example, and prayer. *Where therefore have you put him?* He is hidden in a tomb in the ground, he lies under a stone, and he is not easily found. In that case, it will not be inappropriate to dedicate the fourth sermon to this fellow four days buried, following the example of the Savior when we hear, "*Look, he whom you love is not well*; let us stay here another day."*

*Song 2:14

*see Rom 14:5; 12:3; Isa 59:10; Ps 90:6
†John 11:34

*John 11:3, 6

On the Solemnity of the Assumption of
the Blessed Virgin Mary[1]

Sermon Four

Of the Four Days of Lazarus and the Celebration of the Virgin

1. When the mother of the incarnate Word is taken up into heaven,* it is a time for all people to sing out loud, and all humanity should utter praise without ceasing, for human nature is exalted above all immortal spirits in the Virgin. But although devotion does not permit us to be silent about her glory, mere thought does not conceive anything worthy, nor does untaught speech give birth to it. So it is that the celestial powers when they see so rare a thing cry out in admiration, *Who is this who comes up from the wilderness leaning upon her beloved?* And if they were to speak more clearly, "How great she is! From where flows such richness of love on one who comes from the desert? For such love is not seen among us, though we are made glad in the city of God by flowing waters, and we drink with glory from the fountain of contentment and glory.* Who is this who rises from beneath the sun, where there is nothing but pain, trouble, and vexation of spirit, leaning upon the beloved of her soul?"*

*Wis 3:7

*Song 8:5

*Pss 45:5; 35:9

*Eccl 1:14; Ps 89:10

---

[1] *Sermo in assumptione Beatæ Virginis Mariæ* (Asspt 4).

Why shouldn't I declare delights* about gracious virginity joined to the gift of fruitfulness, the honor of humility, the honeycomb dripping with charity,* the womb of mercy, the fullness of grace, the unique and glorious singularity? The queen of the world, then, rising up from the wilderness,* is made beautiful, as the church sings, and charming in her delights—even to the holy angels.* But let them stop being amazed by the delights of this wilderness, for the Lord has given his blessing, and our earth has brought forth its increase.†

Why are they amazed that from a desert land Mary ascends abounding with delights? Let them rather be amazed that Christ came down from the richness of the heavenly kingdom as a poor man. For it seems a far greater miracle that the Son of God was made a little lower than the angels* than that the Mother of God should be exalted above the angels. But if his emptying* became our fulfillment, his miseries are the world's delights.* Briefly, he who was rich for our sakes became poor so that he might enrich us with his poverty.* Thus the shame of the cross became the glory of believers.*

2. But if you recall, today you are owed a sermon about Lazarus. He who is our life hastens to a tomb to lead out of the tomb someone four days dead.* He seeks Lazarus so he might be sought and found by him. *In this is charity, not that we loved him, but that he first loved us.** Come then, Lord, seek him whom you love,* that you may make him love and seek you. Ask where they have laid him, for he lies captive, bound, and burdened. He lies in the prison of his conscience, he is restrained by the bonds of discipline, and as though by a stone placed upon him he is crushed and oppressed by the burden of penitence. Most of all he lacks the love that is strong as death* and the charity that endures all things.* In addition, in all these things *he now stinks, Lord, for it is the fourth day!**

Margin notes:

Quidni delicias dixerim
*Song 4:11
*Song 3:6
*antiphon *Speciosa* for the Common of the Blessed Virgin Mary
†Ps 84:13
*Heb 2:9
*Phil 2:7
mundi deliciae sunt
*2 Cor 8:9
*1 Cor 1:18
*John 11:38-39
*1 John 4:10
*John 11:3
*Song 8:6
*1 Cor 13:7
*John 11:39

I think the natural wit of many is trying to anticipate and figure out whom I mean by Lazarus. Doubtless it is one who, recently dead to his sins, digs through his own walls to see the many ugly abominations* of his perverse and unsearchable heart!* Or, as another prophet says, he has entered into the rock and in the dust of the earth has hidden himself from the face of the Lord's wrath!*

*Ezek 8:8-9
*Jer 17:9

*Isa 2:10

3. But what of this: *Lord, he now stinks, for it is the fourth day?** Maybe someone doesn't immediately get the meaning of this stinking and of these four days. I think the first day is the day of fear. By its brilliance in our hearts we die to sin and, as it were, are buried in our conscience. The second day, if I am not mistaken, is spent in strife. It is usually true that in the first stages of conversion, temptation to bad habits rises up more fiercely, and the fiery darts of the devil cannot easily be extinguished.* The third seems to be one of grief, when a person looks back upon his life in bitterness of soul* and does not so much work for a change of direction in the future as bewail a lamentable past.

*John 11:39

*Eph 6:16

*Isa 38:15

Are you surprised that I call these days? But such as these are destined for the grave, days of mist and darkness, days of grief and bitterness. There follows a day of shame, not unlike the other three, when the pitiful soul is covered in dreadful confusion while it looks unceasingly at its sins, considering their nature and magnitude, and under the gaze of the heart it keeps mulling over the disgraceful images of its sins. A soul of this kind doesn't dissemble but judges; it piles up everything. A judge stern in her own regard, she does not spare herself. Her sternness works to advantage, and her harshness is deserving of pity; she is quickly reconciled with divine grace, provided that her mind vies against itself with that end in view.

Yet, *Lazarus, come forth*.* Don't stay dead any longer in that stench! For decaying flesh is the closest thing

*John 11:43

to decay itself, and the one who is utterly confounded and wasting away is near to despair. Therefore, *Lazarus, come forth. Deep calls to deep,** the deep of light and pity, the deep of misery and darkness. His goodness is greater than your iniquity,* and where there is abundance of sin, he gives abundance of grace. *Lazarus, come forth*, he says. And if he were to speak more openly, he would say "How long will the darkness of your conscience hold you back? How long will you weep in your bed with a heavy heart? *Come forth*, advance, breathe freely of the light of my pity."* This is what you read in the prophet: *For my praise I restrained my mouth from you, lest you perish.** Another prophet spoke of himself more clearly: *My soul is troubled within me; therefore I will remember you.**

4. But now, what do you understand by the saying *take away the stone*,* and a little later, *unbind him*?† Is it possible that after a visitation of divine, consoling grace he will stop doing penance because *the kingdom of heaven approaches?** Will he set aside discipline, lest God be angry and he perish from the path of the just?* Far from it! Let the stone be taken away, but let penitence remain, not urgent and burdensome now, but strengthening a lively and mature mind or, rather, confirming it; for clearly his food is to do the will of God,* of which he was ignorant before.

Thus discipline no longer binds free people—as it is said, *the law is not given for the righteous**—but it rules their will and directs it into the way of peace.* The prophet sings more plainly in the Psalms about this raising of Lazarus, *you will not leave my soul in hell*,* because, as I remember I said on the second day of the observance of this feast, the consciousness of a guilty mind is an imprisoning hell. *You will not leave your holy one*—not a holiness that is his own, obviously, but yours, the one you yourself make holy—*to see corruption.** Indeed the fourth day is near to corruption, for he began to stink.

*Ps 41:8

*Rom 5:20

*Sir 36:1

*Isa 48:9

*Ps 41:7

*John 11:39
†John 11:44

*Matt 3:2

*Ps 2:12

*John 4:32-42

*1 Tim 1:9
*Luke 1:79

*Ps 15:10

*John 11:39

He was approaching complete decay and entering the abyss of evil where the impious reviles.* But when the powerful voice comes and he is brought back to life by it, he gives thanks, saying, *you have shown me the path of life, you have filled me with joy in your presence.** You have called me to contemplate it; *you have led my soul out of the depths** while my spirit within me was troubled by seeing the dreadful face of my conscience.* *He called with a loud voice,* says the gospel, *Lazarus, come forth:** in a loud voice surely filled not so much with sound as with piety and great strength.

*Prov 18:3

*Ps 15:10

*Ps 29:4
*Ps 142:4
*John 11:43

5. But where have we arrived? Have we not escorted the Virgin, going above the heavens? And here we are going into the depths with Lazarus. From angelic brilliance the discourse has rushed downward to the stench of one four days dead! Why is this, if not because we were being borne down by our own weight, and the topic, as fertile as it is familiar, was getting hold of us? I admit my ignorance; I do not conceal my own cowardice. There is nothing that more delights me yet more terrifies me than passing time talking about the glory of the Virgin Mother. Let me be silent about the unspeakable privilege and thoroughly singular prerogative of her merits.

The fact is that the whole world with devoted affection embraces her, honors her, and receives her, as is right. Let all long to speak of her, yet whatever can be said of her is less welcome, less pleasing, less acceptable than what cannot be said! Is it surprising that whatever of the incomprehensible glory the human mind is able to comprehend should make little sense? I mean, look, if I praise her virginity, there follow many virgins presented to me.* If I speak of her lowliness, maybe a few will be found who, after her son's example, are gentle and lowly of heart. If I wish to make much of her mercy, there are some, both men and women, who are full of mercy.*

*Ps 44:15

*Ps 5:8

There is one thing in which *she is like no one either before or after her, having the joy of motherhood with the honor of virginity.** *Mary chose the best part.*† Truly it was the best, for the fruitfulness of marriage is good, but the chastity of a virgin is better. But, above all, the best is virginal fruitfulness, or fruitful virginity. This is the privilege of Mary; it will be given to no other,* for *it shall not be taken away from her.** It is unique, but because of that it is also found to be ineffable, so that no one should be able to understand it, let alone tell about it. What if you also take into account whose mother she is? What language, even if it be an angel's, can fittingly extol the Virgin Mother's praises, the mother of no one but God? Twofold is the novelty, twofold the prerogative, and twofold the miracle, yet absolutely worthily and fittingly harmonized. What I mean is, no other son adorned a virgin, nor any other birth God.*

*Sir 44:10
†Luke 10:42

*Isa 42:8
*Luke 10:42

**neque enim filius alius virginem, nec Deum decuit partus alter*

6. Yet if you pay close attention you will see that this is not all. Whatever other virtues there are that seem common to all came to be absolutely unique in Mary. For instance, who would dare compare even angelic purity to this virginity that was worthy to become the shrine of the Holy Spirit and the dwelling-place of the Son of God?* If we estimate the value of something by its rarity, then she who first had the idea to lead the angelic life on earth is higher than all. *How shall this be*, she says, *when I have not known a man?** Her intention of virginity cannot be moved, for she did not hesitate, even when the angel promised her a son. *How shall this be?* she says. For it is not like this with others. Simply, *I have not known a man*, showing no desire for a son or any hope of offspring.

*Luke 1:35

*Luke 1:34

7. Yes, how great and precious the virtue of lowliness with such purity and innocence, a conscience completely free from sin, or rather, with such fullness of grace.* From where does your humility—and such

*Luke 1:28

humility—come to you, O blessed one? She upon whom the Lord should look is clearly worthy, whose beauty the King desires, whose pleasant fragrance attracts to her couch him who is from eternity in the father's bosom. See how manifestly our Virgin's canticle and the marriage song agree, she whose womb was the marriage-chamber of her betrothed. Listen to Mary in the gospel: *he has looked upon the lowliness of his handmaid.** Hear her also in the marriage-song: *While the king was on his couch, my nard gave forth its fragrance.** Now nard is a lowly* herb that cleanses the heart, so that it is clear that the name *nard* denotes the humility whose fragrance and beauty found favor with God.

*Luke 1:48
*Song 1:11
*humilis

8. Let him not talk about your mercy, O Virgin without equal, if there is someone who invoked it in his need and is sure it failed. For in your other virtues we your humble servants delight along with you for your sake, but in this one, in ourselves for ours. We praise your virginity, we marvel at your humility, but your mercy tastes sweeter to the miserable, and we embrace your mercy with more affection, reflect on it more often, and invoke it more frequently. For it is your mercy that gained a cure for the whole world and obtained salvation for all. For everyone knows you to have been solicitous for the whole human race, you to whom it was said, *Do not be afraid, Mary, for you have found grace,** the thing you were looking for.

*Luke 1:30

Who then can search out the length and breadth of your mercy, O blessed woman,* or its height or depth?* Its length is such that it comes to the aid of all who call upon it up until the last day. Its breadth fills the terrestrial sphere,* so that the whole earth is full of your mercy. Its height is such that it contrives to bring about the renewal of the heavenly city. And its depth gains redemption for those who sit in darkness and in the shadow of death.* It is through you that heaven is filled, hell is emptied, the ruins of heavenly Jerusalem

*O benedicta
*Eph 3:18

*Ps 32:5

*Luke 1:79

are rebuilt,* and life that has been lost is given to those who wait in misery. So powerful and holy is your love, affectionately compassionate and overflowing in affectionate aid,* equally rich in one as in the other.

9. Let our thirsty soul, therefore, hasten to the fountain; let our misery with all earnestness run to this mound of mercy. See, now, O blessed Virgin, whatever prayers we have been capable of we have launched to you, who have ascended to your son, and we follow, at least at a distance.* May your piety, you who found favor with God, be known to the world; may it through your holy prayers obtain pardon for the guilty, health for the sick, strength for the fainthearted, consolation for the afflicted, and help and deliverance in danger. On this day of solemnity and joy, O merciful Queen, may your Son our Lord shower the gifts of his grace on your servants who call upon the most sweet name of Mary with praise, *who is God above all, blessed forever.**

*Heb 12:22

**affectu compatiendi, et subveniendi abundant affectu*

*Matt 26:58

*Rom 9:5

On the Solemnity of the Assumption of
the Blessed Virgin Mary[1]

Sermon Five

On the Same as Before

1. *Jesus entered into a certain village.** What our Lord and Savior considered worth doing once and for all, openly in one place at a particular time, he accomplishes every day and in all parts of the earth invisibly in the hearts of the chosen. I mean, we hear that Jesus *entered into a certain village, and a certain woman named Martha received him,** and so on, as the gospel just said. What is this village* save the human heart? Before the Lord comes to it, it is encircled by a moat of desires* and shut in by a wall of obstinacy, and, within it, across its whole width, rises the tower of Babylon!*

 Three things are surely most necessary for every town: provisions to sustain the inhabitants, fortifications to protect them, and weapons with which to resist an enemy. So also those who dwell in this town have for a diet bodily pleasure and the greed of the present age* to feed upon. They have protection, too—the hardness of their hearts—so that the powerful arrows of the word of God can scarcely ever penetrate. To repel the enemy, the weapons they are equipped with are the arguments of worldly wisdom.

*Luke 10:38

*Luke 10:38
*castellum

**cupiditatis fossa*
*Gen 11:1-9

*2 Cor 1:12

[1] *Sermo in assumptione Beatæ Virginis Mariæ* (Asspt 5).

That is why it is written, *The children of this world are wiser in their generation than the children of light.** [*Luke 16:8]

2. But when Christ enters and visits this town, it is turned upside down and in its place is built another, one that is new, beautiful, and spiritual, and what was said is fulfilled: *Anyone who is in Christ is a new creature; old things will pass away;* and *Behold, all things are become new.** [*2 Cor 5:17] With greed† [†*cupiditatis*] done away, the enormous capacity of desire is expanded, so that at his approach the mind, which until now was content with earthly things, longs more for heavenly things. Now a wall of self-restraint is set in place, and an outer wall of patience.* [*see Isa 26:1] But this work rises from a foundation of faith, and it grows from love of one's neighbor to the love of God, which is on a higher level and on the towers of that same wall; for without a doubt the strength of self-restraint is perfect when, living together with our neighbors in the unity of faith,* [*Eph 4:13] we restrain ourselves from sin not by the fear of punishment or the desire for human praise but only because we are encircled by divine love. Certainly the love* [*caritas] of God, with which he loves* [*diligit] us, must be higher than the wall, meaning that it fights on behalf of someone practicing self-restraint; for self-restraint cannot continually resist the strength and blows of the tempter unless it is protected by his grace.

Therefore the outer wall of patience is set in place lest the devil should have easy access to attack self-restraint. Those who are protected by patience and make self-restraint a way of life* [*continenter vivunt] may well testify, saying with the apostle, *Who shall separate us from the love of Christ? Shall tribulation, or distress, or persecution, or hunger, or nakedness, or peril, or a sword?** [*Rom 8:35] You see how strong the wall of self-restraint is when *neither death, nor life, nor angels, nor principalities, nor powers, nor things present, nor things to come, nor height, nor depth, nor any other creature can separate us from the love of God, which is in Christ Jesus.** [*Rom 8:38-39]

3. But now let us knock at its gates, I mean the gates of justice, so that they may be opened for us,* and let us see within *the mighty works of the Lord, sought out by all who love him.** That tower,† that mystic tower, is built there by his operation, as though on Mount Sion, and by means of it the saints, with hearts made humble, climb from the valley of tears to heaven. They climb, I say, not by their own merits but by the help and grace of God, as the Holy Spirit said through the prophet David: *Blessed is the one whose strength is in you; he has set his heart on the upward path.* Do you ask where he is? *In the valley of tears,** that is, in the humility of this present life. And he repeats this same grace, saying, *The lawgiver also gives the blessing.* *Ps 117:19

*Ps 110:2
†see Matt 21:33

*Ps 83:6-8

What the goal of this ascending is and to what fruit this grace leads those who are ascending he adds immediately, saying, *They will go from strength to strength, and the God of gods will be seen in Zion.* This—I mean, the vision—is our reward; this is the goal and fruit of our labors. Who would not without hesitation put so great a fruit before all things both seen and unseen? Who is there whose cold heart is not set on fire by this longing? For this is that grace that blessed John the Evangelist commends to us when he says, *And of his fullness we have all received, grace for grace.**

*John 1:16

4. From this we infer that we have received a threefold grace from God. By one we were converted, by a second we are strengthened in temptation, and by a third we are rewarded when we have been tried and tested. The first, by which we are called, initiates us; the second, by which we are justified, carries us; the third, by which we are glorified, brings us to perfection. Of the first it is said, *of his fullness we have received.* Of the remaining two is said *and grace for grace,* that is, the gifts of eternal glory for the reward of temporal struggle. Let the first grace be in the wall of self-restraint to which we are called, let the second be in

the ascent of the tower that we climb, and let the third be at the summit where we finish up. Here, then—that is, on the summit—when those who have done well come to it, they are made into the home and habitation of the Lord.* About such as these it is written, *For there the tribes go up, the tribes of the Lord, as is the testimony of Israel, to give thanks to the name of the Lord, for his seat is there.**

*fiant iam locus et sedes Domino

*Ps 121:4-5

Now while they were on the wall of self-restraint and stood in the fighting-line, they could be attacked, and so in the first place it is as a helper, so to speak, that *God is known in Judah.** But when they take their stand together in that place, there they see the Lord. *In Israel his name is great; his place is in peace, and his dwelling is in Sion. There he broke the power of the archers, the shield, the sword, and the battle,** because no movement of the flesh withstands but is in all ways subject to the spirit. This was the place ardently desired by the prophet when he said, *if I give sleep to my eyes or slumber to my eyelids, or rest to my head, until I have found a place for the Lord.** That is where he longs to fly, saying, *Who will give me wings like those of a dove, that I may fly away and be at rest?**

*Ps 75:2

*Ps 75:2-4

*Ps 131:4-5

*Ps 54:7

5. Now it may be asked about the inhabitants of this fortress what food sustains them, what fortification protects them, or what armor they use to ward off attack. We may reasonably reply that just as the fleshly are nourished by the works of the flesh,* so all the more their food is the fruit of the spirit.* For their food is to do the will of the almighty Father.* Their food is the word of God, on which all the holy ones feed, humans and angels alike. So it is written, *A man shall not live by bread alone, but by every word that comes from the mouth of God.** Their fortification is the wall of self-restraint, as I have said, and the outer wall of patience.* As for armor, they have what the apostle describes: *the breastplate of righteousness, the shield of faith,*

*Gal 5:19
*Gal 5:22
*John 4:34

*Matt 4:4

*Isa 26:1

the helmet of salvation, and the sword of the spirit, which is the word of God.* \hfill *Eph 6:15-17

Let it not disturb anyone that the word is both food and sword, as if that were absurd or impossible. In material matters one thing is for this purpose, another for that; one thing belongs here, another there. But in spiritual matters it is not the case that one thing is better suited for something than another thing is, or that one thing belongs here and another thing there, but in God all things are for us,* and *God is all in all.*† I mean, look. In nature, is there anything so different from one another as a loaf of bread and a stone? And yet if you go back to the mystical sense, they both have the same meaning. For Christ is called bread and also stone: the living bread and the stone that the builders rejected.* Symbolically they both mean the same thing, though they differ in their respective qualities.*

*sed omnia sunt nobis in Deo
†1 Cor 15:28

*see John 6:41; Ps 117:22

*utrumque quidem est per significationem, licet neutrum sit per proprietatem

6. But let us return to the subject. Jesus came into the village, and two sisters, Martha and Mary,† that is, activity and understanding, received him. Received, did I say, or were received? Let it be one or the other, for it is they, not Jesus, who benefit from either one. And when Jesus came to them, he matched one of two qualities, strength and wisdom, to each as best fit her:* strength to activity, wisdom to understanding. So the strength of God and the wisdom of God are both proclaimed by the apostle.†

†Luke 10:38-39

*duo confert congruentia singulis, virtutem et sapientiam
†1 Cor 1:24

But why is it that when he is coming in it is Martha who welcomes him and scurries about and ministers to him, but when he has entered Mary sits at his feet, hanging on his words with her heart, unless action comes first and contemplation afterward? For whoever desires to arrive at contemplation must first exercise himself diligently in good works, as it is written: *My children, if you desire wisdom, hold to righteousness, and God will give her to you.** And elsewhere, *By your precepts I understand,* and *purifying their hearts by faith.**

*Sir 1:33
*Ps 118:104; Acts 15:9

By what faith? Faith working through love.* Martha, while she rightly pushes on, is the model of activity. As for Mary—provided that she sits, is silent, and does not react to distractions—she portrays the image of contemplation. So intent on the word of God with all the force of her mind is she that, spurning all else, she drinks in only the grace of the knowledge of God, to which she is devoted as if she were rendered unconscious of external things, while within she is utterly happy, rapt in the joy of contemplating God. Certainly it is she who speaks in the Song of Songs, *I sleep, but my heart wakes.** [*see Gal 5:6] [*Song 5:2]

7. But Martha receives the Lord in two ways, and she prepares a twofold feast for him, because she had shut him out in two ways. For there are two sorts of deeds that drive God away from us, namely, wrongdoings* and crimes.† We call wrongdoings those things we do against ourselves, and crimes those against our neighbor. Similarly, there are two things that bring him back, self-restraint and kindness, so opposites are corrected by opposites. For it is written, *As you have given your members to serve uncleanness and iniquity to iniquity, so now give your members to righteousness in sanctification.** So while Martha is busy preparing a marvelous meal, her hands full as she carries out her role, she wants Mary, too, that is, her understanding and all her interiority, to get busy and set to work to help her finish her task. And so she complains that she receives no help from her sister, addressing her complaint, though, not to Mary but rather to the Lord: *Lord, do you not care that my sister has left me to serve alone? Then tell her to help me.** Now a certain accusation is highlighted here, as well as respectful solicitude toward the Lord. With him present, Martha does not dare address Mary but rather opens her complaint to him, calling the one Lord who has the power to command her sister to do whatever is necessary. [*flagitia] [†facinora] [*Rom 6:19] [*Luke 10:40]

Let us not be surprised then if we see someone who is toiling and doing good complain of the inactivity of a brother, because we read in the gospel that Martha acted like this toward Mary. But as for Mary complaining about Martha because she wished her to take part in her actions—about this we know nothing. In any case, she would not be able to do both things at the same time, that is, devote herself to external concerns and be empty for the interior desires of wisdom. Of that wisdom it is written, *one who is free from activity will have it*.* Therefore Mary sits and stays, motionless, wanting neither to interrupt the silent repose nor lose the sweet pleasure of contemplation, particularly when within she hears the Lord himself saying, *Be still and know that I am God.** *Sir 38:25

*Ps 45:11

8. Here we should consider the three things that prevent contemplation. The eye of our soul is the intellect. Just as physical light and other physical phenomena are seen with the eye of the body, so God, who is boundless light, and his invisible attributes are in some way perceived by the understanding.* But the outer and inner eyes differ from one another. Exterior physical light acts on the outer eye so that it can see, but the Creator's interior light is poured into the inner eye so that it may discern. There are three things that prevent either eye from seeing. Let us start, then, by reasonably considering external and visible things so that from visible things considered in their due order the intellect may the more easily rise to the things beyond understanding. *Rom 1:20

It can happen that an eye is healthy and receptive, but if external light is lacking it sees nothing. On the other hand it sometimes happens that light is present to it, but because it is irritated by blood or some other thick fluid, it can hardly make things out at all. Again, it often happens that it lacks neither light nor health but is irritated by some dust getting thrown into it, so that its acuity is blunted. So there are three things that obstruct the eye: darkness, thickening of the blood, and dust blowing in. Now it is these very things by which the inner eye is impeded, but they are known by other names. What there is called darkness here is called sin. The sins themselves flow together into the memory as though into some cesspit, and here you have that thickened fluid. And what there is called dust here is known as anxiety about worldly matters. These therefore are the three things that blind the eye of the intellect and shut it off from contemplation of the true light: the darkness of sin, the recalling of those same sins, and anxiety about worldly matters.

The prophet complained that he was afflicted by the first of these diseases when he said, *My strength fails me, and the light of my eyes is also gone.** For when we are deprived of the light of justice, we can see nothing but the darkness of our sins. Likewise he felt that he was weighed down by the second when he said, *I turned in my trouble, when I was pierced by grief.** He laments that he was seized by the third when he says, *I ate ash as though it was bread,** that is, the ashes of activity instead of the bread of contemplation.

*Ps 37:11

*Ps 31:4

*Ps 101:10

Whoever then wishes to apply the eye of the mind to divine contemplation must first cleanse the self of this threefold hindrance. If anyone strives to do this, that person will find a threefold remedy for this threefold disease. The first is healed by confession, the second by prayer, and the third by quiet. Mary would have been hindered from her intention by the third disease, that is, by the anxiety about activity.* So while Martha served she sat and remained quiet.

*cura actionis

9. While this one complains and that one keeps silent, let us hear what the Lord answers for Mary: *Martha,* he says, *you are anxious and troubled about many things.** You are troubled about many things, trying to provide self-restraint for yourself while you see to

*Luke 10:41

everything necessary* for your neighbors. In order to hold on to self-restraint, you are eager for vigils, fasting, and punishing your body! In order to supply for the others, you throw yourself into work; to have something to distribute, you willingly bear with the difficulty involved.* To repeat, you are troubled about many things, *yet one thing is necessary.** For unless you do your work in accord with unity,* it will not be accepted by God who is unity, as he himself testifies.† For it is written, *There is no one who does good, no, not one.** So it is that when the water was moved in the pool, one man was cured;* so it is that when ten lepers were cured, one *returned, praising God in a loud voice.** To this one, while rejecting the others, the Lord bore laudatory witness, saying, *Were not ten healed? Where are the nine? No one is found to return and give glory to God except this stranger.** Paul also said, *All run, but only one receives the prize.** We learn clearly from these and many other passages of Scripture how important single-mindedness is,* particularly from the text we are considering, where the Lord says *yet one thing is necessary.*

    10. But you must know that the unity of the saints, which we have commended from the Scriptures, is one thing; the unity of criminals, which is shown and proved from those same Scriptures, is another, for of this it is written, *The kings of the earth are risen up, and the rulers take counsel together against the Lord and against his Christ.** The evangelist says about the same—*then the Pharisees went away and took counsel so that they might capture him in his words,** and again, *the chief priests and the Pharisees gathered together a council.** Why? As John witnesses, *that they might kill Jesus.** Our Lord himself shows how stubborn this unity of sinners is when he speaks to blessed Job about the body of the devil, saying, *His body is like a compact molten shield and like scales pressed together. They are joined to one another,** and not even

*necessitatis

*Eph 4:28
*Luke 10:22
**opus tuum in unitate feceris*
†Gal 3:20

*Ps 13:3
*John 5:4
*Luke 17:15

*Luke 17:17-18
*1 Cor 9:24

*unitas

*Ps 2:2

*Matt 22:15
*John 11:47
*John 11:53

**una uni coniungitur*

a breath of air comes between them: one clings to another, and holding together, they will not be separated.* Such unity, or rather perversity, is usually seen in brothers who are lukewarm and halfhearted in conversion.* Try to urge them on to a healthy practice, honest and noble: they would sooner put up with the huge expense and most painful difficulty involved in resisting than to desire to reach the goal by an easy shortcut that established practice has proven to be correct. This kind of unity is perverse and accursed!

11. Having excluded this sort of unity from our hearts and conversations, let us follow the sort that is good and pertains to good people. This also is twofold, the one that justifies and the one that glorifies; the one is deserved, the other is a reward. Of the first is written, *and the multitude of believers were of one heart and one soul,** and of the second, *Who clings to the Lord is one spirit.** But since this latter is mostly the object of future hope—for it has more to do with the future than with the present—let us hope to receive it from God but put it aside for the time being rather than discuss it.

Rather, let us take up the unity that justifies and that is now so necessary for us. That is the behavior of sweetness* that the psalmist sweetly extols in sacred song: *Behold, how good and pleasant it is for brothers to live together in unity!** Having sung of the beauty of this unity, the prophet was not silent about its usefulness, for he said, *the Lord has promised blessing and life**—blessing now, and *eternal life in the world to come.*† It is this unity, I tell you, that the apostle handed down to be observed with the greatest love* when he said, *endeavoring to keep the unity of the spirit in the bond of peace.**

12. Now the goodness of this unity is preserved in two ways by those whose job it is to see it preserved. All who are perfect must have unity with regard to

*Job 41:6-8

**tepide ac remisse conversatium*

*Acts 4:32
*1 Cor 6:17

**ipsa est enim decus suavitatis*

*Ps 132:1

*Ps 132:3
†Mark 10:30

**summa diligentia observandam*

*Eph 4:3

themselves and with regard to their neighbors, to themselves through their integrity and to their neighbors through conformity. All creatures, particularly rational ones, ought to imitate their leader. Now our God is one, as Moses said: *Hear, O Israel: the Lord your God is one.** But also, while he is one and the same and perfect in himself, lacking nothing, yet there belongs to him a courtesy toward us and a love born of kindness coming to us. We also, then, each of us, must be one with ourselves through integrity of virtue and one with our neighbors through bonds of love. The apostle John, speaking of love, commends to us this imitation, saying, *As he is, so are we in this world.**

*Deut 6:4; Mark 12:29

*1 John 4:17

But this unity, which we said each one should have toward oneself, can be hindered by three things: excess, cowardice, and capriciousness. There are many who think they can do what they cannot and presume they have received what they have not. Peter was an example of this confidence when at the time of the passion of our Lord he said, *Lord, I am ready to go to prison and to death, with you.** Cowardly people are the opposite of those who indulge in excess. Peter represents these, too, when he says, *Go from me, for I am a sinful man, O Lord.** The capricious and inconstant are *carried away by every wind of doctrine;** what pleased them a short time ago now displeases them, and what they now choose they will disapprove of soon.

*Luke 22:33

*Luke 5:8
*Eph 4:14

But what use is it to enumerate these faults unless we give the remedies by which we can cure ourselves of them? Let us pursue *the enemies of unity,** and let us not turn aside until they give way. Against excess must be put consideration of human frailty, for that is very powerful in casting down hateful presumption. Against cowardice must be set confidence in the power of God, so that what you think you cannot do in your own strength you can do with its help, and you may say with the apostle, *I can do all things in*

*Ps 17:38

him who strengthens me,* Christ. Against capriciousness must be put the advice of a senior, so that you may not be led astray by differing and strange doctrines** but may do what the law of God enjoins of you: *Ask your father, and he will inform you; ask the elders, and they will tell you.**

*Phil 4:13

*Heb 13:9

*Deut 32:7

13. We have talked of that unity that all people have toward themselves; let us now speak of that which each has toward the neighbor. This unity, too, is considered in two ways: when out of love we are inclined toward the other, and when we in turn receive the affection of the other. And this unity is also hindered by two things, obstinacy and suspicion. Obstinacy does not permit us to enter the heart of another, and suspicion does not allow us to believe that we are loved by others. So it comes about that while in our obstinacy we do not love others, and in our suspicion we think we are not loved by others, the unity that we should have with others is hindered. But this twofold disease is cured by twofold charity: that which seeks not its own* and that which believes all things.† Let the obstinate have the charity that seeks not its own and loves others; let the suspicious have the charity that believes all things and believes that it is loved by others, without a shadow of doubt.

*1 Cor 13:5
†1 Cor 13:7

On the Solemnity of the Assumption of
the Blessed Virgin Mary[1]

Sermon Six

To Establish "full of grace" in Mary in Three Ways

1. *H*ail, Mary, *full of grace.** The fullness of grace cannot stand in her virginity alone. Nor in addition does it fall to everyone to receive it. Happy are those who *have not defiled their garments** and who along with our queen glory in the privilege of virginity. But *do you have only one blessing*, O Lady? Indeed *I implore that you bless* me.* That virtue has been wasted by me, and now I cannot even aspire to it. I have lain in rottenness in my filth;* *I have become a beast.** But it cannot be, can it, that you no longer have anything for me? It cannot be that there is nowhere where I can be with you, can it, even though I am not strong enough to follow you wherever you go?* The angel seeks the girl whom the Lord had prepared for the son of his lord.* He drinks water from your jar, delighting in the strength* made known to him. But you won't neglect also to water the beasts, will you? The angel drinks, because you do not know a man;* let the beasts also drink, because you boast of humility in a singular way. *The Lord has regarded*, it says, *the*

*Luke 1:28

*Rev 3:4

*Gen 27:38

*see Joel 1:17
*Ps 72:23

*Rev 14:4

*see Gen 24:14
*virtute

*Luke 1:34

[1] *Sermo in assumptione Beatæ Virginis Mariæ* (Asspt 6).

lowliness of his handmaid.[*] It might be true that virginity without humility *has glory, but not with God.*[*] The Highest always looks upon humility, but the lofty he holds at a distance.[*] He gives grace to the humble but resists the proud.[*]

But perhaps even with these two measures your water jar is not full.[*] There is enough room for a third, so that not only may the angel and the beasts drink but also the master of the feast. The angel servant draws out this good wine that we have kept till now[*] so that he may take it to the master of the feast. I mean the Father, the *principium* of the Trinity, who is rightly called the master of the feast. In commending the fruitfulness of Mary, which is the third measure, the angel reasonably says, *Of you shall be born a savior, who shall be called the son of God,*[*] as if to say, "You have this conception in common with him alone."

Sidenotes:
*Luke 1:48
*Rom 4:2
*Ps 137:6
*1 Pet 5:5
*John 2:6
*John 2:9-10
*Luke 1:35

Sunday within the Octave
of the Assumption[1]

Of the words of the Apocalypse: *A great wonder appeared in heaven, a woman clothed with the sun, and the moon under her feet, and on her head a crown of twelve stars.**

*Rev 12:1

1. My beloved brothers, one man and one woman did us great harm! But thanks be to God, by one man and one woman everything has been restored, though not without a huge gain in grace. The gift is not like the offense,* but the magnitude of the kindness exceeds the appraised value of the damage. So the most prudent artist did not destroy what was ruined* but effectively made it over again entirely. What I mean is, he made the new Adam from the old and transformed Eve into Mary.

*Rom 5:15

*Matt 12:20

Certainly Christ was sufficient for us since now all our sufficiency is of him.* But it was not good for us that man should be alone.* It was most suitable that each sex should take part in our restoration since both had part in its downfall. *The man Christ Jesus* is the faithful and powerful *mediator between God and humankind,** but human beings are in dread of the divine

*2 Cor 3:5
*Gen 2:18

*1 Tim 2:5

---

[1] *Sermo in dominica infra octavam assumptionis* (OAsspt).

majesty in him! Humanity seems to be swallowed up by divinity, not because its substance is changed, but because the disposition is deified.* Not only is Christ's mercy celebrated, but his judgment as well,† because even if he learned compassion from the things that he suffered* so that he was merciful, he had also the power of judgment.* In short, *our God is a consuming fire.** How can sinners not fear to come near? As sure as wax melts when exposed to the fire, won't they perish in the presence of God?*

**sed affectio deificata*
†Ps 100:1

*Heb 5:8
*Heb 2:17
*Heb 12:29

*Ps 67:3

2. So, then, that the woman who is blessed among women* will not be seen to have no purpose,† a place will be found for her in this restoration. For we have need of a mediator to this Mediator, and there is none more expedient for us than Mary. Eve, through whom the old serpent poured his poisonous venom onto humankind,* was very cruel, but Mary, who gave to men and to women the saving antidote to drink, is faithful. The one was the servant of seduction, the other of propitiation. The one instigated rebellion, the other forced in redemption.*

*Luke 1:28
†*ne . . . videbitur otiosa*

*Gen 3:6

**suggessit . . . ingessit*

Why should human frailty waver before Mary? There is no sternness in her, no terror: she is altogether gentle, offering milk and wool to all. Attentively review the entire sequence of gospel events and see whether there is any chiding, any harshness, or any sign of even the slightest anger in Mary, let alone anything that should cause you to be suspicious or afraid to approach her. But if you find that she is full of every kind of pity and grace, of mercy and gentleness, as indeed she is, then give thanks to him who of his tender mercy foresaw your need of such a mediator. In short, she became all things to all, and of her great charity she made herself debtor to all, both wise and foolish.* She opened her bosom of mercy to all, so that of her fullness all might receive:* the captive redemption, the sick healing, the sad consolation, the sinner pardon,

*1 Cor 9:22; Rom 1:14

*John 1:16

the just grace, the angel joy, the whole Trinity glory, and the Son the substance of human flesh, so that no one should be hidden from her warmth.* *Ps 18:7

3. Don't you think that this is the woman clothed with the sun?* Let us suppose that the rest of this prophetic vision shows this image to refer to the present-day church—but surely it is not unsuitable to attribute it to Mary. Surely it is she who clothed herself as with another sun. As that one rises on the good and bad alike,* so too does this one: she does not investigate past deserts* but to all shows herself vulnerable to entreaty, to all renders herself merciful, and pities the needs of all with the greatest feeling.* For every failing† is below her; she surpasses with an incomparable excellence every creature, and whatever there is of weakness or corruption she subdues. Rightly then is the moon said to be beneath her feet!* In any case, it seems that we have said nothing strange in saying that the moon was beneath her feet, since we cannot doubt that she is exalted above the cherubim and seraphim.*

*Rev 12:1

*Matt 5:45
*praeterita non discutit merita
*amplissimo affectu
†defectus

*Rev 12:1

*Antiphon Exaltatum est for the Feast of the Assumption

But the moon represents not only corruption because of its waning but also a foolish way of thinking, and indeed it sometimes represents the church of this time, first because of its changefulness and then because it takes its splendor from elsewhere. In both senses the moon may properly be understood to be beneath Mary's feet, but each in a different way, for *the foolish person changes like the moon, but the wise one stays constant like the sun.** In the sun is heat and abiding splendor; in the moon, only a splendor that is altogether changeable and uncertain and never stays in one phase.*

*Sir 27:12

*Job 14:2

Rightly then is Mary clothed in the garment of the sun, since she has penetrated the boundless abyss of divine wisdom, further than can be believed—so far as the condition of a created being without personal union* permits—and seems to be bathed in inaccessible light.† By that fire surely the lips of the prophet are cleansed, and with that fire the seraphim blaze.# But what Mary merited was something quite different, not to be momentarily touched, but rather covered over, embraced, and as it were enclosed by the fire itself. Yes, this woman's cloak is most radiant but also most ardent,* she whose every quality shines so brightly that, far from any darkness, there is no suspicion of any shadow or anything less than light, and no lukewarmness or anything but the most fervent zeal.

4. All foolishness is far below her feet, so that she has no part with the number of foolish women and the company of foolish virgins.* Rather he, the stubborn prince of all foolishness, who is as changeable as the moon,* lost his wisdom and seemliness and is trampled and bruised beneath the feet of Mary,† suffering wretched servitude. Surely she is the woman promised long ago by God, who was to bruise the head of the ancient serpent with righteous foot, and for whose heel he lay in ambush with many wiles, but in vain.* For she alone crushed all heretical perversity—one propounding as dogma that she did not bring forth Christ of the substance of her flesh, another suggesting that she did not give birth to a baby but just found him, yet another blaspheming that after giving birth she had relations with a man, and another, not able to stand to hear her called the mother of God, scoffing most irreverently at the great name *Theotokos*.

But those who lay in wait were crushed, those who would trip up trampled underfoot, those who would detract confounded—and all generations call her blessed.* Finally the dragon, in the person of Herod,† lay in wait for her when she gave birth,# so that he might take her newborn son and devour him, to revive the enmity between the woman's seed and the dragon.*

Margin notes:

**sine personali unione creaturae condicio*
†1 Tim 6:16
#Isa 6:6

*Gen 3:1

*Job 2:10; Matt 25:2

*Sir 27:12; Exod 28:17
†Gen 3:15

*Gen 3:15

*Luke 1:48
†see Matt 2:3-18
#Rev 12:4

*Gen 3:15

5. Now it might seem better to understand the word *moon* as referring to the church because her radiance is not from herself but from him who says, *Without me you can do nothing.** In that case you have an accurate description of the mediator we just now identified: *A woman*, it says, *clothed with the sun, and with the moon under her feet.** Let us embrace the footprints of Mary, my brothers, and with devout supplication let us prostrate ourselves at her blessed feet. Let us hold her and not let her go until she blesses us,* for she is powerful. Surely she is the fleece standing between the dew and the threshing-floor,* the woman set between the sun and the moon, Mary between Christ and the church.

*John 15:5

*Rev 12:1

*Song 3:4; Gen 32:26

*Judg 6:36-40

Maybe it is less strange to speak of her as a fleece covered with dew than as a woman clothed with the sun. Great is the friendship between them; no, altogether extraordinary, the proximity to one another of the sun and the woman! I mean, how does so fragile a nature stand in such a violent ardor? Rightly did you marvel, blessed Moses, did you desire to stare intently. Truly, *put your shoes from off your feet** and the coverings from your worldly thoughts, if you wish to draw near. *I will turn aside and see this great sight.* It is truly a wonderful sight, a bush burning without being consumed,* a great sign, a woman clothed with the sun remaining inviolate. It is not natural for a bush, covered in flames, to remain and not be burnt; it is not within the power of a woman to stand clothed with the sun. It is not in human power, nor is it in the power of the angels; some higher power is needed. *The Holy Spirit*, he said, *shall come upon you.** And as if he had said that *God is a Spirit** and *our God a consuming fire,** he adds, *the power*—not mine, or yours, but— *of the most high shall overshadow you.** And so there is nothing extraordinary in so excellent a garment being worn by a woman so excellently overshadowed.

*Exod 3:5

*Exod 3:2-3

*Luke 1:35
*John 4:24
*Heb 12:29
*Luke 1:35

6. *A woman*, it says, *clothed with the sun.* Surely she is clothed with light as with a garment.* The carnal will not understand this because it is spiritual; to them it seems foolish.* It did not seem so to the apostle, who said, *Put on the Lord Jesus Christ.** What familiarity you enjoy with him, Lady! How close, even intimate, you have merited to be! What favor you have found with him!* He remains in you and you in him!† You clothe him and are clothed by him! You clothe him with the substance of flesh, and he clothes you with the glory of his majesty.* You clothe the sun with a cloud, and you are yourself clothed with the sun.

*Ps 103:2

*1 Cor 2:14
*Rom 13:14

*Luke 1:30
†John 6:57

*Isa 2:10

The Lord has made a new thing upon the earth: a woman shall encompass a man,* none other than him of whom it was said, *Behold the man. His name is Dawn.** He has made a new thing upon the earth, that a woman should appear clothed with the sun.† And she crowned him, and in turn she was worthy to be crowned by him: *Go forth, O daughter of Zion, and behold King Solomon in the crown with which his mother crowned him.** But this is elsewhere. Go in rather in the meantime and see the queen in the diadem with which her Son crowned her.

*Jer 31:22

*Zech 6:12;
Oriens
†Rev 12:1

*Song 3:11

7. *On her head*, it says, *is a crown of twelve stars.** Indeed her head was worthy to be crowned with stars, since it shone brighter than they and she adorned them rather than they her. Why should not the stars crown her who is clothed in the sun? *As in the days of spring*, it says, *roses surround her, and lilies of the valley.** Surely the left hand of the bridegroom is under her head, and his right hand embraces her.* Who can give a value to her jewels? Who can number the stars with which Mary's royal crown is studded? It is beyond the power of humans to describe that crown and to declare of what it is made. But we, according to the measure of our littleness, avoiding the danger of probing secret matters, may understand by those twelve stars

*Rev 12:1

*Sir 50:8

*Song 2:6

with which Mary is notably adorned twelve singular graces. Indeed in Mary may be found the graces of heaven, the graces of the flesh, the graces of the heart; if those three were multiplied by four, we should have the twelve stars with which our queen's crown shines.

Certainly for me the light flashes first in the birth of Mary, second in the greeting of the angel, third in the overshadowing of the Spirit, and fourth in the conception of the Son of God, which words cannot describe. Likewise the brightness of the star shines forth with glory in these, namely, the stronghold of virginity, fecundity without seduction,* pregnancy without weariness, childbearing without pain. Also gentle modesty shines forth in Mary with particular splendor and devout humility, the generosity of belief and the martyrdom of the heart. It is a mark of your zeal that you look long at each of these. Meanwhile I think I have fulfilled my duty if I have been able to show you these things briefly.

quod sine corruption fecunda

8. Why do stars shine at Mary's birth? Clearly because she comes of a line of kings, of the seed of Abraham, of the noble stock of David.* As if this were not enough, add to it that God granted to that birth by a unique privilege of sanctity to know what had been promised from heaven to the patriarchs long before, foreshadowed by mystic and wonderful signs and foretold by the words of the prophets. For she was prefigured by the rod of the priest,* which flowered without a root, by Gideon's fleece, which was wet in the midst of dry ground,* and by Ezekiel's vision of the gate facing the sunrise, open to no one.* Isaiah in particular promised that a rod should arise from the root of Jesse.* Rightly is it written that a great sign appeared in heaven,* known to be promised long before. *The Lord himself*, he said, *will give you a sign: behold, a virgin shall conceive.** Truly he gave a great sign, because he was great who gave it. Whose keenness

*Response for the Nativity of Mary

*Num 17:8

*Judg 6:36-38
*Ezek 44:1-3

*Isa 11:1
*Rev 12:1

*Isa 7:14

of vision did the brilliance of this privilege not overwhelm exceedingly? She, a woman, was so reverently and courteously greeted by the Archangel*—as if he saw her exalted on her royal throne above all orders of celestial beings, nearly adored by him who until now was accustomed to be adored by humans*—that the supreme merit and singular grace of the Virgin are commended to us.

9. Nevertheless this new type of conception shines forth, a conception not in sin like every other.* Rather, by the Spirit overshadowing her Mary was to conceive, without consort but by sheer sanctification.* For she gave birth to the true God and the Son of God—at once God's son and a human's, fully God and fully man issuing from Mary. This is an abyss of light that I cannot without difficulty declare, the strength of whose brilliance even the eye of the angel does not cloud over. Furthermore, in liberty of spirit transcending the decrees of the Mosaic Law*—as the singular nature of her intention* amply shows—she vowed to God the integral sanctity of both body and spirit, bodily virginity and the practice of virginity.*

It shows the unassailable grounds of her intention† that she replied so resolutely to the angel who had promised her a son, *How shall this be, since I do not know a man?** But first she was *troubled at his word and wondered what kind of salutation this might be*,* hearing that she was blessed among women when what she really had always wanted was to be blessed among virgins. That is why she *wondered what kind of salutation this might be.** She found it bewildering, and when the threat to her virginity became manifest in the promise of a son, she could no longer hide the fact, saying, *How shall this be, as I do not know a man?* She richly deserved the blessing, which she did not forgo, that her virginity should be far more glorious by reason of its fruitfulness, and the fruitfulness far more glorious by

*Luke 1:28

*Gen 19:1

*Ps 50:7

*Luke 1:35; *sola et de sola sanctificatione Maria conciperet*

*2 Cor 3:17

*ipsius propositi novitas

*virginitatem carnis et propositum virginitatis . . . vovit
†propositi
*Luke 1:34
*Luke 1:29

*Luke 1:28

reason of her virginity, and that these two stars should be seen to shine with parallel rays.

For it is a glorious thing to be a virgin, but for a virgin to be a mother is far more glorious on any showing. Indeed the bothersome grief that other pregnant women in labor experience she alone did not experience, for she alone conceived without lustful pleasure. So it was that immediately after her conception, when other women are most miserably afflicted, Mary went up to the hill country in haste so that she might care for Elizabeth.* And she went to Bethlehem when her time had almost come,* carrying that precious burden, carrying that light burden,* carrying him by whom she was carried. So she brought forth a new offspring at a birth that was dazzling and endowed with joy, and alone among women she knew nothing of the usual difficulty and pain of childbirth. If we reckon the value of anything by its rarity, nothing rarer than this can be found. *No one like her was seen before, nor did she have a successor,** and we, if we gaze upon her faithfully, doubtless profess admiration as well as veneration, devotion, and consolation.

*Luke 1:39
*Luke 2:4-5
*Matt 11:30

*Antiphon *Genuit* for the Nativity of the Lord

10. There remain yet to consider some matters that call for imitation. It was not for us before our birth to have been promised by God at sundry times and in diverse manners—preannounced from heaven!—and we were not honored by so novel a greeting as that delivered by the archangel Gabriel. Even less does Mary make common cause with us* in two other things—clearly her secret is her own!† For she is the only one of whom it is said, *What is born of her is of the Holy Spirit,** and she is the only one to whom it is said, *The holy one that shall be born of you shall be called the Son of God.** Let maidens be offered to the king, but after her,* for she alone takes the first place. She outstrips us by far in that she alone conceived without corruption, carried a child without heaviness, and bore a son without pain.

*communicat nobis
†Isa 24:16
*Matt 1:20

*Luke 1:35
*Ps 44:15

None of these things is demanded of us, yet clearly a certain amount is demanded. What I mean is, if we lack gentle modesty or humble heart or magnanimous faith or reasonable compassion,* the uniqueness of her gifts will not be an excuse for our negligence, will it? As a most lovely jewel in a crown, as a star shining on the head*—such is a blush on the face of the modest person.* And really, does anyone think that the one full of grace† was devoid of this grace? Mary blushed.# We can prove this from the gospels. Where does she appear talkative, where presumptuous? She stood at the door asking to speak to her son* and did not interrupt his discourse with motherly advice or enter uninvited into the house in which her son was speaking.

*compassio mentis

*Rev 12:1
**rubor in facie hominis verecundi*
†Luke 1:28
#*pudibunda fuit Maria*
*Matt 12:46

In all the four gospels, if I remember right, Mary is heard to speak only four times: first to the angel but only after he had spoken to her once and yet again;* second to Elizabeth, when the voice of Mary's greeting caused John to leap in her womb and Elizabeth magnified Mary, but Mary was concerned rather to magnify God;* third to her twelve-year-old son when she and his father had been looking for him sorrowing;* and a fourth time at the marriage-feast when she spoke to her son and the servants.* And this speech was the surest evidence of her inherent gentleness and virginal modesty. You can see that she considered the shame* of others as her own and so could not refrain from pointing out the lack of wine. When she was chided by her son, being gentle and humble of heart* she neither answered him nor lost hope but urged the servants to do whatever he commanded them.

*Luke 1:34

*Luke 1:46-55

*Luke 2:48
*John 2:3-5

*verecundia

*Matt 11:29

11. Is it not said that the shepherds came first of all and were the first to find Mary? *They found Mary and Joseph and the child placed in a manger.** And it was not without Mary his mother that the magi, too, if you remember, found the child,* and carrying the Lord of the temple into the temple of the Lord, she heard

*Luke 2:16

*Matt 2:11

many things from Simeon both about him and about herself, for she was slow to speak but swift to listen.* And *Mary kept all these things, pondering in her heart.*† But in all these things you will not find the least word about the sacrament of the Lord's incarnation. How unfortunate we are who have the spirit only in our nostrils!* How unfortunate, we who—being full of cracks, as the comedian says, and leaking out everywhere—release the spirit all at once!†

Often Mary heard her son not only speaking to the people in parables# but also revealing the mysteries of God one by one to the disciples. She saw him doing miracles, she saw him at the last hanging on the cross, dying, rising again, and ascending. But in all these things how often is it mentioned that the voice of the most modest maiden, of the most chaste turtledove,* was heard? Then we read in the Acts of the Apostles that when they returned from Mount Olivet they continued with one accord in prayer. Who did? If Mary was there, she would be mentioned first, since she is above all, as much by virtue of her son as by reason of her own sanctity. *Peter and Andrew*, Scripture says, *and James and John*, and the rest who come after, *all these continued together with the women and with Mary, the mother of Jesus.*

Did she then show herself the lowest of women because she was mentioned last? Truly the disciples, to whom *the Spirit was not yet given, because Jesus was not yet glorified,** were of the flesh when a dispute arose among them about who should be first, whereas Mary, although she was greater, humbled herself, not only among them all, but before them all.* Rightly the last was made first, and since she was first, she made herself last.* Rightly did she become sovereign of all when she showed herself the servant of all. Rightly was she exalted above the angels* when with ineffable gentleness she ranked herself below widows and penitents,

*Luke 2:22-35;
Jas 1:19
†Luke 2:19

*see Isa 2:22;
spiritum habemus in naribus
†Prov 29:11;
see Terence, *The Eunuch*, 105
#Mark 4:11

*Song 2:12

*Acts 1:13-14

*John 7:39

*Luke 22:24

*Matt 19:30

*see the antiphon *Exaltata est* for the Assumption

below her from whom was thrown out seven devils.* I beg you, my sons, imitate this virtue, if you love Mary; if you strive to please her, emulate her modesty. For nothing so befits a human being, nothing is so suitable for a Christian, and nothing is more proper for a monk.

12. It is obvious enough in the Virgin's case that the virtue of humility shines forth from her very gentleness. Doubtless humility and gentleness are, so to speak, sisters sucking at the same breast, completely at one with him who said, *Learn of me, for I am meek and lowly of heart.** For as self-exaltation is the mother of presumption, so true gentleness is only born of true humility. Yet Mary's humility is not only adorned by her silence but sounds clearly in her speech. She had heard the words, *What is born of you shall be called the Son of God,** and she replied that she was nothing but a servant.* Next, when she had come to Elizabeth, immediately the unique glory of the Virgin was revealed to Elizabeth by the Spirit so that she marveled at the one who had come, saying, *Whence is this to me, that the mother of my Lord should come to me?** She added, in praise of the voice of the one greeting her, *As the voice of your greeting sounded in my ears, the child in my womb leapt for joy,** and she blessed the faith of her who believed, saying, *Blessed are you who believed. For the things will be done in you that were spoken to you of the Lord.** These were extraordinary praises! Nevertheless Mary's devout humility let her keep nothing for herself; rather, she poured out everything to him whose privileges were praised in her. "You," it says, "magnify the Mother of the Lord," but she says, *My soul magnifies the Lord.** At the sound of my voice you say that your son leaped for joy, but *my spirit has rejoiced in God my savior,** and he himself, like the friend of the bridegroom, rejoices at the voice of his beloved.* You say she is blessed because she believed, but the reason

*Luke 8:2

*Matt 11:29

*Luke 1:35
*Luke 1:38

*Luke 1:43

*Luke 1:44

*Luke 1:45

*Luke 1:46

*Luke 1:47
*John 3:29

for blessedness and belief is the tender gaze of heaven, so that all generations shall call me blessed,* because God has gazed upon the humility and lowliness of his handmaiden.

*Luke 1:48

13. Nevertheless, brothers, we should not suppose that holy Elizabeth was mistaken in the words that she spoke under the sure inspiration of the Spirit,* should we? In no way. Blessed was she whom God gazed upon, and blessed she who believed.* For here is seen the great fruit of divine regard. By the ineffable skill of the Spirit such greatness, coming upon such humility, drew near to the innermost part of the virgin's heart.* Therefore, when we declare her fruitfulness and wholeness, it is as if these were two stars growing ever brighter under one another's gaze,* for obviously her lowliness does not lessen her greatness, nor her greatness her lowliness. Lowly in her own estimation, she was still great in her ready trust in the promises made to her, so that even though she thought herself to be only a servant girl,* she could not doubt that she was chosen for that incomprehensible mystery, that wonderful transaction, that inscrutable mystery,* and she believed that she would be the true mother of him who was both God and man.†

*Luke 1:25

*Luke 1:45

*Luke 1:35

*Rev 12:1

*Luke 1:38

*incomprehensibile hoc mysterium, admirabile commercium, inscrutabile sacramentum
†Luke 2:34-35; see Saint Leo, S 21 (PL 54:191B)

This is the sure sign of divine grace acting in the hearts of those who are chosen, that humility may not make them cowardly nor greatness of soul make them arrogant. The two work together with the result that greatness does not turn into self-exaltation but rather that humility increases, so that those who are chosen might be found the more devout and not ungrateful to the Giver of gifts, and, likewise, that cowardice does not take anything away from humility. The less one presumes on one's own virtues, the more one trusts in divine strength.

14. The martyrdom of the Virgin—which we named as the twelfth star in her crown, if you remember*—is

*Rev 12:1

mentioned in the prophecy of Simeon as well as in the account of the Lord's passion. For the holy man says of the infant Jesus, *Behold, this child is set for a sign that shall be opposed*, and he said to Mary, *and a sword shall pierce your own soul.** Truly, blessed Mother, a sword has pierced your soul. For unless it had, it would not have penetrated the flesh of your Son. And after your Jesus—he is everyone's, but especially yours—has sent out his spirit,* the cruel lance, not sparing him even after death, although it could harm him no more, opens his side,* and while it clearly cannot touch his soul, it pierces yours. Without a doubt his soul was not there, but clearly yours could not be wrenched away. Yes, a violent grief pierced your soul, so that we may say with good reason that you are more than a martyr, in that your feeling of compassion exceeded physical suffering.*

15. Did not these words wound you more than a sword, truly piercing your soul, reaching even to the division of soul and spirit:* *Woman, behold your son?*† What a substitution! John will be to you as Jesus, the son of Zebedee in place of the Son of Man, a man pure and simple instead of the true God! When you heard this, how could it not pierce your most affectionate soul when ours, although of stone, although of iron, are torn by its very description? Marvel not, brothers, that Mary is called a martyr in soul. Let the one wonder who does not remember hearing that Paul mentioned among the crimes of the heathen that they were without affection.* This was far from the visceral feelings of Mary; so may it also be far from her servants.

But perhaps someone will say "Did she not know that he would die?" Doubtlessly. "Did she not hope that he would rise again at once?" Faithfully. "And yet she grieved when he was crucified?" Exceedingly. Otherwise, what kind of man are you, my brother,

*Luke 2:34-35

*Matt 27:50

*John 19:34

**corporeae sensum passionis excesserit compassionis affectus*
*Heb 4:12
†John 19:26

*Rom 1:31

or where did you get that wisdom, that you should marvel more at Mary's suffering with her son than at Mary's son suffering? For could he die in the body and she not die with him in her heart? A charity greater than anyone possesses brought this about,* charity the like of which has not been seen since. *John 15:13

Now, Mother of mercy, through this very affection of your most pure mind, the moon, lying prone at your feet,* sets you as a mediator between herself and the sun of justice* and supplicates you that in your light she may see light* and win the grace of the Sun by your invocation, for he has loved you above all and honored you, clothing you with the garment of glory and placing the crown of beauty on your head.* You are full of grace, full of heavenly dew, leaning on your beloved, breathing in his fragrance.* Feed today your poor ones, Lady, for even the puppies eat the crumbs,† and give drink of flowing water not only to the son of Abraham, but to the camels,* because you are the daughter chosen and preordained* for the Son of the Most High, *who is God above all, blessed for all ages. Amen.**

*Rev 12:1
*Mal 4:2
*Ps 35:10

*Sir 6:32; Ezek 16:12

*Est 15:17; Song 8:5
†Matt 15:27

*Gen 24:18-20
*Gen 24:14

*Rom 9:5

On the Nativity of Blessed Mary[1]

Of the Bringing of Water

1. The heavens cherish the presence of the fruitful Virgin, and the earth venerates her memory. Thus all her goodness is shown there, and here is found its remembrance: there is fullness, here a poor offering of the firstfruits; there is the substance, here only the name. *Lord*, it says, *your name is forever, and your remembrance from generation to generation.** From generation to generation—not of angels, surely, but of human beings. Would you know why her name and memory are among us and the reality in heaven? *Thus shall you pray,* he said: *Our Father, who are in heaven, hallowed be your name.** Faithful is the prayer whose very beginning reminds us both of our divine adoption and of our sojourning on earth.

*Ps 134:13

*Matt 6:9

We know, then, that as long as we are not in heaven, we sojourn as alienated from the Lord,* and we groan within ourselves, awaiting our adoption as sons* and the presence of our Father. It is worth notice then that when the prophet speaks of Christ he says, *The spirit before our face is Christ our Lord; under his shadow we shall live among the nations.** Now one who lives among celestial blessings is not in the shadow, but rather in splendor. *In the splendor of the saints*, it says, *I brought you from the womb before the daystar arose.** This is what the Father says.

*2 Cor 5:6
*Rom 8:23

*Lam 4:20

*Ps 109:3

---

[1] *Sermo in nativitate Beatæ Virginis Mariæ* (NatBVM).

2. Now it was this very splendor that the Mother gave birth to—in the shadow, yes, but the shadow with which the Most High overshadowed her.* Rightly does the church sing, not that church of the saints in splendor on high, but the one that sojourns in an alien country on earth in the meantime: *Under the shadow of him whom I desired I sat down, and his fruit was sweet to my mouth.** She had asked that the full light of midday,* where the bridegroom finds pasture, should be disclosed to her, but it was kept back, and instead of the full light she received the shadow, and instead of fullness the taste. Now she did not say simply, "Under the shadow of him whom I desired," but *under the shadow of him whom I desired I sat down.* For she had not asked for the shadow but the full noonday itself, full light from full light, *and his fruit,* she said, *was sweet to my mouth,* as if she would say "to my taste." *How long will you not depart from me, nor let me alone until I swallow my spittle?** How long shall this sentence remain: *Taste and see how sweet the Lord is?** Indeed he is pleasant to my taste and sweet to my throat, and therefore it is right that the bride should burst into a song of thanks and praises.

*Luke 1:35

*Song 2:3
*Song 1:6

*Job 7:19
*Ps 33:9

3. But when will it be said, *Eat, my friends, and drink, and be inebriated, my dearest ones?** *The just will feast,* says the prophet, but *in the sight of God,** surely not in the shadow. And he says of himself, *I shall be satisfied when your glory shall appear.** But the Lord says to his apostles, *you are they who have continued with me in my temptations, and I appoint for you a kingdom, as my father has appointed for me, that you may eat and drink with me at my table.* But where? *In my kingdom,* he says.* *Blessed is he who shall eat bread in the kingdom of God.** *Hallowed be your name,** then, because meanwhile *you are among us, Lord,** dwelling in our hearts by faith, because *your name is invoked among us.**

*Song 5:1
*Ps 67:4

*Ps 16:15

*Luke 22:28-30
*Luke 14:15
*Matt 6:9
*Jer 14:9
*Eph 3:17

*Your kingdom come.** By all means let the perfect come and purge what is in part.* *You have your fruit for*

*Matt 6:10
*1 Cor 13:10

holiness, says the apostle, *and its end is eternal life,** eternal life, a never-failing fount, which waters the entire surface of Paradise.* Not only does it water it, but it inebriates it, *a fountain of gardens, a well of living waters that flow with force,** *and the force of its waters makes glad the city of God.**

Who is truly the fount of life* but Christ our Lord?† *When Christ your life shall appear, then shall you also appear with him in glory.** For the fullness† emptied itself# so that it might be to us justice and sanctification and remission,‡ and it did not yet appear to us as life or glory or blessedness.* The fount was dispersed toward us, the waters flowed in the streets, and no stranger may drink from them.*

The celestial artery descended through an aqueduct, not exhibiting the full measure of the fount but just a steady rain of grace upon our thirsty hearts, to one more, to another less. Truly that aqueduct is full so that others may take of its fullness, but not the full measure itself.*

4. You have guessed, I am sure, whom I mean by the aqueduct, who takes its fullness from the heart of the Father himself and gives it to us, not as it is but as we can receive it. You are aware to whom was said, *Hail, full of grace.** Can it be that we are amazed that so great and wonderful an aqueduct could be made, whose head, like the ladder that the patriarch Jacob saw, could touch the heavens,* or indeed pass beyond them and reach the fountain, the living waters, which are above the heavens?* Solomon was also amazed and said, as if in despair, *Who shall find a mighty woman?** Therefore the human race lacked the streams of grace before that time, because the lovely aqueduct of which we speak did not yet intercede. And you will not think it strange that it was awaited so long if you remember how many years Noah,* a just man,† labored in the

*Rom 6:22

*Gen 2:6

*Song 4:15
*Ps 45:5
*Ps 35:10
†Luke 2:11

*Col 3:4
†Col 2:9
#Phil 2:7
‡Cor 1:30
*Col 3:4

*Prov 5:16-17

*John 1:16

*Luke 1:28

*Gen 28:12

*Gen 1:7
*Prov 31:10

*Gen 5:32
†Gen 7:6

making of the ark,* *in which few, that is eight souls, were saved,** and that was enough for a short time. *Gen 6:9 *1 Pet 3:20

5. But how did this our aqueduct reach so sublime a fount? How do you suppose, except by fervent devotion and pure prayer, as it is written, *the prayer of the righteous pierces the heavens?* And who is this just person if not Mary, that just woman from whom the Sun of justice arose for us.* How then did she reach the inaccessible heights of majesty except by knocking, asking, and seeking?*At last she found what she sought,* she to whom it was said, *You have found favor with God.*† But she is full of grace,# and yet she still finds grace? She is truly worthy to find what she seeks, she who was not sufficient to herself and who could not rest content with her own virtue, but—as it is written, *who drinks me still thirsts*—she begs for grace overflowing for the salvation of all humans. *The Holy Spirit*, it says, *shall come upon you,* and that precious ointment shall flow upon you abundantly and copiously in every direction. Thus it is: we feel it, our face shines with oil.* Now we cry, *Your name is as ointment poured out,* and your name is remembered from generation to generation.* Truly this is not an empty promise, for even if the wine is poured out,* it is not wasted. Therefore if young girls, naturally with young minds, love the bridegroom, this is no small thing, and the ointment flows down from his head, reaching not only his beard but the very hem of his garment.* *Sir 35:21 *Mal 4:2 *Matt 7:7 *Song 3:4 †Luke 1:30 #Luke 1:28 *Sir 24:29 *Luke 1:35 *Ps 103:15 *Song 1:2 *Ps 101:13 *Song 1:2 *Ps 132:2

6. Consider, O human, the counsel of God, hear the counsel of Wisdom, the counsel of holiness. He who would water the threshing-floor with dew first pours it upon a fleece;* he is to redeem the human race; he assigns the whole price to Mary. Why? Perhaps so that Eve should be justified by her daughter and so that man's quarrel against woman should henceforth be settled. No more, O Adam, say, *The woman whom* *Judg 6:38-40

you gave me gave to me of the forbidden *tree*;* say rather, "The woman whom you gave me has given me to eat of the fruit of blessedness." No doubt this is a counsel of perfection, but perhaps there is another that is not entirely so. It is this, but it is not enough, I think, for your desires. Milk is sweet, but if we churn it, the fatness of butter results.

Look more carefully, then, to see with what depth of devotion he wished her to be honored by us, he who has put the sum of all good in Mary so that it flows from her, who comes leaning on her beloved.* She is a garden of delights, on which that divine south wind not only breathes at its coming but also blows through and fills with its breeze, so that its scents flow on all sides and give off their odor,* the cloud of her graces. Take away her body, shining like the sun, which gives light to the world: where is the day? Take away Mary, this star of the sea, the sea truly great and wide:* what is left but enveloping darkness and the shadow of death and deep shadows?

7. Let us honor Mary, then, with all the sinews of our being, with all the affections of our hearts and all our prayers, because that is the wish of him who desires us to possess all things through Mary. This, I say, is his wish, but it is for us. For since she knows the course and outcome of all miseries, she soothes our fear, awakens our faith, strengthens our hope, drives away our cowardice, and encourages us when we are timid. You fear to approach the Father? Terrified by the mere sound of his voice,* you flee to the woods. He has given Jesus as a mediator. What can such a Son not gain from such a Father? He will be heard because of his humble submission:* *For the father loves the son.*† Or are you afraid of him too? Your brother is your own flesh,* tempted in all things yet without sin,† *that he might be merciful.*# This is the brother Mary gave to you. But perhaps you fear the divine majesty in him,

because although he became man, yet he remained God.* Do you wish to have an advocate with him? Have recourse to Mary.

*1 John 2:1

Now if the humanity of Mary is pure, it is not only pure from all contamination; it is also pure by the matchlessness of her nature. I say equally surely that she will be heard for her humble submission. The son will listen to his mother and the mother to her son. My little children, she is the ladder for her sinners, she is my great reason for confidence, she is the ground of my hope. Now, can her son drive her away, or support her when she is driven away? Can the son refuse to hear her, or not be heard by her? He can do neither. *You have found favor with God*, said the angel.* How happily! She will always find favor, and her favor is all that we need. The wise virgin* asked not for wisdom, like Solomon,* or riches or power, but grace. And it is by grace alone that we are saved.

*Luke 1:30

*Matt 25:2
*1 Kgs 3:9-11

8. What else do we want, brothers? Let us ask for grace, and let us ask through Mary, because she has found what we seek, and she cannot be disappointed.* Let us ask for grace, but grace from God.* For from humans grace is a delusion.* Let others ask for merit; let us eagerly seek to meet with grace. Why? Is it not because of grace that we are here? Surely *it is of the mercy of God that we are not consumed.* What are we? We are false, murderers, adulterers, thieves, the scum of the earth.* Examine your consciences, brothers, and see that *where sin abounds, there grace abounds all the more.*

*Matt 7:7
*Luke 1:30
*Luke 2:52; Prov 1:30

*Lam 3:22

*1 Cor 4:13
*Rom 5:20

Mary does not claim merit but asks for grace. She trusts grace so much, having no trace of high-mindedness, that she fears the salutation of the angel.* Mary, the gospel says, *wondered what kind of salutation this might be.* For she believed she was unworthy of an angelic salutation. Perhaps she thought, "whence is this, that the angel of my Lord should come to me?"* *Do not be afraid, Mary,* and do not be surprised at the coming

*Rom 11:20

*Luke 1:29

*Luke 1:43
*Luke 1:30

of the angel: a greater one than an angel comes. Do not be surprised at the angel of the Lord, and *the Lord of the angel is with you.** Then why should you not see the angel when you live like an angel? Why should the angel not visit one who has the same way of life? Why should he not greet one of the saints and a close friend of God?* The life of an angel is clearly that of a virgin, and *those who neither marry nor are given in marriage will be like the angels of God.**

9. But you may be sure that it was not for this reason that our aqueduct ascended to heaven, nor was it by her prayer alone that she pierced the heavens,* but by the purity which brought her near to God, as the wise man said,* for she was a maiden *holy in body and spirit,* to whom particularly belongs that saying, *our citizenship is in heaven.** *Holy,* I say, *in a body and spirit,* lest you should have any doubt about this aqueduct. Likewise she is exalted but nevertheless remains unchanged. *A garden enclosed,** *a sealed fountain, a temple of God, a shrine of the Holy Spirit.** For she is not a foolish virgin who has no oil, but there is oil in plenty laid down in her vessel.† *She has set her heart on high paths,*# ascending in her way of life, as I said, as in her prayer. Then *she went up into the hill country with haste, and she greeted Elizabeth,** and she remained serving her for three months,* so that then she, the mother, might say to the mother, as her son said to Elizabeth's son, *Let be: for thus it becomes us to fulfill all righteousness.** She climbed the mountains, she whose just dealing was as the justice of God.* This was the third time the Virgin ascended, so that a threefold cord might not easily be broken.*

If her charity burned in asking for grace, her virginity shone forth in her flesh, and her humility stood out in her obedience. For if *everyone who humbles oneself is exalted,** what is higher than this humility? It is said that Elizabeth marveled that she had come and said, *whence is this to me, that the mother of my Lord should come to me?** But it is more to be wondered at that, like her son, she came not to be ministered unto but to minister.* Rightly did the divine singer, falling down in admiration before her, say, *Who is this who comes forth as the rising dawn, fair as the moon, clear as the sun, and terrible as an army with banners?** She has ascended higher than the whole human race, she has ascended to the angels, and she has gone beyond even them and outstripped every heavenly creature. Surely it is necessary that she drink beyond the angels so that she may give living water to humankind.

*Luke 1:43

*Matt 20:28

*Song 6:9

10. *How shall this be*, she says, *since I do not know a man?** Truly she was *holy in mind and spirit*, having an untouched body and the intention of being untouched.* But the angel said to her in reply, *The Holy Spirit shall come upon you, and the power of the Most High shall overshadow you.** "Do not ask me," he said, "he is above me and I cannot get to him." *The Holy Spirit shall come upon you*, not an angelic being, *and the power of the Most High shall overshadow you*,* not I. You have not stood even among the angels, holy maiden. The thirsty earth waits to be given to drink for something higher than your ministering to it. When you have gone a little past them you will find him whom your soul loves.* A little, I say, not because he is high above all, but because you will find nothing between him and them. Go therefore beyond Virtues and Dominations, beyond Cherubim and Seraphim, that you may come to him of whom they cry in alternate song, *Holy, holy, holy, Lord God of hosts.** *For what shall be born of you is holy; he shall be called the Son of God.*† *The fount of wisdom, word of the Father in the highest.*#

*Luke 1:34

*1 Cor 7:34

*Luke 1:35

*Ps 138:6

*Song 3:4

*Isa 6:3;
Canon of the Mass
†Luke 1:35
#Sir 1:5

This word will become flesh by your agency, the flesh of him who says, *I am in the Father and the Father is in me*,* and may also say, *I came forth and proceeded from God.** *In the beginning*, it says, *was the word.*†

*John 14:10
*John 8:42
†John 1:1

Now the fountain gushes forth, but in the meantime it is contained in itself. Now *the Word was with God*,* dwelling in light inaccessible,* and the Lord said from the beginning, *I think thoughts of peace and not of affliction*.* But your thoughts are for you alone, and we do not know what you think. For who has known the mind of God, and who has been his counselor?† The thought of peace descended as the embodiment of peace: *The word was made flesh and dwelt among us*.* *He lives in our hearts by faith*,* he lives in our memory, he lives in our thought, and he even descends to our imagination itself. For how should a person think of God except by making an image in his heart?

*John 1:1
*1 Tim 6:16

*Jer 29:11;
Introit for
Pentecost 24
†Rom 11:34

*John 1:14
*Eph 3:17

11. He was altogether incomprehensible and inaccessible, nor could he be seen or pictured in the mind. But now he wished to be understood, to be seen, and to be visualized in the mind. Do you ask in what way? Truly by lying in the cradle,* resting in the Virgin's lap,* preaching on the mount,† spending the night in prayer,# or hanging on the cross, growing pale in death, free among the dead‡ and ruling in hell, or rising again on the third day* and showing the apostles the marks of the nails,* the signs of victory, revealing to them for the first time the secrets of heaven. Which of those things is not considered true, holy, and sacred? If I consider any of those things, I consider God, and he is my God in all things.*

*Luke 2:12
*Matt 5:1
†Matt 5–7
#Luke 6:12
‡Ps 87:6
*John 20:20-27
*John 20:25-27

*John 20:28

I said that I thought upon these things, and I judged it prudent to pour out the memory of your goodness, which the high priestly staff brought forth in plenty in nuts of this kind,* which Mary, drinking in the heavens, gave to us in fuller measure. In the heavens, truly, and beyond the angels, she received the Word from the heart of the Father himself, as is written, *Day utters speech to day*.* Surely the Father is the day; indeed day after day shows the salvation of God. Is not the Virgin the day? A splendid one, too. Clearly the day shines

*Num 17:8

*Ps 18:3

forth, *which comes forth like the rising dawn, beautiful as the moon, bright as the sun.**   *Song 6:9

12. See then how she came to the angels with the fullness of grace,* with the Spirit overshadowing her above the angels.* In the angels there is charity, purity, and humility. Which of these is not preeminent in Mary? But it has been shown from above, as far as it can be shown to us; let us follow the highest. To which of the angels has it ever been said,* *The Holy Spirit shall come upon you, and the power of the most high shall overshadow you; therefore what shall be born of you is holy, called the Son of God?* Then *truth shall arise from the earth,** not from the angelic creation. He took not the angels but the seed of Abraham.*

*Luke 1:28
*Luke 1:35

*Heb 1:5

*Ps 84:12
*Heb 2:16

It is a great thing for an angel to be a servant of God; but Mary has deserved something higher, to be his mother. The fruitfulness of the Virgin is her crowning glory, and she is made as much higher than the angels* by a singular gift, as she is different in that she received the name of mother because of her service. She who is full of grace found this grace, to be burning in charity, of untouched virginity and devout humility, with child yet without knowing a man, bearing a child yet without the pains of childbearing women.* That is a little thing; that which is born of her is called holy and is the Son of God.

*Heb 1:4

*Luke 1:35

13. For the rest, brothers, we must take great care that the Word, which came forth from the Father's mouth by the agency of the Virgin, should not return empty,* but still through that same Virgin we return grace for grace.* Let us cry out her memory until we breathe her presence, and may her graces return to the streams of their beginning, that they may flow more abundantly. For unless they return to their spring they will dry up, and we shall be unfaithful in a little* because we do not deserve to receive the greatest. It is little to remember at present, little compared with

*Isa 55:11
*John 1:16;
Ps 144:7

*Luke 19:17

what we desire, but a great deal compared with what we deserve; our desire is far lower, but infinitely higher than our deserts. Wisely then does the bride give no small praise for this small thing. For when she said, *Tell me where you feed your flocks, where you make them rest at midday*,* receiving little for much and pouring out an evening sacrifice* in place of evening pasturage, she murmurs a little, as happens usually, or is sad, but gives thanks and shows herself more devoted in all things. For she knows that if she is faithful in the shadows of memory she will beyond doubt attain to the light of his presence. So *you who call upon the name of the Lord, do not be silent, and give him no rest.*

Those who have God present with them do not lack encouragement, and the words of another prophet— *Praise the Lord, Jerusalem; praise thy God, O Zion**—are words of joy rather than denunciation. Those who walk in faith* need admonition to be silent and to give him no rest. For he speaks, and *he speaks peace to his people, and to his saints, and to those who are converted to the heart.** And *with the Holy you shall be holy, and with an innocent man you shall be innocent*,* and he will hear himself listening and speak to himself speaking. For if you are silent you give him rest. Silent from what? From praise. *Be not silent*, it says, *and give him no rest, until he establishes Jerusalem as praise on the Earth.** Praise the Lord, O Jerusalem, for it is pleasant and comely to praise him,* unless perhaps we suppose the citizens of Jerusalem are gratified by mutual praise and deceive themselves.*

14. *Your will be done*, Father, *as it is in heaven, so too in earth*,* that the praise of Jerusalem be established in earth.* But what kind of thing is it? Does angel seek honor from angel in Jerusalem?* Does a human being seek to be praised by humans on the earth? What dreadful forwardness! But it is held by those who know nothing of God,* *who have forgotten their*

God.* *You who call upon the name of the Lord, do not be silent* in his praise until he is established and made perfect on earth. Yet speech is not good. Otherwise the prophet would not say *it is good* for a person *to wait in silence for the salvation of God.*

It is good to keep silence from boastfulness, from blasphemy, from murmuring and distraction. For one person, worn out by the burden of work and the heat of the day,* murmurs in mind and judges those who watch for his soul* as though they were losing their reason. There is uproar, but above all the silence that the noise of that obdurate soul causes to the voice of him who blasphemes,* which shall not be forgiven in this life* or in the future. A third walks in great matters and in things that are too wonderful for him,* saying, *Our hand is triumphant,* and thinks himself to be something when he is nothing.*

What would he say to the one who speaks peace?* He says, *I am rich and want for nothing.* Then the word of Truth is *Woe to you who are rich, for you have your consolation.* On the contrary, he says, *Blessed are they who mourn, for they shall be comforted.* Therefore let the wicked tongue be silent in us,* the blaspheming and boastful tongue, since *it is good to wait in silence for the salvation of the Lord,* that you may say, *Speak, Lord, for your servant hears.* Words of this kind are not for him but against him; as the lawgiver says to those who murmur, *Your murmuring is not against us, but against the Lord.*

15. Be silent then about these things, but not entirely, so as not to give him peace.* Speak to him in confession against boastfulness, that you may obtain pardon for the past. Speak to him in thankfulness against murmuring, that you may find more grace in the present. Speak in your prayer against lack of faith, that you may obtain glory in the future. Confess the past, I say, and give thanks for the present, and henceforward pray

*Jer 3:21
*Isa 62:6

*Lam 3:26

*Matt 20:12
*Heb 13:17

*Ps 54:9
*Matt 12:31–32
*Ps 130:1
*Deut 32:27
*Gal 6:3
*Zech 9:10
*Rev 3:17

*Luke 6:24
*Matt 5:5
*Ps 11:4

*1 Sam 3:10

*Exod 16:8

*Isa 62:6-7

assiduously for the future, so that not even he can refuse forgiveness for the past, giving gifts in the present and making promises for the future. Be not silent, I say, and give him no peace. Speak, that he may speak and say, *My beloved is mine, and I am his.** His voice is pleasant and his utterance sweet.*

*Song 2:16
*Song 2:14

Truly this is no voice of complaint, but the voice of the turtledove. Do not say, *how shall we sing the Lord's song in a strange land?** For she is not thought foreign of whom the bridegroom says, *The voice of the turtledove is heard in our land.** He heard her saying, *Catch us the little foxes,** and perhaps for that reason she broke forth into a voice of exultation:* *My beloved is mine, and I am his.* Clearly the voice of the turtledove, which clings to its mate through life and death with complete chastity, so that neither life nor death can separate it from the love of Christ!* See then whether anything can separate the beloved from the one he loves, although she sins and perseveres in working against him. Heaping clouds strove to cut off the rays of the sun, so that our iniquities should make a barrier between ourselves and God,* but the sun waxed hot, and they were all melted.* Or when would you have returned to him unless he had persisted and called to you, *Return, O Shulamite, return, return, that we may look upon you?** Therefore do you persevere also, and do not be turned from him by beatings or toil.

*Ps 136:4

*Song 2:12
*Song 2:15
*Ps 41:5

*Rom 8:38-39

*Isa 59:2
*Exod 16:21

*Song 6:12

16. Wrestle with the angel* and do not yield, because *the Kingdom of heaven suffers violence, and the violent take it by storm.** Will you not struggle? *My beloved is mine, and I am his.** Make his love known; may he make trial of yours, for your God tries you in many ways.* He turns aside,† he turns away his face, but not in anger.# This is making trial, not giving judgment. The beloved upholds you; do you uphold the beloved, act with courage.* Your sins have not overcome him; may his blows not overcome you. Then

*Gen 32:24

*Matt 11:12
*Song 2:16

*Deut 13:3
†Song 5:6
#Ps 9:32

*Ps 26:14

you shall obtain blessing. But when will this be? When dawn comes,* when day has broken,† when Jerusalem is made a praise in the earth.# It says, *Behold, the man wrestled with Jacob until morning.*‡

*Let me hear your loving kindness early in the morning, because I have put my hope in you.** I will not be silent, nor will I give you peace, until the morning,* and may you not hunger. For assuredly it is not right that you feed, except among the lilies. *My beloved is mine, and I am his who feeds among the lilies.** And if you remember, it was clearly said in the Song above that the appearance of flowers was accompanied by the sound of the turtledove.* But notice that the place, not the food, is mentioned, nor is it said on what he feeds his flock, but among what. For perhaps he does not nourish them on food but on the presence of the lilies, and he does not feed on the lilies but dwells among them. For lilies please by their smell rather than by their taste and are better suited to be looked at than to be eaten.

17. So *he feeds his flock among the lilies, until the day dawns,** and the beauty of the flowers is followed by the richness of the fruit. Meanwhile it is not the time of flowers or of fruit while we live in hope rather than in fact; *we walk in faith, not in sight,** and we rejoice in expectation rather than in experience. Now think of the tenderness of a flower, and be mindful of the word that the apostle spoke, that *we have this treasure in earthen vessels.** What terrors seem to threaten the flower! How easily the lily is pierced by sharp thorns! Rightly did the beloved sing, *As the lily among the thorns, so is my friend among women.**

Was the one not among thorns who said, *With those who hate peace, I will be peaceful?** So even though the just person grows like a lily, he does not feed his flock on lilies like the bridegroom,* nor is he pleasing to himself alone. Hear him then as he lingers among the lilies: *Where two or three are gathered together in my*

*Gen 32:26
†Song 2:17
#Isa 62:7
‡Luke 9:38; Gen 32:24

*Ps 142:8

*Isa 62:6-7

*Song 2:16

*Song 2:12

*Song 2:17

*2 Cor 5:7

*2 Cor 4:7

*Song 2:2

*Ps 119:7

*Hos 14:6

name, there I am in the midst of them.* Jesus always loves the middle place, but the Son of man, the mediator between God and man,* always rejects hostility and resentment. *My beloved is mine, and I am his, who feeds his flock among the lilies.* Let us take care to keep lilies, my brethren, to root out the thorns and thistles,* and make haste to sow lilies, in case perhaps the beloved should deign to descend to feed us.

18. He surely fed his flock in the presence of Mary, and more abundantly for the cloud of the lilies. Are not lilies the glory of virginity, the sign of humility, the crown of charity?* We also shall have lilies, but how much smaller! But the bridegroom will not even deign to feed among these unless joyfulness of devotion has lit up the thankfulness of which we spoke before, and purity of intention has brightened our prayer, and gentleness purified our confession, as it is written: *If your sins were as scarlet, they shall be white as snow, and if they were red as crimson, they shall be like white wool.**

For the rest, whatever you are preparing to offer, remember to entrust it to Mary, so that grace may return to the bestower of grace by the same aqueduct through which it came. Now God is not powerless to bestow grace without that aqueduct, if he wishes, but he has been pleased to give you this means. Perhaps you have not shaken your hands,* those hands that are covered in blood or stained with bribes, free of all bribes. And so that modest gift that you desire to offer will be pleasing and worthy of all acceptance.* Be sure that you make your offering by the hands of Mary if you do not wish to suffer loss. Certainly some lilies are white, and the lover of lilies will not find fault with anything he finds in Mary's hands.

A Sermon to the Abbots[1]

How Noah, Daniel, and Job Crossed the Sea, Each in His own Way: on a Ship, by a Bridge, by the Shallows

1. This great and wide sea,*—and it is certain that nothing else is signified by it but this present bitter and stormy age—gives passage for three types of people to cross to freedom. These three are Noah, Daniel, and Job;* the first crossed on a ship, the second by a bridge, and the third by the shallows. Now these three men signify three orders in the church: Noah steered the ark* so that it did not perish in the deluge, and in that I see the type of the rulers of the church. Daniel, a man of dreams,* dedicated to abstinence and chastity* and occupied only with God, represents the order of those who are penitent and chaste. Job in marriage ordered well the good things of this world,* and he is the figure of the faithful people who lawfully possess the things of the world.*

*Ps 103:25

*Ezek 14:14

*Gen 7:7

*Dan 9:23
*Dan 1:8

*Job 1:3
*1 John 3:17

Of the first and second we must speak, since there are in our company venerable brethren and our fellow abbots of the rank of prelates, and there are also present monks of the orders of penitents, from whom we

---

[1] *Sermo ad abbates* (Abb).

abbots should not think ourselves distanced, unless—may it not be so—we are unmindful of our profession because of our position. The third, the rank of married men, I pass over briefly, as they have little to do with us. For they cross the mighty sea by the shallows, troubled and dangerous though they are, and the path they take is long, for they take no shortcut. Since the way is dangerous, we grieve that many perish on it, and consequently we see very few who complete the journey. For it is difficult, particularly in these days, since wickedness has lost its stigma, to avoid the whirlpool of vice in the billows of this present age, and the traps of sin and crime.

2. So, then: the continent are those who go by a bridge, which is an easier and shorter way, and everyone knows it is safer. But I am setting the advantages aside and pointing out the dangers, something much better and more profitable to do. Your path is straight, my brothers,* and safer than that of married people, but it is not completely safe. For there is a threefold danger to be feared, namely, if anyone should want to compare himself to another, to look back,* or to stand or even sit down in the middle of the bridge. For the narrowness of the bridge does not allow for any of these three things, and narrow is the way that leads to life.*

Let us then all pray against this danger with the prophet; let not the foot of pride come against us, for they who work iniquity have fallen.* For the one who puts his hand to the plow and then looks back* will certainly fall straightway, and the waters will cover his head. But the one who wishes to stand,* not leaving the Order but pretending to advance in it, must needs fall, driven forth and tripped up by those who follow. For narrow is the way,* and that is a hindrance to those who would advance and travel along it. Thus they assert themselves and are censorious and cannot

*Isa 26:7

*Luke 9:62;
Gen 19:26

*Matt 7:14

*Ps 35:12-13
*Luke 9:62

*1 Cor 10:12

*Matt 7:14

bear the inactivity of tepidity but drive themselves on as though by some goad and push themselves, so that they must necessarily do one of two things, either make some progress or give up entirely. It is not right, then, to halt one's steps; likewise, it is not profitable to look back or to compare oneself with others. Instead, let us run with all humility and make haste, so that we may not be far from him who goes forth as a giant to run a race.* And if we are wise, we shall keep him before our eyes* and, attracted by his aroma,† we shall run more easily and quickly.

*Ps 18:6
*Ps 15:8
†Song 1:3

3. But the pathway over the bridge will not be found too narrow for those who wish to walk along it. For it is made of three kinds of wood, so that the foot of those who wish to rely on it entirely shall not slip on the path. These three are punishment of the body,* poverty of worldly goods, and the humility of obedience. For *by many tribulations we are able to enter into the kingdom of heaven,** and *those who want to be rich* in this world *fall into temptation and the snare of the devil;** the one who has been separated from God by disobedience returns to him by obedience on this straight path. So it is necessary for these three to be linked. For the punishment of the body cannot stand fast among riches, nor can it be easily established without obedience; poverty with pleasure and self-will has no energy, and obedience cannot survive among riches and pleasure, nor can it be deserving of praise.

*poena corporis

*Acts 14:21
*1 Tim 6:9

4. But when these things have been duly linked, see if you have not passed over three perils of this sea: the lust of the flesh, the lust of the eyes, and the pride of life.* Duly linked, I say, so that you are sure that there is not a trace of impatience in the penance, a speck of desire in the poverty, a stain of self-will in the obedience. For those who murmured perished by serpents,* and *those who want to be rich*—not those who are, but *those who want to be rich—fall into the snare of the devil.**

*1 John 2:16

*1 Cor 10:9-10

*1 Tim 6:9

But how does it profit you if you indeed desire not riches but the appearance of poverty, as intensely or even more than people in the world desire wealth? What difference does it make how much property is desired if the affections are corrupt, except that it seems more acceptable that what seems to be greater should be most greatly desired? Also, if anyone makes the excuse, either openly or in secret, that his spiritual father enjoins on him what he desires himself, if he flatters himself on his obedience, he deceives himself.* For in this case it is not he who obeys his superior but the superior who obeys him.

*Gal 6:3

5. But because, according to the saying of the Savior, by the measure with which we measure out it shall be measured to us again,* it is good for people† to give in abundance, so that they may be of the number of those to whose breast others shall give good measure, pressed down, shaken together, and running over.* It is sufficient for the salvation of the body to bear troubles patiently, but it is perfection to embrace them gladly with fervor of spirit. It is sufficient to be able to refrain from asking for superfluous things, and even not to complain if necessary things are lacking, but it is perfection to rejoice and cheerfully look into how another might have what is necessary while you yourself suffer want. It is sufficient for salvation if you choose to bend your reluctant mind to your superior neither unwillingly nor with any manipulation so you can do what you want, but it is perfection to avoid the things by which you feel your own will is gratified, as far as is possible with a good conscience.

*Matt 7:2
†1 Cor 7:26

*Luke 6:38

6. Now the superiors are those *who go down to the sea in ships, doing business in great waters.** They are not confined to clearly marked bridges or footpaths, and they can hasten freely wherever they wish and meet people as is necessary, making their way over bridges or paths, going to set things in order, to search out

*Ps 106:23

perils and avoid them, to rouse the lukewarm and build up the weak. So *they mount up to the heavens, and they descend to the depths,** now making their way across lofty places, now judging the infernal and dreadful deeds of the devil. *Ps 106:26

But what ship can be found that can withstand such mighty waves and remain safe in so great a danger? Surely *love is as strong as death, and jealousy as cruel as the grave,** because, as you read next, *many waters cannot quench love.** This ship is necessary to the superiors, with its three sides compact together, as is always the shape of ships, so that, following the teaching of Paul, it may surely be *charity, from a pure heart and a good conscience and faith unfeigned.** The superior has purity of heart if he desires to benefit rather than to command,* as is his privilege, or seeks nothing of his own in his office except pleasing God and saving souls. *Song 8:6 *Song 8:7 *1 Tim 1:5 *RB 64.8

But his way of life must be blameless, and let him with a pure intention begin to do and to teach* as an example to the flock,* and according to the rule of our Master, whatever he has taught his disciples to be contrary to God's law, let him show by his example is not to be done,* lest the brother whom he was reproving might murmur and say, *Physician, heal thyself.** For such an event does great harm to the superior and is utter ruin to the ones he rules. I do not speak thus as being free from this, but because to me and to all equally the Truth cries out that the one who is in command must be blameless,* so that he may answer his accusers* with the Lord, clear in conscience, *which of you accuses me of sin?** Certainly he cannot be absolutely without sin in this miserable life, but the master should completely avoid what he reproves in his pupils. *Acts 1:1 *1 Pet 5:3 *RB 2.13 *Luke 4:23 *1 Tim 3:2 *Ps 118:42 *John 8:46

7. For this reason people should be in their hidden thoughts what they are in their ordinary life, lest they be humble in appearance but inwardly full of pride,

presuming on their wisdom or virtue or holiness, which is no doubt imaginary, when they do not trust in the goodness of God alone, as the humility of their life would have you believe. And see how exactly these three, purity of heart, a good conscience, and faith unfeigned,* mirror some other words of the apostle, when he says, *it is a small thing that I should be judged by you, or by a human court,** and so on. I do not judge myself, he says, for *I know nothing about myself** that I should seek my own, but the things that are Jesus Christ's.* It is a small thing that I should be judged of you about my good conscience* and blameless life.† *The one who judges me, however, is God,*# he said, to teach us that his hope rested in God alone,‡ since he was humbled under the mighty hand of God.* But be the judge of this, whether the threefold question to Peter, when he was asked, "Do you love me, do you love me, do you love me?"* can be truly applied to these words. You have charity *from a pure heart and a good conscience and faith unfeigned.** Indeed it was from a ship that the question was asked* whether he who was to become fisher of men possessed love.†

*1 Tim 1:5

*1 Cor 4:3
*1 Cor 4:4

*Phil 2:21
*1 Tim 1:5
†1 Tim 3:2
#1 Cor 4:4
‡Ps 72:28
*1 Pet 5:6

*John 21:15-17

*1 Tim 1:5
*see John 21:9-17
†Matt 4:19

On the Feast of Saint Michael[1]

Sermon One

Of the Threefold Reasons that the Angels Care for Us

1. Today is celebrated the memory of the angels, and you require a sermon proper for such a festival. But what are vile worms to say about the angelic spirits? We believe certainly, and hold as an article of faith, that they are blessed by the presence and vision of God, and we rejoice* eternally in the good things that eye has not seen and ear has not heard and that have not entered into the hearts of men.* What is a man to say to men about matters that he cannot encompass in his thought and that they cannot in the least comprehend with their ears? For if *the mouth speaks out of the abundance of the heart,* the tongue must necessarily be quiet from lack of understanding.

*2 Chr 6:41

*1 Cor 2:9

*Matt 12:34

Yet if it is difficult for us to speak of that glorious light in which the holy angels outshine us in themselves, or rather in their God, let us speak of what they reveal to us: grace and love. For in the heavenly spirits is found not only virtue, which we must admire, but also splendor, which we must love. Likewise it is

---

[1] *Sermo in festo sancti Michaëlis* (Mich 1). Saint Michael the Archangel, celebrated Sept. 29.

proper for us, since we deserve no glory, the more to embrace the mercy with which it is certain they overflow, for they are the servants of God, the citizens of heaven,* and the princes of Paradise. That is testified by that apostle who was caught up to the third heaven* and found worthy to have part in that blessed court and to know its secrets, since *they are all ministering spirits, sent to serve those who are the heirs of salvation.**

2. Let no one find this unbelievable, since the Creator, the King of angels, came not to be ministered to but to minister and to give his life for many.* Why should that ministry of angels be rejected by anyone, when he surpasses them to whom they minister with all eagerness and joy? If you still doubt it, know that he who saw it bore witness:* *A thousand thousands ministered unto him, and ten hundred thousand stood before him.** Another prophet, speaking to the Father of the Son, says, *You made him a little lower than the angels.*† So clearly it becomes him who excelled in sublimity thus to excel also in humility and to be lower than the angels inasmuch as he gave himself to a lower ministry, he who was made *as much superior* to the angels *as he has inherited a more excellent name than they.**

But perhaps you ask in what sense he seems lower than the angels, since he came to minister* and they also were sent to minister, as we saw before.* The bride in the Song of Songs rightly says, *Look, he comes leaping upon the mountains, skipping upon the hills.** For he leaped among the angels when he ministered, and when he was ministered to, he skipped over them. For the angels minister, but from another world, offering our good works to God and bringing back to us his grace. Therefore the Scripture says that *the smoke ascended in the sight of God from the angel's hand;** anxiously he offers *the much incense that he has been given.*† It is our sweat, not theirs, that they offer to God, our tears, not theirs; it is his gifts that they bring to us, not theirs.

*Eph 2:19

*2 Cor 12:2

*Heb 1:14

*Matt 20:28

*John 19:35

*Dan 7:10; *decies centena millia*
†Heb 2:7

*Heb 1:4

*Heb 2:9
*Heb 1:14

*Song 2:8

*Rev 8:4; Versicle for the Feast of Saint Michael
†Rev 8:3

3. Not so that minister* who is higher than others but lower than all, who offered himself as a sacrifice of praise* and in offering his soul to the Father† gives us his flesh even today. It is in no way surprising if the holy angels deign to minister to us and indeed do so gladly through the grace of so great a minister, for they love us because Christ loved us.* A common proverb says, "the one who loves me loves my dog." We also, you blessed angels, are the little dogs of that Lord whom you love with such affection, the little dogs, I say, who want to be fed with the crumbs that fall from the table of our masters,* which you are. And for the rest, I say this so that you may have greater confidence in the blessed angels: invoke their help naturally in every need, and lead your lives more worthily in their presence, embracing their grace more and more, holding fast to their kindness, and begging their indulgence. Therefore I think it necessary to lay before your charity other instances that represent the blessed angels as caring for us in our weakness, without anxiety on their part but not without profit to us, not causing any diminution of their felicity but increasing our well-being.

*Rom 15:8

*Heb 9:14
†Ps 49:23

*see 1 John 4:19

*Matt 15:27;
Luke 16:21

4. It is beyond doubt that human souls partake of reason and are capable of blessedness and, if we dare say it, are born of angelic nature. Nor, O blessed Spirits, can you properly disdain the precept of the law, which you must visit,* although, as you see, it has fallen into great wickedness. But I do not think that you, O citizens of heaven, are pleased by the destruction of your country and the ruin of its walls, which as you see are half fallen down. If you desire their renewal, as is right, I beg you often to repeat words of prayer before the throne of glory, saying, *Do good in your good pleasure to Zion, so that the walls of Jerusalem may be built up.** If you love the beauty of God's house,* or rather because you truly love it, let the living and thinking stones*

*Job 5:24

*Ps 50:20
*Ps 25:8
*1 Pet 2:5

experience your zeal, since for the restoration of God's house they can be built up only together with you. This, my brothers, is the threefold rope* by which the love of the angels is drawn from the high habitation* of the heavens to console us, to visit us, and to help us, for the sake of God, for our sake, and for themselves: for the sake of God, particularly, so that they may imitate his heart-filled mercy toward us;* for our sake, so that in us they may look with compassion on his indisputable likeness; and for their own sake, as they long with all desire for their ranks to be renewed by us. The angelic spirits, having the firstfruits of his divine majesty—which is perfected from the mouths of babes,* who feed only on milk and are not yet nourished on solid food*—truly delight in its blessed enjoyment but are moved the more by expectation and longing for its fulfillment.

*Eccl 4:12
*Deut 26:15

*Luke 1:78

*Ps 8:3

*Heb 5:12

5. Therefore, beloved, reflect what need we have of care, that we may show ourselves worthy of the angels' constant presence and thus live in their sight and not perhaps offend the holy ones while gazing upon them. Woe to us indeed if provoked by our sins and negligence they judge us unworthy of their presence and visitation, so that we must lament and say with the prophet, *My friends and my neighbors approached and stood against me, and those who were near me stood at a distance, and those who sought my soul used violence,** and those whose presence could protect us and drive away our enemy drew away from us. And if we have the friendship of the angelic host, which we need so much, we must avoid offending them and must try our best to do those things in which we know they delight. Now there are many things that please them and that they delight to find in us, such as sobriety, chastity, voluntary poverty, frequent longing for heaven, and prayers with tears* and with the heart's desire. But above all these things the angels of peace demand from us unity

*Ps 37:12-13

*RB 52.4

and peace.* Why should they not find much pleasure in those things that show the likeness of their country in us, so that they marvel at the new Jerusalem on earth?* I tell you that insofar as we share in that state,† so shall we feel and speak,# so that there are no divisions among us, but we are all one body.‡

6. On the contrary, nothing causes them such offense and indignation as dissensions and scandals if they are found among us. Let us hear also what Paul says to the people of Corinth: *For whereas jealousy and quarreling are among you, are you not carnal,* and do you not walk according to men?** Likewise in the epistle of Jude the apostle we read, *These are those who separate themselves, being sensual,* lacking the spirit.*† You may see how the soul of humans gives life to all members of the body, bonded together. Take away a part from the whole and see whether it still lives—and so too for everyone who calls Jesus accursed, because no one speaking by the Spirit of God speaks thus, for cursing is separation.* So, I maintain, is everyone who is separated from unity: do not doubt that the spirit of life has gone from him. Rightly, then, do the apostles call those who separate themselves carnal and brutish, not having the spirit of life.* Therefore the holy and blessed spirits, finding scandals and dissensions, say, "What have we to do with this generation, which does not have the spirit of life? For if the Spirit were there, charity would be shed abroad by it,* and unity would not be broken." And they say, "We will not abide with these people forever, for they are carnal;* for what has light to do with darkness?* We belong to the kingdom of unity and peace, and we hoped that these people would come to the same unity and peace. But now what is there to prevent us from being separated from them?" You see how the words of the gospel agree with this solemn saying when they warn us of scandal against little ones, since scandals greatly

*Isa 33:7

*Rev 21:2
†Ps 121:3
#Rom 12:16;
1 Cor 1:10
‡1 Cor 10:17

*carnales
*1 Cor 3:3

*animales
†Jude 19

*1 Cor 12:3

*Gen 6:17;
1 Cor 3:1-3;
Jude 19

*Rom 5:5

*Gen 6:3
*2 Cor 6:14-15

displease the angels: *Whoever causes one of these little ones . . . What follows is hard.**

*Matt 18:6

But the time has gone; we must go to Mass. I hope the adjournment is not troublesome to you: it could in fact be useful if I would follow the present text in greater detail in another sermon.

On the Feast of Saint Michael[1]

Sermon Two

Of the Words of the Lord, *If anyone offends one of these little ones**

*Matt 18:6

1. You have heard, my brethren, a gospel reading that utters terrible thunders against those who offend the weak.* Truth flatters no one, speaks softly to no one, appeals to no one, but utters open denunciations, saying, *Woe to that man through whom the offence comes;** *it were good for him if he had never been born**—born, that is, again,† born to life, born of the spirit,# who ends up in the flesh!‡ *It were better for him* who stirs up offense in this house, in this holy community of friends,* which is pleasing to God and exceedingly dear to his angels, *if a millstone were hanged about his neck,** and instead of the easy yoke and light burden of the Savior, the heavy burden of earthly greed were placed upon his shoulders and *he were drowned in the depth of the sea** by its wide and spacious hands,* which is without doubt the evil world.† It would be less damnable for him to perish in the world than in the monastery. Indeed a man who has no charity must perish, even if he gives his body to be burned.*

*Matt 18:6

*Matt 18:7
*Matt 26:34
†John 3:3
#John 3:8
‡Gal 3:3
*familiari congregatione

*Matt 18:6

*Matt 11:30
*Ps 103:25
†Gal 1:4

*1 Cor 13:3

---

[1] *Sermo in festo sancti Michaëlis* (Mich 2).

I say this, my brothers, not because I do not think well of you, or because this terrible vice seems to rule your lives, but so that you may take care to persevere and grow more and more* in the charity, unity, and peace* in which you stand in the Lord.† *For what is our hope, and our joy, and the crown of glory?*# Is it not your unity, your unanimity, in which I rejoice that you are found to be lovers of your brothers,* having mutual charity among yourselves before all things,* which is the bond of perfection?* For that reason I beg you: *Stand thus fast in the Lord, my dearly beloved.** For by this all will know, even the holy angels, that you are the disciples of Christ, if you have love for one another.*

*1 Thess 4:1
*Eph 4:3
†Phil 4:1
#1 Thess 2:19

*Col 3:14
*1 Pet 4:8
*Col 3:14
*Phil 4:1

*John 13:35

2. If you remember what I told you in the previous sermon about the threefold reason for the love and care of the angels for us, the service of brotherly love can also be greatly praised for the same reason. It is easy to suppose that nothing we said appeals to people who do not love their neighbor. For we will not be loved by the angels for the grace of Christ, will we, if by our lack of mutual love they also know that we are by no means his disciples?* We will not be loved by them for our own sakes, will we, that is, for the likeness to the spiritual nature, if we are found not to love those with whom we share our human nature and if there are disagreements among us,* proving that we are worldly rather than spiritual? Finally, they will not love us for their own sakes, either, will they, and for our part in the future restoration of their city, if, which heaven forbid, the one thing by which alone we can be united with them and built up with them, the cement of charity, is lacking? How will they hope that the walls of their city will be rebuilt if they know, if they see, that we are not living stones* that can cleave together but are rather dust that the wind blows away from the face of the earth,* that is worked up by the breath of a single word to a whirlwind and dispersed

*see John 13:35

*1 Cor 3:3

*1 Pet 2:5

*Ps 1:4

by the slightest breath of suspicion? Let it suffice to repeat the words of the Lord: *if anyone offends one of these little ones.** Truly, I believe you will from now on take great care to avoid this terrible scourge.

3. And who is not moved by what follows in the gospel—*if your eye offends you, pluck it out**—and so on? Surely we are not told to pluck out this bodily eye, or cut off one of these hands, or likewise a foot, are we? Let such a wholly carnal and utterly ridiculous idea be banished from our minds! Rather, after the divine word has warned us sharply against scandals that affect others, as you have heard, he instructs us what we should do about the scandal within, when we find a conflicting law in our members.* For *he knows of what we are made,** so that for us a scandal of this kind is not easily avoided.

Again, daily experience lets us know that this scandal happens in three ways. For instance, sometimes there is in us the single* eye of spiritual intention,† which may be attributed to grace rather than to us. But our eye offends us, and it is truly ours, when our will persistently works another intention that is less holy. But we have besides that the wholesome plan of the Savior: *Pluck it out and throw it from you.** This command will be fulfilled if you do not consent, if you cast it from you, if you resist it. The same thing is true about the hand and foot. For when we are intent on good works and our own will tries to draw us aside to other things, it is our hand that offends us;* it must be plucked off and cast from us so that we do not consent to it.

4. So, then, desiring to advance in holy living* and to climb the steps of the ladder that appeared to Jacob† and, according the words of the psalmist, to go from strength to strength,* we too often suffer offense from the foot* of our cowardice and negligence, for without fail it tries to go downward or at most makes but a

*Matt 18:6

*Matt 18:9

*Rom 7:32
*Ps 102:14

*simplex
†Rom 7:23

*Matt 18:9

*Matt 18:8

**sancta conversatio*
†Gen 28:12; see RB 7.5-9
*Ps 83:8
*Matt 18:8

halfhearted effort to go forward. It must be cut off so that the foot of grace, which stands in an even place,* can run without offense, without scandal, and without hindrance. For when he says that it is better for us to enter into life with one eye or hand or foot than to go into the hell of fire with two,* he is referring to those who follow their own will, whether it be good or ill, and go by two ways, following now the good, now the evil, according as their desire vacillates. For them it would be better cleave to grace in all things and, when their own will* opposed it, cut it off and cast it from them.

*Ps 25:12

*Matt 18:8-9

*propria voluntas

For it is by lengthy training in the cutting off of our own will that we conquer it to a degree, so that our soul may learn not to be proud* but rather to be subject to God without any disgrace or shame. Then it is not necessary to pluck out our eye, since by cleaving to the single eye one becomes single himself.* Surely it is not another eye but one with it, for the apostle bears witness that *the one who is joined to the Lord is one spirit with him.**

*Ps 61:2

*Matt 6:22

*1 Cor 6:17

Now what is said of the eye must also be understood of the hand and the foot. For one whose will clings to grace out of affection* and with desire, so that he does not wish to do what is evil, or do things of a lesser good, or do less well than the promptings of grace suggest—this, clearly, is a perfect man!* Now while this peace pertains of happiness, the silencing of scandals and the victory over temptation are of fortitude. The former pertains to glory, the latter to manhood.*

*ex affectione

*vir; Jas 3:2

*virtus

Sunday of the First Week of November[1]

Sermon One

Of the Vision of Isaiah

1. *I saw the Lord seated upon a throne, high and lifted up, and the whole earth was full of his majesty.** A heavenly vision is described for us in the speech of the prophet. *I saw the Lord seated*, he says. A wonderful sight, my brothers, and blessed were the eyes that saw it.* Who does not desire with his whole heart to look upon the glory of such majesty? This indeed was ever the only desire of all the saints. For it is he *whom the angels have desired to look upon,** whom to see is eternal life.*

But, my brothers, from the same prophet and from the same God, I hear of another, far different vision, because it is Isaiah who says in another place, *We saw him, and he was not beautiful or comely; we esteemed him as a leper,* and so on.* First then we must consider the second vision, and we see that it is given to all, whereas the first seems to be granted only to the prophet. Not without reason is it written there *we saw him,* and here *I saw him,* for you must understand that the one is granted to all, whereas the other is a mark of singular merit. For Herod saw him destitute of form or comeliness,* and the Jews also saw him, those Jews who

*Isa 6:1, 3, as in the responsory *Vidi* for the Sunday following All Saints
*Luke 10:23

*1 Pet 1:2
*John 17:3

*Isa 53:2, 4

*see Luke 23:8

---

[1] *Sermo in dominica I novembris* (1 Nov 1).

counted all his bones.* And now the prophet speaks of this blessed vision, saying in clear condemnation, *Let the wicked be destroyed, lest they see the glory of God.**

2. Therefore it was not only at sundry times and in diverse ways that he spoke through the prophets* but that he was also seen by the prophets. David acknowledged him as lower than the angels,* and Jeremiah saw him speaking with human beings on earth.* Isaiah bears witness that he saw him in one way raised on a lofty throne* and in another way not only lower than the angels or among human beings but as a leper,* that is, not only in the flesh but in the likeness of sinful flesh.* You, too, if you wish to see Jesus lofty,* take care first to see him lowly.* If you wish to see him as a king sitting on a throne, look upon him as the serpent lifted up in the wilderness.* Let this vision humble you so that the other may exalt you when you are humbled. Let the first give respite and healing to your wound, that the other may fulfill and satisfy your desire.* Do you see him emptied out?* Let it not be an indifferent vision, because you will not be able indifferently to see him lifted up. You will be like him when you see him as he is;* be like him now, seeing him for what he became for your sake. For if you do not refuse a likeness in his humility, you will certainly be granted a likeness in his splendor.

He will never allow one who shared in his tribulation to be shut out from the communion of his glory. He has never refused to let one who shares his passion come with him into his kingdom; even on the cross he proclaimed that the thief should be with him in Paradise that day.* So it is that he said to the apostles, *You are those who have remained with me in my tribulations,** and *I will assign a kingdom to you.*† So if we suffer with him we shall also reign with him;# meanwhile let us contemplate Christ and him crucified.‡ Let us set his seal on our hearts, his seal on our arm.* Let us embrace him as it were with the arms of love; let us

*Ps 21:18
*Isa 26:10
*Heb 1:1
*Heb 2:9
*Bar 3:38
*Isa 6:1
*Isa 53:4
*Rom 8:3
*sublimem
*humilem
*John 3:14
*Ps 102:5
*Phil 2:7
*1 John 3:2
*Luke 23:42-43
*Luke 22:28-29
†Rom 8:17
#2 Tim 2:12
‡1 Cor 2:2
*Song 8:6

follow him with the desire for holy living, for this is the way he who is the salvation of God* is shown to us, no longer without beauty or comeliness but in full glory, so that his splendor fills the whole earth.*

*Ps 49:23

*Ps 71:19; Wis 1:7

3. It is fitting that the first vision is seen as if it were still wintertime, not on a throne but farther down and even in an insignificant* dwelling. For a great house usually has two dwelling places, the summer one above, and the winter one below. Therefore, since the very hearts of his disciples were shriveled up by the ice of winter, and Peter, no less cold in his heart than in his body, warmed himself at the coals against the frost,* it was not the time to dwell on the throne, or, rather to be thus manifest. But when a new song shall be sung,* *the winter is over and gone, the flowers have appeared in our land,** then it will be fitting that the Lord should ascend the throne, and should dwell on high.*

*humiliori

*John 18:18

*Ps 95:1

*Song 2:11-12
*Isa 33:5

4. Consider, therefore, that when Isaiah was uttering these words, he foresaw the glory of that time with the eye of prophecy: *I saw the Lord*, he said, *sitting on his throne, high*, and so on.* But what kind of throne are we to suppose that is, my brethren? For the Most High does not dwell in temples made with hands.* No material substance seems fit for such a throne, such an occupier. The spiritual structure, which the true and eternal life has chosen for his dwelling place, must be built of living stones,* so if an angelic creature scarcely suffices for this throne, and sinners even less, he will determinedly raise the needy out of the earth, the poor from the dust, that he may set them among princes and complete the throne of glory.* Perhaps for that reason the one who saw describes the throne not only as high but also as lifted up, so that as the loftiness of the angels should be depicted as stable, so should the merciful lifting up of human beings be. What follows seems to require more careful consideration; let it be enough for today that we have begun.

*Isa 6:1

*Acts 7:48

*1 Pet 2:5

*Ps 113:7-8; 1 Sam 2:8

Sunday of the First Week of November[1]

Sermon Two

*contemplator

*Isa 6:3, as in the responsory *Vidi* for the first Sunday in November
†Matt 6:10
#John 12:31
‡Job 9:24
*Luke 22:53

*Ps 1:4

*Ps 71:19

*Rom 8:21-22

1. *T*he whole earth—so says our contemplative* of the one he saw exalted on his throne—*is full of his majesty*:* Your kingdom come, O Lord, and let the earth be filled with your majesty, even as the heavens are filled.† Why is the prince of this world# everywhere so riotous as at a bacchanalia if not because *the earth is given into the hands of the wicked*?‡ This is his hour and the power of darkness,* but there will certainly be a time when he, who has no place in heaven and will be banished also from the face of the earth, will be found in subterranean caverns. Therefore, as is clear, David, having announced the good fortune of the saints, continued concerning the evil one and his angels or members, saying, *It is not so with the wicked, not so, but they are like the dust that the wind drives from the face of the earth*.* Then there will be no risk of temptation, no chance of disturbance, no possibility of harm. The whole earth will be full of his glory,* for there will be no flouting of his will, but rather creation itself will be set free from the servitude of the corruption with which it groans and is in travail until now.* And there will be a new heaven and a new

---

[1] *Sermo in dominica I novembris* (1 Nov 2).

earth,* so that wherever you turn your eyes, you will see the glory of God shining forth in all things.

2. But there is another earth that is nearer to you, and for it the solicitude is greater and more just. For no one has ever yet hated his own flesh.* Comfort it therefore so that it, too, may rest in hope,* knowing that the whole earth will be filled with the glory of God.* But how will the glory of God fill our human flesh, beloved, since even Paul, who had the firstfruits of the Spirit,* groans in misery and says, *I know that there is no good thing in me, that is, in my flesh?** Now certainly sin did not reign in his mortal body.* Notice that he speaks only of the mortal body and says that sin does not rule completely. For the law of sin,* which the fullness of glory would at its coming completely drive out, was in his members. This is not all, for *the last enemy that shall be destroyed is death.**

This earth of ours will be filled with the glory of God when all consciousness of sin is quite done away,* and with it the debt of death. The whole earth, I say, will be filled with the glory of God when it is clothed with the glory of the resurrection; it will put on the robe of immortality* and will at last be fashioned like the glorious body of Christ. *We await a savior who shall change the body of our humility, that it may be configured to his glorious body.** Why do you still complain, miserable flesh? Why do you rebel and lust against the spirit?*

If he humiliates you, if he punishes you, if he brings you into subjection,* it is no less for your sake than his. Why do you envy those who are not ashamed to beg for glory, which is no glory, from the work of worms and the skins of mice—finery unworthy of men, forbidden even to women, for it dishonors rather than adorns them?* Let them reform, or rather deform, their bodies. As for you, if you are the body of humility, the same artist will reform you who formed you originally. You, if you are wise, will wait for that hand so that it may remake what it has made.

*Rev 21:1

*Eph 5:29
*Ps 15:9

*Ps 71:19

*Rom 8:23
*Rom 7:18
*Rom 6:14, 12

*Rom 7:23

*1 Cor 15:26

*Ps 71:19;
2 Thess 2:7

*1 Cor 15:53

*Phil 3:20-21
*Gal 5:17

*1 Cor 9:27

*1 Pet 3:3;
1 Tim 2:9

3. Now listen to what follows in that prophetic vision. *And those*, he says, *who were under it** *filled the temple.*† Therefore I said, "Humble yourself under the powerful hand of God, that he may exalt you in due time."* See that you are found under him; otherwise you cannot be with him. What, then? Do you think that he would haphazardly admit human beings to so blessed a temple when he did not even let in the angels haphazardly? Or does he who made distinctions among the stars not make distinctions among clumps of earth?* He who weighed gold and tried it will weigh silver also.*

*i.e., the throne
†Isa 6:1
*1 Pet 5:6

*1 Cor 15:41
*Ps 65:10; Wis 3:6

What sort of person do you think must be found to fill the place of a rejected angel? Clearly one who is free from all iniquity, particularly that which was found in that angel and which brought about no light offense or momentary anger, but eternal hatred. For it was pride that once brought disorder to that kingdom, shook its walls, and even destroyed it in part—and in no small part. And then what? You don't think that pride was easily admitted after that, do you? Certainly the city could not but hate it and violently abominate a bane of this kind!

You may be sure, brothers, that he who did not spare the angels in their pride will not spare human beings.* He does not act contrary to his own nature, and he is no respecter of persons:* his judgments are consistent. Humility alone pleases him, either in the angels or in humans, and he who sits upon the throne chooses only those who are submissive to fill the temple.* Indeed it is written, *Who is like the Lord our God, who dwells on high and looks upon the humble in heaven and on earth?** See if this is not the word of Michael, who resisted to his face the one who said in his pride, *I shall be like the most high.** The name *Michael* means "Who is like God?"²

*2 Pet 2:4

*Acts 10:34

*Rev 7:15

*Ps 112:5-6

*Isa 14:14

---

² Jerome, *Liber interpretationis Hebraicorum nominum, s.v. Michahel*, ed. P. de Lagarde, G. Morin, M. Adriaen, CCSL 72 (Turnhout: Brepols, 1959), 82.

4. The prophet was right, then, when he said that he saw the Lord on his throne high and lifted up, lest you should think that the one* who said, *I will rise above the heights of the clouds*,* is said to be high and lifted up, or should use the words *high and lifted up* of those who raise themselves in pride, and when he added, *and those who were under him filled the temple.** By this you should understand clearly that it is not that loftiness that rises up against him* that is commended, but those in the temple, whether before the throne or under it, some raised in steadfast stability, some lifted up from the last place by divine pity. And lest you object that all things are under his rule, or that his saying *those who were under him* should be taken in an inclusive sense, he added the part about the seraphim to show that he approved and recommended only one kind of submission to God, that which is voluntary and proceeds from ardent charity. About the seraphim we shall speak in due course, as God provides.

*i.e., Lucifer
*Isa 13:14

*Isa 6:1

*2 Cor 10:5

5. *And those*, he says, *who were under him filled the temple*. God created the angels from the beginning, that in them the fullness of his blessed temple might be established; yet with most of them God was not pleased,* because *even in his angels*, as it is written, *he found wickedness*.* He was in their ranks who said, *I will set my seat in the North*,* and there were those who entrusted themselves to him. Miserable is the one who has preferred rather to be without God than subject to him; miserable also those who saw a thief and made common cause with him.* They went away unhappy, and their place was left empty for another to take.

*1 Cor 10:5
*Job 4:18
*Isa 14:13

*Ps 49:18

You, my soul, will you not be subject to God?* For in no other way will there be a place in the temple for you, for *those who were under him filled the temple*. In vain will the foolish virgins beat upon the door, in vain will they cry out when the wedding is over and the door shut.* Unhappy the soul who, arriving at that wedding feast, is shut out! Unhappy the one to

*Ps 61:2;
Matt 25:10-12

*Matt 22:10

whom they cry, *Let the wicked be destroyed lest he see the glory of the Lord!** Why then has that wretched person seen the light of this day when he will not deserve to gaze on that glory? Would that my eye had never seen anything if—which God forbid!—it were to be denied that vision. Let the proud go their way; rather, let them become arrogant, let them be elated and puffed up, let them always seek to appear on a cloud, so that when the rule of justice is come they will be cast out into the void!

*Isa 26:10

But as for you, my soul, let that not happen. Rather, be subject to God, subject with all your strength,* subject with the warmth of devotion, for *above it stood the seraphim.** Let us stand with them today, my brothers, and let us not be removed from that temple* in which all say, "Glory!" because they contemplate the glory of Our Lord Jesus Christ, who is *above all, blessed for ever.**

*ex animo

*Isa 6:2

*Ps 28:9

*Rom 9:5

Sunday of the First Week of November[1]

Sermon Three

1. I do not think that I should fail in offering you a sermon today about the two seraphim of which Isaiah speaks. When he had testified that he saw the Lord sitting upon his throne, he added that above it stood the seraphim.* *Seraphim*, as you have often heard, beloved, is the title of one of the seven orders of supernal spirits, the highest and most exalted one. I think that no significance should be given to the fact that only these two seraphim are described in this passage, particularly since there are countless cohorts of them. Now, my brothers, since it is granted to everyone in my position to abound in understanding,* in my reading these two seraphim are to be understood as the rational creatures, both angels and humans. And you will not marvel that the seraphim are made human; remember that the Creator and Lord of the seraphim was made man. It is to your shame, O proud one, that you, who were created one of the angels, did not deserve to stand among the angels.

*Isa 6:2

*Rom 14:5

Look, our king comes to make new angels on the earth! And so that you may agonize even more and be tormented by your own envy, they are not angels of

[1] *Sermo in dominica I novembris* (1 Nov 3).

any lower rank, but seraphim. Hear now what he says: *I have come to bring fire on the earth, and what do I wish but that it be already kindled?** He wants the seraphim to be created so that they may stand where you fell! *The seraphim*, it says, *stood above.** Why did you not stand fast in the truth, O Lucifer, son of the morning,* except that you were not of the seraphim? Seraphim are understood as burning or fiery.² O unhappy one, you had light, but you had no warmth. It had been better for you if you had been a fire-bearer rather than a light-bearer* and not glittering with such an unbridled desire that being frigid yourself you should pick out a frigid region. For you said, *I will ascend above the heights of the clouds; I will sit in the far recesses of the north.**

*Luke 12:49

*Isa 6:2
*Isa 14:12; John 8:44

**ignifer magis . . . quam lucifer*

*Isa 14:14, 13

Why do you hasten to rise in the morning, Lucifer? Why do you vaunt yourself above the stars and seem to shine more brightly than they? Your boasting will be short-lived. The Sun of justice follows,* whom you tried to cast out by false pretense, and by both his raging heat and his splendor you will be brought to nothing and will utterly disappear! Furthermore, your plot to appear at the end of the age as that condemned human being and to be extolled above everything that is called God and revered as God is in vain, for then the Lord will come as the true Sun rising, and at the brightness of his coming you will be utterly destroyed!*

*Mal 4:2

*2 Thess 2:8

2. How much better was John the Baptist, himself a light-bearer.* At least he did not make a fool of himself!* It was by the authority of God the Father and not by his own presumption (lest he should be a thief and a robber)* that he went ahead of the Lord. *Behold, it says, I send my messenger before you.** You have also in

*John 5:35
*Ps 21:3

*John 10:1
*Luke 7:27

---

² See Jerome, *Liber interpretationis Hebraicorum nominum*, s.v. *Seraphim*, ed. P. de Lagarde, G. Morin, M. Adriaen, CCSL 72 (Turnhout: Brepols, 1959), 121–22 (*Seraphim ardentes uel incendentes*).

the Psalms, *I have prepared a lamp for my Christ.** For he was a burning and shining light, and the Jews were willing for a time to rejoice in that light,* but not he. Why? Ask him, let him speak for himself: *The friend of the bridegroom stands and rejoices greatly at the bridegroom's voice.** So John stands, for he is not a reed shaken by the wind.* He stands because he is a friend; he stands because he is burning, just as the seraphim are also described as standing. The friend of the bridegroom does not rival the bridegroom in glory as he comes forth from his chamber;* rather, he prepares the way† and he announces grace so that he himself may deserve to receive of his fullness.*

*Ps 131:17

*John 5:35

*John 3:29
*Matt 11:7

*Ps 18:6
†Matt 3:3

*John 1:16

So John shines as a light, and the more generously he burns, the brighter; the more truly, the less he longs to shine. He is the faithful bearer of light, who did not come to take the place of the Sun of righteousness but to proclaim his glory.* *I am not the Christ,*† he said; *he who comes after me is stronger than I, whose sandals I am not worthy to remove*, and again, *I baptize you with water; he will baptize you with the Holy Spirit and with fire.**

*Mal 4:2
†John 1:20

*Mark 1:7; Matt 3:11

It seems as though the light-bearer openly says, "Why do you stare at my brilliance? I am not the sun. You will see another far off; compared with him I am darkness and not light. I, like the morning star, sprinkle you with morning dew,* but he will shed his rays upon you with warmth and melt the ice; he will dry up the marshy land and warm what is cold; he will be as it were a garment for the poor." The word of the forerunner agrees with that of the judge, but Christ clearly manifests the fire promised by John when he says, *I have come to bring fire on the earth.**

*Wis 11:23

*Luke 12:49
*fervorem

3. Perhaps you may say that just as there is heat* in fire, so there is brilliance. I do not dispute it, as long as the heat is seen to be somehow more essential. Let the Lord himself tell us what he praises most in the fire. *I have come*, he says, *to bring fire on the earth, and what*

do I wish but that it be already kindled?* You know for certain what he wishes, but be certain also that in his will there is life* and that the servant who knows the will of the Lord and does not do it will be beaten with many blows.* Why are you in such a hurry to shine? The time has not yet come when *the just will shine like the sun in the kingdom of their father.** In the meantime this desire to shine is pernicious; it is much better to give off heat.*

But if you so strongly desire brightness, take care to be what you seem and seek to be hot first, and without doubt brightness will be added to you; otherwise you labor for nothing, since brightness without heat is untrustworthy. Light that does not come from fire is borrowed or, more accurately, false. You can borrow for a little while what does not belong to you, but there will be greater confusion if you want it to seem that what is not yours is yours. The moon, they say, has brightness without heat because it borrows it from the sun, and it borrows so frequently—in fact all the time—that it is always changing and never stays in the same state.*

Here is how it is with the perfect and with the fool: *the fool changes like the moon, and the wise stays the same, like the sun.**³ That one is a fool, I say, who has lost wisdom because of his concern for appearances,* that is, who has grown numb through splendor.

4. So Lucifer fell like lightning from heaven,* but the seraphim stand.† Yes, the seraphim stand because *charity never fails.*# They stand in astonishment, rapt in contemplation of him who sits upon the throne. They stand in eternal unchangeableness and unchangeable eternity. You tried to sit on the throne, O accursed

---

³ Bede, "In Samuelem Prophetam," book 1, in *Commentaria in Scripturas Sacras*, ed. J. A. Giles (London, 1844), 371.

one;* therefore your feet have slipped and your footsteps stagger.* It is the Son who sits upon the throne, the Lord of hosts, judging all things with tranquillity.* The singular Trinity sits, who in a singular way has immortality;* that one alone is singular for whom there is no variableness nor shadow of turning.* The seraphim indeed stand immutable, but in their own way, not to be compared with the Trinity. They stand outstretched, leaning toward him* upon whom they desire to look.* He who presumed to sit on the throne was willing to be satisfied with himself; therefore now he hungers only for malice because that is the only thing he has that is his.

*Isa 14:13
*Ps 72:2

*Wis 12:18
*1 Tim 6:16
*Jas 1:17

*Luke 4:20
*1 Pet 1:12

*When he speaks a lie, he speaks from what is his own, because he is a liar and the father of the lie.** When you hear a lying word, know that it is the work of malice. And he may maliciously please himself with malice, yet he cannot find satisfaction in it. For the singular sublime Trinity sits, who is singular in itself and is thus truly singular; it is singular in enjoying itself, singular in lacking nothing, singular in being sufficient unto itself.

*John 8:44

Sunday of the First Week of November[1]

Sermon Four

      1. **W**hen the prophet had said that the seraphim stood above, he added, *The one had six wings, and the other had six wings.**** *Isa 6:2
What is the meaning of these wings, brothers? When the winter has gone* and the king sits on his throne,* must these seraphim still fly to relieve the various needs of various people, to free them from perils that threaten, to bring help to those in difficulties, to console those who find themselves in trouble? God forbid there be any want in that kingdom of eternal beatitude, any danger, any trial or tribulation that requires such measures! What then are these wings? I like it that they stand there; I absolutely desire that they remain like that, and by no means do I allow anything that would deprive me of that stability. But I know that you, O blessed Isaiah, are a prophet* and have the spirit of him who exceeds in abundant goodness not only the merits of human beings but also their vows.[2]

    As regards me, may that stability that I love so much be kept safe, and if these wings increase beatitude, I do

*Isa 6:2
*Song 2:11
*Isa 6:1;
Matt 25:31

*John 4:19

---

[1] *Sermo in dominica I novembris* (1 Nov 4).
[2] Collect for Twelfth Sunday after Pentecost.

not object. Moreover, I believe that just as staying put is preferred when on watch,* so is enthusiasm when it comes to flying; otherwise stability will be thought to be as unfeeling as stone. But you may say, "Even if they must have wings, why do they have so many? What is the meaning of this multiplicity of wings?" Hear what follows: *With two wings they cover their head, with two their feet, and with two they fly.** In those words I think I see that what is said of their staying put is explained more clearly by their flying. For where should the seraphim fly but to him for whom they burn with love? See how a flame flies and stands still at the same time, and you will not find it strange that the seraphim fly while they stand and stand while they fly.

*statione

**Isa 6:2*

2. But because we have said where they fly, your scrupulous desire for knowledge seems to wonder about the wings with which they fly. Those to whom it has been given to see can bear the more trustworthy and convincing witness. Nevertheless, I suppose it is not unreasonable to understand as perception and devotion* these wings by which the seraphim are taken up to him who is above them. The wing of knowledge lifts them, but it alone is not enough. Those who try to fly with only one wing fall the more quickly, and the farther they are raised up, the worse the fall.

**agnitionem et devotionem*

The philosophers of the Gentiles tried to do this, those who while they knew God did not glorify him as God but disappeared into their own thoughts, and their foolish heart was darkened.* They ended up given over to their own depraved thought and fell into consequent dishonorable habits. Thus is proved the truth of the saying *The one who knows the good and does not do it is a sinner.** Such also is zeal without knowledge,* for the faster you run, the harder you fall; the force of the rebound equals the force of the thrust. But when charity goes hand in hand with understanding, and devotion with perception, people fly safely, fly and never stop, because they fly in timelessness.

**Rom 1:21, 28*

**Jas 4:17*
**Rom 10:2*

3. Now about the veiling of head and feet, which has already been mentioned, there is a tradition sanctioned by the Fathers[3] that the head and feet of God are veiled, meaning that what was before the world and what will be after the consummation are both hidden. This tradition is based on what is distinctly written in the Latin codices: *his head and his feet.** But our interpreter says that the word is common in Hebrew and "can be translated *his* or *their,* so that the seraphim, thanks to the ambiguity of the Hebrew word, are said to cover either the face and feet of God or to cover their own face and feet."[4] So it can seem strange—unless he is following Origen's commentary here*—that between these two possible interpretations he has chosen the meaning that the vision's description seems to render less likely: that they fly and at the same time veil the head and feet of him who is sitting.

*Isa 6:2

*Origen, *In Isaiah,* Hom 1.2

4. Draw a picture of what it seems permissible to say about the seraphim: the head and feet would be covered over, and only the middle part of the body would be visible, but even that not entirely, because of the wings they are provided to fly with. This picture leads me to consider my own head, my body, and my feet, in the light of the apostle's words when he says, *Whom God knew before ever they were and ordained that they should be conformed to the likeness of his son, and those whom he predestined he has also called, and those whom he called, he also justified, and those whom he justified he also glorified.** Thus my beginning is an act of grace alone, and I have nothing in myself to which I attribute either predestination or vocation. Of course it is differ-

*Rom 8:29-30

---

[3] Jerome, Ep 18.7 (CSEL 54.83); Ambrose, *De Spiritu Sancto* 3.163 (PL 16:813).
[4] Jerome, *In Isaiah* 3.6.2 (PL 24:93); see also *In Isaiah* 1.10 (PL 24:33).

ent when it comes to the work of justification. There I am no outsider. It is clearly both the work of grace and my own work.

Do you see how the seraphim appear more or less in the middle? At the end is consummation. It is an act of grace alone. There is nothing for me to do in this part or with it, not even to boast in it, as if I would be seen to be a fellow-worker or a partner in it. The seraphim therefore veil their head with two wings if they truly understand and humbly confess that mercy alone goes before them. They veil their feet also with two wings if they are neither ignorant of the mercy that will follow nor ungrateful for it.

How necessary it is not to neglect the veiling of his head and feet but on the contrary to do it all the more carefully now when the Judge sits on his throne,* for he will shine more brightly with the light of truth on the seraphim who are standing near him and will make them burn more ardently with the heat of charity.

*Isa 6:1; Matt 25:31

May that mercy about which we have spoken and which is from everlasting to everlasting on his chosen ones be pleased to place us who are labeled his unworthy servants in their number. For a determined space of time in the middle, free will is on display whereby to merit grace, but on him alone depends the beginning and the ending, so that he may be for us the Lord our God, the Alpha and Omega,* and that we may rightly cry to each other, *Not to us, Lord, not to us, but to your name give glory.** Amen.

*Rev 1:8; 22:13

*Ps 113:9

SUNDAY OF THE FIRST WEEK OF NOVEMBER[1]

SERMON FIVE

1. The sacred writings commend to us that Christ the Lord is from the Father, and in the Father, and with the Father, and by the Father, and for the Father, and even below the Father. In that he is from the Father, his birth is mysterious; in that he is in the Father, it is a unity of substance; as he is with the Father, he is of like majesty. These three are eternal attributes. But if his birth is from the Father, how is he in the Father and with the Father? Perhaps it is not unreasonable that he reclines with the Father when he is described as seated with the Father. Now hear the mode of this sitting together and reclining. For as the sitting expresses the majesty, so the sitting together expresses the equality of majesty, particularly when he is seated at the right hand of the Father,* not beneath his feet* or behind him.† And while sitting down is restful, reposing is more so.

What is to be seen as more delightful and indeed sweeter to the Son, the fact that he is in the Father or that he rules over all things with the Father? In which of these do you think rests the highest peace of God,* which surpasses all perception? Where do you

*Mark 16:19
*1 Cor 15:26
†Sir 46:8

*Phil 4:7

[1] *Sermo in dominica I novembris* (1 Nov 5).

suppose that the rest, which is the inherent quality of the Lord, more properly abides? And if it cannot be expressed with sufficient dignity by the tongue, it may yet be rightly conceived by the heart, so that while his indivisible singleness of being in all things is preserved, a distinction may be made in thought between his equality of glory and his unity of substance, like the distinction between being seated and reclining.

2. It seems that the bride is scarcely to be seen sitting; she must be shown reposing. *Show me*, she says, *you whom my soul loves, where you rest at midday.** But for every soul who savors wisdom, when the apostle says, *The one who is joined to the Lord is one spirit*,* it tastes altogether sweeter than when the apostles are told, *When the king shall sit on the throne of his glory, you too shall be judges.** The reclining is by no means less pleasant than the sitting. *I am in the father*, says the Son, *and the father is in me.** The unity of substance cannot be expressed more distinctly. For since each is in the other, neither can be considered as further out and neither further in than the other, but it must rather be believed that in each there is pure unity of substance.

It is something like the saying, *The one who dwells in charity dwells in God, and God in him*,* except that this is a spiritual union, as we said before: *The one who clings to God* is not indeed one substance with him, but *one spirit*; there indeed a unity of nature rather than of substance is meant. Hence we have in the gospels, *I and the father are one.** So, following the simile we used before, the rest of the Lord is as it were the bedchamber of the Only-begotten. He who has become the Firstborn brings us to his bedchamber* and his rest† in our own measure, through this union of wills and joining of the spirit, which is the work of charity.

3. Now what is said by the Father postulates someone walking, and what he says foretells the coming, at his behest, of the incarnation that we are soon to

*Song 1:6

*1 Cor 6:17

*Matt 19:28

*John 14:10

*1 John 4:16

*John 10:30

*Song 3:4
†Heb 1:6; 3:11

celebrate. Indeed he himself said, *For I have proceeded from God and come from him.** At last he was seen on earth and talked with humans,* and he stood in the midst of us and we knew him not,* and he stood with us, God with us, the true Emmanuel, in the Father's place.* Because he stood with us, he was our helper; because he stood in the Father's place, he represented love. In all things he sought the glory of the Father,* whose will he had come to do.* And if you consider Christ on the cross and imagine him crucified,* you will certainly find that he is below the Father. This is the particular property of the humility of his human nature, concerning which he himself said, *My father is greater than I.** Shall we dare to say that he was ever without the Father? No one would presume to say this if he himself had not first said, *My God, My God, why have you forsaken me?** There was some kind of dereliction there, and there was no show of courage in such tribulation, no demonstration of majesty.

4. We have then Christ Jesus born of the Father, resting in the Father, seated with the Father, walking from the Father, standing in the Father's place, hanging on the cross below the Father, dying in some way without the Father. In which of these ways are we to think that Isaiah saw him when he said, *I saw the Lord sitting on his throne, high and lifted up?** For the vision the same prophet spoke about in another passage was quite different: *We saw him, and he was not beautiful or comely, and we considered him like a leper and struck by God and brought low.** He saw the same man each time, but he did not see him in the same way, and in some sense it was not the same man he saw. For now he saw him bruised by blows, loaded with reproaches, assailed by insults.* He saw him as one despised, hanging on the cross; he saw him dying for us, and he said, *He was bruised for our transgressions; by his wounds we are healed.** It was the least of men who appeared there, the de-

*John 8:42
*Bar 3:38
*John 1:26

*Matt 1:23

*John 7:18
*John 6:38
*1 Cor 2:2

*John 14:28

*Matt 27:46

*Isa 6:1

*Isa 53:2, 4

*Lam 3:30

*Isa 53:5

spised one,* but here the whole earth is full of his majesty.* There he is the man of sorrows, acquainted with grief;* here he is the Lord seated on his throne.†

And the first vision, which was seen by many, is described by a plural word, but the second is as singular as it is sublime. So he is one of many when he says, *We saw,* but he is alone and solitary* when, out of the body, he says, *I saw the Lord sitting.** No doubt the Lord is properly described when he is perceived as seated. For to be seated is the prerogative of one who presides, of one who is lord and ruler. To be seated on a throne is the particular mark of domination. To be simply seated is usually a mark of low degree. Yet as we said before, he who reclines with the Father with delight is seated with the Father as a ruler: on the one hand he is the loving spouse, on the other the ruler who commands respect. There it says, *The Lord is glorious among his saints, wonderful in his majesty.*² *

5. *I saw,* he said, *The Lord sitting upon his throne, high and lifted up, and the whole earth was full of his glory, and who were beneath him filled the temple.*³* Who were beneath him? Surely the throne of which he spoke? Although high and lifted up, still it was beneath him. For if he was sitting on the throne, clearly the throne was beneath him. And how did it fill the temple? Besides, since the whole earth is full of his glory, how is the temple filled, and from where? Know this from what you hear, that the throne is not to be thought of as a physical device, but you must understand it as an angelic creation. If *the soul of the righteous is the seat of wisdom,*⁴* how much more worthy of praise is the seat of a holy angel? This indeed is the seat of his glory, high

*Isa 53:3
*Isa 6:3
*Isa 53:3
†Isa 6:1

*Isa 53:2
*Isa 6:1

*see Ps 67:36;
Exod 15:11

*Isa 6:1-3

*Prov 12:23,
LXX

---

² Gradual *gloriosus* in the common of several martyrs.
³ As in Response *Vidi* in the first Sunday in November.
⁴ See Jean Leclercq, *Recueils d'études sur saint Bernard et ses écrits,* 2 vols. (Rome: Edizioni di storia e letteratura, 1962), 2:308.

up by its nature but lifted up much more by grace. For by nature he has made them exalted, but by grace he has lifted them up, and it is said of them, *By the word of the Lord were the heavens established.**

*Ps 32:6

These cohorts of angels, above which God is seated and which are below him, fill the temple although the whole earth is full of his majesty. For everywhere he reigns, everywhere he governs, his majesty is everywhere; it is a presence of grace, not of wrath. But his good, acceptable, and perfect will* is not, I claim, everywhere, like his power, or why do we say *may your will be done, as in heaven, so on earth?** For his will is done concerning all and through all, but not in all. In the souls of the elect the will of God is done when their will is one with his.*

*Rom 12:2

*Matt 6:10

*1 Cor 6:16-17

That is the spiritual conformity that makes them one spirit, as when we read, *The multitude of believers were of one heart and one soul.** *And those who were beneath him filled the temple.** They filled it with every spiritual blessing,* they filled it with divine consolation,† they filled it with a variety of graces,# they filled it with the fruit of holiness.‡ *Holiness is fitting to your House, Lord.** They filled it with diverse gifts of favor, of counsel and strength, of knowledge and goodness, and they filled it with the fear of the Lord.†

*Acts 4:32
*Isa 6:1
*Eph 1:3
†Acts 9:31
#1 Cor 12:4
‡Rom 6:22
*Ps 92:5, as in the Antiphon *Domum tuam* for Lauds of the Dedication of a Church
†Isa 11:2-3
#Isa 6:2

6. *The seraphim stood above him.*# That is the name of the highest, the loftiest order of angels, who are represented as standing above all the rest; yet although they take precedence over all others, they still stand aside, showing faithful service and complete obedience to God, who is higher than they. For it is clear that the place of the Lord, the place of an angel, and the place of a person are quite different. Christ stands in fervor before the Father, seeking the Father's glory, as his faithful only-begotten son, even the firstborn of the Father,* supporting the adopted sons of the Father by his fervor. So Stephen saw him standing there and ac-

*John 1:14

knowledged him as his helper;* so the prophet called on him to rise and help him, saying, "Arise, Lord; help us."*

Truly the angels stand to serve him, as the prophet says: *Thousands of thousands ministered to him, and ten hundred thousand served him.** For it is the duty of a person to stand, to continue steadfastly in vigor of mind and constancy of purpose. So Moses stood, throwing himself into the breach in the sight of the Lord, to turn away his wrath;* so *Phineas stood and made peace with him.** *The seraphim stood above.* What is the meaning of the prophet's words when he says that he saw not one or many standing there, but two? It is clear from what he says next that two appeared to him: *One had six wings, and the other had six.** And it is well that two stood there: *For woe to one alone, because if he falls he has no one to lift him up.** Woe to you, proud spirit, lover of aloofness and self-confidence: you have not stood firm in the truth; you have been driven out; the foot of pride could not stand.* You wished to be seated alone, and like lightning you fell from heaven* and will have none ever to hold you up.

7. *One had six wings, and the other had six.* What is the reason for this number of wings? *With two*, the prophet says, *they covered his head, with two his feet, and with two they flew.** A great mystery and mighty symbolism! These words require attentive ears on your part, but they demand a much more ready tongue on mine, and a mind spiritually attuned. It is my own opinion I express, however; I am not stating a fact but making some sort of guess and giving an opinion. Is there any reason to doubt that when Lucifer was cast down the seraphim were sent to keep watch, just as when humanity fell God sent the cherubim to keep guard?* And perhaps it is not inappropriate that the flaming sword of the cherubim, fashioned from the tree of life, with its sharp and fiery blade, more terrible

*Acts 7:55-59

*Ps 43:26

*Dan 7:10; *decies centena millia*

*Ps 105:23
*Ps 105:30

*Isa 6:2

*Eccl 4:10

*Ps 35:12
*Luke 10:18; Isa 14:12

*Isa 6:2

*Gen 3:24

than anything else to mortal flesh, is said to have warded off physical hands.

But the seraphim only received wings to ward off a spiritual eye. Then *with two*, he said, *they covered his head, and with two his feet*, so that the wicked person should not be able to look upon the height or depth of God. There will be a time when *the glory of God shall be revealed*,* but this will not happen until what is written is fulfilled: *Let the wicked be destroyed, lest he see the glory of God.** Meanwhile his head is covered and his feet are covered, so that the mid-part is left to be seen by the evil one, but with envy. And they are covered by wings that ward him off but lift and sustain them.

*Isa 40:5

*Isa 26:10

8. But first we must inquire with what wings they are said to fly, for he said, *with two they flew*. Perhaps it is not inappropriate for us to say that these are nature and grace, particularly since the height and position of the throne was told us before. It is said that it is by their naturally sublime intellect and through the burning love that is theirs by grace that they stretch and lean toward him who is above them, but it is through their office that they stand, as we said before,* and by their devotion that they fly. Let it be said that they cover the head of God, and also his feet, but let them not cover them for their own sakes; let them rather fly and hover between them with devotion, following the height and depth of his power and wisdom. They do not look upon his majesty* to be overwhelmed by his glory; the Spirit, who explores the depths of God,* rules and guides them,* and they love no less than they understand.

**diximus;*
see S 1 Nov 3.4

*Prov 25:27
*1 Cor 2:10
*Rom 8:14

Lucifer, that proud one, while choosing the light but having no fire, relies on only one wing and can encompass only a fall, not a flight. For he exulted in his brightness, but he was not burning, not enkindled,⁵* as the prophet describes the seraphim. He did not stand upright, for he was full of contempt, but he could not fly, because he was full of presumption. The strength of his life upheld him, but to his own ruin, for being bereft of grace, he soon fell. That is like the fate of those who have known God but did not glorify him or give thanks, and finally they are punished by being given up to a depraved mind, and their foolish heart is darkened.* Then the veil was finally drawn round the prince of darkness, and he was unable to pierce it by any natural strength to see the head and feet of the one who sits above the throne. Thus the seraphim stand and are at his side, and with two wings they cover his head and with two his feet.

*incensus

*Rom 1:21, 28

9. The substance of the divine being is not composed of flesh, nor is it formed in human shape with physical limbs. *God is spirit,** and what is said of him must be understood in a spiritual manner. Who will unveil for us his head and his feet, which the seraphim cover with two wings, but the Spirit himself, who knows all that is in him and searches out the deep things of God?* For I think that it is those that are meant by the head in this passage. According to this, then, his head is his majesty, his power, his eternal strength, and his divinity.* Concerning his head, as the prophet says, *Your righteousness is like the mountains of God.* And what follows? *Your judgments are a great abyss.** It does not seem unfitting that they should be designated by calling them feet. For they are like his feet, his untraceable ways, his inscrutable judgments,* the depth of his wisdom and his being, faultless but

*John 4:24

*1 Cor 2:10

*Rom 1:20

*Ps 35:7

*Rom 11:33

---

⁵ Jerome, *Liber interpretationis Hebraicorum nominum, s.v. Seraphim,* ed. P. de Lagarde, G. Morin, M. Adriaen, CCSL 72 (Turnhout: Brepols, 1959), 121–22.

incomprehensible. The very mystery of the Lord's incarnation is understood to relate particularly to the feet, and likewise it is connected with the whole operation of our salvation.

The prophet of God marvels to see the nature of that sublime justice, like mountains. For our justice, if such exists, is humble; it is just, perhaps, but it is not pure, unless indeed we think ourselves better than our fathers,* who said with truth and humility, *All our justice is like the cloth of a menstruating woman.** How should our justice be undefiled, when it cannot be faultless? The justice of humans may seem to be pure if they do not consent to sin, so that it does not reign in their mortal body.* For at the beginning, the justice of the first man was not only just but also pure, as long as it was granted to him not to see sin. But since it was not firmly established and easily lost its purity, this justice did not keep its integrity.

Clearly justice among the angels is pure, undefiled, and firmly established, but it is far below that of God. For it is not native to them but is implanted by God, so that their nature, because it is part of them, is shown to be capable not only of justice but also of injustice. For is it not wickedness that we read that true Justice is found in the angels?* For *no living being will be justified in your sight,** says one who was by no means ignorant of the justice of God. He did not say *no person, but no living being,** lest perhaps you should suppose it did not apply to angelic spirits. For they are living beings, and the more just they are, the nearer they stand to him with whom is the fount of life.

Nevertheless they are just, but they derive their justice from him rather than sharing it with him;* it is by his gift, not by affinity with him. For he is justice whose will is not consistent as it is consistency itself, and both are no other than his being. For that is most truly justice, and each is no other than his substance.

*1 Kgs 19:4
*Isa 64:6

*Rom 6:12

*Job 4:18
*Ps 142:2

*homo . . . vivens

*Ps 35:10

For that is truly justice, and it is as pure and firmly established as a mountain, and, as I said, it is even his very being. What depth is concealed in that head! What glory, what sublimity in that shady and secret mountain!⁶ *

*Hab 3:3

10. With what wings do we think that the seraphim cover this head, so that by no loftiness of nature, no light of reason, can the eye penetrate the clarity of its light? With the two wings, if I am right, of glory and delight. If their delight in the wonder of contemplating him is inexpressible, their glory in worshiping him is not less. The evil one, wondering but not worshiping, because he did not wish to seem inferior by worshiping, had not the strength to establish himself in wonder. So he ended by turning his wonder to envy and did not condescend to worship but tried to imitate him. How much better to be the seraphim, delighting in wonder, who have by their worship made themselves worshipful, and who possess true glory in him whom to serve is to reign⁷ and before whom all who exalt themselves are abased.*

*Luke 14:11

And now hear how with these two wings the seraphim seem to cover the very head of the Lord, as we said, so that no unjust person may look upon it. For as often as the evil one casts his eyes above, he comes against the delight and glory of the angels, and a dreadful fog comes before his eyes, like a leaden cloud, and he cannot get past it. Thus indeed the evil one is frustrated as it were by a double veil, so that he cannot see the things above but wastes away with his eyes dazzled, now by the delight, now by the glory of those whom he wretchedly recognizes as higher than himself. For what irritation of the eye is so unbearable

---

⁶ As in the tract *Domine* for the sixth *feria* after Pentecost.
⁷ See Postcommunion Feast of Saint Irenaeus, June 28.

as envy? And his envy and the spite by which he is tortured because of the glory and delight that are not his are not directed at others. Misery, so they say, is free from envy.

11. But the feet of the Lord, by which are meant the impenetrable abyss of his judgments and the untraceable ways of his being,* are also covered by the seraphim with two wings. I call them prudence and felicity.* For since they are faithful and also prudent servants, so they perform the work of God and provide for the salvation of the elect, so that the evil one is absolutely unable to seize them. I think that it is because of this covering that in ignorance he caused the Lord of glory to be crucified,* and consequently every day unknowingly and unwillingly he serves the cause of our salvation, grieving too late because, while he wished to injure us, he found that he had benefitted us.* So he is deceived by the machinations of his own cunning,* because those who are unwilling to reveal him are faithful, and being prudent they know how to conceal the secrets of divine providence and regard for us.

12. So from the two topmost wings we learn that the evil one marveled but did not worship, as we have said; so from the two central ones we know he had spiritual understanding by his nature but not affection by grace, and from those below it is easy to know how he was found bereft of fidelity, but by the same token he was not without prudence. Unless you think it was someone else who was called the serpent, more cunning than all other creatures.* Perhaps we do not inappropriately say, since his fall was so irrevocable and his ruin so irreparable, that from the wings of which we spoke, just as there was no help on the right, so there was no lack of help on the left.

It was not thus with the two who the prophetic vision told us were standing upright* at the side of

*Rom 11:33

*Matt 24:45

*1 Cor 2:8

*Heb 1:14
*2 Cor 2:11

*Gen 3:1

*Isa 6:2

the God of majesty, whose feet, so it is said, they cover with two wings, with faithfulness and felicity, with that very wonder in which they delight, and with the worship in which they glory in their loftiness. Then with two they fly, with the natural power of intellect, as we have said, and the efficacy of grace. But they leave the mid-part uncovered and visible, representing, I suggest, the enduring kindness of God, inviting humans to penitence. For all may see how he makes the sun rise on the just and on the unjust,* and it rains on just and unjust alike.* By this love Solomon, that just man, paved the mid-parts for the daughters of Jerusalem,* so that they should not seek higher or lower things. But in the mid-parts they may occupy themselves and by striving eventually advance to the contemplation of lofty and wonderful things.* But the evil one is tortured bitterly at present by this vision and will be more heavily tormented in the future, first because he grudges the endurance of this kindness toward us, and then because he can in no way see a way by which he himself may be led to penitence.

*Rom 8:4
*Matt 5:45

*Song 3:10

*Sir 3:22

On the Feast of All Saints[1]

Sermon One

Of the Gospel Reading: Jesus Seeing the Crowds

1. The feast of All Saints is celebrated today, and it is right that it should be celebrated with all devotion. Even though the feasts of Saint Stephen or Saint Peter or of anyone else seem great—as they are—how great is that of not only one, but of all? My brothers, you know that it is the custom of those living in the world to prepare festal meals on feast days, and the greater the feast, the more sumptuous they are. What, then? Will not delicacies of the heart be sought for those who are converted at heart* and spiritual favorites prepared for the spiritual?* So our banquet is prepared, brothers; each item has been cooked,* and the hour for sumptuous dining has come.

*Ps 84:9
*1 Cor 2:13
*Matt 22:4

For it is right that the soul* should be satisfied first. Without doubt and without comparison, it is the portion having the better claim, particularly, as is clear, because the solemnities of the saints pertain more to souls than to bodies. Souls more readily receive the things that pertain to souls, since souls are joined to those things by a natural affinity. On such as these, in

*anima

[1] *Sermo in festivitate omnium sanctorum* (OS 1).

fact, the saints have the greater compassion; they desire all the more good things for souls and delight all the more in their restoration, since they like us were capable of suffering.* They complained about the troubles of this pilgrimage, this miserable exile. They bore the heavy burden of the body and the tumult of the world and were tried by the enemy's temptations. No doubt this feast is more welcome and much more acceptable to them, because it offers dishes for the soul, than are those that are celebrated by the worldly who look to satisfy the desires of the flesh.*

*Jas 5:17

*Rom 13:14

2. But really, from whom or from where will there be for us bread for the soul *in a desert land, in a place of horror and vast solitude?** From whom or from where food of the spirit for us under the sun,* where there is nothing except labor and sorrow and affliction of spirit?* But I know who said, *Seek and you shall find,*† and, *If you, being evil, know how to give good gifts to your children, how much more shall your Father in heaven give the good Spirit to those who ask him?** Neither am I ignorant of how resolutely you have entreated all night and all day, begging to be given the living bread from heaven,* not that which fortifies the body but that which strengthens the human heart.* For I dare not say that we are table companions, but rather beggars, living on whatever God supplies. We are beggars, I repeat, lying at the door of a wealthy king, full of sores* and desiring to be satisfied or, rather, just sustained, by the crumbs that fall from the table of our masters,* whose solemnity we celebrate today.

*Deut 32:10
*Eccl 1:14

*Ps 89:10
†John 16:24

*Luke 11:13

*John 6:32, 41
*Ps 103:15

*Luke 16:20

*Matt 15:27

No doubt they abound in good things* and receive good measure, pressed down and running over.* In addition, we trust that there will be someone to give to us, for great is the gulf and exceedingly huge the distance between* the generosity and goodness of God and the cruelty of a rich miser. Therefore our Father is giving us today*—for the Father of mercies†

*Song 8:5
*Luke 6:38

*Luke 16:26

*Matt 6:9
†2 Cor 1:3

must also be the Father of the miserable—he is giving us, I repeat, living bread from heaven* and food in abundance.* I am going to cook it up, and my soul is the kitchen.

    3. All night long, wondering how your courses would be prepared, *My heart grew hot within me, and while I was musing the fire blazed*—doubtless that which the Lord Jesus sent on earth and vehemently wished should be kindled.* For in order to cook spiritual food, one must have spiritual fire. It only remains for me to distribute to you what I have prepared. As for you, consider the Lord, who gives more than his servant who distributes, for I am nothing more than your fellow servant.*

    As God himself knows, I along with you, for you, and for myself beg the bread from heaven and the sustenance of life. Therefore it is not I but your Father who gives you the living bread from heaven;* it is he who feeds you with works, with words, and even with the flesh of the Son, which is real food.* Now concerning works I read, *My food is that I should do the will of my Father,** and concerning words, *Man shall not live by bread alone, but by every word that proceeds from the mouth of God.** So we have his deeds and his words to feed on; afterward, by his grace, we shall receive in its fullness the sacrament of the body of the Lord on the holy table of the altar.

    4. We read in today's gospel that *seeing the crowds, Jesus went up onto the mountain.** For with the Lord preaching, people from the cities and villages followed,* of whom he saved souls and healed bodies,* and they clung to him, delighted as much by his speech as by his face, for his voice was sweet and his countenance comely,* as it is written, *You are fairer than the children of men: grace is poured into your lips.** Such is he whom we follow and cling to; he is altogether lovely,* and not only people but angels desire to look upon him.*

What is there more delightful that we may present to you? Without a doubt, these are the delicacies of angels. So *taste and see how sweet the Lord is.** And this delight, this flavor, this discerning taste,* which in truth is drawn out from hiding—all that can be desired is not to be compared with it.† Do you marvel at the sun's splendor, the beauty of a flower, the taste of bread, and the fruitfulness of the earth? All these things are given by God, yet there can be no doubt that he has kept for himself abundantly more than he has given to creatures.

*Ps 39:9
**huic suavitati, huic sapori, huic sapientiae*
†Prov 3:15

5. Let us not suppose that the fact that he went up onto the mountain* is an idle gesture, since it was foretold so long beforehand by the prophet who long ago cried, *Go up onto a high mountain, you who announce good tidings to Sion.** About this ascension, if you have no better explanation, I think I have one. I mean what blessed Luke records at the beginning of the Acts of the Apostles when he says, *In the former book I wrote of all that Jesus began to do and to teach.** It was not in the fashion of the Pharisees, who bound up unbearably heavy burdens and laid them on people's shoulders but then refused to lift a finger to move them.* Could this be the good bread of the soul, greatly strengthening a people's heart?*

*Matt 5:1

*Isa 40:9

*Acts 1:1, Vulg

*Matt 23:4

*Luke 9:57; Ps 103:15

I follow you faithfully, O Lord, wherever you go, and I will fearlessly run the way of your commandments,* knowing that you yourself are going ahead in them. Carefree, I say, I run the way of your commandments, since I know that you came out from highest heaven to run along this way and that your running to its heights will be along this way.* I cannot keep chewing one thing at a time like this, brothers. Be yourselves clean, cud-chewing animals,²* that it may

*Ps 118:32; RB Prol.49

*Ps 18:7

*Lev 11:3

---

² *Be: estote* (*sum*), but it could also be *eat* (*edo*).

be as it was written: *A desirable treasure rests in the mouth of the wise.** But I must speak as concisely as possible, as there is much to be said in a short time, particularly as the solemn Mass has yet to be celebrated.

6. *Seeing the crowds, Jesus went up into the mountain.** He saw with the eye of pity, because they were like wandering sheep, not having a shepherd.* Why did he go up into the mountain before he began to teach them? Was it not because by so doing he taught them that it was necessary for those who preach the word of God to look toward high and holy things and climb the mountain of virtue with the soul's desires* and a holy way of life?* *And when he had sat down, his disciples came to him.*† "When he had sat down," the writer says. Otherwise, who could approach such a preeminent giant!*

With great condescension he humbled himself* and stopped to sit down, so that he might say to the Father, *You know my sitting and my rising.** He sat down so that even publicans and sinners,* Mary Magdalene,† and the thief on the cross might come to him whom not even the angels could approach when he was standing. *And when he had sat down, his disciples came to him.** They came not so much by their footsteps as by their hearts' devotion and by the imitation of virtue. It is right that the throngs are not said to have come to him, nor any of the people, but the disciples. For it is said that when the Old Testament was given on Mount Sinai, Moses went up alone and the people waited below,* for the mountains give peace to the people and the hills bring righteousness,* and what was said to the apostles in darkness and secrecy should be affirmed afterward in the light, and what was spoken in their ear should be proclaimed from the housetops.* Then it goes on,

7. *And opening his mouth, he taught them.** He opened his mouth—he who first opened the mouths of the prophets. This is what is said in the Psalms, by the

---

*Prov 21:20

*Matt 5:1

*Matt 9:36; 1 Pet 2:25

*desideriis animi
**conversatione sancta*
†Matt 5:1

*Ps 18:6
*Phil 2:7

*Ps 138:2
*Matt 9:10
†Luke 8:44

*Luke 23:42

*Exod 19–31

*Ps 71:3

*Mark 10:27
*Matt 5:2

mouth of the prophet: *Lord, open my lips, and my mouth shall proclaim your praise.** But now he who spoke manifold things in many ways through the prophets† has at last spoken to us with his own voice, as if he would say, *And the one who spoke, see: I am here.*# Blessed are those who heard the word of God‡ that came forth from his mouth. Indeed what they heard has been preserved for us, and we can hear it, though not from the Lord himself.

Opening his mouth he taught them, saying: Blessed are the poor in spirit.* Truly his mouth is opened, and in it treasures of wisdom and knowledge are still hidden.* Actually, this is teaching that he gives in the Apocalypse—*Behold, I make all things new**—and that he had beforehand spoken by the prophets—*I will open my mouth, I will utter things hidden since the foundation of the world.** For what is so secret as that poverty should be blessed? Yet it is the Truth who speaks, who can neither deceive nor be deceived, and it is the Truth who says, *Blessed are the poor in spirit.* So, you foolish sons of Adam, do you seek riches, do you still desire riches, although the blessedness of the poor is praised by God, preached to the world, and believed by human beings?* Let the pagan, who lives without God,† seek them; let the Jew, who has accepted earthly promises, seek them; but what is the attitude, or, better, what is the frame of mind of a Christian who would anxiously seek for riches when Christ has proclaimed that the poor are blessed? How long, alien brothers,* how long will your mouth speak vanity,* saying that those who possess these things,* visible and temporary as they are, are blessed, when the Son of God has opened his mouth and spoken the truth: blessed are the poor, but woe for the rich?*

8. But pay careful attention to the fact that he does not speak simply of the poor, because the general population* is poor through miserable necessity, not

*Ps 50:17; RB 9.1: the verse that opens Vigils
†Heb 1:1
#Isa 52:6
‡Luke 11:28

*Matt 5:2-3
*Col 2:3

*Rev 21:5

*Matt 13:35

*1 Tim 3:16
†Eph 2:12

*Ps 17:46
*Ps 37:13
*Ps 143:15

*Luke 6:24

*plebeios

laudable will. For my part, I hope that the misery of their affliction will be of use to them in the presence of the mercy of God's goodness. But I know that here the Lord was not speaking of people of this kind, but of those who could say with the prophet, *Willingly I will sacrifice to you.** Yet not even every instance of voluntary poverty has praise from God, for it is said that philosophers left all their goods and, freed from the cares of worldly affairs, were able without hindrance to spend their time in the study of vanity, not desiring worldly wealth but preferring the wealth of their own reason.*† He makes a distinction by adding *in spirit*, that is, by the will of the spirit. *Blessed* then *are the poor in spirit**—namely, spiritual intention, spiritual desire for the sake only of God's good pleasure and the salvation of souls—*for theirs is the kingdom of heaven.*

Blessed indeed, *for theirs is the kingdom of heaven*. But who is it who speaks thus, who in this way declares the poor happy, who in this way makes them rich? Do you think it can be true? Without doubt it will be, since he who promises is true and mighty. If the enemy murmurs, he will be answered, "*May I not do what I wish? Is your eye evil because I am good?** If you are justly humiliated because you have desired to exalt yourself against me, shall not those who for my sake humble themselves deserve to be exalted?" Truly, my brethren, if he was cast down from heaven in great misery because he aspired to the highest place, desired to be exalted, and presumed to be above all, does it not follow that they who of their own will give themselves over to the humility of poverty should be blessed and, according to God's promises, possess the kingdom of heaven, which he forfeited? And hear the wise pronouncement of Wisdom, giving the first remedy for the first sin, whether or not she speaks openly: "Do you desire to gain heaven, which was lost by the proud angel who trusted in his own strength and in the mul-

*Ps 53:8

*sensu suo
†Rom 14:5
*Matt 5:3

*Matt 20:15

titude of his own riches?"* Embrace the low estate of poverty, and it shall be yours." He says next, **Ps 48:7*

9. *Blessed are the meek, for they shall possess the earth.** Good. Bravo. For it was right after commending poverty to preach gentleness, because for those who have left all, the first temptation usually concerns unaccustomed bodily trials and fleshly afflictions. What advantage is poverty if, God forbid, a poor person descends to grumbling and becomes irritable and impatient with formation? It is terrific that after the promise of the Kingdom another lesser kingdom is given as an earnest, so that, according to Scripture, we may have the promise of this present life as well as that which is to come,* and our expectation of things to come may be strengthened by our being shown present things. **Matt 5:4*

**1 Tim 4:8*

Blessed are the meek, for they shall possess the earth. This earth I take to be our body, and if the soul wishes to possess it, if she deserves to have mastery over her members, she must herself be meek and subject to her superior, since in the same way that she deals with her inferior, just so will she present herself to her superior. For the creature is armed for avenging the injury done to her Creator. And so the soul that finds her flesh in the rebellion against her knows that it is less subject to its higher powers than it behooves her to be. Let her be meek and humble under the powerful hand of the Most High;* let her be subject to God† and also to those to whom she owes obedience, who are set over her in his place, and she will straightway find her body obedient and subjected. For it is the Truth who says, *Blessed are the meek, for they shall possess the earth.*

**1 Pet 5:6*
†*Ps 61:2*

And see if a second medicine is not provided against the second wound of sin. After the fall of the treacherous angel, it was Eve, stirred up by a restless spirit, who was the first to sin. She rejected the easy yoke and light burden of the Lord,* for she would not wait to receive perfect blessedness from the hand of God, from whom

**Matt 11:29*

she had received other things, but at the serpent's suggestion attempted to snatch it prematurely.* Therefore she lost Paradise, the land of delights; therefore she found in her body a conflicting law.*

*Gen 3:5

*Rom 7:23

But now, perhaps, at this word of the Lord you burn with desire for meekness and bewail your hardness of heart, your beastly—no, rather your savage, untamable emotions! Listen, then, to what follows!

10. *Blessed are they who mourn, for they shall be comforted.** An untamed horse is tamed with whips, a fierce soul by contrition of spirit* and frequent tears. Therefore *in all your doings remember your end.** Never allow the horror of death, the dreadful decision of judgment, or fear of the fires of hell to be far from the eyes of your heart. Consider the misery of your pilgrimage; in the bitterness of soul reflect upon your years,* picture the perils of human life and your own frailty. If you persevere in this sort of meditation,* I assure you that you will hardly notice whatever outside you seems irksome, because you will be wholeheartedly taken up with what is irksome on the inside!

*Matt 5:5
*Isa 65:14
*Sir 7:40

*Isa 38:15

*cogitatione

But the Lord will not suffer you to be without comfort, for he is *the Father of Mercy* and *the God of all comfort,** and what Truth promises will be fulfilled to the uttermost: *Blessed are they who mourn, for they shall be comforted.* The saying of Solomon accords with this: *It is better to go into the house of mourning than the house of feasting.** Therefore, Eve, you would have been happy if after your fault you had sought the comfort of tears; having turned to penitence,* you quickly would have had pardon. Instead, you sought the unhappy comfort of your husband, who was in the same situation. Thus you have infected your offspring with a vile poison, a grotesque vice,* so that to this day when one of them is ruined the other takes comfort! Unhappy indeed the comfort of Eve, and of those who imitate her misery!

*2 Cor 1:3

*Eccl 7:3

*Job 42:10

*Gen 3:6

But *blessed are they who mourn, for they shall be comforted.* What is this comfort but the grace of devotion springing from the hope of pardon, the most attractive delight of the good, the taste—however small—of wisdom, of the one whose soul the kind Lord refreshes in the meantime. But that taste is nothing other than the incitement of desire and motion of love, as it is written, *They who eat me still hunger, and they who drink me still thirst.** Therefore he says,

11. *Blessed are those who hunger and thirst after righteousness, for they shall be satisfied.** Let the one who is hungry hunger more, and the one who desires desire more ardently, because the more we desire, the more we will receive—and not according to the imperfect measure of our desire (since until we possess perfectly, we cannot desire perfectly, but then we cannot even possess perfectly until we desire perfectly!)—but we are going to receive a good measure, pressed down, and running over.* *Blessed are those who hunger and thirst after righteousness, for they shall be satisfied.* To the weak palate of the heart and the fainting soul righteousness still seems hard and tasteless,* but those who taste it—it is they who really know how blessed are those who hunger for it, *for they shall be satisfied.* O truly blessed and glorious satisfaction! O holy feast! O banquet greatly to be desired, where there can be no trouble, no envy, since the greatest satisfaction and the greatest desire will be there!

Blessed are those who hunger and thirst after righteousness, for they shall be satisfied. I believe that this saying was directed against Adam. He seems to have kept some trace of righteousness, in that he had some compassion on his wife,* but if he had thirsted for righteousness, he would doubtless have been anxious to give back what he owed, not only to his wife but much more to his Creator.* For to his wife, as to an inferior, he owed compassion and also education, for

*Sir 24:29

*Matt 5:6

*Luke 6:38

**dura et insipida;* see RB 58.8: *omnia dura et aspera*

*Gen 3:6

**non solum uxori, sed multo magis Creatori;* 1 Cor 7:3

a wife's head is the husband.* But to God he owed obedience and subjection. What are we to think, my brothers, about so many today who judge this fact harshly yet imitate it foolishly? They blame Adam because he obeyed the voice of his wife rather than that of God,* yet they themselves listen every day to Eve, that is, their flesh, rather than to God. Brothers, if we were to see Adam present here and now, torn between his wife's request and his Creator's command, should we not cry out warning him, saying, "Beware, unhappy man! Think what it is you do! Your wife is a temptress; do not do what she asks!" Well, how often has a similar temptation come upon us, and we have not taken that advice?

*Eph 5:23

*Gen 3:17

For *blessed are those who hunger and thirst after righteousness, for they shall be satisfied.* But what can all our righteousness be in God's sight? Is it not reckoned *as a cloth of a menstruating woman*,* in the prophet's words, and, if strictly judged, will not all our righteousness be found unrighteous and inadequate?* What then will be the case of sin when even righteousness cannot defend itself? Therefore, steadfastly proclaiming with the prophet, *Do not enter into judgment with your servant,* Lord, let us in all humility return to mercy, which alone can save our souls,* and consider carefully what follows:

*Isa 64:6

*Dan 5:27

*Ps 142:2

*Jas 1:21

12. *Blessed are the merciful, for they shall obtain mercy.* Now hear how Zacchaeus succinctly covers both in a single sentence when he says, *Half of my goods I give to the poor, and if I have defrauded anyone, I will pay him back fourfold.* You see how much he hungers for righteousness, for whom it is not enough to restore in equal measure; rather he gives back fourfold. His mercy also is great, for he gives half of his goods to the poor.

*Matt 5:7

*Luke 19:8

I will not hide my feelings: *My mouth shall speak the praise of the Lord.* *Of the Lord*: make no mistake, not your own. For it is not to you I give the glory,

*Ps 144:21; as in the Alleluia on the feast of the Holy Name of Jesus

but to the name of the Lord.* Certainly Zacchaeus, *whose praise is in the Gospel*,* gave half of his goods to the poor.* But I can see many Zacchaeuses here who have reserved no part of all their goods for themselves. Who will write the gospel of those Zacchaeuses for me, or indeed of those Peters, who said confidently to the Lord, *Look, we have left all and followed you*?* But it is now written in the everlasting gospel,* it is written and sealed in the book of life,* *Blessed are the merciful, for they shall obtain mercy.*

Now, my brothers, this saying touches on Adam's barbarity. It seems that, out of love* for his wife, he was the first to sin. For look; we know, Adam, that she is bone of your bone and flesh of your flesh,* and you sinned out of love* for her. Let us now see how much you love* her. The Lord comes bearing a fiery sword to avenge wickedness; become on her account your own accuser in the crisis and say, "Lord, the woman is the weaker, the woman was led astray; the iniquity is mine, mine is the sin, let vengeance be visited on me alone."

But he did not speak thus; he said, *The woman whom you gave me, she gave me of the tree and I ate.** What wickedness! You flee from taking the punishment for her, even though you don't deny the guilt! O grief! How you jumble everything up, perniciously merciful when you should have been severe, and savagely pernicious when the right thing was to expend mercy? For you would not have lost out in any way by making satisfaction for her with a willing heart, as you ought to have done.

It follows, brothers, that a person should never sin because of another—that is of righteousness—and one should gladly bear the sins of another—that is of mercy. *Blessed are they who hunger and thirst after righteousness, for they shall be satisfied. Blessed are the merciful, for they shall obtain mercy.** There follows,

*Ps 113:9
*2 Cor 8:18
*Luke 19:8

*Matt 19:27
*Rev 14:6
*Phil 4:3

*amore

*Gen 2:23
*amore
*diligas

*Gen 3:12

*Matt 5:6-7

13. *Blessed are the pure in heart, for they shall see God.** Blessed indeed and altogether blessed who shall see him *whom angels desire to look upon,** whom to see is eternal life.* *My heart speaks to you, my face has sought you: your face, Lord, I seek.** For whom do I have in heaven but you, and besides you what do I desire on earth? *My flesh and my heart fail, but God is the strength of my heart and my portion for ever.** When *will you fill me with the joy of your face?** Disaster for me, because of the uncleanness of heart! It is what prevents me from deserving to be admitted to that happy vision. What care, my brethren, what zeal must we exercise, so that the eye with which we must look upon God may be cleansed? I feel myself defiled by a threefold uncleanness: the desires of the flesh,* the desire for worldly glory, and the consciousness of past faults. For there are in my soul some motions of each desire that I cannot destroy by reason or force as long as I am held in the bondage of this present evil world* and in this body of death.

But against this stain of sin I set the remedy of prayer. Therefore, *as the eyes of servants look to the hand of their lords, so our eyes to the Lord our God, until he shall have mercy on us,** he who alone is pure and can make pure what was conceived from impure seed.* It was for this reason that confession, the remedy for consciousness of sin, was instituted, and all is washed away in confession. See, these are the things that cleanse the eye of the heart, prayer and confession. Indeed *blessed are the pure in heart, for they shall see God.* They shall see him at the end *face to face*; even now they see him, but *in a glass, darkly*, and now they know in part, but then they shall know perfectly.* For everyone in whose conscience sin lives shut up sins either in hope and thinks of God as one who is not greatly displeased by sin, or sins in desperation, feeling that God is without pity. To each of these it may rightly be said, *You thought, wicked one, that I was like you,** since neither of them sees God,

*Matt 5:8

*1 Pet 1:12
*John 17:3
*Ps 26:8

*Ps 72:25-26
*Ps 15:11

*1 John 2:16

*Gal 1:4

*Ps 122:2
*Job 14:4

*1 Cor 13:12

*Ps 49:21

but their iniquity speaks falsely to them,* making for them an idol in place of him, which is not him. *Ps 26:12

Blessed indeed are the pure of heart, since they alone see God; only they feel him in his goodness,* for he is good, and none is good save him.* *Blessed are the pure in heart, for they shall see God.* Unhappy are Adam and Eve, who turn *in words of malice to do wicked deeds** and flee from the cleansing of confession but remain in the uncleanness of their heart and are cast out from the sight of God.* Next follows, *Wis 1:1
*Mark 10:18

*Ps 140:4

*Gen 3:23-24

14. *Blessed are the peacemakers, for they shall be called the sons** *of God.*† Rightly shall they be called sons, since they finish the work of the Son.# For he it is through whom, reconciled,‡ we have peace with God,* and it is he who reconciled all things to himself, both on earth and in heaven:* *the mediator between God and humankind, the man Christ Jesus.** And mark now how in the first three beatitudes the soul is reconciled to itself, in the next two to its neighbor, and in the sixth to God; in the seventh it reconciles others, as though received into the grace of God and granted happy familiarity. For it is by poverty, gentleness, and tears that the eternal likeness and image that embraces all times is renewed in the soul; by poverty it merits the future, by gentleness it claims the present for itself, and by the grief of penitence it even regains the past, as it is written, *I will reflect on you upon all my days in the bitterness of my soul.** As for justice and mercy, we bind them together perfectly when in the name of justice we do not do to others what we do not wish should be done to us,* and in the name of mercy we do to others what we wish that people would do to us.* *filii
†Matt 5:9
#filii
‡Rom 5:10
*Rom 5:1
*Col 1:20
*1 Tim 2:5

*Isa 38:15

*Tob 4:16
*Matt 7:12

Now, reconciled to ourselves, reconciled also to our neighbor, through the cleansing of our heart we trust that we are reconciled to God. Blessed indeed are they who, while not ungrateful for their own reconciliation, are dutifully concerned for their neighbors, striving to reconcile them also, as far as they are able, to themselves and to God. Can you imagine the sort of praise people deserve, or with what affection they should be embraced, who dwell with their brothers without acrimony,* carefully on guard that there be in themselves nothing that others have to put up with while themselves patiently putting up with whatever is irksome in others,* who consider as their own the temptations of others and say with the apostle, *Who is offended and I do not burn? Who is weak, and I am not weak?* * *Blessed are the peacemakers, for they shall be called the sons of God. For God is not of confusion, but of peace,** and so it is right that the sons* of peace be called the sons* of God.

*Phil 3:6

*Gal 6:2

*2 Cor 11:29
*1 Cor 14:33
*filios
*filios

15. Now what follows refers particularly to the martyrs, and though the present, God be thanked, is not a time of persecution, if persecution should be unavoidable it would have to be borne with patience. For *blessed are they who suffer persecution for righteousness' sake, for theirs is the kingdom of heaven.*[3]* But what does it mean that the same promise is made to the poor and to martyrs, except that voluntary poverty is really a kind of martyrdom? *Blessed is the man,* says the prophet, *who has not gone aside after gold or hoped*

*Matt 5:10

---

[3] Two manuscripts contain a different reading for the first two sentences of §15: "Now follows the eighth beatitude, reserved for martyrdom. It seems we have neither the time nor the courage to endure it; rather, justice is honored as long as it is ready at hand, but none or few endure persecution for it! They are happy (if they really are) that the Kingdom of heaven is theirs, as long as nobody persecutes them for it! But if tribulation should be multiplied, then they exult in a multitude of ways, considering not the disagreeable things that are seen but the rewards that are not seen. For the things that are seen are temporal, and those that are not seen eternal. *Blessed,* he says, *are you, when people shall revile you and persecute you and say all manner of evil against you falsely, for my sake. Rejoice and be exceedingly glad on that day, for great is your reward in heaven*" (Luke 6:22-23).

for coin in his treasury. Who is he? We will praise him: he has done wonderful things in his life.* What is more to be wondered at, what martyrdom more painful, than to hunger at a feast, to be cold among much precious clothing, to be oppressed by poverty among the riches that the world offers, the devil shows us, and our appetite desires? Will the person who has striven thus not deserve to be crowned,* throwing away the promise of the world and, what is more glorious, triumphing over himself and crucifying the craving of covetousness?* So the kingdom of heaven is promised alike to martyrs and the poor, because it is bought with poverty but won without delay by suffering for Christ.

*Sir 31:8-9

*2 Tim 2:5

*Col 2:15

On the Feast of All Saints[1]

Sermon Two

Of the State of the Saints before their Resurrection

1. Today, most beloved, we celebrate the festival of All Saints, a commemoration worthy of the greatest devotion. I have in mind to give a sermon* for you about their common happiness, the reward of labor, wherein they enjoy a blessed rest, and the future consummation they await. May the Holy Spirit come to my aid so that I follow not the conjectures of my own opinion but the authority of divine writings, and that I seem not to be prophesying out of my head, but rather as far as possible relying on the witness of Scripture.

*sermonem facere

With the help of God, then, there will be a threefold purpose for this sermon: to the extent that the happy reward of the saints is discerned even in part, we may strive the more ardently to follow in their footsteps, sigh with the most fervent desire for their companionship, and with devotion readily commend ourselves to their patronage. For *this is a faithful saying and worthy to be accepted by all,** that those whom we accompany with solemn veneration we may also follow in conduct, so that while extolling these most

*1 Tim 1:15

---

[1] *Sermo in dominica I novembris* (1 Nov 2).

blessed ones we may with all passion hasten to their beatitude, and while we delight in celebrating them we may be supported by their patronage.

Yes, the festive memorial of the saints will be found to yield no little fruit, for it utterly routs languor, tepidity, and error. By their intercession our weakness is aided and our carelessness corrected; the contemplation* of their blessedness rouses us from carelessness, and by their example our ignorance is dispelled. Therefore, since there is no doubt that you are perfectly equipped, both by today's reading of the holy gospel and by the words of our Lord himself, to follow in the footsteps of the saints, here before your eyes is raised the ladder by which the whole company of saints whom we venerate today ascends.* I am not unaware that most of last night and today have been spent with reverent devotion begging for their favors. Now I shall attempt, however meagerly, to speak of their happiness, as he who magnifies and glorifies those whom he first called and justified* grants me to do.

*consideratione

*Gen 28:12

*Rom 8:30

2. We read in the prophet, *Turn back to your rest, my soul, for the Lord has blessed you: for he has delivered my soul from death, my eyes from tears, and my feet from falling,** and in another psalm, *Our soul has escaped like a bird from the snare of the fowlers.** I seem to have discovered in the course of holy Scripture many similar sayings of people who rejoice with no little amazement that they have been set free, words of perfect confidence and great happiness—an expression of thanksgiving and praise that in my opinion does not accord at all with those who dwell in *houses of clay** and eat *their bread in the sweat of their brow.** For *who* among them *can boast of having a pure heart?**

Who would dare to boast that his snare is broken* and his feet delivered from falling* when the apostle cries out, saying, *Let the one who stands watch lest he*

*Ps 114:7-8
*Ps 123:7

*Job 4:19
*Gen 3:19
*Prov 2:9
*Ps 123:7
*Ps 114:8

fall?* So he says about himself, *I am an unhappy man! Who will deliver me from the body of this death?** And in another place, *Brothers, I do not judge myself to have understood. One thing however I know, that forgetting the things that are behind and stretching toward the things that are before me, I press towards the prize,** and so on, and again, *I run not as without a purpose, I fight not as beating the air, but I chastise my body and keep it under subjection, lest after having preached to others I cause myself to be rejected.** This is clearly a war cry; these are the words of a vigorous commander boldly fighting. Or rather, they seem to be spoken by one who is conquering—who can doubt it?—or, perhaps, not by one who is conquering but by one returning from the battle, having gained the victory and waiting with a joyful and untroubled conscience for the day of great triumph to come.

 3. What do brave soldiers, good servants, say when they return from battle? *Turn again to your rest, my soul!** For while you fight for the Lord in the body of this death* there is no rest, because of both the heat of battle and the danger of an outcome still uncertain. On the one hand the tumult of temptations will incite you, while on the other the fear of falling is even more disturbing. Even if soldiers of Christ had glory,* brothers, it would not yet be fitting for them to have rest. So it is that the brave and extremely strong* soldier whom we mentioned a short time ago said, *This is our glory: the testimony of our conscience.** I do not think the *testimony of the conscience* is to be understood as the conscience bearing witness to itself. *For it is not the one who commends himself who is approved, but the one whom God commends.**

 The *testimony of the conscience*, therefore, of which the apostle boasts, is not something that the conscience makes but what the Spirit of Truth speaks in it,* making a testimony of our spirit, since we are children of

Marginal notes:
- *1 Cor 10:12
- *Rom 7:24
- *palmam; Phil 3:13-14
- *1 Cor 9:26-27
- *Ps 114:7
- *Rom 7:24
- *2 Tim 2:3
- *i.e., Paul
- *2 Cor 1:12
- *2 Cor 10:18
- *John 14:17

God.* For when Truth approves, when righteousness bears witness, it is without doubt the voice of God giving praise and of the Holy Spirit making testimony. In addition, if such soldiers fight manfully, the King, who is standing close by and for whose love and honor they fight, will applaud them with joy, praising their brave deeds and proclaiming that victory is at hand, and will promise them the rewards that are already prepared for them and an eternal crown. It is in this testimony that tried and brave soldiers glory, but they still do not take any rest, instead fighting all the more bravely and valiantly. *Rom 8:16

So while they still go on fighting, the chosen of God rejoice, but only in the firstfruits of the Spirit,* who aids them in their weakness with his power and comforts their feebleness with his witness.* So the apostle of whom we spoke says, *The Kingdom of God is not meat and drink, but righteousness and peace and joy in the Holy Spirit.** *Rom 8:23 *Rom 8:26 *Rom 14:17

4. Now, the time of soldiering served, the saints have joy in their spirit until the day comes when they also have joy in their bodies. For we read in the psalm, *The light of your countenance has shone upon us, Lord; you have put gladness in my heart.** How? Clearly from what follows: *with the fruit of their grain, wine, and oil.** For the soul of such a one heard a voice saying, *Give her of the fruit of her hands, and her works shall praise her in the gates.** Also from what John is bidden to write in the Apocalypse: *Blessed are the dead who die in the Lord.* Why are they blessed? *From now on, says the Spirit, let them rest from their labors.** Also in the same psalm that we quoted a short time ago, these words follow: *In peace in him I will sleep and rest.** And concerning labors, we have in the Apocalypse, *and their works follow them.** Why do they follow them, if not so that *they may praise them in the gates*? Why do they follow them, except to increase them by their fruit, and, as they take *of the* *Ps 4:7 *Ps 4:8 *Prov 31:31 *Rev 14:13 *Ps 4:9 *Rev 14:13

fruit of their hands,* we recognize them as the young fattened cattle set upon the altar when, according to the prophet's testimony, the walls of Jerusalem shall have been rebuilt.*

    Meanwhile, of course, they are under the altar, not on it. He points this out to us himself, whose testimony must be believed.* As he wrote in the Apocalypse, he heard their voices under the altar itself.* Up till now, then, the light of the Lord's countenance is a seal upon them,* and even if it be not complete, the joy they have in their hearts is great, until the day comes when he will fill them with the joy of his countenance.* Meanwhile, I tell you, those souls have turned back to their rest,* until the day comes when they are worthy to enter into the rest of the Lord.* In the meantime, while he is coming, their works continue to praise them in the gates;* then each shall be praised by God. You see, brothers, how great is the unity* of the Scriptures, how they speak of the blessedness of souls with one sense and almost the same words.

    5. Now let none of you suspect as in any way insignificant the peace and joy of those who, now completely free from all trouble, recall their years* in sweetness of soul, rejoicing for the days in which they suffered humiliation, the years when they saw bad things,* who with delighted surprise consider the dangers they escaped, the hardships they endured, and the battles they won, and who, in place of all these, look with sure and certain faith for the blessed hope and the coming of the glory of their great God and Savior* who will raise up and transform their bodies, configuring them to the glory of his own body.*

    6. How great is their happiness, how immeasurable their joy who exult with the threefold joy from the remembrance of virtue performed, the manifestation of rest in the present, and the certain expectation of future consummation! Regarding this future consum-

Marginal references:
*Ps 4:8
*Ps 50:20-21
*Ps 92:5
*Rev 6:9
*Ps 4:7
*Ps 15:11
*Ps 114:7
*Ps 94:11
*Prov 31:31
*1 Cor 4:5
*Isa 38:15
*Ps 89:15
*Titus 2:13
*Phil 3:21

mation, we have their voice at the end of that psalm of which we just spoke. For each of those souls to whom it has been granted to attain to that rest says, *I will sleep and rest, for you alone, Lord, have established me in hope**— each individually, I say—"in hope, no longer between hope and fear where previously, not without concern and great anxiety, I was vacillating."

In the same way, concerning the present rest of the saints, we have it written in another psalm, *Turn again to your rest, O my soul, for the Lord has done good for you.** Good, I say, but not yet the best. Hear then how good: *For he has delivered my soul from death, my eyes from tears, and my feet from falling.** That is, "he has utterly freed me from all sin and punishment for sin, and from the fear and danger of falling again." For this is the soul's most sweet bed, which no one now will wash or wet with tears, when *God shall wipe away all tears from their eyes.** This is the bed in which she no longer feels remorse* nor is turned back to toil when pierced by a thorn.* For she has left that land that produced for her thorns and brambles.* This is the soul's couch, on which she never tosses and turns in her sickness,* for all traces of sickness have passed.

This, I say, is the most pleasant and healthful rest of the soul, a clear, quiet, and secure conscience. Let a clear conscience be a pillow for the blessed soul, let tranquillity be a rest for her head, let confidence be her covering, so that in this meantime she may sleep with pleasure on her couch and may rest in joy.

7. Now about the remembrance of virtue performed, you have their words clearly expressed in the one hundred twenty-third psalm, the words of which I recalled above. For with great wonder they reflect upon and closely consider from what innumerable snares and dangers they have been counted worthy to be freed by divine help, and exulting in God,* they say, *If the Lord had not been with us, let Israel now say, if*

*Ps 4:9-10

*Ps 114:7

*Ps 114:8

*Rev 7:17
*Ps 4:5
*Ps 31:4
*Gen 3:18
*Ps 40:4

*see
Pss 31:11; 32:1

the Lord had not been with us when men rose up against us, they would have swallowed us alive. Our soul would have crossed through a torrent; perhaps our soul would have gone through unendurable water.* And they add, *Blessed be the Lord, who did not give us into the snare of their teeth!* Similarly, the words that the apostle earnestly spoke at the time of his deliverance seem to apply to him much more now that he is at rest. For now he may safely say, *I have fought the good fight, I have finished the course, I have kept the faith: now there is laid up for me a crown of righteousness, which the just judge will give me in that day.*

*Ps 123:1-5
*Ps 123:6

*see
2 Tim 4:6, 7-8

Brothers, these, I tell you, these are all the activities of the saints in the present time; this is their food, this their sleep. Therefore the Holy Spirit desired that these words that we have brought forward—and similar ones, too—should be written, so that from them their situation might in some measure be known to us.

8. But they are affected and much more greatly delighted by meditations like these in ways far different than we can comprehend or our speech express. For hear how the prophet labors, stammering and uttering many words yet not achieving the great effect he intended: *How great is the plenitude of your sweetness, Lord, that you have hidden away for those who fear you!* What did he add? *You have prepared it for those who hope in you, in the sight of humankind.** There is therefore a plenitude of sweetness laid up, great, very great, but not yet complete, since it will be completed openly, not in secret, when the saints no longer rest below the altar* but sit on thrones like judges.* For their holy souls, freed from their bodies, are at once admitted to rest, but this is not the full glory of the kingdom. *The righteous await me*, said the prophet while he was held in the prison of this body, *until you restore me.** And the voice of God summons the holy souls to the resurrection of their

*Ps 30:20

*Rev 6:9
*Luke 22:30

*Ps 141:8

bodies: *Rest a little while, until the number of your brothers shall be completed.*²*   *Rev 6:11

But now the talk must come to an end, for we are summoned to the solemn celebration of the Mass. There is still more to say about this topic; let's keep it for another talk.

---

² As in the responsory *Sub altare* for the feast of the Holy Innocents.

On the Feast of All Saints[1]

Sermon Three

*In What Way Shall They Be without Blemish or Wrinkle?**

*Eph 5:27

1. You will have noticed, I think, from the things that were said in my previous talk, that there are three states of holy souls: the first, in the corruptible body, the second, without the body, and the third, in the body now glorified. The first is in the strife of the church militant, the second in the church at rest, and the third in complete blessedness; the first in the tents of pilgrimage, the second in the courts, and the third in the house of God. *How lovely are your tabernacles, Lord of hosts!** But much more to be desired are the courts, according to what follows: *My soul longs and faints for the courts of the Lord.** But since, as you hear, no one has fainted in those courts, *Blessed are all those who dwell in your house, Lord!** I rejoiced, brothers, *in those who said to me, "We will go into the house of the Lord."**

*Ps 83:2

*Ps 83:3

*Ps 83:5

*Ps 121:1

If you ask why I anticipate this time so confidently, it is doubtless because many of us already stand in these courts, waiting until the number of brothers is made up.* They will not enter that blessed dwelling without us, or without their bodies; that is, the saints will

*Rev 6:11

---

[1] *Sermo in festivitate omnium sanctorum* (OS 3).

not go without the people, nor the spirit without the flesh. For it is fitting neither that complete blessedness should be tendered until the person to whom it is given is complete nor that perfection should be given to an imperfect church. Therefore, although they were awaiting the resurrection of the body, as I said in the previous talk, they received the divine answer,* *Wait a little while, until the number of your brothers is complete.*² * Still, each of them has already received a robe,* but they will not be clothed in double robes* until we also are clothed, as the apostle says of the patriarchs and prophets: *God has provided some better thing for us, so that they should not be made perfect without us.** For the first robe* we spoke of is felicity and rest for the soul, and the second is immortality and glory of the body. Therefore they say, *Avenge, Lord, the blood of your saints that has been poured out,** not through desire for vengeance or zeal for due punishment, but through longing for the resurrection and glorification of their bodies, which they do not doubt must wait till the Day of Judgment.

*Rom 11:4
*Rev 6:11
*singulas stolas
*duplicibus; Rev 6:11; Prov 31:21

*Heb 11:40
*Luke 15:22

*Ps 78:10; see the Tract in the Mass of the Holy Innocents

2. But what is this to you, O unhappy flesh, O foul, O rotten! What is this to you? The souls of the righteous, which God has marked with his own likeness and redeemed with his own blood,* await you; without you their joy cannot be complete nor their glory made perfect nor their blessedness be full. Indeed this natural desire is so strong in them that not all the affection of their souls flows freely toward God; it is to some extent held back and wrinkled as long as they are bent down* by desire for you.

*Gen 1:26

*inclinantur

So blessed John, who by the Spirit unseals many things for us about the state in which the blessed souls rest, says, *They are without blemish before the throne*

---

² Responsory *Sub altare* for the Feast of the Holy Innocents.

of God.* Without blemish, I repeat, but not without wrinkle, until the day comes when Christ shall show forth his glorious church without blemish or wrinkle.* Among those who still strive, the church is not without blemish, for *no one is free from filth, not even an infant whose life on earth is of only one day,** a life that blessed Job alleges is warfare.†

It is among those who rest under the altar of the Lord,* surely, that the church is without blemish, as you read in the psalms: *Lord, who shall dwell in your tabernacle, or who shall rest on your holy mountain? The one,* it says, *who enters without blemish.** So the one who walks without blemish will rest on the mountain of the Lord; they who are without a wrinkle shall be exalted above the mountain. But do you wish to know when the souls of the blessed shall be without a wrinkle? When the heavens are spread out like a skin that is utterly stretched,* so that not the slightest wrinkle is found in it; then, without a doubt, is when they will follow the Lamb wherever he goes.* I mean, truly the souls of those by whom the Lamb is followed everywhere must be stretched and spread out. Where does he go?* *He spans the world from end to end and orders all things sweetly.**

3. Do you wish to know were the Lamb goes, and where the souls of the blessed must follow him? *In all things I sought rest.** Clearly this is the rest of the Lord.† It is not broken off or closed off with regard to any limited thing, since he rejoices and takes pleasure in all and seeks and finds rest[#] in all. For good things are pleasing to him in themselves, and no less does he find delight in the good intention of the wicked. *He loves mercy and righteousness,** so he takes pleasure not only in the glory of the good but also in the punishments of the wicked, insofar as they are just.

What then? Do you think that a human soul can enter into the joy of its Lord* and into his rest,† so that

---

Margin notes:
*Rev 14:5
*Eph 5:27
*Job 14:4, from an ancient version
†Job 7:1
*Rev 6:9
*Ps 14:1–2
*Ps 103:2
*Rev 14:4
*John 13:36
*Wis 8:1
*Sir 24:11, as in the Epistle read for the Feast of the Assumption
†Exod 35:2
#Luke 11:24
*Ps 32:5
*Matt 25:21
†Ps 94:11

it too may delight in all things, and not be gathered into a wrinkle by any affection of its own* but may pass into a universal and divine love?* No doubt it can if it is found faithful with regard to the few things† that it undertook in its time of combat, that is, with regard to its body's members, with regard to its senses, and with regard to its instinctive desires that it undertook to rule over, so that it could be shown how faithful it was to its Lord. Let the servant of Christ *know how to possess his vessel in sanctification*;* let him glorify and bear God in his body,* having no doubt that the Lord who is bountiful and rich will set him over many things* because he has been faithful in a few things:* *he made him lord of his house, and prince of all his possessions.**

*privata affectione
*affectum;
Ps 72:7
†Matt 25:21

*1 Thess 4:4
*1 Cor 6:20
*Luke 19:17
*Matt 25:21
*Ps 104:21

Let this not seem to you hard to believe, my brothers, as if I speak of my own accord, since the Truth itself makes these promises openly, and of his promises there can be no possible doubt.* *Blessed is that servant*, he says, *whom the Lord, when he comes, shall find so doing. Truly I say to you, he shall set him over all his goods.** The faithful servants are set over all their master's goods when they are counted worthy to enter into his joy* and then to rejoice with him in everything, to delight in all, and to take pleasure in everyone. For according to the witness of the apostle, *The one who cleaves to the Lord is made one spirit*,* and his will,† cleaving in all things to the divine will,# becomes one with it, so that now nothing may be found in any created thing that is against it, but rather that all things may come about in accordance with, or rather remain in, his decision.*

*John 7:17

*Matt 24:46-47

*Matt 25:21

*1 Cor 6:17
†voluntas
#divinae voluntati

*arbitrio

4. This then is the blessed hope that the holy souls look for,* and although they occupy themselves with thanks for the happiness in which they now rest, they call to God, begging him for the completion that they await. So we say that although they are without the blemish of the past,* yet they are not without the constricting wrinkle. They are seen to have arrived at

*Titus 2:13

*Eph 5:27

thanksgiving but not yet at the voice of praise.* That is because it becomes the perfect ones to praise the Perfect One, so that he may be praised by his inheritance* when they shall praise him, and at the same time each one will receive praise from God.* So it is significant that the prophet uses the future tense when he says, *Blessed are they who dwell in your house, Lord; they shall praise you forever.** Blessed John in the Apocalypse heard not so much the voice of praise as the voice of prayer, for you read, *I heard under the altar the voices of the slain.** What cries? *Avenge, Lord, the blood of your saints that has been poured out.** This is the voice of prayer, not of praise. But how long shall we stand around the altar and fear to approach? Your charity desires, if I am not mistaken, to hear the mystery* of that altar and to know its holy and hidden secret.* But who am I to dare to burst into the chamber of the saints and rashly rummage around? Haven't I read that anyone who probes into majesty shall be crushed by glory?*

But let us stop there for today, for perhaps at our knocking those holy souls who dwell there will deign to reveal the altar's secret, not for any merit of ours but for the sake of him *who loved us and washed us from our sins in his blood*,* for we know that we too are citizens and members of God's household, not like strangers and foreigners, who would expect to be driven away from that secret dwelling-place.*

*Isa 51:3

*Ps 105:5
*1 Cor 4:5

*Ps 83:5

*Rev 6:9
*Ps 78:10

*sacramentum
*mysterium

*see Prov 25:27

*Rev 1:5

*Eph 2:19

On the Feast of All Saints[1]

Sermon Four

Of Abraham's bosom, and of the altar beneath which Blessed John heard the voices of such souls of the saints, and of the seven loaves from which we read that the same number of baskets remained

1. As I think you will remember, when the sermon started digging into the altar beneath which Blessed John heard the voices of the saints,* we broke up so that, with prayer preceding, a more sure approach to the sacred and secret chamber might lie open to us. It is time that I should tell you of the experience that has been granted to me, allowing, of course, that it may have been revealed to others in another way.

*Rev 6:9

First, then, we can reflect on the meaning of Blessed John's assertion that he heard the voices of the souls of the saints beneath the altar, while in the gospel the Savior, speaking of the soul of Lazarus, says that it has been borne by angels not beneath the altar, but to Abraham's bosom.* Likewise it seems that Job, a holy

*Luke 16:22

[1] *Sermo in festivitate omnium sanctorum* (OS 4).

man, in no way dared to hope to approach the altar of God, since he said, *Who will allow to me that you will protect me in the depths and hide me until your anger passes, and that you will appoint a time to remember me?** But when Blessed John heard the voices of the saints beneath the altar, the time for which blessed Job asked had already come; the time of reckoning, the time of mercy had already come.*

For until he who was longed for came* to cancel the decree of our damnation† with his own blood and quench the fiery sword,# opening the kingdom of heaven to those who believe, no way to it lay open to any of the saints. Rather, God had provided a place of rest and refuge for them below, and a great gulf was fixed* between those holy souls and the souls of the wicked. For although both were in darkness, they were not both undergoing punishment; the wicked were in torment and the righteous in consultation.* But that they were in darkness we learn from the testimony of Blessed Job, who said that he himself would go to a place of darkness, covered with the shadow of death.* And this place, dark indeed but restful, the Lord called the bosom of Abraham because, I suppose, they rested in faith and expectation of the Savior. For Abraham's faith was so clearly proved and approved* that he was the first to be counted worthy to receive the promise of the coming incarnation of Christ.*

Now the Savior, descending to this place, *broke the gates of brass and shattered the bars of iron** and led from their prison those who had been bound;* they were indeed seated, that is, at rest, but in the shadow of death.[2]* Then he set them beneath the altar of God,† hiding them in his tabernacle in the time of trouble and keeping them safe in the secret place of his dwell-

---

[2] See the antiphon *O Clavis David* for Dec. 18.

ing* until the time should come when they should go forth, when the number of their brothers should be complete,* and they should see the kingdom prepared for them from the beginning of the world.

And if it is true that now in any place whatsoever the rest of the saints is called the bosom of Abraham*—a custom clearly arising from the gospel—it is no less clear that no one should doubt that the one bosom is quite different from the other, since the one was in darkness, the other in full light; the one was in the lower regions, the other in the heavens. Yet it does not seem strange that the children of the patriarchs should be received into the bosom of their father, since they merited to pass over from this world to their fellowship.*

2. Further, the altar we are going to talk about may, I think, rightly be supposed to be nothing other than the very body of our Lord and Savior. Moreover, I think this interpretation of mine agrees with his,* particularly when I hear him saying in the gospel, *Where the body is, there the vultures will gather.** So in this interim time the saints rest in joy under the human nature of Christ, a thing that the angels themselves long to look upon,* until the time comes when they no longer lie beneath the altar but are raised above the altar.

But what have I said? No one, neither human beings nor angels, can attain—let alone surpass—the glory of Christ's human nature, right? How then can I say that those who are now at rest beneath the altar are to be raised above the altar? By vision and by contemplation, not by authority! For the Son, as he promised, will show us himself,* not in the form of a servant but in the form of God.* He will also show us the Father and the Holy Spirit, and without that vision nothing will satisfy us, since this is life eternal, that we should know the Father,* the true God, and Jesus Christ whom he sent,* and in them, without doubt, the Spirit that is of both.

*Ps 26:5

*Rev 6:11

*Matt 25:34

*Heb 5:11

*1 Cor 2:16

*Luke 17:37

*1 Pet 1:12

*John 14:21
*see Phil 2:6-7

*John 14:8-9
*John 17:3

In our contemplation of him, he will while passing by certainly serve to us* deep within new delights previously quite unknown to us. So Blessed John says in his epistle, *Now we are the children of God, but it does not yet appear what we shall be.* And he adds, *But we know that when he appears we shall be like him, because we shall see him as he is.** Now hear the bride in the Song of Songs speaking boldly and with certain hope, because already set above the altar: *His left hand* (doubtless that of the Bridegroom) *under my head, and with his right hand he embraces me.** For the blessed soul goes beyond Christ's incarnation and humanity, which may justly be called his left hand, so that she may contemplate his sublime divinity and majesty, which may not unfittingly be called his right hand.

3. We shall then, brothers, in that eternal and perfect beatitude enjoy God in three ways: seeing him in every creature, holding him within ourselves, and, what is ineffably more cleansing and blessed than all these, knowing the very Trinity in itself and contemplating it with the pure eye of the heart* and without any enigma.† In this will be eternal and complete life, that we may know the Father and the Son# with the Holy Spirit, and that we may see God as he is, not only as he dwells in us and in other created beings but as he is in himself.* So the first two things we mentioned seem to be like the husk surrounding a grain of wheat, while this truly great knowledge of beatitude is the kernel of the wheat, the fat of the grain* with which Jerusalem, the holy city, is nourished.*

Truly how great is that beatitude, so hidden from our eyes,* that ear has not heard, nor eye seen, nor has it entered the human heart* what brightness, what pleasure, what joy awaits us in that knowledge. It is the peace of God that surpasses all understanding.* How much more does it surpass our power of speech? To experience it is given to no one, nor may any try

*Luke 12:37

*1 John 3:2

*Song 2:6

*Matt 5:8;
Eph 1:18
†1 Cor 13:12
#John 17:3

*1 John 3:2

*Deut 32:14
*Ps 147:3

*Luke 19:42
*1 Cor 2:9

*Phil 4:7

to express it. *Full measure*, says the Lord, *pressed down, shaken together, and running over shall they pour into your lap.** Full measure in the whole of creation, pressed down in the inmost part of our humanity, shaken together in the outer part, and running over in God himself. Here is the sum of happiness,* here the towering glory, here the overflowing of blessedness.*

*Luke 6:38

*felicitatis
*beatitudo

4. How he will be seen in creatures and how held by us, we can now guess to some extent from the firstfruits of the Spirit that we have already received.* But that knowledge* is still altogether unknown† to us. It is a wonderful thing, a mighty thing, so that we cannot attain to it. True, we can understand to some extent how he will be seen in created things, particularly since he is even now sometimes seen in them.* So according to the witness of the apostle, philosophers caught sight of the invisible things of God through the things that are made.*

*Rom 8:23
*cognitio
† incognita

*Ps 138:6

*Rom 1:20

Nevertheless, however much we may succeed in glimpsing how powerfully, how prudently, how benevolently the eternal majesty created all things, brooded over all things, and set everything in order, we will end up understanding only a tiny bit of it. But, as I said in the previous talk, the time will come when we shall follow the Lamb wherever he goes,* and we will comprehend him in every creature so that we may rejoice in all things, which is *the joy of the Lord*.* So, yes, let us rejoice in everything, but only for his sake and none other, just as he delights not in others but in himself!

*Rev 14:4

*Neh 8:10

5. He is held by us even now, in fact, and how that is so, we can to some extent imagine. For it is agreed that the nature of souls is threefold. As the wise of this world* have reported, and as even without them nature and daily experience teach, the human soul is possessed of a threefold power: rational, irascible, and concupiscible. Everyone agrees that both knowledge

*1 Cor 1:20

and ignorance correspond to our rationality, depending on whether we put it into practice or not. Similarly, desire and contempt correspond to our concupiscence, and joy and anger to our irascibility. Therefore God will fill our rationality with the light of wisdom, so that knowledge will in no way be lacking to us.*

*1 Cor 1:7

He will fill our concupiscence with the fount of righteousness,* so that we may in all things desire righteousness and be completely filled with it, [as it is written, *Blessed are those who hunger and thirst for righteousness, for they shall be satisfied.*]* For nothing else can fill the soul's desire; nothing other than righteousness can make the soul happy.† And when he has filled our concupiscence with righteousness, the soul will spurn whatever it ought to spurn, and whatever it ought to yearn for* it will yearn for, and it will greatly strive after* whatever it should greatly strive after. Since, then, it is clearly on the basis of the object of our desire* that we are considered either just or unjust, we rightly attribute righteousness to it. Finally, when God has filled what is called irascibility, then perfect tranquillity will be in us, and in the greatest charm and gladness we will be filled with divine peace.

*iustitiae

*Matt 5:6, added in two manuscripts
†beatificare

*concupiscere
*apetet

*concupiscibili nostro

Furthermore, when you rightly consider the soul, notice that the perfect beatitude of the soul consists in these three, when because of justice knowledge does not puff up* and because of gladness it does not sadden, so that the proverb is nullified that says, *The one who serves up knowledge also serves up grief,** when knowledge ensures that justice does not lose its ability to discern and gladness ensures that it does not become burdensome, when knowledge keeps gladness from being foolish, and justice keeps it pure.

*1 Cor 8:1

*Eccl 1:18 (an ancient version)

6. But as regards all these things, until now our exterior person has received nothing. Therefore, so that *glory may even now dwell in our land** and, as another prophet has it, the majesty of the Lord may fill the

*Ps 84:10

whole earth,* four things are required, obviously composed of the four elements that make them up. Do not marvel that the one who is more wretched seems to need more, when you read in the psalm the prophet saying, *My soul thirsts for you; how greatly my flesh thirsts for you!** Therefore our earth has immortality, lest one fear that it will return again to dust. For our body, rising, can no longer die, for death has no more power over it.* But what good is it if one lives always in the misery and suffering of the mortality by which this corruptible body* is incessantly afflicted, and dies not once but constantly? For even water has impassibility.

    *Ps 71:19

    *Ps 62:2

    *see Rom 6:9

    *1 Cor 15:53

They say that suffering comes from disordered humors. But now our body desires lightness, doubtless from air, one of the elements of which it is composed. It is to be believed that in the future the lightness and agility of the bodies of the blessed will be such that they can, if they wish, follow our thoughts everywhere without delay or difficulty and with all rapidity. What more is lacking to the perfect happiness of the body? Only beauty everywhere. Now that perfection that we must have we cannot unreasonably attribute to the part that we have from fire. For as the apostle says, *We await the Savior, who will conform the body of our humiliation into the likeness of his body's glory.** So he accomplishes what he promised, that *the righteous will shine like the sun in the kingdom of their Father.** Thus God will completely fill our souls when he gives us perfect knowledge, perfect righteousness, and perfect joy. So his majesty will fill the whole earth, when the body will be incorruptible, impassible, and agile, conformed to the glorious body of Jesus Christ.

    *Phil 3:20-21

    *Matt 13:43

And see if perhaps these things[3] are the seven breads with which we read that the Savior satisfied four

---

[3] Knowledge, justice, joy, majesty, incorruptibility, impassibility, and agility.

thousand people, the morsels of which the apostles gathered up in the same number of full wicker baskets.* For we are nourished on this bread when in joyful meditation we reflect in blessed hope, until the day *when he shall come*,* when no longer in hope but rejoicing in the reality that we will be shown, we may merit to receive as many full baskets in place of each of our breads.

*Matt 15:32-38

*1 Cor 11:26

On the Feast of All Saints[1]

Sermon Five

Of the Advantage of Their Memory

1. This day is a festival for us, and today's solemnity is counted among the principal feasts. What shall we say of it? Which apostle, which martyr, which saint does it commemorate? Not any one in particular, but all equally. We all know that the feast that we celebrate today is called the feast of All Saints, and indeed it is so. Of all saints, I repeat, either of heaven or of earth. For there are saints of heaven, and there are saints of earth, and among those of earth some are still on earth, while some are already in heaven! So we celebrate a festival of all these together, but not necessarily in the same way for each. This fact is not to be wondered at, since the sanctity of all is not the same in each, but there is considerable difference between one saint and another. I do not mean that one is more holy than another, for that would be a difference of degree rather than of character. It is not a matter of greater and lesser; rather, they are all rightly and truly said to be saints, but for different reasons.

[1] *Sermo in festivitate omnium sanctorum* (OS 5).

And perhaps this diversity of holiness and renown can be attributed equally to angels and humans. For while those who have never been known to fight cannot be honored as though they had won a victory, yet they are to be greatly honored in another way—as your friends,* O God, who clung to your will with as much happiness as ease. But maybe this was their way of fighting, that they stood their ground firmly when others were giving way to sin and did not enter into the council of the ungodly,* but with one voice they all said, *It is good for me to cling to God.** So what is to be celebrated in them is the sweet blessing of prevenient grace;* what is honored is the goodness of God—not that he led them to repentance,* but that he led them away from everything for which repentance would be required; not because he delivered them from temptation, but because he preserved them from temptation.

2. There is another kind of holiness, in its own way clearly worthy of honor, among these who have come from great tribulation, who have washed their robes white in the blood of the Lamb* and who after many agonies now reign triumphant in heaven, for they have contended according to the rules.*

Is there yet a third kind of holiness among the saints? There is, but it is hidden. For there are saints who still strive, still fight, still run, but have not yet received the prize.* Perhaps it seems that I am rash to call them saints, yet I know that one of them did not hesitate to say to God, *Preserve my soul, for I am holy.** So also the apostle who knew the secrets of God said openly, *We know that all things work together for good to those who love God, to those who are called saints according to his purpose.**

There is then a diversity in the way human beings are called saints, for some are so called because they have finished their course, others because they are as yet predestined to do so. Sanctity of this kind is hidden with God; it is concealed, and it is celebrated in a

*Ps 138:17

*Ps 1:1
*Ps 72:28

*Ps 20:4
*Rom 2:4

*Rev 7:14

*2 Tim 2:5

*1 Cor 9:24; Phil 3:13

*Ps 85:2

*Rom 8:28

concealed way. For *a person does not know whether he is worthy of love or hate,** but all are kept in uncertainty for the future. Therefore let the renown of those saints lie in the heart of God, for *the Lord knows his own,** and he himself knows whom he has chosen from the beginning.* So let it be with those ministering spirits who are sent to serve those who are heirs of salvation.*   *Eccl 9:1   *2 Tim 2:19   *John 13:18   *Heb 1:14

As for us, we are forbidden to sing the praises of human beings in their lifetime.* For how shall praise be assured when life is not assured? *He shall not be crowned unless he has contended according to the rules,** says that heavenly trumpet. And hear the rules of the contest from the lawgiver himself: *The one who perseveres to the end is the one who shall be saved.** You do not know who will persevere, you do not know who will contend according to the rules, you do not know who will receive a crown.   *Sir 11:30   *2 Tim 2:5   *Matt 10:22

3. Praise their virtue whose victory is now assured; extol with faithful voices those in whose crowns you can safely rejoice. We have sung to the saints tonight, saying, *Fear the Lord, all his saints,** but not to these. I mean, it is not those who have persevered to the end whom we have exhorted to fear, for it is written, *There shall no longer be any fear within our borders.** Rather, we were speaking to those saints who need much protection because of their many perils. They *fight not only against flesh and blood but against principalities and powers, against the rulers of the darkness of this world, against spiritual wickedness in the heavens.** They have need of protection, which is sought in various ways both near and far. And where there are so many battles without, fears ought not be lacking within,* so that it may rightly be said to them, *Fear the Lord, all his saints.*   *Ps 33:10   *see 2 Kgs 2:21; Rev 21:4   *Eph 6:12   *2 Cor 7:5

In the meantime, all our happiness is to fear God, as the Scriptures say: *Happy the one who fears always.** And again the psalmist says, *Happy are all those who fear the Lord, who walk in his ways.** It is far otherwise   *Prov 28:14   *Ps 127:1

with the blessed, in whom perfect charity has cast out fear;* walking in his ways, they no longer fear but rather praise him while they dwell at home, as the same writer says: *Blessed are those who dwell in your house, Lord. They will praise you forever and ever.** Meanwhile our joy, our festivity, is in the fear of the Lord, for theirs is turned more into exultation and praise.

4. This is what human beings may surely be praised for, that they do not live their own lives but that of God, for the life of a human being is temptation.* There is a double security in this praise—unless perhaps it seems, if we consider it carefully, that the one is contained in the other. Accordingly, we should not fear to praise those who are truly and certainly praiseworthy nor hesitate to give glory to those who are rapt in glory, even if they can in no way be moved by our praise: vanity has no way to enter a place that truth has already fully occupied.

You will ask, "But where in the world is the glory of the saints? For they do not each glorify themselves, do they, since it is written, *May not your own mouth praise you.** And they do not praise each other, because they are intent and alert in praise of the Creator, in whom all their blessedness reposes, never finding time for mutual praise. As the prophet says, and as we mentioned before, *Blessed are those who dwell in your house, Lord; they will praise you forever and ever!*"*

All that may be so, but I do not subscribe to the belief that the saints are bereft of glory, especially in the view of what the apostle says: *Our momentary light affliction works for us a far greater and eternal weight of glory.** And the prophet says, *Visit us with your salvation, that we may see the good of your chosen ones and rejoice with your people who rejoice, so that you may be praised with your inheritance.** For he did not say, "so that you may be praised by your inheritance," but *with your inheritance*, so that the praise to come may be understood

*1 John 4:18

*Ps 83:5

*see Gal 2:20; Job 7:1

*see Prov 27:2

*Ps 83:5

*2 Cor 4:17

*Ps 105:4-5

as praise in common. For while the inheritance itself praises the Lord, let us hear from the apostle who it is who praises the inheritance: *Then*, he says, *there will be praise for each one*. From whom? *From God.** A great praise-giver, and a praise to be energetically embraced! A happy exchange of praise, where blessedness is in both praising and being praised.

*1 Cor 4:5

5. What to the saints, then, is our praise, what our glorifying, what this very solemnity of ours? What are earthly honors when the heavenly Father honors them according to the true promise of his son?* What to them is our celebration? They are fulfilled. It is quite clear, brothers: the saints do not need to be honored by us, nor is anything added to them by our devotion. We venerate their memory to our advantage, not to theirs. Do you wish to know how greatly that is to our advantage? I confess that a great longing flares up in me when I think of them, a threefold longing. People say, "What the eye does not see, the heart does not grieve for." My memory is my eye! To reflect on the saints is in some way to see them. This is our portion in the land of the living,* and it is no mean portion if affection accompanies memory, as it should. Thus, I say, our citizenship* is in heaven,† but ours is not like theirs. They are there in fact, but we in desire. They are there in reality; we are there through memory. When shall we be joined to the company of our ancestors?* When shall we in all our being be present with them?

*John 12:26

*Ps 141:6

*conversatio
†Phil 3:20

*Acts 13:36

This, then, is the first desire that the thought of the saints either rouses or urges in us, that we may enjoy their long-desired company and be found worthy to be fellow citizens and companions of the blessed spirits, to mingle with the ranks of the patriarchs, the fellowship of the prophets, the company of the apostles, the great army of martyrs, the company of confessors, the choirs of virgins—in short, to be gathered into and rejoice together with the communion of saints.

6. The recollection of each one of them, as if each were a spark or, better, a blazing torch, inflames the minds of the devout so that they long for the sight of them and for their embrace; they imagine themselves among them, their hearts pulsing strongly with eagerness, now for all together, now for these, now for those.

So what is this negligence of ours, this laziness, or, better, this madness of ours that we are not with continual sighs and burning affection trying to break out from here to be cast in among those happy ranks? What misery, the hardness of our hearts!* What misery, the sin of the people, whom the apostle calls to mind as being *without affection*.* The church of the firstborn is waiting for us, and we do nothing about it;† the saints long for us, and we think little of it; the righteous await us, and we take no notice. Let us awake, brothers; let us rise again with Christ, let us seek the things that are above, let us taste the things that are above.* Let us desire with great desire,† let us hasten in expectation, let us occupy our souls with prayer. I mean, admit it, there is no security in our community life, no perfection, no peace! Yet he says, *How good and pleasant it is for brothers to live in unity!** The point is, whatever trouble befalls, whether within or without, we will find it to be all the more bearable because of the fellowship of true brothers, with whom we are of one soul and one mind in God.* How much sweeter a union will it be, how much more pleasant, how much more blessed, when there is no suspicion, no occasion for disagreement, when perfect charity will bind all in an indissoluble bond, where we shall be one even as the Father and Son are one!*

7. We must desire not only the company of the saints but also their joy, for when we feel the lack of their presence, the more zealously fervent is our ambition for glory. This is no pernicious ambition, nor is this

*Matt 19:8

*Rom 1:31;
2 Tim 3:3
†Heb 12:23

*Col 3:1-2
†Luke 22:15

*Ps 132:1

*Acts 4:32

*John 17:22

striving for their glory in any way dangerous. When we said, *Not to us, Lord, not to us, but to your name give glory,** we were referring to this life. The angels sing the same thing: *Glory to God in the highest, and on earth peace to people of good will.** *Do not touch me*, he says, *for I have not yet ascended to the Father.** It is the Word of glory. Of course, *the wise son knows the glory of his father,** So *do not*, says Glory, *do not touch me.* That means "do not seek glory; better, flee from it, and don't dare to touch me" until she shall come to the Father, where all glorying is totally secure. There *In the Lord my soul will be praised; the humble will hear and rejoice.** Doesn't it seem that the one saying, *Do not touch me; I have not yet ascended to the Father*, has heard her who in the Song of Songs cries out, *Fly, my beloved, fly?** This is what we cited before: *Not to us, Lord, not to us, but to your name give glory.* That is why we sang in one of the hymns today, together with one of the choirs of angels, "Give peace to your servants; / We also give glory / To you for all the ages."[2]

*Ps 113:9

*Luke 2:14
*John 20:17

*Prov 13:1;
after an ancient version

*Ps 33:3

*Song 8:14

8. Again, since *the life of a human being on earth is a trial,** it makes more sense to seek peace than glory: peace with God, peace with your neighbor, peace with yourself. *O guardian of humans, why have you placed me against you, and I am made a burden to myself?** An internal rebellion much to be mourned is at hand! Not a civil war but a domestic one, the desire of the spirit against that of the flesh and of the flesh against that of the spirit.* How has this come about, except that *you have placed me against you*? I mean, you are true freedom, you are life, you are glory, you are fullness, you are blessedness, while I am poor and wretched and pitiable, altogether mixed up and brought low, dead

*Job 7:1
(an ancient version)

*Job 7:20

*Gal 5:17

---

[2] Hymn for the memorial of several martyrs (*Des pacem famulis, / Nos quoque gloriam / Per cuncta tibi sæcula*).

on account of sin, sold under sin!* In short, you, complete and holy delight and rest for the spirits of the blessed, you from the beginning placed me in opposition to Eden, which means "delight,"³ in work and even drudgery.

Still, you say, *Return to me with all your heart.** That makes it clear that we are turned away, we whom you exhort to turn back; that makes it clear that we are against you, we whom you call back that we might convert. But how? *In fasting*, it says, *and tears and mourning.** What a marvelous thing! You don't go around fasting, do you, or spend your time in tears, or live in mourning? No, all of these things are far from you, and even more certainly are you far from them! Clearly your kingdom is in Jerusalem, which you satisfy with the choicest grain,* where there is no weeping or wailing or any sort of sorrow,* but rather thanksgiving and the voice of praise.* *Let the righteous*, it says, *feast in the presence of God and take delight in joy and exultation.**

So how shall we be converted to him in fasting, tears, and mourning? Can it really be that the righteous will find him in joy and exultation but the one who is not righteous only in fasting, tears, and mourning? Clearly it can be, but the righteous who has already attained the sight of God, not the one who is still living by faith.* When the Lord says, *I am with him in tribulation,** he is clearly referring to the one walking by faith, not to one who has already reached his face.* While it is true that there is one head for all the members, yet it is not manifested in the same way for each of them. To those the Head shows himself with

---

³ See Jerome, "*Hebraicae Quaestiones in Libro Geneseos*," in *S. Hieronymi Presbyteri Opera,* Pars 1.1, ed. P. de Lagarde, G. Morin, M. Adriaen, CCSL 72 (Turnhout: Brepols, 1959), 4, re. Gen 2.8 (*Porro* eden *deliciae interpretantur*).

Margin notes:
- *Rom 8:10; 7:14
- *Joel 2:12
- *Joel 2:12, read at Terce during Lent
- *Ps 147:14
- *Rev 21:4
- *Eph 5:4; Isa 51:3
- *Ps 67:4
- *Rom 1:17
- *Ps 90:15
- *2 Cor 5:7; 1 Cor 13:12

bristly thorns, hanging on a cross, so they may likewise be humble and together be stung with remorse, and to these he appears glorious so that they themselves may be glorified and may glory in having been made like him, for they see him as he is.* *1 John 3:2

9. This, then, is the second desire that blazes up in us from the commemoration of the saints: that just as he is to them, so to us Christ should be manifested as our life so that we too may appear with him in glory.* *Col 3:4 In the meantime, of course, he is not like this, but rather he is seen as he became for us, our Head, crowned not with glory but wrapped round with the thorns of our sins, as Scripture says: *Come out, O daughters of Sion, and see King Solomon in the diadem with which his mother crowned him.** *Song 3:11 O King, O diadem! Supposing the mother is the Synagogue, she who crowned our King with a crown of thorns is not a mother at all, but a stepmother. Let the members be ashamed if they follow after glory seeing that their Head was so displayed as inglorious, having no beauty or comeliness or anything of that sort.* Without a doubt it is Solomon, the truly peaceful one,† who in this present time is neither blessed nor glorious, so that in all things that angelic hymn might be verified, that is, peace on earth, glory in heaven.* *Isa 53:2; Eph 5:27 †1 Chron 22:9; Song 8:11 *Luke 2:14

It would be a shameful thing if the members were to be pampered when the Head is being pierced by thorns, the one who was clothed by everyone with purple not for honor but derision.* Yet you see in *Mark 15:17-20 many places where today's feast is celebrated as a kind of Bacchanalia and an opportunity to rub shoulders with the influential. I'm not to be judged wrong for saying that, am I? They themselves can see that this is what they do. It is they themselves, not the saints, whom they celebrate in this way. Whatever they do, it is for themselves, not for the saints. When Christ shall come, it will not be so that his death may be announced again,* but so that we might know that we have died with him and our life is hidden with him.* The glorious Head will appear, and with him his glorified members will flash forth, that is, when our body of humiliation shall be configured to the glorious Head,* who is Christ himself. This glory is the prudent way of rubbing shoulders with the influential! Let us eagerly desire it, lest we should hear, *The glory that you seek is from one another, and the glory that comes from God alone you do not want.**

*1 Cor 11:26
*Col 3:3
*Phil 3:21
*see John 5:44

10. So that we might hope for this glory and aspire to such beatitude, we must also surpassingly desire the prayers of the saints, so that their intercession may win for us what is outside the realm of possibility for us to attain on our own. *Have mercy on me, have mercy on me, at least you, my friends.** You yourselves know our danger, you know our fictitiousness,* you know our ignorance and the cunning of adversaries, you know their fury and our fragility. It is to you I am speaking, who were in these very same temptations, who overcame these very same conflicts, who evaded these very same snares, and who learned compassion from the things you suffered.* In addition, I rely on the angels, that they may not refuse to visit their own species but rather, as it is written, *You will visit your own species and not sin.** All the same, even though I think I can presume on the similarity of spiritual substance and rational form, my confidence is even more inspired by those who are human just like me: they will by rights feel pity for one of their own species and family, who is bone of their bone and flesh of their flesh.*

*Job 19:21
*Ps 102:14; figmentum

*see Heb 5:8

*Job 5:24

*Gen 2:23

11. Finally, having crossed over from this world to the Father,* they left behind holy pledges for us. Even if we see their bodies buried here in peace, their names live forever;* that is, their glory is never buried. God forbid, O holy ones, God forbid that you should be like that cruel Egyptian, Pharaoh's cupbearer, who

*John 13:1

*Sir 44:14

once reinstated in his former position immediately forgot holy Joseph, who was kept in prison!* I mean, the members were not united with the head, nor did the faithful share anything with the unfaithful, nor did Israel have any affinity with Egypt, any more than light does with darkness.* Egypt is interpreted "darkness," while Israel is the one who sees God.[4] Even more, wherever Israel was, there was light. Our Lord Jesus was not like that cupbearer; he could not forget the thief crucified with him. Without a doubt what he promised was done:* in one and the same day he shared his sufferings and he reigned with him.* *Gen 40:14, 23

*2 Cor 6:14-15

*Luke 23:40-43
*2 Tim 2:12

As for us, if we are not members of the same Head as the saints, then what is the point of today's solemn liturgies, and why do we greet each other so warmly? Yet the one who said, *If one member is honored, all members rejoice with it,* likewise said, *If one member suffers, all the members suffer with it.** What we do is consistent with what they do: we rejoice together with them, and they suffer along with us; through devout meditation, we reign with them, while they by devoutly intervening fight with us and in us. For we cannot doubt their devout solicitude for us. As we said above, because they will not attain their fullness without us,* they cannot but hope for us to obtain our reward,* so that in that last great day of solemn festivity* all members will assemble together with their most excellent head to form one perfect man,* and Jesus Christ our Lord will be praised along with his inheritance,* our Lord, *who is above all things, God blessed* and praised and glorified for ever.*

*1 Cor 12:26

*Heb 11:40
*Ps 141:8
*John 7:37

*Eph 4:13
*Ps 105:5
*Rom 9:5
*Dan 3:56

---

[4] See Jerome, *Liber nom hebr,* CCSL 72:143 (*Aegyptus tenebrae uel tribulatio*), 75, s.v. *Israhel* (*Israhel est uidere deum siue uir aut mens uidens deum*).

For the Dedication of a Church[1]

Sermon One

Of the Five Sacraments of the Dedication

1. Because today's festival, my brothers, is entirely a family affair, it should be all the more dear to us. For while we have all the other feasts of the saints in common with other churches, this one is our own, so obviously if we do not celebrate it, no one will. It is ours because it concerns our church; even more, because it concerns us. Are you surprised and embarrassed that a feast for yourselves be celebrated? But *do not be like horse and mule, which have no understanding.** For what sanctity can these stones have that we should celebrate their festival?

*Ps 31:9

They do indeed have sanctity, but it is because of your bodies.* Who can doubt that your bodies are holy, since they are the temple of the Holy Spirit, *that every one of you should know how to possess his vessel in sanctification?** And so your souls are holy *on account of the Spirit of God living in you,** your bodies are holy because of your souls, and this house is holy because of

*1 Cor 6:15, 19

*1 Thess 4:4
*Rom 8:11

---

1 *Sermo in dedicatione ecclesiæ* (Ded 1). The solemn dedication of the church at Clairvaux was probably performed in 1138, according to Elphège Vacandard, *Vie de S. Bernard*, 2 vols. (Paris: Gabalda, 1895), 1:418–19. For the relationship of its date to the placement of these sermons, see the Introduction to this volume, pp. xxviii–xxx.

your bodies. A person who was still held in corruptible flesh* and in a body of sin, and whose soul gave itself to the grave sin of adultery, nevertheless said, *Preserve my soul, for I am holy!** Truly *God is wonderful in his saints*,* not only in those in heaven, but in those on earth, too. In both places he has saints, and in both he is wonderful, blessing those and sanctifying these.

*Rom 6:6
*Ps 85:2
*Ps 67:36

2. Do you demand proof* of the sanctity of which I speak? Do you wish some miracles of those saints to be shown to you? Certainly many of you have manfully* abandoned sins and vices in which they rotted* like beasts in their own dung, and every day you tirelessly resist their opponents, following the apostle, who says this of the saints: *Out of weakness they became strong and were made valiant in war.** What is more wonderful than that one who could scarcely abstain for two days from extravagance, from drunkenness, from inebriation, from debauchery, from promiscuity,* and from other similar—and dissimilar!—vices now refrains from them for many years, even for his whole life? What is more miraculous than that so many youths, so many young adults, so many of noble birth, in fact all whom I see here, are held as it were in an open prison without chains, fixed by the fear of God* alone, that they persevere in such penitential torment, beyond human strength, above nature, and against custom?

*2 Cor 13:3
*viriliter
*Joel 1:17

*Heb 11:34

*Rom 13:13

*Ps 118:120

I think you can see what great wonders we could find if each of us was to examine in detail his own exodus from Egypt* and his sojourn in the desert—that is, his renunciation of the world—his entering the monastery and his way of life* in the monastery. What are these except the manifest proofs of the Holy Spirit dwelling in you?* For the activity of the body proves that the soul dwells in the body, and the spiritual life proves that the Spirit dwells in the soul. The one is discerned by sight and hearing, the other by charity and humility and all the other virtues.

*Ps 113:1

*conversationem

*Rom 8:11

3. So it is your festival today, my dear brothers, your very own. You are dedicated to the Lord; he has chosen you and made you his own: *The poor has abandoned himself to you; you will be the helper of the orphan.** What a good trade you've made, beloved! By renouncing whatever you might have possessed in the world, you have merited to belong to the Creator of the world and to possess him for your own, since he is without doubt the portion* and inheritance† of his people. For it is not the case, as the children of iniquity said, that *Blessed are the people who possess such things,** storing them up for their future in this life, *whose barns are overflowing from one to another and whose flocks multiply,** and so on; it is not, I say, *Blessed are the people who possess such things,* but *Blessed are the people whose God is the Lord.**

See then if it is not fitting that we should celebrate a feast day because he made us his own and has used us as his ministers and deputies in order to bring about what he himself had promised: I, he said, will be their God in the midst of them,* *for we are his people and the sheep of his pasture.*† When this house was dedicated to the Lord by the hands of a bishop, there is no doubt that it was done for us—and not only for us who were present, but for whoever will fight for the Lord in this place until the end of the age.*

4. Those things that have visibly taken place within these walls should therefore be fulfilled in us spiritually. And if you wish to know what they are, they are these: the sprinkling, the inscription, the anointing, the illuminating, and the blessing. Bishops did these things in this visible building; *Christ having taken his place as the high priest of the good things to come** works invisibly in us from day to day. First he sprinkled us with hyssop, so that we might be cleansed, washed, and made white* and so that it might be said of us, *Who is this who ascends* all white?* He washes us, I say, in confes-

---

*Ps 9:35

*Ps 141:6
†Ps 15:5

*Ps 143:15

*Ps 143:13

*Ps 143:15

*Rev 21:3;
Zech 2:10
†Ps 94:7

*RB Prol. 3,
Prol. 40

*Heb 9:11

*Ps 50:9
**dealbata;*
see Song 3:6

sion, he washes us in the tears that flow, he washes us in the sweat of penitence, but he washes us even more in that precious water that flows from the fountain of holiness, that is, from his side.* He sprinkles us with hyssop,* which is a lowly† herb that cleanses the breast, *with the water of the knowledge of salvation,*# which is the fear of the Lord, the beginning of wisdom,‡ and the fountain of life,* even mixing it with the savor of salt so that it shall not be a fear that is flavorless,† without hope, without devotion.

    That is not all. He inscribes with the finger of God, with which he expelled demons,* doubtless through the Holy Spirit. He writes his law, I say, not now on stone tablets *but on tablets that are hearts of flesh,** fulfilling the prophetic promise* that he would take away the stony heart and give instead a heart of flesh, not a stubborn one, not a Jewish one, but a godly* one, a meek one, a cooperative* one, a devout one. *Blessed is the one you instruct, Lord, and teach by means of your law!** Blessed, I say, are those who are taught and *are mindful of his commandments, to do them.** Otherwise, *to those who know how to do good but do not do it, to them it is sin,** and *the servant who knows the will of his lord and does not do it shall be beaten with many strokes.**

    5. It is necessary therefore that the spiritual unction of grace should help our weakness,* rubbing its grace over the crosses of the observances and the manifold acts of penitence of our religious practice. For no one can follow Christ without the cross, and who can bear the bitterness of the cross without this anointing? So it is that many detest and shun penitence, for they see the cross but not the unction. You who have experienced it, you know firsthand* that our cross is truly anointed, and through the grace of the Spirit that helps us, our penitence is pleasant and delightful, and I may say our bitterness* is very sweet! But where the unction of this grace has gone before, Christ does not put his

*John 19:34
*Ps 50:9
†*humilis*
#Sir 15:3
‡Ps 110:10; Prov 9:10
*Prov 14:27
†Matt 5:13

*Luke 11:20

*2 Cor 3:3
*Ezek 11:19

*pium
*tractabile
*Ps 93:12

*Ps 102:18
*Jas 4:17

*Luke 12:47

*Rom 8:26

*ecce ipsi scitis

*Isa 38:17

light under a bushel but on a candlestick, because it is time that our light should shine among people so that they may see our good works and glorify our Father who is in heaven.* *Matt 5:15-16

6. Now then, truly let us expect a blessing at the end, when he shall open his hand and fill all things living with a blessing.* *Ps 144:16 For in the first four things[2] there are benefits, but in a blessing there are rewards.* *praemia In a blessing the entire grace of sanctification will be perfected when we have entered *the house not made with hands*, but the *eternal one in the heavens*.* *2 Cor 5:1 That house is built of living stones,* *1 Pet 2:5 of angels and humans. For the building and dedication will be completed together. When the wood and the stones are separated,* *disiuncta they do not make a house, nor can anyone live in it. It is only their union* *coniunctio that makes the house. So the perfect unity of heavenly spirits, joined together* *sibi . . . connexa without any division, makes a habitation whole and pleasing to God, which the indwelling of his glorious majesty* *Isa 2:10 blesses beyond words. For who better would know all the counsels of kings or be aware of all their words and deeds than the wood and the stones of their palaces,* *1 Pet 2:2, 5 if they did not lack the faculty of intelligence? And so the living and reasoning stones of that heavenly court participate in the divine counsels, and they know the mystery of the Trinity and hear the ineffable words* *2 Cor 12:4 that humans are not permitted to speak. *Blessed are they who dwell in your house, Lord! They will praise you forever.** *Ps 83:5 For to the extent that they see, understand, and know, so much the more do they love, so much the more do they praise, and so much the more greatly are they astonished.

---

[2] *Praemissis*: the sprinkling, the inscription, the anointing, the illuminating.

7. But because we have already said that his house was perfectly in harmony and joined together,* it remains for us to press as far as we can that connection and close union.* We read in Isaiah, *the soldering† is sound.*# So the stones are in harmony with each other‡ through the twofold solder of full understanding and perfect love. To the degree that they stand together in charity itself, which is God,* so too do they cling together† with greater love.# And no distrust can separate them from each other, because the ray of truth that penetrates all things allows nothing among them to be concealed. Since *the one who clings to the Lord is one spirit** with him, there is no doubt that the blessed spirits, who cling to him together with him and in him, penetrate all things.

**cohaerere . . . connexam esse*

**iuncturam et connexionem;* Eph 4:16
†*glutino*
#Isa 41:7
‡*sibi cohaerent*
*1 John 4:16
†*invicem . . . copulantur*
#*dilectione*

*1 Cor 6:17

If you desire to reach this house, let your heart long and grow weak to enter the courts of the Lord,* just as the prophet proclaims: *One thing have I asked of the Lord, this I request, that I may dwell in the house of the Lord all the days of my life.** Moreover, be like the prophet: *Thus he swore to the Lord, made an oath to the God of Jacob: if I go into the tabernacle of my house,* and so on.*

*Ps 83:3

*Ps 26:4

*Ps 131:2-3

But what follows from here will be dealt with in another sermon as God himself will grant.

For the Dedication of a Church[1]

Sermon Two

How We Should Cling to Ourselves and Others

1. Once upon a time that glorious king and prophet of the Lord, holy David, began to be disturbed by a religious consideration, judging it intolerable that he himself lived in a house worthy of a king but the Lord of Hosts had as yet no house on earth.* We also, brothers, should consider this same matter faithfully and manfully. (Although this idea of the prophet found approval with God, yet the execution of the work was left to Solomon—but this is another topic, and a short hour is not enough time for us to expound it.)

*2 Sam 7:2

Now, O soul, you live in a lofty house that was built for you by God. I mean this body that he shaped, prepared, and ordained so that you might live in it with delight and glory. But even for your very body too he made a lofty house, totally suited to it and beautiful. I am referring, of course, to this perceptible and inhabitable universe. Do you not therefore think it intolerable that while he has made a house for you, you should fail* to make a temple for him? Certainly you have a house now, but be sure that your house will

*dissimules

[1] *Sermo in dedicatione ecclesiæ* (Ded 2).

fall down before long, and unless you make preparations for another one, you will be exposed to rain, wind, and cold!* *Who shall stand before his cold?*† Happy indeed a thousand times over the soul who can say, *For we know that if our earthly house of this habitation is dissolved, we have a building from God, a house not made with hands, eternal in heaven.** Therefore, my soul, give no sleep to your eyes nor slumber to your eyelids until you find a dwelling-place for the Lord, a tabernacle for the God of Jacob!*

*Matt 7:27
†Ps 147:17

*2 Cor 5:1

*Ps 131:4–5

2. But what shall we think, brothers? Where shall a place be found for this building, and who can be its architect? For this visible temple has certainly been made for us, and for our dwelling, *yet the Most High does not dwell in buildings made by hands.** What temple shall we build for him who says, and says rightly, *I fill heaven and earth?** I should indeed be troubled and my spirit be vexed within me* if I didn't hear him saying somewhere, *The Father and I will come to him and will make our home with him.** Therefore I know that even if a house is prepared for him, it will not hold him, but only his image. The soul is able to hold him, for she is created in his image.

*Acts 7:48

*Jer 23:24
*Ps 142:4

*John 14:23

Hasten then; *adorn your bedchamber, Sion,*² for the Lord has found pleasure in you* and your land will be inhabited.* *Rejoice greatly, O daughter of Sion;*† your God will dwell in you.# Say with Mary, *Behold the handmaid of the Lord: let it be done to me according to your word.*‡ Speak next the words of blessed Elizabeth: *How does is it happen to me that the majesty of my Lord should come to me?** How great then is the courtesy of God, how great the honor, how great the excellence, and how great the glory of souls, that the Lord of all, who has need of nothing, should order a temple for himself to be made among them!

*see Luke 1:30
*Isa 62:4
†Zach 9:9
#Isa 62:4;
Rev 21:3
‡Luke 1:38
*Luke 1:43

---

² Response *Adorna* for the Feast of the Purification.

3. So, my brothers, let us strive with every desire and with great thankfulness to build a temple for him in ourselves, concerned in the first place that he should dwell in us as individuals, then in all of us together, because he spurns neither the part nor the whole. First then let all take care not to be at odds with themselves, for *every kingdom divided against itself will be brought to desolation, and a house shall fall upon a house,** and Christ will not enter a house where the walls are fallen and the fences broken down.* For doesn't the soul want the house of its body to be whole, and won't it necessarily leave if its limbs are scattered?

*Luke 11:17

*Ps 61:4

Let the soul be watchful then, if it desires Christ to dwell by faith in its heart,* that is, within itself; let it take great care that its members, that is, reason, will, and memory, are not at variance with each other. Let reason therefore be without error, so that it may be agreeable to the will, for that is what the will loves. Let the will be without iniquity, since that is what reason approves. Otherwise, if the soul passes sentence on itself because of the perversity of its will in a matter that it approves by reason, there is internal war and dangerous disagreement, for reason often taunts such a will, accusing it, judging and condemning it. It is for this reason that the evangelist says in the gospel, *Agree with your adversary quickly, while you are on the way with him, lest he deliver you to the judge and the judge deliver you to the torturer,** and so on. But let memory be without stain, so that no sin remain in it that may not be canceled by a sincere confession and by the fruits worthy of repentance.* Otherwise the will will hate and the reason detest the conscience in which lurks hidden sin. A person prepares a good dwelling for God when reason is not deceived nor will perverted nor memory stained.

*Eph 3:17

*Matt 5:25

*Matt 3:8

4. Now, since each one of us is of the same mind, we must be linked and bonded together* by mutual

*connecti . . . conglutinari

charity, which is the bond of perfection.* For perfect understanding is not to be had in this life, and maybe it shouldn't be. In the house of heaven, understanding is the nourishment of love, but here it could be its undoing. For *who can boast that he has a pure heart?** So it is easy both for the knowing to be confounded and for the knower to be harmed. Where knowing brings delight,* there will be no longer any error. Then that house will be more the firmly joined together and, as it were, will last forever. This one, though, like the tents of soldiers, doesn't hold together so well. That one is a house of joy, this one of warfare; that one is a house of praise, this other of prayer. This one, I say, is *our strong city*,* that other, our city of rest.† So if we are victorious here, we will be glorious there, with a crown in place of a helmet, a scepter and palm instead of a sword, a cloak decked with gold instead of a shield, and the garment of joy in place of a breastplate.*

In the meantime,* it seems without a doubt better to be hard pressed* than made to perish,† and to bear the weight of a shield and breastplate rather than be wounded by the fiery darts of the evil one,* from which may he shield us with his divine protection, he who is blessed forever.†

*Col 3:14

*Prov 20:9

**iucunda erit*

*Isa 26:1
†Sir 36:15

*Eph 6:16-17
*interim
*premi
†*perimi*
*see 1 Sam 17:5-6, 38-39
†Rom 1:25

For the Dedication of a Church[1]

Sermon Three

Of Three Sorts of Equipment We Possess for Godly Vigilance

1. This house, my brethren, is the fortified town of the eternal king, but it is besieged by enemies. As many of us then who are sworn to defend it and have enlisted in its army know that we need equipment to guard this camp: a fort, weapons, and rations. What, then, is the fort? *Our Sion is a strong city*, says the prophet; *the savior shall place in it walls and bulwarks.** Its wall is continence, its bulwarks patience. Good is the wall of continence, which surrounds and encircles it in such a way that death may not enter by the windows of the eyes* or by any of the other senses.

*Isa 26:1

*Jer 9:21

Good is the bulwark of patience, which holds off the first attacks of the enemy, so that we stand strongly together unarmed among many trials and persevere, always indestructible. To hold patience before oneself is the sole remedy when continence is shaken and begins to faint and, when the urge to sin rages, to refuse agreement with it altogether: *In your patience you shall possess your souls.** Therefore the Savior himself shall become the walls and bulwark of his city,* being made

*Luke 21:19
*Isa 26:1

---

[1] *Sermo in dedicatione ecclesiæ* (Ded 3).

righteousness for us by God the Father* and patience, of which the prophet speaks when he says, *My God is my patience.** The wall, I say, shall be set up in our way of life,* the bulwark in suffering, in abstaining from all fleshly lusts and the enticements of this present life and holding fast against them in every way. *1 Cor 1:30
*Ps 70:5
**conversatione*

2. We must therefore prepare weapons, spiritual weapons, powerful for God, not only to resist but to fight against and even storm the enemy with great strength. *Put on the armor of God,** says Paul, and so on. *Eph 6:11

Let us consider the matter, brothers. The enemy's temptation is a burden to us, but our prayer to God is far more burdensome to the enemy! His iniquity and cunning injure us, but our simplicity and cries for mercy torture him much more. He cannot bear our humility; he is burnt by our charity and racked by our meekness and obedience. Now we cannot be threatened by hunger so as to be compelled to hand over the fortress to the enemy, since, thanks be to God, the terrible curse of the prophet, or rather of God through the prophet—hunger and thirst, but not for food and water but for the word of God—does not come upon us.* On the contrary, we know that *people do not live by bread alone, but by every word that comes from the mouth of God.** *Amos 8:11

*Matt 4:4

So we do not lack nourishment, since we often hear sermons, and even more often we hear the reading of the sacred writings, and from time to time we taste the delights of spiritual devotion, like puppies that eat from the crumbs that fall from their masters' table:* I speak of those celestial feasts that are supplied from the wealth of the house of God.* We also have the bread of tears,* which, although less sweet, makes strong the human heart.* And we have the bread of obedience, of which the Lord spoke to his disciples when he said, *My food is to do the will of my Father.** Above all we have the living bread from heaven, the body of our Lord *Matt 15:27

*Ps 35:9
*Ps 79:6
*Ps 103:15

*John 4:34, according to an ancient version

and Savior,* in the strength of which† all the darts of the enemy are overcome.

*John 6:41
†1 Kgs 19:8

3. In this way, then, the strength of the Lord's camp is secured so that it need fear nothing if we are willing to act faithfully and bravely and are not found traitorous or cowardly or slothful. For they become traitors who plot to bring the Lord's enemies into his camp—those who belittle, who are hateful to God,* who sow discord* and cultivate scandals.† For the Lord's place is established in peace,# but the devil's place is shown to be in discord.

*Rom 1:30
*Prov 6:19
†RB 65.2
#Ps 75:3

Do not be surprised, my brothers, if I seem to speak somewhat harshly, since the truth flatters no one. Those who try to introduce vices into this house and make it a den of demons* know that they are nothing but traitors. Thanks be to God, we do not find many of this kind here, but occasionally by chance we discover some who have conversation with the enemy and make a covenant with death;* that is, they endeavor, as far as they can, to diminish the discipline of the order, to cool its ardor, disturb its peace, and breach its charity. Let us avoid them as far as we can, as it is written of such, *But Jesus would not trust himself to them.** But I tell you that even though they are borne with for a little while, they will bear judgment upon themselves unless they quickly make amends, since they had plotted to bring about a great evil.

*Matt 21:13

*Isa 28:15

*John 2:24

What then, my brother? Do you through works preserve faith with vanity or lukewarmness or some other vice but lie to God with the tonsure?* Certainly you have taken from Christ a most excellent camp if you hand over Clairvaux to his enemies. From there year after year he receives revenue excellent and precious in his eyes.* He is accustomed to lay up in this place, this fort of his, the abundant booty he seizes from the enemy, and he has confidence in its great strength. Right here are *those whom he has redeemed from*

*RB 1.7

*1 Sam 26:21

the hand of the enemy and gathered from many lands, from the rising of the sun and its setting, from the north and from the sea.* To what kinds of punishments therefore do you think should be subjected the one who betrays this camp when he has been caught red-handed and seized, being able neither to hide nor to escape? You can be certain that he will not be condemned to an ordinary death; no, it is necessary for him to die by select torments.

*Ps 106:2-3

But I will not dwell upon these things any longer. I think it better that we keep away from such terrible treason, taking greater care in the future not to attract but to repel vices, of whatever sort they are, whether they be of the flesh or of the world, so that we do not deserve to incur the disgrace or punishment of a traitor.

4. In the second place we should take care lest anyone should either flee from the fort, dismayed by cowardice and trembling for fear where there is no fear,* or, in insane rashness, feel secure where there is great danger. Those who run away expose themselves to the hands and swords of the enemy, not only unaware that they are totally lacking in mercy and cruel toward others, yes, but also that they are very cruel toward their own, and most cruel to themselves.

*Ps 52:6

5. And now, because time passes, I touch briefly on the third peril. Passionate as I am,* and as you deserve, for your salvation, I try to find different remedies for different moral weaknesses. What advantage is there to your not betraying the camp, or not wanting to abandon it, if you keep on being lazy and slothful within it? Let us strive, beloved, with all our mind and with all our strength,* to hold the camp of our Lord and King that has been entrusted to us, being careful to resist all the wiles of the enemy and aware of all his machinations, as it is written: *Resist the devil, and he will flee from you.** But since we know who said, *Unless the*

*cupidus

*see Deut 6:5;
Matt 22:37;
Mark 12:30;
Luke 10:27

*Jas 4:7

*Lord keeps watch over the city, in vain does the watchman stay awake,** let us be humbled under the mighty hand of the highest, with complete devotion committing ourselves and this house to his mercy, that he may keep us safe from all snares of the enemy,* to the praise and glory of his name, which is blessed forever.*

*Ps 126:1

*1 Pet 5:6
*Ps 71:17

For the Dedication of a Church[1]

Sermon Four

Of the Threefold Dwelling-Place

1. We celebrate this day with due praises, and we honor it with festive delights. But because it is not fitting for monks or becoming for wise people to be ignorant of what they venerate or to celebrate what they do not understand, we must ask ourselves what this is all about, or for which of the holy ones this commemoration is held. Not presuming that I myself am reliable, let another speak first, one whose testimony is greater and held to be most trustworthy.*

*1 John 5:9

Perhaps you wonder why I begin this way when, as you see for yourselves, this very church, the anniversary of whose dedication is being celebrated, makes it clear. Who can hesitate to say that its walls are holy when the consecrated hands of bishops have sanctified them with so many rites? Ever since that time it is well known that frequent readings of the holy Scriptures re-echo in that place, the devout whispers of holy prayers are murmured, the blessed presence of holy relics are honored, and holy spirits tirelessly stand on watch keeping vigil.

[1] *Sermo in dedicatione ecclesiæ* (Ded 4).

Perhaps you say, "All these things are evident, but who boasts to have seen angelic guardians keeping guard?" Well, even if *you* do not see, there is one who does see, that is, who sends. Who is that? Surely the one who said by the prophet, *I have set guards upon your walls, O Jerusalem.** There is a Jerusalem on high that is free and is our mother,* but I do not believe that the watchmen were set above *her* walls, in praise of whom the prophet sang, *Who places peace on your borders.** If you think that this is a small matter, go on and listen to what immediately follows that text: *All the day and all the night they shall not be silent.**

*Isa 62:6
*Gal 4:26
*Ps 147:3
*Isa 62:6

Accordingly you will see that this is not the Jerusalem of which you have read, *Its gates shall not be shut by day, for there shall be no night in her,*[2]* For that Jerusalem suffers no mishaps, nor does it need guards, but our Jerusalem needs guards allotted to it by day and night: *I have set guards upon your walls, O Jerusalem.**

*Rev 21:25
*Isa 62:5

2. You are kind, O Lord; you cannot be content with this fragile protection of our walls, but over those who are themselves over others you have set an angelic guard so that they may defend both the walls and those who are contained within the circuit of the walls. So, Father, as it is pleasing to you,* so it is necessary for us. For our ministry falls short unless you send ministering spirits to be with us and for us in our ministry so that we may inherit salvation.* What if we do not see the service as long as we experience the help, if we do not deserve to see the face yet still feel the effect? We learn certainly from this that invisible things are preferable to visible. *For the things that are seen are temporal, but the things that are not seen are eternal.** So the cause of visible things lies in the invisible,

*Matt 11:26
*Heb 1:14
2 Cor 4:18

---

[2] As in the Responsory "Haec est Jerusalem" at the consecration of a church.

as, according to the apostle, *The invisible things of God are seen by his creatures, being understood by the things he has made.** So indeed, once when the Jews were blaspheming the Holy One of Israel concerning remission of invisible sins, he refuted them with the visible sign of physical health: *But that you may know that the Son of Man has power on earth to forgive sins, then he said to the paralytic, Get up, take your bed, and go to your home.**

*Rom 1:20

*Matt 9:6

3. He did the same with the Pharisee who had complained about the doctor who healed and had passed judgment on the sick woman who received salvation: he challenged him with manifest proofs, enumerating her attentive gestures. For the Pharisee was mistaken, having until then been shrinking back as if she were a sinner—she who, clinging to the divine feet, bathed them with tears, wiped them dry with her hair, pressed her mouth against them, and anointed them with ointment.* Who is he to make a list of sins now forgiven, to judge someone for touching, to reckon her a sinner who while deploring the things she has done hates iniquity and while kissing the Lord's feet loves justice,* and, again, while wiping them dry with her hair shows humility and while anointing them with ointment exhibits gentleness?

*Luke 7:36-50

*Ps 44:8

It is not possible, is it, for sin to reign in a contrite soul and an anguished spirit?* Does charity not cover a multitude of sins?* *Many sins are forgiven her, because she loved much.** Rightly then, O Pharisee, she will no longer be called a sinner, as your opinion would have it, but instead holy and a disciple of Christ, from whom in such a short time she learned to be gentle and lowly of heart.* Surely this is what you read in the prophet, but perhaps you overlooked it: *Turn the wicked, and they will be no more!**

*Rom 6:12
*1 Pet 4:8
*Luke 7:47

*Matt 11:29

*Prov 12:7

Thus, my beloved, thus also if that old accuser of the brothers* reproaches you about your past, about things that make you to blush,* you will hear the apostle

*Rev 12:10
*Rom 6:21

giving you inestimable consolation, saying, *Some of you were like this, but you have been washed and are sanctified,** *1 Cor 6:11
and also, *You have your fruit in sanctification, and your end indeed in everlasting life;** speaking openly, he says, *The temple of God is holy, which temple you are.** *Rom 6:22 / *1 Cor 3:17

4. Surely it was in deference to him* that we allowed him the first word at the beginning of this sermon when we were asking who these holy people were whose sanctity we celebrate with solemn devotion. For although we call these walls holy—and the consecration by bishops makes them so, as do the frequent repetition of the Scriptures, insistent prayers, relics of the saints, and visitation of angels—yet the holiness these things have in themselves is not enough for them to be held to be worthy of honor, nor are they considered to be holy because of themselves. Rather, a house is holy because of the bodies within it, and the bodies because of the souls, and the souls because of the Spirit dwelling within them.* Therefore, lest anyone doubt, let a visible sign of favor be done for us as well as his invisible grace.* I say, moreover, that here you rise like the paralytic in the gospel, that you so easily take up your bed—your body, in which you were lying sick*—and that you then go to your house, that house, yes, in which you rejoice, saying with the prophet, *We will go into the house of the Lord.**

O wonderful house, to be preferred to the beloved tabernacles and to the courts most desired! *How beloved are your tabernacles, Lord of hosts! My soul desires and faints in the courts of the Lord.** But they are even more blessed who dwell in your house, Lord. They will be always praising you.** Glorious things are spoken of you, house of God.* In your tents is the sighing of penitence, in your courts the taste of joy, in you the fullness of glory. This place below is the house of prayer, the one in the middle the house of expectation, and you the house of thanksgiving and praise. Happy then is the one who

*Saint Paul

*Rom 8:11

*Ps 85:17

*Mark 2:11-12

*Ps 121:1

*Ps 83:2-3

*Ps 83:5
*Ps 86:5

flees from evil, that is, from error, and does good,* so that that one may be freed from evil, that is, punishment, and in you receive favor.

For here are the firstfruits of the Spirit,* there the riches, and in you the fullness, where that good measure, pressed down, shaken together, and running over may be poured into our laps!* Here people become saints, there they are safe, and in you they are blessed. These indeed are the firstfruits of the Spirit that are supplied in the meantime to those who strive: holiness in their way of life,* piety in intention, and courage in the struggle. By holiness of their way of life understand the fruits of penitence and the bodily practice of the divine commandments.

But since these things cannot be simple* unless the eye is simple,* holiness of intention and purity of heart are of necessity called forth; nor must the desire for honor or the passion for praise creep in, but that only should be desired that alone fulfills desire, and let every grace we have received be returned to the fount from which it sprang. Remember that perseverance, alone of all things, shall be crowned, and it will not easily be acquired among so many dangers unless you maintain manifold courage in manifold strife. So much for living in tents.

5. Next, with regard to the courts that receive those who come to be comforted with pleasure and joy after bitter conflicts—there already the riches of the Spirit are being paid out, there is rest from their labors, freedom from anxieties, and peace from enemies. For *from now on, says the Spirit, let them rest from their labors,** the Spirit that up to now has so ardently forbidden leisure and enjoined labor. That same Spirit that only lately was inciting them to plans of action and causing them to be anxious about many things* will make them free from care and insulate them from all anxiety.* When the victory is won the very same Spirit

*Ps 36:27

*Rom 8:23

*Luke 6:38

*in conversatione

*simplicia
*simplex;
Matt 6:22

*Rev 14:13

*Luke 10:41

*Ps 12:2

will allow them to sleep in sweet peace together with itself,* though while the lion was roaring† it roused them to watchfulness and girded them for battle.

But as we mentioned above,* freedom from evil is better than reward for good. Nevertheless, the hard experience of our life forces us to value the absence of evil as the summit of the good, just as our conscience reckons it the fullness of sanctity when no one is accusing us of anything! How far we are from the highest good, we who say there is justice only because there is no guilt, and happiness just because there is not misery!

6. But God forbid that anyone think that such is the fruitfulness of that house and the torrent of delights,* and whatever else there is that *eye has not seen, nor ear heard, nor has it arisen into the human heart what God has prepared for those who love him.** Do not wish to hear, O human, what the human ear has not heard, nor ask of a human about what the human eye has not seen nor the mind* conceived. At the same time, though, let us not be completely silent, for even now as we greet our native land from afar,* we seem to get a whiff of the threefold promise guaranteed: I mean, the power, the splendor, and the glory. For it was a man, and a child of this captivity,* who said, *I will come into the power of the Lord.** We can understand what it would be like to be without weakness, surrounded as we are by weakness.* But what it would be like to be clothed in strength* and to come into power†—and not merely power, but great power, even omnipotence!—in this in-between stage* we cannot know.

The faithful witness* cries that *those whom he justified, he also glorified.** In the meantime, the glory† that ought especially to come from that greatness# of which there is neither limit nor quantity—let us in our weakness at least hope for it, without, though, trying to comprehend* it.

*Ps 4:9
†1 Pet 5:8

*Ded 4.4

*Ps 35:9

*1 Cor 2:9

*animus

*Heb 11:13

*Dan 5:13
*Ps 70:15

*Heb 5:2
*Luke 24:49
†Ps 70:15

*interim
*Rev 1:5
**magnificavit;*
Rom 8:30
†*magnificentiam*
#*magnitudine*

**aestimare non licet*

Truly, there is no need either to fear or to be suspicious of the promise of glory.* Then you will drink of glory with joy and confidence even though in the meantime you are detoured by the many threats to your desire. But then there will be for everyone praise from God,* totally secure and eternal, limitless and without distinction, as it is written, *Praise is pleasant and fitting.**

gloriae

*1 Cor 4:5

*Ps 146:1

Well, then, brothers! In this interim, let us fight bravely in the tabernacles so that we may rest pleasantly in the courts and may at last enjoy sublime glory in the house, when this light and momentary affliction of ours will work in us an exceeding and eternal weight of glory* and we will be praised in the Lord the livelong day,* but in truth,† not in vainglory.#

*2 Cor 4:17

*Ps 43:9
†*veritate*
#*vanitate*

For the Dedication of a Church[1]

Sermon Five

Of the Twofold Consideration of Oneself

1. Today, my brothers, we celebrate a festival, and a glorious one. But maybe I said that too easily, because if you go on to ask which of the saints we celebrate, the answer does not come so readily. For as often as the memory of any apostle or martyr or confessor is commemorated—for example, of blessed Peter, of glorious Stephen, of our holy Father Benedict, or of any other of the great princes of the great court in heaven—it is not difficult to say whose feast day it is. The present solemnity, though, doesn't have to do with any of these, even though it is a major solemnity—major, not minor. If you are willing to hear it, it is the feast of the house of God, of the temple of God, of the city of the eternal King, of the bride of Christ.

No one is in any doubt that the bride of the Holy One is herself holy and worthy of all celebration and honor. And who can doubt the holiness of the house of God, of which it is said, *Holiness is fitting to your house*?* So his temple is holy, wonderful in symmetry;† but John bears witness that he also saw the holy city:

*Ps 92:5
†Ps 64:5-6

[1] *Sermo in dedicatione ecclesiæ* (Ded 5).

*I saw the holy city, the new Jerusalem, coming down from God out of heaven, adorned as a bride for her husband.*²*   *Rev 21:2
And in those words is the beginning of my disclosing what up to now I have wished to hide. What I mean is, that very bride, who is the city, is at the same time the temple and the house. And this is not to be wondered at, especially since he himself is one, he who deigns to show himself all at the same time to be King and God and also *Paterfamilias*.

2. You will not be satisfied, I think, until you have further learned who in the world it is who should merit to be called and to be the house of this *Paterfamilias*, the temple of God, the city of this King, and indeed the bride of this glorious Bridegroom. Yet I am not a little fearful to express my opinion about this, lest any of you, as heaven forbid, chance to hear it with insufficient humility or faith, and lest anyone should go away from this gathering either haughty because of the magnitude of glory or incredulous because of a timid spirit!* I hope   *Ps 54:9
that you will always be found both faithful and humble, both of which are absolutely necessary for salvation. For it is only to the humble that he gives grace,* and it is   *1 Pet 5:5
impossible to please him without faith.*   *Heb 11:6

I hope, then, and in all ways I desire that you hasten to show yourself to him as both small and great, or rather—that you may be all the more astounded—as both nothing and something or, again, as something great. For without magnanimity* you will not be   *magno animo
able to lay hold of those great goods or to perpetrate violence with regard to the Kingdom of heaven;*   *Matt 11:12
nor will you be able to enter that same Kingdom of heaven unless you are converted and become as little children.*   *Matt 18:3

---

²As in the Responsory "This is Jerusalem," for the Consecration of a Church.

I am not a man of deep experience,* so I cannot belch out to you what I have not had a taste of. Having said that, I will say what I sometimes experience being acted out in me so that if others should judge it useful for themselves they can imitate me. For I am convinced that if I should but once have mercy on my own soul it would please my God!* I frequently think about my soul; if only I might do so more extensively and always! For there was a time when it was acted upon, but just a little, or even less, of course because I loved it just a little or really hardly at all. For how can it be said that someone loves that whose death he loves? Because if—this is true and beyond dispute—wickedness is the death of the soul, then the truth in the saying *the one who loves iniquity hates his own soul** is proved absolutely. I used to hate my soul and would still if he who first loved my soul had not bestowed on me this, the beginnings of his love.*

*profundi sensus

*2 Kgs 1:14

*Ps 10:6

*1 John 4:10

3. By his goodness, sometimes when I think about my soul, I confess that it seems to me that I find two contrary things in it. If I consider it exactly as it is in and of itself and according to its truth,* I can perceive nothing to be more true about it than that it has been reduced to nothing.* What use is there in listing all the ways it is wretched, how it is burdened with sin, overspread with darkness, entangled in enticements, aroused by sexual desires, subject to passions, full of illusions, inclined always to evil,* leaning toward every vice, and, finally, full of every kind of disorder and disgrace? For if all our righteousness, seen in the light of truth, seems to be like the rag of a menstruating woman,* how will our unrighteousness be reckoned! If the light that is in us is darkness, how great is that darkness!*

*iuxta rei veritatem

*Ps 72:22

*Gen 8:21

*Isa 64:6

*Luke 11:35

It is easy for all of us, if we examine all our ways completely and without dissembling, and if we judge impartially, to bear witness to the apostolic truth in everything and freely proclaim: *The one who thinks he is something when he is nothing deceives himself.** *What is man that you magnify him*, says a faithful and devout witness, *or that you set your heart upon him?** What? Surely man* is made as an emptiness,† man is brought to nothing,# man is nothing. But how is one nothing whom God magnifies? How is one nothing upon whom God has set his heart?

*Gal 6:3

*Job 7:17
*homo
†Ps 143:4
#Ps 72:22

4. Let us breathe a bit, my brothers, and if we are nothing in our own hearts, perhaps in the heart of God something different about us lies hidden. Father of mercies,* Father of the miserable, why do you set your heart upon them? I know, I know! *Where your treasure is, there your heart is also.** How then can we be nothing if we are your treasure? All peoples are before you as though they did not exist* and are considered as nothing and empty. Before you, indeed, but not within you. That is how they are in the justice of your truth, but not in the affection of your tenderness.*

*2 Cor 1:3

*Matt 6:21

*Isa 40:17

*pietatis

For you summon the things that do not exist as if they did exist.* So they are not, because you summon the things that are not, but they are, because you summon them. Granted that they may not exist in themselves, yet with you by all means they do exist, according to the apostle, *not by works, but by the one calling.** For this is how without a doubt in your tenderness you will console those whom in your righteousness you humbled,* so that those who are deservedly restricted in their own hearts may be nobly unrestricted in yours.* For all your ways are mercy and truth to those who seek your covenant and your testimonies, the covenant of tenderness and the testimonies of truth.*

*Rom 4:17

*Rom 9:12

*Ps 118:75

*2 Cor 6:12-13

*Ps 24:10

5. Mortal, read in your heart, read within yourself the testimony of truth concerning yourself, and even in this ordinary light you will declare it undeserved. Read in the heart of God the covenant that has been

established in the blood of the Mediator,* and you will find how different it is to possess a thing in hope than to hold it in fact! *What is man*, it says, *that you magnify him?** Great†, certainly, but because of God, since it is by him that he is magnified. How are humans not great to him who has such great care for them? *His care is for us*, says the apostle Peter.* And the prophet says, *As for me, I am needy and poor, but the Lord is solicitous for me.** Clearly there is a clever connection between the two points of view,* so that at one and the same time a person both descends and ascends, seeing both himself as poor and needy and God as being solicitous for him.

This is angelic, to ascend and descend at the same time: *You will see*, he says, *angels ascending and descending upon the Son of Man.** They suffer no such hardship whether ascending or descending. By God's merciful foresight,* they are sent at one and the same time both to minister to those who shall be heirs of salvation* and to serve before the Face of Majesty. Why? So that we should have consolation and they no tribulation. Otherwise, how could they calmly let themselves be separated for our sakes, for even a little bit, from that face of glory on which they always desire to look?* Now hear Truth itself in the gospel: *Their angels*, he said—no doubt those of little children—*always see the face of the Father in heaven.** Thus those deputed as guardians of the little ones are deprived in no way of their beatitude.

Thus it was that Saint John saw the city of Jerusalem coming down,* and he could not see it standing still. And notice that he spoke of it coming down, not falling. What I mean is, at a certain time no small part of that city did fall, though it was the least sacred part,* and you can see how great a fall it was, because the city became an enemy of all holiness.*

*Heb 9:15-17

*Job 7:17
†*magnus*

*1 Pet 5:7

*Ps 39:18
utriusque considerationis

*John 1:51

*Heb 11:40
*Heb 1:14

*1 Pet 1:12

*Matt 18:10

*Rev 21:2

*Rev 11:13

*Acts 13:10

6. Now John could not see this catastrophe, this terrible fall, because it was not yet; but the Word, who was in the beginning,* saw it;† he saw the prince,# about whom he said to the apostles,‡ *I saw Satan as lightning falling from heaven.** And so that part that fell will be repaired by God when he restores the ruins and rebuilds the walls of Jerusalem,* but not from those parts that fell. This city that was seen coming down has already been prepared, as it says in what follows: *prepared by God.** Now if in fact the holy angels descend, not fall, it is because God so prepared it ahead of time, preparing for them, evidently, both the will and ability. So the apostle testifies that they have been sent not only as helpers but as messengers in ministry.*

*in principio
†John 1:1
#*principium*
‡John 8:25
*Luke 10:18
*Ps 109:6

*Rev 21:2

*Heb 1:14

For why should he not send angels to those to whom he himself had willed to be sent by the Father? Why should he not bend the heavens to those to whom he, the King of heaven, bent down, so that he should write on the earth with his finger?* *Lord, bend down your heavens**—that is a small thing—*and come down*! Is there more? That those to whom he bent down he should also make ascend with him! Also, as we have said, the ascent and descent of the angels was free from alteration.

*John 8:6
*Ps 143:5

As for us, though, we have to be turned now this way, now that way, for we are not allowed to stay above, nor is it in our interest to remain long below. *They rise up to the heaven and descend to the deeps: their soul melts away in trouble.** Why does it say that? Because surely in this interim period their soul melts away in mischief* more than it delights in good things;* the former things are present realities while those others they have only in hope. *Who then can be saved?** the disciples ask their Savior. And he says, *With people this is impossible, but not with God.** This is all our confidence, this is our only consolation, this is the whole ground of our hope.*

*Ps 106:26
*malis
*bonis

*Matt 19:25

*Mark 10:27
**ratio spei nostrae*

7. But now that we are certain of the possibility, what shall we do about the will? *Who knows whether he is worthy of love or of hatred?** *Who has known the mind of the Lord, or who has been his counselor?** Here we must be helped by faith, here piety must run to help us, so that what lies hidden in the Father's heart concerning us may be revealed to us by his Spirit, and his Spirit may bear witness and persuade our spirit that we are the children of God.* Persuade, that is, by calling, and justifying freely by grace;* without a doubt, here is the crossing-over point, as it were, from eternal predestination to the future glorification.*

*Eccl 9:1
*Rom 11:34

*Rom 8:16
*Rom 3:24

*magnificationem

Therefore, clearly, about these two points of view* we believe that the one can be said to be of judging and truth and the other, not unfittingly, of faith and tenderness.* And you will not be surprised that among human qualities such dissimilar ones are found if you but take into account the degree to which a diversity of natures seem to come together in the same substance. For what is more exalted than the life-giving spirit yet more humble than the slime of the earth?* This cohering in the human creature of things so mutually incoherent does not escape the notice of the wise of this age, who define the human as a reasonable animal.³ The linking together of reason and death* is remarkable indeed, as is the union of discretion and corruption. Indeed, in human customs, affections, and pursuits, the contrast is found to be not less but greater, so that if you look at all human depravity and then consider in detail everything that is found there to be good, you would think it wholly miraculous that such opposites should exist together.

*geminam illam considerationem

*pietatis

*Gen 2:7

*rationis et mortis

---

³ Saint Ambrose offers a similar definition concerning Noah 4:10 in *De Noe* 4.10 (CSEL 32:420), a passage read at the Second Nocturn on Sexagesima Sunday.

Thus a man comes to hear himself called now the son of Jonas, now Satan himself. Stop being surprised by this: just refresh your memory of the gospel and to whom it was said—both truthfully spoken, because both by the Truth—first, *Blessed are you, Simon, Son of Jonas,** and then a little later, *Get behind me, Satan!*† One man was both, even if both did not have the same origin. I mean, the one was from the Father, the other of human origin, yet the same man was both. Why Son of Jonas? Because it was not flesh and blood but the Father who revealed to him what he said.* Why Satan? Because he savored human things and not the things of God.*

*Matt 16:17; Bar-Jonas
†Mark 8:33

*Matt 16:17

*Mark 8:33

Now if we carefully examine ourselves to see what we are from each point of view—that in the one case we are nothing while in the other highly praised, since, as you see, so great a majesty had such care for us and set his heart upon us*—I think that our boasting will be a little tempered. But if it is instead increased and strengthened, it is because we glory not in ourselves but in the Lord,* we from whom this one thing only can be looked for, that we say, "If he has determined to save us, we shall be set free without delay."*

*Job 7:17

*1 Cor 1:31

*Esth 13:9

8. Now either by moving on from what we find in those imitations to something superior or else devoting a bit more attention to them, let us ask what is the house of God, let us ask what is the temple, let us ask what is the city, let us ask what is the bride. I have not forgotten,* but I say it with fear and reverence: "We are." "We are," I say, "but in the heart of God"; we are, but by his respect for us, not by our respectability. Let not human beings usurp what belongs to God so as not to presume to make themselves great.* Otherwise the God who makes us what we are will bring low those who exalt themselves.* And even if in our childish impetuosity we wanted to be saved cheaply,* we would rightly not be saved. Pretense shuts off mercy

**neque enim oblitus sum*

*Ps 9:39

*Matt 23:12
*gratis

from misery, just as there is no place for respect where respect is presumed.

On the other hand, the humble confession of disease calls forth compassion. Yes, it is this alone that makes God like the wealthy *paterfamilias* who nourishes in times of famine* and in whose care we have bread in abundance.* So we are his house, where there is never any lack of the nourishment of life. And remember that he designed his house to be a house of prayer;* this seems to agree with what the prophet says when he declares that we surely receive from him in our prayers the bread of tears to eat and, in our tears, drink.* In addition, according to the same prophet, as we said before, holiness is fitting to this house.* Clearly, then, when the purity of continence accompanies the tears of penitence, what is now his house becomes henceforth the temple of God. *Be holy*, he says, *as I your Lord God am holy.** And the apostle says, *Do you not know that your bodies are temples of the Holy Spirit, and the Holy Spirit dwells in you?** *If anyone defiles the temple of God, God will destroy that one!**

*Ps 32:19
*Luke 15:17

*Matt 21:13

*Ps 79:6
*Ps 92:5

*Lev 19:2

*1 Cor 6:15-19
*1 Cor 3:16-17

9. Nevertheless, holiness isn't enough, is it? Peace is necessary too, on the evidence of the apostle who said, *Pursue peace and holiness, without which no one will see the Lord.** This is what makes brothers of a single way of life* to live in unity,† building a new city for our King, the Peaceful one, called the true Jerusalem,# that is, vision of peace.[4] For where many people are gathered but with no bond of peace, no observance of the law, no discipline, and no one in charge, that's not a people but a mob; it's not a city but confusion.* It is Babylon and has nothing to do with Jerusalem.

*see Heb 12:14
*unius moris
†Pss 67:7; 132:1
#Rev 3:12;
1 Chr 22:9

*Gen 11:9

---

[4] See Jerome, *Int Heb nom, s.v. Ierusalem*, CCSL 72:121 (*Ierusalem uisio pacis*).

But how will it come about that so great a king will become a bridegroom and the city will come to be his bride?* It is possible only for that to which nothing is impossible: *Love is strong as death.** How is it that he does not lift her up easily, her who is already inclining toward him? Indeed from now on, that first way of looking at yourself that we mentioned is not at all your consideration. Here the greater the faith, the more generously it is put into practice.

*Rev 21:2
*Song 8:6

Finally he himself says, *I will betroth you to me in faith, I will betroth you in judgment and righteousness*—his, not yours, understand—*I will betroth you in loving-kindness and compassion.** If he did not do this as a bridegroom, if he did not love as a bridegroom, if he was not as jealous as a bridegroom, do not agree to be considered his bride!

*Hos 2:19-20

10. And so, my brothers, if through an abundant spread of food we are found to be the true house of the great *Paterfamilias*, if through sanctification the temple of God, if the city of the mighty King through the communion of a shared life, if the bride of the immortal bridegroom through delighted love,* I think that there is no reason for me to hesitate to proclaim us ourselves to be the solemnity. You will not be surprised that this celebration takes place on earth, since it also takes place in heaven. But if, as the Truth says—and it cannot not be true—there is joy in heaven over one sinner who repents,* even among the angels of God,* then there is no doubt that it is multiplied by the penitence of so many sinners! Do you still wish to hear more? *The joy of the Lord is our strength!** Let us therefore rejoice with the angels of God; let us rejoice together with God! And let this solemnity be celebrated with thankfulness, because the more it is a family affair, the more devoutly celebrated it should be.

*dilectionem

*Luke 15:7
*Luke 15:10

Neh 8:10

For the Dedication of a Church

Sermon Six

Concerning the word of Jacob: *Truly the Lord is in this place**

*Gen 28:16

*domus

1. The dedication of our house* is for us a family celebration. Even more of a family affair, though, is the dedication of us. Indeed it is our sprinkling, our blessing, our consecration, celebrated through the hands of holy bishops, that today's anniversary calls to mind with due praises. God isn't concerned about stones, is he?* It is human beings, not walls, who say, *His care is for us.** One such human was Jacob, who while he was asleep saw angels descending and ascending.* This is a small thing; he also bears witness that the Lord of angels was there, saying, *Truly the Lord is in this place, and I knew it not.**

*1 Cor 9:9
*1 Pet 5:7

*Gen 28:12

*Gen 28:16

*Gen 28:17

*Matt 18:20

*1 Cor 2:12

One marvels at the grace and is awestruck at the greatness of glory. *How frightful is this place,** how evident and certain that the Lord is in this place, where not only two or three* but a great multitude is gathered together and perseveres in his name! Let no one be unaware; let none of you be ignorant. For *we have not received the spirit of this world but the Spirit that is from God, that we may know what God has given us.** That place is indeed frightful and worthy of all rev-

---

[1] *Sermo in dedicatione ecclesiæ* (Ded 6).

erence that people of faith inhabit, where holy angels congregate, and that the Lord himself honors with his presence.

2. How could so great a patriarch have been unaware that there is no place where God is not? But perhaps he was marveling at something else when he said, *Truly the Lord is in this place*. It is there that he truly is and is truly the Lord, where in his name angels and humans gather together. Although he is in every place, he to whom no place is closed (yet we expressly say, *Our father, who art in heaven*),* he may show himself as present there in some other way that is particularly his own—though not because he himself is different, but because each one distinguishes different things. *Matt 6:9

He is, therefore, in every place, embracing all things and disposing all things* but in far different ways. To the wicked he is present but hiding,* to the elect he is both acting and watching;† he both feeds and rests beside# those above, and those below he accuses and condemns. He makes his sun to rise even over the wicked,* but where dissimulation exists among the wicked, the truth is not present. So, if one can say so, with the wicked he is in hiding,* with the righteous in truth, with the angels in felicity, and with those below he is in his ferocity.*
*Wis 8:1
*see Wis 11:24; *dissmulans*
†*operans et servans*
#Song 1:6
*Matt 5:45

*dissimulatione

*feritate sua

Does it sound hard to you that I speak about ferocity? Indeed I respect both his wrath and his rage. *Lord, reprove me not in your rage,** and, *Truly*, it says, *the Lord is in this place*. For where he makes it rain on the just and on the unjust,* he is our father and the father of mercies,* hoping for people to repent. When he condemns the stiff-necked, he is judge, and *It is dreadful to fall into the hands of the living God.** Where he takes his rest, he is spouse,* and happy is the soul whom he takes into his chamber.*
*Ps 6:2

*Matt 5:45
*2 Cor 1:3

*Heb 10:31
*Song 1:6
*see Song 1:3

3. Still, *truly the Lord is in this place* if we serve him *in spirit and in truth.** For the Lord was not truly with *John 4:24

those to whom he said, *Why do you call me Lord, Lord, and do not do what I say?*[*Luke 6:46] The sacred writings give testimony that Adam was first set in Paradise to tend and guard.[*Gen 2:15] Likewise the second Adam,[†1 Cor 15:47] in the assembly[#ecclesia] of the saints,[‡Ps 88:6] in the congregation of his own, *in the garden of delights*[*Gen 2:8, according to an ancient version]—indeed his delight is to be with the sons of men[†Prov 8:31]—he himself, I say, *is Lord in this place*, to tend and guard.

In any case, just as *unless the Lord builds the house, they labor in vain who build it*, so also *unless it is he who guards the city, the ones guarding it keep watch in vain*.[*Ps 126:1] Further, the vision of the patriarch itself shows that angels were ascending and descending in that place,[*Gen 28:12] ascending to see the face of the Father,[*Matt 18:10] descending to care for us.

What, then? In what way ought we to be here, in such great reverence standing in the very place where God is, working and serving, and where the angels are, ascending and descending? Clearly, it behooves us to be penitent and expectant. That is, to forget what lies behind[*Phil 3:13]—to ignore, reject, and reflect upon those years in the bitterness of our souls[*Isa 38:15]—and then, with equal intention and passion, to stretch ourselves out toward to what lies ahead.[*Phil 3:13] We have come to this place; here we stand fast. These things are demanded of us:[*see 1 Pet 2:8] penitence for past sins and expectation of future rewards.

On the Feast of Saint Martin, Bishop[1]

Of Examples of Obedience

1. Your assembly demands of me a sermon, as does the arrival of these august personages who have come from afar and whom we are pleased to greet. Truly it is I who would gladly listen to them, but since they choose, or rather demand, that I speak, they must be obeyed. And really, their word is as living to us* as their gentleness is great; clearly they are more august in merit, more superior in dignity, more richly endowed with wisdom, so that they might rightly refuse not only to visit us but also to listen to us! Their learning is effective* and their teaching worthy of all acceptance!* Accordingly, not in word and tongue but in deed and truth* they urge us to be their imitators as they are the imitators of Christ* and to learn what they themselves learned from him: to be gentle and humble of heart.*

So Mary reached out to Elizabeth, the virgin to the married woman, the mistress to her handmaid, the mother of the Judge to the mother of the Forerunner, the mother of God to the mother of the servant.* So later on Jesus went to John to be baptized, that he might fulfill all righteousness.* In the same way, reverend fathers, you do not demean yourselves by being swifter to listen than to speak,* even in the company

*Heb 4:12

*Heb 4:12
*1 Tim 1:15
*1 John 3:18

*1 Cor 4:16
*Matt 11:29

*Luke 1:39-56

*Matt 3:13-17

*Jas 1:19

---

[1] *Sermo in festivitate sancti Martini episcopi* (Mart). Saint Martin, Bishop of Tours, 316–97; his feast day is Nov. 11.

of those who have great need of your example. And we, because we cannot fulfill all righteousness,* take care to show you a little, knowing that it is right for one who is lower to obey his superiors.

2. But from where shall we speak? *The one who is from the earth speaks about the earth,** says the voice of one crying out.* Let us then speak from the earth, because we have our being from the earth and with regard to the earth. *Hear, you dwellers upon earth and you sons of humans:** it is to you we speak, and about you. We are born on earth, we live on earth, we die on earth, returning to the place from which we arose!* Here the entrance is narrow, the pause short, and only death is certain! Adam is forced to bear the judgment that he deserved.* He increased vigorously, he multiplied, and he filled the earth.* Yet whether he wishes it or not, however he may kick against it,* he still always bears the judgment he received: *Earth you are*, it says, *and into earth you will go!**

It is a heavy sentence, but not without some measure of great mercy. It is very hard, but if you consider what is deserved, full of leniency. For otherwise the sinner might be told, with as much justice, "You were earth, but from it you will go under the earth!" It would be just, and the Lord too would be just and greatly to be praised.* It is fitting that he be praised, but I am not qualified to praise him. That being the case, still the fact is that I should be speaking truly if I said, *You are just, O Lord, and your judgments are right.** *The depths cannot confess you and death cannot praise you,** but *we who live, we bless the Lord!**

Therefore you have spared your creature, you have spared the glory of your name* in that you did not suffer the man coming down from Jerusalem to be carried off even in the smallest way to Jericho.* Until now abandoned half alive on the road, I can halfway praise; there where I will come alive again, all of me

*Matt 3:15

*John 3:31
*Matt 3:3

*Ps 48:2-3

*Gen 3:19

*Deut 32:15
*Gen 1:28
*Deut 32:15

*Gen 3:19, according to an ancient version

*Ps 47:2

*Ps 118:137
*Isa 38:18
*Ps 113:26

*Ezek 36:21

*Luke 10:30

will live in praise, and *all my bones shall say: Lord, who is like you?** Therefore when you were angry you remembered your mercy,* not condemning a mortal in the place of perdition but humbling him in the place of affliction.* Why do you defend yourself, man? Why do you risk a harsher sentence? You are a slave of earth, you are made of earth,* so that earth itself is your native land, it is your matter.

3. But, you say, I would rather hear it said, "because you are spirit and to spirit you will go." Surely I am spirit, inasmuch as my soul is concerned; nor would I doubt that this is the stronger part of me. For I have heard from the apostle that *the Lord is spirit** and from the Lord himself that *God is a spirit.** Not only spirit, but the father of spirits.* Why, then, if my mother according to the flesh preserves me, since I am partly flesh, would not the Father of spirits receive me, since I am partly spirit? I know, I know: it is a matter not so much of the substance itself as of the fault. For as those who sin according to the spirit inhabit the windy middle ground between heaven and earth, from which they are called powers of the air,* so *our iniquities come between us and God,** between the Creator, the Father of Spirits,† and the spiritual creature. For the body draws the soul into its own country, and, see, by overpowering it oppresses the pilgrim soul. For the body has become a leaden weight,* but only because iniquity sits upon it. *For the body weighs down the soul,** but certainly *because it is corrupt*—corrupt, or rather, according to the apostle, *it is dead on account of sin.**

So granted that a person is in some sense heavenly—being without doubt like the heavenly spirits, both in substance and in form, since spiritual in substance and rational in form—these two are still not enough to raise him and make him worthy to hear, "you are heavenly, and to heaven you shall go." It's no use boasting of free will,* which is in the mind;† the

*Ps 34:10
*Hab 3:2

*Ps 43:20

*Gen 2:7

*2 Cor 3:17
*John 4:24
*Heb 12:9

*Eph 2:2
*Isa 59:2, according to an ancient version
†Heb 12:9

*Zech 5:7-8
*Wis 9:15

*Rom 8:10

**libertate arbitrii*
† *mente*

person is led captive into the law of sin, which is of the flesh.* For example: say one twofold cord could be shown to prevail over another that is equally twofold; even so, those whom the earth rightfully claims for itself under a twofold law, being both their native land and their matter—nevertheless, because of the twofold likeness of form and substance mentioned before, they may likewise receive heaven so as to become heavenly. Only now it becomes triple when sin is added to that lower cord that pulls them downward, and unless grace opposes it, it will not be broken.* But when grace arrives, doubtless it is easily broken, that heavy bond of iniquity by which we are dragged, or rather that we drag. This grace comes between us and God—not separating us, though, but renewing and joining.

*Rom 7:23

*Eccl 4:12

4. And so I will betake myself to the mountain of grace and the hills of mercy, whose treasures, I hear, are all stored up in the keeping of Christ.* I will go to him who is full of grace and truth,* in the chance that I may receive of that fullness* or, rather, in the chance that I may be received into that fullness, so that with the other parts of the body I may finally come *to the measure of the age of the fullness of Christ.* *No one ascends into heaven but the one who came down from heaven.** He is a faithful and bounteous mediator who has not caused division but *has made both one, breaking down the middle wall of partition between us,** forgiving us all our sins, blotting out the written decree that was against us, that was hostile to us, and he has taken it out of the way, fixing it to the cross; despoiling principalities and powers, he has made a show of them openly, triumphing over them,* and *making peace through his blood of those who are on earth and those who are above the earth.** Therefore on account of this salvation, which he will work in the midst of the earth,* he has been quick not to set human creatures under the earth, as they deserved for their sins, but on the earth.

*Col 2:3
*John 1:14
*John 1:16

*Eph 4:13
*John 3:13

*Eph 2:14

*Col 2:13-15

*Col 1:20
*Ps 73:12

Since then while still in the interim established upon earth we have breathing room and nothing to despair over, we can look to heaven and look to the good and perfect gifts from above, from the Father of lights,* from the Father of spirits,† from the Father of mercies.# For this reason he made the human being upright,‡ yes, the body itself, and he put humans' mouth in the highest position, so that while the rest of living things, being prone, look at the earth, humans, having raised their face to the stars, may sigh for that place, higher still, where their blessed and eternal dwelling-place is.

*Jas 1:17
†Heb 12:9
#2 Cor 1:3
‡Ezek 7:30

5. The vision of that most luminous country is certainly a most vehement incentive to love and a stimulus of most burning desire for us who stare with faith and devotion, is it not? The stars of the sky are not like the clods of dirt! Between the sun's splendor and the murkiness on the ground there is no little distance! There are any number of things here that look beautiful seen with other things like them, but they are unfailingly mixed up with things that are not beautiful, like gold in mud, a jewel in dung,* a lily among thorns.* *You are altogether lovely,*† *my homeland, and there is no spot in you:* you are altogether lovely—*apart from what lies hidden within.** What is that? Surely those angelic spirits, and the souls of the saints who have been worthy to enter *the place of the marvelous tabernacle, up to the house of God.** For there are terrestrial bodies, and likewise celestial bodies, but different by far is the celestial glory from the terrestrial;* likewise there are celestial and terrestrial spirits, and there is no little distance between them. Angels, Archangels, Virtues, Principalities, Powers, Dominations, Thrones, Cherubim, and Seraphim: well have I learned their names, but that seems to be the extent of it. For what shall I, a dweller on earth, comprehend of the heavenly, I, a man of flesh, of the spiritual and divine?

*Ezek 7:19
*Song 2:2
†Song 4:7
*Song 4:1

*Ps 41:5

*1 Cor 15:40

Yet even if I do not know what lies hidden in all those titles, this I have learned for sure: that something great and wonderful lies hidden and sealed under the majesty of all these words. Not without reason is it called heaven:* of the extraordinary thing hidden† in it I am obviously ignorant. It is hidden, I say, yet in no way is it denied to faith. I mean, as it is given to us on earth to see the exterior beauty of heaven but not to reach it, likewise, regarding the glory of its inward secrets, although it is not granted us to grasp it, it is granted to hear about it. We see the fatherland, but we greet it from afar;* we get a whiff of those joys but do not taste them.

*caelum
†celatur

*Heb 11:13-14

6. Yet while we dwell in this region of the shadow of death,* it is not without reason that the Only-begotten himself, who is in the bosom of the Father,* both explains to us through faith about the glory of the heavenly spirits and reveals it to us through the visual beauty of bodies.

*Isa 9:2
*John 1:18

*Ps 44:11

*Heb 5:8
†Ps 2:12

*Phil 3:3
*Ps 25:8

*2 Cor 3:18
†Ps 44:12

*Ps 44:11
†obaudire

Hear, O daughter, he says, *and see!* * It is true. Where? *Incline your ear*, he says, *and forget your people and your father's house*. He wishes us to lay aside stubbornness, to learn obedience,* and to embrace discipline.† He wishes us to forget the things that are behind, despise the things that are below, give up earthly behaviors and innate vices, taste heavenly things, strive for the things that are above, and long for the things that are to come.* He wishes his noble creature to desire the great beauty of his house,* in which the creature *might be transformed in his image from glory to glory, even by the spirit of the Lord;** and likewise the king may desire† his glory, surely a spiritual one. But where, you will say, is he either seen or heard bidding me to incline my ear* and listen?† At least it is clear what desire it gives rise to.

7. Consider closely, then, the heavenly bodies in all their glory; how they continually obey the divine

laws, so that in uninterrupted motion they never go out of the set cycles of the seasons, nor do they go beyond the fixed limits of space. But those sublime spirits themselves, understand, are all performing acts of service and are sent to fulfill a most worthy ministry* (or should I say unworthy?). I think that you will not find anywhere in the Scriptures that any of them contradict the one who sent them or were ever in the slightest way stirred against their inferiors, those to whom they were sent to serve. They are models of obedience, and, consequently, if you pay close attention, they are all the more acceptable as they are of a more worthy substance.

*Heb 1:14

But human sensibility and reason, I know, always inclining to evil,* are murmuring about this under the breath: "Why do you propose to me the obedience of heaven's elemental beings," you say, "as though there were any sensibility in them, or as if any reasonable deliberation flourished in them and they did not so much seem to act as to be urged? Why do you thus commend the obedience of the very angels? The angels perceive, but only pleasant things; they obey the Creator, but with a will as happy as it is spontaneous. Why are they obedient? *They always look upon the face of the Father*,* to see whom is perfect beatitude, eternal glory, and the highest pleasure.

*Gen 8:21

*Matt 18:10

8. Set before us, O Lord, the patriarchs and prophets, men obedient to your precepts, obedient in conformity with your will, obedient contrary to their own will. So it was done. Here is presented to us—for the sake of brevity I'll omit the others—Abraham, leaving his own land at the Lord's command,* turning away his handmaid and her son,* even prepared to sacrifice his son Isaac.† What can human cleverness mock here? Perhaps one may reply that because God appeared to them in many different ways,* so he was received in hospitality; he joined in meals, encouraged in conversation, instructed

*Gen 12:1-4
*Gen 21:10-14
†Gen 22:1-10

*Heb 1:1

with advice,* gave sons, imparted glory through victories,* and gave riches.† What shall you say, seeing that Christ *was made obedient* to the Father *even unto death, even the death of the cross?**

Much, as it is said, *in every way!** For when shall I presume to emulate the only-begotten Son of God, *Christ the power of God and the wisdom of God?** *He offered himself because he wished it*;* he suffered at the time and to the extent of his own choosing, true man as he was, but no less true God. I don't even want you to bring forward the obedience of the apostles, those to whom, yes, according to the prophetic promise, it was granted to see the Teacher with their own eyes* and with their own ears to hear him teaching. One of them in his writing said quite clearly, *what we saw and heard, and what we looked upon with our eyes and touched with our hands: the word of life.** Why shouldn't they have left everything?* Why shouldn't they have followed in every way such a majestic presence? What would I not have done if an opportunity like that had been presented to *me*! But *he has not dealt so with all the nations*,* either before or since. Indeed, just as many kings have desired to see and have not seen,* so the days have already come when we desired to see one day of the Son of Man,* yet I was not worthy.

9. So it is advantageous that Martin takes center stage, so that from the one in the center* there may be an opportunity for sinners. For today he is seen like us in all things,* endowed with feeling and subject to suffering. He lived long after the times of the visions of patriarchs and prophets. He was pure human being, having nothing of the divine nature but believing in one whom he had not seen, full of the fruit of obedience, and rich in virtues. He forsook earth and strove after heaven, entrusting to earth what he had from earth and directing his spirit to the Father of spirits,* whom he served faithfully in the spirit of adoption.*

He was not a heavenly body; nor was he a heavenly spirit. He was a rational animal, a mortal, an earth-dweller, a son of man.* He was born on earth, brought up on earth, on earth trained and tested, on earth, too, accomplished. He was not a patriarch or one of the prophets,* of whom Truth in the gospel said *the law and the prophets were until John.** He was not by any means Christ, though without a doubt Christ was in him by faith and faith alone.

*Ps 48:3

*Matt 16:14
*Luke 16:16

10. And now in the same way *the word is near you, in your heart and in your ear,** if only you seek him with an upright heart. Indeed this is the apostle's interpretation of what Moses said: this is the *word of faith.** And the same apostle says in another place, *Jesus Christ is the same yesterday, today, and forever.** *Yesterday* refers to the time from the beginning to the Ascension of the Lord,* *today* from now to the end of the world,† and again *tomorrow* is eternity, after the common resurrection. Christ is not absent from any of these; from none is Jesus absent, from none is anointing absent, from none salvation. He was shown to the patriarchs and prophets in visions, to the apostles in humanity, to Martin by faith, to angels as beauty. He promised that he would reveal himself as this same beauty to the elect—not today, of course, but in eternity. Indeed, yesterday has passed on, and this, our today, has dawned, as the apostle said: *although we have known Christ after the flesh, we do so no longer.** For in this morning it seems that some of the flesh of the Lamb has been reserved,* but let what is left be given to the fire; that is, up until today that same flesh is intended for us, but in a spiritual, not a carnal, way.

*Rom 10:8

*Deut 30:14

*Heb 13:8

*Matt 24:21
†Matt 28:20

*2 Cor 5:16

*Exod 12:10

11. And there is no reason for us to object that our era has been deprived either of the apparitions granted to the ancestors of the Old Testament or of the bodily presence that was displayed to the apostles. Indeed for those who contemplate in faith, neither case will hold

true. For right now, today, without any doubt whatsoever, the true substance of his flesh is present to us in the sacrament. There really are revelations, but as they pertain to the spirit and to power,* so that in the time of grace, which is now, no grace should be found lacking to any.* Finally, *eye has not seen, nor ear heard, nor has it entered into the heart of men the things that God has prepared for those who love him; but to us he has revealed by his spirit.** Don't marvel at the fact that carnal things are shown to them who are ready for the coming of his flesh. For to us it is necessary that grace be so much the more efficacious and revelation so much the more worthy, because what we await is so much the more excellent!

*Luke 1:17

*1 Cor 1:7

*1 Cor 2:9-10

12. So, as we said before, Martin was not that Christ, yet he possessed Christ, not as the angels do in the presence of his glory, nor as the apostles do in the vision of his humanity, nor as he once spoke to his saints in visions,* but in the way in which the church now possesses him, in faith and sacraments. It was said of John, *He himself was not the light,** but *a lamp* clearly *burning and shining,** but I think that if I bring him into the discussion, you will say, "He was the greatest of men, more than a prophet.* In fact, he was the angel of God the Father, as he himself attests, *Behold, I send my angel,*" * and so forth.

*Ps 88:20

*John 1:8
*John 5:35

*Matt 11:9-11

*Mal 3:1

Martin, too, was *a burning and shining light*, and it does not offend him in the least to be imitated, but imitated in the things that can be imitated, not in what is manifestly extraordinary. Today you are seated at the rich man's table;* *consider carefully what is put before you.** Distinguish between food and the vessels that hold food. You are bidden to take the former, but not the latter. Martin is the rich man, rich in merit, rich in miracles, rich in virtues, rich in signs. *Consider carefully*, then, *what is put before you*, what is for admiration and what for imitation, or, as this text of Scripture goes on

*Luke 16:21
*Prov 23:1, according to an ancient version

to say, *because it behooves you to prepare yourself for such things, consider carefully.**   *Prov 23:2, from an ancient version

Martin raised three dead people to life, the same number he had read that the Savior raised.² He restored sight to the blind, hearing to the deaf, speech to the mute, walking to the lame, and health to the withered. He escaped from danger by divine power, he repulsed flames hurled at his body, he laid low the immense structure of a sacrilegious siege engine coming down from the sky like a column; he cleansed a leper with a kiss, cured a paralytic with oil, conquered demons, saw angels, and foresaw the future.*   *Luke 7:14-15; Matt 18:25; John 11:43-44

13. Truly, these and the other most noble mighty deeds like them that he performed†—why should I not call them the marvelous vessels of this rich man, heavy with gold, flashing with gems, equally precious in material and workmanship? Do not expect to find flavor in these things, but marvel at their splendor. Let us let our lamp shine* in this way so that in his light you may see that light* that, being pure in itself, you cannot look upon. For he is not that light, but he came to bear witness to that light,* and God appears to you glorious in his saint,³* as long as you cannot attain to his glory as it is in itself.   †Ps 70:19   *John 5:35   *Ps 35:10   *John 1:8   *Ps 67:36

Nevertheless, you should not imagine that Martin's lamps while trimmed are found to be empty! He is not a foolish virgin; he has oil in his vessels.* He has wine in his jars;* he has plenty of food in those serving bowls, spiritual dainties that poor men may not only see and wonder at but eat and be satisfied, and in these things they may praise the Lord,* and in them   *Matt 25:7-8   *Amos 6:6   *Ps 21:27

---

² Sulpicius Severus, *Vita Sancti Martini, Episcopi et Confessoris* in *Opera*, ed. C. Halm, CSEL 1:108–37 (Salzburg, 1866), 117–34, chaps. 7–24 (hereafter V Mart); "Dialogus Secundus (Tertius)," in *Opera*, ed. C. Halm, CSEL 1:180–216 (Salzburg, 1866), 198, 216.

³ See the gradual *Gloriosus* in the common for several martyrs.

their hearts may live. Otherwise, how should the dead praise you, O Lord?*

That the praise of admiration be pleasant and fitting,* let them also live in imitation, so that they may partake of his delicacies more eagerly and may contemplate his riches more diligently. In this way, as we run about in the brilliance and ardor of this lamp with certain mutually penetrating affections, the one will make us appreciate the other all the more, and the intermingling of both will augment their charm. So this Martin was humble and poor in spirit,* showing the effects of divine grace, which God would not have given in such measure except to one of such humility.

14. Let me give you a few examples of his virtue. The blessed Hilarion knew Martin to be poor in spirit when, trying to lay on him the office of deacon and not succeeding because of protests of unworthiness, he ordered Martin to become an exorcist, which in that place was seen as an insult, for Hilarion knew that Martin would not refuse the humbler order.* He was a poor man, with dirty clothes, disheveled hair, and contemptible appearance, and, although at his election certain malevolent persons threw these things in his teeth, he made no changes in them at all, so it is written.* In short, because Martin was truly poor in spirit he deserved to be called poor and simple.

But mark his gentleness, as his friend Sulpicius writes about it.* He showed so much patience in the face of all injuries that when while he was bishop† he was injured with impunity by the lowest clergy, he did not for that reason at any time remove them from office or banish anyone from his affection if he could avoid it. I think you all remember how he openly showed this in the case of Briccius. For he chose him out of everyone as his successor, warned him of the great adversity to come, and then *for his fidelity and meekness he consecrated him,** even though Martin had

*Ps 113:25

*Ps 146:1

*Matt 5:3

*V Mart 5 (CSEL 1:115–16)

*V Mart 10 (CSEL 1:119–20)

*V Mart 26 (CSEL 1:136)
†*esset summus sacerdos*

*Sir 45:4

heard him answering someone who had asked him about Martin, "If you are looking for that mad fellow, look over there; see, he is in the habit of looking at the sky like that as though he were out of his mind!"

Indeed, the man of God, given that he looked down at the earth, was always looking up to heaven! For he knew that this was the reason that he was made upright of body, as I said before.* He knew that his treasure was there,† he knew that his Christ sat there at the right hand of God,# he knew that he would never attain to what he desired until he reached that place. As for on earth being called mad, he took no notice, for his conversation* was in heaven,† and his eyes were in his head.# Of course tears were on his cheeks;‡ they were always welling up. Many were those who openly criticized him, however, just as he always abounded in tears, weeping for their sins.*

*see Mart 4 above
†Matt 6:21
#Mark 16:19

*conversatio
†Phil 3:20
#Eccl 2:14
‡Lam 1:2

*V Mart 27
(CSEL 1:137)

15. But the extent to which he hungered for righteousness* is shown in other deeds of his, particularly in the searching out of idolatry, the destruction of temples, the pulling down of statues, and the cutting down of sacred groves. He was never afraid to put himself at risk, so that the occasion of so great an offense should be destroyed at the root.* And the Savior himself boasted among the angels about Martin's showing himself merciful to a poor man, displaying the half-garment that Martin had given to him.*

*Matt 5:6

*V Mart 11–13
(CSEL 1:121–23)

*V Mart 3
(CSEL 1:113)

If only before the most high Judge into whose marvelous dwelling he has entered* he would think to show us, pitiable as we are, the same mercy with which he rescued those condemned to death and destined to all kinds of torments, of whom it is written that he lay at midnight before the door of an earthly judge! How will he not hear him now, he whom he allowed to be heard then? Further, this most especially demonstrates his purity of heart,* that he is not defeated when he speaks with his enemy in the gate:*

*Ps 41:5

*Matt 5:8
*Ps 126:5

"O calamitous one, you will find nothing in me! The bosom of Abraham has received me."⁴ For when he had happily completed his peacemaking labors*—permitted to know the end of his days—he met formerly dissenting priests among whom peace had been made—he himself fell asleep in peace.

*Matt 5:9

16. For the rest, it would take too long to recount the persecutions he suffered for righteousness' sake*—how he was fearless in the presence of Julius Augustus in the city of the Vangiones or, rather, how he stood firm when terrorized at having been handed over to prison, defenselessly to face the opposition of barbarians on the next day;* how in the Alps he was completely at ease under the ax that a robber brandished over his head;* how at Milan Auxentius the Arian made a furious attack on him and, after inflicting many injuries upon him, ended by driving him out of the city; how elsewhere, fighting fiercely against the priests' treachery, he was first afflicted with tortures and beaten publicly with rods, then finally driven out of the place; how at the destruction of some temple a godless person attacked him with a sword, and he offered his neck to the smiter, and his attacker, when he raised his right arm for the blow, fell down flat; how when another man wished to strike him with a knife, it fell from his hands and suddenly disappeared.⁵ There is no doubt that he received many crowns for these things; even if he was never a martyr by the effect of perfect suffering, yet he was a martyr by the affection of a most zealous will.

*Matt 5:10

*V Mart 4 (CSEL 1:114)

*V Mart 5 (CSEL 1:115)

*Song 5:1
*Isa 38:16

*Eat, friends, drink, and be intoxicated, most beloved!** In such things as these the life of* your *spirit is made alive.** It

---

⁴ Sulpicius Severus, "Epistula 3," in *Opera*, ed. C. Halm, CSEL 1:146–51 (Salzburg, 1866), 149.

⁵ Sulpicius Severus, "Epistula 3," in *Opera*, ed. C. Halm, CSEL 1:146–51 (Salzburg, 1866), 148.

isn't those who raise the dead, give sight to the blind, heal the sick, cleanse lepers, cure paralytics, win mastery over demons, foretell the future, and shine with their miracles whom the divine Word calls blessed, is it? Isn't it rather the poor in spirit, the meek, those who mourn and who hunger and thirst after righteousness, the merciful, the pure in heart, the peacemakers, and those who suffer persecution for righteousness' sake?* *Matt 5:3-12

17. Pardon me, brothers: I have somewhat neglected Martin's example of obedience, the only thing in the plan of this discourse that it is fitting for us to make known. Yes, we are prolonging things, but, as I see it, *it is good for us to be here*!* In any case, trust me; we *Matt 17:4 are gradually getting to Martin today! "Lord," he said, "if I am needed by your people, I do not refuse the toil. Your will be done!"* O truly holy soul! O measureless charity! O obedience without equal! You have fought the good fight, you have kept the faith; there remains for you a crown of righteousness, with which the just Judge shall repay you this day,* and you still *2 Tim 4:7-8 say, "I do not refuse the toil; your will be done!" You have offered Isaac;* you have slit the throat of him *Gen 22:11 you loved, as far as you could; you have sacrificed your only joy with pious devotion and are ready to return again to danger, to fight the battles again, to undergo the toil afresh, to undertake the tribulation, to prolong the temptation, and then to be kept longer from that felicity and long-desired company of the blessed spirits, to be recalled from the very portal of glory to the troubles of this mortal life, finally, and above all, to continue still longer alienated from your Christ if he desire it.* *2 Cor 5:6*

There is no doubt either that one who shows himself ready to obey an order even before it is given merits more grace than the one who is ready to obey an order after it is given. O holy angels, your obedience is great, but if you will allow me to say so, I do not know if there could ever be found among you one ready to be sent on a mission* on which it was necessary not to see the Father's face.* It is a great thing, Peter, that you left all to follow the Lord;* but I heard you saying on the mountain when he was transfigured before you, *Lord, it is good for us to be here; let us build three tabernacles.** That is far from "If I am still needed by your people, I do not refuse the toil." Your heart is ready, O Martin, your heart is ready,* either to remain in the body, or to die and be with Christ!*

*Heb 1:14
*Matt 18:10
*Matt 19:27

*Matt 17:4

*Ps 56:8
*Phil 1:23-24

18. Great indeed is the security in the face of a death not dreadful; great is the perfection to be found in the vision of Christ desired so fervently and single-mindedly. But this is far greater in every way: you who are not afraid to die—no, more, you who with such great desire long for the presence of the Lord, do not refuse to live and even be worn out by the most tiresome suspense. I mean, could he not have obeyed in some other way, he who with such devotion cried out at that moment, "Your will be done"?

May it be our part, brothers, in today's feast diligently to consider the obedience served up to us at the table of the poor, or rather of this rich man,* knowing that it is this very thing that is demanded of us, the very thing that we must make ready, so that each of us may say, *I am ready, and I am not troubled, so that I may keep your word.** Not only once or in part, but *God, my heart is ready, my heart is ready,** ready for whatever and not setting conditions on any purpose of yours. Perhaps I desire this one thing particularly, even greatly, but I do not refuse the other: *let your will be done as it is in heaven!** I desire rest, but I do not shun toil: your will be done!

*Prov 23:1-2

*Ps 118:60
*Ps 56:8

*1 Macc 3:60;
Matt 6:10

ON THE FEAST OF SAINT CLEMENT[1]

Of the Three Waters

1. *P**recious in the sight of the Lord is the death of his saints.** *Let the wicked hear it and be angry, gnash his teeth, and fade away!** *He is taken in his own craftiness,** *he has fallen into the pit that he dug,** been caught in the snare he laid. *Through the devil's envy death came into the world,** but consider how *precious is the death of his saints!* Hear then, enemy of life; listen, author of death. Over whom does your fraud have power, whom does your cunning hurt? On the contrary, in order to add to your woe, these things work together *for good for those who, called according to his purpose, are holy.** This means nothing other than this: today the blessed martyr whose solemnity we celebrate triumphed over the death of the body, which is your work.

*Ps 115:6
*Ps 111:10
*Job 5:13
*Ps 7:16
*Wis 2:24

*Rom 8:28

Thus he made a virtue of necessity, exchanged the penalty of sin for the reward of glory,* and proved himself faithful in a little thing so that he might be found worthy to be set over a great matter.* For it was a little thing, utterly little, whatever it was that blessed soul had gained, in comparison with the glory that he merited from the present passion. For all pleasure

*Luke 19:17
Matt 25:21

---

[1] *Sermo in natali sancti Clementis* (Clem). Pope Clement I, d. 99; his feast is celebrated on November 23. See *Bibliotheca hagiographica latina antiquae et mediae aetatis*, ed. Société des Bollandistes (Brussels, 1898–1957), 278–79.

of this world, all its glory, whatever is desirable in it* is small in comparison with that felicity, that glory, and that blessedness—if it can be called small, and not rather nothing, *a vapor that appears for a moment.**

Blessed Clement was of high birth, a man of many possessions, a great inheritance, and considerable learning, so much so that he was considered the foremost philosopher of his time.² All these things he had received from the Lord. For they are the gifts of God.* He showed himself faithful to the one who had given him these things when he spurned them all for love of God, counting all things but loss and thinking of them as dung, that he might win Christ.*

2. But perhaps the enemy is complaining, saying, *Skin for skin! All that a man has he will give in exchange for his soul!** What then? Do you suppose that he will be found faithless in the very life of his body, a life he has received from the Lord, so that he prefers it to the Lord? See, you have the power: attack him by means of your accomplices* so that he is hard pressed from both sides and compelled to choose to be separated either from the Lord or from the body. Come up with a variety of brutal torments, but know that you are making crowns for our martyr! For just as he scorned the adornments and trappings of this life, so he scorned life itself! His whole body he exposes to you in death, and he curses you to your face;* he even blasphemes your idols with his holy mouth. He proclaims the Lord his God freely even in the midst of your torments and frankly acknowledges him. Therefore he will be crowned,* because he fought according to the rules; he conquered faithfully and could not be separated from the love of Christ* either by the temptations of this life or by the fear of death.

*1 John 2:16
*Jas 4:15
*Eph 2:8
*Phil 3:8
*Job 2:4
*Phil 1:23
*Job 1:11
*2 Tim 2:5
*Rom 8:39

---

² "Legenda S. Clementis," in *Bibliotheca Casinensis* 4, Florilegium (Monte Cassino, 1880), 374–78.

Tell us, I beg you, holy soul, who thus exposed your body to punishments, I implore you—did you love it, or not? "Surely I loved it," he said, *for no one ever hated his own flesh.** So I loved it, but I loved it very little, like a servant-girl, and I loved the Lord God much more. As a proof of this love and an example of the toil,* I willingly embraced the very death of the body for his glory.

3. What are we to say to this, brothers? We rejoice with the martyr, but his glory does not exist apart from our shame! I mean, look, Clement was *a man like us, subject to suffering,** compassed by the same infirmity and bound to his flesh by the same bond of natural affection.* If then he thus glorified Christ in his body† and received the cup of salvation,# what shall we give back to the Lord for all he has given to us?‡ He has marked us with the same sign, he has redeemed us with the same blood* and called us to the same inheritance, incorruptible, undefiled, eternal, reserved in the heavens.* Why can we not drink the cup of Christ with blessed Clement?* But perhaps some will say, "We can!—It's just that there's no opportunity; the time of persecution is past."

But I confess I don't give much credence to those who say these things. Why? Well, every day you shrink before the prick of a needle; do you suppose you can stand against a sword? Show in small conflicts how valiantly you can stand in a great struggle. See, I do not say to you, "Sacrifice to idols, and you shall live; if you are not willing to do so, you shall die with many tortures." The Lord knows of what we are made,* and he does not devise such a hard struggle for us. To blessed Clement he gave *a hard struggle so that he might conquer and learn that wisdom is more powerful than anything.**

4. But what is your struggle, my brothers? Every day suggestions enter your heart: Break your rule! Murmur! Malign people! Slack off! Pretend to be sick! To

*Eph 5:29

*Gregory the Great, *Hom in Ev* 30.1

*Jas 5:17

*Heb 5:2
†1 Cor 6:20
#Ps 115:4
‡Ps 115:3

*Rev 5:9

*1 Pet 1:4
*Matt 20:22

*Ps 102:14

*Wis 10:12

satisfy your feelings, answer back to someone who might have spoken harshly! But no one is told, "If you don't do it, you will die!" Yet only with difficulty and labor will you make a firm stand against them in your soul.

"Who could bear up with things so great?" This is the reply we usually give those encouraging us, either through the exterior man or through the Holy Spirit within. If we test ourselves in a struggle of this kind, if we barely resist, if now and then we give in—what should we do in so great a trial as that one? If our weakness gives way to a flimsy straw, how shall we resist spears? Do you see how we are reduced to nothing* and, like women and children, praise others who fight but are unable to fight ourselves? What are we to do then? Surely we are all called to the feast of the Lamb,* and in his sight we may not appear empty.†

*Ps 72:22

*Rev 19:9
†Exod 23:15

Let us then consider carefully what is set before us,* since it behooves us to prepare ourselves for such great things. Blessed Clement reflected on the fact that wine had been set before him by the Lord, and he himself, being a rich man, likewise brought wine to the feast by the shedding of his own blood. "But we are poor, Lord, and we have no wine."* Yet he said, *Fill your jars with water.* "So, then, if we present water, will it be accepted?" Indeed it will be. Not only that, but he who, following the advice of Wisdom, carefully reflected on what was set before him*—he, that is, *who came not only in water, but in water and blood*—he will see to it that that very water along with wine is set before us. He who saw it bore testimony that from the open side of the Lord sleeping on the cross came forth blood and water.*

*Prov 23:1-2

*John 2:3
*John 2:7

*Prov 23:1
*1 John 5:6

*John 19:34-35

5. And therefore, my brothers, that we may prove ourselves faithful to our God, if we have not the martyrdom of blood—for martyrdom is evidence*—let us ask the evidence of water, and God will not despise it.

*testimonium

There are three things that bear witness on earth: spirit, water, and blood.* Blessed are those for whom a threefold testimony is sufficient, because *a threefold cord is not easily broken.** If we do not have the testimony of blood, let us hold on to the Spirit and water, since without the Spirit neither blood nor water is sufficient. Or, more correctly, if there is just the Spirit, without water or blood, its testimony is enough because it is the Spirit of truth;* neither blood nor water is of any use by itself, but it is the Spirit who testifies in them. Having said that, though, I think that seldom or never will you find the Spirit without water and blood.

  *1 John 5:8

  *Eccl 4:12

  *John 14:17

Therefore, beloved brothers, let us who don't have blood seek water! And since we mentioned the water jars above, let us seek after those two or three measures that each of those jars contained!* For Christ puts before us a triple measure of water, and perfect is he among us who can do as he has, that is, who can contain three measures. This is why the disjunctive was used, two *or* three, so that it may be understood that at least two are necessary, but the third is not demanded of everyone.

  *John 2:6

6. Receive therefore the triple measure of water that the Savior himself sets before you. He weeps for Lazarus* and over the city of Jerusalem,† and this is the first water. He sweats as the hour of his passion approaches, and this is the second water, not from his eyes only but flowing from his whole body, since this was red and of the color of blood, as it is written, *and his sweat was like drops of blood falling onto the earth.** And again clearly the third is the one we already mentioned, the water that together with blood flowed from his side.*

  *John 11:35
  †Luke 19:41

  *Luke 22:44

  *John 19:34

Therefore you too have the first if you irrigate with your tears the bed of your conscience* and wash the spots of past sins with the pain of compunction. You have the second water if you eat your bread in the

  *Ps 6:7

sweat of your brow,* punishing your body with the labor of penitence* and restraining the flame of concupiscence. And it is the color of blood either because of the labor or because of the fire of concupiscence that it extinguishes.

*Gen 3:19
*1 Cor 9:27

And then, without a doubt, if you can attain to the grace of devotion, you will be given to drink of the water of saving wisdom,* and the Spirit of Christ,† which is sweeter than honey,# *will become* in you *a fount of the water of wisdom to eternal life*.‡ And remember that this is the water that proceeds from the side of a man* and streams unimpeded. Now the one who wishes to take delight in this grace must be dead to the world!

*Sir 15:3
†Rom 8:9
#Ps 18:11
‡John 4:14
*John 19:34

Therefore, if I may briefly repeat myself: the first water cleanses the conscience of past sins; the second, so that you may avoid them in the future, extinguishes concupiscence; and the third, if you merit to attain to it, gives drink to the thirsty soul.

Sermon on the Passing of Saint Malachy the Bishop[1]

1. My most dearly beloved, an abundant blessing has descended on you from heaven this day. You should suffer loss, but I would be in danger had I not faithfully apportioned it, for it seems to me that this duty has been entrusted to me. Still I fear for your loss and my damnation, in case it be said, *The little ones ask for bread, and no one offers to them.** I know how necessary for you is the consolation coming down from heaven, since it is certain that you have manfully* sworn off all carnal pleasures and earthly allurements. No one could entertain a doubt that it was all a gift from heaven and in the divine plan* that Bishop Malachy should fall asleep among you today and be buried here as he had desired.[2]* When not a single leaf of a tree falls to the ground without God's will,* is anyone so stupid that he does not plainly see in the coming and the passing of this man a truly great plan of divine goodness?

*Lam 4:4

*viriliter

*see Acts 2:23

*V Mal 67
*see Matt 10:29

---

[1] *Sermo in transitu sancti Malachiæ episcopi* (Mal). Malachy, archbishop of Armagh (Ireland), died at Clairvaux on Nov. 2, 1148, and was buried there.

[2] Bernard, *Vita Sancti Malachiae Episcopi* 67, ed. Jean Leclercq and H. M. Rochais, SBOp 3 (Rome: Editiones Cistercienses, 1963), 295–378, here 371–72; *The Life and Death of Saint Malachy the Irishman*, trans. Robert T. Meyer, CF 10 (Kalamazoo, MI: Cistercian Publications, 1978), 1–93, here 85. For Meyer's translation of this sermon, see CF 10:107–12.

He came from the ends of the earth to be buried here in our earth. He was bent upon another errand, to be sure, but because of his special love for us, we know it was that which he desired most of all. Certainly he experienced many delays on the journey itself, having been denied permission to sail until the time of his consummation was approaching, and the goal that could not be reached.* We received him who had come to us by many hardships as an angel sent from God,* out of reverence for his holiness. And he received us out of his deeply ingrained humility and gentleness* with love far greater than we deserved. Then he spent but a few days with us in good health, awaiting his brethren who were still scattered about England, because the ill-founded suspicions of the king impeded the man of God. But when they had all come together and he was preparing for the journey to Rome, for which he had come, he was suddenly overtaken by sickness, and he sensed at once that he was being called instead to the heavenly court. God foresaw something better for us, lest Malachy in going away from us should be perfected elsewhere.*

2. To the physicians there appeared no sign of serious illness, much less of death. But he, in high spirits, said that it was completely befitting that Malachy should pass from this life in this year.* Great effort was taken against it, both in fervent prayers to God and in every way we could, but his merits so won the day that his heart's desire was granted him and the request of his lips was not withdrawn.* So it was that everything happened to concur with his own wishes: that he had chosen for himself this of all places by divine inspiration and that he had long desired as the day of his burial that day on which the general commemoration of all the faithful is celebrated.*

But this has also quite rightly increased our joy: that the same day had been chosen, by God's instigation,

*Sir 39:34; Job 14:5
*Gal 4:14
*Eph 4:2

*Heb 11:40

*V Mal 71

*Ps 20:3

*V Mal 67, 71

for the reburial of the bones of our brethren, which had been brought from the earlier cemetery. As we were bringing in the remains and singing the customary psalms, the holy man kept saying how greatly this chant delighted him. And not long afterward he himself followed, sunk into a blissful and refreshing sleep. We give thanks therefore to God for all his dispositions: that he deigned to honor us though unworthy with the presence of Malachy's holy death, that he enriched his poor men with the very precious treasure of his body, and that he chose to support us who are weak by so great a pillar of his church.* Because one or another of two signs proves a thing was done for our good,* either that this place is pleasing to God or that he wishes to render it pleasing to himself, he led this man of outstanding holiness *from the ends of the earth** here to die and here to be buried.

*see Gal 2:9

*Ps 85:17

*Matt 12:42

3. Our very love for this holy father compels us to grieve more deeply along with that people and to shudder more violently at the cruelty of death, which has not refrained from afflicting the church with so terrible a wound. Death surely is awful and inexorable, which has penalized such a great crowd of people by striking down one. Blind and improvident, it has tied Malachy's tongue, shackled his footsteps, relaxed his hands, and closed his eyes. Those faithful eyes, I say, that by their tender, loving tears used to bring divine grace to sinners; those undefiled hands that had always loved to be exercised in laborious and humble deeds, which had so often offered up for sinners the saving host of the Lord's body and were *lifted up to heaven in prayer without anger or contention*,* which are known to have conferred many blessings on the sick and to have shone with various signs; *the beautiful steps of the one who preached the gospel of peace and brought glad tidings of good things*;* those feet that were so often wearied in the eagerness of loving mercy; those footsteps,

*1 Tim 2:8

*Rom 10:15; Isa 52:7

always worthy to be pressed with devout kisses; and then those holy *lips of the priest that guarded knowledge;** *the mouth of the righteous, which meditated wisdom, and his tongue, which, speaking righteousness** or rather *mercy*,† used to cure such great wounds of souls.

Nor should we wonder, brothers, that death is full of iniquity when *iniquity itself brought forth death,** that it is a thoughtless thing, born as it was of seduction.* Nor should we marvel, I repeat, if it strikes without discernment, when it came from a transgression,* if it is cruel and heedless when it has come forth from the trickery of *the old serpent** and from the folly of the woman. But why do we dispute that it dared to assail Malachy, a faithful *member of Christ,** when it also attacked Malachy's head and the head of all the chosen people as well?* It rushed upon the guiltless one who was not to suffer, but it did not escape guiltless. *Death* struck against life, but life came to grips with death and *was swallowed up in life.** It gobbled up the hook for itself. Thereafter it began to be held by him whom it seemed to have held.³

4. But perhaps someone may say, "How does death seem to be overcome by the head if it still rages in freedom against the members? If death is dead,⁴* how did it kill Malachy? If conquered, how does it still prevail over everyone, *and there is no man who shall live and not see death?*"* Clearly death has been conquered—the work of the devil* and the penalty of sin. Sin—the cause of death—has likewise been conquered. The wicked one—himself the author of sin and death—is conquered.* Not only are they conquered; they have already been judged and condemned.

*Mal 2:7

*Pss 36:30; 100:1
†Prov 31:26

*Jas 1:15
*2 Cor 11:3

*1 Tim 2:14

*Rev 12:9; 20:2

*1 Cor 6:15

*Eph 4:15

*1 Cor 15:54;
2 Cor 5:4

*see Hos 13:14

*Ps 88:49
*1 John 2:13-14

*1 John 2:13-14

---

³ See Bernard, SC 26.11 (SBOp 1:78; CF 7:70–71). Bernard's source for this metaphor may be Rufinus, *Commentarius in symbolum apostolorum* 16, or Gregory, *Moralia in Iob* 33.7.
⁴ Antiphon for First Vespers of the Feast of the Exaltation of the Holy Cross.

Their sentence is divided certainly, but not yet publicly proclaimed. *The fire is* already *prepared for the devil,** even though he is not yet cast into it. He is still allowed to continue his evil practices for a short while longer.* He has been made the hammer of the Heavenly Artificer, the *hammer of the whole earth.** He bruises the elect for their profit and the evil for their condemnation. Therefore *as it is for the master of the household, so for those of his household,** that is, sin and death. It is not to be doubted that although sin was nailed to the cross with Christ,* it was allowed for a while not to rule but to reside in the apostle himself while he lived. I am lying if he does not himself say, *Now it is no more I who act, but the sin that dwells in me.** So too death itself is not yet compelled to depart, but it is forced not to do harm. There will be a time, however, when it will be said, *Death, where is your victory?** *Death is surely the last enemy that shall be destroyed.** Now indeed since he rules who has *the power of life and death** and even confines the sea within the fixed boundaries of its shores,* death itself is to the Lord's beloved but a refreshing sleep. To this the prophet witnesses, who says, *When he gives sleep to his beloved, behold the inheritance of* the Lord.* *Terrible is the death of the sinful,*† whose birth is evil and their life worse. *But precious is the death of the saints.** Clearly it is precious, for it is the end of their labors,* the consummation of victory, as it were, the gate of life, and the entrance to perfect security.

5. Therefore, brothers, let us be glad, let us rejoice, as is fitting, with our father, for it is an act of devotion to mourn Malachy dead and a much greater devotion to rejoice with him alive. Is he not alive? Happily alive! To the eyes of the foolish he seemed to be dead,[5]* of course, but he is at peace, now at last *a fellow citizen*

*Matt 25:41

*Rev 12:12
*Jer 50:23

*Matt 10:25

*Col 2:14

*Rom 7:17

*1 Cor 15:55
*1 Cor 15:26
*Wis 16:13
*see Ps 103:6-9;
Job 38:8

*Ps 126:2-3
†Ps 33:22
*Ps 115:15
*Rev 14:13

*Wis 3:2

---

[5] See Mass for the Vigil of All Saints (*Missale Romanum* 734).

of the saints and a member of the household of God.* He sings with them, and he gives thanks, saying, *We have passed through fire and water, and you have brought us out into a place of refreshment.** He passed through manfully, it is evident, and he went through happily. The true Hebrew celebrated Passover in spirit, and in departing he said to us, *With desire I have desired to eat this Passover with you.** *We passed through fire and water, and you led us into a place of refreshment*, he whom sadness could not break nor ease detain. There is below us a place that fire claims so entirely as its own that the miserable rich man there could not have even a single drop of water from the finger of Lazarus.* And above there is *the City of God, which the streams of the river make glad,** *a torrent of pleasure,** *a cup that inebriates* richly.† Here in its very midst is contained *the knowledge of good and evil*,* and here one undergoes *the experience of pleasure and tribulation.** Eve the unfortunate brought us into these vicissitudes. Here, of course, are day and night, but in hell there is only night, and in heaven only day.* Happy the soul therefore who passes through both, neither succumbing to pleasure nor fainting at tribulation.*

6. I think I should tell you briefly about some of the noble miracles of this man, by which we recognize that he *passed* bravely *through fire and water.** A tyrannical race claimed the metropolitan see of Patrick, the great apostle of the Irish, creating archbishops in regular succession,* *possessing the sanctuary of God by heredity.** Our beloved Malachy, begged by the faithful to stand up to such great evils, *took his life in his hands** and went forward bravely. He took on the bishopric, putting himself in great danger so that he might put an end to so great an injustice. He ruled the church amid perils, but once the perils were gone he immediately ordained someone else to succeed him in true canonical fashion. For it was on this stipulation that

*Eph 2:19

*Ps 65:12

*Luke 22:15

*Luke 16:24-26
*Ps 45:5
*Ps 35:9
†Ps 22:5
*Gen 2:9
*2 Cor 8:2

*Rev 21:25; 22:5

*Eph 3:13

*Ps 65:12

*V Mal 19–22
*Ps 82:13
*see 1 Sam 19:5; Ps 118:109

he had accepted the office, so that later on, once the fury of persecution had passed, he would be able to appoint someone else. He wanted to be allowed to return again to his own see,* where he lived in the religious community that he had himself founded, without ecclesiastical or worldly benefices. Until now he has lived among them as one of them without any goods of his own. Thus the fire of tribulation tried the man of God, but it did not consume him.* Surely he was gold. Likewise pleasure did not tempt and destroy him, nor did he stand still as an idle spectator on the road, heedless of his own pilgrimage.

*V Mal 19–31

*examinavit non exinanivit; Pss 16:3; 65:10-11

7. Which one of you, brothers, would not passionately desire to imitate his holiness, if one dared even to hope for it? I believe that you will listen more eagerly if I tell you what made Malachy holy. But should my testimony seem less than acceptable, listen to what Scripture has to say: *He made him holy in faith and meekness.** By faith he trampled the world underfoot, as John witnesses, who said, *This is the victory that overcomes the world, our faith.** For *in the spirit of meekness*† he endured with good cheer everything that was hard and contrary. Like Christ he walked upon the seas* so that he would not be snared by enticements, and he *possessed his soul in patience** so that he would not be crushed by troubles. Of both these things you have examples in the Psalms: *A thousand shall fall by your side and ten thousand at your right hand.** For how many more fall to the false promises of prosperity than to the scourge of adversity?

*Sir 45:4

*1 John 5:4
†Gal 6:1

*John 6:19; Matt 14:25

*Luke 21:19

*Ps 90:7

Dear brothers, let none of us be deceived by the level surface of an easier way into imagining that the path of the sea would be more comfortable for us. Here the plain holds great mountains, imperceptible to be sure, but more dangerous for that very reason. The way among steep hills and rugged rocks may seem far more laborious, but to the experienced it is found to be far safer and more desirable. On both paths there is struggle, on both there is danger everywhere, as he well knew who said, *by the weapons of righteousness on the right and on the left.*^{*} Thus we may rejoice with those who *have passed through fire and water and* have come into *a place of refreshment.*^{*} Do you want to hear about this place of refreshment? If only someone else would tell you about it! For I cannot belch forth what I have never tasted.

8. Today I seem to hear Malachy speaking to me about that place of refreshment: *Turn, my soul, to your rest; for the Lord has been generous to you, for he has delivered my soul from death,* and so on.* Listen to what few words I have to say, *for the day is far spent,*^{*} and this sermon has gone on longer than I had hoped, because I am unwillingly torn away from the sweet name of our father, and my tongue dreads to cease speaking of Malachy. My brothers, the death of the soul is sin,⁶* unless perhaps what you read in the prophet has escaped you: *The soul that sins, it shall die.*^{*} Threefold then is the rejoicing of the man who has been freed from all sin and labor and danger. From now on neither is *sin* said *to dwell in him,*^{*} nor is the sorrow of penitence* declared, nor from then on is he warned to guard himself lest he should fall. Elijah has put down his pallium.* It was not what he feared: it was not that he feared it be touched or even taken by an adulteress.* He climbs into the chariot.† Now he is not afraid he may fall.# He mounts up joyfully, not laboring to fly under his own power, but sitting in a swift chariot. Let us, beloved, run to this place of refreshment, eager in spirit, *in the odor of the ointments*^{*} of our blessed father, whom we see this day to have stirred up our sluggish spirits to a burning, ardent desire. *Let us run*

*2 Cor 6:7

*Ps 65:12

*Ps 114:7-8
*Luke 24:29

*Ps 114:8

*Ezek 18:4

*Rom 7:17–20
*2 Cor 7:10

*2 Kgs 2:8

*Gen 39:12, 15
†2 Kgs 2:11
#Ps 116:8

*Song 1:3

---

⁶ See John Chrysostom, S for Easter (PG 50:437).

after him, I say, crying out continuously, *Draw us after you.** In the affection of our hearts and the perfection of our conversion, let us return devout thanks to the Almighty and Merciful One that he has willed that we, unworthy servants, utterly without merits of our own, are at least never without the prayers of another.

*Song 1:3-4

On the Vigil of Saint Andrew

the Apostle[1]

How We Should Prepare for the Solemnities of the Saints with Fasting

1. The authority of the Fathers has ordained that the feasts of the saints be preceded by prayerful fasting. It would be expedient for us, then, and in no way foolish,* if we did as we were advised. For since we commit sins every day and *offend in many things*,* it is quite inappropriate for us to engage in the celebration of holy festivities, particularly important ones, unless first we undergo the purification of abstinence, by which we may be found the more worthy and more able to receive spiritual consolation. For *the righteous is the first to accuse himself*,* and people do not start to praise others without first blaming themselves. And if just people, apprehensive, are afraid to anticipate the one who is prepared to pass judgment on their righteous deeds,* what are we to do whose sins in this interval of time are hidden

*Ps 21:3

*Jas 3:2

*Prov 18:17, according to an ancient version

*Ps 74:3

---

[1] *Sermo in vigilia sancti Andreæ* (VAnd).

and not judged?* Truly we must fear lest our deeds be found out and brought to judgment.*

*Ps 31:1
*1 Tim 5:24

If not even the just person presumes to praise the saints without modesty and shame, how much more should the sinner, in whose mouth is no fitting praise,* always be afraid of that inevitable word, *Why do you recite my statutes?** Or *Friends, how did you come here, not having a wedding garment?** Blessed are they who have been at pains to keep their robes,* that is, the glory of a good conscience,* ever spotless and always show them shining. But because there are few who keep their heart with all diligence,* and there are fewer, if indeed there can be fewer, who keep it in all holiness, they must try to wash away their stains by constant abstinence, particularly when it is time for some particular solemnity to be celebrated.

*Sir 15:9

*Ps 49:16
*Matt 22:12
*Rev 22:14
*2 Cor 1:12

*Prov 4:23

2. Not only is the observance of the fast a preparation for the festivity to come, but it is also an admonition, and no minor instruction. From it we learn what the true way of the eternal feast is. For why should we anticipate solemnities by a fast except that *through many tribulations we enter the kingdom of God?** Indeed, the person who does not observe the abstinence prescribed for the vigil is not worthy of the solemn joy. Truly, I say, if you will not afflict your soul during the vigil, you will rightly be judged unworthy of the rest and joy of the feast,* for the entire time of this present penitence is a vigil of the great feast and eternal sabbath* that we are waiting for! And you will not quibble at a longer vigil if you await an eternity of rejoicing. Although solemnities that last a day call for a day's preparation, that one, even though it is eternal, does not demand an eternal preparation! But where does it take us to, the delightful memorial—for such this festival is often called, perhaps all the more worthily—of this feast? We must return to what is at hand.

*Acts 14:21

*Isa 58:5

*Heb 4:9

3. So the reason for today's fast, and for the joy and solemnity that pertain to what we await, is the passion of Blessed Andrew the apostle. For it is right that if we cannot hang with him, we should fast with him. Indeed, who can doubt that he fasted when he hung on the cross for two days? Let us be found, therefore, to share in his passion,* even if only a little, and if we are not nailed to the cross with him, yet we fast with him, so that by the mercy of God we may also be sharers in his crown and companions of his spiritual joys in this present life. For how shall we not exult in the memory of his triumph when we know that he exulted greatly at the time of his torture? Will not the feast be one of gladness when the cross itself is so full of joy? Since we usually call an occasion of joy a festival, so a cross is so called from crucifixion, or certainly crucifixion from cross.

*1 Pet 4:13

With what exultation of the whole earth* shall the miracle of a new beginning, a great work of divine strength, be celebrated? Andrew was human like us,* and with what strong spiritual ardor did he thirst for the cross; with what joy unheard of by the world did he dance when he saw afar the cross prepared for him! "O cross," he said, "so long desired² and now prepared for my eager mind! I come to you fearless and rejoicing so that you, exulting too, may take me up!"* Do you see that he cannot contain himself before so great a joy? "Come," he says, "so that you, too, may exult!" The measure of exultation is so great, isn't it, that the cross itself exults—not as if having a motive for happiness, but as being total happiness. What is less customary, beyond all reason, and against nature than for

*Ps 47:3

*Jas 5:17

*suscipias

---

²Antiphon *Cum pervenisset* for the *Magnificat* of the Second Vespers of Saint Andrew, from the legends of Saint Andrew. For the legend of Saint Andrew, see *Bibliographia hagiographia latina antiquae et mediae aetatis*, ed. Socii Bollandiani (Brussels, 1898–99), no. 428.

one crucified to rejoice like the cross? Nature cancels any sense of happiness in the one; as for the other, if it prevails over someone, it wipes out all joy and heaps up pain. "I was always your lover," he says, "and I have desired to embrace you."³

Brothers, this is flashing fire! It is not a talking tongue, or if it is a tongue, it is certainly fiery—coals of that fire that Christ sent down from heaven to the martyr's bones.* And would that they might purify us, consuming and burning all carnal affection there is in us.* What indeed are those sparks, and from what interior fire do they shine?

*Lam 1:13

*Ps 119:4

4. Clearly, blessed Andrew, your faith is like a mustard seed,* which, when you begin to rub it, all unexpectedly starts to give off heat. What if it were rubbed a little more? What soul could bear that heat, what act of hearing could bear the words? As long as Ægeas⁴ is only slightly threatening, Andrew seems a contemptible grain of mustard seed. "The Lord," he says, "sent me to this province, in which I have acquired no small population." But let the threatening pestle approach, and then his taste will be sharper and he will speak more resolutely. Ægeas expects him to be afraid when he threatens the torture of the cross, but it is not so. On the contrary, he is set ablaze by these words, and he cries out without restraint, "If I were afraid of the cross, I should not proclaim its glory!" So when he saw that the wood was prepared for him, his heart burned within him, and he extolled it and caressed it as his beloved! He greeted it most courteously, gazed at most devotedly, and praised it most loftily, and he

*Matt 17:19

---

³ Antiphon *Videns Andreas* for Nocturns of the Feast of Saint Andrew.

⁴ Jacobus de Voragine, *The Golden Legend*, trans. William Granger Ryan, 2 vols. (Princeton: Princeton University Press, 1993), 1:13–20.

took pride in his proclamation, crying out with the affections rather than the voice, "Hail, O most precious cross, you who received glory and beauty from the limbs of the Lord! Hail, O cross, you who have been sanctified by the body of the Lord and adorned with his limbs as with pearls!"

Servants of the cross, whoever they may be, are right to venerate the lover of the cross, but he rightly deserves greater devotion from those who in a particular way promised to take up his cross. It is to you and about you, my brothers, that I say this, you who with no deaf ear have heard the trumpet of the gospel: *The one who does not carry his cross and follow me cannot be my disciple.** Be prepared to apply your mind with all diligence to this solemnity, and celebrate it with all your heart, because in it an altogether great treasure of consolation and exhortation is laid up for you, if only you will dig for it and probe into it.

*Luke 14:27

On the Feast of Saint Andrew[1]

Sermon One

Concerning Clean Fish

1. In our celebrations today of the glorious triumph of blessed Andrew, we have exulted and rejoiced in the words of grace that proceeded from his mouth,* for there could be no place for sadness when he himself rejoiced so greatly. None of us has suffered with someone who suffered like this, none has dared to weep for someone rejoicing.* Otherwise it would have made complete sense for him to say to us what the Savior said to those who were following him and weeping when he was carrying the cross: *Daughters of Jerusalem, do not weep for me, but weep for yourselves.** As it turned out, when blessed Andrew himself was led to the cross, the people, who grieved that such a holy and just man should be unjustly condemned, wished to stop him from being punished. Instead, he stopped them with urgent prayer,* lest he should lose his crown or, rather, should not suffer.[2]

    He desired if at all possible to depart and to be with Christ,* but on the cross that he had always loved; he desired to enter the kingdom, but by the gibbet. For what does he say to this one whom he loved? "Through you," he says, "may he receive me, for

*Ps 89:14; Luke 4:22

*see Rom 12:15

*John 19:17; Luke 23:28

instantissima preces; see RB Pro.4: *instantissima oratione*
*Phil 1:23

---

[1] *Sermo in natali sancti Andreæ* (And 1).
[2] See Antiphons and Responses for the Feast of Saint Andrew.

through you he redeemed me." So if we love him we rejoice with him,* not only because he is crowned but also because he is crucified, because the Lord gave him his heart's desire and put on his head a crown of precious stones.* Yet while we acclaim him because he was counted worthy to delight in the embrace of the cross he desired, it would be strange if we did not also marvel at his joy, which we acclaim.

*John 14:28

*Ps 20:3-4

2. As we keep this night of vigil and take pleasure in singing words of such great exultation, you would think that none of us had any reason to reflect and say, "What is the meaning of this new rejoicing, and where does it spring from? Is the cross truly precious and can it really be loved, and is there really any reason to exult in it?" Yes, it is true, my brothers! If you reflect, the wood of the cross always brings forth life, produces the fruit of delight, distills the oil of pleasantness, and gives forth the ointment of spiritual blessings.* It is not a tree of the woodlands: *it is the tree of life for those who grasp it.** It is a life-giving tree; otherwise why should it grow in the Master's land?* I call that the most precious lump of soil to which it is fixed by the nails as if by roots. If it were not more precious than them all and more fruitful than any other, it would never have been planted in that garden, nor would it have been allowed to live in that vineyard.

*Ps 44:8

*Prov 3:18
*Luke 13:7

Why should it be a matter for wonder that he should give sweetness to the cross, he who gave it also to fire?[3] Why should the cross seem tasteless when the flame has savor? Why did Laurence find savor in the fire, laughing at his executioners and mocking his judge? How shall we answer this, my brothers? Why do we not find savor in tribulation that is for Christ or

---

[3] Antiphon *Beatus Laurentius* for the *Magnificat* at the feast of Saint Laurence.

taste what is hidden in manna?* For by that means the devil is utterly conquered, and there is nothing at all he can take from us. Let this one thing be enough for us against the twofold malice of the enemy. *Rev 2:17

3. For that most wicked one has snares; he has darts, too, since he is the most cunning* hunter of human beings, thirsting only for the lifeblood of souls. Some he attacks cunningly with the weapons of any kind of suggestive thought, and he wounds many of those whose patience is fragile. Others he strives to net with pleasures, and among them he encloses a great number* of those who creep on the ground and flutter near it. *Gen 3:1 *Luke 5:6

So let there be joy in tribulation,* and the wicked one will have no means of alluring them, no way to bring them down. We are set free from the snare of the hunter and equally from the harsh word.* *The enemy, if he makes a suggestion of carnal pleasure, shall not prevail against the one* whose delight is in the cross of Christ, and if the enemy tries to use any bitterness to wear down his soul, the son of wickedness shall not afflict him.* Those who are fed by fasting have no desire for delicacies; how much less are they likely to murmur about the one they delight in. Clearly *he has made the Lord his refuge*,* so that neither the enemy's trap nor his arrow should be feared. Rather, he is a clean fish, having scales and fins,* for just as *the net is surely spread in vain before the eyes of birds*,* so the dart is hurled fruitlessly against those wearing a corselet of scales. The law decrees that fish like this are clean, those that are supported by fins and protected by scales, whether they be in the sea, in a river, or in a pond.* This great and wide sea holds clean fish that are worthy of the master's table,* for out of those who in thought and behavior live according to this present age, he keeps for himself many thousands*—those whom the apostolic dragnet hauls in so that once brought in they are separated from the wicked.* There without a doubt *2 Cor 7:4 *Ps 90:3 *Ps 88:23 *Ps 90:9 *Lev 11:9 *Prov 1:17 *Lev 11:9 *Ps 103:25 *Rom 11:4 *Matt 13:47-49 our fisher of men will sit* and draw all Achaia after him.⁴ [*Matt 4:19]

The river also contains clean fish, those who are found faithful stewards.* And the river is the Order of Preachers, who do not stay in the same place but stream forth and surge out to water many lands. And there are also clean fish in the ponds, those who serve the Lord in cloisters,* in spirit and power.† It is right that monasteries should be compared to ponds, where the fish are to some extent enclosed and have no freedom to wander but are always ready for the spiritual feast,* saying among themselves, "When will he come, he who shall bear me away? *I wait through all the days, in which I am now a soldier, until my change comes*."* [*1 Cor 4:2; *Phil 3:13; †Luke 1:17; *see RB 22.6; *Job 14:14]

4. Moving on, as we remember from the law quoted above, those fish are clean that have scales and fins.* There are many scales, but out of them is woven as it were a single coat of mail, for the virtue of patience is one, even though in different trials we see it manifested in different ways. And indeed I think that as scales are compared to patience, so fins may be not unreasonably compared to joy. For joy lifts up and lightens, so that anyone who is joyful seems to take a leap into the depths! But in order that we may have two fins, we require a twofold joy. It is perhaps because of that that the apostle teaches—for he indeed had fins, by which he was caught up to the third heaven and flew also to Paradise*—not only to boast in hope but also to boast in suffering.* Without a doubt, that person, whoever it may be, flies on high who delights not only in the expectation of future goods but also in the actual evils of the present. Therefore let such a one boast even in these. [*Lev 11:9; *2 Cor 12:2-4; *Rom 5:2-3]

---

⁴ Lesson for the second Nocturn on the Feast of Saint Andrew.

Such a one we find the blessed apostle to be: such a one we marvel at, such a one we deservedly acclaim.

5. This brings us to consider three stages: of beginners, of practitioners, and of the accomplished.* For *the fear of the Lord is the beginning of wisdom,*† hope is in the middle, and the fulfillment is charity; and indeed, listen to the apostle to the effect that *charity is the fulfillment of the law.** The one who begins with fear bears the cross of Christ with patience,* the practitioner carries it gladly in hope, and the perfected embraces it ardently out of love. He is the only one who can say, "I have always been your lover, and I have desired to embrace you."⁵

*incipientium, proficientium, perfectorum
†Ps 110:10

*Rom 13:10
*see Luke 14:27; Mark 15:21

That saying is far from his who bears the cross but would choose, if it were possible, that he should not come to that hour.* Also, if I do not appear to speak too boldly, it is far from that word, *Father, if it be possible, let this cup pass from me.** What do I mean? He even had mounted an ass's colt* so he would not be abandoned to his enemies. I am completely aware of the fear of cowardice in the war leader, I am aware of the cry of the sick in the doctor, I am aware that the hen becomes sick along with her chicks;* I reflect on his charity, I am astounded by his compassion, I am frightened by the respect he shows. The merciful Lord does not take for himself the robust condition* of blessed Andrew, for *those who are whole have no need of a physician, but those who are sick.** But if anyone is offended by this show of condescension, that one clearly needs to hear, *Is your eye evil, because I am good?** For to that person the aroma of life is death.*

*John 12:27

*Matt 26:39
*John 12:14

*see Matt 23:37

*affectum

*Matt 9:12

*Matt 20:15
*2 Cor 2:16

6. How great would it have been, Lord Jesus, if at the approach of the hour for which you had come*

*John 12:27

---

⁵ Antiphon *Videns Andreas* at Vigils for the Feast of Saint Andrew.

you had stood unfazed as one who had the power to put down his life and no one should take it from you?* Wasn't it far more glorious, since it was all done for us, that not only the body's suffering but also the heart's affection should act on our behalf, and that not only would your death bring people back to life but also your fear would make them strong, your grief happy, your loathing eager, your agitation calm, and your desolation consoled? At the resurrection of Lazarus I find that *he groaned in spirit and was troubled in himself.** But let it be for the interim that he allowed himself to be troubled not out of the exigencies of his condition but by the goodness of his own will.

In addition there is something further that I hear. Up to this point the *love* that *is as strong as death** has prevailed in such a superior way that the angel of God had to strengthen the Christ! Who, and whom? Hear the evangelist: *An angel*, he says, *appeared, strengthening him.** Whom? Surely him for whom the Virgin's womb, which had been closed, opened to give birth,* him at whose bidding water was changed to wine,* at whose touch leprosy was put to flight,* beneath whose feet the sea stood firm,* and at whose voice the dead were raised,* him who upholds all things by the word of his power,* by whom all things were made,† and through whom all things subsist, himself an angel. What do I mean? Who is he? I should marvel less if he were not utterly unutterable. The one who comforted him, then, could not himself grasp the majesty of him who was comforted.

7. I ask you, Angel, whom do you console? You are not ignorant, are you, of who it is to whom you came to bring consolation? Certainly he is a consoler, certainly he is a comforter; otherwise he would not have said that another Comforter would be sent to the apostles by the Father,* if he were not himself a comforter. So I see in him a very great comforter, who

*John 10:18

*John 11:33

*Song 8:6

*Luke 22:43
*Matt 1:22-23
*John 2:7-9
*Mark 1:41-42
*Matt 14:25
*John 11:43-44
*Heb 1:3
†John 1:3

*John 14:16

is near to those who are of a broken heart.* I am not in despair, O Lord, although the tribulation I suffer seems grievous to me; even though I am fainthearted, even though I desire that the cup pass from me.* I am not in despair, I say, provided that I may add, *But not what I will, but as you will.** I have learned from him not to rely on fleshly or on faltering consolation but on the angelic, the spiritual, the heavenly. I accept this, but now only if I don't complain, because that would mean complete separation from you, if I didn't immediately come to my senses again; I do not refuse, even though I have need of consolation. What then? Do I recognize my own cry in the Savior and yet have no hope of salvation? Clearly *in patience I will possess my soul!**

*Ps 33:19

*Mark 14:36

*Matt 26:39

*Luke 21:19

8. Yet I wish to go on practicing* and not be content with the safety already attained. *The one who fears God will do good,** says Wisdom. But it is not enough, for it is written, *Depart from evil and do good,** *seek peace and pursue it.** Do not be content with safety: seek peace, lest your very safety be in danger. Hear the angel, then, who when he who became our peace was born* exulted and sang, *Peace on earth to people of good will.** For what is good will but a well-ordered mind? What is that, you say? Surely one that is in accord with reason, with that which says that *the sufferings of this present time are not worthy to be compared with the glory that shall be revealed in us.** Now if you have begun to feel thus, doubtless you would willingly bear the cross of the Lord, and you would say, *I am prepared to keep your commandments, and I am not troubled.**

*proficere

*Sir 15:1

*Ps 36:27
*Ps 33:15

*Eph 2:14
*Luke 2:14

*Rom 8:18

*Ps 118:60

9. But *if you would be perfect,** one thing is necessary.* What is that, you say? Assuredly it is *joy in the Holy Spirit.*† For truly those who are restrained by fear are patient, and those who are prudently directed by hope are kind, but if they were not *fervent in spirit,** they could easily slip. Also, the charity that is spread

*Matt 19:21
*Mark 10:21;
see Luke 10:42
†Rom 14:17

*Rom 12:11

abroad by the Spirit* is patient and kind† and furthermore will never disappear.# In the first command that was given to our parents,‡ if you consider it carefully, Eve was patient and Adam was kind. But both of them fell, probably because neither he nor she was steadfast of purpose. *The woman saw the tree, that it was pleasing to sight and sweet for food.**

Do you not think that it was difficult for her to restrain her hand? When she was asked by the serpent, see whether her words did not suggest that the command had been hard for her: "We eat of every tree in the garden, but of the tree of the knowledge of good and evil he told us not to eat."* She does not say "This is the will of the Creator: he knows why it is so; it is sufficient for us to obey him, because our life is in his will."* And so the woman was easily seduced, so that she trusted in his promise and agreed to his suggestion. For his part, the man did not suffer seduction, but subversion by his love for the woman. For he would have chosen to obey the command, which he thought was in his interests, if the woman had not persuaded him otherwise. And it does not seem that he found difficulty in keeping the commandment, but however good his will was, he had no fortitude because he had no fervor.

10. Indeed *love** *is as strong as death*,† not patience or hope, but love; not fear or reason, but the spirit of strength. Patience says, "This is what should be done," because it is driven by fear. Good will says, "This is what is expedient, and this should be done," because it is drawn by the reasonableness of hope.* But charity,† inflamed by the Spirit, says neither "this is what should be done" nor "this is what is expedient," but "This is what I wish, what I long for, what I strongly desire."* You see what is the sublimity, the security, and the pleasantness of charity. Happy the soul who comes to that state of charity!

---

*Rom 5:5
†1 Cor 13:4
#1 Cor 13:8
‡ Gen 2:16-17

*Gen 3:6;
see Gen 2:9

*Gen 3:2-3;
2:16-17

*Ps 29:6

*dilectio
†Song 8:6

*Isa 11:2
†*caritas*

**Sic volo . . . cupio, . . . desidero vehementer*

Let us not lose hope, then, since the memory of him who reached it is especially celebrated so that we might invoke his help and be urged on by his example. I say more: it seems to me that I see some of us at that stage! If you say, "Blessed Andrew was an apostle," then it is not possible for you who are weak to follow in his footsteps; but what a loss of face if you don't imitate someone right next to you! No one reaches the top in an instant; the top of the ladder is reached by climbing, not by flying. Let us climb, therefore, as it were with two feet: meditation and prayer.* Meditation teaches us what is lacking; prayer takes care that it is not lacking. The one shows the way; the other takes you along it. By meditation we learn the dangers that threaten us; by prayer we avoid them, by the help of our Lord Jesus Christ.

*Gen 28:12

On the Feast of Saint Andrew[1]

Sermon Two

Of the Four Arms of the Cross

1. Today is the celebration of the solemnity of Saint Andrew, and if we examine it carefully and conscientiously, we shall find in it much that will strengthen our souls. Indeed, at the very beginning of his conversion he affords us a great example of perfect obedience. This is a virtue essential to all Christians, but we must embrace it particularly closely, for by our very profession we are bound to obedience. He is a wise banker, or rather he is Wisdom itself, to whom we must return the coin of obedience, and he will not receive it unless it is found to be whole, without any deceit. For if we deliberate, if we weigh the matter and obey this commandment but not that, the coin is broken; Christ, to whom as debtors we are bound to render sound currency, will not accept it. For in all simplicity all of us have promised unconditional obedience. And if anyone gives that obedience insincerely and only in appearance but grumbles in private, the coin is false. It consists of lead, not silver, and injustice rests upon lead coinage. He acts deceitfully,* but in the sight of God, for *God is not mocked.*†

*Ps 35:3
†Gal 6:7

---

[1] *Sermo in natali sancti Andreæ* (And 2).

2. Do you desire to hear the shape of perfect obedience? *The Lord saw Peter and Andrew,* says the evangelist, *casting their net into the sea, and he said to them, "Come after me: I will make you fishers of men."** "I will turn fishermen into fishers of men," he says, "or rather preachers";* *and they immediately,* without weighing the matter or hesitating, without worrying about how they would live or how unlettered and unpolished men were to become preachers, asking no question and making no delay, *leaving their nets* and ship, *they followed him.**

*Matt 4:18-19

**Faciam . . . de piscatoribus piscatores, immo praedicatores*

*Matt 4:20

Be sure, my brethren, that these words were written for your sake and are recited year by year in the church so that you should know the shape of true obedience and should chasten your hearts in the obedience of charity.* It is this alone that commends the coinage of obedience, silver coinage, proved and cleansed.* It is charity alone that makes the coinage pleasing and acceptable to God. Indeed *the Lord loves a cheerful giver.** And likewise, *if I give my body to be burnt but have not charity, it profits me nothing.**

*1 Pet 1:22
*Ps 11:7

*2 Cor 9:7

*1 Cor 13:3

3. Do you wish us to speak about the passion of this blessed apostle, which we celebrate today, for the praise of Christ and for your edification? Certainly you have heard how when blessed Andrew came to the place where the cross had been made ready, he was strengthened in the Lord and through the Spirit, which with the other apostles he had received in tongues of fire; he spoke words of true fire.* So, seeing from afar off that the cross had been made ready, he did not grow pale, as mortal weakness would seem to demand, nor did his blood grow cold; his hair did not stand on end, nor did his voice stick in his throat; his body did not tremble, nor was his mind disturbed; his understanding did not desert him, as usually happens. His mouth spoke out of the fullness of his heart,* and he uttered as it were fiery sparks through the burning charity of

*Acts 2:3

*Matt 12:34

his heart. For what did blessed Andrew utter when, as I said, he saw from afar the cross made ready for him? "O cross," he said, "long desired, and now awaited by my longing heart! In serenity and gladness I come to you;[2] lift me up in joy, the disciple of him who hung upon you, because I have always been your lover, and I have desired to embrace you."[3]

I ask you, my brothers, is it a man who speaks thus? Or is it an angel or some other creature? He is a man like us, subject to suffering.* Truly his passion proves that he is subject to suffering, yet when it is near he exults with great joy. When was there such unheard-of exultation, such strange joy, in a human? When was there such constancy in such weakness? When was there such a spiritual mind in a human, such burning charity, such strength of mind? Let us never imagine that such valor had its origin in him alone. It was a gift, the work of God, coming down from the Father of lights,* from him *who alone does great marvels.*†

4. Clearly it was the Spirit, beloved, who helped him in his weakness,* and it was through the Spirit that into his heart was poured love as strong as death,* or rather, stronger than death.* Would that we too might be found partakers of it! For see, the work of penitence is grievous for us, the affliction of the body is a heavy burden, abstinence is irksome. Our soul is bored to sleep during Vigils through our weariness,* for no other reason than lack of the Spirit. If the Spirit were present, doubtless it would help us in our weakness,* and, just as it did with blessed Andrew's cross and even his death, it would cause our fatigue and our penitence to be not only free from annoyance but also

*Jas 5:17

*Jas 1:17
†Ps 135:4

*Rom 8:26
*Rom 5:5
*Song 8:6

*Ps 118:28

*Rom 8:26

---

[2] Antiphon *Cum pervenisset* at the *Magnificat* on the feast of Saint Andrew.
[3] Antiphon *Videns Andreas* for Nocturns at the feast of Saint Andrew.

desirable and altogether delightful to us. *For my spirit, says the Lord, is sweeter than honey,** so that not even the bitterness of death,* though it may be very bitter, can be stronger than the sweetness of the Spirit.

*Sir 24:27
*Isa 38:17

What will this sweetness not transform when it makes death itself most sweet? What roughness can withstand an ointment that makes even death most pleasant? *When he shall give sleep to his beloved, behold the heritage of the Lord.** What trouble will not be driven out by the joy that makes death itself delightful? Let us seek this spirit, my brothers; let us strive with all diligence to be found worthy to possess this spirit, so that the one whom we already possess we may possess more abundantly. *For whoever does not have the spirit of God, he is none of his.** *For we have not received the spirit of this world, but the spirit that is of God, that we might know the things which are freely given to us by God.** His works of salvation and the deeds of his life give us a proof of his presence, for we can do nothing of ourselves unless the life-giving Spirit,* the Spirit of the Savior, is with us.

*Ps 126:2-3

*Rom 8:9

*1 Cor 2:12

*John 6:64

Let us ask then that God should multiply his gifts in us and increase his Spirit, which has already given its firstfruits. For there is no more certain proof of his presence* than the desire for greater grace, for he himself has said, *Those who eat of me hunger still, and those who drink of me still thirst.**

*Rom 8:23

*Sir 24:29

5. But perhaps the consciences of many will reply to us, "We desire this Spirit to aid us in our infirmity, but we cannot find him."* And I say, "you do not find him because you do not seek him; you do not receive him because you do not ask."* You ask and do not receive because you ask indifferently. God awaits nothing else, asks for nothing else, but that he should be sought ceaselessly and with longing. In short, how will he ever deny those who ask when he challenges and cheers on those who don't ask! *If you,* he says, *being*

*Rom 8:26

*see Matt 7:7-8

evil, *know how to give good things to your children, how much more will your Father in heaven give the good spirit to those who seek him?** Ask then, beloved, ask without ceasing, ask without hesitating,* and in all your doings call upon the presence and help of this sweet and pleasant Spirit.*

And we, brothers, must take up our cross with blessed Andrew, or rather, with him whom he followed, our Lord and Savior. For that was why Andrew rejoiced and exulted, and indeed he seemed to die not only for the Lord but with him, and was marked with the likeness of his death,* so that suffering with him he might also reign with him.* For we too, brothers, must bear our cross with the blessed Andrew, or rather with him. Let us too be crucified with him in the same way;* let us attend with the ears of our heart to the voice saying,* *Whoever wishes to follow me, let him deny himself and take up his cross and follow me.** It is as though he said, "The person who desires me, let him despise himself; who wishes to do my will, let him learn to crush his own."

6. But enemies wage war without letup, are unceasingly armed against us. Let us too arm ourselves against them: let us imitate the weapons of our king by also taking up our cross, with which we triumph over all our enemies. For I have heard what the psalmist promised, or rather the Holy Spirit through his mouth: *His truth will surround you as a shield.** It is doubtless the shield of the Highest; certainly he was speaking of him, as the previous words of the psalm itself clearly shows. Why, brothers, are we surrounded by a shield if not because wars surround us on every side? In short, listen to why he surrounds you as a shield: *His truth*, it says, *will surround you as a shield.* Why? *You shall not fear*, he says, *the terror by night nor the arrow that flies in the daytime, the pestilence that walks in the darkness nor the sickness that destroys at noon.**

You see, don't you, how necessary it is that his truth should surround you like a shield when the weapons of the enemy surround you? The terror by night comes from below, the arrow that flies in the daytime is on the left, the pestilence that walks in darkness is on the right, and—so that there should be no breathing space—the sickness that destroys at noon falls from above! We are poor and pitiable: even though with so many serpents nearby and weapons darting about everywhere and enemies rising up on all sides, we sleep in dangerous heedlessness and negligence, we are lethargic from leisure, we indulge in pointless occupations and entertainments, slothful in our spiritual exercises, as if peace and safety* were already here and as if human life on earth were not warfare.* \hfill *1 Thess 5:3 \newline *Job 7:1

It is this, I tell you, beloved, that causes me great terror, and it pierces my soul with a sword of mighty fear: that we clearly lack fear, though surrounded by such great perils, and are less careful than we ought to be. Indeed this negligence of ours proves one of two things: either that we have surrendered ourselves entirely to our enemies without knowing it or, if we have been preserved in these perils, that we are ungrateful to him who watches over us. It is clear enough that each of these holds some peril. Therefore I beg you, beloved, that the malignant watchfulness of our enemies and the ever-present malice that makes them so watchful, so eager to overcome us, should make us careful and vigilant, that we may work out our salvation with fear and trembling.* \hfill *Phil 2:2

7. Look, what I mean is, in the cross is our salvation; that is why we should manfully fasten ourselves to it. *The word of the cross,* says the apostle, *is foolishness to those who perish, but to those who are saved, that is, to us, it is the power of God.** This is the shield by which we are surrounded, that its four arms may repel the fourfold weapon of the enemy. Let the lower arm be set against \hfill *1 Cor 1:18

the night's terror, that is, against the cowardice that comes from the flesh's sufferings, so that what is below us—the body—we may manfully strive to correct and even subject to servitude!* Whoever curses us to our face* or tries to induce us to evil is the arrow that flies by day;* he is on the left and must be warded off by the left arm of the cross.

*1 Cor 9:27
*1 Cor 11:20
*Ps 90:6-7

But if someone is a sycophant and under the guise of confidentiality tries to get me to drink the poison of slander-mongering against the brothers and to sow hatred—in short, tries to persuade a just person to do anything wicked—he is on the right hand; indeed he is Judas approaching me with a kiss,* he is the enemy that walks in darkness,* and so it is by the right arm of the cross that he must be warded off.

*Luke 22:48
*Ps 90:6

But look! Here is the sickness that destroys at noonday, the spirit of pride that often rises up against us subtly in a shining array of virtues. We take care frequently to point out to you how pernicious this is. For *the beginning of all sin* and the cause of all damnation *is pride.** Because of that, whoever you are who desire to work out your salvation, remember to ward this off with the arm of the cross above the head, so that you not be lifted up by pride, your heart not be haughty, and you not busy yourself with great matters or marvels that are beyond you,* and the arm of the cross that stands high above your head will ward off the weapons that come from above. Yes, it is only on this arm that the title of salvation and of sovereignty is inscribed,* because only the one who humbles himself merits to be saved and lifted up.*

*Sir 10:15

*Ps 130:1

*Mark 15:26
*Matt 23:12

8. Now let me briefly repeat: these four arms are moderation,* patience, prudence, and humility. Happy is the soul who boasts in this cross, who triumphs in this cross! Let him persevere, and he will be strong enough not to be overcome by any temptation. So let him pray, whoever carries this cross, let him pray with

*continentia

blessed Andrew to his Lord and Master that he may not suffer him to be taken down from the cross. For what does the evil one not dare, what does the wicked one not presume to attempt? What he had thought to inflict on the disciple at the hands of Ægeas, he had intended to do to his master by the tongues of the Jews.* But in each case he was led to regret it and went away confounded and defeated. If only he might go from us, too, conquered by him who has won the victory in both himself and his disciple! May he make us worthy too, victoriously to carry to the end whatever cross of repentance we have taken up in his name, *he who is God above all, blessed through the ages.**

*Legend of Saint Andrew, in the second Nocturn of the feast of Saint Andrew

*Rom 9:5

On the Death of Master Humbert[1]

1. **H**umbert, the servant of the Lord, is dead, a devoted servant and faithful follower. You saw yourselves how he expired last night in our arms, as if he were a worm of the earth. For three days he suffered the weariness of death, which devoured him with its jaws to satiate its thirst for his blood. Ah, it did what it could: it killed the flesh, and there it is concealed in the heart of the earth.* It took from us a dear friend, a wise counselor, a strong helper. The slayer of human beings, unsatisfied, spared neither you nor me, but spared me far less. Is it thus that you separate us, O bitter death?* O cruel slayer! O bitterness most bitter!* O terror and horror of the sons

*Matt 12:40

*1 Sam 15:32
*Isa 38:17

---

[1] *Sermo in obitu domni Humberti* (Humb). Humbert was a monk of La Chaise-Dieu for twenty years before going to Clairvaux in 1117. He became prior of Clairvaux in 1125, and in 1128 abbot of Igny. He returned to Clairvaux in 1138 and died there ten years later. Bernard addressed his Ep 141 to Humbert as abbot of Igny. On Humbert, see Conrad of Eberbach, *Exordium Magnum cisterciense sive Narratio de initio Cisterciensis ordinis* 3.4, ed. Bruno Griesser, SSOC 2 (Rome: Editiones Cistercienses, 1961), 146–49; Conrad of Eberbach, *The Great Beginning of Cîteaux: The* Exordium Magnum *of Conrad of Eberbach*, trans. Benedicta Ward and Paul Savage, ed. E. Rozanne Elder, CF 72 (St. John's, MN: Cistercian Publications, 2012), 219–22.

of Adam! What have you done? You have slain him, you have taken possession of him.

But to what end? It is only the flesh you have taken; you have no power over the soul.* It flies to its Creator, whom it had desired so ardently and followed so faithfully all the days of its life. That very body that you think you possess will be taken from you, but when you, the last enemy,* have been destroyed, then you too will be swallowed up in victory.* You will give it back, without a doubt; one day you will give back that body that yesterday, greatly rejoicing and applauding,* you entangled in your nets,* that as a sign of your arrival you filled with spittle and curses, with squalor and dirt. The Only-begotten of the Father will come with great power and glory to seek Humbert and to configure this cadaver to the body of his brilliance.* But what of you? Assuredly, as it is written in Jeremiah, at the end of days you will still be foolish;* while Humbert goes on living eternally, you will go on dying. The sea creature vomited up Jonah, whom it had swallowed,* and you will give back Humbert, whom you think to have confined deep within your vast belly.

*Luke 12:4

*1 Cor 15:26
*1 Cor 15:54

*Isa 35:2
*Luke 21:27

*Phil 3:21

*Jer 17:11

*Jonah 2:11

2. For the rest, brothers, this servant of God displayed for you a sermon composed of every kind of holiness, a sermon long and broad, as long as the length of his life, as broad as his life was sublime. It is not necessary for me to open my mouth any further on this subject if you well retain his sermon, if you have engraved it on your hearts. For fifty years and more he lived in the service of him whom to serve is to reign, for from his boyhood years he was to be found in the sanctuary of God. He lived with us for thirty years, almost from the foundation of this monastery, not only blameless* but even with grace, so that his memory will be a blessing* not only to us but to the generation that is to come.*

*Phil 3:6
*Sir 45:1
*Ps 70:18

He passed his life as a stranger and pilgrim,* since he knew that he was not of this world.* Here he had

*Gen 23:4
*John 17:14

no abiding city,* and it was as if he had no family,† but looking to the future he advanced toward the prize of his upward call.* There was nothing in him that the world might rightfully claim either as its own or from him, because the world did not please him, nor he the world. He accepted from its resources as little as he could and would have taken less if he had not been constrained by obedience. He had food and clothing and was content with these*—and not a superfluity, but according to need, although he often objected that even what was necessary was superfluous!

If I remember correctly, a few days ago while we were speaking together he said that he was a freeloader in this monastery and that he grazed in the house of God while being as good as nothing to anyone. He was truly gentle and lowly of heart,* and while he flourished with other virtues, he had a special grasp on gracious mildness. Because he showed himself lovable and affable to all, he was intensely lovable.

3. But to return to what I was saying, in all these things you all know full well how circumcised in mouth and tongue he was,* you who for so long saw his way of life and heard his sermon. Did anyone ever hear any petty remark from his mouth, any unkind word, boastful utterance, or envious comment? Did anyone ever hear him judge others or agree with anyone who did? Did anyone hear him indulging in foolish talk? Indeed, who did not dread being overheard by him if they chanced to talk in that way? Truly he guarded his ways that he should not offend with his tongue,* knowing that the one who does not offend in word is a perfect man.*

Far from you, Humbert, was that evangelical woe: Woe to you who laugh now, for you shall weep!* Did any of you ever come upon him laughing, even when he was in the company of many others who were laughing? He always showed a bright countenance so as not to be a burden, but, if you remember, he did not completely give way to laughter. What is more, you not only saw his fervor in the worship of God both by day and by night and right up to the day of his death, but you marveled at it. When he arrived at the age of debility, he was worn out and enfeebled in addition to having the many grave infirmities of old age, as many of you know; however, as it is said, spirit is the conqueror of years and knows not how to yield to weakness.

To say it briefly, in cold weather as well as hot, ascending and descending hills and valleys, he performed the work of young men to the admiration and astonishment of all. If I ever detained him for the favor of his counsel on the quantity of business I had, he was sad and gloomy until he was returned to your fellowship. It was rare if he ever missed the solemn Vigils—which, though, he not rarely anticipated—and he was very rarely absent from the other hours of the chanted office except from necessity, when sickness was tailing him and he was under the sentence of imminent death.*   *2 Cor 1:9

4. Then he hardly touched the community's food in the refectory, and if anything else was put before him, he either refused to accept it or accepted it so disagreeably that it frequently worried the community. He would have made it a rule always to drink water if I had not strenuously dissuaded him. If ever he was forced to drink wine, he diluted it so much that it was wine more in color than in taste. He scarcely ever entered the infirmary, and then only when compelled by obedience, and when he did enter it, he could scarcely be kept there. I confess that the insufficient obedience in this respect was because his great authority overwhelmed me. Am I to praise him? I do not praise him in this,* because, as you know, he persisted too obstinately in this kind of thing. I think that if he regretted anything, it was that he was at variance with us about his physical needs.   *1 Cor 11:22

But what was he like in giving advice? He was clear and discreet, as I know well because I often tapped his soul. But it was not only I who knew this; all of you knew it. Who was ever afflicted by many great temptations and did not hear from his mouth both the root of the temptation and the remedy for its cure? For he used to pass quickly through all the corners of an ailing conscience so that the man who sought his counsel could well believe that he saw everything and was present to all.

5. What of his charity? He had so put on the bowels of mercy* that he found excuses for everyone, he intervened on everyone's behalf, even if those for whom he was speaking did not know it,* for he cared not for personalities but for necessities. He was lowly of heart, mild in speech,* diligent in his work, burning in charity, faithful in what he was entrusted with, thoughtful and prudent in counsel. Of all the men I used to see in those days, he was the most balanced,* being the same every hour of every day. Clearly he planted his footsteps in the way of Jesus Christ until he finished the course of his life.*

He was poor as Jesus was poor. He lived his life in labor as the Lord did. One was crucified, and the other, fastened to many great crosses, bore the marks of Jesus in his own flesh,* making up in his own body what was lacking in the sufferings of Christ.* The one rose again; the other will rise. The one ascended into heaven; the other, we think, will ascend. Assuredly he will ascend when the King of Glory* descends on our account, in the same way he first ascended, that he may make known his power,* for it is no less marvelous to descend through clouds than to ascend by means of a cloud. For thus did the angels foretell: this Jesus who ascended from you into heaven shall likewise come as you saw him going into heaven.*

*Col 3:12

*Acts 10:34

*Matt 11:29

*compositus

*2 Tim 4:7

*Gal 6:17
*Col 1:24

*Ps 23:7

*Ps 105:8

*Acts 1:11

Do not praise a person in his life,* says the Scripture, because there is no sure praise except after death. I too was careful to practice this with regard to him, for during his lifetime I did not speak in that way lest perhaps I should incur a charge of flattery or he commit the fault of vanity. But henceforth neither of these things is to be feared, for I do not see him, and perhaps he does not hear me. But even if he is to hear me he is not affected by human words, for he clings firmly and in blessedness to the Word of God. The enemy shall not be able to do anything against him, and the author of vanity shall not hurt him.*

*Sir 11:30, according to an ancient version

*Ps 88:23

6. Look, most sweet father: he is before your eyes, that fount of purity for whom you thirsted with such intensity of spirit. See, you are plunged into that depth of godly goodness, the memory of whose abundant sweetness you were accustomed so devotedly to bring forth!* When did you ever speak words that did not resonate with true purity, or in which the holy goodness of God was not heard? Therefore I do not grieve for you,* Humbert, for God gave you your heart's desire.* Rather, I grieve for myself that your sweet counsel has been taken away, your great help, a man of sympathetic mind,* one after my own heart.†

*Ps 144:7

*2 Sam 1:26
*Ps 20:3

*Ps 54:14
†Acts 13:22

All these evils have reverted upon me, Lord Jesus, and your terrors have overpowered me.* You have sent far away from me my friends and my neighbors and my acquaintances, away from misery!* You have taken from me my relations in the flesh, my relations in the spirit, who were wise both in your affairs and in worldly matters, in accordance with your will. You have taken away one after another of those who carried my burden, the great burden, that you laid on me. One man, Humbert, almost alone of all my companions, was left to me;* he was all the dearer to me as he was older, and you took him, because he was yours.

*Ps 87:17

*Ps 87:19

*Job 6:13

And I, I alone am left to face the blows, I die in every one, and all your waves have gone over me.* If only you would kill the one you scourge instead of keeping the wretch alive for so many bitter deaths!

I do not contradict the words of the saint,* but if only he who has begun would finish me off, it would be a consolation to me; let him not spare whom he afflicts with sorrow!* I am ready for scourges,† but perhaps my loving Father will exchange scourges for favors. Therefore it is not with murmuring that my words are full, but with grief.* I do not weep for Humbert—there can be no weeping for him who has been called to the rich man's table*—but for me and for you, for this house, and for all our brothers, who sought advice from his mouth.

So when the women who had followed our Savior from Galilee were lamenting over him, he, carrying his cross like a criminal carrying his noose, looked back at them and said, Daughters of Jerusalem, do not weep for me, but weep for yourselves and for your children,* for the things concerning me have an end.* The things you see awaiting me are temporary; the things you do not see are eternal.* If they are temporary, then they are passing away, and if they are passing away, then they are mortal. All the proof necessary that they are passing away and dying is that they can be seen. The things that we saw at the death of Humbert are temporal,* but now he has joy and gladness for all eternity.*

7. We must not grieve, then, for one who has neither grief nor pain.* Nor must we complain that he has been taken from us; let us rather give thanks that he was granted to us for so long. Indeed, I think that he lived only for us for the last ten years, and I fear he may have been taken away because we were not worthy of his company.* Who knows whether he has been taken away so he might protect us by his intercession before the Father? Would that it were so! For if when he was

*Ps 87:8

*Job 6:10

*Job 6:9-10
†Ps 37:18

*Job 6:3

*Luke 16:21

*Luke 23:28
*Luke 22:37

*2 Cor 4:18

*Isa 35:10
*Dan 12:3

*Rev 21:4

*Wis 4:10

with us his charity was so great that when it came to bodily needs he gladly gave me what was his, how much more now that he cleaves to the greatest charity—I mean God*—will he show even greater love and charity toward me. But maybe now he knows the whole truth about me and my way of life* and doesn't show compassion as he used to do but instead scorns me so that I might fear. But if it is on account of our sins that God has taken him from us, let him himself prevail with God that they be mercifully forgiven, so that we do not receive one punishment upon another.*

8. For the rest, my brethren, I tell you that if you were following in his footsteps you would not so easily slide along with empty thoughts and idle conversation, joking and off-color humor; you waste much of our life and much time in these things! Time flies and cannot be recalled, and while you think you are avoiding a light punishment, you incur a greater one! For be sure of this, that after this life what has been neglected here will in the place of purging be paid for a hundredfold, to the uttermost farthing.*

I myself know that it is hard for someone who is negligent to embrace discipline,* for a talkative person, silence, for one who is used to going here and there, stability; but it will be harder, much harder, to bear those future troubles. And as I myself have always known, that person who is buried here endured many temptations of this kind at first, but he fought bravely and was victorious. Then it was hard for him to maintain the fight in the midst of temptations; afterward, though, it would have been harder for him to return to those frivolities, because good habits had become natural to him.

Practice these teachings and aim for the example that you saw and heard in him* so that you may come to him to whom he himself has come, who is God, blessed forever.*

*1 John 4:16

*conversatione

*2 Cor 2:3

*Matt 5:26

*Ps 2:12

*Phil 3:17

*Rom 9:5

Index of Scriptural References in Bernard's Liturgical Sermons (CF 51–54)

Column 1 indicates the book of the Bible, with the cited chapter and verses. Column two identifies the sermons and paragraphs where the citations appear, grouped by the number of the volumes of English translations in the Cistercian Fathers series (**51, 52, 53, 54**). Abbreviations for the names of the sermons appear on pages lxxi–lxxiii above.

Genesis (Gen)	
1:1	**51**: Nat 2.1
1:2	**51**: VNat 5.2
1:5	**51**: Circ 3.5; **52**: Palm 2.1
1:7	**54**: NatBVM 4
1:16	**53**: PP 1.1
1:26	**51**: Adv 3.1, Nat 2.4; **52**: Ann 1.7, Ann 1(alt).7, Pasc 1.8; **53**: Asc 4.5; **54**: OS 3.2
1:26-27	**51**: Nat 2.3
1:27	**51**: Nat 1.2
1:27-28	**51**: Adv 1.5
1:28	**54**: Mart 2
1:31	**52**: Pasc 1.8
2:4	**53**: Pent 2.4
2:6	**54**: NatBVM 3
2:7	**51**: VNat 3:8, VNat 4.7, Nat 2.1; **54**: Ded 5.7, Mart 2
2:8	**54**: Ded 6.3
2:9	**52**: Ann 1.8, Ann 1 (alt).8; **54**: Mal 5
2:10	**51**: Nat 1.6
2:15	**52**: 4 HM 11; **54**: Ded 6.3
2:16-17	**51**: Circ 1.1; **54**: And 1.9
2:17	**51**: Adv 2.2; **52**: Ann 1.8, Ann 1 (alt).10, Ann 1 (alt).11
2:18	**54**: OAsspt 1
2:19	**52**: Sept 2.2
2:21	**52**: Sept. 2.1
2:21-22	**51**: P Epi 2.3; **52**: Sept 2.1
2:23	**52**: Sept. 2.1; **54**: OS 1.12
2:24	**52**: Sept 2.1, Ann 1 (alt).8
3:1	**52**: Ann 2.3; **53**: 6 p P 2.5; **54**: OAsspt 3, 1 Nov 5.12, And 1.3
3:1-6	**53**: Pent 2.3

3:1-7	**52**: Ann 1.8	3.22	**51**: Adv 2.1, Adv 2.2, Epi 3.7
3:2-3	**54**: And 1.9		
3:3	**52**: Ann 1.8	3:23-24	**52**: Ann 1 (alt).8; **54**: OS 1.13
3:4	**51**: Adv 2.4, Nat 2.3; **52**: Ann 1.8	3:24	**51**: Nat 1.3; **54**: 1 Nov 5.7, OS 4.1
3:5	**51**: VNat 2.2, Nat 2.3; **52**: Ann 1.8, Ann 1 (alt).8; **53**: Asc 4.4, Asc 4.5; **54**: OS 1.9	3:29	**51**: VNat 6.3
		4:7	**52**: Quad 5.3; **53**: Asc 4.12, 6 p P 2.1
3:5-6	**51**: Adv 1.3 (2x)	4:9	**51**: Adv 3.6; **53**: JB 9
3:6	**52**: Ann 1.8, Ann 1 (alt).8; **54**: OAsspt 2, OS 1.10, OS 1.11, And 1:9	4:10	**52**: Ann 14
		4:13	**52**: 4 HM 8
		5:22	**53**: Asc 6.9 (2x)
		5:24	**53**: Asc 3.2
3:7	**52**: Pasc 1 (alt).4	5:32	**54**: NatBVM 4
3:7-8	**54**: NatBVM 7	6:3	**52**: Pasc 2.1; **53**: Asc 3.8; **54**: Mich 1.6
3:8	**51**: Epi 1.3; **52**: 4 HM 11	6:7	**52**: Ann 1.14, Ann 1 (Alt).14
3:9	**52**: Ann 1 (alt).8		
3:9-13	**52**: Ann 1.8	6:8	**54**: Asspt 3.5
3:10	**51**: Nat 1.3; **52**: Ann 1.8	6:9	**54**: NatBVM 4
		6:14	**52**: Palm 1.4
3:12	**54**: NatBVM 6, OS 1.12	6:17	**52**: Quad 1.1; **54**: Mich 1.6
3:15	**52**: Quad 1.1; **54**: Asspt 2.9, OAsspt 4 (2x)	7:3	**51**: VNat 5.2
		7:6	**54**: NatBVM 4
3:16	**51**: VNat 1.1, VNat 4.3, Circ 3.10; **52**: Ann 2.1, 4 HM 6	7:7	**54**: Abb 1
		7:15	**52**: Quad 1.1
		7:19	**52**: 4 HM 5
3:17	**51**: Circ 3.10; **52**: Ann 1 (alt).8; **54**: OS 1.11	8:21	**52**: 4 HM 13, Pasc 1 (alt).2; **54**: Ded 5.3, Mart 7
3:18	**52**: Palm 2.5, Pasc 2.7; **53**: PP 2.3; **54**: NatBVM 17, OS 2.6	9:6	**52**: Ann 1.7, Ann 1 (alt).7
		11:1-9	**54**: Asspt 5.1
3:19	**51**: Nat 1.3, Nat 3.5, P Epi 2.7; **52**: Sept 1.3; **54**: OS 2.2, Mart 2, Clem 6	11:4-9	**53**: Asc 4.5
		11:9	**54**: Ded 5.9
		12:1	**51**: Epi 2.2
		12:1-4	**54**: Mart 8
3:21	**51**: Nat 3.1	12:10	**51**: VNat 6.10

14:13-16	**54**: Mart 8	32:12	**53**: PP 1.1
15:6	**54**: OS 4.1	32:24	**54**: NatBVM 16 (2x)
15:9-10	**52**: Sept 2.3	32:26	**52**: 4 HM 14; **54**:
16:12	**53**: 6 p P 1.3		NatBVM 16,
17:11	**51**: Circ 1.1		OAsspt 5
17:12	**51**: Circ 1.2, Circ 3.5	32:30	**51**:VNat 3.2
17:14	**51**: Circ 3.3, OEpi 2	35:18	**51**:VNat 6:9
17:16	**54**: OS 4.1	37:3	**52**: Quad 2.6
18	**54**: Mart 8	37:20	**52**: Pasc 3.3
19:1	**54**: OAsspt 8	37:23	**52**: Quad 2.6
19:11	**51**: SP 3	37:27	**54**: NatBVM 7
20:9	**53**: PP 1.1	38:27-30	**51**:VNat 4.7
21:10-14	**54**: Mart 8	39:12	**54**: Mal 8
22:1-10	**54**: Mart 8	39:15	**54**: Mal 8
22:11	**54**: Mart 17	40:13	**53**: PP 3.2
22:17	**51**:VNat 2.1	40:13-14	**51**: Adv 6.4
23:4	**53**: Asc 3.6; **54**: Humb 2	40:14	**51**: Adv 6.5
		40:15	**51**: Adv 1.5
24:2-3	**51**:VNat 6.4	41:41	**53**: Asc 3.2
24:14	**54**: Asspt 6, OAsspt 15	41:52	**51**:VNat 6.9
24:18-20	**54**: OAsspt 15	42:27	**51**: Nat 1.8
24:35	**54**: Mart 8	43:15	**53**: 6 p P 1.2
26:27	**53**: Rog 1	47:9	**51**:VNat 3.2
27:1	**51**: Adv 1:8, Epi 3.3	48:10	**51**: Adv 1.8
27:8	**52**: OPasc 1.3	49:8-12	**51**:VNat 1.4
27:28	**53**: Pent 2.6	49:10	**51**:VNat 1.4
27:30	**51**: P Epi 2.1	49:17	**52**: Ben 4
27:38	**54**: Asspt 6	49:26	**54**: OS 4.1
28:12	**53**: Asc 4.10, JB 1; **54**: Mich 2.4, And 1.10, Ded 6.1, Ded 6.3, NatBVM 4, OS 2.1	49:27	**52**: Pasc 3.3
		Exodus (Exod)	
		1:15-22	**51**: Epi 3.3
		1:16	**52**: OPasc 1.5
28:16	**54**: Ded 6.1	2:3-5	**52**: OPasc 1.5
28:17	**53**: JB 1; **54**: Ded 6.1	2:10	**52**: OPasc 1.4
29:16-30	**51**: P Epi 2.8	2:21	**51**: P Epi 2.2
29:18-26	**54**: Asspt 3.1	3:2-3	**54**: OAsspt 5
30:33	**51**:VNat 2.2, VNat 5.3	3:5	**54**: OAsspt 5
		3:18	**53**: 6 p P 1.2
32:7	**52**: OPasc 1.7	5:7	**51**: P Epi 1.5

6:12	**54**: Humb 3	9:3	**51**: Epi 1.6
7:12	**53**: Asc 3.9, Asc 6.11	10:1	**52**: Pur 2.2
8:26	**51**: VNat 1.5; **53**: PP 2.2	10:14	**52**: Palm 3.5
		11:2-3	**51**: Epi 3.1
12:5	**51**: Circ 2.1, P Epi 2.1	11:3	**54**: OS 1.5
12:10	**54**: Mart 10	11:9	**54**: And 1.3, And 1.4
12:11	**52**: Pasc 1.14	12:2	**52**: Pur 3.1
13:2	**52**: Pur 3.1	12:2-4	**52**: Pur 3.1
13:3	**53**: 4 p P 2	12:6-8	**52**: Pur 3.1
13:12-13	**52**: Pur 3.1	14:10	**51**: Circ 2.1
15:11	**54**: 1 Nov 5.4	14:40	**51**: VNat 6.11
15:18	**51**: VNat 6:3	18:5	**51**: Nat 1.2
16:8	**54**: NatBVM 14	18:6	**51**: Nat 1.2
16:21	**54**: NatBVM 15	18:21	**51**: Nat 1.2
19–31	**54**: OS 1.6	19:2	**51**: VNat 5.1; **54**: Ded 5.8
19:14	**53**: Asc 4.6		
20:7	**51**: Circ 2.3	19:9	**54**: Asspt 2.3
23:15	**52**: Pur 2.2; **54**: Clem 4	19:12	**51**: Nat 1.2
		21:11	**51**: Circ 2.1
25:30	**51**: VNat 6.8	25:10	**53**: Pent 3.8
28:2	**52**: Palm 1.3	25:10-11	**53**: Pent 1.6
28:17	**54**: OAsspt 4	25:35	**53**: Asc 3.6
28:40	**52**: Palm 1.3		
29:22	**52**: Pasc 1 (alt).2	**Numbers (Num)**	
29:41	**52**: Pur 3.2	5:8	**52**: Pur 3.3
31:18	**52**: Ann 3.2	5:13	**53**: JB 11
32:9	**51**: OEpi 1; **52**: Pasc 2.5	7:9	**52**: VNat 3.1
		12:1	**52**: P Epi 2.2 (2x); **52**: Pur 2.1
33:11	**52**: Quad 3.2, Palm 2.7	12:6-8	**52**: Palm 2.7
33:20	**52**: Palm 2.7	14:3-4	**53**: 6 p P 1.1
33:23	**52**: Palm 2.7	17:8	**54**: OAsspt 8, NatBVM 11
34:9	**51**: Adv 1.5		
34.24	**51**: Nat 1.2	18:12	**52**: P Epi 2.1
34:28	**52**: Quad 3.2	20:17	**51**: VNat 3.6; **52**: Quad 6.1; **53**: Pent 2.5, VPP 2
35:2	**54**: OS 3.3		
		21:8-9	**52**: Pasc 1.3
Leviticus (Lev)		21:22	**52**: Adv 2.5; **53**: VPP 2
3:9	**52**: Pasc 1 (alt).2		
5:11	**52**: Pur 3.1		

24:16	**53**: PP 3.2	33:2	**53**: Pent 1.2
24:17	**53**: Asc 2.4	33:12	**53**: Pent 3.5
28:2	**52**: Pur 2.1		
28:8	**52**: Pur 3.2	**Joshua (Josh)**	
29:12	**52**: 4 HM 1	1:14	**53**: 4 p P 2
32:33	**52**: VNat 6.8	2:1	**54**: Asspt 2.2
		5:2	**51**: Circ 2.1, OEpi 1
Deuteronomy (Deut)		10:24	**51**: Adv 2.1
2:27	**52**: Quad 6.1	22:4	**51**: VNat 6.8
5:32	**52**: Ann 1.5	22:7	**51**: VNat 6.8
6:4	**54**: Asspt 5.12		
6:5	**54**: Ded 3.5	**Judges (Judg)**	
6:16	**51**: Circ 3.6	1:8	**51**: SP 8
7:16	**51**: Adv 1.4	1:15	**54**: In lab mess 2.3
8:4	**53**: PP 3.6	5:31	**53**: Asc 3.1
13:3	**54**: NatBVM 16	6:36-38	**54**: OAsspt 8
14:8	**52**: Ben 5 (2x)	6:36-40	**54**: OAsspt 5
15:19	**52**: Ben 6	6:37-40	**52**: Ann 3.8
24:1	**51**: P Epi 2.7	6:38-40	**54**: NatBVM 6
25:5	**53**: PP 3.6		
26:8	**51**: Nat 1.2	**First Samuel (1 Sam)**	
26:15	**54**: Mich 1.4	2:3	**51**: Adv 5.3; **53**: Asc 1.3
30:13	**51**: Adv 1.10		
30:14	**51**: Adv 5.3; **52**: Pur 1.4; **54**: Mart 10	3:10	**51**: SP 6; **54**: NatBVM 14
32:4	**52**: Pasc 1.4, Pasc 1 (alt).4	7:3	**51**: VNat 4.1
		13:14	**51**: Nat 5.5
32:5	**54**: Asspt 2.3	15:23	**52**: Pasc 3.4
32:7	**54**: Asspt 5.12	15:32	**54**: Humb 1
32:10	**54**: OS 1.2	16:7	**51**: Adv 2.1, Circ 2.5
32:13	**51**: OEpi 5; **53**: Pent 2.7	17	**53**: 4 p P 1
		17:33	**53**: 4 p P 3
32:14	**53**: 4 p P 2; **54**: OS 4.3	17:34-35	**53**: 4 p P 2
		17:37	**53**: 4 p P 3
32:15	**54**: Mart 2 (2x)	17:38-39	**53**: 4 p P 3
32:27	**54**: In lab mess 3.7, NatBVM 14	17:39	**53**: 4 p P 3
		17:40	**53**: 4 p P 3
32:29	**53**: PP 2.7, PP 2.8	17:49	**52**: Ann 3.2; **53**: 4 p P 4
32:31	**54**: In lab mess 1.3	17:51	**53**: 4 p P 5
32:43	**51**: Adv 1.4	18:30	**51**: VNat 1.4

19:5	**54**: Mal 6	26:21	**54**: Ded 3.3

Second Samuel (1 Sam)
2:3   **51**: Adv 5.3; **53**: Asc 1.3
3:10   **51**: SP 6; **54**: NatBVM 14
7:3   **51**: VNat 4.1
13:14   **51**: Nat 5.5
15:23   **52**: Pasc 3.4
15:32   **54**: Humb 1
16:7   **51**: Adv 2.1, Circ 2.5
17   **53**: 4 p P 1
17:33   **53**: 4 p P 3
17:34–35   **53**: 4 p P 2
17:37   **53**: 4 p P 3
17:38–39   **53**: 4 p P 3
17:39   **53**: 4 p P 3
17:40   **53**: 4 p P 3
17:49   **52**: Ann 3.2; **53**: 4 p P 4
17:51   **53**: 4 p P 5
18:30   **51**: VNat 1.4
19:5   **54**: Mal 6

First Kings (1 Kgs)
1:20   **53**: Pent 2.4
2:8   **54**: 1 Nov 1.4
3:9   **51**: Adv 7.1
3:9–11   **54**: NatBVM 7
3:26   **51**: VNat 6.11
8:27   **54**: Asspt 1.3
17:5–6   **54**: Ded 2.4
17:38–39   **54**: Ded 2.4
19:4   **54**: 1 Nov 5.9
19:7   **51**: Adv 1.6
19:7–8   **51**: P Epi 1.5
19:8   **52**: Quad 3.2; **54**: Ded 3.2
21:7   **54**: Mal 7
22:14   **54**: Asspt 3.3

Second Kings (2 Kgs)
1:14   **54**: Ded 5.2
1:26   **54**: Humb 6
2:8   **54**: Mal 8
2:9   **53**: Asc 6.14 (2x)
2:9–10   **53**: Asc 3.5
2:10   **53**: Asc 6.14
2:11   **52**: Quad 3.2; **53**: Asc 6.9; **54**: Mal 8
4:2   **53**: JB 12
4:3   **53**: Asc 3.7
4:3–6   **53**: Asc 6.8
4:6   **53**: Asc 3.7
4:35   **52**: Pasc 1.7, Pasc 1 (alt).7
4:40–41   **53**: Pent 2.6
5:10   **52**: Pasc 3.1
7:2   **54**: Ded 2.1
16:5   **52**: Pur 3.2
16:5–13   **54**: In lab mess 1.4
16:15   **52**: Pasc 1.2, Pasc 1 (alt).2
22:1   **51**: Epi 2.2

First Chronicles (1 Chr)
22:9   **51**: Epi 2.2; **52**: Ann 1 (alt).11; **54**: Ded 5.9
25:8   **51**: Adv 4.3
29:15   **51**: Adv 6.4

Second Chronicles (2 Chr)
6:41   **54**: Mich 1.1
23:7   **52**: Pur 3.1

Ezra (Ezra)
3:4   **52**: Sept 1.4
3:18   **52**: Pur 2.2
9:4   **52**: Res 1.2, Res 1 (alt).2

Nehemiah (Neh) [2 Esdras]
8:10   **54**: OS 4.4, Ded 5.10

Tobit (Tob)
1:3   **53**: PP 3.2
4:16   **53**: Pent 3.7; **54**: OS 1.14
13:11 **51**: Epi 3.3
13:22 **51**:VNat 1.4

Judith (Jdt)
8:22   **51**: Circ 1.1
16:5   **53**:Asc 3.5
19   **52**: Pur 2.2

Esther (Esth)
13:9   **54**: Ded 5.7

Job
1:3   **54**:Abb 1
1:11   **54**: Clem 2
1:17   **52**: OPasc 1.7
2:4   **54**: Clem 2
2:10   **52**: Quad 1.1; **54**: OAsspt 4
3:1   **51**:VNat 3.2
3:3   **51**:VNat 2.2
3:5   **53**:Asc 6.7
3:9   **51**: Adv 1.3
3:24   **52**: Sept 2.3
3:26   **51**: Epi 1.7
4:12   **54**:Asspt 3.7
4:18   **52**:Ann 1 (alt).13; **54**: 1 Nov 2.5, 1 Nov 5.9
4:19   **51**:VNat 6.7; **54**: Asspt 3.1, OS 2.2
4:18   **52**:Ann 1 (alt).13
5:7   **54**: In lab mess 2.1
5:13   **51**: Adv 2.1; **54**: Clem 1

5:24   **54**: Mich 1.4
6:3   **54**: Humb 6
6:9-10 **54**: Humb 6
6:10   **54**: Humb 6
6:13   **54**: Humb 6
6:14   **52**:Ann 3.9
7:1   **54**: OS 3.2, OS 5.3, OS 5.4, And 2.6
7:17   **51**: Adv 1.7, Epi 1.2; **54**: Ded 5.3, Ded 5.5, Ded 5.7
7:18   **52**: Palm 2.1
7:19   **52**: Sept 1.3; **54**: NatBVM 2
8:22   **52**: Ben 11
9:24   **54**: 1 Nov 2.1
10:21 **54**: OS 4.1
10:22 **53**:Asc 6.7
13:35 **53**: PP 2.1
14:1   **52**: 4 HM 6
14:2   **51**:VNat 6.10; **52**: Pur 2.3; **53**:JB 3; **54**: OAsspt 3, 1 Nov 3.3
14:4   **51**:VNat 4.2,VNat 4.5, Nat 1.1, Nat 1.7, P Epi 2.6; **52**: Ann 1.1, Ann 1.13, 4 HM 6, 5 HM 2; **53**: Pent 2.1; **54**: OS 1.13, OS 3.2
14:13 **54**: OS 4.1
14:14 **54**:And 1.3
15:15 **51**:VNat 4.8
15:31 **51**: Adv 1.3
17:2   **53**:Asc 4.5
19:23 **53**:Asc 4.7
22:22 **53**:Asc 4.10
23:11 **52**: 4 HM 11
26:13 **51**:VNat 1.5; **53**: Pent 2.3

28:18	**51**: Nat 3.2	4:7	**53**: Pent 2.6; **54**: OS 2.4
28:28	**51**: Nat 4.2		
31:19-20	**52**: Palm 1.4	4:8	**52**: Pasc 1 (alt).8; **54**: OS 2.4
33:6	**53**:VPP 3		
38:8	**54**: Mal 4	4:9	**54**: OS 2.4, Ded 4.5
40:12	**52**: Pasc 1.17	4:9-10	**54**: OS 2.6
41:1-2	**52**: Ann 1.12	5:8	**54**: Asspt 4.5
41:6-8	**54**: Asspt 5.10		
41:25	**52**: Quad 2.1	**Proverbs (Prov)**	
41:34	**51**:VNat 4.9	1:2	**53**: Asc 6.15
42:10	**51**:VNat 2.6; **54**: OS 1.10	1:10	**52**: Pasc 1 (alt).2
		1:17	**54**: And 1.3
		1:30	**54**: NatBVM 8
Psalms (Pss)		1:32	**52**: Palm 2.2, Palm 3.2
1:1	**54**: In lab mess 3.8, OS 5.1	2:11	**53**: 6 p P 1.4
1:2	**53**: Asc 4.10, Asc 6.7	2:14	**51**:VNat 3.3 **52**: Quad 2.3, Ann 3.3; **53**:VPP 1, 6 p P 1.1
1:3	**51**:VNat 2.1; **52**: Ben 4 (2x)		
1:4	**51**: Adv 6.5, Nat 2.2, Circ 2.1; **52**: Ben 1.1, Ann 1 (alt).8; **53**:VPP 1, 6 p P 1.1, 6 p P 1.3; **54**: Mich 2.2, 1 Nov 2.1	3:15	**54**: OS 1.4
		3:16	**51**: Adv 4.1, VNat 1.5, VNat 4.2; **52**: Pasc 1 (alt).14
		3:17	**51**: Adv 1.11
		3:18	**54**: And 1.2
		3:32	**54**: In lab mess 3.9
1:5	**51**: Adv 4.3	3:34	**51**:VNat 4.6, VNat 4.9, Nat 4.2
2:1	**51**: SP 8		
2:2	**54**: Asspt 5.10	4:23	**54**: Asspt 2.2, VAnd 1
2:8	**51**:VNat 2.7; **52**: Pasc 1 (alt).3	4:37	**52**: Ann 1.5
		5:15-17	**52**: Pur 1.2
2:8-9	**52**: Pasc 1.9	5:16-17	**54**: NatBVM 3
2:9	**53**: PP 3.3	5:20	**52**: Pasc 2.2
2:11	**52**: Palm 2.5	6:3	**53**: Rog 1
2:12	**52**: Palm 2.5; **54**: Asspt 4.4, Mart 6, Humb 8	6:19	**54**: Ded 3.3
		6:27	**52**: Pasc 2.2
		7:18	**51**: Circ 3.7
4:3	**53**: Asc 4.4, Asc 4.8	8:31	**54**: Ded 6.3
4:4	**53**: Asc 4.8, Asc 4.9	9:1	**51**: Adv 3.4, Adv 3.7
4:5	**53**: PP 3.4; **54**: In lab mess 1.4, OS 2.6	9:10	**54**: Ded 1.4
		10:28	**53**: Pent 2.1

11:26	**53**: 6 p P 2.1	31:19	**51**: P Epi 1.5; **53**: Asc 6.7
12:3 (LXX)	**52**: Pur 1.4, Ben 3		
12:7	**54**: Ded 4.3	31:21	**51**:VNat 2.1,VNat 2.5; **54**: OS 3.1
12:16	**51**: Adv 1.4		
12:23	**54**: 1 Nov 5.5	31:26	**54**: Mal 3
13	**51**:VNat 1.2	31:31	**54**: OS 2.4
13:1	**52**: Ann 1.6		
13:4	**51**:VNat 5.2	**Ecclesiastes (Eccl)**	
13:14	**51**: P Epi 2.8	1:2	**53**: JB 7
14:13	**52**: Palm 2.1; **53**:VPP 3	1:3	**53**: JB 7
		1:4	**53**: 4 p P 3
14:27	**51**: P Epi 1.4; **54**: Ded 1.4	1:7	**51**:VNat 3.6; **52**: Quad 1.3
16:4	**53**: Pent 3.4	1:8	**51**:VNat 5.2
16:32	**51**: Circ 3.9	1:14	**53**: Asc 6.2; **54**: Asspt 4.1, OS 1.2
18:3	**54**: Asspt 4.4		
18:17	**54**:VAnd 1	1:18	**51**:VNat 3.4; **54**: OS 4.5
18:19	**52**: Quad 4.2		
20:9	**54**: OS 2.2, Ded 2.4	2:14	**54**: Mart 14
20:23	**51**: Adv 4.5	3:1	**51**: Adv 6.3
21:20	**54**: OS 1.5	3:18-19	**53**: Asc 4.12
22:28	**51**:VNat 3.6	4:8	**53**: 6 p P 1.3
23:1	**51**: Nat 3.1; **54**: Mart 12, Clem 4	4:10	**51**: Circ 3.6; **54**: 1 Nov 5.6
23:1-2	**54**: Mart 18, Clem 4	4:12	**52**: Ann 1.8, Ann 1 (alt).8, 4 HM 5; **53**: PP 2.8, 6 p P 2.6; **54**: NatBVM 9, Mich 1.4, Mart 3, Clem 5
23:2	**54**: Mart 12		
25:27	**51**: Nat 1.2; **54**: 1 Nov 5.8, OS 3.4		
26:11	**51**:VNat 5.1		
26:15	**52**: Pasc 2.11		
26:16	**53**: 6 p P 2.6	7:3	**52**: Palm 2.2; **54**: OS 1.10
27:2	**51**: Nat 3.2; **54**: OS 5.4		
		7:4	**52**: Quad 1.4
28:9	**51**: Epi 3.5	7:7	**52**: Palm 2.2
29:11	**54**: OAsspt 11	7:30	**53**: 6 p P 3.1; **54**: Mart 4
30:30	**52**: Pasc 1.9, Pasc 1 (alt).9		
		9:1	**52**: Sept 1.1; **53**: Asc 2.5; **54**: OS 5.2, Ded 5.7
31:10	**52**: Quad 1.1; **54**: Asspt 2.9, NatBVM 4		
		10:1	**52**: 4 HM 6
31:18	**54**: Asspt 2.9	10:4	**52**: Ben 4

11:30	**54**: OS 5.2	2:12	**51**: VNat 1.1, Nat 1.3; **52**: Ann 3.7; **54**: OAsspt 11, Nat BVM 15, NatBVM 16
12:7	**52**: Ann 1 (alt).9		
12:12	**51**: Epi 3.6		

Song of Songs (Song)

1:1	**54**: Asspt 1.4, Asspt 4.7	2:14	**53**: Pent 1.5; **54**: Asspt 3.7, OS 1.4
1:2	**52**: 4 HM 14; **54**: NatBVM 5 (2x)	2:15	**54**: NatBVM 15
1:3	**51**: VNat 1.2, Circ 1.4; **52**: Quad 1.3; **54**: In lab mess 3.4, Asspt 1.1, Abb 2, Ded 6.2, Mal 8	2:16	**51**: Adv 2.3; **52**: Ann 3.7; **54**: NatBVM 15, NatBVM 16 (2x)
		2:17	**54**: NatBVM 16, NatBVM 17
1:3-4	**54**: Mal 8		
1:4	**53**: Asc 2.6 (2x), Asc 4.9	3:2	**53**: Pent 3.1
		3:4	**52**: 4 HM 14; **54**: OAsspt 5, NatBVM 5, NatBVM 10, 1 Nov 5.2
1:6	**53**: PP 2.3; **54**: NatBVM 2, NatBVM 13, 1 Nov 5.2, Ded 6.2		
		3:6	**54**: Asspt 4.1, Ded 1.4
1:7	**51**: Adv 1.11	3:10	**54**: 1 Nov 5.12
1:12	**51**: VNat 3.1	3:11	**51**: VNat 6.11, Epi 2.1; **54**: OAsspt 6
2:1	**51**: Adv 2.4; **52**: Ann 3.7	4:1	**54**: Mart 5
2:2	**54**: NatBVM 17, Mart 5	4:7	**54**: Mart 5
		4:9	**51**: VNat 3.1
2:3	**53**: 6 p P 2.6; **54**: NatBVM 2	4:11	**54**: Asspt 4.1
		4:12	**54**: NatBVM 9
2:4	**53**: Pent 3.1, 6 p P 1.2	4:12-16	**54**: NatBVM 6
2:6	**51**: Adv 4.1, VNat 4.1; **54**: OAsspt 7, OS 4.2	4:15	**54**: NatBVM 3
		4:16	**54**: Asspt 2.2
		5:1	**54**: NatBVM 3, Mart 16
2:8	**51**: Adv 1.11; **53**: Asc 4.6, Asc 4.11; **54**: Mich 1.2	5:2	**52**: Sept 2.1; **54**: Asspt 5.6
2:9	**51**: VNat 4.10, P Epi 1.1; **53**: JB 2	5:3	**51**: P Epi 1.3; **52**: Pasc 1.15
2:10	**54**: Asspt 3.5	5:6	**51**: VNat 1.1, VNat 6.1; **54**: In lab mess 3.1, NatBVM 16
2:11	**54**: 1 Nov 4.1		
2:11-12	**54**: 1 Nov 1.3		

5:10	**51**: Adv 2.4; **52**: Pasc 1.5	3:5	**53**: Asc 3.9
		3:6	**54**: 1 Nov 2.3
5:16	**51**: P Epi 2.1; **54**: OS 1.4	3:7	**51**: Adv 4.3; **54**: Asspt 4.1
6:3	**51**: Circ 3.6	4:1	**51**: VNat 4.2
6:9	**54**: Asspt 2.9, NatBVM 9, NatBVM 11	4:10	**54**: Humb 7
		4:11	**53**: Asc 3.2, Asc 6.9
		4:13	**51**: Circ 3.10
6:12	**52**: Ann 3.10; **54**: NatBVM 15	4:15	**52**: Ann 3.10
		5:6	**53**: PP 1.4
8:1	**51**: Epi 2.1	5:21	**51**: Epi 2.3
8:5	**51**: VNat 5.5; **54**: Asspt 4.1, OAsspt 15, NatBVM 6, OS 1.2	6:7	**51**: SP 3; **53**: Asc 4.5
		6:20	**54**: In lab mess 3.5, NatBVM 9
		7:6	**51**: Epi 3.3
8:6	**51**: Adv 5.3; **52**: Ann 1.12; **53**: Asc 6.15, Pent 3.1; **54**: Asspt 4.2, Abb 5, 1 Nov 1.2, Ded 5.9, And 1.6, And 1.10, And 2.4	7:13	**53**: 6 p P 2.1
		7:22	**52**: Quad 2.5
		7:26	**51**: VNat 4.9, P Epi 2.1
		7:30	**52**: 4 HM 8, Pasc 1.1; **53**: Asc 6.9
		8:1	**51**: Adv 1.9, Nat 1.2, SP 7; **52**: Pasc 1.1; **54**: OS 3.2, Ded 6.2
8:7	**54**: Abb 5		
Wisdom (Wis)			
1:1	**53**: Pent 3.4; **54**: In lab mess 3.9, OS 1.13	9:15	**51**: VNat 2.3; **52**: Pur 1.4, Sept 1.5, Sept 2.2, 4 HM 14; **53**: Rog 2, Asc 2.3, Asc 3.1, Asc 6.2, Asc 6.9; **54**: Asspt 3.1, Mart 3
1:3	**53**: Pent 3.6		
1:4	**53**: Pent 3.5		
1:5	**54**: Asspt 2.5		
1:6	**52**: OPasc 2.4		
1.7	**54**: 1 Nov 1.2	10:12	**54**: Clem 3
1:13	**54**: In lab mess 2.1	11:20	**52**: Sept 1.3
2:16	**53**: PP 2.6	11:21	**51**: Circ 1.1; **52**: Palm 3.1
2:20	**51**: VNat 4.3; **52**: 4 HM 3		
		11:23	**52**: Ann 3.5; **54**: 1 Nov 3.2
2:24	**54**: In lab mess 2.1, Clem 1		
		11:24	**53**: 6 p P 2.2; **54**: Ded 6.2
3.2	**53**: PP 2.5; **54**: Mal 5		

12:18	**51**:VNat 6.1; **53**: Pent 2.8; **54**: 1 Nov 3.4	17:12	**54**: 1 Nov 3.3
		18:17	**52**: Adv 4.6
		18:30	**52**: Ben 8
16:13	**53**: PP 2.4, 6 p P 2.3; **54**: Mal 4	19:2	**53**: Pent 3.1
		19:23	**51**:VNat 6.5
16:20	**52**: Ben 10, Ann 3.1; **53**: 6 p P 2.1	20:30	**51**: Nat 2.5
		20:31	**51**: Nat 2.5
16:33	**54**: Mal 4	22:2	**53**: PP 2.3, 4 p P 2
18:15	**51**:VNat 1.5	23:5	**53**: 4 p P 2; **54**: In lab mess 2.2
19:16	**53**: Asc 6.2		
		24:5	**52**: Ann 1 (alt).13
Sirach (Sir) [Ecclesiasticus]		24:11	**51**: Adv 2.1; **54**: OS 3.3
1:5	**54**: NatBVM 10		
1:16	**51**: P Epi 2.8	24:27	**53**: Asc 3.9; **54**: And 2.4
1:27	**53**: PP 2.6		
1:33	**54**: Asspt 5.6	24:29	**53**: 6 p P 2.6; **54**: In lab mess 3.4, NatBVM 5, OS 1.10, And 2.4
2:10	**51**: Circ 3.9		
2:14	**54**: In lab mess 3.9		
3:22	**54**: 1 Nov 5.12		
3:30	**51**: P Epi 2.9	24:45	**51**: Adv 1.6
3:33	**51**: P Epi 2.9	25:1	**52**: Quad 1.5 **53**: 6 p P 1.2
6:32	**54**: OAsspt 15		
7:40	**53**: PP 2.6; **54**: OS 1.10	27:12	**53**: JB 3; **54**: Asspt 2.2, OAsspt 3, OAsspt 4
10:9	**51**: Adv 1.2		
10:13	**51**: Adv 1.3	30:24	**54**: In lab mess 2.1
10:15	**51**: Adv 1.3; **54**: And 2.7	31:8–9	**54**: OS 1.15
		34:28	**51**:VNat 3.4
11:25	**52**: Palm 2.1, Palm 2.2	34:30	**51**:VNat 3.4
11:30	**54**: Humb 5	35:17–21	**53**: Asc 5.1
14:5	**52**: Ann 1 (alt).8	35:21	**51**: Adv 1.10, Epi 3.5 **52**: Quad 4.2; **54**: NatBVM 5, NatBVM 9
14:22	**51**: Nat 1.5		
15:1	**51**: Adv 5.2; **54**: And 1.8		
15:3	**51**: Nat 1.5, P Epi 2.8 **52**: Ann 2.4; **53**: 6 p P 1.4; **54**: Ded 1.4, Clem 6	36:1	**53**: Asc 3.6; **54**: Asspt 4.3
		36:6	**51**:VNat 4.3, VNat 4.4
15:5	**53**: Asc 6.15	36:15	**54**: Ded 2.4
15:9	**54**:VAnd 1	36:15–18	**53**: Pent 2.4
17:5–6	**53**: Asc 6.15	36:18	**52**: Ann 1.14

38:25	**54**: Asspt 5.7	3:1	**51**: Nat 1.3
40:1	**51**: Nat 3.3; **52**: Sept 2.2, 4 HM 6, 4 HM 14	3:7	**51**:VNat 6.8; **53**: Rog 1
		3:8	**51**: Epi 1.7
40:20	**53**: Pent 3.1	3:14	**51**: Epi 2.3
42:14	**54**: Asspt 3.3	4:2	**52**: Pur 2.1; **53**: Asc 6.1, Pent 2.1; **54**: Asspt 1.2
44:10	**53**: PP 3.1, PP 3.4, PP 3.5; **54**: Asspt 4.5		
44:11	**53**: PP 3.6	4:4	**53**: Asc 2.6, Pent 2.1
44:12	**53**: PP 3.6	4:14	**51**: Adv 1.11
44:16	**53**: Asc 6.9	5:4	**51**: SP 6; **53**: Pent 2.8
45:1	**54**: Humb 2	5:7	**52**: OPasc 2.2
45:4	**51**:VNat 5.4; **54**: Mart 14, Mal 7	5:22	**53**:VPP 1
		6:1	**54**: 1 Nov 1.1, 1 Nov 1.2, 1 Nov 1.4, 1 Nov 2.3, 1 Nov 2.4, 1 Nov 4.4, 1 Nov 5.4 (3x), 1 Nov 5.5
45:7-8	**53**: Asc 3.1		
45:17	**51**: Nat 1.6		
46:8	**54**: 1 Nov 5.1		
48:9	**53**: Asc 6.9		
48:14	**51**: Circ 1.5		
50:3	**53**: Pent 2.8	6:1-2	**52**: OPasc 2.2
50:8	**54**: OAsspt 7	6:1-3	**54**: 1 Nov 5.5
51:9	**53**: Asc 6.7	6:2	**54**: 1 Nov 2.5, 1 Nov 3.1 (2x), 1 Nov 3.4, 1 Nov 4.1, 1 Nov 4.3, 1 Nov 5.6 (2x), 1 Nov 5.7, 1 Nov 5.12
51:41	**52**: Pur 1.2		
Isaiah (Isa)			
1:2	**51**:VNat 1.1		
1:3	**51**: Circ 3.2		
1:5	**52**: Pasc 1.17	6:3	**53**: Pent 1.6; **54**: NatBVM 10, 1 Nov 1.1, 1 Nov 2.1, 1 Nov 5.4
1:6	**51**: Circ 2.3; **52**: 4 HM 6; **53**: Pent 2.3		
1:13	**53**: JB 1		
1:18	**54**: NatBVM 18	6:6	**54**: OAsspt 3
1:23	**51**: Adv 1.3	7:10-12	**51**: Adv 2.1
1:66	**51**: Adv 1.5	7:12	**51**: Adv 2.1
2:2	**53**: Asc 4.6	7:13	**51**: Adv 2.1 (2x)
2:3	**53**: Asc 4.6	7:14	**51**: Adv 2.1, Nat 5.1; **54**: OAsspt 8
2:10	**51**: Circ 2.2; **54**: Asspt 4.2, OAsspt 6, Ded 1.6		
		7:14-15	**51**: Nat 3.2
		7:15	**51**: Adv 2.2
2:19	**51**: Circ 2.2	8:4	**51**:VNat 1.4
2:22	**54**: OAsspt 11	9:2	**51**: Adv 7.1, Nat 3.1;

	53: Asc 6.10; **54**: Mart 6	14:13-14	**52**: Ben 11, OPasc 2.1
9:4	**51**: Adv 6.2	14:14	**51**: Adv 1.3, VNat 4.9; **52**: Ben 11; **54**: 1 Nov 2.3, 1 Nov 3.1
9:6	**51**: Adv 2.5, VNat 4.1, VNat 5.3, VNat 6.3, VNat 6.7, VNat 6.8, Innoc 2, Circ 1.3, Circ 1.4, Epi 1.2, Epi 1.4, Epi 2.2, Quad 2.1, Palm 1.3, Pasc 4.1; **53**: Asc 4.2	15:9	**51**: Circ 2.3
		19:1	**51**: Adv 1.9; **53**: Asc 6.11
		20:3	**52**: Quad 2.6
		21:11	**51**: Adv 3.6
		21:12	**54**: In lab mess 3.9
9:7	**51**: Circ 1.5	24:2	**51**: SP 3
9:16	**52**: Quad 1.5	24:16	**54**: OAsspt 10
10:22-23	**51**: Circ 2.3	26:1	**54**: Asspt 5.5, Ded 2.4, Ded 3.1
10:27	**51**: Adv 6.2, VNat 1.2	26:7	**53**: VPP 2; **54**: Abb 2
11:1	**52**: Ann 3.7; **53**: Asc 6.1; **54**: OAsspt 8	26:9	**51**: VNat 6.1
		26:10	**54**: 1 Nov 1.1, 1 Nov 2.5, 1 Nov 5.7
11:1-2	**51**: Adv 1.11, Adv 2.4	26:18	**51**: P Epi 2.8
11:1-3	**52**: Ann 2.5	26:19	**51**: VNat 1.2, VNat 3.1
11:2	**51**: VNat 4.9; **52**: Sept 2.3; **53**: PP 2.8; **54**: And 1.10	27:1	**51**: Circ 2.3
		28:5	**51**: Epi 2.3
11:2-3	**52**: Pasc 3.6; **54**: 1 Nov 5.5	28:15	**54**: Asspt 2.3, Ded 3.3
		28:16	**51**: OEpi 1
11:2-4	**52**: OPasc 2.1; **53**: Pent 3.1	28:18	**54**: Mart 2
11:3	**51**: P Epi 2.8 **52**: Ann 2.3 (2x)	28:21	**52**: 4 HM 2
		29:13	**52**: Quad 2.2
11:4	**52**: Ann 3.6	29:15	**52**: Quad 4.3
11:5	**51**: Nat 1.4	30:5	**51**: Adv 1.1
12:3	**51**: Nat 1.6	30:20-21	**54**: Mart 8
12:4	**51**: Nat 1.6	30:26	**51**: Adv 4.3
12:6	**52**: Quad 2.1	30:27	**51**: Adv 1.6
14:12	**51**: Adv 1.2; **54**: 1 Nov 3.1, 1 Nov 3.4, 1 Nov 5.6	32:30	**52**: Ben 9
		33:5	**54**: 1 Nov 1.3
		33:7	**51**: Adv 3.5, Epi 1.1; **52**: Ann 1.10, Ann 1 (alt).10; **54**: Mich 1.5
14:12-14	**53**: Asc 4.3		
14:13	**53**: Asc 4.3; **54**: 1 Nov 2.5, 1 Nov 3.1, 1 Nov 3.4	33:15	**54**: NatBVM 18

33:17	**53**: Asc 4.13	49:6	**51**: VNat 1.4
33:22	**52**: OPasc 1.5	49:13	**51**: VNat 1.1
35:2	**54**: Humb 1	49:15	**52**: Ann 1 (alt).9
35:10	**54**: Humb 6	50:5	**53**: JB 2
38:10	**51**: VNat 2.6, P Epi 1.4; **52**: Ann 3.3; **53**: 6 p P 2.3	51:3	**51**: VNat 4.8; **52**: Palm 2.2, 4 HM 14; **54**: Asspt 1.1, OS 3.4
38:15	**53**: PP 2.7; **54**: Asspt 3.4, Asspt 4.3, OS 1.10, OS 1.14, OS 2.5, Ded 6.3	51:10	**52**: Ann 1.13
		51:13	**51**: VNat 6.8
		51:23	**53**: 6 p P 3.1
38:16	**53**: Rog 2; **54**: Mart 16	52:3	**51**: P Epi 1.3
38:17	**54**: Ded 1.5, And 2.4, Humb 1	52:6	**54**: OS 1.7
		52:7	**51**: VNat 4.8, P Epi 2.1; **54**: Mal 3
40:1	**51**: Nat 5.1		
40:5	**51**: Adv 5.1; **54**: 1 Nov 5.7	53:1	**51**: Epi 1.1
		53:2	**53**: Asc 4.9; **54**: 1 Nov 1.1, 1 Nov 5.4 (2x)
40:6	**51**: Circ 3.3, Epi 1.2; **52**: Palm 1.1; **53**: 4 p P 3	53:2-4	**52**: 4 HM 3
		53:3	**52**: 4 HM 11; **54**: Asspt 3.5, 1 Nov 5.4 (2x)
40:8	**53**: 4 p P 3		
40:9	**54**: OS 1.5		
40:17	**51**: VNat 3.2; **54**: Ded 5.4	53:4	**51**: VNat 4.3; **52**: Quad 1.2, 4 HM 3, 4 HM 11; **54**: 1 Nov 1.1, 1 Nov 1.2, 1 Nov 5.4
41:7	**52**: Quad 1.2; **54**: Ded 1.7		
42:3	**52**: Pasc 2.5		
42:7	**51**: Circ 3.4; **54**: Asspt 2.4, OS 4.1	53:5	**54**: 1 Nov 5.4
		53:7	**51**: Adv 4.7, Circ 2.1; **52**: Pur 3.2, Palm 2.3, 4 HM 2, 4 HM 4, Pasc 3.2; **53**: Pent 2.7; **54**: Mart 8
42:8	**51**: Nat 4.2; **54**: Asspt 4.5		
43:2	**52**: Quad 1.2		
45:19	**53**: Pent 1.5; **54**: In lab mess 3.9		
		53:7	**52**: Pasc 3.5
46:5	**51**: Epi 2.3	53:8	**51**: VNat 1.1; **53**: Pent 1.1; **54**: Asspt 1.4
46:8	**52**: Pasc 1.17; **53**: Rog 1		
46:12	**52**: Palm 2.7	53:12	**52**: Palm 1.1, 4 HM 3, 4 HM 4 (2x), 4 HM 8; **53**: Asc 4.6
48:9	**54**: Asspt 4.3		
48:20	**53**: Asc 2.4		
48:22	**52**: Ann 1.8, Ann 1 (alt).8	55:1	**52**: Pasc 2.7
		55:2	**51**: Adv 5.2

55:6	**52**: Quad 3.3	64:1	**51**:VNat 6.4
55:7	**51**: Epi 1.4; **52**: Ann 3.3, 4 HM 9	64:4	**51**:VNat 3.10
		64:6	**54**: 1 Nov 5.9, OS 1.11, Ded 5.3
55:9	**52**: 4 HM 9		
55:11	**52**: 4 HM 8; **54**: NatBVM 13	65:14	**54**: OS 1.10
		66:1	**53**: JB 1
55:12	**51**:VNat 1.1	66:2	**51**:VNat 6.10; **53**: Pent 3.1
57:21	**52**: Ann 1.8		
58:1	**52**: Quad 4.4		
58:2	**52**: Quad 4.4	**Jeremiah (Jer)**	
58:3	**52**: Quad 3.4; **54**: Asspt 3.5	1:5	**54**: Asspt 2.8
		1:14	**53**: 6 p P 2.5
58:5	**54**:VAnd 2	2:13	**53**: Pent 3.1
58:7	**51**: Nat 2.5	3:1	**53**: JB 11 (2x)
59:1	**53**: Asc 3.6	3:21	**54**: NatBVM 14
59:2	**54**: NatBVM 15, Mart 3	4:10	**51**: SP 3
		4:22	**52**: Ann 1 (alt).1, Palm 2.7
59:2	**51**:VNat 3.2		
59:10	**54**: Asspt 3.7	6:14	**51**: Epi 1.1
60:5	**51**:VNat 5.6; **53**: Asc 3.8	9:1	**52**: OPasc 1.8
		9:20-21	**53**: Asc 6.8
61:1	**51**:VNat 1.2,VNat 2.8; **52**: Quad 1.3	9:21	**53**: 6 p P 2.5; **54**: Ded 3.1
61:4	**51**: Adv 1.5	11:9	**51**: OEpi 1
61:7	**51**:VNat 3.5; **52**: Ben 11	13:23	**51**: P Epi 2.2
		14:9	**54**: NatBVM 3
61:10	**52**: Ann 1.6, Ann 1 (alt).1	17:9	**52**: Quad 4.3; **54**: Asspt 4.2
62:3	**51**: Epi 2.3	17:11	**54**: Humb 1
62:4	**54**: Ded 2.2	17:14	**51**:VNat 1.2
62:5	**54**: Ded 4.1	18:20	**52**: 4 HM 8
62:6	**54**: NatBVM 14, Ded 4.1	20:7	**52**: Pasc 1.12
		20:14	**51**:VNat 2.2,VNat 3.2
62:6-7	**54**: NatBVM 13 (2x), NatBVM 15, NatBVM 16	23:24	**51**: Nat 1.1; **54**: Ded 2.2
62:7	**54**: NatBVM 14, NatBVM 16	24:7	**53**: Pent 3.8
		25:11-12	**52**: Sept 1.4
63:1	**53**: Asc 2.3, Asc 2.4, Asc 3.5, JB 2	25:38	**52**: Pasc 1.9, Pasc 1 (alt).9

29:10	**52**: Sept 1.4	3:56	**51**: Epi 3.6
29:11	**52**: Ben 10, Ann 1.9;	4:1	**53**: PP 3.2
	53: Pent 2.2; **54**:	4:2	**53**: Pent 3.1
	NatBVM 10	4:4	**52**: Pasc 2.9; **54**:
30:14	**51**: Adv 1.4		Mal 1
31:2	**54**: OAsspt 6	4:5	**53**: PP 3.2; **54**: In lab
31:22	**52**: Pur 3.1		mess 2.3
33:11	**51**: VNat 1.1	4:20	**53**: Asc 3.3, Asc 6.11,
48:10	**53**: 6 p P 3.4; **54**: In		Pent 3.2; **54**:
	lab mess 3.9		NatBVM 1
48:29	**51**: Adv 1.5	4:20	**51**: Adv 1.10
50:9	**52**: Quad 4.4		
50:23	**53**: 6 p P 2.5; **54**:	**Baruch (Bar)**	
	Mal 4	3:11	**53**: PP 1.4
51:9	**52**: Pasc 4.1	3:14	**51**: VNat 1.5
		3:24	**54**: Asspt 2.1
Lamentations (Lam)		3:25	**51**: VNat 3.9
1:2	**54**: Mart 14	3:37	**52**: Ann 1.6, Palm 3.1
1:12	**52**: 4 HM 11, Pasc 1	3:38	**51**: Adv 1.6, Adv 5.1
	(alt).4	3:38	**53**: Asc 2.1, Asc 2.3,
1:13	**54**: VAnd 3		Asc 6.10, Asc 6.11,
2:13	**51**: Epi 2.3		Pent 2.7, Pent 2.8,
3:9	**53**: 6 p P 2.5		VPP 2; **54**: 1 Nov
3:15	**51**: VNat 5.2		1.2, 1 Nov 5.3
3:16	**54**: Asspt 3.7	4:36	**53**: Asc 4.7
3:22	**54**: NatBVM 8	5:5	**53**: Asc 4.7
3:25	**51**: Adv 3.3; **54**: In lab		
	mess 3.3	**Ezekiel (Ezek)**	
3:26	**51**: Nat 5.5; **54**:	1:4	**53**: 6 p P 2.5
	NatBVM 14	1:12	**54**: In lab mess 3.6
3:27-28	**53**: PP 1.5	1:24	**52**: Palm 1.3
3:28	**53**: Asc 4.12	3:7	**52**: Palm 2.7, Pasc 2.5
3:30	**52**: 4 HM 3, Pasc 1	3:26	**52**: Pasc 2.9
	(alt).3; **54**: 1 Nov	7:19	**54**: Mart 5
	5.4	7:30	**54**: Mart 4
3:40	**52**: Ann 3.3	8:8-9	**54**: Asspt 4.2
3:40-41	**53**: Asc 3.9	10:3	**52**: Ben 11
3:41	**53**: Asc 4.9, Asc 6.2,	11:19	**51**: VNat 1.1, OEpi
	Asc 6.3, Asc 6.8		1; **52**: Ann 3.2; **54**:
3:51	**52**: Quad 3.4		Ded 1.4

14:14	**52**: Palm 1.4; **54**: Asspt 3.4, Abb 1	13:8	**52**: Ann 1.8, Ann 1 (alt).8
14:20	**51**:VNat 6.8; **54**: Asspt 3.4	13:21	**52**: Ann 3.4
		13:22	**52**: Ann 1 (alt).9, Ann 3.5
16:5	**51**: Adv 1.4		
16:19	**51**:VNat 6.9	13:30	**52**: Ann 3.4
18:4	**54**: Mal 8	13:45	**53**: 4 p P 1
18:22	**51**: P Epi 1.4	13:55	**52**: Ann 1 (alt).8
18:23	**51**: Nat 5.3	13:59	**51**: P Epi 2.3; **52**: Ann 1 (alt).8
18:24	**53**: PP 3.6		
20:28	**51**:VNat 6.9	**Hosea (Hos)**	
24:6	**51**: Circ 2.1	2:7	**53**: JB 11
28:17	**54**: 1 Nov 3.3	2:19-20	**54**: Ded 5.9
33:11	**52**: Pur 3.3	6:2	**51**: Adv 1.11; **52**: Pasc 1.8, Pasc 1 (alt).8
36:21	**54**: Mart 2		
36:22	**51**:VNat 2.7	6:3	**51**:VNat 2.2 (2x)
36:26	**51**:VNat 1.1, Nat 3.3, OEpi 1	6:5	**53**:VPP 4
		7:9	**52**: Quad 2.2; **54**: Asspt 2.6
44:1-3	**54**: OAsspt 8		
44:2	**52**: Pur 3.1	10:11	**54**: Asspt 2.6
47:5	**53**: Asc 3.2	10:12	**51**:VNat 3.3; **53**: Pent 2.7
Daniel (Dan)			
1:8	**54**: Abb 1	13:14	**54**: Mal 4
1:8-16	**52**: Palm 1.4	14:6	**54**: NatBVM 17
2:43	**51**:VNat 3.9	**Joel**	
3:26	**52**: Quad 1.2	1:17	**52**: Pur 1.1, Pasc 1.9, Pasc 1 (alt).9; **54**: Asspt 6, Ded 1.2
3:52	**51**: Innoc 1		
5:13	**54**: Ded 4.6		
5:27	**54**: OS 1.11	2:12	**52**: Quad 2.2, Quad 2.4
7:9	**53**: Asc 6.1		
7:10	**52**: Ben 11, OPasc 2.2; **54**: Mich 1.2, 1 Nov 5.6	2:12-13	**52**: Quad 2.1
		2:13	**52**: Quad 2.5, Ann 1 (alt).9, Ann 3.3
9:19	**52**: Ann 1 (alt).9	2:15	**52**: Quad 4.1, Quad 4.2
9:23	**54**: Asspt 3.5, Abb 1		
12:3	**51**: Adv 1.11, VNat 3.2; **54**: Humb 6	**Amos**	
		3:8	**52**: Pasc 1.9, Pasc 1 (alt).9
13	**52**: Ann 3.1		
13:5	**51**: SP 3		

Index of Scriptural References

5:1	**53**: PP 3.3	**Haggai (Hag)**	
5:2	**52**: Pasc 1.6	1:6	**51**: Adv 4.2
6:6	**53**: 4 p P 1; **54**: Mart 13	2:8	**51**: Nat 4.1; **52**: OPasc 2.4; **54**: OS 4.1
8:11	**54**: Ded 3.2	2:15	**54**: Asspt 3.5

Jonah

Zechariah (Zech)

1:3	**52**: 4 HM 11	1:13	**53**: PP 2.3
1:12	**51**: Adv 1.4	2:10	**54**: Ded 1.3
2:11	**54**: Humb 2	3:1-3	**51**: Nat 4.1
		5:7-8	**54**: Mart 3

Micah (Mic)

1:3	**51**: Adv 1.11	6:12	**51**: Epi 1.5; **54**: OAsspt 6
1:9	**54**: In lab mess 3.8	8:19	**52**: Quad 4.2
4:1	**53**: Asc 4.6	9:9	**54**: Ded 2.2
4:2	**53**: Asc 4.6	9:10	**54**: NatBVM 14
5:2	**51**: VNat 1.4, VNat 6.7, Epi 3.4	9:11	**52**: 4 HM 11
5:5	**52**: Ann 1 (alt).11	9:17	**53**: Pent 3.1
6:8	**51**: VNat 3.4; **53**: Pent 2.8	12:10	**51**: Adv 5.1

Malachi (Mal)

7:5	**53**: 6 p P 2.5	1:6	**52**: OPasc 2.1
7:6	**53**: 6 p P 2.5	2:7	**54**: Mal 3
7:19	**51**: VNat 3.1	3:1	**53**: JB 6; **54**: Mart 12
		3:2	**51**: Adv 6.5

Nahum (Nah)

1:9	**51**: Circ 2.5	4:2	**51**: Adv 1.9, VNat 3.2, VNat 5.3, VNat 6.8, Circ 3.5, Epi 1.5, Epi 3.3; **53**: Asc 4.1; **54**: OAsspt 15, NatBVM 5, 1 Nov 3.1, 1 Nov 3.2
2:7	**51**: Circ 3.8		

Habakkuk (Hab)

2:3	**51**: SP 7; **53**: Asc 5.1, Asc 6.14
2:4	**51**: VNat 6.4
3:2	**54**: Mart 2
3:3	**54**: 1 Nov 5.9

Susanna (Sus)

1-64	**52**: Ann 3.1
5	**51**: SP 3
8	**52**: Ann 1.8, Ann 1 (alt).8

Zephaniah (Zeph)

1:15	**51**: VNat 2.2; **54**: Asspt 4.3	22	**52**: Ann 1 (alt).9
3:8	**52**: Pasc 1.4, Pasc 1 (alt).4	55	**52**: Ann 1 (alt).8

59	**51**: P Epi 2.3; **52**: Ann 1 (alt).8	2:9-10	**51**: Epi 3.4
		2:11	**51**: Nat 5.2, Epi 1.5, Epi 3.5; **54**: OAsspt 11
First Maccabees (1 Macc)			
3:3	**53**: Pent 3.1	2:13	**52**: Pasc 1.11, Pasc 1 (alt).11
3:15	**51**: Adv 7.2		
3:60	**51**: VNat 2.8; **54**: Mart 18	2:15	**51**: Epi 1.6
		2:16	**52**: OPasc 1.5
11:3	**51**: Nat 1.3	2:16-18	**52**: Palm 1.3
16:3	**51**: Epi 1.1	2:23	**51**: SP 6
		3:2	**51**: Nat 3.3; **54**: Asspt 4.4
Second Maccabees (2 Macc)			
3:32	**52**: Palm 3.5; **54**: Mal 3	3:3	**52**: Palm 2.5; **54**: 1 Nov 3.2, Mart 2
9:5	**51**: Adv. 1.4	3:4	**53**: JB 6
12:5	**52**: Ann 3.5	3:8	**54**: Ded 2.3
14:35	**53**: Asc 2.1, Asc 2.2	3:10	**52**: Ben 5
15:3	**52**: Ben 7	3:11	**54**: 1 Nov 3.2
15:14	**51**: VNat 3.6	3:13-17	**51**: Epi 2.1, Epi 3.2, SP 2; **54**: Mart 1
Matthew (Matt)			
1:2-16	**51**: Adv 1.11	3:14	**51**: Epi 2.1, OEpi 4; **53**: JB 10
1:19	**51**: Nat 4.2		
1:20	**54**: OAsspt 10	3:15	**51**: OEpi 4, OEpi 5; **52**: Palm 3.2; **54**: NatBVM 9, Mart 1
1:21	**51**: VNat 1.2, Nat 5.5, Circ 1.3, Epi 1.3		
		3:16	**51**: Epi 1.7
1:22-23	**54**: And 1.6	3:16-17	**51**: Epi 3.7; **52**: Quad 1.3
1:23	**51**: Adv 1.11, Adv 2.1, VNat 6.6, Nat 5.1; **54**: 1 Nov 5.3	3:17	**51**: Nat 5.1, Circ 3.3, Epi 1.7; **52**: Pur 1.1, Quad 1.3, Ann 3.7
2:1	**51**: VNat 6.9, Epi 1.5		
2:1-2	**51**: Epi 3.3		
2:1-12	**51**: Epi 2.1, Epi 3.2	4:2	**52**: Quad 3.2
2:2	**51**: Circ 2.2, Epi 3.3	4:3	**52**: Pasc 1.11; **53**: Asc 6.1
2:3-18	**54**: OAsspt 4		
2:4-5	**51**: Epi 3.4	4:4	**51**: VNat 6.10; **52**: Ben 12, Ann 2.4; **53**: JB 7, 6 p P 1.4; **54**: Asspt 5.5, OS 1.3, Ded 3.2
2:6	**51**: VNat 6.7		
2:7	**51**: Adv 1.10, VNat 1.5		
2:8	**51**: Adv 1.10		
2:9	**51**: Epi 3.4		

4:5-6	**52**: Pasc 1 (alt).4	5:10	**51**: Circ 1.2; **53**: Asc 4.10; **54**: OS 1.15, Mart 16
4:6	**52**: Pasc 1.11		
4:7	**51**: Circ 3.6		
4:9	**52**: Pasc 1.11, Pasc 1 (alt).11	5:13	**54**: Ded 1.4
		5:15	**53**: Asc 4.2, JB 4
4:18	**53**: PP 1.3	5:15-16	**54**: Ded 1.5
4:18-19	**54**: And 2.2	5:16	**52**: Quad 1.4; **53**: JB 4
4:19	**54**: Abb 6, And 1.3	5:17	**51**: OEpi 4; **52**: Quad 3.3
4:20	**54**: And 2.2		
4:21-22	**54**: In lab mess 3.7	5:18	**51**: VNat 1.1; **52**: Palm 3.1
5:1	**54**: NatBVM 11, OS 1.4, OS 1.5, OS 1.6 (2x)		
		5:20	**52**: Ann 3.4
		5:25	**54**: Ded 2.3
5:1-2	**53**: Asc 4.11	5:26	**54**: Humb 8
5:2	**54**: OS 1.7	5:45	**53**: Pent 3.8; **54**: OAsspt 3, 1 Nov 5.12, Ded 6.2
5:2-3	**54**: OS 1.7		
5:3	**51**: Adv 4.5, VNat 4.6, VNat 6.7, Circ 1.2; **53**: PP 2.8; **54**: OS 1.8, Mart 13		
		6:2	**53**: PP 3.6; **54**: Asspt 3.5
		6:4	**52**: OPasc 1.8; **53**: JB 3
5:3-12	**54**: Mart 16		
5:4	**51**: Adv 4.5; **53**: PP 2.8; **54**: OS 1.9	6:6	**53**: Asc 4.11
		6:9	**54**: NatBVM 1, NatBVM 3, OS 1.2, Ded 6.2
5:5	**53**: PP 2.8; **54**: NatBVM 14, OS 1.10		
		6:10	**51**: VNat 2.8; **52**: Pasc 3.5; **54**: NatBVM 3, NatBVM 14, 1 Nov 2.1, 1 Nov 5.5, Mart 17
5:6	**51**: Adv 4.5, Adv 4.7, VNat 1.6; **52**: Ann 3.1, Ann 3.5; **53**: 6 p P 3.4; **54**: OS 1.11, Mart 15		
5:6-7	**54**: OS 1.12	6:12	**51**: VNat 6.10, P Epi 1.4
5:7	**51**: Adv 4.6; **54**: OS 1.12		
		6:12-13	**51**: 5 HM 5
5:8	**51**: Adv 4.6, VNat 5.1, VNat 5.5; **54**: OS 1.13, OS 4.3, Mart 15	6:16	**51**: Adv 4.2; **52**: Quad 1.4 (2x), Quad 1.5
		6:17	**52**: Quad 1.1, Quad 1.3, Quad 1.5
5:9	**51**: Adv 4.6; **54**: OS 1.14, Mart 15	6:21	**52**: Ann 3.7; **54**: Ded 5.4, Mart 14

6:22	**51**:VNat 3.6; **54**: Asspt 3.5, Mich 2.4, Ded 4.4	9:9	**53**: 6 p P 2.4
		9:10	**54**: OS 1.6
		9:12	**51**: Circ 2.1, Epi 1.6; **54**: And 1.5
6:24	**54**: In lab mess 3.9		
6:34	**51**:VNat 6.1	9:15	**53**: Asc 1.1, Asc 2.3, Asc 3.9, Asc 6.1
7:2	**53**: PP 1.1; **54**: Abb 5		
7:6	**51**:VNat 4.6, VNat 5.1; **52**: Pasc 4.2	9:17	**51**:VNat 1.6; **53**: Asc 3.7, Pent 3.1
7:7	**54**: NatBVM 5, NatBVM 8	9:30	**52**: Pasc 3.2
		9:35	**54**: OS 1.4
7:7-8	**51**: SP 7; **53**: Asc 6.14; **54**: And 2.5	9:36	**54**: OS 1.6
		10:8	**52**: Ben 3, Palm 1.4; **53**: Asc 6.11
7:8	**53**: Rog 1; **54**: In lab mess 3.9		
		10:15	**51**:VNat 2.8
7:11	**52**: OPasc 2.5	10:22	**52**: Pasc 1.2, Pasc 1 (alt).2; **54**: OS 5.2
7:12	**52**: Quad 1.5; **53**: Pent 3.7; **54**: OS 1.14		
		10:25	**54**: Mal 4
		10:27	**51**:VNat 6.10; **53**: JB 4
7:14	**53**: Asc 2.6; **54**: Abb 2 (2x)		
		10:29	**54**: Mal 1
7:22	**53**: Asc 1.2	10:36	**53**: 6 p P 2.5
7:23	**53**: PP 3.6	11:5	**53**: Asc 2.1
7:27	**54**: Ded 2.1	11:7	**53**: JB 6; **54**: 1 Nov 3.2
7:29	**52**: Palm 3.1		
8:1	**53**: Asc 4.6	11:8	**53**: JB 6
8:3	**52**: Quad 2.1	11:9-11	**54**: Mart 12
8:8	**53**: JB 12	11:10	**53**: JB 6
8:10	**51**: Epi 3.4; **53**: 4 p P 1	11:11	**52**: Pasc 1.10, Pasc 1 (alt).10; **53**: JB 6
8:11	**51**:VNat 6.9		
8:12	**52**: Palm 2.2; **53**: 6 p P 1.2	11:12	**52**: Sept 2.3; **54**: NatBVM 16, Ded 5.2
8:19	**52**: Quad 1.2		
8:20	**51**: Adv 2.1 (2x); **52**: 4 HM 13; **53**: Asc 6.1	11:15	**52**: Sept. 1.2
		11:18	**53**: JB 6, JB 8
		11:25	**51**: Adv 1.1; **53**: PP 1.5
8:25	**53**: 6 p P 2.5	11:26	**54**: Ded 4.2
9:2	**51**: Adv 1.8	11:29	**51**: Adv 4.4, VNat 4.10, VNat 5.6, Nat 1.1, Nat 4.3, Epi 1.7; **52**: Quad
9:5	**52**: Ann 1.3		
9:6	**54**: Ded 4.2		
9:8	**53**: Asc 6.11		

Index of Scriptural References 297

	2.1, 4 HM 3, Pasc 1.3, Pasc 1 (alt).3; **53**: Asc 6.11; **54**: OAsspt 10, O Asspt 12, OS 1.9, Ded 4.3, Mart 1, Humb 2, Humb 5	13:42	**52**: Palm 2.2
		13:43	**51**: Adv 4.3; **54**: 1 Nov 3.3
		13:44	**51**: VNat 4.6, Nat 2.5, Nat 3.2
		13:46	**54**: In lab mess 3.5
		13.46-57	**54**: And 1.3
11:30	**52**: Ann 2.4, 5 HM 2; **53**: Asc 3.6, PP 3.2; **54**: OAsspt 9, Mich 2.1	13:49	**51**: Epi 2.3
		13:55	**51**: Epi 1.7
		14:4	**53**: JB 9
		14:23	**53**: Asc 4.11 (2x)
12:20	**54**: OAsspt 1	14:25	**53**: Asc 6.11; **54**: Mal 7, And 1.6
12:24	**54**: Asspt 2.2		
12:27	**52**: Pasc 1.12	14:25-26	**53**: Asc 2.1
12:29	**51**: Nat 1.4; **52**: Ann 1.12, Pasc 1 (alt).5; **53**: Pent 3.1; **54**: Asspt 2.1, Asspt 2.4	14:28-30	**53**: 4 p P 3
		14:29	**53**: PP 1.2
		14:29-30	**53**: Asc 2.3
		14:30	**53**: 4 p P 3, 6 p P 2.5
12:31-32	**54**: NatBVM 14	15:8	**51**: Adv 3.2; **52**: Quad 2.2
12:34	**54**: Mich 1.1, And 2.3		
12:39	**51**: VNat 6.11; **52**: Pasc 1.4, Pasc 1.5	15:24	**52**: Pasc 1.3, Pasc 1 (alt).4
12:39-41	**52**: Pasc 1.12	15:27	**52**: Sept 1.3; **54**: In lab mess 2.2, OAsspt 15, Mich 1.3, OS 1.2, Ded 3.2
12:40	**54**: Humb 1		
12:42	**52**: OPasc 1.5; **54**: Mal 2		
12:44	**54**: Asspt 2.2, Asspt 2.4 (2x), Asspt 2.7	15:32-38	**54**: OS 4.6
		16:1	**52**: Pasc 2.1
12:44-45	**52**: Quad 1.2; **54**: Asspt 2.5	16:4	**54**: In lab mess 3.3
		16:6	**54**: In lab mess 3.9
12:45	**52**: Pur 1.3; **53**: Asc 1.3	16:14	**54**: Mart 9
12:46	**54**: OAsspt 10	16:17	**53**: PP 1.2; **54**: Ded 5.7
13:16	**53**: Asc 1.1, Asc 6.11 (2x)		
		16:18	**53**: Pent 3.1
13:16-17	**54**: Asspt 3.7	16:19	**53**: VPP 4, PP 1.2
13:27-28	**53**: PP 2.3	16:22	**52**: Pasc 1 (alt).2; **54**: Mich 2.4
13:33	**51**: Nat 2.4 (2x)		
13:34	**52**: Quad 2.1	16:24	**51**: Epi 3.6; **52**: Pasc 1 (alt).2, Pasc 1 (alt).8; **54**: And 2.5
13:35	**54**: OS 1.7		
13:41	**51**: Adv 3.5, Epi 2.3		

16:26	**52**: Ann 2.4, Pasc 2.7	19:8	**52**: Ann 3.2; **54**: OS 5.6
16:27	**51**: VNat 3.3, Circ 3.5, OEpi 4	19:14	**51**: Innoc 2; **52**: Palm 1.3
17:1	**53**: Asc 4.7		
17:1-5	**51**: SP 2	19:16	**52**: Ann 1.3
17:2	**53**: Asc 4.7, Asc 4.11	19:21	**51**: Epi 3.6; **54**: And 1.9
17:4	**51**: VNat 6.10; **53**: Asc 4.8, Asc 4.9, Asc 6.1, 6 p P 2.5; **54**: Mart 17 (2x)	19:25	**54**: Ded 5.6
		19:27	**52**: 4 HM 12; **53**: Asc 2.3, Asc 3.4, Asc 6.11, Asc 6.12, V PP 1; **54**: In lab mess 3.7, OS 1.12, Mart 8, Mart 17
17:5	**51**: Epi 1.7 (2x); **52**: Pur 3.2		
17:6	**53**: Asc 4.9		
17:19	**54**: VAnd 4		
17:27	**53**: Asc 2.1	19:27-29	**53**: PP 1.5
18	**54**: Mart 12	19:28	**52**: Ben 11 (3x); **53**: 1 Nov 5.2
18:3	**51**: VNat 4.9, VNat 5.3, VNat 6.7; **54**: Ded 5.2		
		19:30	**54**: OAsspt 11
		20:6-7	**52**: Pur 2.2
18:6	**51**: SP 4; **52**: Palm 2.6; **54**: Mich 1.6, Mich 2.1 (2x), Mich 2.2	20:12	**54**: NatBVM 14
		20:15	**51**: Epi 1.3; **54**: OS 1.8, And 1.5
		20:16	**52**: Pur 2.1
18:7	**54**: Mich 2.1	20:22	**54**: Clem 3
18:8	**54**: Mich 2.3, Mich 2.4	20:23	**51**: Innoc 1; **52**: Ben 11
18:8-9	**54**: Mich 2.4		
18:9	**54**: Mich 2.3 (2x)	20:28	**54**: NatBVM 9, Mich 1.2
18:10	**54**: Ded 6.3, Ded 5.5, Mart 7, Mart 17		
		21:2-7	**53**: Asc 4.12
18:12	**51**: Adv 1.7, Adv 2.2; **53**: Asc 6.13, Pent 2.5	21:3	**52**: Palm 3.2
		21:5	**52**: Ann 1.14, Ann 1 (alt).14
18:16	**51**: Circ 2.3; **52**: OPasc 2.2	21:7	**53**: PP 3.6
		21:8	**52**: Ben 3 (2x)
18:17	**52**: Pasc 3.4	21:9	**52**: Pur 1.1, Palm 1.2, Palm 2.4, Palm 2.5
18:20	**53**: JB 2; **54**: NatBVM 17, Ded 6.1		
		21:13	**54**: Ded 3.3, Ded 5.8
		21:33	**54**: Asspt 5.3
18:28	**51**: Adv 3.5	21:37	**51**: Nat 5.1
19:4	**51**: Adv 1.5, Adv 3.1	21:38	**51**: VNat 1.3,

	Circ 3.4		**52**: Pasc 4.2
21:41	**52**: Pasc 1.9	24:23	**51**:VNat 3.3
22:4	**54**: OS 1.1	24:28	**53**: Asc 4.1, JB 2
22:8	**51**:VNat 2.7	24:43	**51**:VNat 3.3
22:9	**51**: P Epi 2.2	24:45	**54**: 1 Nov 5.11
22:10	**54**: 1 Nov 2.5	24:46-47	**54**: OS 3.3
22:11-12	**52**: Ann 1.7, Ann 1 (alt).7	25	**54**: Mart 12
		25:1-13	**54**: Asspt 2.9
22:12	**51**: Adv 3.3; **54**: VAnd 1	25:2	**54**: NatBVM 7, OAsspt 4
22:15	**54**: Asspt 5.10	25:3	**51**: P Epi 2.9
22:30	**54**: In lab mess 3.5, NatBVM 8	25:3-4	**54**: NatBVM 9
		25:6	**51**: Adv 4.2; **52**: Palm 2.3
22:37	**54**: Ded 3.5		
22:40	**51**:VNat 5.2	25:7-8	**54**: Mart 13
22:42-43	**52**: Ann 3.7	25:8	**51**: Adv 4.2; **52**: Quad 1.5; **54**: Asspt 2.9
22:43-44	**52**: Pasc 1.10		
22:44	**53**: Asc 6.1	25:10-12	**54**: 1 Nov 2.5
22:45	**53**: Asc 6.1	25:11-12	**54**: Asspt 2.9
23:3	**51**: SP 3	25:12	**51**: Adv 4.2
23:4	**52**: Pasc 2.11; **54**: OS 1.5	25:21	**54**: OS 3.3, Clem 1
		25:26	**52**: 4 HM 10
23:6	**51**: Nat 5.5, SP 3	25:31	**54**: 1 Nov 4.4
23:10	**53**: JB 1	25:31-36	**51**:VNat 6.9
23:11	**54**: Asspt 3.3	25:31-46	**54**: Asspt 3.6
23:15	**54**: Asspt 2.5, Ded 5.8, And 2.7	25:34	**54**: OS 4.1
		25:41	**52**: Ben 11; **54**: Mal 4
23:21	**54**: Asspt 3.3	26:7-10	**52**: Quad 1.2
23:24	**54**: Asspt 2.6	26:8	**54**: Asspt 3.2
23:25	**54**: Asspt 2.5	26:8-9	**53**: 6 p P 2.4
23:27	**54**: Asspt 2.5 (2x)	26:10	**53**: Asc 1.3
23:33	**54**: In lab mess 3.3	26:24	**52**: Ann 1.11; **53**: PP 2.1
23:35	**52**: 4 HM 11		
23:37	**51**:VNat 2.1; **54**: And 1.5	26:28	**52**: 4 HM 11
		26:31-35	**52**: Palm 3.5
24:12	**51**: Adv 1.9; **52**: Ann 3.9, Pasc 2.1	26:34	**52**: Pasc 3.6; **54**: Mich 2.1
24:21	**52**: Sept 1.4; **54**: Mart 10	26:39	**52**: Pasc 3.5; **54**: And 1.5, And 1.7
24:22	**51**: Nat 5.1, Circ 1.3;	26:42	**52**: Ann 1.14

26:44	**52**: Palm 3.4	**Mark**	
26:50	**52**: 4 HM 7	1:7	**54**: 1 Nov 3.2
26:56	**53**: Pent 1.2	1:11	**51**: SP 2
26:58	**54**: Asspt 4.9	1:26	**51**: Adv 6.2
26:67	**52**: 4 HM 3	1:41-42	**54**: And 1.6
26:69-72	**53**: Pent 1.2	2:4	**51**: VNat 6.1
26:69-74	**53**: 6 p P 2.4	2:7	**51**: Circ 1.5
26:69-75	**53**: PP 1.1	2:11	**52**: 4 HM 14
26:75	**53**: PP 3.3	2:11-12	**54**: Ded 4.4
27:5	**52**: 4 HM 4	3:29	**51**: SP 5
27:6	**51**: VNat 2.7	3:33	**51**: P Epi 2.5
27:14	**52**: 4 HM 3	4:11	**54**: OAsspt 11
27:19	**52**: Pasc 1.3	4:28	**52**: Ben 4
27:32	**52**: Ben 6	5:7	**51**: Nat 3.4
27:34	**53**: Asc 1.3	5:8	**51**: P Epi 2.1
27:35	**52**: Palm 2.4	5:9-13	**52**: Ben 5
27:38	**52**: Palm 3.3	6:20	**53**: JB 9
27:42	**52**: Pasc 1.1, Pasc 1.2, Pasc 1.3, Pasc 1.13, Pasc 1 (alt).1, Pasc 1 (alt).2, Pasc 1 (alt).4	6:39-40	**53**: 6 p P 1.3
		7:34	**53**: Asc 6.7
		7:37	**53**: JB 1
		8:1-9	**53**: 6 p P 1.1
		8:2	**53**: 6 p P 1.1 (2x)
27:46	**54**: 1 Nov 5.3	8:2-3	**51**: SP 7
27:50	**54**: OAsspt 14	8:3	**53**: 6 p P 1.3
27:51-52	**52**: 4 HM 1, 5 HM 1	8:5	**53**: 6 p P 1.4
27:52	**52**: Pasc 1.6, Pasc 1 (alt).6	8:6	**53**: 6 p P 1.2, 6 p P 2.1
		8:8	**53**: 6 p P 2.1
27:53	**54**: Asspt 1.3	8:33	**52**: Pasc 1 (alt).3; **54**: Ded 5.7
27:63	**52**: Pasc 1.12 (2x)		
27:64	**53**: Asc 4.4	8:36	**52**: Ann 2.4
27:66	**52**: Pasc 1.5, Pasc 1.12	8:38	**51**: Adv 5.1
28:1-5	**52**: Pasc 3.6	10:18	**54**: OS 1.13
28:1-7	**52**: Pasc 1 (alt).6	10:21	**54**: And 1.9
28:2	**52**: Pasc 1.5	10:27	**54**: OS 1.6, Ded 5.6
28:3	**52**: Pasc 1.5	10:29	**51**: P Epi 1.5
28:6	**52**: Pasc 2.12	10:30	**51**: P Epi 1.5; **54**: Asspt 5.11
28:18	**52**: Pasc 1.9		
28:20	**51**: VNat 4.7, VNat 4.10; **53**: JB 1; **54**: Mart 10	10:47	**51**: Circ 3.4
		10:51	**51**: SP 6
		11:9	**52**: Palm 2.5

Index of Scriptural References   301

11:24	**52**: Quad 5.5	1:28	**51**:VNat 4.3,VNat 6.11; **52**: Ann 2.1, 4 HM 6; **54**: Asspt 2.2, Asspt 4.7, OAsspt 2, OAsspt 8, OAsspt 9, OAsspt 10, NatBVM 4, NatBVM 5, NatBVM 8, NatBVM 12
12:29	**54**: Asspt 5.12		
12:30	**54**: Ded 3.5		
12:42	**52**: Pur 3.3		
14:36	**54**: And 1.7		
14:55	**52**: Ann 3.3		
14:58	**51**:VNat 3.5		
15:17-20	**54**: OS 5.9		
15:21	**54**: And 1.5		
15:26	**54**: And 2.7		
15:29	**52**: Pasc 1.1	1:29	**54**: OAsspt 9, NatBVM 8, OS 4.1
15:32	**52**: Pasc 1.1, Pasc 1 (alt).1	1:30	**51**: Adv 2.5,VNat 6.1; **54**: Asspt 4.8, OAsspt 6, NatBVM 5, NatBVM 7, NatBVM 8 (2x), Ded 2.2
15:39	**51**: Epi 2.3, Epi 2.4		
16:1	**52**: Pasc 2.3		
16:1-7	**52**: Pasc 1 (alt).6		
16:2	**53**: JB 12		
16:3	**52**: Pasc 2.12		
16:3-4	**52**: Pasc 1.5		
16:14	**53**: Asc 1.1 (2x)	1:31	**51**: Epi 1.3
16:16	**51**:VNat 3.10; **53**: Asc 1.2 (2x)	1:32	**51**: Adv 1.3,VNat 1.1,VNat 4.6, Nat 4.3
16:17	**53**: Asc 1.2		
16:17-18	**53**: Asc 1.2	1:34	**52**: Ann 1.12; **54**: Asspt 4.6, Asspt 6, OAsspt 9, OAsspt 10, NatBVM 10
16:18	**53**: Asc 1.3 (2x)		
16:19	**53**: Asc 2.3; **54**: 1 Nov 5.1, Mart 14		
		1:34-35	**52**: Ann 2.1
Luke		1:35	**51**:VNat 1.1,VNat 4.6,VNat 5.3, VNat 6.11, Nat 2.4, Innoc 1; **53**: Asc 3.3, Asc 6.11, Asc 6.12, Pent 3.1, JB 4; **54**: Asspt 2.2, Asspt 4.6, Asspt 6, OAsspt 5, OAsspt 9, OAsspt 10, OAsspt 12, OAsspt 13, NatBVM 2,
1:13-17	**53**: JB 6		
1:14	**53**: JB 6, JB 7		
1:15	**53**: JB 4, JB 6, PP 2.4; **54**: Asspt 2.8		
1:17	**51**: Adv 5.1; **54**: Mart 11, And 1.3		
1:24	**53**: JB 6		
1:25	**54**: OAsspt 13		
1:26	**52**: Ann 3.7		
1:26-35	**51**: Epi 1.3		
1:26-38	**53**: Pent 2.3		

	NatBVM 5, NatBVM 10 (2x), NatBVM 12 (2x)	1:76 1:76-77 1:77	**52**: Palm 2.5 **53**: JB 11 **53**: JB 11
1:38	**54**: OAsspt 12, OAsspt 13, Ded 2.2	1:78	**51**: VNat 4.10; **53**: Asc 6.11; **54**: Mich 1.4
1:39	**54**: OAsspt 9		
1:39-40	**54**: NatBVM 9	1:79	**51**: VNat 4.8; **52**: Palm 2.5; **54**: Asspt 4.4, Asspt 4.8, OS 4.1
1:39-56	**54**: Mart 1		
1:41	**51**: Epi 1.6; **53**: JB 4		
1:42	**51**: VNat 3.10, Nat 2.4, P Epi 2.5; **52**: Pur 3.2, Ann 3.8; **53**: Asc 6.1	2:1	**51**: Adv 1.9
		2:4	**51**: VNat 6.4
		2:4-5	**54**: OAsspt 9
1:43	**53**: JB 4; **54**: OAsspt 12, NatBVM 8, NatBVM 9, Ded 2.2	2:7	**51**: VNat 4.6, Nat 1.1, Nat 1.3, Nat 3.1, Nat 5.1, Circ 2.2, Epi 1.5, Epi 2.1; **52**: Pasc 3.1; **53**: Asc 6.13
1:44	**51**: VNat 6.5; **53**: JB 4 (2x), JB 10; **54**: OAsspt 12		
		2:8	**51**: Nat 3.5
1:45	**51**: Nat 2.4; **54**: OAsspt 12, OAsspt 13	2:8-11	**51**: Nat 5.5, Epi 1.3
		2:9-13	**51**: Nat 4.1
		2:9	**51**: Circ 2.2
1:46	**54**: In lab mess 3.7, OAsspt 12	2:10	**51**: VNat 6.8, Epi 2.2
		2:10-11	**51**: VNat 6.2
1:46-55	**54**: OAsspt 10	2:10-18	**51**: Nat 3.1
1:47	**54**: In lab mess 3.4, OAsspt 12	2:11	**51**: Nat 5.5, Circ 1.3; **54**: NatBVM 3
1:48	**51**: VNat 1.4, Nat 4.2; **52**: Ann 3.7, Ann 3.9, Palm 2.6; **53**: Pent 2.4; **54**: Asspt 4.7, Asspt 6, OAsspt 4, OAsspt 12	2:12	**51**: Nat 4.1, Nat 4.2; **54**: NatBVM 11
		2:13	**51**: Nat 3.2, Epi 2.2
		2:14	**51**: VNat 4.1, VNat 4.8, Nat 4.2, Innoc 2; **52**: Ann 1.14, Ann 2.3; **54**: And 1.8
1:49	**53**: 6 p P 2.5 (2x); **54**: In lab mess 3.7	2:15	**51**: VNat 6.7, VNat 6.10
1:56	**54**: Asspt 2.8, NatBVM 9	2:16	**51**: Nat 4.2; **54**: OAsspt 11
1:68	**54**: Asspt 2.4		

2:19	**51**:VNat 3.10; **54**: Asspt 2.8, OAsspt 11	3:23	**51**: Circ 3.7, Epi 1.7; **52**: Pur 3.3
2:21	**51**: Circ 1.1, Circ 1.3 (2x), Circ 2.1, Circ 2.2, Circ 2.3, Circ 3.5, Circ 3.11	4:15	**53**:JB 3
		4:18	**51**:VNat 1.2; **52**: Quad 1.3; **53**:Asc 6.10
		4:20	**54**: 1 Nov 3..4
2:22	**52**: Pur 3.1	4:22	**54**:And 1.1
2:22-35	**54**: OAsspt 11	4:23	**54**:Abb 5
2:22-36	**52**: Pur 1.1	4:34-35	**52**: Pasc 3.2
2:22-38	**52**: Pur 2.1	5:5	**53**: 4 p P 3
2:26	**52**: Pur 1.2, Pasc 1 (alt).11	5:6	**54**:And 1.3
		5:8	**54**:Asspt 5.12
2:28	**51**: Nat 5.2	6:1	**51**:Adv 4.7
2:29	**52**: Pur 1.2	6:12	**51**:Adv 4.7; **53**:Asc 4.11; **54**: NatBVM 11
2:34	**51**: Nat 4.1; **52**: Pasc 1.17		
2:34-35	**54**: OAsspt 13, OAsspt 14	6:17	**53**:Asc 2.1
		6:24	**51**: Nat 3.5, Nat 5.5; **54**: NatBVM 14, OS 1.7
2:37	**52**: Pur 1.4		
2:40	**51**: Circ 3.7		
2:41-52	**51**: Circ 3.7	6:25	**54**: Humb 3
2:42	**51**: P Epi 2.5	6:38	**51**:VNat 5.7; **52**: Sept 1.4, 4 HM 14; **53**:Asc 5.2, Asc 6.4, Pent 1.6; **54**:Abb 5, OS 1.2, OS 1.11, OS 4.3, Ded 4.4
2:46-51	**52**: Pasc 3.4		
2:48	**51**: Circ 2.4; **54**: OAsspt 10		
2:49	**52**: Pasc 3.5		
2:51	**51**: P Epi 2.5; **52**: Pasc 3.4		
		6:42	**51**:VNat 4.5
2:52	**54**: NatBVM 8	6:46	**54**: Ded 6.3
3:6	**51**: Nat 5.5	7:14-15	**54**: Mart 12
3:7	**53**:JB 9	7:27	**54**: 1 Nov 3.2
3:8	**51**: Adv 3.6; **52**:Ann 3.9, OPasc 2.5; **53**: JB 9	7:31	**51**:Adv 1.1
		7:36-50	**53**: 6 p P 2.4; **54**: Ded 4.3
3:9	**53**: PP 2.1, PP 2.3; **54**: Asspt 2.6	7:39	**53**: 6 p P 2.4; **54**: Asspt 3.2
3:16	**51**: Nat 2.5; **52**: Pasc 1.10, Pasc 1 (alt).10	7:47	**54**: Ded 4.3
		8:2	**54**: OAsspt 11
3:22	**51**: Epi 3.8	8:5	**52**: Ben 10

8:7	**52**: Palm 2.5		2.4 (2x), Asspt 2.7,
8:13	**54**: In lab mess 3.9		Asspt 2.9, Asspt 3.1,
8:14	**52**: Palm 2.5		Asspt 3.6, Asspt 5.1
8:44	**54**: OS 1.6	10:38-39	**54**: Asspt 5.6
9:26	**51**: Adv 5.1, Innoc 3;	10:38-42	**54**: Asspt 1.3
	52: Ann 1.8, Ann 1	10:39	**54**: Asspt 3.2
	(alt).8	10:40	**53**: 6 p P 2.4; **54**:
9:38	**54**: NatBVM 16		Asspt 2.7, Asspt 3.2
9:54	**51**: Adv 2.3		(2x), Asspt 5.7
9:56	**51**: Nat 1.3; **53**: Asc 2.4	10:41	**51**: P Epi 2.2; **54**:
9:57	**54**: OS 1.5		Asspt 3.2, Asspt 3.4,
9:58	**51**: Adv 4.7; **52**: Pasc		Asspt 3.6, Asspt 5.9,
	3.1		Ded 4.5
9:62	**52**: Pasc 1.15; **53**: PP	10:41-42	**52**: Sept 2.3
	3.2; **54**: Abb 2 (2x)	10:42	**52**: Palm 2.5; **54**:
10:1	**52**: Pur 2.2		Asspt 3.1, Asspt 3.2,
10:18	**51**: Adv 1.2; **52**: Ben		Asspt 4.5, And 1.9
	11; **53**: Asc 4.3; **54**:	11:3	**51**: VNat 6.10, Nat
	In lab mess 3.8,		1.7, P Epi 1.5; **53**:
	Asspt 2.1, 1 Nov		Asc 4.11
	3.4, 1 Nov 5.6,	11:4	**53**: Rog 1
	Ded 5.6	11:5	**53**: Rog 1
10:20	**53**: Asc 2.5	11:5-6	**51**: VNat 6.8
10:22	**54**: Asspt 5.9	11:6	**53**: Rog 1 (2x)
10:23	**51**: VNat 6.4, P Epi	11:10	**53**: Rog 1
	2.1; **53**: Asc 6.11;	11:13	**52**: OPasc 2.5; **53**:
	54: 1 Nov 1.1		Asc 3.9, Pent 2.1;
10:24	**54**: Mart 8		**54**: OS 1.2, And 2.5
10:27	**53**: JB 10; **54**: Ded 3.5	11:17	**53**: Asc 6.5; **54**: Ded
10:30	**51**: VNat 6.1; **52**: Ann		2.3
	1.7, Ann 1 (alt).7;	11:20	**54**: Ded 1.4
	53: Asc 4.4, Asc 4.8;	11:21	**51**: Circ 1.5; **52**: Ann
	54: Mart 2		1.12, Pasc 1.1,
10:33-34	**52**: Pasc 2.6		OPasc 1.2; **54**: Asspt
10:35	**52**: Sept 1.2		2.1
10:36-37	**52**: Quad 3.3	11:22	**54**: Asspt. 2.4
10:37	**51**: Adv 6.3; **53**: Asc	11:23	**51**: SP 4
	2.6, PP 3.4	11:24	**53**: Pent 2.5; **54**: OS
10:38	**54**: Asspt 1.3, Asspt		3.3
	1.4, Asspt 2.2, Asspt	11:26	**51**: Circ 1.5

11:28	**51**: Adv 5.2; **54**: OS 1.7	15:7	**54**: Ded 5.10
11:35	**54**: Ded 5.3	15:10	**52**: Ben 10; **54**: Ded 5.10
11:41	**51**: P Epi 1.4	15:14-17	**51**:VNat 6.10
11:52	**51**: Adv 1.3	15:17	**51**:VNat 6.10; **52**: Sept 1.3; **54**: Ded 5.8
12:4	**54**: Humb 1		
12:4-5	**52**: Ann 3.5		
12:6	**53**: PP 3.6	15:22	**54**: OS 3.1
12:8	**52**: OPasc 1.8	15:25-28	**52**: Pasc 1.13
12:32	**53**: Asc 5.1	15:32	**54**: In lab mess 3.2
12:35	**51**:VNat 3.6; **52**: Pur 2.2	16:8	**53**:VPP 1; **54**: Asspt 5.1
12:35-36	**53**: Asc 6.4	16:15	**52**: Pasc 1.4
12:36	**51**: P Epi 1.1	16:16	**54**: In lab mess 3.6, Mart 9
12:37	**54**: OS 4.2		
12:38-40	**51**:VNat 3.6	16:17	**54**: In lab mess 3.9
12:40	**51**:VNat 3.5	16:19	**53**: Pent 3.5, JB 6
12:47	**52**: 4 HM 10; **54**: 1 Nov 3.3, Ded 1.4	16:20	**54**: OS 1.2
		16:21	**54**: Mich 1.3, Mart 12, Humb 6
12:49	**52**: Pur 2.2; **53**: Asc 6.15, JB 3; **54**: 1 Nov 3.1, 1 Nov 3.2, 1 Nov 3.3, OS 1.3	16:22	**54**: OS 4.1
		16:24	**52**: Quad 4.1
		16:24-25	**54**: Mal 5
		16:25	**54**: OS 4.1
13:6-9	**53**: PP 2.1	16:26	**52**: Ann 1.12; **54**: OS 1.2, OS 4.1
13:7	**54**: And 1.2		
13:8	**53**: PP 2.3	17:10	**51**: Adv 3.7; **52**: Ann 1.13, Palm 3.2; **53**: Pent 2.6
13:23	**51**:VNat 3.3		
13:27	**53**: Asc 1.2		
13:32	**51**: Adv 2.1	17:15	**54**: Asspt 5.9
14:11	**51**: Nat 2.6; **53**: Asc 2.6; **54**: NatBVM 9, 1 Nov 5.10	17:17-18	**54**: Asspt 5.9
		17:22	**54**: Mart 8
		17:37	**54**: OS 4.2
14:15	**54**: NatBVM 3	18:11	**52**: Ann 1.5, Pasc 3.4
14:22	**51**:VNat 2.7	18:11-12	**52**: Quad 4.2, Ann 1.1
14:27	**54**:VAnd 4, And 1.5	18:11-14	**52**: Ann 3.10
14:29	**51**: Adv 1.9; **53**: 6 p P 1.2	18:13	**52**: Quad 4.4; **53**: Asc 6.15
14:31	**52**: Ann 1.2		
14:33	**51**: Epi 3.6	18:14	**51**: Adv 4.2; **53**: Asc 2.6
15:5	**51**:VNat 3.1		

18:38	**51**: Circ 3.4	22:53	**54**: 1 Nov 2.1
19:8	**54**: OS 1.12 (2x)	23:8	**54**: 1 Nov 1.1
19:10	**51**: Adv 4.1, VNat 1.2	23:21	**52**: 4 HM 9
		23:24	**52**: 4 HM 9
19:14-15	**52**: Pasc 1.9	23:26	**52**: Ben 6
19:17	**54**: NatBVM 13, OS 3.3, Clem 1	23:27	**52**: Palm 3.5 (2x)
		23:27-28	**52**: Pasc 2.4
19:21-22	**52**: Ben 11	23:28	**54**: And 1.1, Humb 6
19:27-28	**52**: Palm 3.1	23:33	**52**: Pasc 1.11, Pasc 1 (alt).11
19:41	**51**: Adv 4.7, VNat 2.1; **54**: Clem 6	23:34	**51**: Adv 4.7; **52**: Palm 2.3, 4 HM 8
19:42	**54**: OS 4.3		
19:44	**51**: Adv 6.1	23:42	**51**: Epi 2.3; **54**: OS 1.6
21:19	**53**: Asc 2.6; **54**: Ded 3.1, Mal 7, And 1.7	23:42-43	**54**: 1 Nov 1.2
		23:43	**52**: Palm 1.2
21:27	**53**: Asc 2.4; **54**: Humb 1	23:50	**52**: Pasc 1 (alt).8
		24:7	**53**: Asc 4.12
21:34	**53**: Asc 4.9 (2x)	24:13	**52**: Pasc 3.6
22:15	**52**: Palm 3.3, Pasc 1 (alt).4; **54**: Mal 5	24:20	**52**: 5 HM 3
		24:21	**52**: Pasc 1.11, Pasc 1 (alt).2
22:24	**54**: OAsspt 11		
22:25	**53**: Asc 4.3	24:25-27	**53**: Asc 3.3
22:28-29	**54**: 1 Nov 1.2	24:26	**51**: Epi 2.3
22:28-30	**54**: NatBVM 3	24:27	**52**: Pasc 3.6
22:29	**54**: In lab mess 2.2	24:29	**51**: Adv 7.2 (2x); **54**: Asspt 2.4, Mal 8
22:29-30	**52**: Quad 1.1		
22:30	**54**: OS 2.7	24:32	**53**: Asc 6.10
22:31	**52**: Palm 3.3	24:34	**52**: Pasc 3.6
22:33	**54**: Asspt 5.12	24:44	**52**: Ann 1.6
22:37	**51**: Circ 2.1; **52**: Ann 1.10, Palm 3.5, Pasc 1.11, Pasc 1 (alt).4; **54**: Humb 6	24:45	**52**: Pasc 3.6
		24:45-46	**53**: Asc 3.3
		24:46	**53**: Asc 4.3, Asc 4.12
		24:49	**53**: Asc 2.3, Asc 4.1, Pent 1.2, Pent 3.1; **54**: Ded 4.6
22:42	**52**: Pasc 3.3, Pasc 3.5; **54**: Asspt 3.5		
22:43	**52**: Palm 2.3, Palm 3.4; **54**: And 1.6	24:50-51	**53**: Asc 2.3
		24:51	**53**: Asc 3.4, Asc 6.15
22:44	**52**: 4 HM 8; **54**: Clem 6	**John**	
		1:1	**51**: Nat 3.1; **54**: In lab
22:48	**54**: And 2.7		

	mess 3.4, NatBVM		Mart 4
	10 (2x), Ded 5.6	1:17	**52**: Ben 10, Ann 3.2
1:1-2	**51**: Nat 2.4	1:18	**51**:VNat 2.7; **52**: 4
1:3	**54**: Asspt 1.3, And 1.6		HM 14; **53**: Asc
1:5	**51**: Adv 1.6; **52**: Pur		6.11; **54**: Mart 6
	1.2	1:19	**52**: Ann 1.3
1:6	**53**: JB 6	1:20	**53**: JB 10; **54**: 1 Nov
1:6-7	**53**: PP 2.4		3.2
1:8	**53**: JB 11 (2x); **54**:	1:26	**52**: Pur 1.2; **54**: 1
	Mart 12, Mart 13		Nov 5.3
1:8-9	**53**: JB 8	1:27	**53**: JB 10
1:9	**51**:VNat 4.9; **52**:	1:29	**51**: Adv 6.1,VNat
	Pasc 3.1		4.5, Nat 5.4, Circ
1:10	**51**: Adv 3.1		3.4, Epi 1.6; **52**: 4
1:12	**52**: OPasc 1.1; **54**: In		HM 5; **53**: Asc
	lab mess 1.1		6.11, JB 11
1:13	**52**: Sept 1.1, Palm 3.4	1:32	**51**: Epi 1.7
1:14	**51**:VNat 1.2,VNat	1:36	**51**: Circ 3.4
	1.3,VNat 4.1,VNat	1:46	**51**:VNat 1.4
	4.6,VNat 6.3,	1:48	**53**: JB 4
	VNat 6.6, Nat 1.1,	1:51	**51**: Adv 3.1; **53**: JB 1;
	Nat 2.6, Nat 3.3,		**54**: Ded 5.5
	Circ 2.3, Circ 3.2,	2:1-11	**51**: P Epi 1.1, P Epi
	Circ 3.3; **52**: Quad		2.2
	1.3, Ann 1.6, Ann	2:2-11	**51**: Epi 2.1, Epi 3.2
	2.1, 4 HM 2, 4	2:3	**51**: P Epi 1.2, P Epi
	HM 13, OPasc 2.1;		2.4; **54**: Clem 4
	53: Asc 3.3, Pent	2:3-5	**54**: OAsspt 10
	2.3; **54**: Asspt 1.3,	2:4	**51**: P Epi 2.5
	NatBVM 10, 1 Nov	2:5	**51**: P Epi 1.2
	5.6, Mart 4	2:6	**51**: P Epi 1.3, P Epi
1:15	**51**: Nat 3.2		1.5, P Epi 2.8; **54**:
1:16	**51**:VNat 5.3,VNat		Asspt 6, Clem 5
	6.1; **52**: Quad 1.2;	2:7	**51**: P Epi 2.8; **54**:
	53: JB 10 (2), JB		Clem 4
	12; **54**: Asspt 2.2,	2:7-9	**54**: And 1.6
	Asspt 5.3, Asspt 5.4,	2:9-10	**54**: Asspt 6
	OAsspt 2, NatBVM	2:11	**51**: Epi 1.8
	3, NatBVM 13,	2:15	**52**: OPasc 1.2
	1 Nov 3.2,	2:19	**51**: Nat 2.5

2:24	**54**: Ded 3.3	4:32-42	**54**: Asspt 4.4
2:25	**52**: Palm 2.3	4:34	**52**: Palm 3.4; **53**: 6 p
3:3	**54**: Mich 2.1		P 1.4; **54**: Asspt 5.5,
3:4	**54**: In lab mess 3.3		OS 1.3, Ded 3.2
3:5	**51**: OEpi 2; **54**: In	5:4	**54**: Asspt 5.9
	lab mess 3.2	5:13	**52**: Palm 3.1, Pasc 1.3
3:7	**54**: In lab mess 3.3	5:14	**51**: VNat 3.4
3:8	**51**: VNat 3.5; **53**:	5:20	**51**: Adv 1.4; **52**: Quad
	Pent 1.1; **54**: Mich		1.3, Pasc 1 (alt).4;
	2.1		**54**: NatBVM 7
3:12	**51**: Nat 1.6	5:22	**51**: Adv 2.3; **52**: Ann
3:13	**54**: Mart 4		1.11, Ann 1 (alt).11
3:14	**54**: 1 Nov 1.2	5:31	**52**: Ann 1.5
3:17	**51**: Adv 2.3, Nat 1.3,	5:34	**51**: Circ 2.3
	Epi 1.3	5:35	**51**: VNat 3.2, VNat
3:18	**52**: OPasc 1.1, O		3.5; **53**: JB 3, JB 5,
	Pasc 1.3		JB 8, JB 10; **54**: 1
3:19	**51**: Adv 7.2; **52**: Pur		Nov 3.2 (2x), Mart
	1.2		12, Mart 13
3:20	**52**: Ann 1 (alt).8; **53**:	5:36	**52**: Pasc 2.1
	6 p P 1.3	5:44	**51**: Adv 4.2; **52**: Ann
3:29	**53**: Asc 6.1, JB 8, JB		1.4; **54**: NatBVM
	10, JB 11; **54**:		14
	OAsspt 12,	6:10	**53**: 6 p P 1.2
	1 Nov 3.2	6:12	**51**: Epi 3.1; **53**: 6 p P
3:30	**53**: JB 12		2.4, PP 2.1
3:31	**54**: Mart 2	6:15	**51**: Adv 4.4; **52**: Palm
3:34	**53**: Asc 5.2, JB 10, JB		3.1
	12	6:19	**54**: Mal 7
4:11	**52**: Ann 2.1	6:27	**53**: JB 7
4:14	**51**: VNat 4.9; **54**:	6:32	**54**: OS 1.2 (2x), OS
	Clem 6		1.3
4:19	**54**: 1 Nov 4.1	6:35	**51**: VNat 6.10
4:22	**51**: VNat 1.4	6:37-38	**52**: Palm 3.4
4:23	**51**: Circ 2.3; **53**: VPP	6:38	**51**: SP 6; **52**: Pasc 3.3;
	1		**54**: 1 Nov 5.3
4:23-24	**53**: Pent 3.2	6:39	**52**: Pasc 3.5
4:24	**53**: Asc 3.3 (2x); **54**:	6:41	**51**: Circ 3.2; **54**: Asspt
	In lab mess 3.9,		5.5, OS 1.2, Ded
	OAsspt 5, 1 Nov 5.9,		3.2
	Ded 6.3, Mart 3	6:44	**54**: In lab mess 3.4

Index of Scriptural References

6:51	**51**: Adv 5.2, Circ 3.2; **52**: Palm 3.4; **53**: 6 p P 1.4		3.2, Ann 3.4
		8:9	**52**: Ann 3.4 (2x)
		8:11	**52**: Ann 3.6
6:54	**52**: Pasc 1.17	8:13	**52**: Ann 1.5
6:55	**52**: Palm 3.4	8:21	**53**: Asc 6.12
6:56	**54**: OS 1.3	8:22	**51**: Adv 1.3
6:57	**54**: OAsspt 6	8:25	**54**: Ded 5.6
6:60	**52**: Ben 12; **53**: Asc 4.11	8:29	**51**: Epi 1.7
		8:32	**51**: Adv 1.1, Adv 1.5
6:61-68	**52**: Ben 12	8:34	**52**: OPasc 2.5
6:63	**52**: Pasc 2.2, Pasc 3.6, OPasc 1.6	8:37	**51**: P Epi 1.4
		8:42	**54**: NatBVM 10, 1 Nov 5.3
6:64	**51**: P Epi 2.1; **54**: And 2.4	8:44	**51**: Adv 1.2; **52**: Ann 2.3, Pasc 1.1, O Pasc 2.1; **53**: JB 9; **54**: 1 Nov 3.1, 1 Nov 3.4
6:65	**52**: Pasc 3.5, OPasc 2.3		
6:66	**52**: Ben 12		
6:68	**52**: Ben 12 (2x); **54**: In lab mess 3.8		
		8:46	**51**: Circ 2.1; **54**: Abb 5
6:68-69	**53**: Asc 2.6		
6:69	**53**: Asc 6.11	8:47	**52**: Sept 1.1, Sept 1.2
7:1	**52**: Palm 3.1	8:50	**52**: Pasc 3.2
7:8	**52**: Ann 1 (alt).10	8:56	**51**: VNat 6.4, VNat 6:5, Circ 1.4; **52**: Pur 1.2; **54**: In lab mess 3.6
7:17	**54**: OS 3.3		
7:18	**52**: Quad 1.4, Quad 1.5, Pasc 1.1; **54**: 1 Nov 5.3		
		8:59	**52**: Palm 3.1
7:23	**51**: Adv 5.3, Nat 5.4; **52**: Palm 3.5	9:4	**51**: VNat 5.1
		9:6	**51**: VNat 4.5
7:24	**52**: Quad 5.5; **53**: JB 1, PP 2.5	9:24	**53**: Pent 1.5
		9:32	**51**: VNat 3.9
7:34	**53**: Asc 2.3	9:34	**51**: Circ 3.5
7:37	**54**: OS 5.11	10:1	**54**: 1 Nov 3.2
7:39	**53**: Pent 1.3; **54**: OAsspt 11	10:17-18	**51**: Nat 2.5
		10:18	**52**: 4 HM 4; **54**: And 1.6
8:3-11	**52**: Ann 3.1		
8:5	**52**: Ann 3.2	10:30	**52**: OPasc 1.8; **54**: 1 Nov 5.2
8:6	**52**: Ann 1.12, Ann 1 (alt).12, Ann 3.2 (2x); **54**: Ded 5.6	10:36	**52**: Pur 2.2
		10:38	**52**: Pasc 1.4
8:7	**51**: Epi 1.6; **52**: Ann	11:3	**54**: Asspt 3.7, Asspt 4.2

11:4	**51**: Nat 3.4	12:32	**51**:VNat 6.11 (2x);
11:11	**53**: PP 2.5		**52**: Pasc 1.3; **53**:
11:33	**54**: And 1.6		Asc 4.12, Asc 4.13
11:34	**54**: Asspt 3.7	12:35	**53**: Asc 6.10
11:35	**51**: Adv 4.7; **54**: Clem 6	12:38	**51**: Epi 1.1
		13:1	**52**: Palm 3.1, Palm 3.3, Pasc 1 (alt).3
11:38	**54**: Asspt 3.5		
11:38-39	**54**: Asspt 4.2	13:4-5	**52**: Palm 3.4
11:39	**52**: Pasc 1.8, Pasc 1 (alt).8, Pasc 2.3; **54**: Asspt 4.2, Asspt 4.3, Asspt 4.4 (2x)	13:7	**52**: 5 HM 4
		13:8	**52**: Palm 3.4, 5 HM 4, 5 HM 5
		13:9	**52**: 5 HM 4
11:39-43	**54**: Asspt 2.7	13:10	**52**: 5 HM 4; **53**: Pent 3.5
11:43	**53**: Asc 2.1; **54** Asspt 4.3, Asspt 4.4		
		13:12	**53**: 6 p P 2.1
11:43-44	**54**: Mart 12	13:15	**51**: Nat 1.1, Nat 4.1; **52**: Ben 11, 5 HM 4, Pasc 3.5
11:44	**54**: Asspt 4.4		
11:47	**54**: Asspt 5.10		
11:49-50	**52**: Ann 1.14	13:16	**51**: Circ 3.7
11:50	**52**: Pasc 1.1	13:18	**52**: OPasc 2.3; **54**: OS 5.2
11:51	**52**: Pasc 1.1		
11:51-52	**52**: OPasc 1.5	13:27	**52**: Pasc 1.17
11:53	**54**: Asspt 5.10	13:33	**53**: Asc 6.12
11:54	**52**: Palm 3.1	13:35	**54**: Mich 2.1, Mich 2.2
12:13	**52**: Palm 2.3, Palm 2.4, Palm 3.1		
		13:36	**53**: Asc 2.3; **54**: OS 3.2
12:14	**52**: Ben 3; **54**: And 1.5		
		13:37	**54**: Asspt 3.5
12:23	**54**: Ded 2.2	14:2	**53**: Asc 2.3, Asc 4.9 (2x)
12:24-25	**52**: Pasc 3.5		
12:25	**51**:VNat 5.5; **52**: Ben 9	14:2-3	**53**: Asc 4.1
		14:3	**52**: Pasc 1 (alt).14; **53**: Asc 4.14
12:26	**52**: Pasc 1 (alt).14; **54**: Asspt 3.3, OS 5.5		
		14:4	**53**: Asc 4.10 (2x)
12:27	**52**: Quad 4.3; **54**: And 1.5, And 1.6	14:6	**51**: OEpi 5; **52**: Sept 2.1; **53**: Asc 2.6, VPP 2
12:31	**51**: Adv 4.3, Nat 3.1; **52**: OPasc 1.2; **54**: Asspt 2.1, 1 Nov 2.1		
		14:8	**51**:VNat 4.8; **53**: JB 2
		14:8-9	**54**: OS 4.2

14:10	**54**: NatBVM 10, 1 Nov 5.2	16:5	**53**: Asc 6.15
14:12	**53**: Asc 3.5	16:6	**53**: Asc 3.4, Asc 3.8, Asc 6.12
14:16	**54**: And 1.7	16:7	**52**: Pasc 1 (alt).3, Pasc 4.2; **53**: Asc 2.3, Asc 3.4, Asc 4.1, Asc 6.12, Asc 6.13, Pent 3.2
14:16-17	**53**: Asc 6.12		
14:17	**51**: Adv 4.2; **54**: OS 2.3, Clem 5		
14:18	**53**: Asc 2.3, Asc 3.6		
14:21	**54**: OS 4.2	16:8	**53**: Pent 1.3
14:23	**51**: Adv 3.4, Adv 5.2; **53**: Asc 3.9	16:12	**52**: 5 HM 4
		16:13	**53**: Asc 3.9
14:26	**53**: Pent 1.5, Pent 2.6, Pent 2.7	16:20	**53**: Asc 3.4 (2x), Asc 3.8
14:27	**51**: VNat 4.8	16:24	**54**: OS 1.2
14:28	**54**: Asspt 1.3, 1 Nov 5.3, And 1.1	16:27	**51**: VNat 2.7
		16:28	**51**: P Epi 2.3; **52**: Ben 10
14:30	**51**: Nat 2.5		
14:31	**51**: Adv 1.4; **52**: Pasc 1 (alt).3	16:33	**52**: OPasc 1.1
		17:2	**52**: Pasc 1 (alt).3
15:1	**53**: Pent 3.1	17:3	**51**: VNat 5.6, Innoc 3; **53**: Pent 1.1; **54**: 1 Nov 1.1, OS 1.13, OS 4.2, OS 4.3
15:3	**51**: P Epi 1.4		
15:5	**54**: OAsspt 5		
15:11	**51**: VNat 5.7		
15:13	**51**: Adv 2.1, VNat 4.7; **52**: Ann 1.13, 4 HM 4, Pasc 1.3, Pasc 1 (alt).3 (2x); **53**: Rog 1; **54**: OAsspt 15	17:4	**52**: 4 HM 2, Pasc 1.3
		17:5	**53**: Asc 6.1
		17:12	**51**: Circ 1.5
		17:14	**54**: Humb 2
		17:22	**54**: OS 5.6
15:15	**52**: Ann 1.13; **53**: Asc 6.11	17:24	**52**: Pasc 1 (alt).14
		18:4	**51**: Adv 4.4
15:16	**51**: VNat 6.9	18:6	**51**: VNat 2.6
15:18	**52**: OPasc 1.1	18:18	**54**: 1 Nov 1.3
15:22	**51**: Adv 3.3	18:22	**53**: Asc 2.1
15:24	**51**: Adv 5.1, Circ 3.4	18:23	**52**: Ann 1.11
15:26	**51**: Adv 4.2; **52**: Ann 1.3, OPasc 1.6; **53**: Asc 3.9, Pent 2.1, Pent 2.6, Pent 2.7	18:27	**53**: PP 2.4
		18:36	**51**: Epi 2.2
		18:37	**51**: Adv 7.2, Epi 2.2
		19:2	**51**: Epi 2.3
		19:5	**51**: Epi 2.3

19:14	**51**: Epi 2.3	20:27	**52**: Pasc 1 (alt).14
19:15	**52**: Palm 2.4 (2x), Pasc 1.9	20:28	**54**: NatBVM 11
		20:29	**51**:VNat 6.5; **54**: In lab mess 3.7
19:17	**54**: And 1.1		
19:19-22	**52**: Pasc 1.2	21:6	**52**: Pasc 3.6
19:21-22	**52**: Pasc 1.2	21:9-17	**54**: Abb 6
19:23	**52**: Ann 1 (alt).7; **53**: Asc 2.2, Asc 2.3	21:15-17	**52**: Pasc 2.3; **53**: 6 p P 2.4; **54**: Abb 6
19:23-24	**52**: Ann 1.7	21:19-20	**51**: Innoc 1
19:24	**52**: Ann 1 (alt).7	21:22	**51**: Innoc 1
19:26	**52**: 4 HM 6; **54**: OAsspt 15		
		Acts	
19:30	**51**: Nat 1.8; **52**: 4 HM 4 (2x), Pasc 1.3	1:1	**51**: Nat 1.1; **54**: Abb 5, OS 1.5
19:34	**51**: Nat 1.8, P Epi 1.3, P Epi 2.3; **52**: OPasc 1.5; **54**: OAsspt 14, Ded 1.4, Clem 6 (2x)	1:3	**52**: Pasc 3.1, Pasc 3.6; **53**: Asc 6.10
		1:9	**52**: Pasc 3.6; **53**: Asc 2.2, Asc 3.4, Asc 3.5, Asc 4.1, Asc 6.15
19:34-35	**52**: Pasc 1.5; **54**: Clem 4		
19:35	**52**: OPasc 1.5; **54**: Mich 1.2	1:11	**53**: Asc 2.4; **54**: Humb 5
19:37	**51**: Adv 5.1	1:13-14	**54**: OAsspt 11
20:5-7	**52**: Ann 2.1	1:14	**53**: Asc 5.1, Asc 6.14, Asc 6.15
20:14-17	**53**: 6 p P 2.4		
20:17	**52**: Pasc 3.6; **53**: PP 3.6	2:1	**53**: Pent 1.6, Pent 3.8
		2:2	**52**: Quad 4.4; **53**: Asc 3.4, Asc 3.9, Asc 6.13, Asc 6.15, Pent 1.2
20:19	**51**:VNat 6.4; **52**: Pasc 1.5; **53**: Asc 6.15, Pent 1.2		
20:19-20	**52**: Pasc 3.6	2:2-3	**53**: Pent 1.6, Pent 3.1
20:20-27	**54**: NatBVM 11	2:3	**52**: Ben 10; **53**: Pent 1.2, Pent 2.7; **54**: And 2.3
20:22	**53**: Asc 6.15		
20:22-23	**53**: Pent 1.4		
20:24-25	**53**: Asc 6.13	2:5	**51**:VNat 5.2
20:25	**53**: Asc 2.4, Asc 4.6	2:7	**51**: Adv 1.2
20:25-27	**54**: NatBVM 11	2:12	**51**: Adv 1.2
20:26	**52**: Pasc 1.5; **53**: Asc 6.13	2:13	**53**: Pent 3.1
		2:23	**54**: Mal 1

2:25	**51**:VNat 6.8	9:15	**51**:VNat 4.1, SP 1; **53**: JB 4, PP 1.1, PP 3.1
2:27	**51**:Adv 1.6		
2:33	**52**: Pasc 1 (alt).14		
2:44	**53**: Pent 3.2	9:16	**53**: PP 3.1
3:18	**52**:Ann 1.6	9:31	**53**:Asc 5.1, PP 3.254: 1 Nov 5.5
3:19	**53**:Asc 1.3		
4:25	**52**: Sept 2.3	9:40	**53**: PP 1.2, PP 2.4
4:32	**52**: Sept 2.3; **53**: Pent 3.2; **54**:Asspt 5.11, 1 Nov 5.5, OS 5.6	10:34	**54**: 1 Nov 2.3, Humb 5
		10:38	**51**:Adv 1.6; **53**:Asc 2.1
4:33	**53**:Asc 1.1		
5:1-11	**53**:VPP 4	12:3-11	**53**: PP 2.4
5:11	**53**: PP 2.4	12:10	**53**: PP 1.2
5:15	**53**:Asc 3.5	12:23	**53**: Pent 1.5
5:39	**53**: PP 3.6	13:10	**54**: Ded 5.5
5:41	**53**:Asc 3.9, Pent 1.2	13:22	**51**: Nat 5.5; **52**: Quad 2.5, Ann 1.2; **54**: Humb 6
7:48	**54**: 1 Nov 1.4, Ded 2.2		
7:51	**52**: OPasc 24	13:26	**53**: PP 2.1
7:55-59	**54**: 1 Nov 5.6	13:32	**51**:VNat 1.4
7:59-60	**51**: Innoc 2	13:35	**51**:VNat 4.6,VNat 4.3,VNat 6.6, Circ 2.1
8:18-24	**53**: PP 1.2		
8:32	**51**:Adv 4.7; **52**: Palm 2.3, Pasc 3.2; **53**: Pent 2.7		
		13:36	**54**: OS 5.5
		13:47	**51**:VNat 1.4
8:33	**52**: 4 HM 3	13:48	**52**: Pur 1.2
9	**51**: SP 1	14:21	**54**: Abb 3,VAnd 2
9:1	**51**: SP 1; **53**: PP 3.11	14:22	**52**: Palm 3.5, Pasc 2.11
9:1-2	**53**: PP 1.1		
9:1-30	**53**: PP 2.4	15:9	**51**:VNat 5.5
9:3	**51**: SP 2	16:2	**51**: Circ 2.5
9:4	**51**: SP 2 (2x); **52**:Ann 1.11	17:30	**53**:Asc 6.10
		18:3	**53**: PP 1.3
9:4-6	**53**: PP 1.1	20:28	**51**:VNat 2.7
9:5	**51**: SP 5, SP 6	21:15	**51**:Adv 6.5
9:6	**53**: PP 3.1	22:7	**52**:Ann 1.11
9:6-7	**51**: SP 7	22:8	**51**: SP 6
9:9	**51**: SP 7	24:4	**53**: 6 p P 1.4
9:13	**53**: PP 3.1	24:25	**53**:Asc 6.4
9:13-14	**51**: SP 8	26:6	**51**:VNat 1.4

Romans (Rom)

1:5	**51**: Nat 1.5	3:23	**51**: Nat 1.7, Circ 3.2; **53**: PP 3.1
1:8	**51**: SP 1	3:24	**52**: Ann 1.3; **54**: Ded 5.7
1:11	**53**: Asc 6.8		
1:14	**52**: Ann 1 (alt).10; **54**: OAsspt 2	3:25	**51**: Circ 1.5
		3:28	**52**: Ann 1.3
1:16	**51**: Adv 7.2, Epi 2.4; **52**: Palm 3.2	3:34	**51**: Adv 3.7
		4:2	**51**: VNat 1.6; **54**: In lab mess 3.7, Asspt 6
1:17	**51**: VNat 1.6, VNat 6.4; **52**: Quad 5.5, OPasc 1.2; **54**: In lab mess 3.6	4:5	**53**: Pent 2.8
		4:8	**52**: Sept 1.1
		4:11	**52**: Pasc 1.11
1:19	**51**: Nat 1.2	4:15	**54**: Asspt 3.7
1:20	**51**: VNat 3.2; **53**: Asc 3.3, Pent 1.1; **54**: Asspt 5.8, 1 Nov 5.9, OS 4.4, Ded 4.2	4:17	**54**: Ded 5.4
		4:21	**52**: Ann 1.4
		4:25	**51**: Circ 1.3; **52**: Ann 1.4, 4 HM 4, Pasc 1 (alt).14, Pasc 1.16
1:21	**54**: 1 Nov 4.2, 1 Nov 5.8	5:1	**51**: VNat 2.1, Nat 5.1; **54**: OS 1.14
1:25	**54**: Ded 2.4	5:2	**53**: Asc 4.8
1:28	**54**: 1 Nov 4.2, 1 Nov 5.8	5:2-3	**53**: Pent 3.8; **54**: And 1.4
1:30	**54**: Ded 3.3	5:3	**52**: Quad 1.6
1:31	**54**: OAsspt 15, OS 5.6	5:5	**52**: Ben 10, Pasc 2.1, OPasc 1.6; **53**: Asc 4.1, Pent 1.5; **54**: Mich 1.6, And 1.9, And 2.4
1:32	**53**: JB 9		
2:4	**51**: Epi 1.4; **52**: 4 HM 9; **53**: Pent 1.1; **54**: OS 5.1		
		5:6	**51**: Circ 3.2
2:6	**53**: Asc 1.2	5:7	**51**: Adv 2.1; **52**: Ann 1 (alt).12, 4 HM 4
2:15	**52**: Quad 1.5		
2:21	**52**: Pasc 2.11	5:8	**52**: 4 HM 4; **53**: Asc 4.6
2:23	**51**: Adv 1.4; **52**: Ann 3.4	5:9	**52**: Pur 1.3
2:28-29	**51**: VNat 2.1; **52**: Pasc 1 (alt).14	5:10	**51**: Nat 5.1; **52**: Ann 1 (alt).14, 4 HM 4; **54**: OS 1.14
3:2	**51**: P Epi 2.5; **52**: 4 HM 8; **54**: Mart 8	5:12	**51**: P Epi 1.3; **52**: 4 HM 6, OPasc 2.4
3:21	**52**: 4 HM 4		

Index of Scriptural References

5:14	**51**: P Epi 1.3; **53**: Pent 2.1	6:22	**51**: VNat 5.6; **53**: PP 2.3; **54**: NatBVM 3, 1 Nov 5.5, Ded 4.3
5:15	**51**: P Epi 1.3; **52**: 4 HM 7; **54**: OAsspt 1	6:23	**52**: Ann 3.7
5:16	**52**: 4 HM 7	7:1	**53**: PP 3.6
5:20	**51**: VNat 1.5, P Epi 1.3; **52**: Pasc 3.6; **53**: 6 p P 2.4; **54**: Asspt 4.3, Nat BVM 8	7:6	**53**: Pent 3.6
		7:13	**53**: PP 1.1
		7:14	**53**: 4 p P 2
		7:17	**54**: Mal 4, Mal 8
		7:18	**54**: 1 Nov 2.2
6:1	**51**: Adv 1.5	7:20	**54**: Mal 8
6:4	**51**: Circ 3.5; **52**: Pasc 1.14, Pasc 1.18; **53**: Asc 6.3, Asc 6.4, Pent 3.6	7:21	**52**: Ann 1.8
		7:23	**52**: Ann 1.8, Ann 1 (alt).1, 4 HM 13, Pasc 2.12; **53**: Asc 4.12; **54**: NatBVM 3, Mich 2.3, 1 Nov 2.2, OS 1.9, Mart 3
6:5	**51**: Circ 2.3; **52**: 5 HM 2, Pasc 1.15; **54**: And 2.5		
6:6	**51**: Adv 5.3; **52**: 5 HM 4; **53**: Asc 6.3; **54**: Ded 1.1, And 2.5	7:23-24	**51**: VNat 6.1
		7:24	**51**: Adv 6.2, VNat 2.3, VNat 4.10; **52**: Sept 2.3; **54**: OS 2.2, OS 2.3
6:9	**52**: Pasc 1.6, Pasc 1 (alt).6	7:32	**54**: Mich 2.3
6:10	**52**: Pasc 1.6, Pasc 1.14, Pasc 1 (alt).6	8:1	**51**: Adv 6.2; **52**: Pur 1.4, 5 HM 5; **53**: Asc 1.3
6:12	**52**: OPasc 2.5; **54**: Asspt 2.3, 1 Nov 2.2, 1 Nov 5.9, Ded 4.3	8:3	**51**: Adv 2.1; **52**: 4 HM 7; **53**: Pent 2.1; **54**: 1 Nov 1.2
6:12-13	**51**: Adv 3.6, Adv 6.2 (2x)	8:4	**51**: SP 1; **52**: Pur 1.4; **54**: 1 Nov 5.12
6:13	**52**: 4 HM 7	8:5	**53**: Asc 6.13
6:14	**54**: 1 Nov 2.2	8:6-7	**51**: Nat 1.5; **52**: Ben 12
6:17	**52**: 4 HM 10	8:7	**51**: Nat 3.1
6:19	**53**: Asc 4.6; **54**: Asspt 5.7	8:8	**51**: SP 1
		8:9	**54**: Clem 6, And 2.4
6:19-21	**51**: VNat 5.2	8:10	**51**: Epi 3.6; **52**: 4 HM 14; **54**: Mart 3
6:21	**54**: Ded 4.3		

8:11	**51**: Nat 1.4; **54**: Ded 1.1, Ded 1.2, Ded 4.4	8:26-27	**53**: Pent 1.4
		8:28	**51**:VNat 6.4; **54**: In lab mess 1.1, In lab mess 1.2, In lab mess 1.3, OS 5.2, Clem 1
8:13	**52**: Pasc 2.2; **53**: 6 p P 3.4		
8:14	**54**: 1 Nov 5.8		
8:15	**51**: Innoc 2; **52**: OPasc 1.2; **53**: Pent 1.4; **54**: Mart 9	8:29	**51**:VNat 1.3; **52**: Sept 1.1, Ann 2.2, 4 HM 12, Pasc 3.5, OPasc 1.1
8:15-16	**51**: Epi 3.8		
8:16	**51**: Adv 4.2; **52**: Ann 1.1; **53**: Pent 2.6, Pent 3.8; **54**: OS 2.3, Ded 5.7	8:29-30	**54**: 1 Nov 4.4
		8:30	**51**:VNat 4.1; **54**: OS 2.1, Ded 4.6
		8:31	**51**: Adv 7.2, VNat 2.8; **52**: Pasc 1.14; **54**: In lab mess 1.3
8:17	**51**: Adv 6.3, VNat 1.2; **52**: Ann 2.2, Pasc 1.16; **53** Asc 6.4; **54**: 1 Nov 1.2, And 2.5		
		8:32	**51**: Adv 2.4, VNat 1.3; **52**: 4 HM 4; **53**: Pent 2.7
8:18	**52**: Ann 1.2; **53**: Asc 4.7 (2x); **54**: And 1.8	8:33	**51**:VNat 2.8, Epi 1.3
		8:33-34	**51**:VNat 1.2
8:20	**51**:VNat 2.4	9:1	**52**: Quad 1.5
8:21	**52**: Sept 1.4; **53**: Asc 4.8	9:4	**51**: Innoc 2
		9:5	**51**: Adv 2.5, Adv 6.5, Nat 3.5, Nat 5.5, Innoc 3; **52**: 4 HM 14, Pasc 1.18; **53**: Asc 2.6, Asc 4.14, VPP 4, 6 p P 2.6; **54**: Asspt 1.4, Asspt 4.9, OAsspt 15, 1 Nov 2.5, And 2.8, Humb 8
8:21-22	**54**: 1 Nov 2.1		
8:22	**51**:VNat 2.5		
8:23	**51**: Innoc 2; **52**: OPasc 1.1; **54**: NatBVM 1, 1 Nov 2.2, OS 2.3, OS 4.4, Ded 4.4, And 2.4		
8:26	**51**: Adv 7.2; **52**: Sept 1.5, Quad 5.5, OPasc 2.4; **53**: Pent 1.3, Pent 1.5, Pent 2.5, Pent 2.7, Pent 3.8; **54**: OS 2.3, Ded 1.5, And 2.4, And 2.5		
		9:11	**53**: Asc 2.5
		9:12	**54**: Ded 5.4
		9:15	**53**: Pent 3.8
		9:18	**51**: Nat 5.3
		9:19	**51**:VNat 1.2
		9:21	**54**: Asspt 2.4
		9:23	**53**: Asc 2.6

9:28	**51**: Circ 2.3; **52**: Ann 3.2	12:3	**51**:VNat 5.2; **54**: Asspt 3.7
9:29	**53**: Asc 4.1	12:4	**52**: Sept 2.3
9:30	**51**:VNat 1.6	12:6	**51**: SP 7; **52**: Sept 2.3
10:2	**52**: Ann 1.11, Pasc 3.4; **54**: 1 Nov 4.2	12:10	**52**: Pur 2.3
		12:11	**52**: Ann 3.9; **53**: Asc 6.7; **54**: And 1.9
10:3	**52**: Pasc 3.4		
10:5	**52**: Ann 1.14, Ann 1 (alt).14	12:15	**52**: Quad 2.3; **54**: And 1.1
10:6	**52**: Ann 1.14, Ann 1 (alt). 14	12:16	**54**: Mich 1.5
		12:17	**51**: Circ 2.5; **52**: Quad 4.2, Ben 10
10:6-7	**52**: Pasc 1.1		
10:8	**51**: Adv 1.10, Adv 5.3 (2x); **52**: Pur 1.4; **54**: Mart 10	12:19	**51**: Adv 1.2; **52**: Ann 3.6
		12:21	**52**: 4 HM 9; **53**: 6 p P 3.3
10:10	**51**:VNat 1.6; **53**: Asc 1.3		
		13:1	**51**: Adv 3.4; **53**: Asc 4.2
10:14-15	**51**: Epi 3.1		
10:15	**51**:VNat 4.8, P Epi 2.1; **54**: Mal 3	13:10	**54**: And 1.5
		13:12	**51**: Nat 5.5, P Epi 2.7; **53**:VPP 1
10:16	**51**: Epi 1.1		
10:17	**51**:VNat 4.8, SP 5	13:12-13	**51**:VNat 5.2
11:4	**54**: OS 3.1, And 1.3	13:13	**52**: Pasc 1.16; **54**: Ded 1.2
11:8	**52**: Pasc 1.10		
11:20	**51**: Circ 3:9; **52**: Quad 2.1; **54**: NatBVM 8	13:14	**51**:VNat 5.5, Epi 3.3; **53**: Asc 1.1; **54**: OAsspt 6, OS 1.1
11:33	**51**:VNat 4.1; **54**: 1 Nov 5.9, 1 Nov 5.11	14:5	**51**: Nat 1.2, Nat 1.5; **54**: 1 Nov 3.1, OS 1.8
11:34	**51**: Adv 1.2, Nat 3.3, Circ 3.5; **52**: Ann 2.2; **54**: NatBVM 10, Ded 5.7	14:9	**53**: Asc 6.3
		14:17	**52**: Pur 2.3; **54**: OS 2.3, And 1.9
		15:4	**53**: PP 2.2; **54**: In lab mess 1.1
11:36	**52**: Sept 1.1; **53**: Pent 3.2		
		15:8	**51**:VNat 6.4; **54**: Mich 1.3
12:1	**52**: Pur 2.1, Pur 3.2, Pur 3.3; **53**: Asc 4.9		
		15:13	**52**: Sept 1.2
12:2	**51**: Nat 1.5; **54**: 1 Nov 5.5	15:19	**52**: Sept 1.2
		15:30	**53**: Asc 4.9

16:4	**51**:VNat 6.11	2:2	**51**:VNat 4.7, P Epi 2.1; **54**: 1 Nov 1.2, 1 Nov 5.3
16:20	**51**: Adv 7.2; **53**: 6 p P 2.5 (2x)		
16:23	**52**: Quad 3.1	2:3	**52**: Sept 1.1
16:27	**53**: Asc 6.15	2:4	**51**: Adv 2.1
		2:6	**51**: P Epi 2.1
First Corinthians (1 Cor)		2:6-8	**53**: PP 1.5
1:4	**52**: Ann 1.6	2:8	**51**: Adv 3.3; **52**: 4 HM 10, Pasc 1.12; **54**: 1 Nov 5:11
1:7	**54**: OS 4.5, Mart 11		
1:10	**54**: Mich 1.5		
1:12	**53**: PP 3.6	2:9	**51**:VNat 3.10,VNat 4.8, Nat 2.6; **53**: Asc 4.14; **54**: Asspt 1.4, Mich 1.1, Ded 4.6, OS 4.3
1:18	**51**: Adv 7.2; **52**: Pasc 1.13; **54**: Asspt 4.1, And 2.7		
1:19	**53**: Asc 4.4, Asc 4.5		
1:20	**52**:Ann 1 (alt).10; **54**: OS 4.5	2:9-10	**54**: Mart 11
		2:10	**51**: Circ 3.5; **53**: Pent 2.8; **54**: 1 Nov 5.8, 1 Nov 5.9
1:21	**51**: Adv 7.2, Epi 1.5; **52**: Pasc 3.6; **53**:Asc 4:6		
		2:12	**51**: Circ 3.2; **52**: Ann 3.9; **53**: 6 p P 2.5; **54**: In lab mess 1.1, In lab mess 3.5, Ded 6.1, Ded 6.2, And 2.4
1:22	**52**: Pasc 1.4 (2x)		
1:23	**52**: Pasc 1.13		
1:24	**51**: Adv 7.2, Nat 1.3, Nat 3.1, Epi 1.7; **52**: Ben 3, Palm 3.2, Pasc 1 (alt).10; **53**: Asc 3.1, Asc 4.2, Asc 6.10; **54**: Asspt 5.6, Mart 8		
		2:13	**51**: Innoc 2; **52**: Ann 1 (alt).11, Palm 1.2; **54**: OS 1.1
		2:14	**51**: Nat 3.3; **52**: Ann 2.4; **54**: OAsspt 6
1:25	**52**: 4 HM 4	2:15	**52**: Palm 2.2
1:26	**51**: Nat 3.5	2:16	**54**: OS 4.2
1:27	**53**:Asc 4.4	3:1-3	**54**: Mich 1.6
1:30	**51**: Adv 5.1,VNat 5.3, OEpi 5; **52**: Pur 1.3, Ann 3.10, 4 HM 13; **54**: NatBVM 3, Ded 3.1	3:3	**54**: Mich 1.6, Mich 2.2
		3:9	**51**: SP 4; **52**: Quad 1.1
		3:10	**51**: SP 7
		3:16-17	**54**: Ded 5.8
1:31	**52**: OPasc 1.2; **54**: In lab mess 3.7, Ded 5.7	3:17	**52**: Pur 1.4; **54**: Ded 4.3

3:18	**51**: Epi 1.5; **54**: Asspt 3.4		Asspt 5.11, Mich 2.4, 1 Nov 5.2, OS 3.3, Ded 1.7
3:19	**51**: Adv 2.1, Nat 1.5, Nat 3.1; **52**: Ben 12, Pur 1.4	6:18	**51**: Nat 4.2; **52**: Pasc 2.11
4:2	**52**: Pasc 1 (alt).14; **54**: Asspt 3.5, Asspt 3.6, And 1.3	6:19	**54**: Ded 1.1
		6:20	**54**: Asspt 3.1, OS 3.3, Clem 3
4:3	**54**: Abb 6	6:20	**52**: Palm 1.4
4:3-4	**53**: JB 3	7:3	**54**: OS 1.11
4:4	**54**: Abb 6 (2x)	7:7	**54**: In lab 2.2
4:5	**51**: Adv 4.2, VNat 5.3; **54**: OS 2.4, OS 3.4, OS 5.4, Ded 4.6	7:24	**52**: Palm 2.6
		7:26	**54**: Abb 5
		7:31	**53**: Pent 3.4, 4 p P 4
		7:34	**54**: NatBVM 10
4:9	**51**: VNat 2.5; **52**: Ben 9	7:40	**51**: Epi 1.3; **52**: Pasc 3.4
		8:1	**51**: Adv 5.2; **53**: Asc 4.4, Asc 4.5; **54**: OS 4.5
4:12	**52**: Ann 3.6		
4:13	**54**: NatBVM 8		
4:15	**53**: PP 3.6	9:9	**51**: Adv 1.4; **54**: Ded 6.1
4:16	**54**: Mart 1		
5:7	**52**: Ann 2.5, Pasc 1.13	9:17	**51**: SP 8; **54**: Asspt 3.4
5:8	**51**: Adv 1.4, Adv 2.2; **52**: Pasc 1.13	9:22	**51**: VNat 5.6; **54**: OAsspt 2
5:12	**52**: Pasc 1.18	9:24	**54**: Asspt 5.9, OS 5.2
5:20	**52**: Pasc 1.6	9:26	**51**: VNat 2.8, Epi 2.4; **53**: PP 2.1
5:23	**52**: Pasc 1.6		
6:3	**52**: Ben 11	9:26-27	**54**: Asspt 2.3, OS 2.2
6:11	**51**: VNat 5.2; **53**: PP 3.1; **54**: Ded 4.3	9:27	**51**: Adv 3.6, Epi 3.6; **52**: OPasc 1.7; **54**: 1 Nov 2.2, Clem 6, And 2.7
6:15	**51**: Adv 6.1, VNat 2.7, SP 2; **52**: Quad 1.2, Pasc 2.11; **54**: Ded 1.1, Mal 3		
		10:5	**54**: 1 Nov 2.5
		10:9-10	**54**: Abb 4
6:15-19	**54**: Ded 5.8	10:12	**52**: Sept 1.1; **54**: In lab 3.8, Abb 2, OS 2.2
6:16	**51**: P Epi 2.3		
6:16-17	**510**: Nat 2.6; **54**: 1 Nov 5.5	10:13	**51**: Adv 1.5, Innoc 3, P Epi 2.6; **53**: Asc 6.14, JB 8
6:17	**52**: Ben 12, Ann 3.8, OPasc 1.8; **54**:		

10:17	**53**: 6 p P 1.4; **54**: Mich 1.5	13:10	**51**: VNat 3.5; **54**: In lab mess 3.6, NatBVM 3
10:31	**53**: Asc 1.1		
11:3	**51**: P Epi 2.1	13:12	**51**: VNat 5.3; **53**: Asc 3.3, Asc 4.2; **54**: OS 1.13, OS 4.3
11:20	**54**: And 2.7		
11:22	**54**: Humb 4		
11:20-22	**53**: JB 1	14:15	**51**: Nat 4.1; **53**: 4 p P 3
11:26	**51**: VNat 6.6; **54**: OS 4.6		
		14:19	**53**: 4 p P 4
11:27	**52**: OPasc 2.4	14:33	**53**: Asc 5.1; **54**: OS 1.4
11:29	**52**: Pasc 1.17		
11:30	**52**: Pasc 1.17	15:2	**54**: Asspt 6
11:31	**51**: Adv 3.7	15:3	**51**: Adv 4.7
12:3	**53**: 6 p P 1.3; **54**: Mich 1.6	15:8	**51**: VNat 6.11
		15:9	**53**: PP 3.1
12:4	**51**: Adv 7.1; **53**: Pent 1.3; **54**: 1 Nov 5.5	15:10	**53**: Pent 1.5, 6 p P 2.4; **54**: In lab mess 3.5
12:7	**53**: Pent 1.2; **54**: Mal 4		
		15:19	**53**: 6 p P 1.2
12:11	**53**: Pent 1.2	15:20	**51**: Nat 1.4; **52**: Pasc 1.8, Pasc 1 (alt).6
12:23-24	**53**: Asc 2.4		
12:31	**52**: Pasc 4.2	15:22	**51**: Adv 1.4, P Epi 1.3
13:1	**54**: Asspt 1.3	15:23	**52**: Pasc 1 (alt).6
13:3	**51**: Nat 2.6; **52**: OPasc 1.6; **54**: Mich 2.1, And 2.2	15:24	**51**: VNat 2.7, Circ 1.5; **52**: Palm 2.7
		15:25	**51**: Nat 2.6
13:4	**52**: 4 HM 9, Pasc 2.8; **54**: And 1.9	15:26	**51**: VNat 2.7, Nat 1.4; **52**: Ann 1.12; **54**: 1 Nov 2.2, 1 Nov 5.1, Mal 4, Humb 1
13:5	**51**: Nat 1.5; **52**: 4 HM 8; **54**: Asspt 1.3, Asspt 5.13		
		15:28	**51**: VNat 5.7; **54**: Asspt 5.5
13:6	**52**: Pasc 2.8		
13:7	**54**: Asspt 4.2, Asspt 5.13	15:32	**51**: Adv 3.3, VNat 3.5
		15:34	**52**: Pur 1.2; **54**: NatBVM 14
13:8	**52**: 4 HM 8, OPasc 1.8; **54**: 1 Nov 3.4, And 1.9		
		15:40	**54**: Mart 5
13:9	**53**: Pent 1.1; **54**: In lab mess 3.6	15:41	**54**: 1 Nov 2.3
		15:44	**52**: Ben 8, Ben 9; **53**: Asc 6.2, Pent 1.6
13:9-12	**52**: Sept 1.1		

15:45	**51**:VNat 6.3	3:5	**54**: OAsspt 1
15:45-46	**52**:Ann 1 (alt).7	3:6	**51**: P Epi 1.3; **53**: 4 p P 3
15:46	**52**: Palm 1.1		
15:47	**54**: Ded 6.3	3:10	**53**: Asc 2.4
15:49	**51**:Adv 5.3	3:15-16	**53**: Asc 6.10
15:50	**52**: OPasc 1.8; **53**: PP 2.6	3:17	**54**: Asspt 3.1, OAsspt 9, Mart 3
15:52	**51**:Adv 1.2	3:18	**53**:Asc 4.9; **54**:Asspt 3.5, Mart 6
15:53	**51**:VNat 4.4; **54**: 1 Nov 2.2, OS 4.6	4:1	**52**: Pur 1.3
15:54	**51**:VNat 3.2; **54**: Mal 3, Humb 1	4:4	**51**: Nat 2.4
		4:7	**51**:Adv 3.6; **54**: In lab mess 3.7, NatBVM 17
15:55	**52**: Pasc 1.1; **54**: Mal 4		
15:56	**52**:Ann 1 (alt).14		
		4:11	**52**: Palm 1.1
Second Corinthians (2 Cor)		4:15	**53**: Pent 3.4
1:3	**52**:Ann 1 (alt).9; **54**: OS 1.2, OS 1.10, Ded 5.4, Ded 6.2, Mart 4	4:17	**52**: Sept 1.4; **54**: OS 5.4, Ded 4.6
		4:18	**51**:VNat 6.8; **53**: JB 1; **54**: In lab mess 3.6, In lab mess 3.7, Ded 4.2, Humb 6
1:3-4	**51**: Nat 5.1		
1:5	**51**: Adv 5.1, Epi 1.1		
1:5-6	**51**:VNat 4.1	5:1	**51**:VNat 2.2; **54**: Asspt 3.1, Ded 1.6, Ded 2.1
1:6	**51**: Nat 3.5		
1:7	**53**: Asc 6.7		
1:9	**54**: Humb 3	5:4	**51**:VNat 3.5; **54**: Mal 3
1:12	**51**:Adv 4.2; **52**:Ann 1.1, Ann 1.5; **54**: Asspt 5.1, OS 2.3, VAnd 1	5:6	**54**: In lab mess 3.5, NatBVM 1, Mart 17
2:3	**54**: Humb 7	5:7	**51**:VNat 4.8; **54**: NatBVM 13, NatBVM 17
2:7	**51**:VNat 3.5		
2:10	**53**:VPP 4		
2:11	**51**: Circ 3.6; **54**: 1 Nov 5.11	5:13	**52**: Ben 9
		5:15	**53**:Asc 6.9, PP 3.5
2:14-15	**52**: Quad 1.4	5:16	**51**: P Epi 2.1; **53**:Asc 6.12; **54**: Mart 10
2:15	**53**:Asc 2.5		
2:16	**52**: Pasc 1.13, Pasc 2.3; **54**: And 1.5	5:17	**51**:Adv 5.3; **54**: Asspt 5.2
3:3	**54**: Ded 1.4	5:19	**52**: 4 HM 2

5:21	**52**: 4 HM 7		2.6, VPP 4 **54**: In
6:5	**53**: Pent 2.6		lab mess 2.1
6:7	**52**: Sept 1.5; **54**: Mal 7	11:28	**54**: Asspt 3.6
6:10	**53**: JB 7	11:29	**54**: OS 1.14
6:12-13	**54**: Ded 5.4	12:2	**52**: Quad 6.3, OPasc
6:14-15	**52**: Pasc 1.16; **54**: Mich 1.6, OS 5.11		2.2; **53**: Asc 2.6 (2x), Asc 6.14, PP 1.2; **54**: Mich 1.1
6:14-16	**53**: Asc 6.13	12:2-4	**54**: And 1.4
7:4	**53**: Asc 6.7; **54**: In lab mess 3.1, And 1.3	12:4	**52**: Ann 1.10; **54**: Ded 1.6
7:5	**52**: Ann 1.6, Ann 1 (alt).9; **54**: OS 5.3	12:6	**51**: Adv 1.7
7:8-10	**52**: Quad 1.4	12:19	**53**: Asc 4.2
7:10	**52**: Quad 2.3, Ben 12; **54**: Mal 8	12:21	**53**: PP 1.2
7:15	**52**: Sept 1.1	13:3	**53**: JB 2; **54**: In lab mess 3.4, Ded 1.2
8:2	**54**: Mal 5	13:7	**53**: Pent 1.3
8:9	**52**: Pasc 3.1; **54**: Asspt 4.1	**Galatians (Gal)**	
8:18	**51**: Nat 4.2; **54**: OS 1.2	1:4	**51**: Adv 4.7, VNat 2.2, Circ 3.6; **52**: Quad 6.1; **53**: Asc 3.9, Asc 4.7, Asc 6.10, 6 p P 1.1, 6 p P 2.5 (2x); **54**: Mich 2.1, OS 1.13
8:21	**51**: VNat 5.4		
9:2	**53**: 6 p P 1.1		
9:7	**51**: Nat 1.7; **52**: Pur 23, Quad 3.1; **54**: And 2.2		
10:1	**51**: SP 8	2:9	**54**: Mal 2
10:5	**54**: 1 Nov 2.4	2:20	**51**: Nat 1.8; **52**: Quad 6.2, Pasc 1.14; **54**: OS 5.3
10:7	**53**: JB 1, PP 25		
10:18	**52**: Pasc 3.2; **54**: OS 2.3	3:3	**52**: Ann 3.9; **54**: Mich 2.1
11:2	**51**: Circ 2.4		
11:3	**52**: Pasc 1.3	3:5	**53**: Pent 1.2
11:13	**54**: Mal 3	3:11	**51**: VNat 6.4, VNat 6.10; **52**: Quad 5.5, OPasc 1.2
11:14	**51**: Circ 3.11; **54**: Asspt 2.9		
11:23	**51**: Adv 6.5; **53**: Asc 2.1	3:20	**54**: Asspt 5.9
		3:29	**51**: VNat 2.1
11:26	**52**: Sept 1.5	4:4	**51**: Adv 1.9, Nat 5.1, Circ 2.2, Circ 3.4,
11:27	**51**: Adv 6.5; **53**: Pent		

	OEpi 3; **52**: 4 HM 6	6:8	**51**:VNat 5.3; **52**: Ben 9; **53**: Asc 6.13, JB 7
4:5	**51**: Innoc 2; **52**: Ann 2.2; **54**: In lab mess 3.3	6:9	**51**: Adv 7.1
		6:14	**51**:VNat 4.7, Circ 3.2; **52**: Quad 6.3, Pasc 1.13; **53**: Asc 4.13
4:13	**53**: Asc 2.4, Asc 4.6		
4:14	**54**: Mal 1		
4:19	**51**:VNat 6.11	6:16	**51**: Adv 5.3
4:20	**53**: 6 p P 1.1	6:17	**54**: Humb 5
4:22-24	**52**: Palm 3.2		
4:26	**53**: Asc 6.4, Asc 6.5; **54**: Ded 4.1	**Ephesians (Eph)**	
		1:3	**54**: 1 Nov 5.5
4:30	**52**: Palm 3.2; **53**: Asc 6.13	1:4	**53**: Pent 2.1
		1:5	**51**: Innoc 2; **52**: Ann 2.2
5:6	**52**: Pasc 2.1, Pasc 2.2; **53**: Asc 1.3; **54**: Asspt 5.6	1:6	**51**:VNat 6.6
		1:9	**52**: Ann 1.13, Ann 1 (alt).12
5:11	**52**: Pasc 1.13		
5:13	**51**: Adv 3.2; **53**: Asc 1.2	1:18	**51**:VNat 2.1; **52**: Quad 1.2; **53**: Asc 2.6, Asc 6.10; **54**: OS 4.3
5:16	**52**: Pur 1.4; **54**: In lab mess 3.6		
5:17	**52**: Ann 1.6, Ann 2.5; **53**: Rog 2, Asc 3.7, Asc 6.5, 6 p P 2.5; **54**: 1 Nov 2.2	1:21	**53**: PP 1.2
		1:23	**53**: Asc 2.2
		2:2	**51**: Nat 1.2; **54**: Mart 3
5:19	**54**: Asspt 5.5	2:3	**52**: Pur 1.3, Quad 1.1; **53**: Pent 2.1
5:22	**51**:VNat 2.7; **52**: Pur 2.3, Ann 3.7; **54**: Asspt 5.5		
		2:4	**51**:VNat 2.7, Nat 5.1; **52**: 4 HM 4; **53**: 6 p P 2.2, 6 p P 2.6
5:24	**51**: Epi 3.6; **53**: 6 p P 2.5		
5:25	**52**: Pur 1.4	2:8	**54**: Clem 1
6:1	**51**: Adv 3.3, Adv 7.2; **52**: Pasc 2.4; **54**: Mal 7	2:10	**52**: Pasc 2.1
		2:12	**51**:VNat 5.2; **54**: OS 1.7
6:2	**54**: OS 1.14	2:14	**51**:VNat 4.9; **52**: Pur 1.2, Ann 1.12; **53**: Pent 2.2; **54**: Mart 4, And 1.8
6:3	**54**: NatBVM 14, Abb 4, Ded 5.3		
6:7	**54**: Asspt 2.6, And 2.1		

2:17	**53**: Pent 2.2	4:15	**54**: Mal 3
2:18	**51**: Adv 2.4, Adv 2.5	4:15-16	**52**: Pasc 1 (alt).8
2:19	**52**: Quad 6.4; **54**: In lab mess 3.5, NatBVM 8, Mich 1.1, OS 3.4, Mal 5	4:16	**52**: Quad 1.2; **54**: Ded 1.7
		4:20	**53**: VPP 1
		4:22-24	**53**: Pent 3.6
2:20	**51**: OEpi 1	4:23	**51**: Nat 1.1
3:10	**51**: Epi 1.6	4:28	**54**: Asspt 5.9
3:13	**54**: Mal 5	4:30	**51**: SP 4; **52**: OPasc 2.2
3:15	**53**: Pent 2.4		
3:17	**51**: Adv 7.2, VNat 6.10; **52**: Pur 1.2, Pur 1.4 (2x), Ben 4, Ann 1.4, Pasc 2.1, OPasc 1.4; **54**: NatBVM 3, NatBVM 10, Ded 2.3	5:2	**52**: Pasc 1 (alt).3; **53**: Pent 2.7
		5:18	**53**: Pent 3.1
		5:19	**51**: Nat 4.1
		5:23	**54**: OS 1.11
		5:26-27	**51**: P Epi 1.3
		5:27	**51**: P Epi 2.6; **53**: JB 11; **54**: OS 3.1, OS 3.2, OS 3.4
3:18	**54**: Asspt 2.1, Asspt 4.8		
3:19	**54**: NatBVM 18, Mich 1.4	5:29	**51**: Circ 3.7; **53**: Asc 6.13; **54**: 1 Nov 2.2, Clem 2
4:2	**54**: Mal 1		
4:3	**52**: Pur 2.2, Sept 2.3, Quad 4.2, Ann 1.5, OPasc 2.2; **54**: Asspt 5.11, Mich 2.1	5:30	**52**: Sept 2.1
		5:31	**51**: VNat 6.3, VNat 6.11; **52**: Sept 2.1
		5:32	**51**: Adv 1.1, VNat 6.3; **52**: Ann 1 (alt).1
4:8	**51**: VNat 1.4; **54**: Asspt 1.2		
		6:11	**54**: Ded 3.2
4:9	**53**: Asc 2.6	6:12	**51**: VNat 2.2; **52**: Pasc 1.3; **53**: 6 p P 2.5; **54**: OS 5.3
4:9-10	**53**: Asc 4.1		
4:10	**51**: Adv 1.6; **53**: Asc 2.1, Asc 2.2, Asc 2.3, Asc 2.4, Asc 4.3, Asc 4.6, Asc 4.14		
		6:13	**51**: Adv 7.1
		6:14	**52**: OPasc 2.1
		6:15-17	**54**: Asspt 5.5
		6:16	**51**: P Epi 1.4; **53**: 6 p P 2.5; **54**: Asspt 3.5, Asspt 4.3
4:13	**51**: Circ 2.3; **52**: Quad 1.1; **54**: Asspt 5.2, Mart 4		
		6:16-17	**54**: Ded 2.4
4:14	**53**: 6 p P 1.3; **54**: Asspt 5.12	6:17	**52**: Quad 2.5

Philippians (Phil)

1:11	**53**: Pent 3.8
1:23	**51**: Adv 6.2, VNat 2.2, VNat 2.3, VNat 4.10; **53**: Asc 3.6, Asc 4.14; **54**: Clem 2, And 1.1
1:23-24	**54**: Mart 17
1:24	**53**: Asc 6.12
2:2	**54**: And 2.6
2:2-3	**52**: Sept 2.3
2:5-7	**52**: Ben 9
2:6	**51**: Adv 1.2; **52**: OPasc 2.1; **54**: OS 4.2
2:6-7	**51**: Nat 1.2; **52**: Pasc 4.1, OPasc 1.1
2:7	**51**: Adv 4.4, VNat 4.6, Nat 3.5, Circ 3.3; **52**: Ann 3.8, Ann 3.10, 4 HM; **53**: Asc 4.6, Asc 6.15; **54**: Asspt 4.1, NatBVM 3, 1 Nov 1.2, OS 1.6, OS 4.2
2:7-8	**51**: Nat 1.1
2:8	**52**: 4 HM 4, Pasc 1.3, Pasc 1 (alt).3 (2x); **54**: Mart 8
2:9	**51**: Circ 2.2; **53**: Asc 2.6
2:9-10	**51**: Circ 1.4
2:10-11	**53**: Asc 2.2
2:12	**54**: And 2.6
2:21	**51**: VNat 6.8, Nat 1.5; **54**: Asspt 3.5, Abb 6
2:24	**51**: Epi 3.3
3:3	**54**: Mart 6
3:6	**54**: OS 1.14, Humb 2
3:8	**54**: In lab mess 2.3, Clem 1
3:13	**51**: VNat 4.8, VNat 6.8, VNat 6.9; **52**: Pur 2.3; **53**: 6 p P 3.2; **54**: In lab mess 3.6, OS 5.2, Ded 6.3 (2x), And 1.3
3:13-14	**54**: In lab mess 1.2, OS 2.2, Humb 2
3:17	**54**: Humb 8
3:18	**52**: Pasc 1.16
3:19	**51**: Adv 3.2
3:20	**53**: Asc 4.1 (2x); **54**: In lab mess 3.6, NatBVM 9, OS 5.5, Mart 14
3:20-21	**51**: Adv 4.3, Adv 6.1; **54**: 1 Nov 2.2, OS 4.6
3:21	**51**: Nat 5.4; **52**: Pasc 1.8; **53**: Asc 2.4; **54**: OS 2.5, Humb 1
4:1	**54**: Mich 2.1 (2x)
4:3	**54**: OS 1.12
4:4	**51**: VNat 4.1, VNat 4.10
4:5	**51**: VNat 4.10
4:6	**51**: VNat 4.10
4:7	**51**: Adv 6.5, VNat 2.1, VNat 4.8; **52**: Ann 1 (alt).14; **53**: Asc 6.4; **54**: 1 Nov 5.1, OS 4.3
4:8-9	**53**: Asc 6.6
4:12	**52**: Palm 3.2
4:13	**52**: OPasc 1.2; **53**: Asc 5.2, PP 2.4; **54**: Asspt 5.12

Colossians (Col)

1:9	**53**: Asc 6.14

1:15	**51**: Nat 2.4	3:5	**53**: Asc 6.3
1:18	**51**: Nat 1.4; **53**: JB 1	3:9-10	**53**: Pent 3.6
1:20	**52**: Pur 1.3; **53**: Asc 4.13, PP 1.1; **54**: OS 1.14, Mart 4	3:12	**52**: Quad 1.3; **53**: Asc 2.3, VPP 2; **54**: Humb 5
1:24	**51**: SP 2; **52**: Palm 3.4; **54**: Humb 5	3:14	**52**: Ann 1.5; **53**: Asc 5.2; **54**: Mich 2.1 (2x), Ded 2.4
2:3	**51**: Adv 1.3; **53**: Asc 2.2; **54**: OS 1.7, Mart 4	3:16	**51**: Nat 4.1; **52**: Ann 3.9
2:4	**52**: 5 HM 3	3:25	**52**: Pur 1.2
2:9	**51**: VNat 4.1, VNat 4.9, Epi 1.2; **52**: Palm 3.2, 4 HM 2; **53**: Asc 2.2; **54**: NatBVM 3	8:9	**51**: VNat 6.7

First Thessalonians (1 Thess)

		2:5	**52**: Sept 1.5
2:13	**53**: Pent 1.4	2:13	**53**: PP 2.3
2:13-15	**54**: Mart 4	2:19	**54**: Mich 2.1
2:14	**51**: SP 2; **54**: OS 4.1, Mal 4	3:13	**52**: Ann 2.4, Ann 3.1
		4:1	**54**: Mich 2.1
		4:3	**52**: Palm 3.4
2:14-15	**53**: Asc 2.1	4:4	**54**: OS 3.3, Ded 1.1
2:15	**54**: OS 1.15	4:4-5	**53**: Pent 3.7
2:18	**51**: Epi 2.2; **53**: 4 p P 2	4:16-17	**51**: Adv 6.5
		4:17	**51**: VNat 2.3; **52**: Palm 1.2; **53**: Asc 6.2
2:19	**52**: Quad 1.2		
3:1	**51**: Adv 1.6; **53**: Asc 2.2, Asc 4.14		
		5:3	**54**: And 2.6
3:1-2	**51**: VNat 2.3; **52**: Pasc 1.18; **53**: Asc 6.3, Asc 6.4, Asc 6.5, Asc 6.8; **54**: In lab mess 3.6, OS 5.6	5:4-5	**53**: VPP 1
		5:5	**51**: VNat 5.2 (2x)
		5:7	**51**: VNat 5.2; **53**: VPP 1
		5:8	**51**: VNat 6.1
3:2	**51**: VNat 6.8; **53**: Asc 6.14	5:14	**52**: Pasc 1.2
		5:17	**51**: SP 7; **54**: And 2.5
3:3	**52**: Quad 6.2	5:19	**53**: JB 10
3:3-4	**51**: Nat 2.5		
3:4	**51**: Adv 5.1, VNat 5.3, OEpi 5; **52**: OPasc 1.4; **54**: NatBVM 3 (2x)		

Second Thessalonians (2 Thess)

		1:11	**53**: Asc 1.3
		2:4	**51**: VNat 4.9, OEpi 5

2:7	**52**: Ann 3.9; **54**: 1 Nov 2.2, Mart 9	5:9	**52**: Ann 1.13
2:8	**54**: 1 Nov 3.1	5:14	**52**: Ann 1.6
3:13	**51**: VNat 4.10	5:17	**53**: JB 7
		5:22	**51**: SP 8
		5:24	**54**: Asspt 2.6, VAnd 1
First Timothy (1 Tim)		6:5	**51**: SP 3
1:5	**54**: Abb 5, Abb 6 (3x)	6:8	**51**: Circ 2.4; **53**: JB 6; **54**: Humb 2
1:9	**54**: Asspt 4.4	6:9	**54**: Abb 3, Abb 4
1:13	**51**: SP 5; **53**: PP 3.1, PP 3.2	6:11	**52**: Ann 1.14
1:15	**51**: VNat 1.1, Nat 3.5, SP 6; **52**: Ann 1.13, 4 HM 4, O Pasc 2.3; **53**: PP 3.1; **54**: NatBVM 18, OS 2.1, Mart 1	6:16	**51**: Adv 1.8, Adv 3.1, VNat 4.8, VNat 6.3, Nat 3.3; **53**: Asc 4.1, Pent 1.1; **54**: OAsspt 3, NatBVM 10, 1 Nov 3.4
1:17	**51**: SP 8; **53**: Asc 3.2		
2:4	**51**: Innoc 3	**Titus**	
2:5	**51**: Circ 2.2; **52**: Ann 1.13, Ann 2.2; **54**: OAsspt 1, NatBVM 17, OS 1.14	1:2	**53**: Asc 6.4
		1:16	**51**: VNat 2.1, VNat 3.3
		2:11-12	**51**: Nat 4.3
2:7	**51**: SP 1	2:11-13	**51**: Nat 4.3
2:8	**53**: Asc 6.7, Asc 6.15; **54**: Mal 3	2:12	**51**: VNat 5.2, Nat 4.3; **52**: Pasc 2.11; **53**: Asc 6.8, PP 2.7
2:9	**54**: 1 Nov 2.2		
2:14	**54**: Mal 3	2:13	**51**: VNat 4.10; **52**: Pasc 1.8; **53**: 6 p P 2.6; **54**: OS 2.5, OS 3.4
3:2	**54**: Abb 5, Abb 6		
3:16	**51**: VNat 3.10, VNat 6.5, Innoc 2, Circ 2.1, Epi 2.1; **52**: 4 HM 10, Pasc 1.11, Pasc 1 (alt).11; **53**: JB 4; **54**: In lab 3.3, OS 1.7	2:14	**53**: Asc 6.7
		3:1	**52**: Ann 2.4
		3:4	**51**: Nat 1.2, Epi 3.7; **52**: Palm 3.3; **53**: Asc 1.1
4:8	**53**: PP 2.7; **54**: Asspt 2.6, OS 1.9	3:5	**51**: Nat 1.5; **52**: Ann 1.5
4:9	**51**: Nat 3.5; **52**: 4 HM 4	3:6	**53**: Pent 2.8
		3:7	**53**: Asc 6.4

Hebrews (Heb)

1:1	**51**:VNat 6.4, Epi 1.1, SP 3; **52**:Ann 1.6; **53**:Asc 3.1; **54**: 1 Nov 1.2, OS 1.7, Mart 8
1:3	**51**: Nat 2.4, Circ 2.1, Circ 3.3, P Epi 1.3; **52**: Pur 3.2; **53**: JB 12; **54**: In lab 3.4, And 1.6
1:4	**51**:VNat 6.2; **54**: Asspt 3.7, NatBVM 12, Mich 1.2
1:5	**54**: NatBVM 12
1:6	**54**: 1 Nov 5.2
1:9	**51**:VNat 6.1; **52**: 4 HM 8; **54**: Asspt 2.9
1:12	**51**: Epi 1.6
1:14	**51**:VNat 2.6; **52**: Ben 11, OPasc 2.2; **54**: Mich 1.1, Mich 1.2, 1 Nov 5.11, OS 5.2, Ded 4.2, Ded 5.5, Ded 5.6, Mart 7, Mart 17
2:7	**51**: Nat 2.4, Circ 2.1; **52**: Pur 1.3; **54**: Mich 1.2
2:9	**51**: Nat 2.4, Circ 2.1, Circ 3.3; **52**: Pur 1.3, Ann 3.8; **54**: Asspt 4.1, Mich 1.2, 1 Nov 1.2
2:10	**51**: Adv 1.6
2:14	**52**: Pasc 1.1
2:16	**54**: NatBVM 12
2:17	**54**: NatBVM 7, OAsspt 1
2:18	**52**: Pur 2.2
3:11	
4:3	
4:9	
4:11	
4:12	
4:15	
4:16	
5:2	
5:7	
5:8	
5:11	
5:12	
5:14	
6:5	
6:7-8	
7:4	
7:24	
9:2-3	
9:10	
9:11	
9:11-12	
9:12	
9:14	
9:15-17	
9:19	
9:28	

3:11	**54**: 1 Nov 5.2
4:3	**52**: Palm 3.5
4:9	**54**:VAnd 2
4:11	**54**: Asspt 2.1
4:12	**51**: Nat 3.5, SP 6; **52**: Ann 1.11, Ann 3.2, Pasc 2.11; **53**: Asc 6.7, Pent 2.8; **54**: OAsspt 15, Mart 1
4:15	**52**: Palm 3.1, 4 HM 11; **54**: NatBVM 7
4:16	**53**: JB 12
5:2	**53**: Asc 4.6; **54**: Ded 4.6, Clem 3
5:7	**51**:VNat 3.10; **52**: 4 HM 9; **54**: NatBVM 7
5:8	**54**: OAsspt 1, Mart 6
5:11	**54**: OS 4.1
5:12	**51**: P Epi 2.1; **52**: Ann 3.1, Pasc 4.2; **54**: Mich 1.4
5:14	**51**: Circ 3.10, P Epi 2.1
6:5	**53**: Asc 6.10
6:7-8	**53**: PP 2.1
7:4	**51**: Adv 1.2
7:24	**54**: Asspt 3.3
9:2-3	**53**: Asc 3.8
9:10	**51**:VNat 5.1
9:11	**53**: Asc 6.1; **54**: Ded 1.4
9:11-12	**51**:VNat 3.5
9:12	**51**: SP 2; **52**: Pur 3.2
9:14	**51**: Adv 4.4; **54**: Asspt 2.8, Mich 1.3
9:15-17	**54**: Ded 5.5
9:19	**53**: JB 11
9:28	**52**: 4 HM 10; **53**: Asc 6.1

10:7	**52**: Ann 1.14, Ann 1 (alt).14; **53**: Rog 2	13:17	**51**: Adv 3.6; **54**: NatBVM 14
10:31	**52**: Ann 3.5; **53**: JB 8, PP 1.1; **54**: Ded 6.2	**James (Jas)**	
10:37	**51**: SP 7	1:6	**51**: Epi 3.3; **53**: Pent 1.4; **54**: And 2.5
11:6	**51**: VNat 5.4; **52**: OPasc 1.3; **53**: Asc 1.2, Asc 3.5; **54**: Ded 5.2	1:8	**54**: In lab mess 3.9
		1:14	**52**: Pur 1.3, Ann 1.8, Ann 1 (alt).8; **53**: Asc 3.7
11:13	**54**: Ded 4.6		
11:13-14	**51**: Epi 1.1; **54**: Mart 5	1:15	**54**: Mal 3
11:26	**53**: PP 2.2	1:17	**52**: Ann 1.10, Ann 1 (alt).10, Pasc 2.9; **53**: PP 2.7; **54**: 1 Asspt 1.2, Nov 3.4, Mart 4, And 2.3
11:33	**52**: OPasc 1.2		
11:34	**54**: Ded 1.2		
11:39	**51**: VNat 6.5		
11:40	**51**: VNat 2.5; **53**: VPP 2; **54**: OS 3.1, Ded 5.5, Mal 1	1:18	**54**: In lab mess 3.3, In lab mess 3.4
12:7	**53**: Asc 2.6	1:19	**51**: Epi 1.7; **54**: OAsspt 11, Mart 1
12:9	**53**: Pent 2.4, Pent 3.7; **54**: Mart 3, Mart 4, Mart 9	1:21	**51**: Adv 1.1, Nat 1.1; **53**: PP 2.8; **54**: OS 1.11
12:13	**52**: Ben 7		
12:14	**52**: Quad 4.2, Ann 1.5; **53**: Pent 3.5; **54**: Ded 5.9	1:23-24	**53**: 6 p P 1.1
		1:27	**52**: Quad 6.1
		2:17	**52**: Pasc 2.1, OPasc 1.3
12:15	**52**: Quad 1.1; **53**: PP 2.3		
		2:18	**52**: Pasc 2.1
12:22	**52**: Palm 1.2; **53**: Asc 5.2; **54**: Asspt 4.8	2:19	**52**: OPasc 1.3
		2:20	**51**: VNat 3.3; **52**: Pasc 2.1, OPasc 1.3
12:23	**54**: OS 5.6		
12:24	**52**: Ann 1.4	2:26	**52**: Pur 2.2, Pasc 2.12
12:29	**54**: OAsspt 1, OAsspt 5	3:2	**51**: Nat 1.7, Circ 2.5; **52**: 5 HM 4; **54**: Mich 2.4, VAnd 1, Humb 3
13:8	**51**: VNat 6.3; **52**: Pur 1.2; **54**: Mart 10		
		3:5-12	**51**: P Epi 2.7
13:9	**54**: Asspt 5:12	3:8	**52**: Pasc 2.9
13:13	**53**: 6 p P 1.1	3:17	**51**: Nat 1.5; **52**: Pasc 3.5
13:14	**52**: Quad 6.1; **54**: Asspt 1.1, Humb 2		

4:2	**51**:VNat 2.4		**54**: Mich 1.4, Mich
4:4	**52**: Pur 1.4		2.2, 1 Nov 1.4,
4:6	**51**:VNat 4.6, Nat		Ded 1.6
	4.2, Circ 3.9; **52**:	2:6	**52**: Pur 1.3
	Ben 4, Ann 3.9	2:8	**54**: Ded 6.3
4:7	**52**: Pur 1.4; **54**: Ded	2:9	**54**: In lab mess 3.2
	3.5	2:11	**52**: Quad 6.1 (2x); **53**:
4:14	**53**:JB 7		Asc 4.12
4:15	**54**: Clem 1	2:17	**52**: Quad 4.2
4:16	**51**:VNat 4.9	2:21	**53**:VPP 3
4:17	**52**: Ann 1.6, Ann 1	2:22	**51**: Adv 4.7, Circ 2.1,
	(alt).1; **53**:Asc 4.11,		Circ 3.4; **53**: PP 1.1
	Pent 1.5; **54**: 1 Nov	2:23	**52**: Palm 2.3, Pasc 3.2
	4.2, Ded 1.4	2:24	**53**: Asc 6.3
5:17	**51**: Adv 2.1, Epi 3.7;	2:25	**54**: OS 1.6
	53:VPP 3; **54**: OS	3:3	**54**: 1 Nov 2.2
	1.1, Mart 9, Clem	3:9	**52**:Ann 3.6
	3,VAnd 5, And 2.3	3:13	**53**: 6 p P 3.3
5:20	**52**: Pur 1.1, 4 HM 9	3:20	**51**: Adv 5.1; **54**:
			NatBVM 4
First Peter (1 Pet)		4:8	**51**: Adv 2.5; **52**: Quad
1:2	**54**: 1 Nov 1.1		2.6; **54**: Mich 2.1,
1:3	**51**: Nat 2.5; **52**: Quad		Ded 4.3
	1.1; **54**: In lab mess	4:13	**52**: Pasc 1.15; **54**:
	3.3		VAnd 3
1:4	**54**: Clem 3	4:17	**51**: Adv 4.3
1:9	**51**: SP 3	4:18	**54**: In lab mess 3.9
1:12	**51**: Adv 2.4, P Epi	5:3	**54**:Abb 5
	2.3; **52**: Quad 1.2;	5:5	**51**: Adv 2.1,VNat
	54: 1 Nov 3.4, OS		4.6,VNat 4.9; **53**:
	1.4, OS 1.13, OS		6 p P 3.4; **54**: Asspt
	4.2, Ded 5.5		6, Ded 5.2
1:18	**52**: OPasc 1.5	5:6	**52**: Sept 1.1; **53**: PP
1:18-19	**53**: Pent 2.8		3.1; **54**: In lab mess
1:19	**51**: Circ 2.1		2.1, Abb 7, 1 Nov
1:22	**54**:And 2.2		2.3, OS 1.9, Ded
1:24	**53**: 4 p P 3		3.5
1:24-25	**53**:JB 7	5:7	**51**: Adv 3.3,VNat
2:2	**54**: Ded 1.6		5.5; **53**: Asc 5.1; **54**:
2:5	**51**:VNat 2.6 (2x);		Ded 5.5, Ded 6.1

5:8	**51**:VNat 5.2; **52**: Pur 2.2, Sept 1.5; **54**: Asspt 2.4, Ded 4.5	2:15	**52**: Pasc 2.2
		2:15-16	**52**: OPasc 1.7
		2:16	**52**: Ann 1.8, Ann 1 (alt).8, 4 HM 5; **53**: Asc 1.3, Asc 1.8; **54**: Abb 4, OS 1.13, Clem 1
5:8-9	**52**: OPasc 1.2		
5:9	**51**:VNat 6.10		
5:12	**54**: In lab mess 3.8		
		2:17	**53**: 4 p P 4

Second Peter (2 Pet)

1:3	**51**: P Epi 1.4	2:20	**51**:VNat 6.10
1:9	**52**: 5 HM 2	2:27	**53**: Asc 3.9
2:4	**54**: 1 Nov 2.3	3:2	**51**:VNat 5.3; **54**: 1 Nov 1.2, OS 4.2, OS 4.3
2:19	**52**: Pur 1.4		
2:20	**53**: Asc 1.3; **54**: In lab mess 3.3	3:13	**52**: OPasc 1.1
		3:17	**52**: Palm 1.4; **54**: Abb 1
2:22	**51**:VNat 2.6, VNat 5.1, VNat 6.10; **52**: Pasc 2.2; **54**: In lab mess 3.9, Asspt 2.5 (2x)	3:18	**51**: Adv 3.5; **52**: O Pasc 1.8; **54**: Mart 1
		4:2	**51**: Adv 1.10, Epi 1.2
		4:8	**52**: Pasc 3.3
3:3	**51**:VNat 5.2	4:10	**54**: Asspt 4.2, Ded 5.2
3:4	**51**: Circ 2.2	4:16	**52**: Sept 2.1; **54**: 1 Nov 5.2, Ded 1.7, Humb 7

First John (1 John)

1:1	**51**:VNat 6.4; **52**: 4 HM 13; **54**: Mart 8	4:17	**54**: Asspt 5.12
		4:18	**51**: P Epi 1.4, P Epi 2.8, P Epi 2.9; **54**: OS 5.3
1:8	**51**:VNat 6.10, Nat 1.7, P Epi 2.6; **52**: 5 HM 4		
		4:19	**54**: Mich 1.3
1:9	**51**: P Epi 2.6; **53**: JB 8, PP 3.3	4:20	**51**: Adv 3.3
		5:4	**51**:VNat 6.4; **52**: OPasc 1.1, OPasc 1.2; **54**: Mal 7
1:12	**52**: OPasc 1.4		
2.1	**53**: Pent 1.4, PP 3.3; **54**: NatBVM 7	5:5	**52**: OPasc 1.3, OPasc 1.7
2:4	**51**:VNat 3.3; **52**: OPasc 1.3	5:6	**52**: OPasc 1.4; **54**: Clem 4
2:5	**52**: Pasc 1.3		
2:6	**51**:VNat 2.3	5:7	**52**: OPasc 1.8 (2x)
2:13	**52**: OPasc 1.2	5:7-8	**52**: OPasc 1.8, OPasc 2.1
2:13-14	**54**: Mal 4 (2x)		

5:8	**52**: OPasc 1.6, OPasc 2.4; **54**: Clem 5	5:4–5	**51**: Nat 2.5
		5:4–7	**52**: Pasc 1.10
5:9	**54**: Ded 4.1	5:5	**52**: Pasc 1.1, Pasc 1.5, Pasc 1.9, Pasc 1.10 (2x), Pasc 1 (alt).1, Pasc 1 (alt).9, Pasc 1 (alt).10 (2x)
5:16	**52**: 5 HM 4		
5:18	**52**: Sept 1.1		
5:19	**53**: Asc 6.10		

Second John (2 John)

4	**53**: Pent 1.3	5:8	**51**: Epi 3.5
		5:9	**52**: Pur 3.2, Pasc 1 (alt).10; **54**: Clem 3

Third John (3 John)

9	**51**: SP 3	5:12	**52**: Pasc 1.9, Pasc 1.10, Pasc 1.12, Pasc 1 (alt).9, Pasc 1 (alt).12, 4 HM 5

Jude

9	**51**: Nat 4.1		
12	**52**: Ben 5	5:13	**53**: Asc 6.1
19	**53**: 6 p P 1.3; **54**: Mich 1.6 (2x)	6:9	**54**: OS 2.4, OS 2.7, OS 3.2, OS 3.4, OS 4.1 (2x)
		6:11	**51**: VNat 2.5; **54**: OS 2.7, OS 3.1, OS 4.1

Revelation (Rev)

1:5	**54**: OS 3.4, Ded 4.6		
1:8	**54**: 1 Nov 4.4	7:4–8	**51**: Nat 4.1
2:7	**52**: Pasc 3.5	7:14	**51**: Adv 4.7, Circ 3.4; **52**: OPasc 1.5, Pasc 1.5; **54**: OS 5.2
2:17	**53**: Rog 2; **54**: And 1.2		
3:4	**54**: Asspt 6	7:15	**54**: 1 Nov 2.3
3:12	**54**: Ded 5.9	7:17	**54**: OS 2.6
3:15–16	**54**: Asspt 3.5	8:3	**53**: Asc 4.9; **54**: Mich 1.2
3:16	**52**: Pur 2.2; **53**: Asc 3.7, Asc 6.7, PP 3.6, 4 p P 2; **54**: In lab mess 3.9	8:4	**54**: Mich 1.2
		9:9	**51**: Nat 4.1
		11:12	**52**: Palm 2.7
		11:13	**54**: Ded 5.5
3:17	**54**: Asspt 2.6, NatBVM 14	12:1	**54**: OAsspt 1, O Asspt 3 (2x), O Asspt 5, OAsspt 6, OAsspt 7, OAsspt 10, OAsspt 13, O Asspt 14, OAsspt 15
3:20	**54**: Asspt 2.2		
4:10	**51**: Adv 2.4; **52**: Palm 1.3; **53**: Asc 4.9		
5:1	**52**: Pasc 1.10, Pasc 1.11		
5:1–2	**52**: Pasc 1 (alt).11	12:2	**54**: Mal 4
5:3–4	**52**: Pasc 1 (alt).12	12:4	**54**: OAsspt 4

12:9	**54**: Mal 3	20:14	**53**: Pent 2.5
12:10	**51**: Circ 2.5; **54**: Ded 4.3	21:1	**54**: 1 Nov 2.1
14:3	**52**: Pasc 1 (alt).8; **53**: Asc 4.9	21:2	**51**:VNat 2.1; **54**: Mich 1.5, Ded 5.1, Ded 5.5, Ded 5.6, Ded 5.9
14:4	**52**: Quad 1.1, 4 HM 12; **53**:Asc 4.9, Asc 6.3; **54**: Asspt 6, OS 3.2	21:3	**54**: Ded 1.3, Ded 2.2
		21:4	**54**: OS 5.8, Humb 7
		21:5	**51**: Adv 5.3, VNat 4.3; **54**: OS 1.7
14:5	**54**: OS 3.2		
14:6	**54**: OS 1.12	21:25	**54**: Ded 4.1, Mal 5
14:13	**52**: Palm 3.5; **53**: Pent 1.6; **54**: OS 2.4, Ded 4.5	22:5	**54**: Mal 5
		22:11	**51**: P Epi 2.9; **52**: Pasc 2.9; **53**: PP 3.2
17:15	**52**: OPasc 1.5	22:12	**52**: OPasc 1.5
19:9	**54**: Clem 4	22:13	**54**: 1 Nov 4.4
19:10	**54**: OS 1.3	22:14	**54**:VAnd 1
20:2	**53**: Asc 2.1; **54**: Mal 3		

Index of Subjects in Bernard's Liturgical Sermons (CF 51–54)

This selective index indicates subjects in Bernard's Liturgical Sermons, identified in each case by abbreviation of the sermon name, sermon number if more than one sermon has the same name, and paragraph number, organized according to their appearance in the four volumes of English translations in the Cistercian Fathers series (e.g., Nat 1.6 = Sermo in nativitate domini [On the Lord's Birthday] sermon 1, paragraph 6; Ben 2 = Sermo in natali sancti Benedicti [The Feast of Saint Benedict], paragraph 2). Abbreviations for the names of the sermons and their locations in the CF volumes appear on pages lxxi–lxxiii above. God, Christ, and Jesus are not included in the index.

Aaron   Nat 1.6, P Epi 2.2, Pur 2.2
Abbot   Ben 2, 5 HM 2; *see also* Superior
Abel   Ann 1.4
Abraham   Adv 1.11, VNat 2.1, VNat 6.4, VNat 6.5, VNat 6.9, Circ 1.1, Sept 2.3, Ben 12, Ann 1.14, Ann 1 (alt).14, Palm 1.4, OAsspt 8, OAsspt 15, NatBVM 12, OS 4.1, Mart 8, Mart 15
Abstinence   Nat 1.7, P Epi 1.4, P Epi 2.7, Quad 1.6, Quad 3.1, Palm 1.4, Pasc 1.15, Asc 6.4, 6 p P 2.5, In lab mess 3.5, Asspt 4.3, Abb 1, Ded 1.2, VAnd 1, VAnd 2, And 2.4
Adam   Adv 1.1, Adv 1.4, Adv 1.9, Adv 2.1, Adv 2.2, Adv 4.1, Adv 5.3, VNat 2.2, VNat 2.4, VNat 3.2, Nat 3.1, Nat 3.3, Nat 3.5, Circ 3.4, Epi 1.2, Epi 1.3, P Epi 1.3, Sept 1.3, Sept 2.1, Sept 2.2, Ben 10, Ann 1.4, Ann 1.8, Ann 1.10, Ann 1.12, Ann 1 (alt).6, Ann 1 (alt).8, Ann 1 (alt).9, Ann 1 (alt).10, Ann 1 (alt).11, Ann 1 (alt).12, Ann 2.3, 4 HM 6, 4 HM 11, Pasc 1.9, Pasc 1 (alt).9, OPasc 1.5, OAsspt 1, NatBVM 6, OS 1.7, OS 1.11, OS 1.12, OS 1.13, Ded 6.3, Mart 2, And 1.9, Humb 1

Index of Subjects 335

Adultery   P Epi 2.1, Ann 1.5, Ann 3.1, Ann 3.2, Ann 3.4, Ann 3.10
Adversary   Pur 2.2, Sept 1.5, Quad 4.3, Pasc 4.2, OPasc 1.2, In lab mess 3.6, OS 5.10, Ded 2.3
Adversity   Sept 1.5, Quad 2.5, Palm 2.1, Palm 2.2, Palm 3.1, Palm 3.2, Mart 14, Mal 7
Affection   Adv 2.1, Adv 3.3, VNat 2.4, Nat 1.6, Nat 3.3, Circ 3.2, P Epi 2.3, Sept 2.1, Quad 1.3, Quad 4.4, Ann 1 (alt).9, Ann 1 (alt).10, Ann 2.4, Palm 3.2, Pasc 2.3, In lab mess 1.1, Asspt 1.4, Asspt 4.5, Asspt 4.8, Asspt 5.13, OAsspt 15, NatBVM 7, Mich 1.3, 1 Nov 5.12, OS 1.14, OS 3.2, OS 3.3, OS 5.5, OS 5.6, Ded 5.4, Mart 3, Mart 14, Clem 3, Mal 8, VAnd 3, And 1.6
Alms   P Epi 1.4, Palm 1.4, Pasc 1.16
Altar   Nat 4.1, Pasc 2.10, OS 1.3, OS 2.4, OS 2.8, OS 3.2, OS 3.4, OS 4.1, OS 4.2
Ambition   Pur 2.2, Ann 1 (alt).8, Pasc 1.16, OPasc 1.7
Ananias   SP 8
Anchorites   Circ 3.6
Andrew   OAsspt 11, VAnd *passim*, And 1 *passim*, And 2 *passim*
Angels   Adv 1 *passim,* Adv 2.3, Adv 2.4, Adv 3.1, Adv 3.5, Adv 6.5, VNat 1.1, VNat 2.5, VNat 2.6, VNat 2.7, VNat 4.1, VNat 4.3, VNat 6.2, VNat 6.5, VNat 6.8, Nat 2.4, Nat 3.1, Nat 3.2, Nat 3.5, Nat 4.1, Nat 4.2, Nat 5.5, Innoc 2, Circ 1.3, Circ 1.4, Circ 2.1, Circ 2.2, Circ 2.4, Circ 3.2, Circ 3.3, Circ 3.11, Epi 1.3, Epi 2.2, Epi 2.3, P Epi 2.3, Pur 1.3, Ben 9, Ben 10, Ben 11, Ann 1.13, Ann 1 (alt).13, Ann 2.1, Ann 2.3, Ann 3.7, Ann 3.8, Palm 1.2, 4 HM 10, Pasc 1.5, Pasc 1.8, Pasc 1 (alt).6, Pasc 1 (alt).8, Pasc 2.12, Pasc 3.4, Pasc 3.6, OPasc 1.8, OPasc 2.1, OPasc 2.2, Asc 1.1, Asc 2.3, Asc 2.4, Asc 2.6, Asc 4.9, Asc 6.12, Pent 2.1, Pent 2.3, Pent 2.8, Pent 3.1, JB 4, JB 6, In lab mess 3.5, In lab mess 3.8, Asspt 2.2, Asspt 4.1, Asspt 4.6, Asspt 5.5, Asspt 6.1, OAsspt *passim*, NatBVM *passim*, Mich 1 *passim*, Mich 2.1, Mich 2.2, 1 Nov 1.1, 1 Nov 1.2, 1 Nov 1.4, 1 Nov 2.1, 1 Nov 2.3, 1 Nov 2.5, 1 Nov 3.1, 1 Nov 5.5, 1 Nov 5.6, 1 Nov 5.9, 1 Nov 5.10, OS 1.4, OS 1.6, OS 1.8, OS 1.9, OS 1.13, OS 4.1, OS 4.2, OS 5.1, OS 5.7, OS 5.10, Ded 1.6, Ded 4.1, Ded 4.4, Ded 5.5, Ded 5.6, Ded 5.10, Ded 6.1, Ded 6.2, Ded 6.3, Mart *passim*, Mal 1, And 1.6, And 1.7, And 1.8, And 2.3, Humb 5
Anger   P Epi 1.1, Ann 1.9, Ann 1 (alt).9, Ann 1 (alt).10, 4 HM 8, 5 HM 3, Pasc 1.9, Pasc 1 (alt).9
Animal   Epi 3.1, Epi 3.7, Pur 1.1, Pur 2.2, Sept 2.3, Ben 5, Ann 1.6, Ann 1 (alt).6, Palm 3.2, Ded 5.7, Mart 9

Anna   Pur 1.1, Pur 1.4, Pur 2.1
Annunciation   Ann 2.1, Ann 3.1
Antichrist   SP 3
Apocalypse   Epi 3.5
Apostasy   Ben 11
Apostles   Adv 1.2, Adv 1.6, Adv 1.9, Adv 4.2, Adv 5.2, Adv 6.1, Adv 6.2, VNat 1.6, VNat 2.5, VNat 3.3, VNat 4.7, VNat 4.9, VNat 4.10, VNat 5.2, VNat 6.3, VNat 6.4, VNat 6.6, Nat 1.2, Nat 1.5, Nat 5.4, Circ 2.3, Circ 2.4, Circ 2.5, Circ 3.2, Circ 3.6, Epi 1.2, Epi 1.3, Epi 1.5, Epi 3.6, Epi 3.7, OEpi 3, P Epi 2.1, SP 6, Pur 1.4, Sept 1.4, Sept 2.1, Quad 1.6, Quad 2.1, Quad 4.2, Quad 6.2, Quad 6.4, Ben *passim*, Ann 1.1, Ann 1.3, Ann 1.5, Ann 2.3, Ann 3.2, Ann 3.9, Palm 1.4, Palm 2.3, Palm 3.4, 5 HM 5, Pasc 1.13, Pasc 1.17, Pasc 1 (alt).3, Pasc 1 (alt).14, Pasc 2.1, Pasc 2.2, Pasc 2.4, Pasc 2.11, Pasc 4.2, OPasc 1.1, OPasc 1.4, OPasc 1.6, OPasc 2.2, Asc 1.1, Asc 2.1, Asc 3 *passim*, Asc 4.9, Asc 5.1, Asc 5.2, Asc 6.10, Asc 6.12–14, Pent 1.2, Pent 2.1, In lab mess 1.1–2, In lab mess 3.5, In lab mess 3.6–8, Asspt 2.3, Asspt 3.1, Asspt 3.6, Asspt 5 *passim*, OAsspt 6, OAsspt 11, NatBVM 3, NatBVM 11, NatBVM 17, Abb 7, Mich 1.1, Mich 1.6, Mich 2.4, 1 Nov 1.2, 1 Nov 4.4, 1 Nov 5.2, OS 1.5, OS 1.6, OS 1.14, OS 2.2, OS 2.3, OS 2.7, OS 3.1, OS 3.3, OS 4.4, OS 4.6, OS 5.2, OS 5.4, OS 5.5, OS 5.6, Ded 1.2, Ded 5.1, Ded 5.4–9, Mart *passim*, Mal 4, VAnd 3, And 1.4, And 1.5, And 1.7, And 1.10, And 2.3, And 2.7
Ark   Palm 1.4
Arm   Circ 3.3, P Epi 2.3, Pasc 1 (alt).3
Army   Circ 3.6, Quad 6.4
Ascension   Adv 1.6, VNat 3.8, Ann 1.4, Pasc 1 (alt).14, Asc 2.1, Asc 4.1, In lab mess 3.8, Asspt 1.4, Asspt 4.1, OAsspt 11, 1 Nov 1.3, 1 Nov 3.1, OS 1.5, Mart 10, Humb 5
Ass   Ben 3, Palm 2.3, Palm 3.2
Assumption   Asspt 1.1, Asspt 1.4
Authority   Adv 3.4, VNat 6.9, Circ 1.5, Circ 2.5, Sept 2.2, Ann 2.3, Palm 3.1, Pasc 1.9

Baby, Babies   Adv 2.2, VNat 1.1, VNat 4.6, Nat 1.3, Nat 3.1, Nat 3.3, Nat 5.1, Epi 2.4, Epi 3.4, OEpi 4, OPasc 1.5
Babylon   VNat 6.8, Epi 3.3, Sept 1.4, Pasc 4.1, OPasc 2.3
Baptism   Innoc 2, Circ 3.5, Epi 1.6, Epi 3.8, OEpi 1, OEpi 2, P Epi 1.3, Quad 1.3, Palm 1.3, 5 HM 2, 5 HM 3, Pasc 1.15, OPasc 1.6, OPasc 1.7, Asspt 2.8

Index of Subjects 337

Beasts VNat 3.8, VNat 6.7, Nat 2.3, Nat 5.1, Circ 3.2, Pur 1.1, Ben 3,
  Ben 6, Ann 1.6, Ann 1.7, Ann 1 (alt).7, Palm 1.3, Palm 1.4, Palm 2.5,
  Palm 2.6, Palm 2.7, Palm 3.1, Pasc 1.9, Pasc 1 (alt).9, Pasc 3.3, OPasc
  2.2, Asspt 6.1, Ded 1.2
Beatitude Circ 1.2, Quad 2.4, Ann 1.14, 1 Nov 4.1, OS 1.14, OS 2.1,
  OS 4.3, OS 4.5, OS 5.10, Ded 5.5, Mart 7
Beauty Adv 2.4, VNat 2.4, VNat 3.8, Nat 1.4, Nat 2.2, Nat 4.1, P Epi 2.1,
  P Epi 2.2, P Epi 2.3, Ann 1.12, Ann 3.7, Pasc 2.10, Asspt 4.7, Asspt
  5.11, OAsspt 15, NatBVM 17, Mich 1.4, 1 Nov 1.2, OS 1.4, OS 4.6,
  OS 5.9, Mart 5, Mart 6, Mart 10, VAnd 4
Belief Pasc 1.3, Asc 1.2, Asc 1.3, OAsspt 7, OAsspt 12
Belly Adv 3.2, Quad 3.4, Pasc 1.12
Benedict Ben *passim* 2, Palm 2.6, Ded 5.1
Benjamin VNat 6.8, VNat 6.9
Bernard Nat 3.3, Nat 3.4, Nat 3.6, Quad 5.1, Ben 2, Ann 2.1, Rog 1, Asc
  1.1, Asc 4.2, PP 2.3, 6 p P 1.2, In lab mess 2.2, In lab mess 3.1, Asspt
  2.3, Asspt 3.6, Asspt 4.5, OAsspt 7, NatBVM 11, Abb 6, Mich 1.6, 1
  Nov 4.4, OS 1.3, OS 1.13, OS 2.1, Ded 5.2, Ded 5.3, Mart 8, Mal 8,
  Humb 1, Humb 6, Humb 7
Bethlehem VNat 1 *passim*, VNat 6 *passim*, Epi 1.5, OAsspt 9
Betrothal VNat 4.6, P Epi 2.4, P Epi 2.6, Pasc 1.11, Pasc 1 (alt).11
Bird, Birds Adv 2.1, Circ 3.11, Epi 1.7, Pur 3.2, Sept 2.3, Palm 1.3
Birth Adv 1.3, Adv 2.5, Adv 3.2, VNat 1.1, VNat 1.2, VNat 3.9, VNat 4
  passim, VNat 5.1, VNat 6 *passim*, Nat 1.1, Nat 1.8, Nat 2.4, Nat 3.1,
  Innoc 1, Circ 2.2, Circ 3.3, Circ 3.4, Epi 1.3, Epi 3.2, Epi 3.4, P Epi
  2.8, Pur 3.1, Pur 3.2, Sept 1.1, Ann 1.10, Ann 1 (alt).10, Ann 2.1,
  Ann 2.3, 4 HM 6, Pasc 1.5, Pasc 1.11, Pasc 1 (alt).11, Pasc 2.4, OPasc
  1.1, OPasc 1.2, In lab mess 2.1, Asspt 2.8, Asspt 4.5, OAsspt *passim*,
  NatBVM 2, 1 Nov 5.1, Mal 4, And 1.6
Bishop Palm 1.4, 5 HM 2, Ded 1.3, Ded 1.4, Ded 4.1, Ded 4.4, Ded 6.1,
  Mart 14, Mal 1, Mal 6
Blasphemy SP 5, Pur 3.1, 4 HM 3, 4 HM 8, Pasc 1.1, Pasc 1.3, Pasc 1.4
Blessed OPasc 2.1, In lab mess 3.7, In lab mess 3.8, Asspt 1.1, Asspt 1.2,
  Asspt 1.4, 1 Nov 1.1, 1 Nov 2.3, 1 Nov 2.5, 1 Nov 4.1, OS 4.6, OS
  5.3, OS 5.8, Ded 1.3, Mart 16
Blessedness Adv 1.4, Adv 2.5, VNat 2.5, Asspt 2.1, NatBVM 6, Mich 1.4,
  OS 1.7, OS 1.9, OS 2.1, OS 2.4, OS 3.1, OS 3.2, OS 4.3, OS 5.4,
  Clem 1
Blessing Adv 2.2, VNat 4.1, VNat 4.3, Ben 1, Ann 2.1, Ann 3.1, 4 HM 14,
  In lab mess 3.4, Asspt 1.3, Asspt 1.4, Asspt 5.11, Asspt 6.1, NatBVM

1, NatBVM 16, Ded 1.4, Ded 1.6, Ded 6.1, Mal 1, Mal 3, And 1.2, Humb 2

Blindness   Adv 7.2, SP 6, SP 7, Ann 3.10, Pasc 3.2, Asspt 3.3, Asspt 5.8, Mart 12, Mart 16

Blood   Adv 3.6, VNat 2.7, VNat 4.7, Nat 3.3, Nat 3.4, Circ 1.3, Circ 3.1, Circ 3.4, SP 2, Pur 1.3, Pur 3.2, Quad 4.2, Quad 5.2, Ben 12, Ann 1.4, Palm 3.4, 4 HM 8, 4 HM 11, 5 HM 3, Pasc 1.5, Pasc 1.17, OPasc 1.4, OPasc 1.5, OPasc 1.6, OPasc 1.7, OPasc 1.8, OPasc 2.1, OPasc 2.4, OPasc 2.5, Asspt 5.8, NatBVM 18, OS 3.1, OS 4.1, OS 5.2, Ded 5.5, Ded 5.7, Mart 4, Clem 3, Clem 4, Clem 5, Clem 6, And 2.3, Humb 1

Body   Adv 1.6, Adv 1.8, Adv 3 *passim*, Adv 4.2, Adv 4.3, Adv 4.4, Adv 5.2, Adv 6 *passim*, Adv 7.1, VNat 1.6, VNat 2.3, VNat 2.4, VNat 2.5, VNat 3.4, VNat 3.5, VNat 4.4, VNat 4.10, VNat 5.1, VNat 5.3, VNat 6.1, VNat 6.5, Nat 1.4, Nat 2.1, Nat 2.2, Nat 3.1, Nat 3.2, Nat 4.1, Nat 4.2, Nat 5.4, Nat 5.5, Innoc 1, Circ 1.1, Circ 2.3, Circ 3.7, Circ 3.11, Epi 1.4, Epi 2.4, SP 2, Pur 1.1, Pur 1.4, Pur 3.3, Sept 1.3, Sept 1.5, Sept 2.2, Sept 2.3, Quad 1.2, Quad 2.2, Quad 2.4, Quad 5.8, Ben 12, Ann 3.5, Palm 1.4, Palm 3.3, Palm 3.4, Palm 3.5, 4 HM 6, 4 HM 8, 4 HM 13, 4 HM 14, 5 HM 3, 5 HM 4, Pasc 1 *passim*, Pasc 1 (alt).3, Pasc 1 (alt).4, Pasc 2.1, Pasc 2.2, Pasc 2.11, Pasc 3.1, OPasc 1.7, OPasc 2.5, Rog 1, Rog 2, Asc 2.3, Asc 3.1, Asc 3.6, Asc 4.8, Asc 4.12, Asc 6.2, Asc 6.3, Asc 6.5, Asc 6.9, Pent 3.6, 6 p P 2.5, In lab mess 1.2, In lab mess 2.1, In lab mess 2.2, Asspt 2.3, Asspt 2.5, Asspt 5.8, Asspt 5.9, Asspt 5.10, OAsspt 9, OAsspt 15, NatBVM 6, NatBVM 9, NatBVM 10, Abb 3, Abb 5, Mich 1.5, Mich 1.6, Mich 2.1, 1 Nov 1.3, 1 Nov 2.2, 1 Nov 4.4, 1 Nov 5.4, OS 1 *passim*, OS 2 *passim*, OS 3.1, OS 3.3, OS 4.2, OS 4.6, OS 5.9, OS 5.11, Ded 1.1, Ded 1.2, Ded 2.1, Ded 2.3, Ded 3.2, Ded 4.4, Ded 5.8, Mart *passim*, Clem *passim*, Mal 2, Mal 3, VAnd 4, And 1.6, And 2 *passim*, Humb 1, Humb 5

Bone   VNat 2.1, VNat 2.4, VNat 6.6, Sept 2.1, Quad 2.2, 4 HM 2, Pasc 1.10, Pasc 1 (alt).10

Book   Nat 2.5, Quad 5.5, 5 HM 2, Pasc 1.10, Pasc 1.11, Pasc 1.12, Pasc 1 (alt).10, Pasc 1 (alt).11, Pasc 1 (alt).12

Bread   Adv 5.2, VNat 1.6, VNat 6.8, VNat 6.10, Nat 1.3, Nat 1.7, Nat 2.4, Nat 2.5, Nat 3.5, Circ 3.2, P Epi 1.5, P Epi 2.7, Sept 1.3, Quad 2.4, Quad 5.7, Ben 10, Ann 2.4, Ann 3.1, Palm 3.4, 4 HM 14, Pasc 1.11, Pasc 1.13, Rog 1, Rog 2, JB 7, 6 p P 1.4, 6 p P 2 *passim*, Asspt 5.5, Asspt 5.8, OS 1 *passim*, OS 4.6, Ded 3.2, Ded 5.8, Clem 6, Mal 1

Breasts   Epi 1.8, Epi 2.1, P Epi 2.5, 4 HM 8, 5 HM 1
Breath   Nat 2.1, Nat 2.2
Brethren, *see* Brothers
Bride   Adv 1.11, Adv 4.1, VNat 4.10, Circ 1.4, P Epi 2 *passim*, 4 HM 14, Pasc 1.5, Asc 4.11, Asspt 3.5, NatBVM 2, NatBVM 13, Mich 1.2, 1 Nov 5.2, OS 4.2, Ded 5 *passim*
Bridegroom   Adv 2.5, Adv 4.1, VNat 3.1, VNat 4.10, P Epi 2 *passim*, Ann 3.7, Palm 1.1, Asc 2.3, Asc 3.9, Asc 6.1, JB 10, JB 11, PP 2.5, Asspt 2.9, Asspt 3.5, OAsspt 7, OAsspt 12, NatBVM *passim*, 1 Nov 3.2, OS 4.2, Ded 5.2, Ded 5.9, Ded 5.10
Brother   Epi 3.7, P Epi 2.5, SP 4, Quad 2.3, Quad 4.2, Ann 2.2, 4 HM 4, Pasc 1.13, Pasc 1.16, Pasc 2 *passim*, OPasc 1.1, OPasc 1.8
Brotherhood   Quad 4.2
Brothers   Adv 3.5, Adv 3.6, VNat 1.3, VNat 2.5, VNat 3.6, VNat 6.11, Circ 2.5, Sept 1.5, Ben 9, Pasc 3.3, In lab mess 2.2, In lab mess 3.2, In lab mess 3.5, In lab mess 3.9, Asspt 1.3, Asspt 2.7, Asspt 3.4, Asspt 3.5, Asspt 3.6, Asspt 5.7, Asspt 5.11, OAsspt 1, NatBVM 7, Abb 6, Mich 2.1, 1 Nov 1.1, 1 Nov 2.3, 1 Nov 2.5, 1 Nov 3.1, 1 Nov 4.1, OS 1.14, OS 3.1, OS 4.1, OS 5.6, Ded 4.3, Ded 5.9, And 2.7, Humb 6
Burden   Adv 2.1, Adv 3.6, Adv 4.6, Nat 4.1, Sept 1.5, Sept 2.2, Sept 2.3, Quad 3.1, Quad 6.2, Palm 2.6, 4 HM 6, 4 HM 14, 5 HM 2, Pasc 1.14, Pasc 2.11, In lab mess 1.4, Asspt 3.1, Asspt 3.6, Asspt 4.2, Asspt 4.4, OAsspt 9, NatBVM 14, Mich 2.1, OS 1.1, OS 1.5, OS 1.9, OS 5.8, Ded 3.2, And 2.4, Humb 3, Humb 6
Burial   Palm 3.1, 4 HM 6, Pasc 1.11, Pasc 1 (alt).11

Caesar   Palm 2.4, Pasc 1.9
Cain   Adv 3.6
Caiphas   Pasc 1.1
Calumny   Sept 1.5, 4 HM 13, Pasc 1.6
Cana   P Epi 2.4
Canaan   Ann 3.4
Captive   VNat 2.8, 4 HM 4
Captivity   Sept 1.4, Pasc 1.1
Celibacy   Nat 1.7, In lab mess 3.
Centurion   Epi 2.3, Epi 2.4
Charity   Pasc 1.3, Pasc 1.13, Pasc 1 (alt).3, Rog 1, Rog 2, Asc 5.2, Asc 6.15, Pent 1.5, Pent 1.6, Pent 2.5, JB 10, 6 p P 2.6, Asspt 1.3, Asspt 3.4, Asspt 3.5, Asspt 3.6, Asspt 4.2, Asspt 5.13, OAsspt 2, OAsspt 15,

NatBVM 9, NatBVM 12, NatBVM 18, Abb 6, Abb 7, Mich 1.3, Mich 1.6, Mich 2.1, Mich 2.2, 1 Nov 2.4, 1 Nov 3.4, 1 Nov 4.2, 1 Nov 4.4, 1 Nov 5.2, OS 3.4, OS 5.3, OS 5.6, Ded 1.2, Ded 1.7, Ded 2.4, Ded 3.2, Ded 3.3, Ded 4.3, Mart 17, And 1.5, And 1.9, And 1.10, And 2.2, And 2.3, Humb 5, Humb 7

Chastity   Adv 5.3, P Epi 2.7, Pur 3.3, Quad 5.6, Palm 1.4, In lab mess 3.5, In lab mess 3.7, Asspt 4.5, NatBVM 15, Abb 1, Mich 1.5

Cherubim   VNat 6.8, Ben 11, Ann 1.11, Ann 1 (alt).11, OAsspt 3, NatBVM 10, 1 Nov 5.7, Mart 5

Child   Adv 2.2, Adv 2.3, VNat 1.2, VNat 1.3, VNat 2.8, VNat 3.9, VNat 4.1, VNat 4.3, VNat 4.5, VNat 4.6, VNat 4.9, VNat 5.3, VNat 6.3, VNat 6.7, Nat 1.3, Nat 1.4, Nat 1.5, Nat 3.1, Nat 3.2, Nat 4.1, Nat 4.2, Nat 4.3, Nat 5.2, Circ 1 *passim*, Circ 2.1, Circ 3.3, Circ 3.5, Epi 1.2, Epi 1.4, Epi 1.5, Epi 2.3, Epi 3.2, Epi 3.7, Epi 3.8, OEpi 1, OEpi 3, P Epi 2.5, P Epi 2.6, Pur 3.2, Quad 1.1, Quad 2.1, Quad 2.2, Quad 5.7, Ann 1.6, Ann 1 (alt).9, Palm 1.3, Palm 2.6, Palm 3.2, 5 HM 1, Pasc 3.4, Pasc 4.1

Childbearing   VNat 3.10, VNat 4.3

Childbirth   VNat 1.1

Childhood   Epi 3.8

Children   Adv 1.1, Adv 1.7, Adv 1.9, VNat 2.1, VNat 4.1, VNat 5.2, VNat 6.11, Nat 3.3, Nat 5.3, Innoc 2, Epi 3.7, Epi 3.8, OEpi 1, SP 6, Pur 1.3, Sept 1.1, Sept 2.2, Quad 4.2, Ann 1 (alt).8, Palm 1.3, Pasc 2.4, Pasc 3.5, OPasc 1.1, OPasc 1.8, In lab mess 1.1, OAsspt 10, OAsspt 11, OAsspt 12, NatBVM 7, NatBVM 12, OS 4.2, Ded 4.6, Ded 5.2, Ded 5.5, Ded 5.7, Clem 4, And 2.5

Choice   Pur 1.3, Ann 1 (alt).7

Christians   Circ 1.3, SP 3, Sept 2.1, Quad 1.1, Quad 3.2, 4 HM 1, 4 HM 12, Pasc 1.5, Pasc 1.16

Church   Adv 1.1, Adv 3.2, VNat 3.1, VNat 6.3, VNat 6.9, VNat 6.11, Nat 1.7, Circ 2.5, OEpi 3, P Epi 1.3, P Epi 2.2, P Epi 2.6, SP 2, SP 3, Pur 2.1, Pur 2.2, Sept 1.3, Sept 2.1, Sept 2.3, Quad 1.1, Quad 3.1, Palm 1.1, Palm 3.4, 4 HM 1, Pasc 1.3, Pasc 3.4, Pasc 3.5, OPasc 1.5, Asc 6.15, Asspt 3.6, OAsspt 3, OAsspt 5, NatBVM 2, Abb 1, 1 Nov 5.5, OS 3.1, OS 3.2, OS 5.6, Ded 1.1, Ded 4.1, Ded 5.1, Mart 12, Mal 2, Mal 3, Mal 6, And 2.2

Circumcision   VNat 4.6, Innoc 2, Circ 1.2, Circ 2.1, Circ 2.2, Circ 2.4, Circ 3.1, Circ 3.3, Circ 3.5, OEpi 1, OEpi 2, Pur 3.2, 5 HM 2, Pasc 1.11, Pasc 1 (alt).11, Asspt 2.8

Citizen   Quad 5.3, Quad 6.1, Quad 6.4, OPasc 2.3

Index of Subjects   341

City   Adv 3.6, Adv 4.7, VNat 1.4, VNat 4.1, VNat 6.11, Epi 3.3, SP 7, Pur 1.3, Pur 3.2, Sept 1.3, Sept 1.4, Sept 2.3, Quad 2.1, Palm 1.4, Pasc 4.2
Clairvaux   Ded 3.3
Clay   VNat 3.9, VNat 6.7
Cleansing   5 HM 2, Pasc 3.6
Clement   Clem 1, Clem 2
Clergy   Quad 3.1
Cloister   Palm 2.5
Cloth   Ann 2.1, Pasc 2.12
Clothing   Adv 3.2, VNat 4.6, Nat 1.3, Nat 1.4, Nat 3.1, Nat 4.1, Nat 4.2, Nat 5.1, Nat 5.5, Circ 2.2, Circ 2.4, Epi 1.5, Epi 2.1, Epi 2.4, Sept 1.5, Quad 6.1, Ann 1.7, Palm 1.3, Pasc 2.10, Pasc 3.1, Pasc 3.2
Cloud   Adv 1.8, Adv 1.10, Ann 1.10, Ann 1 (alt).10, Pasc 1.12
Comfort   Adv 1.1, Quad 2.4, In lab mess 3.1, 1 Nov 2.2, OS 1.10, And 1.7
Coming   Adv 5.1, Adv 5.2, Adv 5.3, Adv 6.6, VNat 2.5, VNat 3.3, VNat 3.6, Nat 4.3, Pasc 1.8, OPasc 1.6
Command   Ben 5, Palm 3.2, Pasc 1 (alt).4, Pasc 2.3, OPasc 1.3, Asspt 3.3, Mich 2.3, 1 Nov 5.4, Mart 8, And 1.9
Commandments   Adv 3.7, VNat 2.4, VNat 3.3, VNat 5.1, VNat 5.2, VNat 6.8, Circ 1.1, Circ 2.3, Circ 3.10, Epi 3.6, P Epi 2.9, SP 6, Sept 1.4, Sept 1.5, Quad 2.1, Quad 2.2, Quad 2.5, OS 1.5, Ded 1.4, Ded 4.4, And 1.8, And 1.9, And 2.1
Communion   1 Nov 1.2, OS 5.5, Ded 5.10
Community   VNat 3.6, Circ 2.4, Circ 2.5, Circ 3.6, Circ 3.7, OEpi 3, SP 7, Pur 2.2, Quad 1.2, Pasc 3.4, Asspt 3.2, Mich 2.1, OS 5.6, Mal 6, Humb 4
Compassion   Adv 1.7, Adv 4.6, VNat 2.6, Nat 1.3, Innoc 2, Epi 3.8, P Epi 1.2, Pur 1.1, Sept 1.3, Sept 2.1, Quad 1.3, Quad 2.6, Quad 6.3, Ben 2, Ann 1.8, Ann 1.9, Ann 1.10, Ann 2.3, Ann 3.3, Palm 3.5, 4 HM 8, 4 HM 11, Pasc 2.4, Pasc 2.5, Pasc 2.6, Pasc 2.8, Asc 6.11, 6 p P 1.1, 6 p P 1.2, 6 p P 2.1, OAsspt 1, OAsspt 10, OAsspt 14, Mich 1.4, OS 1.1, OS 1.11, OS 5.10, Ded 5.8, Ded 5.9, And 1.5, Humb 7
Complaint   P Epi 2.4, Ann 1.12, 4 HM 2, Pasc 3.2, Asspt 5.7, NatBVM 15, 1 Nov 2.2, And 1.7, Humb 7
Conception   VNat 4.2, VNat 4.3, VNat 4.6, Pur 3.2, Pasc 1.11, Pasc 1 (alt).11, Asspt 6.1, OAsspt 7, OAsspt 9
Concord   Ann 1.5, Asc 5.1, Asc 5.2, 6 p P 1.4
Concupiscence   Circ 1.2, Circ 3.7, 5 HM 3, 5 HM 5, Pasc 1.16, OS 4.5, Clem 6

Condemnation   Adv 1.4, Adv 6.2, SP 6, Ann 3.3, 4 HM 7, 5 HM 3, 5 HM 5
Condescension   Adv 1.6, Adv 1.7, Adv 3.1, Adv 3.2, Adv 4.1, Adv 7.1, Adv 7.2, VNat 3.8, SP 2, SP 6, Palm 3.2
Confession   Adv 1.10, Adv 3.7, Adv 4.6, Adv 5.3, VNat 1.6, VNat 2.1, VNat 2.4, VNat 6.8, VNat 6.11, P Epi 1.4, Quad 2.6, Ann 1.5, Ann 1 (alt).8, Ann 3.9, 5 HM 1, Pasc 1.15, Pasc 2.10, Asc 1.3, PP 3.3, Asspt 2.5, Asspt 5.8, NatBVM 15, NatBVM 18, 1 Nov 4.4, OS 1.13, Ded 1.4, Ded 2.3, Ded 5.8
Confessors   VNat 2.1, Ben 4, Ben 12
Conscience   Adv 1.10, Adv 3.3, Adv 3.6, Adv 4.2, VNat 3.3, VNat 3.5, VNat 5.1, OEpi 5, Quad 1.5, Quad 1.6, Quad 2.4, Quad 3.1, Quad 4.4, Quad 5.4, Quad 5.6, Ann 1.5, Ann 1 (alt).9, Ann 3.4, Palm 3.4, Pasc 2.2, Pasc 4.1, Asc 4.9, In lab mess 1.4, Asspt 2.4, Asspt 2.8, Asspt 4.2, Asspt 4.3, Asspt 4.7, NatBVM 8, Abb 5, Abb 6, Abb 7, OS 1.13, OS 2.2, OS 2.3, OS 2.6, Ded 2.3, Ded 4.5, Clem 6, VAnd 1, And 2.5, Humb 4
Consolation   Adv 4.1, Adv 5.1, VNat 2.2, VNat 2.8, VNat 4.1, Nat 3.5, Nat 5.4, Nat 5.5, Epi 1.1, Epi 1.3, Epi 1.5, SP 7, Quad 5.3, Ben 7, Ann 3.3, Palm 1.4, Pasc 1.18, Pasc 4.2, OPasc 2.3, In lab mess 1.1, In lab mess 1.2, Asspt 3.3, OAsspt 2, 1 Nov 4.1, Ded 4.3, Ded 5.5, Ded 5.6, Mal 1, VAnd 1, VAnd 4, And 1.7, Humb 6
Consummation   VNat 4.7, VNat 4.10, Nat 2.6, Pasc 1.14, 1 Nov 4.3, 1 Nov 4.4, OS 2.1, OS 2.6, Mal 1, Mal 4
Contemplation   VNat 5.3, Sept 2.1, Sept 2.3, Asspt 3.1, Asspt 3.3, Asspt 3.4, Asspt 4.4, Asspt 5.6, Asspt 5.7, Asspt 5.8, 1 Nov 1.2, 1 Nov 2.1, 1 Nov 2.5, 1 Nov 3.4, 1 Nov 5.10, 1 Nov 5.12, OS 2.1, OS 4.2
Contemplative   Palm 2.7
Continence   Nat 4.2, Pasc 2.11, Pasc 2.12
Conversion   VNat 5.1, Epi 3.8, SP 1, SP 6, Quad 2.3, Ben 6, Ann 3.9, Asspt 4.3, Asspt 5.4, Asspt 5.10, Mal 8, And 2.1
Cord, triple   Ann 1.8, Ann 1 (alt).8, 4 HM 5
Corrosion   OEpi 1, 5 HM 2
Corruption   Adv 1.6, Adv 6.4, VNat 4.4, VNat 4.6, VNat 5.3, VNat 6.6, Nat 2.4, Circ 2.1, Sept 2.2, Ben 9, 4 HM 14, Pasc 1.9, Pasc 1 (alt).8, Pasc 1 (alt).9, Pasc 3.3
Counsel   Pasc 1.4, Pasc 1 (alt).3, Pasc 3.4, Pasc 3.5, Pasc 3.6, OPasc 1.3
Courage   VNat 6.10, 4 HM 11, Pasc 3.6, Asc 5.1, Asc 5.2, NatBVM 16, 1 Nov 5.3, Ded 4.4
Covenant   4 HM 11, OPasc 2.1, Ded 5.4, Ded 5.5

Cowardice   Quad 4.3, In lab mess 1.1, Asspt 4.5, Asspt 5.12, OAsspt 13, NatBVM 7, Mich 2.4, Ded 3.4, And 1.5, And 2.7
Creation   Adv 5.3, VNat 2.4, VNat 3.8, Nat 2.1, Nat 2.2, Circ 2.2, Pent 3.3, In lab mess 2.1, In lab mess 3.3, Asspt 1.3, 1 Nov 2.1, 1 Nov 2.5, 1 Nov 3.1, 1 Nov 5.5, OS 4.3
Creator   Adv 2.4, Adv 3.1, Adv 6.5, VNat 2.7, VNat 6.8, Ann 1.6, Pasc 3.3, Asspt 2.1, Asspt 5.8, Mich 1.2, 1 Nov 3.1, OS 1.9, OS 1.11, Ded 1.3, Mart 7, And 1.9, Humb 1
Crime   Innoc 2, SP 1, SP 3, Ben 5, Ben 11, Pasc 3.4
Cross   Adv 3.6, Adv 4.7, VNat 2.7, VNat 4.7, Nat 1.8, Circ 3.2, Epi 2.3, Epi 2.4, Epi 3.6, P Epi 2.3, SP 2, Pur 3.2, Quad 6.3, Ben 6, Palm 1.2, Palm 2.4, Palm 3.5, 4 HM 6, 4 HM 8, Pasc 1 *passim*, Pasc 1 (alt) *passim*, Pasc 2.4, OPasc 1.5, OAsspt 11, NatBVM 11, 1 Nov 1.2, 1 Nov 5.3, 1 Nov 5.4, OS 5.8, Ded 1.5, Mart 4, Mart 8, Clem 4, Mal 4, VAnd 3, VAnd 4, And 1 *passim*, And 2 *passim*, Humb 5, Humb 6
Crown   VNat 2.8, VNat 5.6, Innoc 2, Circ 1.2, Epi 2.1, Epi 2.3, Pasc 1.2, Pasc 1 (alt).2, OAsspt 6, OAsspt 7, OAsspt 10, OAsspt 14, OAsspt 15, NatBVM 18, OS 2.3, OS 2.7, OS 5.2, OS 5.3, OS 5.9, Ded 2.4, Mart 16, Mart 17, Clem 2, VAnd 3, And 1.1
Crucifixion   VNat 3.9, Quad 6.3, Palm 2.4, Palm 3.3, 4 HM 10, OAsspt 15, VAnd 3
Curiosity   Adv 1.1, VNat 2.3, Circ 3.7, SP 4, Ann 1.8, Ann 1 (alt).6, Ann 1 (alt).8, Ann 3.9, 4 HM 5, 5 HM 4, OPasc 1.7

Damnation   VNat 1.3, Pur 1.2, Pasc 1 (alt).4, OPasc 2.4, OS 4.1, Mal 1, And 2.7
Danger   Adv 7.2, VNat 6.5, Nat 3.4, Circ 3.6, Sept 1.5, Sept 2.3, Quad 5.1, Quad 5.3, Pasc 1.17
Daniel   VNat 6.8, Nat 1.7, Palm 1.4, OPasc 2.2, Asspt 3.4, Asspt 3.5, Abb 1
Darkness   Adv 7.2, VNat 3.2, VNat 3.3, VNat 6.3, Quad 4.3, Pasc 1.16
Daughters   Epi 2.2, P Epi 2.3, Quad 2.6, Ann 1 (alt).10, Pasc 2.4, OPasc 1.5
David   Adv 1.3, Adv 2.1, VNat 6.4, P Epi 2.1, Pur 1.2, Quad 2.5, Quad 5.6, Ann 1.5, Ann 3.7, Pasc 1.10, Pasc 1 (alt).1, Pasc 1 (alt).10, 4 p P 1, 4 p P 2, 4 p P 3, 4 p P 4, In lab mess 1.4, Asspt 3.3, Asspt 5.3, OAsspt 8, 1 Nov 1.2, 1 Nov 2.1, Ded 2.1
Days   VNat 3.2, VNat 5.2, VNat 5.4, VNat 6.1, VNat 6.5, Circ 3.5, Circ 3.6, Circ 3.8, Circ 3.10, Quad 6.4, Pasc 1.8, Pasc 1.9, Pasc 1 (alt).4, Pasc 1 (alt).5, Pasc 1 (alt).8

Death   Adv 1.6, Adv 6.2, Adv 7.1, VNat 2.7, VNat 3.2, VNat 3.9, VNat 4.3, VNat 6.1, VNat 6.6, Nat 1.4, Nat 1.5, Nat 1.8, Nat 2.3, Nat 2.5, Nat 3.3, Nat 3.4, Innoc 2, Circ 1.5, Circ 2.1, Circ 2.3, Epi 2.4, P Epi 2.3, Pur 1.2, Pur 3.3, Sept 2.1, Sept 2.3, Quad 2.3, Quad 3.2, Quad 6.2, Quad 6.3, Ben 11, Ann 1 *passim*, Ann 1 (alt).7, Ann 1 (alt).8, Ann 1 (alt).12, Ann 1 (alt).13, Ann 1 (alt).14, Ann 3.5, 4 HM *passim*, 5 HM 2, 5 HM 3, 5 HM 4, Pasc 1 *passim*, Pasc 1 (alt).3, Pasc 1 (alt).8, Pasc 2.2, Pasc 2.3, Pasc 4.1, Pasc 4.2, PP 2.4, PP 2.5, In lab mess 2.1, Asspt 2.3, Asspt 5.12, OAsspt 14, NatBVM 6, NatBVM 11, Abb 6, 1 Nov 2.2, OS 1.10, OS 1.13, OS 2.2, OS 2.3, OS 4.1, OS 4.6, OS 5.9, Ded 3.1, Ded 3.3, Ded 5.2, Ded 5.7, Ded 5.9, Mart *passim*, Clem 1, Clem 2, Mal *passim*, And 1.5, And 1.6, And 1.10, And 2.4, And 2.5, Humb *passim*

Deceit   Adv 1.3, Adv 5.3, VNat 6.5, Nat 2.3, Pasc 1.12, 1 Nov 5.11

Delight   Adv 5.1, VNat 4.1, VNat 5.5, VNat 5.6, Nat 3.3, Circ 3.10, Circ 3.11, P Epi 2.4, Sept 1.3, Quad 1.6, Quad 5.6, Quad 5.7, Ben 12, Asspt 3.4, Mich 1.5, 1 Nov 5.4, 1 Nov 5.10, 1 Nov 5.12, OS 1.4, OS 1.10, OS 3.3, OS 4.2, OS 5.8, Ded 2.4, Ded 4.6, Ded 6.3, Clem 6, And 1.2, And 1.3

Demons   Adv 6.2, Circ 3.11, Quad 1.2, Pasc 1 (alt).4, Pasc 3.2, OPasc 1.3, Asc 1.2, Asc 6.11, Mart 12, Mart 16

Depravity   Ann 1 (alt).12, Pasc 1.16

Desert   VNat 5.5, P Epi 2.5, Pasc 1.3, Pasc 1.11, 6 p P 1.1, 6 p P 1.2, Asspt 4.1, Ded 1.2

Desires   Adv 5.3, Adv 6.2, VNat 1.2, VNat 2.3, VNat 2.4, VNat 3.5, VNat 5.2, VNat 5.7, Nat 3.5, Nat 4.3, Circ 1.1, Circ 1.5, Epi 3.6, P Epi 1.4, P Epi 2.9, Pur 2.2, Quad 2.4, Quad 5.3, Quad 5.8, Ben 9, Ann 1.8, Ann 1 (alt).8, Ann 2.1, Palm 3.5, 4 HM 1, 4 HM 5, 4 HM 14, 5 HM 3, Pasc 1.10, Pasc 1.18, Pasc 1 (alt).10, Pasc 3.3, Pasc 4.1, OPasc 1.7, Asspt 2.3, Asspt 5.1, Asspt 5.2, Abb 4, Mich 1.5, Mich 2.4, 1 Nov 1.1, 1 Nov 1.2, 1 Nov 3.1, 1 Nov 3.3, 1 Nov 3.4, 1 Nov 4.1, 1 Nov 4.2, OS 1.6, OS 1 *passim*, OS 2.1, OS 3.2, OS 3.3, OS 4.5, OS 5.5, OS 5.6, OS 5.8, OS 5.9, Ded 4.4, Ded 5.3, Mart 5, Mart 6, Mart 18, Mal 2, Mal 8, And 1.1, And 1.3, And 2.4, Humb 6

Despair   Adv 1.9, Ben 6, Palm 3.5, Pasc 1.11, Pasc 1 (alt).11, In lab mess 1.1, Asspt 4.3, And 1.7

Devils   Adv 1 *passim*, VNat 3.5, Nat 4.1, Circ 3.6, Pur 1.3, Pur 1.4, Quad 5.3, Ann 2.3, 4 HM 10, Pasc 1.1, Pasc 1 (alt).3, Pasc 1 (alt).11, OPasc 1.2, In lab mess 2.1, Asspt 3.5, Asspt 3.7, Asspt 4.3, Asspt 5.2, Asspt 5.10, OAsspt 11, Abb 3, Abb 4, Abb 6, OS 1.15, Ded 3.3, Ded 3.5, Clem 1, Mal 4, And 1.2

Index of Subjects   345

Devotion   Adv 1.1, Adv 3.2, Adv 4.1, Adv 7.1, VNat 1.3, VNat 1.6, VNat 6.2, VNat 6.5, Nat 1.6, Nat 1.7, Innoc 1, Innoc 2, Circ 3.10, Circ 3.11, Epi 2.3, Epi 3.8, P Epi 2.4, P Epi 2.8, Quad 3.1, Quad 4.1, Quad 6.4, Palm 2.5, Pasc 1.14, Pasc 1.18, Pasc 4.2, In lab mess 1.1, In lab mess 2.3, OAsspt 9, NatBVM 6, NatBVM 18, 1 Nov 2.5, 1 Nov 4.2, 1 Nov 5.8, OS 1.1, OS 1.6, OS 1.10, OS 2.1, OS 5.5, Ded 1.4, Ded 3.2, Ded 3.5, Ded 4.4, Mart 5, Mart 17, Mart 18, Clem 6, Mal 5, VAnd 4
Diadem   VNat 6.11, Nat 1.3, Nat 3.4, Epi 2.1
Disciples   Adv 2.3, Adv 4.7, VNat 5.2, Innoc 1, Circ 2.5, Circ 3.7, Epi 3.2, Epi 3.6, P Epi 1.2, P Epi 1.4, SP 1, SP 8, Pur 2.2, Quad 1.2, Quad 1.4, Ben 10, Ben 11, Ben 12, Ann 3.4, Palm 2.5, Palm 3.4, Palm 3.5, 5 HM 2, Pasc 1.2, Pasc 1.5, Pasc 1.11, Pasc 1 (alt).2, Pasc 1 (alt).3, OPasc 1.8, In lab mess 3.6, Asspt 3.2, OAsspt 11, Abb 6, Mich 2.1, 1 Nov 1.3, OS 1.6, Ded 3.2, Ded 4.3, Ded 5.6, VAnd 4, And 2.3, And 2.8
Discipline   Circ 2.4, Circ 3.11, P Epi 2.7, Quad 5.1, Ann 3.9, Palm 2.5, Palm 2.6, Pasc 2.6
Discord   6 p P 1.3
Discretion   Circ 3.11, Pasc 2.4, Pasc 2.6, Pasc 2.8
Disease   Adv 6.1, Adv 7.1, VNat 1.3, VNat 3.1, Nat 3.5, 4 HM 1, Pasc 1.11, Pasc 3.4, Mich 2.3, 1 Nov 2.4, 1 Nov 5.5, 1 Nov 5.9, 1 Nov 5.11, Ded 5.8
Disobedience   P Epi 1.3, Ann 1 (alt).8, Pasc 2.12
Divinity   Adv 4.4, VNat 3.8, VNat 4.1, Circ 2.1, Epi 1.2, Epi 3.2, OEpi 4, 4 HM 2, Pasc 1.10, OAsspt 1, OS 4.2
Divorce   Nat 2.3, P Epi 2.7
Doctor   Nat 3.5, Circ 2.1, Pasc 2.9, Pasc 3.1
Dogs   VNat 4.6, VNat 5.1, Pasc 2.2
Doubt   Sept 1.1, In lab mess 2.1, Asspt 5.2, 1 Nov 3.3, 1 Nov 5.4, 1 Nov 5.7
Dove   Epi 1.7, Epi 3.7, SP 2, Quad 1.3, Pasc 1.9, Pasc 1 (alt).9, Asspt 3.5, Asspt 5.4
Dream   SP 8, Palm 2.7, Pasc 1.3
Dung   Adv 1.10, VNat 6.7, Pur 1.1, Pasc 1.9, Pasc 1 (alt).9, PP 1.1, PP 1.2, PP 1.3, 4 p P 2, In lab mess 2.3, Ded 1.2, Mart 5, Clem 1; *see also* Manure
Dust   VNat 1.2, VNat 2.6, VNat 3.8, Nat 2.1, Nat 2.2, 5 HM 4

Ear   Adv 6.4, VNat 3.10, VNat 4.8, VNat 4.9, VNat 5.2, Nat 2.6, Epi 3.6, SP 2, Sept 1.2, Quad 3.4, Ann 1 (alt).14, Pasc 2.12, In lab mess 2.1,

Asspt 1.4, Asspt 3.7, Mich 1.1, 1 Nov 5.7, OS 1.6, OS 4.3, Mart *passim*, VAnd 4, And 2.5

Earth   Adv 1 *passim*, Adv 4.1, Adv 4.7, Adv 5.1, Adv 6.6, VNat 1.5, VNat 3.7, VNat 4.1, VNat 4.5, VNat 6.8, Nat 1.3, Nat 2.1, Pur 1.3, Ann 3.2, Ann 3.7, 5 HM 1, Pasc 1.3, Pasc 1.12, Pasc 3.5, Pasc 3.6, Pasc 4.2, OPasc 1.8, OPasc 2.1, OPasc 2.3, In lab mess 3.5, In lab mess 3.6, In lab mess 3.9, Asspt 1.2, Asspt 1.4, Asspt 2.1, Asspt 3.1, Asspt 4.2, Asspt 5.1, OAsspt 6, NatBVM 10, NatBVM 12, NatBVM 14, NatBVM 16, Mich 1.5, 1 Nov 1.1, 1 Nov 1.4, 1 Nov 2.1, 1 Nov 2.2, 1 Nov 3.1, 1 Nov 3.3, 1 Nov 5.3, 1 Nov 5.4, 1 Nov 5.5, OS 1.4, OS 1.9, OS 1.13, OS 1.14, OS 4.6, OS 5.1, Ded 2.2, Ded 5.6, Ded 5.7, Ded 5.10, Mart *passim*, Clem 5, Mal 1, Mal 4, VAnd 3, And 2.6, Humb 1

Earthquake   Pasc 1 (alt).6

Easter   Palm 3.5

Ecclesiastes   Epi 2.2

Eden   OS 5.8

Egypt   Adv 1.8, VNat 1.5, VNat 3.9, VNat 6.10, Epi 3.3, P Epi 1.5, Pasc 1.11, Pasc 1 (alt).11, Pasc 2.2, OPasc 1.5, 6 p P 1.1, 6 p P 1.2, OS 5.11, Ded 1.2

Elders   Palm 1.3, Pasc 1.10, Pasc 1 (alt).10, Asspt 5.12

Elect   Nat 5.1, Circ 2.3, Sept 1.1, Quad 5.8, Ann 1.4, 4 HM 5, OPasc 2.3

Elijah   Quad 3.2, Asc 3.2, Asc 3.5, Asc 6.9, Asc 6.14, Mal 8

Elisha   Pasc 1.7, Pasc 1 (alt).7, Pasc 3.1, Asc 3.5, Asc 6.14

Elizabeth   Nat 2.4, Asspt 2.8, OAsspt 10, OAsspt 12, OAsspt 13, NatBVM 9, Ded 2.2, Mart 1

Emmanuel   Adv 1.11, Adv 2.1, VNat 6.6, Nat 5.1, 1 Nov 5.3

Emmaus   Pasc 3.6

Enemies   Adv 4.7, VNat 2.2, VNat 2.7, Nat 1.3, Nat 1.4, Nat 2.4, Nat 4.1, Circ 3.6, P Epi 1.4, Pur 1.4, Quad 3.1, Quad 5.1, Quad 5.3, Quad 5.4, Quad 6.4, Ben 11, Ann 2.3, Ann 3.3, 4 HM 4, Pasc 1 *passim*, Pasc 1 (alt).2, Pasc 1 (alt).4, OPasc 2.2, In lab mess 1.3, In lab mess 1.4, Asspt 2.3, Asspt 2.5, Asspt 5.1, Asspt 5.12, Mich 1.5, 1 Nov 2.2, OS 1.1, OS 1.8, Ded 3 *passim*, Ded 4.5, Ded 5.5, Mart 15, Clem 1, Clem 2, Mal 4, And 1.2, And 1.3, And 1.5, And 2.6, And 2.7, Humb 1, Humb 5

Enoch   Asc 3.2, Asc 6.9

Envy   P Epi 2.9, Pur 2.2, Sept 1.5, Palm 3.1, 5 HM 3, OPasc 2.2, In lab mess 3.2, 1 Nov 2.2, 1 Nov 3.1, 1 Nov 5.7, 1 Nov 5.10, Clem 1

Epiphany   Epi 3.2

Eucharist   5 HM 2, 6 p P 1.4
Evangelist   Nat 4.2, Circ 1.4, Circ 2.2, Epi 1.6, Epi 1.7, Epi 1.8, Epi 3.5, P Epi 2.8, Asspt 5.3, Asspt 5.10, Ded 2.3, And 1.6, And 2.2
Eve   Adv 1.4, VNat 4.3, VNat 4.5, Ann 1.8, Ann 1 (alt).8, Ann 2.3, OAsspt 1, OAsspt 2, NatBVM 6, OS 1 *passim*, Mal 5, And 1.9
Evil   Adv 1 *passim*, Adv 2.2, Adv 3.3, Adv 6.2, Adv 7.1, VNat 2.2, VNat 3.2, VNat 3.5, VNat 3.8, VNat 5.2, VNat 6.1, Nat 1.7, Nat 2.3, Nat 3.2, Circ 1.5, Circ 2.3, Circ 2.5, Circ 3.6, Circ 3.10, Epi 3.3, SP 1, SP 2, Pur 1.4, Sept 1.5, Quad 1.2, Quad 2.3, Quad 5.2, Ben 5, Ann 1 *passim*, Ann 1 (alt).6, Ann 1 (alt).8, Ann 1 (alt).9, Ann 3.3, Ann 3.4, Ann 3.6, Palm 2.7, 4 HM 8, 4 HM 13, 5 HM 3, 5 HM 4, Pasc 1.1, Pasc 1.2, Pasc 1.4, Pasc 1.17, Pasc 1 (alt).2, In lab mess 1.2, In lab mess 1.4, In lab mess 3.3, Asspt 2.8, Asspt 4.4, Mich 2.4, 1 Nov 2.1, 1 Nov 5.7, 1 Nov 5.10, 1 Nov 5.11, 1 Nov 5.12, OS 1.2, OS 1.8, OS 1.13, Ded 2.4, Ded 3.3, Ded 4.4, Ded 4.5, Ded 5.3, Mart 7, Mal 4, Mal 6, And 1 *passim*, And 2.5, And 2.7, And 2.8, Humb 6
Exile   Adv 1.2, Adv 6.3, Adv 6.4, VNat 4.1, Nat 1.3, Epi 1.1, Epi 2.2, Quad 5.3, Quad 6.1, Ann 1 (alt).9, 4 HM 4, OPasc 2.3
Exodus   Ded 1.2
Eyes   Adv 1.4, Adv 1.8, Adv 3.2, Adv 6.1, Adv 6.2, Adv 6.4, VNat 2.1, VNat 2.2, VNat 2.4, VNat 3 *passim*, VNat 4.5, VNat 4.8, VNat 4.9, VNat 5.2, VNat 6.4, Nat 2.6, Nat 4.2, Epi 1.1, Epi 3.3, P Epi 2.1, SP 2, SP 7, Sept 1.2, Quad 1.2, Quad 2.1, Quad 3.4, Quad 4.3, Ann 1.8, Ann 1 (alt).8, Ann 3.7, Palm 2.7, Palm 3.4, 4 HM *passim*, Pasc 2.8, Pasc 3.2, OPasc 1.7, In lab mess 2.1, In lab mess 3.1, Asspt 1.4, Asspt 2.3, Asspt 3.5, Asspt 3.7, Asspt 5.8, OAsspt 9, Abb 2, Abb 4, Mich 1.1, Mich 2.3, Mich 2.4, 1 Nov 1.1, 1 Nov 1.4, 1 Nov 2.1, 1 Nov 2.5, 1 Nov 5.7, 1 Nov 5.10, OS 1.8, OS 1.13, OS 4.3, OS 5.5, Ded 2.1, Ded 3.1, Ded 3.3, Ded 4.4, Ded 4.6, Mart 8, Mart 11, Mart 14, Mal 3, And 1.5, Humb 6

Face   Adv 6.4, VNat 3.2, Nat 1.3, SP 5, Quad 1.4, Quad 1.5, Quad 1.6, Quad 3.2, Ann 1.14, Ann 1 (alt).10, Palm 2.7, Pasc 2.12
Faith   Adv 7.2, VNat 1.6, VNat 3 *passim*, VNat 4.8, VNat 5.4, VNat 5.5, VNat 6.4, VNat 6.5, VNat 6.10, Nat 2.4, Epi 2.4, SP 5, Pur 1.2, Pur 1.4, Pur 2.2, Quad 1.1, Quad 5.5, Ann 1.3, Ann 1.14, Ann 1 (alt).14, Ann 3.3, Ann 3.9, Palm 1.4, Pasc 1.4, Pasc 2 *passim*, OPasc 1 *passim*, Asc 5.2, Asc 6.8, Pent 1.4, In lab mess 3.3, In lab mess 3.4, In lab mess 3.6, Asspt 5.2, Asspt 5.6, OAsspt 10, NatBVM *passim*, Abb 6, Abb 7, Mich 1.1, OS 2.5, OS 2.7, OS 4.1, OS 5.8, Ded 2.3, Ded 3.3, Ded 5.2, Ded 5.7, Ded 5.9, Ded 6.1, Mart *passim*, Mal 7, VAnd 4

Fasting   P Epi 2.7, Quad 1.1, Quad 1.6, Quad 2.2, Quad 2.4, Quad 3
  passim, Quad 4.1, Quad 4.2, Quad 4.3, Ann 3.10, 4 HM 11
Father   Adv 1 *passim*, Adv 2.3, Adv 3.4, Adv 5.2, Adv 5.3, VNat 1.2, VNat
  2.7, VNat 4.1, VNat 4.6, VNat 6 *passim*, Nat 5.2, Nat 5.3, Circ 1.5,
  Circ 2.1, Circ 2.4, Circ 3.4, Epi 1.6, Epi 2.3, Epi 3.8, P Epi 2.3, Pur
  2.2, Sept 2.1, Quad 1.2, Quad 1.3, Quad 5.7, Ben 10, Ann 1.6, Ann
  1 (alt).9, Ann 1 (alt).10, Ann 1 (alt).11, Ann 2.2, Ann 2.3, Ann 3.7,
  Palm 3.4, 4 HM *passim*, Pasc 1 *passim*, Pasc 1 (alt).3, Pasc 2.1, Pasc
  3.4, Pasc 3.5, Pasc 3.6, OPasc 1.1, OPasc 1.8, OPasc 2.1
Fear   Adv 2.1, Adv 3.6, VNat 3.5, Nat 3.4, Circ 3.5, P Epi 1.4, P Epi 1.5,
  P Epi 2.8, P Epi 2.9, Sept 1.1, Quad 2.3, Quad 4.3, Ann 1.14, Ann
  2.3, Ann 3.3, Ann 3.9, Pasc 2.11, Pasc 3.6, OPasc 2.3, Asc 2.3, Asc
  2.5, Asspt 4.3, NatBVM 7, 1 Nov 5.5, OS 2.3, OS 2.6, OS 5.3, Ded
  1.2, Ded 1.4, Ded 3.4, Clem 2, And 1 *passim*, And 2.6
Feast   Nat 1.1, Innoc 1, Circ 1.2, Epi 3.1, Ben 5, Ann 2.1, Ann 3.1, Pasc
  1.14, In lab mess 2.2, Asspt 2.9, Asspt 5.7, Asspt 6.1, OAsspt 10,
  NatBVM 3, 1 Nov 2.5, OS 1.1, OS 1.11, OS 1.15, OS 5.1, OS 5.8,
  OS 5.9, Ded 1.1, Ded 1.3, Ded 3.2, Ded 5.1, Mart 18, Clem 4, VAnd
  1, VAnd 2, VAnd 3, And 1.3
Feet   VNat 2.3, VNat 4.8, Nat 1.8, Circ 2.3, P Epi 1.3, P Epi 2.1, SP 3,
  Ben 3, Ben 7, Palm 3.1, Palm 3.4, 4 HM 2, 5 HM 2, 5 HM 4, Pasc
  1.4, Pasc 1 (alt).3, Asspt 3.2, Asspt 3.7, Asspt 5.6, OAsspt 3, OAsspt 4,
  OAsspt 5, Abb 2, Mich 2.3, Mich 2.4, 1 Nov 3.4, 1 Nov 4.1, 1 Nov
  4.3, 1 Nov 4.4, 1 Nov 5 *passim*, OS 2.2, Ded 4.3, Mal 3, And 1.6
Fervor   P Epi 2.8, Pur 2.2, Sept 1.2, Pasc 2.1, Asc 6.15, Pent 1.3
Festival   4 HM 1, Pasc 1.16
Fire   Adv 2.3, VNat 3.5, Nat 1.6, Nat 2.4, OEpi 5, P Epi 1.4, P Epi 2.9,
  Pur 2.1, Pur 2.2, Quad 1.2, Quad 5.2, Ben 10, Ben 11, Ann 1 (alt).9,
  Pasc 2.2, Pasc 2.5, Asc 3.7, Asc 6.13, Asc 6.15, Pent 1.1, Pent 1.2,
  Pent 1.6, Pent 2.8, Pent 3.8, JB 3, JB 4, Asspt 2.4, Asspt 5.3, OAsspt
  1, OAsspt 3, OAsspt 5, Mich 2.4, 1 Nov 3.1, 1 Nov 3.2, 1 Nov 3.3,
  1 Nov 4.1, 1 Nov 5.7, 1 Nov 5.8, OS 1.3, OS 1.10, OS 4.6, Mart
  10, Mart 12, Clem 6, Mal *passim*, VAnd 3, And 1.2, And 2.3
Firstborn   OPasc 1.1, 1 Nov 5.2, 1 Nov 5.6
Fish   And 1.3, And 1.4
Fishers   Abb 6, And 1.3, And 2.2
Fishing   Pasc 3.6
Flesh   Adv 1.10, Adv 2.1, Adv 3.2, Adv 4.4, Adv 5.1, Adv 5.3, Adv 6
  passim, VNat 1.3, VNat 1.6, VNat 2.1, VNat 2.2, VNat 2.7, VNat 3.5,
  VNat 3.7, VNat 3.8, VNat 4.4, VNat 5.2, VNat 5.5, VNat 6 *passim*,

Nat 1.1, Nat 1.5, Nat 1.8, Nat 2 *passim*, Nat 3 *passim*, Nat 4.2, Circ 1.1, Circ 1.2, Circ 2.1, Circ 2.3, Circ 3.3, Epi 1.2, Epi 2.2, Epi 3.2, Epi 3.6, Epi 3.7, P Epi 2.1, P Epi 2.5, SP 1, Pur 1.4, Sept 2.2, Quad 2.3, Quad 4.2, Quad 5 *passim*, Quad 6.3, Ben *passim*, Ann 1.5, Ann 1.6, Ann 1.8, Ann 1 (alt).8, Ann 2.2, Ann 2.5, Ann 3.9, Palm 1.1, Palm 2.5, Palm 3.4, 4 HM 5, 4 HM 10, 4 HM 13, Pasc 1 *passim*, Pasc 1 (alt).8, Pasc 1 (alt).11, Pasc 2.1, Pasc 2.2, Pasc 2.11, OPasc 1.7, Rog 1, Rog 2, Asc 1.2, Asc 1.3, Asc 2.4, Asc 3 *passim*, Asc 4.1, Asc 4.2, Asc 6 *passim*, Pent 1.1, Pent 3.2, Pent 3.5, Pent 3.6, JB 7, 6 p P 2.5, In lab mess 3.7, In lab mess 3.8, Asspt 1.3, Asspt 2.3, Asspt 3.2, Asspt 4.3, Asspt 5.4, Asspt 5.5, OAsspt *passim*, NatBVM 7, NatBVM 9, NatBVM 10, Abb 4, Mich 1.3, Mich 2.1, 1 Nov 1.2, 1 Nov 2.2, 1 Nov 5.7, 1 Nov 5.9, OS 1 *passim*, OS 3.1, OS 3.2, OS 4.6, OS 5.3, OS 5.8, OS 5.10, Ded 1.1, Ded 1.4, Ded 3.3, Ded 5.7, Mart *passim*, Clem 2, Clem 3, And 1.7, And 2.7, Humb 1, Humb 5, Humb 6

Flock   VNat 3.6, Ben 8, Pasc 2.3

Flower   Adv 2.3, Adv 2.4, VNat 3.8, Ben 6, Ben 7, Ann 2.1, Ann 2.5, Ann 3.7, Palm 2.4

Food   Adv 2.2, Adv 3.2, Adv 5.2, Adv 6.5, VNat 1.6, VNat 6.9, Nat 1.6, Nat 3.1, Nat 5.1, Circ 2.4, Epi 3.1, P Epi 1.5, P Epi 2.1, SP 7, Sept 1.3, Sept 1.5, Quad 2.4, Quad 4.1, Quad 5.3, Quad 5.6, Quad 6.1, Ann 2.4, Ann 3.1, Palm 1.4, Palm 3.4, 5 HM 1, Pasc 3.1, Pasc 3.6, Pasc 4.2, Asspt 4.4, Asspt 5.5, NatBVM 16, OS 1.2, OS 1.3, OS 2.7, Ded 3.2, Ded 5.10, Mart 12, Mart 13, And 1.9, Humb 2, Humb 4

Forbearance   5 HM 5, Asc 5.1, Asc 5.2, 6 p P 2.2

Foreskin   Circ 1.1, Circ 3.3, OEpi 2

Forgiveness   Adv 4.6, Nat 1.6, Circ 1.5, P Epi 1.4, Quad 4.4, Ann 3.3, Pent 1.3, Pent 1.4, 6 p P 2.4

Fornication   Nat 4.2, Pasc 1.16

Fountain   P Epi 1.2, P Epi 2.8, OPasc 1.8, Asspt 4.1, Asspt 4.9, NatBVM *passim*, 1 Nov 5.9, OS 4.5, Ded 1.4, Ded 4.4, Clem 6, Humb 6

Frankincense   VNat 6.9, Epi 2.1, Epi 2.4, Epi 3.5

Freedom   Sept 2.2, OPasc 1.7, Abb 1, OS 5.8, Ded 4.5

Friends   Adv 2.1, VNat 3.5, VNat 4.7, VNat 6.8, Circ 1.1, SP 3, Pur 1.4, Ann 3.5, 4 HM 4, Pasc 1.3, Pasc 1 (alt).3, Pasc 2.3, Rog 1, Asspt 3.5, NatBVM 8, NatBVM 17, Mich 1.5, 1 Nov 3.2, OS 5.1, OS 5.10, Humb 1, Humb 6

Friendship   Ann 1.14, Asspt 1.2, Mich 1.5

Fruit   Adv 2.4, Adv 3.6, VNat 1.2, VNat 2.7, VNat 3.8, VNat 3.10, VNat 5.6, VNat 6 *passim*, Nat 1.4, Innoc 1, Circ 1.1, Circ 2.2, Circ 3.11,

Epi 3.2, P Epi 2.5, Pur 2.1, Pur 2.3, Pur 3.2, Sept 1.2, Quad 5.5, Ben *passim*, Ann 1.10, Ann 2.4, Ann 3.7, Ann 3.8, Ann 3.9, 4 HM 1, 4 HM 12, Pasc 1.6, Pasc 1.8, Pasc 1 (alt).6, Pasc 3.5, OPasc 2.4, PP 2.1, Asspt 5.3, Asspt 5.5, OAsspt 13, NatBVM 2, NatBVM 3, NatBVM 6, NatBVM 17, Mich 1.4, 1 Nov 2.2, 1 Nov 5.5, OS 2.1, OS 2.3, OS 2.4, OS 4.4, Ded 2.3, Ded 4.3, Ded 4.4, Mart 9, And 1.2, And 2.4
Future   Adv 4.5, VNat 6.4, VNat 6.8, P Epi 1.5, P Epi 2.9, Sept 1.1, Quad 4.1, Ben 2, Ann 3.7, Asspt 5.11, NatBVM 14, NatBVM 15, Mich 2.2, 1 Nov 5.12, OS 1.14, OS 2.6, OS 3.4, OS 4.6, OS 5.2, Ded 3.3, Ded 6.3, Mart 12, Mart 16, Clem 6, And 1.4, Humb 2, Humb 8

Gabriel   Adv 1.2, VNat 4.3, VNat 4.6, VNat 5.3, Nat 4.3, Epi 1.3, Ann 1.14, Ann 1 (alt).14, Ann 2.1, Ann 3.7, OAsspt 10
Galilee   Pasc 1.14, Pasc 1.18, Humb 6
Garden   Adv 2.4, Nat 1.6, Circ 1.1, Ben 5
Garments   VNat 2.1, VNat 2.4, VNat 2.5, Nat 4.1, Nat 5.5, P Epi 1.3, Quad 1.2, Quad 2.5, Quad 2.6, Ben 3, Ann 1.6, Ann 1 (alt).6, Ann 1 (alt).7, Palm 1.4, Palm 2.3, Palm 2.4, Pasc 1.15, Pasc 2.10
Generation   Adv 1.1, Adv 1.11, VNat 1.1, Circ 3.6, 4 HM 8, Pasc 1.5, Pasc 1 (alt).5, In lab mess 3 *passim*, Asspt 1.4, Asspt 5.1, OAsspt 4, OAsspt 12, NatBVM 1, NatBVM 5, Mich 1.6, Humb 2
Generosity   Epi 1.1, P Epi 1.2, Pasc 2.9, OAsspt 7, OS 1.2
Gentile   VNat 6.5, Epi 3.2, Pasc 1.2
Gibbet   Nat 5.2, Epi 2.4, SP 2, Pasc 1.5, Pasc 1.8
Gifts   Adv 3.7, Adv 4.6, Adv 7.1, VNat 1.1, VNat 1.4, VNat 3.10, VNat 4.1, VNat 5.3, VNat 6.2, VNat 6.10, Circ 3.1, Epi 2.4, P Epi 1.3, Pur 3.1, Sept 2.3, Quad 1.2, Quad 1.3, Quad 2.3, Quad 5.7, Quad 5.9, Ann 1.2, Ann 1.3, Ann 3.1, Ann 3.7, Ann 3.9, Palm 1.3, 4 HM 7, Pasc 1.3, Pasc 1.18, Pasc 2.9, Pasc 2.12, Pasc 3.6, Pasc 4.2, Asc 5.2, Pent 2.1, In lab mess 3.5, In lab mess 3.7, Asspt 1.2, Asspt 5.4, OAsspt 1, OAsspt 10, OAsspt 13, NatBVM 12, NatBVM 15, NatBVM 18, Mich 1.2, 1 Nov 5.5, 1 Nov 5.9, OS 1.2, Mart 4, Clem 1, Mal 1, And 2.3, And 2.4
Gladness   VNat 1.1, VNat 4.10, VNat 6.1, Quad 1.2, Ben 12, 4 HM 8, OS 4.5, VAnd 3, Humb 6
Glory   Adv 1.7, Adv 2.4, Adv 2.5, Adv 3.2, Adv 3.3, Adv 4 *passim*, Adv 5.1, Adv 5.3, Adv 6.4, Adv 6.5, Adv 6.6, VNat 1.2, VNat 1.5, VNat 3.7, VNat 4 *passim*, VNat 5.3, Circ 3.2, Ann 1.12, Pasc 1 (alt).14, Pasc 2.10, OPasc 2.1, Asc 2.1, Asc 2.4, Asc 2.6, Asc 3.1, Asc 3.3, Asc 4

passim, Asc 6 *passim,* In lab mess 1.1, Asspt 1.3, Asspt 1.4, Asspt 2.9, Asspt 3.5, Asspt 3.7, Asspt 4.5, Asspt 5.4, Asspt 5.9, Asspt 6.1, OAsspt *passim,* NatBVM 3, NatBVM 12, NatBVM 15, Mich 1.1, Mich 1.4, Mich 2.4, 1 Nov 1.1, 1 Nov 1.2, 1 Nov 1.4, 1 Nov 2.1, 1 Nov 2.2, 1 Nov 2.5, 1 Nov 3.2, 1 Nov 5 *passim,* OS 1.12, OS 2.3, OS 2.5, OS 2.8, OS 3 *passim,* OS 4.2, OS 4.3, OS 4.6, OS 5 *passim,* Ded 2.2, Ded 4.4, Ded 4.6, Ded 5.2, Ded 5.5, Ded 5.7, Ded 6.1, Mart *passim,* Clem *passim,* VAnd 1, VAnd 4, And 1.8, Humb 1, Humb 5
Gold Adv 4.4, VNat 6.9, Nat 3.1, Nat 4.1, Epi 1.5, Epi 2.1, Epi 3.5
Goliath 4 p P *passim*
Goodness VNat 2.1, Nat 1.2, Circ 3.4, Quad 1.3, Quad 1.5, Ben 10, Ann 1.1, Ann 1 (alt).9, 4 HM 1, Pasc 2.6, Asspt 2.6, Asspt 4.3, NatBVM 11, Abb 7, 1 Nov 4.1, 1 Nov 5.5, OS 1.2, OS 1.13, OS 5.1, Ded 4.5, Ded 5.7, Mal 1, Humb 6
Gospel Adv 4.3, Nat 2.4, Nat 4.2, Circ 1.3, Circ 2.3, Epi 1.8, OEpi 2, SP 6, Pur 2.2, Quad 1.3, Quad 3.3, Quad 5.5, Ben 5, Ben 11, Pasc 1.3, Pasc 1 (alt).3, OPasc 1.1, 6 p P 1.1, Asspt 4.4, Asspt 5.1, Asspt 5.7, OAsspt 2, OAsspt 10, NatBVM 8, Mich 1.6, Mich 2.1, Mich 2.3, 1 Nov 5.2, OS 1.4, OS 1.12, OS 2.1, OS 4.1, OS 4.2, Ded 2.3, Ded 4.4, Ded 5.7, Mart 9, Mal 3, VAnd 4
Grace Adv 2.2, Adv 2.5, Adv 3.7, VNat 1.1, VNat 2.6, VNat 3.6, VNat 4.9, VNat 5.3, VNat 6.6, VNat 6.11, Nat 1.6, Nat 1.7, Nat 4.2, Nat 4.3, Circ 3.10, Ann 2.1, Ann 3 *passim,* 5 HM 2, 5 HM 5, Pasc 2.7, Pasc 2.9, Pasc 2.12, Pasc 3.6, Pasc 4.2, Asc 6.8, Asc 6.14, Asc 6.15, JB 11, PP 3.1, PP 3.2, 6 p P 2.1, 6 p P 2.4, 6 p P 2.6, In lab mess 3 *passim,* Asspt 1.3, Asspt 1.4, Asspt 2.5, Asspt 2.8, Asspt 2.9, Asspt 3.6, Asspt 4 *passim,* Asspt 5 *passim,* Asspt 6.1, OAsspt *passim,* NatBVM *passim,* Mich 1.1, Mich 1.2, Mich 1.3, Mich 2.2, Mich 2.3, Mich 2.4, 1 Nov 3.2, 1 Nov 4.4, 1 Nov 5.5, 1 Nov 5.8, 1 Nov 5.12, OS 1.3, OS 1.10, OS 1.14, OS 5.1, Ded 1.5, Ded 1.6, Ded 4.4, Ded 5.2, Ded 5.7, Ded 6.1, Mart *passim,* Clem 6, Mal 3, And 1.1, And 2.4, Humb 2
Graces Asspt 2.2, NatBVM 6
Grain Adv 4.7, Ben 4, Pasc 3.5
Grass Nat 1.7, Circ 3.2, Circ 3.3, Epi 1.2
Greed Ben 5, Pasc 1.16, Pasc 3.3, Asspt 2.6, Asspt 5.1, Asspt 5.2, Mich 2.1
Grief Quad 1.2, Quad 2.3, Ann 3.5, Palm 2.1, Palm 3.5, Pasc 1.12, Asspt 4.3, Asspt 5.8, OAsspt 9, OAsspt 14, OAsspt 15, 1 Nov 5.11, OS 1.14, And 1.6, Humb 6, Humb 7
Guilt Adv 2.5, Adv 6.1, P Epi 1.3, 4 HM 7, In lab mess 1.4, Asspt 2.4, OS 1.12, Ded 4.5

Hand, Hands   Adv 4.1, Adv 4.7, Adv 5.3, Adv 6.1, Adv 6.2, VNat 1.4,
    VNat 3.5, VNat 4 *passim*, VNat 6.4, VNat 6.9, Nat 1.8, Nat 4.2, Circ
    3.4, P Epi 1.3, P Epi 1.5, SP 3, SP 7, SP 8, Sept 1.4, Sept 1.5, Quad
    3.4, Quad 5.2, Ann 1.5, Ann 1.6, Ann 1 (alt).9, Ann 2.3, Ann 3.5,
    Palm 1.3, 4 HM *passim*, 5 HM 4, Pasc 1 *passim*, Pasc 2 *passim*, Pasc
    3.6, OPasc 2.1, In lab mess 2.1, In lab mess 2.2, In lab mess 2.3,
    In lab mess 3.4, Asspt 1.1, Asspt 1.4, Asspt 2.6, Asspt 3.1, OAsspt 7,
    NatBVM 14, NatBVM 18, Abb 7, Mich 2.3, Mich 2.4, 1 Nov 2.1,
    1 Nov 2.2, 1 Nov 2.3, 1 Nov 4.2, 1 Nov 5.1, 1 Nov 5.4, 1 Nov 5.7,
    OS 1.9, OS 1.13, OS 4.2, Ded 1.6, Ded 2.1, Ded 2.2, Ded 6.1, Ded
    6.2, Mart 8, Mal 3, And 1.9
Handmaiden   Nat 4.2, Ann 3.7, Ann 3.9
Happiness   Adv 6.6, VNat 3.5, Quad 5.7, Quad 5.8, Palm 2.1, Mich 2.4,
    OS 2.1, OS 2.2, OS 2.6, OS 3.4, OS 4.3, OS 4.6, OS 5.1, OS 5.3,
    Ded 4.5, VAnd 3
Hardship   Circ 3.8, Ben 11, Palm 2.2, Pasc 4.1
Hatred   Circ 3.4, Circ 3.5, SP 2, Pasc 1.16, Pasc 2.8, OPasc 2.3, Asspt 2.5,
    1 Nov 2.2, 1 Nov 2.3, Ded 5.7, And 2.7
Head   Adv 1.10, Adv 6.1, Nat 1.3, Nat 4.1, Circ 2.3, Circ 3.3, Epi 1.6,
    P Epi 2.1, SP 3, Quad 1 *passim*, Quad 2.1, 5 HM 4, Pasc 1.1, Pasc
    1.3, Pasc 1.8, Pasc 1 (alt).1, Pasc 1 (alt).8, Pasc 1 (alt).14, OAsspt 7,
    OAsspt 15, NatBVM 4, 1 Nov 4.1, 1 Nov 4.3, 1 Nov 4.4, 1 Nov
    5 *passim*, OS 4.2, OS 5.8, OS 5.9, OS 5.11, Mart 14, Mal 3, Mal 4,
    And 2.7
Heart   Adv 1.6, Adv 1.10, Adv 2.1, Adv 2.2, Adv 3.2, Adv 3.3, Adv 3.4,
    Adv 4 *passim*, Adv 5.2, Adv 5.3, Adv 6.2, VNat 1.6, VNat 2.1, VNat 3
    passim, VNat 4 *passim*, VNat 5.1, VNat 5.5, VNat 5.6, VNat 6 *passim*,
    Nat 2.4, Nat 2.6, Nat 3.3, Nat 3.6, Nat 4.2, Nat 4.3, Nat 5.4, Circ
    3.2, Circ 3.8, P Epi 2.8, SP 6, Pur 1.2, Pur 1.4, Sept 1.2, Sept 1.5,
    Sept 2.3, Quad 1.2, Quad 1.6, Quad 2 *passim*, Quad 4.2, Quad 4.3,
    Quad 4.4, Quad 5.7, Ben 10, Ann 1.9, Ann 1 (alt).9, Ann 1 (alt).11,
    Ann 2.4, Ann 3 *passim*, Palm 2.2, Palm 3.3, Palm 3.4, 4 HM 6, 4
    HM 8, 5 HM 1, Pasc 1 *passim*, Pasc 1 (alt).3, Pasc 1 (alt).4, Pasc 2
    passim, Pasc 3.1, Pasc 3.3, OPasc 1.4, OPasc 1.7, Rog 1, Rog 2, Asc
    4.9, Asc 4.14, Asc 6 *passim*, Pent 2.8, Pent 3.5, 6 p P 2.1, 6 p P 2.3,
    In lab mess 1.1, In lab mess 1.2, In lab mess 1.4, In lab mess 3.8, In
    lab mess 3.9, Asspt 2.5, Asspt 2.6, Asspt 2.8, Asspt 3.3, Asspt 4.3, Asspt
    4.7, Asspt 5 *passim*, OAsspt *passim*, NatBVM *passim*, Abb 6, Abb 7,
    Mich 1.1, Mich 1.5, 1 Nov 1.1, 1 Nov 1.2, 1 Nov 1.3, 1 Nov 4.2,
    1 Nov 5.1, 1 Nov 5.5, 1 Nov 5.8, OS 1 *passim*, OS 2.2, OS 2.4, OS

Index of Subjects 353

    4.3, OS 5.2, OS 5.5, OS 5.6, Ded 1.4, Ded 1.7, Ded 2.3, Ded 2.4, Ded 3.2, Ded 4.3, Ded 4.6, Ded 5 *passim*, Mart *passim*, Clem 4, Mal 2, Mal 8, VAnd 1, VAnd 4, And 1.6, And 1.7, And 2 *passim*, Humb *passim*

Heaven   Adv 1.2, Adv 1.6, Adv 2.1, Adv 4.5, VNat 3.5, VNat 4.1, VNat 4.6, VNat 6.8, Nat 1.6, Nat 2.4, Nat 4.2, Pur 1.3, Quad 6.3, Ben 2, Ben 9, Ann 1.13, Ann 1 (alt).10, Ann 1 (alt).13, Ann 3.7, Palm 1.3, 4 HM 13, 5 HM 1, Pasc 1.9, Pasc 1 (alt).6, Pasc 3.1, OPasc 1.8, OPasc 2.1, OPasc 2.2, OPasc 2.3, OPasc 2.5, In lab mess 2.2, In lab mess 2.3, In lab mess 3.5, In lab mess 3.6, In lab mess 3.8, In lab mess 3.9, Asspt 1 *passim*, Asspt 3.1, Asspt 4.1, Asspt 4.8, OAsspt 8, OAsspt 10, OAsspt 12, NatBVM *passim*, Mich 1.1, Mich 1.4, Mich 1.5, Mich 2.2, 1 Nov 2.1, 1 Nov 2.3, 1 Nov 5.5, OS 1 *passim*, OS 4.1, OS 5.1, OS 5.2, OS 5.5, Ded 1.6, Ded 2.2, Ded 2.4, Ded 5.1, Ded 5.2, Ded 5.6, Ded 5.10, Ded 6.2, Mart 3, Mart *passim*, Clem 3, Mal 1, Mal 3, Mal 5, VAnd 3, And 1.4, And 2.5, Humb 5

Hell   Adv 1.6, Adv 2.1, VNat 2.2, VNat 2.6, P Epi 1.4, P Epi 1.5, P Epi 2.8, Quad 4.1, Ann 1.7, Ann 1 (alt).7, Ann 2.3, Ann 3.5, 4 HM 9, Pasc 1.5, Pasc 3.3, Asc 2.1, Asc 3.6, Asc 4.1, Asc 6.7, Pent 1.5, Pent 2.6, Pent 3.1, Pent 3.8

Herod   Innoc 2, Epi 3.3, Epi 3.4, Pasc 1.11, Pasc 1 (alt).11, OPasc 1.5, 1 Nov 1.1

Holiness   VNat 1.1, VNat 3.4, VNat 5 *passim*, Innoc 1, Innoc 2, Innoc 3, Ann 1.5, NatBVM 6, Abb 7, 1 Nov 5.5, OS 5.1, OS 5.2, Ded 1.4, Ded 4.4, Ded 5.8, Ded 5.9, Mal 1, Mal 2, Mal 7, Humb 2

Holy Spirit   Adv 1 *passim*, Adv 2.4, Adv 4.2, VNat 1.1, VNat 2.7, VNat 2.8, VNat 3.2, VNat 3.10, VNat 4.9, VNat 6.10, VNat 6.11, Nat 2.4, Nat 2.6, Nat 5.2, Circ 1.2, Circ 3.2, Circ 3.5, Epi 1.3, Epi 1.5, Epi 3.7, OEpi 2, SP 5, Pur 2.2, Pur 2.3, Pur 3.2, Sept 1.2, Sept 1.5, Quad 1.3, Quad 2.3, Quad 2.5, Ben 10, Ann 1.1, Ann 1.3, Ann 1.5, Ann 2 *passim*, Ann 3.7, Ann 3.9, Palm 3.5, 5 HM 2, Pasc 1.8, Pasc 1.18, Pasc 2.1, Pasc 2.2, Pasc 3.5, Pasc 3.6, Pasc 4.1, Pasc 4.2, OPasc 1.6, OPasc 1.8, OPasc 2 *passim*, Asc 3 *passim*, Asc 4.1, Asc 5.2, Asc 6 *passim*, Pent 1 *passim*, Pent 2 *passim*, Pent 3 *passim*, Asspt 1.3, Asspt 2.2, Asspt 2.8, Asspt 4.6, Asspt 5.3, OAsspt *passim*, NatBVM *passim*, 1 Nov 3.2, OS 2 *passim*, OS 3.2, OS 4.2, OS 4.3, OS 4.4, Ded 1 *passim*, Ded 4.4, Ded 4.5, Ded 5.7, Ded 5.8, Ded 6.1, Clem 4, Clem 5, And 1.9, And 2 *passim*

Honey   Adv 2.3, OEpi 5, Quad 5.7, Pasc 1.3, Pasc 1 (alt).3

Honor   VNat 5.7, Nat 4.1, Pur 2.3, Quad 6.2, Ann 2.2, OPasc 2.1

Hope   Adv 2.3, Adv 3.3, Adv 6.6, VNat 4.1, VNat 4.10, VNat 6.1, Nat 2.5,
   Nat 3.5, Nat 4.3, SP 1, Sept 1.1, Sept 1.2, Quad 1.1, Quad 6.4, Ann
   3.3, Ann 3.7, Pasc 1.8, Pasc 1 (alt).14, OPasc 2.3, Asc 4.1, Asc 4.7, Asc
   5.2, Pent 1.4, 6 p P 2.6, In lab mess 1.2, In lab mess 1.4, In lab mess
   3.1, In lab mess 3.8, Asspt 2.1, Asspt 5.11, NatBVM 7, NatBVM 16,
   NatBVM 17, Abb 7, Mich 2.2, OS 1.10, OS 1.13, OS 2.5, OS 2.6,
   OS 3.4, OS 4.6, Ded 1.4, Ded 5.5, Ded 5.6, And 1 *passim*
House   Adv 2.1, Adv 3.4, Adv 3.7, Adv 6.3, VNat 1.6, VNat 2.4, VNat 2.7,
   VNat 3.5, VNat 4.8, VNat 6.7, VNat 6.8, VNat 6.10, Nat 1.6, Circ
   3.7, Epi 1.3, Epi 3.7, P Epi 2.3, P Epi 2.4, Sept 1.3, 4 HM 12, Pasc
   3.1, OPasc 2.2, Asspt 2 *passim*, Asspt 3 *passim*, OAsspt 10, Mich 1.4,
   Mich 2.1, 1 Nov 1.3, 1 Nov 5.5, OS 1.10, OS 3.1, OS 5.3, Ded 1
   passim, Ded 2 *passim*, Ded 3.1, Ded 3.3, Ded 3.5, Ded 4.4, Ded 4.6,
   Ded 5 *passim*, Ded 6.1, Ded 6.3, Mart 5, Mart 6, Humb 2, Humb 6
Human   Adv 1 *passim*, Adv 2.1, Adv 2.2, Adv 2.3, Adv 3 *passim*, Adv 4.1,
   Adv 4.4, Adv 5.1, Adv 5.3, Adv 7.1, VNat 1 *passim*, VNat 2.4, VNat
   3 *passim*, VNat 4 *passim*, VNat 5.3, VNat 6.6, VNat 6.10, Nat 1.2, Nat
   1.3, Nat 1.4, Nat 2 *passim*, Nat 3 *passim*, Nat 4.1, Nat 5.4, Innoc 2,
   Circ 1.1, Circ 1.2, Circ 2.1, Circ 2.2, Circ 3.2, Circ 3.3, Circ 3.5,
   Epi 1 *passim*, Epi 3.7, P Epi 1.3, P Epi 2.1, SP 7, Pur 2.2, Pur 3.1,
   Sept 1.5, Quad 1.5, Quad 2.1, Quad 4.2, Ann 1.1, Ann 1.7, Ann 2.1,
   Ann 2.2, Ann 2.3, Ann 3.5, Palm 2.6, Palm 3.1, Palm 3.2, Palm 3.5,
   4 HM *passim*, Pasc 1 *passim*, Pasc 1 (alt).3, Pasc 2.4, Pasc 2.7, Pasc
   2.8, Pasc 3.3, OPasc 1.1, OPasc 1.8, OPasc 2.1, Asc 2.3, Asc 4.12,
   Asc 6.11, Pent 2.7, V PP 3, 6 p P 2.1, 6 p P 3.1, In lab mess 1.2, In
   lab mess 2.1, In lab mess 3.2, Asspt 1.2, Asspt 4.1, Asspt 4.5, Asspt
   4.8, Asspt 5.1, Asspt 5.5, Asspt 5.12, OAsspt *passim*, NatBVM *passim*,
   Mich 1.4, Mich 1.6, Mich 2.2, 1 Nov 1.2, 1 Nov 1.4, 1 Nov 2.2, 1
   Nov 2.3, 1 Nov 3.1, 1 Nov 4.1, 1 Nov 5 *passim*, OS 1.7, OS 1.10,
   OS 1.14, OS 3.3, OS 4.2, OS 4.3, OS 4.5, OS 5 *passim*, Ded 1.6,
   Ded 4.6, Ded 5.5, Ded 5.7, Ded 5.8, Ded 6.1, Ded 6.2, Mart *passim*,
   VAnd 3, And 2.3, And 2.6, Humb 1, Humb 5
Humble   OPasc 2.1
Humiliation   Adv 4.3, Adv 4.4, Adv 6.1, Nat 5.5, Ben 11, Palm 1.1, 4
   HM 3, OS 2.5, OS 4.6, OS 5.9
Humility   Adv 2.4, Adv 2.5, Adv 3.2, Adv 4.4, Adv 5.3, VNat 1.5, VNat
   4.6, VNat 5.5, VNat 6.5, VNat 6.6, Nat 1.1, Nat 2.6, Nat 4.2, Nat
   4.3, Circ 2.1, Circ 3.1, Circ 3.9, Epi 1.6, Epi 1.7, Epi 2.3, Epi 2.4,
   OEpi 3, OEpi 4, SP 8, Pur 2.3, Pur 3.3, Quad 2.2, Quad 5.4, Quad
   5.6, Quad 5.9, Ben 4, Ann 3.9, Palm 2.3, Palm 2.6, 4 HM 2, 4 HM

5, Pasc 1.3, Pasc 1.13, Pasc 1 (alt).3, Pasc 3.5, Pasc 4.1, Asc 2.6, Pent 2.5, PP 1.4, 4 p P 6, Asspt 4.7, Asspt 4.8, Asspt 5.3, Asspt 6.1, OAsspt 7, OAsspt 12, OAsspt 13, NatBVM 9, NatBVM 12, NatBVM 18, Abb 2, Abb 3, Abb 7, Mich 1.2, 1 Nov 1.2, 1 Nov 2.2, 1 Nov 2.3, 1 Nov 5.3, 1 Nov 5.9, OS 1.8, OS 1.11, Ded 1.2, Ded 3.2, Ded 4.3, Ded 5.2, Mart 13, Mal 1, And 2.8

Hunger   Adv 4.7, Adv 6.5, Sept 1.3, Sept 1.5, Pasc 1 (alt).11, Pasc 3.3, In lab mess 3.4, OS 1.11, Ded 3.2

Husband   VNat 3.9, Circ 2.4, Ann 1.8, Ann 1 (alt).8, Ann 2.1, Ann 3.5

Hypocrites   Quad 1.4, Quad 1.5, Ben 6

Ignorance   Adv 3.3, Adv 3.5, SP 5, Pur 1.2, Pur 1.3, Sept 1.5, Quad 5.5, 4 HM 10, Asspt 4.5, 1 Nov 5.11, OS 2.1, OS 4.5, OS 5.10

Ignorant   Adv 7.2, 1 Nov 4.4, 1 Nov 5.9, Ded 4.1, Ded 6.1, Mart 5

Image   Adv 5.3, Adv 6.3, Ann 1.7, Ann 1 (alt).7, OPasc 1.1

Imitate   Adv 4.7, Innoc 1, Circ 2.4, Circ 3.1, OEpi 5, 4 HM 11, OAsspt 11, 1 Nov 5.10, OS 1.11, Ded 5.2, Mal 7, And 1.10, And 2.6

Imitation   Nat 1.2, Nat 3.1, Quad 2.1, 4 HM 12, Asc 5.2, JB 5, PP 3.4, Asspt 5.12, OAsspt 10, OS 1.6, Ded 5.8, Mart 12, Mart 13

Impatience   SP 4, Sept 1.5, Quad 1.6, Palm 2.2, 4 HM 8, Pasc 1 (alt).2, Pasc 2.9, Pasc 2.11

Incarnation   Circ 2.2, Ann 2.1, Ann 2.2, Ann 3.8, Pasc 3.1, OAsspt 11, 1 Nov 5.3, 1 Nov 5.9, OS 4.1, OS 4.2

Incorruption   VNat 4.4, VNat 4.6, Nat 2.5, Circ 2.1

Infancy   Nat 4.2, Nat 5.2, Nat 5.5, Circ 3.1, Epi 1.7, Pur 2.1

Infants   Nat 1.1, Nat 3.1, Nat 3.2, Nat 3.3, Nat 5.1, Innoc 2, Innoc 3, Epi 1.5, Epi 1.8, Epi 3.5, Epi 3.7

Inheritance   Adv 4.5, VNat 2.5, Ann 2.2, Palm 3.2, 4 HM 11, Pasc 1.9

Iniquity   VNat 1.2, Nat 2.3, Nat 2.4, Epi 1.6, P Epi 1.1, P Epi 2.6, Pur 2.2, Quad 4.3, Ann 1.5, Ann 3.3, 4 HM 8, 5 HM 4, Pasc 1.4, Pasc 1 (alt).4, Pasc 2.8, Asspt 5.7, Abb 2, 1 Nov 2.3, OS 1.12, OS 1.13, Ded 1.3, Ded 2.3, Ded 3.2, Ded 4.3, Ded 5.2, Mart 3, Mal 3

Injustice   4 HM 6, 1 Nov 5.9, Mal 6

Innocence   Adv 1.5, Adv 5.3, VNat 2.4, VNat 4.6, Circ 2.1, Pasc 2.10

Innocents   Innoc 1, Innoc 2, Circ 3.6, Ann 2.3, Ann 3.4, Palm 1.3

Investiture   5 HM 2

Isaac   Adv 1.11, VNat 6.9, Mart 8, Mart 17

Isaiah   Adv 1.3, Adv 2.1, VNat 4.3, Nat 1.6, Nat 3.2, Circ 1.4, Quad 1.2, Ann 2.5, 4 HM 2, Pasc 1.2, OPasc 2.2, OAsspt 8, 1 Nov 1.1, 1 Nov 1.2, 1 Nov 1.4, 1 Nov 3.1, 1 Nov 4.1, 1 Nov 5.4, Ded 1.7

Israel   VNat 3.6, VNat 5.1, VNat 6.8, Epi 3.3, Epi 3.4, Sept 1.4, Quad 2.1,
    Ben 11, Palm 2.4, Palm 3.1, 4 HM 2, Pasc 1 *passim*, Pasc 1 (alt).1,
    Pasc 1 (alt).2, Pasc 1 (alt).4, Asspt 2.1, OS 2.7, OS 5.11, Ded 4.2
Israelite   OPasc 1.5

Jacob   Adv 1.11, VNat 2.2, VNat 5.3, VNat 6.9, P Epi 2.1, P Epi 2.8,
    Quad 2.6, OPasc 1.7, Asspt 3.1, NatBVM 4, NatBVM 16, Ded 1.7,
    Ded 6.1
James   Nat 1.5, Innoc 1, Palm 3.3, Pasc 2.9, OAsspt 11
Jeremiah   VNat 2.2, Pur 3.1, Asspt 2.8, 1 Nov 1.2, Humb 1
Jericho   VNat 6.1, Ann 1.7, Ann 1 (alt).7, Asspt 2.2, Mart 1
Jerusalem   Adv 1.5, Adv 5.3, VNat 1.4, VNat 2.1, VNat 2.4, VNat 2.6,
    VNat 3.6, Circ 3.7, Epi 3.3, P Epi 2.5, Sept 1.3, Sept 1.4, Sept 2.3,
    Quad 2.5, Ann 1.7, Ann 1 (alt).7, Palm 1.2, Palm 3.1, Pasc 2.4, Asspt
    4.8, NatBVM 13, NatBVM 14, NatBVM 16, Mich 1.4, Mich 1.5,
    OS 2.4, OS 4.3, OS 5.8, Ded 4.1, Ded 5.1, Ded 5.5, Ded 5.6, Ded
    5.9, Mart 2, Clem 6
Jesse   Adv 1.11, Adv 2.4, Ann 2.5, Ann 3.7
Jews   VNat 1.4, VNat 2.1, VNat 5.2, Nat 1.2, Nat 2.5, Nat 5.1, Circ 2.3,
    Circ 3.4, Epi 3.3, Epi 3.4, P Epi 1.3, P Epi 2.6, SP 2, Pur 3.2, Pur
    3.3, Quad 2.5, Ben 5, Ann 3.2, Ann 3.5, Palm 3.1, 4 HM 9, 4 HM
    11, Pasc 1.1, Pasc 1 *passim*, Pasc 1 (alt) *passim*, Asc 1.1, Asc 2.3, Asc
    6.15, Pent 1.2, JB 1, 1 Nov 1.1, 1 Nov 3.2, OS 1.7, Ded 1.4, Ded
    4.2, And 2.8
Joachim   Ann 3.4, Ann 3.5
Job   VNat 6.8, Nat 1.7, Palm 1.4, 4 HM 6, Asspt 3.4, Asspt 3.5, Asspt 5.10,
    OAsspt 10, Abb 1, OS 3.2, OS 4.1
John the Baptist   Adv 6.1, Nat 2.5, Epi 1.6, Epi 1.7, OEpi 4, Pasc 1.10, JB
    passim, In lab mess 3.6, Asspt 2.8, 1 Nov 3.2, Mart 1, Mart 9, Mart 12
John the Evangelist   Innoc 1, Innoc 2, Epi 3.5, Sept 1.1, Sept 2.1, Palm
    3.3, 5 HM 4, Pasc 1.10, Pasc 1.12, Pasc 1 (alt).10, Pasc 1 (alt).12,
    OPasc 1 *passim*, OPasc 2.1, In lab mess 3.4, Asspt 5.3, Asspt 5.10,
    Asspt 5.12, OAsspt 11, OAsspt 15, 1 Nov 3.2, OS 2.4, OS 3.2, OS
    3.4, OS 4.1, OS 4.2, Ded 5.1, Ded 5.5, Ded 5.6, Mal 7
Jonah   Adv 1.4, Pasc 1.5, Pasc 1.12, Pasc 1 (alt).5, Humb 1
Jonas   Ded 5.7
Jordan   VNat 6.8, VNat 6.9, Epi 3.2, SP 2, Pasc 3 *passim*
Joseph   VNat 3.10, Nat 4.2, Nat 4.3, Circ 2.4, Circ 3.7, Epi 1.3, Epi 1.5,
    Epi 1.7, Pur 1.1, Pur 2.1, Pur 3.3, Quad 2.6, Palm 1.4, OAsspt 11,
    OS 5.11

Index of Subjects   357

Joshua   OEpi 1
Joy   VNat 1.1, VNat 2.6, VNat 2.8, VNat 3.4, VNat 3.5, VNat 4.1, VNat
    4.4, VNat 5.7, VNat 6 *passim*, Nat 3.1, Nat 3.5, Nat 4.1, Circ 3.5, Epi
    2.2, OEpi 5, Pur 2.1, Pur 2.3, Quad 2.3, Ben 10, Ann 3.3, Palm 1.1,
    Palm 1.2, Palm 2.1, Palm 3.1, Pasc 1.16, Pasc 1.18, Asspt 1.1, Asspt
    4.5, Asspt 4.9, Asspt 5.6, OAsspt 2, OAsspt 9, NatBVM 13, Mich 1.2,
    OS 1.13, OS 2 *passim*, OS 3.2, OS 3.3, OS 4 *passim*, OS 5.3, OS 5.7,
    OS 5.8, Ded 2.4, Ded 4.5, Ded 4.6, Ded 5.10, Mart 5, Mart 17, Mal
    2, VAnd 2, VAnd 3, And 1 *passim*, And 2.3, And 2.4, Humb 6
Judah   VNat 1.4, VNat 1.6, VNat 2.1, VNat 2.4, VNat 6 *passim*, Ann 3.4,
    Pasc 1 *passim*, Pasc 1 (alt).1, Pasc 1 (alt).9, Pasc 1 (alt).10
Judas   4 HM 4, Pasc 1.17, And 2.7
Judea   VNat 1 *passim*, VNat 6.7, VNat 6.8, Epi 3.3, Palm 3.1
Judge   Adv 4.3, VNat 3.5, VNat 5.6, VNat 6.9, SP 5, Ann 1.11, Ann 1.12,
    Ann 1 (alt).11, Ann 3.5, Pasc 1.12, 1 Nov 3.2, 1 Nov 4.4, OS 2.7,
    OS 2.8, Ded 2.3, Ded 6.2, Mart 1, Mart 15, Mart 17, And 1.2
Judgment   Adv 1.4, Adv 2.3, Adv 3.4, Adv 3.7, Adv 4.3, Adv 4.5, VNat
    2.5, VNat 2.6, VNat 2.8, Nat 1.2, Nat 1.4, Nat 1.5, Nat 3.2, Nat 3.4,
    Nat 5.3, Circ 3.3, Circ 3.5, Epi 1.4, Epi 2.2, OEpi 4, P Epi 1.3, P
    Epi 2.7, SP 3, Sept 2.3, Quad 5.5, Ben 11, Ann 1.11, Ann 1.14, Ann
    1 (alt).11, Ann 1 (alt).14, Ann 2.2, Ann 3.6, Pasc 1.12, Pasc 1.17, Pasc
    3.4, PP 1.2, In lab mess 2.2, Asspt 2.6, OAsspt 1, NatBVM 16, 1 Nov
    2.3, 1 Nov 5.9, 1 Nov 5.11, OS 1.10, OS 1.11, OS 3.1, Ded 3.3,
    Ded 5.9, Mart 2, VAnd 1
Justice   Adv 2.3, Adv 3.6, VNat 3.2, Nat 2.3, Nat 4.2, Nat 5.3, Epi 1.4,
    Quad 4.2, Ben 12, Ann 2.2, Ann 3 *passim*, Palm 3.1, 4 HM 10, Pasc
    3.3, Asspt 5.3, OAsspt 15, NatBVM 5, 1 Nov 2.5, 1 Nov 3.1, 1 Nov
    5.9, OS 1.14, OS 4.5, Ded 4.3, Ded 4.5, Ded 5.4, Mart 2

Kindness   Adv 2.1, Adv 6.5, Circ 3.2, P Epi 1.2, Quad 1.3, Quad 4.3,
    Palm 3.3, 4 HM 9, 4 HM 10, Pasc 3.6, In lab mess 3.3, Asspt 5.7,
    Asspt 5.12, OAsspt 1, NatBVM 16, Mich 1.3, 1 Nov 5.12, And 1.9
King   Adv 1.2, Adv 1.4, Adv 2.1, Adv 3.2, Adv 4.5, Adv 5.1, Adv 6.5,
    VNat 1.5, VNat 2.8, VNat 4.6, VNat 4.9, VNat 5.4, VNat 6.11, Nat
    3.4, Nat 4.1, Circ 3.4, Epi 1.5, Epi 2.1, Epi 2.2, Epi 2.4, Epi 3.3, Epi
    3.4, Pur 1.2, Sept 1.3, Quad 2.5, Quad 3.1, Ann 1.14, Ann 1 (alt).14,
    Ann 3.7, Ann 3.8, Palm 2.4, Palm 3.1, 4 HM 4, 4 HM 7, Pasc 1
    passim, Pasc 1 (alt).1, Pasc 1 (alt).11, Asspt 2.9, Asspt 4.7, Asspt 5.10,
    OAsspt 6, OAsspt 8, OAsspt 10, 1 Nov 1.2, 1 Nov 3.1, 1 Nov 4.1, 1

Nov 5.2, OS 2.3, OS 5.9, Ded 1.6, Ded 3.1, Ded 5 *passim*, Mart 6, Mart 8, Mal 1, And 2.6, Humb 5

Kingdom   Adv 3.5, Adv 4.4, VNat 6.7, Nat 2.6, Epi 2.3, Ann 1.14, Palm 1.2, 4 HM 7, 5 HM 4, Pasc 1.9, Pasc 2.11, OPasc 1.2, OPasc 1.8, In lab mess 2.2, NatBVM 3, NatBVM 16, Mich 1.6, 1 Nov 1.2, 1 Nov 2.1, 1 Nov 2.3, 1 Nov 3.3, 1 Nov 4.1, OS 1.9, OS 1.15, OS 4.1, OS 5.8, Ded 2.3, Ded 5.2, And 1.1

Knowledge   Adv 1.3, Adv 1.4, Adv 1.9, Adv 3.3, Adv 5.2, VNat 3 *passim*, VNat 5.5, Nat 2.3, Circ 1.5, Ann 2.3, Pasc 2.6, Pasc 3.4, Pasc 3.6, Asc 1.2, Asc 4.4, Asc 4.5, Asc 4.6, Pent 2.7, PP 1.3, In lab mess 3.3, In lab mess 3.6, 1 Nov 4.2, 1 Nov 5.5, OS 4.4, OS 4.5, OS 4.6, Mal 5, And 1.9

Labor   Adv 7.2, VNat 2.5, VNat 6.11, Nat 3.6, Circ 3.10, P Epi 2.7, Ann 2.4, Palm 3.5, 4 HM 11, 4 HM 12, 4 HM 14, Pasc 1.8, Pasc 1.9, Pasc 1 (alt).8, Pasc 1 (alt).9, Asc 3.9, Asc 6.7, 6 p P 1.4, In lab mess 2.1, OAsspt 9, 1 Nov 3.3, OS 1.2, OS 2.1, OS 2.4, OS 2.8, Ded 4.5, Ded 6.3, Mart 15, Clem 4, Clem 6, Mal 4, Mal 8, Humb 5

Lamb   Adv 4.7, Adv 6.1, VNat 4.3, VNat 4.5, Nat 2.5, Circ 2.1, Circ 3.4, Epi 1.6, Epi 1.7, OEpi 1, P Epi 2.1, Palm 1.3, Palm 2.3, 4 HM 2, 4 HM 5, 5 HM 2, Pasc 1 *passim*, Pasc 1 (alt).9, Pasc 1 (alt).10, Pasc 1 (alt).12, OS 3.2, OS 3.3, OS 4.4, OS 5.2, Mart 10, Clem 4

Laughter   Adv 4.5, Adv 4.7, VNat 3.4, Nat 5.5, Humb 3

Law   Adv 6.2, VNat 4.6, VNat 5.2, VNat 6.1, Nat 1.2, Circ 1.1, Circ 2.1, Circ 3.4, Circ 3.5, Epi 3.5, OEpi 2, OEpi 3, OEpi 4, SP 6, Pur 3.1, Pur 3.2, Quad 2.1, Quad 2.5, Quad 3.3, Ben 6, Ann 1.8, Ann 1.14, Ann 1 (alt).6, Ann 1 (alt).14, Ann 3 *passim*, 4 HM 13, 5 HM 3, Pasc 2.12, In lab mess 3.6, Asspt 4.4, Asspt 5.12, Mich 1.4, Mich 2.3, 1 Nov 2.2, OS 1.9, Ded 1.4, Ded 5.9, Mart 3, Mart 7, Mart 9, And 1.3, And 1.4, And 1.5

Lawgiver   OPasc 1.5

Lazarus   Adv 4.7, Pasc 1.8, Asspt 2.7, Asspt 2.8, Asspt 3.4, Asspt 3.6, Asspt 3.7, Asspt 4 *passim*, OS 4.1, Clem 6, Mal 5, And 1.6

Leah   P Epi 2.8, Asspt 3.1

Lent   Quad 1.1, Quad 3.3, Quad 3.4, Quad 6.4, Ann 3.1

Lepers   4 HM 3, Pasc 3.1, Asspt 5.9, 1 Nov 1.1, 1 Nov 5.4, Mart 12, Mart 16, And 1.6

Leprosy   Pasc 3 *passim*

Leviathan   Circ 1.1, Circ 2.3, Ann 1.12

Life   Adv 1.5, Adv 2.5, Adv 3.4, Adv 5.1, Adv 6.4, VNat 3.5, VNat 5.3, VNat 5.5, VNat 5.6, VNat 6.4, VNat 6.10, Nat 1.8, Nat 2.1, Nat 2.5,

P Epi 1.5, P Epi 2.8, Pur 3.3, Sept 2.1, Sept 2.2, Quad 1.1, Quad 3.3, Ben 12, Ann 1.3, Ann 1.12, Ann 1 (alt).14, Palm 1.2, 4 HM 13, Pasc 1.5, Pasc 1.18, Pasc 2.3, OPasc 1.4, OPasc 2.3, In lab mess 3.3, In lab mess 3.5, In lab mess 3.9, Asspt 4.8, Asspt 5.11, Abb 2, Mich 1.6, Mich 2.4, 1 Nov 1.4, 1 Nov 5.7, 1 Nov 5.8, 1 Nov 5.9, OS 1.3, OS 1.6, OS 1.9, OS 1.13, OS 4.2, OS 4.3, OS 5.2, OS 5.4, OS 5.7, OS 5.8, Ded 3.1, Ded 4.3, Ded 5.9, Mart 8, Mart 12, Clem 1, Clem 2, Clem 6, Mal 2, Mal 3, Mal 4, And 1.5, And 1.6, And 2.4, And 2.6, Humb *passim*

Light   Adv 1.6, Adv 1.8, Adv 3.1, VNat 3.2, VNat 3.7, VNat 4.8, VNat 4.9, VNat 5.1, VNat 5.2, VNat 6.3, Nat 3.5, Nat 5.5, Circ 3.10, SP 2, Pur 1.2, Quad 4.3, Ann 1.10, Ann 1 (alt).8, Ann 1 (alt).10, Pasc 1.16, Asspt 2.9, Asspt 3.7, Asspt 4.3, Asspt 5.8, OAsspt *passim*, NatBVM *passim*, Mich 1.1, Mich 1.6, 1 Nov 2.3, 1 Nov 2.5, 1 Nov 3.1, 1 Nov 3.2, 1 Nov 3.3, 1 Nov 4.4, 1 Nov 5.8, 1 Nov 5.10, OS 1.6, OS 2.4, OS 4.5, OS 5.11, Ded 1.5, Ded 5.3, Ded 5.5, Mart 4, Mart 12, Mart 13

Lily   Ann 3.7

Lion   VNat 1.4, Sept 1.5, Sept 2.1, Pasc 1 *passim*, Pasc 1 (alt) *passim*, Pasc 3.3, OPasc 1.2

Love   Adv 1 *passim*, Adv 2.1, Adv 2.5, Adv 3.1, Adv 3.2, Adv 3.5, Adv 4.1, Adv 5.2, Adv 5.3, VNat 2.7, VNat 3.7, VNat 3.8, VNat 4.7, Nat 1.2, Nat 1.6, Nat 2.2, Nat 2.6, Nat 5.1, Innoc 3, Circ 3.1, Circ 3.2, Epi 2.4, Epi 3.1, P Epi 1.4, P Epi 2.4, P Epi 2.9, Pur 2.3, Sept 2.1, Sept 2.3, Quad 1.2, Quad 2.3, Quad 2.6, Quad 5.6, Ben 10, Ann 1.12, Ann 1.13, Ann 1.14, Ann 3.9, 4 HM 2, 4 HM 4, 4 HM 5, 4 HM 9, Pasc 1.3, Pasc 1.18, Pasc 1 (alt).3, Pasc 2 *passim*, Pasc 3.3, Pasc 3.4, Pasc 4.2, OPasc 1.6, OPasc 1.8, OPasc 2.2, OPasc 2.3, Asc 4.1, Asc 4.14, Asc 6 *passim*, In lab mess 1.1, In lab mess 1.2, In lab mess 2.3, Asspt 1.2, Asspt 3.7, Asspt 4.1, Asspt 4.8, Asspt 5 *passim*, NatBVM 16, Abb 6, Abb 7, Mich 1.1, Mich 1.3, Mich 1.4, Mich 2.2, 1 Nov 1.2, 1 Nov 4.1, 1 Nov 5.3, 1 Nov 5.8, 1 Nov 5.12, OS 1.10, OS 1.12, OS 3.3, Ded 1.7, Ded 2.4, Ded 5.2, Ded 5.7, Ded 5.9, Ded 5.10, Mart 5, Clem 1, Clem 2, Mal 1, Mal 3, And 1.5, And 1.6, And 1.9, And 1.10, And 2.4, Humb 7

Lucifer   Adv 1.3, VNat 4.9, Ben 11, OPasc 2.1, 1 Nov 2.4, 1 Nov 3.1, 1 Nov 3.4, 1 Nov 5.7, 1 Nov 5.8

Luke   Adv 1.2, Epi 1.7, SP 2, OS 1.5

Lukewarmness   Circ 3.11, Pur 2.2, Quad 4.4, Ann 3.10, Pasc 1.17, Asc 3.6, Asc 3.7, Asc 6.7, PP 3.2, PP 3.6, 4 p P 2, Asspt 3.5, Asspt 5.10, OAsspt 3, Abb 6, Ded 3.3

Lust   Adv 6.2, VNat 3.4, Quad 2.4, Quad 5.2, Quad 5.3, Ben 12, Ann 1.6, Ann 1 (alt).6, Ann 2.5, 4 HM 14, 5 HM 3, OAsspt 9, Abb 4, 1 Nov 2.2, Ded 3.1

Magi   VNat 6.9, Epi 1.5, Epi 2.1, Epi 2.3, Epi 2.4, Epi 3 *passim*, OAsspt 11
Majesty   Adv 1.6, Adv 1.7, NatBVM 5, 1 Nov 1.1, 1 Nov 2.1, 1 Nov 5 *passim*, OS 3.4, OS 4.2, OS 4.4, Ded 5.5, Mart 5
Malachi   Mal *passim*
Malice   Pur 1.3
Man   Adv 3.1, Pur 3.1, In lab mess 3.9, Asspt 1.3, OAsspt 1, OAsspt 15, NatBVM 6, 1 Nov 3.1, 1 Nov 5.4, 1 Nov 5.9, 1 Nov 5.12, OS 5.11, Ded 4.6, Ded 5.5, Ded 5.7, Mart 8, Mart 9, Clem 3
Manger   VNat 1.4, VNat 3.9, VNat 4.6, VNat 6.7, Nat 1.1, Nat 3.1, Nat 3.2, Nat 3.3, Nat 4.1, Nat 4.2, Nat 4.3, Nat 5.1, Nat 5.2, Nat 5.5, Circ 2.2, Circ 3.2, Epi 1.5, Epi 3.4, Pasc 3.1
Manure   Adv 2.4, PP 2.3; *see also* Dung
Marriage   Circ 2.4, P Epi 2.3, Asspt 2.9, Asspt 3.1, Asspt 3.5, Asspt 4.5, Asspt 4.7, OAsspt 10, NatBVM 8, Abb 1
Martha   Sept 2.3, Asspt 2.7, Asspt 2.8, Asspt 2.9, Asspt 3 *passim*, Asspt 5 *passim*
Martin   Mart *passim*
Martyrdom   Innoc 1, Innoc 2, Innoc 3, OPasc 1.6, OPasc 1.7, OAsspt 7, OAsspt 14, OS 1.15, OS 5.5, Clem 5, VAnd 3
Martyrs   Adv 4.7, VNat 2.5, Innoc 2, Ben 12, OAsspt 14, OAsspt 15, Ded 5.1, Mart 16, Clem 1, Clem 2, Clem 3
Mary   P Epi 2.2, Quad 1.2, Pasc 1.12, Asspt 2.7, Asspt 2.8, Asspt 2.9, Asspt 3 *passim*, Asspt 5 *passim*, OS 1.6, *see also* Virgin Mary
Master   Nat 4.2, Circ 3.8
Matthew   6 p P 2.4
Mediator, Mediatrix   Adv 2.5, Nat 5.1, Circ 2.2, Epi 2.4, Pur 1.3, Ann 2.2, Ann 2.3, Asspt 2.2, Asspt 3.6, OAsspt *passim*, NatBVM 7, NatBVM 17, OS 1.14, Ded 5.5, Mart 4
Meekness   Adv 4.5, Nat 4.3, SP 8, Ann 3.6, Palm 1.4
Memory   Adv 5.2, Ben 8, Pasc 1.11, Pasc 1.18, Pent 1.5, JB 11, 4 p P 4, Asspt 2.4, Asspt 5.8, NatBVM 10, NatBVM 11, NatBVM 13, Mich 1.1, OS 5.5, Ded 2.3, Ded 5.1, Ded 5.7, VAnd 3, And 1.10, Humb 2, Humb 6
Mercy   Adv 1.4, Adv 1.7, Adv 2.3, Adv 2.5, Adv 3.3, Adv 3.7, Adv 4.6, Adv 6.6, VNat 1.2, VNat 2.4, VNat 2.8, VNat 3.2, VNat 5.6, Nat 1

passim, Nat 2.5, Nat 5.2, Nat 5.3, Circ 3.4, P Epi 1.1, Pur 1.3, Pur 1.4, Quad 3.3, Ann 1 *passim*, Ann 1 (alt). *passim*, Ann 2.2, Ann 2.3, Ann 3 *passim*, 4 HM 8, 4 HM 9, Pasc 1.18, Pasc 2.6, Pasc 2.11, Pasc 2.12, OPasc 1.8, OPasc 2.1, Asc 2.5, Asc 2.6, Pent 1.4, Pent 2.7, JB 11, PP 3 *passim*, 6 p P 2.3, In lab mess 3.3, Asspt 2.2, Asspt 4.5, Asspt 4.8, Asspt 4.9, OAsspt *passim*, NatBVM 8, Mich 1.1, Mich 1.4, 1 Nov 4.4, OS 1 *passim*, OS 3.3, OS 4.1, OS 5.10, Ded 3.2, Ded 3.4, Ded 3.5, Ded 5.2, Ded 5.4, Ded 5.8, Ded 6.2, Mart 2, Mart 4, Mart 15, Mal 3, VAnd 3, Humb 5

Michael Mich *passim*, 1 Nov 2.3

Milk Adv 2.2, Epi 2.4, OEpi 1, Quad 2.5, Pasc 2.7, Pasc 4.2, In lab mess 2.3, OAsspt 2, NatBVM 6, Mich 1.4

Mind Adv 5.2, Adv 6.1, VNat 2.3, VNat 4.2, VNat 6.5, Circ 2.5, Circ 3.6, Circ 3.8, Pur 1.4, Sept 1.1, Sept 1.5, Sept 2.3, Quad 1.5, Quad 1.6, 4 HM 13, 4 HM 14, 5 HM 4, Pasc 1.2, Pasc 2.3, Pasc 2.4, Pasc 2.8, Asc 3.1, Asc 6.9, In lab mess 3.1, Asspt 3.7, Asspt 4.4, Asspt 4.5, Asspt 5.2, Asspt 5.6, Asspt 5.8, OAsspt 15, NatBVM 10, NatBVM 11, NatBVM 14, Abb 5, Mich 2.3, 1 Nov 5.6, 1 Nov 5.7, 1 Nov 5.8, OS 5.6, Ded 4.6, Ded 5.7, Mart 3, VAnd 3, VAnd 4, And 1.8, And 2.3, Humb 6

Minister Circ 2.4, P Epi 2.8, SP 1, SP 3

Ministry Ben 2, 5 HM 1, Pasc 1 (alt).14, Asspt 3.6, Mich 1.2, Ded 4.2, Ded 5.6, Mart 7

Miracle VNat 1.1, Epi 2.3, P Epi 2.2, Ben 7, Pasc 1.6, Pasc 1 (alt).6, Pasc 2.12, Asspt 4.1, Asspt 4.5, OAsspt 11, Ded 1.2, Mart 12, Mart 16, Mal 6

Misery Adv 7.1, VNat 2.3, Nat 2.4, Nat 5.4, Circ 3.5, Epi 1.1, Epi 1.2, Epi 2.3, P Epi 1.3, Pur 1.3, Sept 1.2, Quad 4.3, Ann 1.10, Ann 1 (alt).8, Ann 1 (alt).10, 4 HM 6, 4 HM 8, 4 HM 10, In lab mess 2.3, Asspt 4.3, Asspt 4.8, Asspt 4.9, NatBVM 7, 1 Nov 2.2, 1 Nov 5.10, OS 1.8, OS 1.10, OS 4.6, OS 5.6, Ded 4.5, Ded 5.4, Ded 5.8, Humb 6

Moderation VNat 4.10, Circ 1.1

Modesty Epi 1.7, Epi 3.8, P Epi 2.5, Palm 3.2, OAsspt 7, OAsspt 10, OAsspt 11, VAnd 1

Monastery Asspt 3.2, Mich 2.1, Ded 1.2, And 1.3, Humb 2

Monastic Circ 3.6, Ben 2, Palm 3.2, Asspt 1.4, Asspt 2.4, Asspt 2.5

Monk Circ 3.7, Quad 3.2, OAsspt 11, Abb 1, Ded 4.1

Moon Asspt 2.2, Asspt 2.9, OAsspt *passim*, NatBVM 9, NatBVM 11, 1 Nov 3.3

Mortification   VNat 6.9, Ann 1.5, OPasc 1.7
Moses   P Epi 2.2, Pur 3.1, Quad 3.2, Ann 1.14, Ann 3.2, Palm 1.4, Palm 2.7, Pasc 3.6, OPasc 1.4, OPasc 1.5, Asspt 5.12, OAsspt 5, 1 Nov 5.6, OS 1.6, Mart 10
Mother   Adv 1.6, Adv 2.4, Adv 2.5, VNat 3.7, VNat 3.9, VNat 3.10, VNat 4 *passim*, VNat 6.3, VNat 6.11, Nat 1.3, Nat 3.1, Circ 2.1, Circ 2.4, Circ 3.3, Epi 1.6, Epi 1.8, Epi 2.1, Epi 3 *passim*, P Epi 1.2, P Epi 2.3, P Epi 2.5, Pur 3.1, Pur 3.3, Sept 2.1, Quad 1.1, Ben 10, Ann 1.8, Ann 1 (alt).8, Ann 1 (alt).9, Ann 2.1, Ann 3.7, Palm 2.6, 4 HM 6, 4 HM 14, 5 HM 1, Pasc 1.11, Pasc 1 (alt).11, Pasc 3.4, In lab mess 2.1, In lab mess 3.2, In lab mess 3.3, Asspt 1.1, Asspt 1.2, Asspt 1.4, Asspt 4.1, Asspt 4.5, OAsspt *passim*, NatBVM *passim*, OS 5.9, Ded 4.1, Mart 1, Mart 3
Mountain   Adv 1.7, Adv 1.11, Adv 2.2, VNat 1.1, VNat 6.3, SP 2, Ben 4, Pasc 1.11, OPasc 2.1, Asspt 1.1, NatBVM 9, NatBVM 11, 1 Nov 5.9, OS 1.5, OS 1.6, OS 3.2, Mart 4, Mart 17, Mal 7
Mourning   Adv 4.5, Nat 5.5, Quad 2.4, Pasc 1.15, NatBVM 14, OS 1.10, OS 5.8
Mouth   Adv 4.7, Adv 5.3, VNat 1.6, VNat 2.1, VNat 2.4, VNat 6.10, Nat 3.2, Epi 1.7, Pur 1.4, Quad 5.5, Ann 2.1, Ann 2.4, Palm 2.3, 4 HM 2, 4 HM 14, Pasc 1 (alt).3, Pasc 1 (alt).4, Pasc 2.3, Pasc 2.9, Pasc 2.11, Pasc 3.1, Pasc 3.2
Myrrh   VNat 6.9, Epi 2.1, Epi 3.5, Epi 3.6
Mystery   Adv 1.1, VNat 1.1, VNat 3.8, VNat 3.10, VNat 4.1, VNat 5.1, VNat 6.3, VNat 6.5, Nat 1.8, Nat 2.4, Innoc 2, Circ 2.1, Circ 2.2, Circ 3.3, Circ 3.5, OEpi 1, Sept 2.1, Quad 2.1, Quad 3.1, Quad 3.4, Ann 1.6, Ann 1 (alt).6, Ann 2.1, Ann 2.2, Palm 3.1, 4 HM 10, 5 HM 4, Pasc 1.11, Pasc 1 (alt).3, Pasc 1 (alt).11, OAsspt 11, OAsspt 13, 1 Nov 5.7, 1 Nov 5.9, OS 3.4, Ded 1.6

Nativity   VNat 4.6
Nature   Adv 2.2, Adv 2.3, VNat 1.1, Nat 5.2, Nat 5.3, Nat 5.4, Circ 1.3, Circ 2.1, Circ 3.4, Epi 1.8, P Epi 2.2, Pur 1.3, Ann 1 (alt).7, 4 HM 10, In lab mess 3.9, Asspt 5.5, NatBVM 7, Mich 2.2, 1 Nov 2.3, 1 Nov 5 *passim*, OS 4.2, OS 4.5, Ded 5.7, Mart 9, VAnd 3
Nazarene   SP 6
Nazareth   Adv 2.3, Ann 3.7
Neighbor   Nat 4.2, SP 3, Quad 2.1, Quad 2.3, Quad 2.6, Quad 3.3, Ann 2.3, Pasc 2.11, JB 5, JB 9, Asspt 3.3, Asspt 3.4, Asspt 5 *passim*, Mich 1.5, Mich 2.2, OS 1.14, OS 5.8, Humb 6

Night   Adv 1.9, Adv 3.6, VNat 5.2, Nat 3.1, Nat 3.2, Nat 4.1, Mal 5, And 2.7
Nineveh   Pasc 1.12
Noah   VNat 6.8, Nat 1.7, Palm 1.4, Asspt 3.4, NatBVM 4, Abb 1

Obedience   Adv 3.4, Adv 3.5, Adv 3.6, VNat 4.9, Circ 3.7, Circ 3.8, Circ 3.11, P Epi 1.3, P Epi 1.4, SP 6, Sept 1.4, Quad 2.6, Palm 1.4, 4 HM 7, Pasc 1.3, Pasc 1.13, Pasc 1 (alt).3, Pasc 2.12, Asc 6.7, 6 p P 1.4, NatBVM 9, Abb 3, Abb 4, 1 Nov 5.6, OS 1.9, OS 1.11, Ded 3.2, Mart *passim*, And 2.1, And 2.2, Humb 2, Humb 4
Obstinacy   Quad 2.5, Pasc 2.12, 6 p P 1.3, Asspt 5.1, Asspt 5.13
Offering   Nat 1.6, Epi 3.5, Epi 3.6, Pur 3.2, Pur 3.3, NatBVM 18, 1 Nov 3.1
Oil   Adv 6.2, VNat 1.2, VNat 6.1, Circ 1.4, OEpi 5, P Epi 2.9, Quad 1 *passim,* Ann 3.3, 4 HM 8, 4 HM 9, Pasc 2.6, Asc 3.7, Asc 6.8, PP 2.3, Asspt 2.9, NatBVM 5, NatBVM 9, Mart 12, Mart 13, And 1.2
Ointment   VNat 1.2, VNat 6.2, Quad 1.2, 4 HM 8, NatBVM 5, Ded 4.3, Mal 8, And 1.2, And 2.4
Outcast   Pasc 1 (alt).3, Pasc 3.2

Pain   VNat 4.3, VNat 4.4, Circ 3.10, Sept 2.3, 4 HM 8, Pasc 4.2, OAsspt 9, Clem 6, VAnd 3, Humb 7
Parable   Nat 2.4, Circ 2.3, Quad 2.1, Ann 1.9, Asspt 2.9, OAsspt 11
Paraclete   Palm 3.4
Paradise   VNat 2.6, VNat 4.7, Nat 1.6, Ann 1 (alt).8, Palm 1.2, 4 HM 11, NatBVM 3, Mich 1.1, 1 Nov 1.2, OS 1.9, Ded 6.3, And 1.4
Passion   Adv 4.7, VNat 4.7, VNat 5.4, Nat 1.4, Nat 1.8, Innoc 1, Innoc 2, Epi 1.2, Quad 1.2, Ben 3, Ann 1.4, Palm 1.1, Palm 1.2, Palm 2.1, Palm 2.3, Palm 2.4, Palm 3 *passim*, 4 HM *passim*, 5 HM 1, 5 HM 2, 5 HM 3, Pasc 1 *passim*, Pasc 1 (alt).4, Pasc 1 (alt).14, Pasc 3 *passim*, OPasc 1.3, Asspt 5.12, OAsspt 14, 1 Nov 1.2, Clem 1, Clem 6, VAnd 3, And 2.3
Passover   OEpi 1, Palm 3.3, Pasc 1.14, Mal 5
Patience   Circ 3.1, Circ 3.8, Circ 3.9, SP 4, SP 7, Ann 3.6, Ann 3.9, Palm 2.3, Palm 2.6, 4 HM 2, 4 HM 5, 4 HM 9, Pasc 1.3, Pasc 1.13, Pasc 1 (alt).3, Pasc 2.5, Pasc 2.11, Pasc 2.12, Pasc 3.2, In lab mess 1.1, In lab mess 1.2, Asspt 2.3, Asspt 5.2, Asspt 5.5, OS 1.15, Ded 3.1, Mart 14, Mal 7, And 1 *passim*, And 2.8
Patriarchs   Adv 1.11, VNat 2.5, VNat 3.2, VNat 5.3, VNat 6.4, Quad 2.6, 4 HM 14, OAsspt 8, OS 3.1, OS 4.1, OS 5.5, Ded 6.2, Ded 6.3, Mart 8, Mart 9, Mart 10

Paul   VNat 4.1, VNat 4.8, VNat 4.10, VNat 6.11, Epi 1.3, P Epi 2.1, SP *passim*, Quad 1.4, 4 HM 10, OPasc 1.2, OPasc 1.6, Asc 6.4, V PP 4, PP 1.1, PP 2.1, PP 3.1, 6 p P 2.4, In lab mess 1.2, Asspt 2.3, Asspt 5.9, OAsspt 15, Abb 6, Mich 1.6, 1 Nov 2.2, Ded 3.2, Ded 4.4

Peace   Adv 1.9, Adv 3.5, Adv 4.6, Adv 6.6, VNat 2.1, VNat 2.2, VNat 2.4, VNat 4.1, VNat 4.8, VNat 4.9, Nat 4.2, Nat 5.1, Epi 1.1, Epi 1.2, Pur 1.2, Pur 1.3, Pur 1.4, Pur 2.2, Sept 2.3, Quad 1.6, Ann 1 *passim*, Ann 1 (alt) *passim*, Pasc 1 (alt).8, Pasc 3.4, OPasc 2.1, OPasc 2.2, Asc 6.4, Asc 6.5, Pent 2.2, JB 11, PP 1.1, In lab mess 1.1, In lab mess 1.2, Asspt 3.6, Asspt 4.4, Asspt 5.11, NatBVM *passim*, Mich 1.5, Mich 1.6, Mich 2.1, Mich 2.4, 1 Nov 5.1, 1 Nov 5.6, OS 1.14, OS 2.5, OS 4.3, OS 4.5, OS 5.7, OS 5.8, OS 5.9, Ded 3.3, Ded 4.1, Ded 4.5, Ded 5.9, Mart 15, Mal 3, Mal 5, And 1.8, And 2.6

Peacemakers   Adv 4.6, VNat 5.3, Epi 2.2, OS 1.14, Mart 16

Penitence   Ann 1.5, Ann 1.8, Pasc 1.17, Pasc 1 (alt).8, Pasc 4.2, In lab mess 1.4, Asspt 2.8, Asspt 3.4, Asspt 3.6, Asspt 4.2, Asspt 4.4, 1 Nov 5.12, OS 1.14, Ded 1.4, Ded 1.5, Ded 4.4, Ded 5.8, Ded 5.10, Ded 6.3, Clem 6, Mal 8, VAnd 2, And 2.4

Penitent   Asspt 2.7, OAsspt 11, Abb 1

Pentecost   VNat 5.2

Persecution   SP 1, SP 3, SP 4, Ann 3.6, Palm 3.1, Pasc 2.11, OS 1.15, Mart 16, Clem 3, Mal 6

Peter   Innoc 1, Ben 12, Palm 3.3, 5 HM 4, 5 HM 5, Pasc 1 (alt).2, Pasc 2.3, OPasc 1.2, Asc 2.3, Asc 3.3, Asc 3.5, Asc 4.8, Asc 6.1, V PP 4, PP 1.1, PP 2.1, PP 3.1, 4 p P 3, 6 p P 2.4, Asspt 5.12, OAsspt 11, Abb 7, 1 Nov 1.3, OS 1.1, OS 1.12, Ded 5.1, Ded 5.5, Mart 17, And 2.2

Pharaoh   OPasc 1.5

Pharisee   Adv 4.2, Quad 4.2, Ann 1.1, Ann 1.5, Ann 3 *passim*, Asspt 5.10, OS 1.5, Ded 4.3

Philosopher   Nat 1.2, Pent 3.4

Phineas   1 Nov 5.6

Physician   Adv 1.10, VNat 3.1, VNat 4.2, VNat 6.1, Nat 3.5

Pilate   Pasc 1.2, Pasc 1.3

Pilgrim   Adv 6.3, Adv 6.4, Epi 1.1, Quad 5.3, Quad 6.1, Quad 6.2, Quad 6.3, In lab mess 3.5, Asspt 3.6, Mart 3, Humb 2

Pilgrimage   OS 1.10, OS 3.1, Mal 6

Pity   Adv 3.3, Adv 4.2, Ann 1.10, In lab mess 2.1, In lab mess 2.2, In lab mess 2.3, Asspt 1.1, Asspt 4.3, OAsspt 2, 1 Nov 2.4, OS 1.6, OS 1.13, OS 5.10

Index of Subjects 365

Pleasure   Adv 3.2, Adv 3.3, Adv 6.4, VNat 2.3, VNat 3.4, VNat 4.2, VNat 5.1, VNat 5.7, Nat 3.3, Circ 1.1, Circ 3.7, Circ 3.10, Sept 1.4, Sept 2.2, Quad 1.1, Quad 2.4, Quad 5.9, Quad 6.1, Quad 6.2, Quad 6.3, Ann 1.8, Ann 1 (alt).8, Ann 1 (alt).12, Ann 2.4, Palm 2.5, 4 HM 13, 5 HM 4, Pasc 1.9, Pasc 1.16, Pasc 1.18, Pasc 2.11, Pasc 3.1, Pasc 3.2, OPasc 1.7, In lab mess 2.3, Asspt 1.1, Asspt 5.1, Asspt 5.7, OAsspt 9, Abb 3, Mich 1.5, OS 3.3, OS 4.3, Ded 2.2, Ded 4.5, Mart 7, Clem 1, Mal 1, Mal 5, Mal 6, And 1.3
Poison   Circ 1.1, Circ 2.3, P Epi 2.9, SP 4, Quad 2.6, Ann 2.1, 4 HM 6, Pasc 1 (alt).1
Poor   Adv 1.8, Nat 5.5, Quad 1.3, Palm 1.4, Pasc 2.11, 1 Nov 1.4, 1 Nov 3.2, OS 1 *passim*, Ded 1.3, Mart 16, Humb 5
Postulates   1 Nov 5.3
Poverty   Adv 4.5, Adv 4.7, VNat 1.5, VNat 4.6, Nat 3.1, Nat 4.1, Circ 2.4, Epi 1.5, Epi 2.3, Ann 3.8, Palm 2.2, 4 HM 12, Pasc 3.1, In lab mess 2.1, Asspt 2.3, Asspt 4.1, Abb 3, Abb 4, Mich 1.5, OS 1 *passim*
Power   Adv 1.10, Adv 2.1, Adv 5.1, Adv 6.5, Adv 7.2, VNat 1.1, VNat 3.8, VNat 4.2, VNat 5.7, VNat 6.6, Nat 1.2, Nat 2.1, Nat 2.2, Nat 2.4, Nat 3.1, Nat 5.4, Epi 2.4, Epi 3.3, Epi 3.7, SP 2, Sept 2.1, Ben 3, Ann 1.6, Palm 3.2, 4 HM 4, 4 HM 5, 5 HM 5, Pasc 1.1, Pasc 1.7, Pasc 1.13, Pasc 1 (alt).3, Pasc 1 (alt).4, Pasc 3.3, Pasc 4.2, OPasc 1.1, In lab mess 3.7, Asspt 1.2, Asspt 1.3, 1 Nov 2.1, 1 Nov 5 *passim*, OS 2.3, OS 4.3, Ded 4.6, Mart 8, Mart 11, Mart 12, Clem 1, Clem 2, And 1.3, And 1.6, And 2.7, Humb 1, Humb 5
Praise   VNat 2.1, VNat 5.3, Pur 3.3, Sept 1.5, Pasc 1 (alt).10, In lab mess 3.3, Asspt 2.3, Asspt 2.8, Asspt 2.9, Asspt 4.5, Asspt 4.9, NatBVM 13, NatBVM 14, NatBVM 16, 1 Nov 3.3, 1 Nov 5.5, OS 1.12, OS 1.14, OS 2.2, OS 2.3, OS 3.4, OS 5 *passim*, Ded 2.4, Ded 4.4, Ded 4.6, Ded 6.1, Mart 2, Mart 13, And 2.3, Humb 4, Humb 5
Prayer   Adv 4.6, Adv 4.7, Adv 6.5, Circ 3.5, Epi 3.5, Epi 3.6, SP 1, SP 7, Quad 4.2, Quad 4.3, Quad 4.4, Quad 5.4, Quad 5.5, Quad 5.9, Ben 8, Ann 1 (alt).9, Palm 3.4, 4 HM 11, 5 HM 5, Pasc 1.15, Pasc 2.3, Pasc 4.2, Asc 1.1, Asc 4.11, Asc 5.1, Asc 6.7, Asc 6.14, Asspt 3.7, Asspt 5.8, OAsspt 11, NatBVM 1, NatBVM 5, NatBVM 9, NatBVM 11, NatBVM 15, NatBVM 18, Mich 1.4, Mich 1.5, OS 1.13, OS 3.4, OS 5.6, OS 5.10, Ded 2.4, Ded 3.2, Ded 4.1, Ded 4.4, Ded 5.8, Mal 2, Mal 3, Mal 8, And 1.1, And 1.10
Preachers   Pasc 1.2, And 1.3, And 2.2
Preaching   SP 1, 4 HM 11, Pasc 2.11, Pasc 3.6

Predestination   Sept 1.1, OPasc 2.3, Asc 2.5, Pent 2.6, 6 p P 2.2, 1 Nov 4.4, Ded 5.7

Pride   Adv 1.2, Adv 1.3, Adv 1.5, Adv 3.2, VNat 3.4, VNat 4.9, Nat 4.2, Circ 3.7, Circ 3.9, Epi 1.7, OEpi 4, Quad 5.9, Ann 1.8, Palm 2.2, 4 HM 5, Pasc 1.11, Pasc 1.16, Pasc 3.1, Pasc 3.4, OPasc 2.2, 4 p P 2, In lab mess 2.2, In lab mess 2.3, In lab mess 3.7, Abb 2, Abb 4, Abb 7, 1 Nov 2.3, 1 Nov 2.4, 1 Nov 5.6, And 2.7

Priest   Nat 4.1, Circ 2.1, P Epi 2.2, SP 3, Palm 3.1, Asspt 5.10, OAsspt 8, Ded 1.4, Mart 15, Mart 16, Mal 3

Princes   Adv 1.2, Nat 2.5, Circ 1.5, Quad 3.1, Asspt 2.1, OAsspt 4, Mich 1.1, 1 Nov 1.4, 1 Nov 2.1, 1 Nov 5.8, Ded 5.1, Ded 5.6

Prison   Adv 1.6, VNat 2.2, VNat 2.3, VNat 3.2, VNat 4.10, Nat 2.5, Circ 3.1, Circ 3.4, Pur 1.3, Pasc 1.5, OPasc 2.4, Asspt 2.4, Asspt 4.2, Asspt 5.12, OS 2.8, OS 4.1, OS 5.11, Ded 1.2, Mart 16

Prisoner   Circ 3.4

Procession   Pur 1.1, Pur 2.1, Pur 2.3, Ben 3, Palm 1 *passim*, Palm 2 *passim*, Palm 3.1, Palm 3.2

Promise   Adv 4.5, VNat 1.4, VNat 2.1, VNat 2.7, VNat 4.1, VNat 4.8, VNat 5.3, VNat 5.6, VNat 6.4, Nat 1.6, Circ 1.2, Palm 3.4, Pasc 1.4, OPasc 1.3, OAsspt 13, NatBVM 5, NatBVM 15, OS 1.9, OS 1.15, OS 3.3, OS 5.5, Ded 1.4, Ded 4.6, Mart 8, Mal 7, And 1.9

Prophecy, Prophet   Adv 1 *passim*, Adv 2.3, Adv 3.2, Adv 3.6, Adv 5.1, Adv 5.2, Adv 5.3, Adv 6.6, VNat 1.4, VNat 2.1, VNat 2.5, VNat 2.7, VNat 3.3, VNat 4.5, VNat 4.10, VNat 5.2, VNat 6 *passim*, Nat 1.1, Nat 1.6, Nat 1.8, Nat 2.1, Nat 5.4, Circ 1.4, Circ 2.3, Circ 3.6, Circ 3.7, Circ 3.9, Epi 1.1, Epi 3.4, Epi 3.5, Pur 1.2, Pur 3.1, Pur 3.2, Sept 1.4, Quad 1.5, Quad 2.2, Quad 2.4, Quad 2.5, Quad 3.2, Quad 3.3, Quad 4.4, Quad 5.6, Quad 5.7, Ben 3, Ben 12, Ann 1 *passim*, Ann 1 (alt).14, Ann 3.3, Palm 1.1, Palm 1.4, Palm 2.6, Palm 2.7, Pasc 1 *passim*, Pasc 1 (alt).1, Pasc 1 (alt).5, Pasc 2.6, Pasc 2.7, Pasc 2.11, Pasc 3.6, OPasc 1.7, In lab mess 2.1, In lab mess 2.3, In lab mess 3 *passim*, Asspt 2.1, Asspt 2.6, Asspt 3.2, Asspt 3.4, Asspt 4.2, Asspt 4.3, Asspt 4.4, Asspt 5.4, Asspt 5.8, Asspt 5.11, OAsspt 3, OAsspt 8, NatBVM *passim*, Abb 2, Mich 1.5, 1 Nov 1.1, 1 Nov 1.2, 1 Nov 2.4, 1 Nov 4.1, 1 Nov 5 *passim*, OS 1 *passim*, OS 2.2, OS 2.4, OS 2.8, OS 3.1, OS 3.4, OS 4.6, OS 5.4, OS 5.5, Ded 1.7, Ded 2.1, Ded 3.1, Ded 3.2, Ded 4.1, Ded 4.3, Ded 4.4, Ded 5.5, Ded 5.8, Mart *passim*, Mal 4, Mal 8

Prosperity   Sept 1.5, Quad 2.5, Palm 2.1, Palm 2.2, Palm 3.2

Proud   Adv 2.1, Nat 4.2, Nat 5.5, 1 Nov 2.5, 1 Nov 3.1, 1 Nov 5.6, 1 Nov 5.8

Proverb   Asspt 2.2, Mich 1.3
Prudence, prudent   Circ 1.5, Circ 3.6, Asc 4.5, PP 2.7, PP 2.8, 1 Nov 5.11, 1 Nov 5.12, And 2.8
Psalmist   Epi 2.3, Quad 2.2, Ann 1.6, Asspt 5.11, Mich 2.4, And 2.6
Psalms   Adv 2.2, VNat 4.7, VNat 4.10, Nat 4.1, Nat 5.3, Epi 3.5, P Epi 2.2, Quad 2.2, Quad 5.6, Ben 10, Ann 1.4, Ann 1 (alt).10, Palm 2.2, Pasc 1.9, Pasc 1 (alt).3, In lab mess 3.1, In lab mess 3.4, Asspt 4.4, 1 Nov 3.2, OS 1.7, OS 2.4, OS 2.6, OS 2.7, OS 3.2, OS 4.6, Mal 2, Mal 7, And 2.6
Punishment   Adv 6.1, Adv 6.6, VNat 2.1, Circ 1.5, Quad 4.1, Quad 4.4, Ann 1.8, Ann 1.9, Ann 1.14, Ann 1 (alt).9, Ann 3.2, JB 9, 6 p P 2.3, 6 p P 2.4, In lab mess 1.4, In lab mess 2.1, Abb 3, OS 1.12, OS 2.6, OS 3.1, OS 3.3, OS 4.1, Ded 3.3, Ded 4.4, Clem 2, Humb 7, Humb 8
Purification   VNat 4.6, Circ 2.1, Circ 3.3, P Epi 1.3, P Epi 1.4, P Epi 2.6, P Epi 2.8, Pur 3.1, Pur 3.2
Purity   Adv 1.10, P Epi 1.3, Sept 2.2, Quad 6.4, Pasc 1.11, In lab mess 3.5, Asspt 4.6, Asspt 4.7, NatBVM 9, NatBVM 12, NatBVM 18, Abb 6, Abb 7, 1 Nov 5.9, Ded 4.4, Ded 5.8, Mart 15, Humb 6

Queen   VNat 3.10, Asspt 1.1, Asspt 1.2, Asspt 1.4, Asspt 4.1, Asspt 4.9, Asspt 6.1, OAsspt 6

Rachel   P Epi 2.8, Asspt 3.1
Rain   Ben 1, Asc 4.6, PP 2.2, NatBVM 3, 1 Nov 5.12, Ded 6.2
Reason   Adv 1.1, Adv 1.4, VNat 3.2, VNat 3.8, VNat 4.9, Sept 2.3, Pasc 1.11, Rog 1, Rog 2, Asc 6.7, Asc 6.8, Pent 1.5, Pent 1.6, 6 p P 1.2, In lab mess 3.3, Asspt 1.1, Asspt 2.4, NatBVM 14, Mich 1.4, Mich 2.2, 1 Nov 1.1, 1 Nov 1.4, 1 Nov 5.7, 1 Nov 5.10, OS 1.8, OS 1.13, Ded 2.3, Ded 5.7, Mart 7, And 1.8, And 1.10
Reconciler   Ann 2.3
Reconciliation   Adv 6.4, VNat 2.4, Nat 5.1, Epi 1.4, Pur 3.2, Ann 1.14, Ann 1 (alt).14, Ann 2.2
Redeemer   Pur 2.1, Ann 3.1
Redemption   Adv 5.1, Nat 1.8, Nat 2.1, Nat 2.5, SP 2, Pur 1.3, Pur 3.2, Ann 2.3, 4 HM 8, Pasc 1.2, OPasc 1.5, OPasc 2.4, OPasc 2.5, Asspt 4.8, OAsspt 2
Reformation   Adv 6.3
Remedy   Adv 1.5, Adv 7.1, VNat 3.10, VNat 6.1, VNat 6.5, Nat 3.4, Nat 3.5, Quad 5.3, Ann 3.3, Pasc 1.11, Pasc 1 (alt).11, In lab mess 3.2, Asspt 5.8, Asspt 5.12, OS 1.13, Ded 3.1, Ded 3.5, Humb 4

Remembrance Adv 3.2
Repentance Adv 1.5, Adv 3.6, Adv 4.6, VNat 2.1, VNat 2.6, VNat 3.4,
   Nat 3.5, Circ 1.5, Circ 2.4, Epi 1.4, Epi 3.8, SP 1, Quad 2.4, Quad
   3.3, Quad 3.4, Ann 1 (alt).8, Ann 3.9, Ann 3.10, 4 HM 9, 5 HM 1,
   Pasc 1.9, Pasc 1.15, Pasc 1.18, Pasc 1 (alt).9, OPasc 2.5, 6 p P 1.4, OS
   5.1, Ded 2.3, And 2.8
Resurrection VNat 1.6, Nat 1.4, Nat 2.5, Ann 1.4, Palm 3.1, Palm 3.4,
   Palm 3.5, 4 HM 1, Pasc 1 *passim*, Pasc 1 (alt) *passim*, Pasc 2.12, Pasc
   3.1, Pasc 3.6, In lab mess 3.5, 1 Nov 2.2, OS 2.8, OS 3.1, Mart 10,
   And 1.6
Rewards Adv 4.2, VNat 4.1, Epi 2.2, OEpi 5, P Epi 2.9, Quad 1.4, Quad
   1.5, Ann 1.4, Ann 3.7, Pasc 1.18, Pasc 1 (alt).14, Asspt 5.4, Asspt 5.11,
   OS 2.1, OS 2.3, OS 5.11, Ded 1.6, Ded 4.5, Ded 6.3, Clem 1
Righteous Adv 4.3, Epi 3.5, Ann 3.5, OPasc 2.1, NatBVM 5, 1 Nov 5.5,
   OS 3.2, OS 5.8, Ded 6.2, Mal 3, VAnd 1
Righteousness Adv 1.9, Adv 3.4, Adv 3.7, Adv 4.5, Adv 4.7, VNat 1.6,
   VNat 2.4, VNat 5.3, VNat 5.6, Nat 1.4, Nat 1.5, OEpi 4, OEpi 5,
   Pur 2.3, Sept 1.5, Ben 3, Ben 7, Ann 1 *passim*, Ann 1 (alt) *passim*, Ann
   3.6, 4 HM 13, 4 HM 14, Pasc 2.5, Pasc 2.6, Pasc 2.8, Pasc 3.4, Asc
   6.4, Asspt 5.5, Asspt 5.6, NatBVM 9, 1 Nov 3.2, 1 Nov 5.9, OS 1
   passim, OS 2.3, OS 2.7, OS 3.3, OS 4.5, OS 4.6, Ded 3.1, Ded 5.3,
   Ded 5.4, Ded 5.9, Mart *passim*, Mal 7
River P Epi 2.4, Sept 1.3, Quad 1.4, Pasc 3.1
Root Adv 6.2, VNat 4.2, SP 1, Ben 4, Ben 5, Ben 7, Ann 2.5, Ann 3.7,
   Pasc 1.3, Pasc 1.10, Pasc 1 (alt).1, Pasc 1 (alt).3, Pasc 1 (alt).10

Sabbath VNat 3.7, Circ 3.10, Palm 3.5, Pasc 1.8
Sacrament Circ 1.1, Ben 12, Palm 3.4, 5 HM *passim*, Pasc 1.17, Pasc 1
   (alt).3, Pasc 2.10, In lab mess 3.3, OAsspt 11, OS 1.3, Mart 11, Mart
   12
Sacrifice Nat 1.6, Epi 3.6, Pur 2.1, Pur 3.2, Pur 3.3, Quad 3.1, Ben 5,
   Palm 3.3, 4 HM 9, Pasc 1.2, Pasc 1 (alt).2
Sadness VNat 3.5, Sept 2.2, Quad 1.4, Quad 2.3, Pasc 1.12, Pasc 1.18,
   Asc 1.1, Asc 3.4, Asc 3.8
Saints VNat 3.2, VNat 3.5, VNat 6.3, Sept 2.2, Ben 3, Ann 1.12, Palm 1.4,
   OPasc 1.2, In lab mess 1.2, Asspt 2.1, Asspt 5.3, Asspt 5.10, NatBVM
   2, NatBVM 8, NatBVM 13, 1 Nov 1.1, 1 Nov 2.1, 1 Nov 5.4, OS
   1.1, OS 2 *passim*, OS 3.1, OS 3.4, OS 4.1, OS 4.2, OS 5 *passim*, Ded
   1.1, Ded 1.2, Ded 4.4, Ded 5.1, Ded 6.3, Mart 5, Mart 12, Clem 1,
   Mal 4, Mal 5, VAnd 1, Humb 6

Salvation   Adv 1.1, Adv 1.6, Adv 1.10, Adv 2.4, Adv 2.5, Adv 5.1, Adv 6.3,
VNat 1 *passim*, VNat 2.6, VNat 3.10, VNat 4 *passim*, VNat 5.3, VNat
5.4, VNat 6 *passim*, Nat 2.5, Nat 3.6, Innoc 1, Innoc 3, Circ 1.3,
Circ 1.5, Circ 2.3, Circ 2.4, Circ 2.5, Circ 3.4, Circ 3.11, Epi 3.3,
P Epi 1.3, P Epi 2.8, SP 3, SP 4, Pur 3.2, Sept 1.1, Sept 1.2, Quad
1.1, Quad 1.4, Quad 2.1, Quad 2.3, Ann 1.6, Ann 1 (alt).6, Ann 2.1,
Palm 2.6, Palm 3.2, Palm 3.3, 4 HM 1, 4 HM 11, 5 HM 4, Pasc 1
passim, Pasc 1 (alt) *passim*, Pasc 3.1, OPasc 2.3, Asc 1.3, Asc 2.1, Pent
2.6, Pent 2.7, Pent 3.8, JB 10, JB 11, PP 2.8, PP 3.4, In lab mess 3.6,
Asspt 1.1, Asspt 3.1, Asspt 3.6, Asspt 4.8, NatBVM 5, NatBVM 11,
NatBVM 14, Abb 5, 1 Nov 1.2, 1 Nov 5.9, 1 Nov 5.11, OS 1.8, OS
5.2, Ded 3.5, Ded 4.2, Ded 4.3, Ded 5.2, Ded 5.5, Mart 4, Mart 10,
Clem 3, And 1.7, And 2.4, And 2.6, And 2.7
Samaritans   Pasc 2.6
Samuel   SP 6
Sanctification   Palm 3.4, Ded 1.6, Ded 4.3, Ded 5.10
Sanctity   Ben 3, Ben 7
Satan   Adv 1.2, Adv 7.2, Nat 2.3, Circ 3.11, Quad 1.2, Palm 3.3, Pasc
1.17, Pasc 1 (alt).2, Pasc 4.2, Asc 2.1, Asc 4.3, Asc 6.10, Pent 2.3, 6 p
P 2.5, In lab mess 3.8, Ded 5.6, Ded 5.7
Saul   SP *passim*
Savior   Adv 1.8, Adv 1.9, Adv 2.5, Adv 4.3, Adv 4.4, Adv 6.1, Adv 6.6,
Adv 7.2, VNat 3.4, VNat 3.5, VNat 4.6, VNat 6 *passim*, Nat 1.2, Nat
3.1, Nat 4.1, Nat 5.2, Nat 5.5, Innoc 3, Circ 1.3, Circ 1.5, Circ 2.2,
Circ 3.1, Epi 1.1, Epi 1.3, Epi 3.5, SP 3, SP 4, SP 6, Pur 2.2, Quad
1.2, Ann 1 (alt).14, Ann 2.5, Palm 1.4, 4 HM 2, 4 HM 5, 4 HM 12,
Pasc 1 *passim*, Pasc 1 (alt).2, Pasc 1 (alt).4, Pasc 1 (alt).6, Pasc 4.1,
Asspt 1.4, Asspt 2 *passim*, Asspt 3.7, Asspt 5.1, Asspt 6.1, Abb 5, Mich
2.1, Mich 2.3, 1 Nov 2.2, OS 2.5, OS 4.1, OS 4.2, OS 4.6, Ded 3.1,
Ded 5.6, Mart 12, Mart 15, Clem 6, And 1.1, And 1.7, And 2.4, And
2.5, Humb 6
Scriptures   Adv 6.5, VNat 1.4, VNat 2.8, VNat 3.1, VNat 3.4, VNat 4.6,
VNat 4.8, VNat 4.9, VNat 5.2, VNat 5.4, VNat 6.8, VNat 6.10, Nat
4.1, P Epi 2.1, Sept 1.1, Ben 4, Ben 6, Ben 9, Ann 1.11, Ann 1.12,
Ann 3.1, Ann 3.2, Palm 1.3, Palm 2.7, Palm 3.2, Pasc 1.17, Pasc 1
(alt).4, Pasc 3.6, 4 p P 2, 4 p P 3, In lab mess 1.1, In lab mess 1.2, In
lab mess 2.1, In lab mess 3.5, Asspt 1.4, Asspt 5.9, Asspt 5.10, OAsspt
11, Mich 1.2, OS 1.9, OS 2.1, OS 2.2, OS 2.4, OS 5.3, OS 5.9, Ded
4.1, Ded 4.4, Mart 7, Mart 12, Mal 7, Humb 5
Seas   Adv 1.10, VNat 6.11, Ann 1.12

Secret   Adv 4.2, Quad 2.1, OPasc 1.8, OAsspt 10, NatBVM 11, Mich 1.1,
   1 Nov 5.9, 1 Nov 5.11, OS 1.7, OS 3.4, OS 5.2, Mart 5
Seraphim   OPasc 2.2, OAsspt 3, NatBVM 10, 1 Nov 2.4, 1 Nov 3.1, 1
   Nov 3.2, 1 Nov 3.4, 1 Nov 4 *passim*, 1 Nov 5 *passim*, Mart 5
Serpents   Adv 1.4, Adv 2.4, Quad 1.2, Quad 5.2, Ben 4, Ann 1.6, Ann
   1.8, Ann 1 (alt).8, Ann 2.1, Ann 2.3, Pasc 1.1, Pasc 1 (alt).4, Asc 1.2,
   Asc 1.3, Asc 3.9, Asc 6.11, Pent 2.3, Asspt 2.9, OAsspt 2, OAsspt 4,
   Abb 4, 1 Nov 1.2, 1 Nov 5.12, OS 1.9, And 1.9, And 2.6
Servants   Adv 3.7, Adv 4.4, Adv 6.5, VNat 2.6, VNat 4.6, VNat 6.2, VNat
   6.4, Nat 1.2, Nat 1.3, Nat 3.4, Nat 3.6, Nat 4.2, Circ 2.4, Circ 3.7,
   OEpi 4, P Epi 2.5, P Epi 2.8, SP 4, SP 6, Pur 1.4, Sept 1.3, Quad
   1.5, Quad 3.2, Quad 5.3, Quad 5.7, Quad 6.4, Ann 1.13, Ann 2.2,
   Ann 3.5, Palm 2.2, Palm 2.5, Palm 3.2, Palm 3.3, 4 HM 4, Pasc 1
   (alt).14, Pasc 4.1
Shame   Adv 3.2, VNat 1.1, VNat 4.2, VNat 4.3, VNat 4.4, Nat 3.4, Epi
   3.8, Ben 11, Ann 1.8, Pasc 2.11, Asspt 4.1, Asspt 4.3, OAsspt 10,
   Mich 2.4, 1 Nov 3.1, Clem 3, VAnd 1
Sheep   Adv 1.7, Adv 2.2, Adv 4.7, Nat 4.1, Quad 2.5, Ben 6, Ann 3.4,
   Ann 3.5, Palm 1.4, Palm 2.3, 4 HM 2, Pasc 1.3, Pasc 1 (alt).4, Pasc
   3.2, OPasc 1.2
Shepherds   Adv 2.2, VNat 6.2, VNat 6.7, Nat 3.1, Nat 3.5, Nat 4.1, Nat
   4.2, Nat 5.5, Epi 1.3, Epi 2.2, Quad 2.5, Ben 7, OPasc 1.2
Shulamite   Ann 3.10, NatBVM 15
Silence   Adv 1.9, P Epi 2.7, Quad 3.4, JB 9, Asspt 3.7, OAsspt 12,
   NatBVM 14, Humb 8
Simeon   Nat 5.2, Pur 1.2, Pur 2.1, Pur 3.2, OAsspt 11, OAsspt 14
Simon   Ben 6, Pasc 3.6, Ded 5.7
Sin   Adv 1.3, Adv 1.5, Adv 2.2, Adv 2.3, Adv 2.5, Adv 3.6, Adv 4.5, Adv
   4.6, Adv 4.7, Adv 6.1, Adv 6.2, VNat 1.2, VNat 1.3, VNat 2.1, VNat
   2.2, VNat 2.3, VNat 3.1, VNat 3.2, VNat 3.4, VNat 4.5, VNat 5.2,
   VNat 6.1, VNat 6.10, Nat 1.4, Nat 1.5, Nat 1.7, Nat 2.3, Nat 3.3,
   Nat 4.2, Nat 5.4, Nat 5.5, Innoc 3, Circ 1.3, Circ 2.1, Circ 2.5, Circ
   3 *passim*, Epi 1.3, Epi 1.6, Epi 3.6, Epi 3.8, OEpi 1, OEpi 4, P Epi
   1.3, P Epi 2 *passim*, SP 5, Pur 1.1, Pur 3.1, Sept 1.1, Quad 2.3, Quad
   2.4, Quad 2.6, Quad 3.4, Quad 4.1, Quad 4.4, Quad 5.1, Quad 5.2,
   Ann 1 *passim*, Ann 1 (alt).6, Ann 1 (alt).8, Ann 1 (alt).14, Ann 2.3,
   Ann 3 *passim*, Palm 2.4, Palm 2.7, Palm 3.1, 4 HM *passim*, 5 HM
   passim, Pasc 1.6, Pasc 1 *passim*, Pasc 1 (alt).14, Pasc 2 *passim*, Pasc 3.3,
   Pasc 3.4, OPasc 2.5, Asc 1.3, Asc 6.13, Pent 1.4, JB 11, 6 p P 2.1, In
   lab mess 1.4, In lab mess 2.1, In lab mess 2.2, In lab mess 3.2, Asspt

Index of Subjects 371

    2 *passim*, Asspt 4.2, Asspt 4.3, Asspt 4.7, Asspt 5.2, Asspt 5.8, OAsspt 9, NatBVM 8, NatBVM 16, NatBVM 18, Abb 1, Abb 6, Mich 1.5, 1 Nov 2.2, 1 Nov 5.9, OS 1 *passim*, OS 2.6, OS 5 *passim*, Ded 1.1, Ded 1.2, Ded 1.4, Ded 2.3, Ded 3.1, Ded 4.2, Ded 4.3, Ded 5.3, Ded 6.3, Mart 3, Mart 4, Mart 14, Clem 1, Clem 6, Mal 4, Mal 8, VAnd 1, And 2.7, Humb 7

Sin, Original   4 HM 6, 5 HM 2, OPasc 2.4

Sinai   OS 1.6

Sinners   Adv 2.3, Adv 4.7, VNat 1.1, VNat 2.1, Nat 5.3, Circ 2.1, Circ 3.3, P Epi 1.4, SP 1, Pur 3.3, Quad 1.5, Quad 1.6, Quad 4.2, Quad 4.4, Ann 3.2, 4 HM 4, Pasc 1 (alt).11, OPasc 2.5, In lab mess 3.8, In lab mess 3.9, Asspt 5.10, OAsspt 1, OAsspt 2, NatBVM 7, 1 Nov 1.4, OS 1.6, Ded 4.3, Ded 5.10, Mart 2, Mart 9, Mal 3, VAnd 1

Sion   Ann 1.14, Ann 1 (alt).14, Asspt 5.3, Asspt 5.4, OS 1.5, OS 5.9, Ded 3.1

Sisters   Ann 1.10, Ann 1.11, Ann 1 (alt).10, Ann 2.2, OPasc 1.8, Asspt 2.7, Asspt 3 *passim*, Asspt 5.6, Asspt 5.7, OAsspt 12

Sleep   Adv 5.1, VNat 5.2, P Epi 2.3, Sept 1.5, Sept 2.1, Sept 2.2, Sept 2.3, Quad 5.6, 4 HM 4, 4 HM 6, 5 HM 5, Pasc 1.8

Solomon   VNat 4.6, VNat 6.11, Circ 3.9, Epi 2.2, Ann 1.11, Ann 1 (alt).11, OAsspt 6, NatBVM 4, NatBVM 7, 1 Nov 5.12, OS 1.10, OS 5.9, Ded 2.1

Son   Adv 1 *passim*, Adv 2 *passim*, Adv 3.1, Adv 5.3, VNat 1.5, VNat 2.7, VNat 4.5, VNat 4.6, VNat 4.9, VNat 5.3, VNat 6 *passim*, Nat 3.4, Nat 5.1, Nat 5.2, Nat 5.4, Circ 2.1, Circ 3.3, Circ 3.4, Circ 3.5, Epi 1.3, Epi 1.4, Epi 1.8, Epi 2.4, Epi 3.7, P Epi 1.2, P Epi 2.4, Pur 1.1, Pur 3.1, Pur 3.2, Pur 3.3, Sept 1.1, Quad 1.3, Ben 10, Ann 1.11, Ann 1 (alt).11, Ann 2.1, Ann 2.2, Ann 3.7, Ann 3.8, 4 HM *passim*, Pasc 1.10, Pasc 1.11, Pasc 1.17, Pasc 1 (alt).11, Pasc 3.1, Pasc 3.2, Pasc 3.6, OPasc 1 *passim*, OPasc 2.1, In lab mess 3.4, In lab mess 3.8, Asspt 1.2, Asspt 1.3, Asspt 1.4, Asspt 2.2, Asspt 2.8, Asspt 2.9, Asspt 3.7, Asspt 4.5, Asspt 4.6, Asspt 4.9, Asspt 6.1, OAsspt *passim*, NatBVM *passim*, Mich 1.2, 1 Nov 3.1, 1 Nov 3.4, 1 Nov 4.4, 1 Nov 5.1, 1 Nov 5.2, 1 Nov 5.6, OS 1.3, OS 1.14, OS 4.2, OS 5.6, OS 5.7, Ded 5.5, Ded 5.7, Mart 8, Mart 9

Soul   Adv 1 *passim*, Adv 3 *passim*, Adv 5.1, Adv 5.2, Adv 6 *passim*, VNat 1 *passim*, VNat 2.3, VNat 2.4, VNat 3.5, VNat 3.8, VNat 4.10, VNat 5.2, VNat 5.5, VNat 6 *passim*, Nat 1.1, Nat 1.4, Nat 1.8, Nat 2 *passim*, Nat 5.4, Circ 3.3, Circ 3.5, OEpi 2, P Epi 1.4, P Epi 1.5, P Epi 2.2, SP 3, SP 4, Pur 1.2, Pur 1.4, Pur 3.3, Sept 1.3, Sept 1.5, Sept 2.2,

Quad 2.4, Quad 3.4, Quad 4.3, Quad 4.4, Quad 5.2, Quad 5.8, Ann 1.7, Ann 1 (alt).7, Ann 2.4, Ann 3 *passim*, Palm 1.1, 4 HM 4, 4 HM 11, 4 HM 13, 5 HM 4, Pasc 1.11, Pasc 2.1, Pasc 2.3, Pasc 2.10, Pasc 4.1, OPasc 1.7, OPasc 2.3, Asc 2.3, Asc 3.7, Asc 4.6, Asc 4.8, Asc 5.2, Asc 6.2, Asc 6.5, Asc 6.9, Pent 1.5, Pent 1.6, PP 1.5, In lab mess 1.2, In lab mess 1.4, In lab mess 2.1, In lab mess 2.2, In lab mess 2.3, In lab mess 3.1, In lab mess 3.7, Asspt 2.3, Asspt 2.4, Asspt 3 *passim*, Asspt 4.3, Asspt 4.9, Asspt 5.8, Asspt 5.11, OAsspt 13, OAsspt 14, OAsspt 15, NatBVM 10, NatBVM 14, Mich 1 *passim*, Mich 2.4, 1 Nov 2.5, 1 Nov 5.2, 1 Nov 5.5, OS 1 *passim*, OS 2 *passim*, OS 3 *passim*, OS 4.2, OS 4.5, OS 4.6, OS 5.6, Ded 1.1, Ded 1.2, Ded 2.1, Ded 2.2, Ded 2.3, Ded 4.3, Ded 4.4, Ded 5.2, Ded 5.3, Ded 5.6, Ded 6.2, Ded 6.3, Mart 3, Mart 5, Mart 17, Clem *passim*, Mal 5, Mal 7, Mal 8, VAnd 2, VAnd 4, And 1.3, And 1.7, And 1.10, And 2 *passim*, Humb 1, Humb 4

Spirit   Adv 3.6, Adv 4.2, Adv 5.1, VNat 2.1, VNat 2.3, VNat 3.9, VNat 6.1, VNat 6.2, VNat 6.5, Nat 1.3, Nat 1.8, Nat 2.6, Nat 4.1, Innoc 1, Circ 2.3, Circ 3.2, Circ 3.9, P Epi 2.3, Pur 1.4, Sept 1.3, Quad 3.1, Quad 3.4, Quad 4.3, Quad 5.1, Ben 5, Ann 1.6, Ann 1 (alt).9, Ann 2.3, Ann 2.5, Ann 3.8, Ann 3.9, 4 HM 4, 4 HM 11, 4 HM 14, Pasc 1.3, Pasc 1.4, Pasc 1 (alt).14, Pasc 2.1, Pasc 2.2, Pasc 2.4, Pasc 3.6, OPasc 2.1, OPasc 2.2, OPasc 2.3, In lab mess 1.1, In lab mess 3.1, In lab mess 3.4, Asspt 3.1, Asspt 3.3, Asspt 3.5, Asspt 5.4, Asspt 5.5, Asspt 5.11, OAsspt *passim*, NatBVM 9, NatBVM 10, Abb 5, Mich 1.1, Mich 1.4, Mich 1.6, Mich 2.1, Mich 2.4, 1 Nov 3.1, 1 Nov 3.2, 1 Nov 4.1, 1 Nov 5 *passim*, OS 1.2, OS 1.8, OS 1.10, OS 2.3, OS 2.4, OS 3.1, OS 5.2, OS 5.8, Ded 1.6, Ded 1.7, Ded 2.2, Ded 4.1, Ded 4.2, Ded 4.3, Ded 5.2, Ded 5.7, Ded 6.1, Ded 6.3, Mart *passim*, Clem 5, Clem 6, Mal 7, Mal 8, And 1.3, And 1.6, And 1.10, And 2.4, And 2.5, And 2.7, Humb 3, Humb 6

Star   Adv 1.3, VNat 3.3, VNat 6.11, Circ 2.2, Epi 1.5, Epi 3.2, Epi 3.4, OAsspt *passim*, NatBVM 6, 1 Nov 2.3, 1 Nov 3.1, 1 Nov 3.2, Mart 4, Mart 5

Stephen   Innoc 1, Innoc 2, 1 Nov 5.6, OS 1.1, Ded 5.1

Strength   Nat 2.4, Pur 2.3, Quad 2.2, Ann 1 (alt).9, 4 HM 4, Pasc 1.10, Pasc 1 (alt).10, OPasc 1.2, OPasc 1.4, In lab mess 3 *passim*, Asspt 2.6, Asspt 4.4, Asspt 5.6, Asspt 5.8, Asspt 5.12, Asspt 6.1, OAsspt 13, Mich 2.4, 1 Nov 5 *passim*, OS 1.8, OS 1.13, Ded 1.2, Ded 3.3, Ded 4.6, Ded 5.10, VAnd 3, And 1.10, And 2.3

Struggle   Adv 7.2, VNat 3.5, Sept 1.5, Quad 5.4, Asspt 5.4, NatBVM 16, Ded 4.4, Clem 3, Clem 4, Mal 7
Suffering   Adv 2.1, Adv 2.3, Adv 4.4, VNat 4.6, Nat 3.3, Innoc 1, Innoc 2, Epi 1.2, Quad 6.3, Ben 12, Palm 1.2, Palm 3.1, Palm 3.3, 4 HM 11, 4 HM 13, 4 HM 14, Pasc 1.15, Pasc 3.3, OPasc 1.7, OAsspt 14, OAsspt 15, OS 1.15, OS 4.6, Ded 3.1, Mart 9, Mart 16, Clem 3, And 1.4, And 1.6, And 1.8, And 2.3, Humb 5
Sun   Adv 1.9, Adv 4.3, VNat 3.2, VNat 4.6, VNat 5.3, VNat 6.8, Circ 3.5, Epi 1.5, Epi 3.3, Asspt 4.1, OAsspt *passim*, NatBVM *passim*, 1 Nov 3.1, 1 Nov 3.2, 1 Nov 3.3, 1 Nov 5.12, OS 1.4, OS 4.6, Ded 6.2, Mart 5
Superior   Adv 3.4, Circ 3.8, OEpi 4, SP 6, Quad 4.2, Abb 5, Abb 6
Susanna   Ann 3.1, Ann 3.4, Ann 3.5
Sweetness   Adv 3.2, Adv 6.5, VNat 1.1, Nat 1.6, Circ 3.10, Epi 2.1, OEpi 5, Pur 2.1, Sept 2.2, Quad 6.4, Ann 3.7, 4 HM 8, 4 HM 9, Pasc 2.7, In lab mess 2.1, Asspt 5.11, NatBVM 2, OS 2.5, OS 2.8, And 1.2, And 2.4, Humb 6
Sword   VNat 6.11, Nat 1.3, Quad 2.5, Ann 3.2, 4 HM 13, Pasc 1 (alt).1
Synagogues   VNat 6.11, Nat 5.5, P Epi 2.2, P Epi 2.3

Tabernacle   OS 3.1, OS 4.1, Ded 1.7, Ded 2.1, Ded 4.4, Ded 4.6, Mart 5, Mart 17
Teacher   Adv 7.2, Circ 3.6, Circ 3.7, Circ 3.8, SP 1, Ben 2, Ben 6, Ann 1.6, Pasc 3.4
Teaching   SP 3, Ben 7, Ben 8, Ben 12, Pasc 3.4
Tears   Adv 4.5, Nat 3.1, Nat 3.3, Nat 3.4, Nat 5.1, Nat 5.5, Epi 3.8, Sept 1.3, Quad 2.4, Palm 3.4, 4 HM 11, 4 HM 14, Pasc 1.15, Pasc 1.18, OPasc 1.7, OPasc 1.8, OPasc 2.5, 6 p P 1.4, 6 p P 2.1, In lab mess 2.2, In lab mess 2.3, Asspt 5.3, Mich 1.2, Mich 1.5, OS 1.10, OS 1.14, OS 2.6, OS 5.8, Ded 1.4, Ded 3.2, Ded 4.3, Ded 5.8, Mart 14, Clem 6, Mal 3
Temperance   Circ 3.7, Ben 12, Palm 3.1
Temple   Nat 2.5, Nat 4.1, Nat 5.2, Pur 1.2, Pur 1.3, Pur 1.4, Pur 2.1, Pur 3.1, Pur 3.2, Sept 1.4, Pasc 1 (alt).4, Asspt 1.3, OAsspt 11, NatBVM 9, 1 Nov 1.4, 1 Nov 2.3, 1 Nov 2.4, 1 Nov 2.5, 1 Nov 5.5, Ded 1.1, Ded 2.1, Ded 2.2, Ded 2.3, Ded 4.3, Ded 5 *passim*, Mart 15, Mart 16
Temptation   Adv 7.1, VNat 2.8, VNat 3.5, Innoc 3, P Epi 2.9, Sept 1.5, Quad 5.3, Quad 5.4, Quad 5.7, Ben 4, Ben 6, Ben 7, Palm 3.3, 4 HM 11, Pasc 1.11, Pasc 1 (alt).4, Pasc 1 (alt).11, OPasc 1.2, OPasc

1.7, 6 p P 1.1, 6 p P 2.5, In lab mess 3.9, Asspt 4.3, Asspt 5.4, NatBVM 3, Abb 3, Mich 2.4, 1 Nov 2.1, OS 1 *passim*, OS 2.3, OS 5.1, OS 5.4, OS 5.10, Ded 3.2, Mart 17, Clem 2, And 2.8, Humb 4, Humb 8

Testament, Old Testament   P Epi 2, Palm 1.2, OPasc 1.5

Testimony   VNat 1.3, VNat 6.5, VNat 6.8, VNat 6.10, Circ 2.3, Circ 2.4, Circ 2.5, Epi 1.6, Epi 1.7, Epi 3.7, Epi 3.8, Ann 1.1, Ann 1.5, OPasc 1.5, OPasc 1.6, OPasc 1.7, Ded 4.1, Ded 5.4, Ded 5.5, Ded 6.3, Clem 4, Clem 5, Mal 7

Thanksgiving   VNat 4.8, P Epi 2.2, Pur 1.3, Quad 5.7, 4 HM 14, Pasc 1.10, OS 2.2, OS 3.4, OS 5.8, Ded 4.4

Thieves   Adv 1.3, Adv 1.4, Adv 5.2, Nat 1.3, Nat 2.3, Nat 5.1, Epi 2.3, Epi 2.4, Quad 3.3, Ann 1.7, Ann 1 (alt).7, Palm 1.2, 4 HM 12, Pasc 1.11, Pasc 1 (alt).11, NatBVM 8, 1 Nov 1.2, 1 Nov 2.5, 1 Nov 3.2, OS 1.6, OS 5.11, VAnd 3

Thomas   In lab mess 3.7

Thorns   Epi 2.3, Ben 6, Palm 2.4, Palm 2.5, 4 HM 8, Pasc 2.7

Throne   Adv 1.9, Adv 2.1, Adv 2.4, VNat 1.5, VNat 4.3, VNat 4.6, Epi 1.5, Pur 1.4, Ben 11, Ann 1.14, Ann 1 (alt).14, Palm 3.5, Pasc 1.10

Tomb   Nat 5.2, Quad 6.2, 5 HM 1, Pasc 1 *passim* Pasc 1 (alt).5, Pasc 1 (alt).6, Pasc 1 (alt).8, Pasc 2.3, Pasc 2.10, Pasc 2.12, Pasc 3.6

Transgressions   Adv 3.3, Circ 1.3, Circ 2.1, Circ 3.3, Epi 1.6, Pur 3.2, Sept 1.5, 4 HM 6, 4 HM 7, 5 HM 2, Pasc 1 (alt).14, Pasc 3.6

Transgressors   Ann 1.10, Ann 1.11, Ann 1 (alt).10, Ann 2.3, Palm 1.1, 4 HM *passim*, Pasc 1.17

Tree   Adv 1.3, Adv 2.2, Adv 2.4, VNat 1.1, VNat 3.8, Circ 1.1, Ben *passim*, Ann 1.8, Ann 1 (alt).8, Ann 1 (alt).10, Ann 1 (alt).11, Palm 1.3, Palm 1.4, Pasc 1.1, Pasc 1.2, Pasc 1 (alt).1, Asspt 2.6, NatBVM 6, 1 Nov 5.7, OS 1.12, Mal 1, And 1.2, And 1.9

Tribulation   VNat 4.1, Quad 1.6, Palm 1.2, Palm 3.5, Pasc 2.11, 1 Nov 1.2, 1 Nov 4.1, 1 Nov 5.3, OS 5.2, OS 5.8, Ded 5.5, Mart 17, Mal 5, Mal 6, VAnd 2, And 1.2, And 1.3, And 1.7

Triduum   5 HM 2, Pasc 1.9

Trinity   Adv 1.2, VNat 3.8, Nat 2.4, Ben 10, Ann 2.2, OPasc 1.8, OPasc 2.1, Asc 6.15, Pent 1.1, Pent 2.3, Pent 3.2, Asspt 6.1, OAsspt 2, 1 Nov 3.4, OS 4.3, Ded 1.6

Truth   Adv 1.1, Adv 1.2, Adv 1.5, Adv 2.4, Adv 3.5, Adv 3.7, Adv 4.2, VNat 3.2, VNat 4.1, VNat 4.5, VNat 5.6, VNat 6.4, VNat 6.10, Nat 2.3, Nat 5.3, Circ 2.3, P Epi 2.6, SP 2, Sept 2.1, Quad 1.2, Quad 1.5, Ben 9, Ben 10, Ann 1 *passim*, Ann 1 (alt) *passim*, Ann 2.4, Ann 3.2,

Ann 3.3, Ann 3.4, 5 HM 4, Pasc 1.13, Pasc 3.4, OPasc 1.6, OPasc 1.8, OPasc 2.1, Rog 1, Rog 2, Asc 3.9, Asc 4.10, Asc 6 *passim*, Pent 1.6, 6 p P 2.6, In lab mess 3 *passim*, NatBVM 12, NatBVM 14, Abb 6, Mich 2.1, 1 Nov 3.1, 1 Nov 4.2, 1 Nov 4.4, 1 Nov 5.6, 1 Nov 5.9, OS 1.7, OS 1.9, OS 1.10, OS 2.3, OS 3.3, OS 5.4, Ded 1.7, Ded 3.3, Ded 4.6, Ded 5 *passim*, Ded 6.2, Ded 6.3, Mart 1, Mart 4, Mart 9, Clem 5, And 2.6, Humb 7

Understanding   Pasc 3.6, Asc 3 *passim*, Asc 4.14, Asc 6 *passim*, PP 2.7, PP 2.8, Asspt 5.6, Asspt 5.7, Asspt 5.8, 1 Nov 4.2, 1 Nov 5.12, OS 4.3, Ded 2.4, And 2.3
Union   VNat 3.9, VNat 3.10, Nat 2 *passim*, 1 Nov 5.2, Ded 1.6, Ded 1.7, Ded 5.7
Unity   VNat 3.6, VNat 3.8, Nat 2.3, Nat 2.4, OEpi 3, Pur 2.2, Sept 1.3, Sept 2.3, Quad 1.1, Quad 1.2, Quad 2.5, Quad 2.6, Quad 4.2, Ann 1.5, Pasc 3.4, OPasc 2.1, OPasc 2.2, Asspt 5 *passim*, Mich 1.5, Mich 1.6, Mich 2.1, 1 Nov 5.1, 1 Nov 5.2, OS 5.6, Ded 1.6, Ded 5.9

Vanity   VNat 2.3, Nat 3.2, Epi 1.7, P Epi 2.9, Quad 1.5, Quad 1.6, Ann 1.8, Ann 1 (alt).8, 4 HM 5, 5 HM 4, Pasc 3.4, OPasc 1.7, In lab mess 3.3, 1 Nov 2.5, 1 Nov 3.1, OS 1.7, OS 1.8, OS 5.4, Ded 3.3, Humb 5
Vices   VNat 1.3, Epi 3.6, SP 8, Sept 1.2, Sept 1.5, Quad 1.6, Quad 2.4, Quad 3.4, Quad 4.1, Quad 4.4, Quad 6.3, Ben 5, Ann 3.9, Ann 3.10, 4 HM 5, 4 HM 13, Pasc 1.15, Pasc 3.4, OPasc 2.2, 4 p P 2, 6 p P 2.5, Asspt 2.6, Abb 1, Mich 2.1, OS 1.10, Ded 1.2, Ded 3.3, Ded 5.3, Mart 6
Victory   VNat 3.2, VNat 6.4, Quad 6.4, Ann 1.13, Palm 1.2, Pasc 1.1, Pasc 1.3, Pasc 4.2, OPasc 1.2, OPasc 1.4, In lab mess 1.2, NatBVM 11, Mich 2.4, OS 2.2, OS 2.3, Ded 4.5, Mart 8, Mal 4, Mal 7, And 2.8, Humb 1
Vigils   Nat 4.1, P Epi 2.7, Asc 3.6, Asc 4.12, Asc 6.7, V PP 1, In lab mess 2.1, Asspt 5.9, Ded 4.1, VAnd 2, And 1.2, And 2.4, Humb 3
Virgin   Adv 1.11, Adv 2.1, Adv 4.2, VNat 1.1, VNat 3.7, VNat 3.9, VNat 3.10, VNat 4.4, VNat 4.6, VNat 6.11, Nat 3.1, Circ 2.1, Circ 2.4, Epi 1.6, Epi 3.8, P Epi 2.9, Quad 1.5, Ben 12, Pasc 1.11, Asspt 1 *passim*, Asspt 2.2, Asspt 2.9, Asspt 4.5, OAsspt 4, OAsspt 8, OAsspt 9, NatBVM 7, NatBVM 8, NatBVM 9, 1 Nov 2.5, OS 5.5, Mart 13
Virgin Mary   Adv 1.6, Adv 2.4, Adv 2.5, VNat 1.1, VNat 3.9, VNat 3.10, VNat 4.3, VNat 4.6, VNat 5.3, Nat 2.4, Nat 3.4, Nat 4.2, Nat 4.3,

376   *Sermons for the Autumn Season*

        Innoc 1, Circ 2.4, Circ 3.3, Circ 3.7, Epi 1.3, Epi 1.5, Epi 3.7, P Epi 1.2, P Epi 2.4, Pur 1.1, Pur 2.1, Pur 3.1, Pur 3.2, Ann 2.1, Ann 2.2, Ann 2.5, Ann 3.1, Ann 3.7, Ann 3.8, 4 HM 6, Pasc 1.5, Pasc 1.9, Pasc 3.4, Asc 3.3, Asc 3.4, Asc 6.1, Asc 6.11, Pent 2.2, Pent 2.3, Pent 2.4, Pent 3.1, JB 4, Asspt 1 *passim*, Asspt 2.8, Asspt 2.9, Asspt 4 *passim*, Asspt 6.1, OAsspt *passim*, NatBVM *passim*, Ded 2.2, Mart 1, And 1.6
Virginity   Adv 2.3, VNat 3.10, VNat 4.5, Circ 2.2, Epi 1.7, Asspt 4.5, Asspt 4.6, Asspt 4.8, Asspt 6.1, OAsspt 7, OAsspt 9, NatBVM 9, NatBVM 12, NatBVM 18
Virtue   Adv 3.4, Adv 4.2, Adv 4.4, Adv 4.5, VNat 2.8, Nat 1.1, Nat 2.6, Nat 4.2, Circ 3.1, Circ 3.8, Circ 3.11, Epi 3.8, Pur 1.3, Quad 2.6, Quad 5.7, Quad 5.8, Quad 5.9, Ann 1 *passim*, Ann 1 (alt) *passim*, Ann 2.1, Palm 1.3, Palm 1.4, Palm 3.2, 4 HM 6, Pasc 1.3, Pasc 1.13, Pasc 1 (alt).2, Pasc 1 (alt).3, Pasc 1 (alt).14, Pasc 2.7, OPasc 1.7, Asc 5.1, Asc 5.2, 6 p P 2.1, In lab mess 3.7, Asspt 4.6, Asspt 4.8, Asspt 5.12, Asspt 6.1, OAsspt 11, OAsspt 13, NatBVM 5, NatBVM 10, Abb 7, Mich 1.1, OS 1.6, OS 2.6, OS 2.7, OS 5.3, Mart 9, Mart 12, Mart 14, Clem 1, And 2.1, And 2.7, Humb 2
Voice   VNat 1.1, VNat 5.5, Nat 1.3, Nat 2.2, Epi 1.7, Epi 3.7, Epi 3.8, SP 2, SP 5, Quad 1.3, Quad 4.4, Ann 1 (alt).8, Ann 1 (alt).9, Ann 1 (alt).10, Ann 2.3, Pasc 1.5, Pasc 2.12

War   Quad 6.4, 4 HM 13, Pasc 3.3, OS 2.2, OS 5.8, Ded 1.2, Ded 2.3, Ded 2.4, And 1.5, And 2.6
Water   Adv 1.1, VNat 4.9, Nat 1.5, Nat 1.6, Epi 1.6, Epi 1.8, Epi 3.2, Epi 3.8, OEpi 1, OEpi 2, P Epi 1.3, P Epi 1.4, P Epi 1.5, P Epi 2 *passim*, Pur 1.2, Quad 1.3, Quad 1.4, Quad 2.2, Quad 4.1, Ben 4, Ben 9, Ann 2.1, Ann 2.4, Palm 3.4, 4 HM 11, 5 HM 2, Pasc 1.5, OPasc 1 *passim*, OPasc 2.1, OPasc 2.4, OPasc 2.5, In lab mess 3.2, Asspt 1.1, Asspt 3.5, Asspt 4.1, Asspt 5.9, Asspt 6.1, OAsspt 15, NatBVM 3, NatBVM 4, NatBVM 9, Abb 2, Abb 6, 1 Nov 3.2, OS 2.7, OS 4.6, Ded 1.4, Ded 3.2, Clem 4, Clem 5, Clem 6, Mal 5, Mal 6, Mal 7, And 1.3, And 1.6, Humb 4
Wedding   VNat 2.7, VNat 2.8, Epi 1.8, Epi 3.2, P Epi 1.1, P Epi 1.2, P Epi 2 *passim*, Quad 6.1
Weeping   Circ 3.5, Quad 2.4, OPasc 1.7
Wife   VNat 6.3, VNat 6.11, Sept 2.1, Ann 1 (alt).8, Ann 2.3, Pasc 1.3, OS 1.11, OS 1.12
Will   Adv 4.6, VNat 1.2, VNat 2.3, VNat 2.8, VNat 4.9, Nat 1.5, Nat 5.3, Innoc 1, Innoc 2, Innoc 3, Circ 1.2, Circ 1.5, Circ 3.7, SP 6, SP 7,

Index of Subjects 377

Quad 2.5, Quad 3.4, Palm 3.4, 4 HM 4, 4 HM 5, 4 HM 12, 5 HM 3, Pasc 1.11, Pasc 1 (alt).14, Pasc 2.8, Pasc 3.3, Pasc 3.4, Pasc 3.5, Rog 1, Rog 2, Asc 3.6, Pent 1.5, Pent 1.6, In lab mess 3.3, Asspt 2.6, Asspt 3.5, Asspt 4.4, Asspt 5.5, NatBVM 14, Abb 5, Mich 2.2, Mich 2.3, Mich 2.4, 1 Nov 1.2, 1 Nov 1.3, 1 Nov 1.4, 1 Nov 2 *passim*, 1 Nov 3.1, 1 Nov 3.2, 1 Nov 3.3, 1 Nov 4.1, 1 Nov 4.3, 1 Nov 4.4, 1 Nov 5 *passim*, OS 1.8, OS 3.3, OS 5.1, Ded 1.4, Ded 2.3, Ded 3.2, Ded 5.6, Ded 5.7, Mart *passim*, And 1.6, And 1.9, And 2.5, Humb 6

Wind   VNat 3.5, Quad 4.4, 4 HM 14, Pasc 2.5

Wine   VNat 1.6, Epi 1.8, Epi 3.2, Epi 3.8, P Epi 1.1, P Epi 1.2, P Epi 1.4, P Epi 2.4, P Epi 2.8, Sept 2.1, Pasc 2.6, Pasc 2.7, Asc 3.7, Pent 3.1, Pent 3.2, Asspt 6.1, OAsspt 10, NatBVM 5, Mart 13, Clem 4, And 1.6, Humb 4

Wisdom   Adv 1.3, Adv 1.9, Adv 2.1, Adv 3.4, Adv 3.6, Adv 3.7, Adv 7.2, VNat 3.8, Nat 1 *passim*, Nat 2.2, Nat 2.5, Nat 3 *passim*, Nat 5.2, Epi 1.5, P Epi 2.1, P Epi 2.8, SP 7, Pur 1.3, Pur 1.4, Sept 1.4, Sept 2.1, Sept 2.3, Quad 1.5, Quad 2.5, Ben 3, Ben 11, Ben 12, Ann 1.6, Ann 1.12, Ann 1 (alt).11, Ann 2.4, Ann 3.10, Palm 2.2, Palm 3.2, 4 HM 8, 4 HM 13, 5 HM 1, Pasc 1.10, Pasc 1.11, Pasc 1 (alt).11, Pasc 1 (alt).12, Pasc 1 (alt).14, Pasc 3.3, Pasc 3.4, Pasc 3.5, Asc 3.1, Asc 4.1, Asc 4.5, Asc 6.2, Asc 6.9, Asc 6.15, PP 2.6, PP 2.7, PP 2.8, 6 p P 1.4, In lab mess 3.4, Asspt 2.2, Asspt 5.6, Asspt 5.7, OAsspt 3, OAsspt 15, NatBVM 6, NatBVM 7, NatBVM 10, Abb 7, OS 1.7, OS 1.8, OS 1.10, OS 4.5, Ded 1.4, Mart 1, Mart 8, Clem 3, Clem 4, Clem 6, Mal 3, And 1.8, And 2.1

Wombs   Adv 1.6, Adv 2.4, Adv 2.5, VNat 1.1, VNat 3.10, VNat 6.4, Nat 2.4, Circ 1.3, Circ 2.1, Circ 2.2, Circ 3.3, Epi 1.6, P Epi 1.2, P Epi 2.4, P Epi 2.5, Pur 3.1, Pur 3.2, Ben 10, Ann 1 (alt).9, Ann 3.8, 4 HM 6, Pasc 1.5, Pasc 1.12, In lab mess 3.3, Asspt 1.1, Asspt 1.2, Asspt 1.3, Asspt 2.2, Asspt 2.8, Asspt 4.7, NatBVM 1, And 1.6

Woman, Women   VNat 4.3, Nat 2.4, Nat 4.1, Circ 2.2, P Epi 2.2, Pur 1.3, Pur 3.1, Pur 3.2, Sept 2.1, Quad 1.1, Ann 1.8, Ann 1 (alt).8, Ann 2.1, Ann 3 *passim*, Palm 3.2, Palm 3.5, 4 HM 6, Pasc 1.5, Pasc 1.10, Pasc 1 (alt).6, Pasc 1 (alt).10, Pasc 2.3, Pasc 2.4, Pasc 3.6, Asspt 1.3, Asspt 1.4, Asspt 2 *passim*, Asspt 3.1, Asspt 3.3, Asspt 3.6, Asspt 4.5, Asspt 4.8, OAsspt *passim*, NatBVM *passim*, 1 Nov 2.2, 1 Nov 5.9, OS 1.11, OS 1.12, Ded 4.3, Ded 5.3, Clem 4, Mal 3, And 1.9, Humb 6

Word   Adv 1.9, Adv 1.10, Adv 3.4, Adv 3.5, Adv 4.6, Adv 5.2, Adv 5.3, VNat 1.1, VNat 1.3, VNat 1.6, VNat 3.8, VNat 4.8, VNat 6 *passim*, Nat 1.1, Nat 2.4, Nat 2.5, Nat 2.6, Nat 3.2, Nat 3.3, Nat 5.1, Nat

5.4, Circ 2.1, Circ 2.2, Circ 2.3, Circ 3.3, P Epi 1.4, P Epi 2.2, SP 6, Pur 1.4, Quad 2.1, Quad 2.5, Ben 1, Ben 7, Ben 10, Ann 1.6, Ann 1.10, Ann 1.11, Ann 1 (alt).11, Ann 2.4, Ann 3.2, Ann 3.9, Palm 1.4, 4 HM 8, 4 HM 13, Pasc 1.1, Pasc 1.17, Pasc 1.18, Pasc 2.9, Pasc 2.11, Pasc 3.4, OPasc 1.8, OPasc 2.2, PP 2.1, 6 p P 1.4, In lab mess 3.3, In lab mess 3.4, In lab mess 3.7, Asspt 1.3, Asspt 3.2, Asspt 5.1, Asspt 5.5, Asspt 5.6, NatBVM *passim*, Mich 2.2, Mich 2.3, 1 Nov 2.3, 1 Nov 3.2, 1 Nov 3.4, 1 Nov 4.3, 1 Nov 5.4, 1 Nov 5.5, OS 1.7, OS 1.9, OS 5.7, Ded 3.2, Ded 5.6, Mart *passim*, VAnd 1, And 1.5, And 1.6, And 2.7, Humb 3, Humb 5

Words   Adv 1.7, Adv 3.2, Adv 4.5, Adv 5.2, VNat 3.1, VNat 3.4, VNat 3.10, VNat 6.10, Nat 1.1, Nat 3.6, Circ 2.1, Epi 1.7, P Epi 1.1, P Epi 2.7, Sept 1.1, Sept 1.2, Sept 2.1, Quad 3.4, Ben 12, Ann 1.8, Ann 1.12, Ann 1 (alt).10, Ann 3.3, 4 HM 6, 4 HM 13, Pasc 1 *passim*, Pasc 1 (alt).3, Pasc 1 (alt).4, Pasc 2.9, OPasc 1.1, OPasc 1.4, Asspt 1.4, Asspt 2.7, Asspt 3.6, Asspt 3.7, OAsspt 15, Mich 2.2, Mich 2.4, 1 Nov 1.4, 1 Nov 2.4, 1 Nov 4.1, 1 Nov 4.4, 1 Nov 5.6, 1 Nov 5.7, OS 1.3, OS 2 *passim*, Ded 1.6, VAnd 4, And 1.1, And 1.2, And 1.9, And 2.2, And 2.3, Humb 6

Works   Adv 1.7, VNat 2.1, VNat 3.3, Nat 1.6, Nat 2.1, Epi 1.7, Pur 2.2, Ben 10, Ann 1.1, Ann 1.4, Ann 3.9, 4 HM 8, Pasc 1.4, Pasc 1 (alt).4, Pasc 1 (alt).10, Pasc 2.1, Pasc 3.4, Pasc 4.2, OPasc 1.3, OPasc 2.5, Asspt 5.3, Mich 1.2, Mich 2.3, OS 1.3, OS 2.4, Ded 1.5, Ded 3.3, Ded 5.4, And 2.4

World   Adv 1.9, Adv 3.1, Adv 3.3, Adv 6.1, VNat 3.3, VNat 3.5, VNat 5.2, Circ 3.6, Epi 3.6, Pur 1.4, Sept 1.5, Quad 6.2, Quad 6.3, Ben 12, Ann 1.13, Ann 1 (alt).13, 4 HM 5, Pasc 1.16, Pasc 2.2, Pasc 3.1, Pasc 3.2, Pasc 3.3, OPasc 1 *passim*, Asc 1.2, Asc 3.9, Asc 4.9, Asc 4.13, Asc 6.8, Asc 6.10, Pent 3.2, Pent 3.3, In lab mess 2.2, Asspt 1.1, Asspt 1.3, Asspt 1.4, Asspt 2.1, Asspt 4.8, Asspt 4.9, Asspt 5.1, Abb 1, Mich 2.1, 1 Nov 4.3, OS 1.1, OS 1.13, OS 4.5, OS 5.3, OS 5.11, Ded 1.2, Ded 1.3, Ded 3.3, Clem 1, Mal 7, Humb 2

Wound   Nat 3.4, Nat 5.1, Circ 2.1, OEpi 3, Quad 1.6, Quad 2.4, Pasc 1.3

Wrath   Epi 1.4, P Epi 1.1, Pur 1.3, Quad 1.1, Ann 1.8

Yoke   Adv 6.2, VNat 1.2, Nat 3.3, Sept 2.2, Ann 2.4, 4 HM 6, 5 HM 2

Zeal   Adv 1.4, Adv 4.5, Nat 1.6, Nat 1.7, Circ 1.5, Quad 3.4, Ann 1 *passim*, Ann 1 (alt).9, Ann 2.2, Pasc 1.3, Pasc 2 *passim*, Pasc 3.4, OPasc 2.1

Zion   VNat 1.5, VNat 6.11, Epi 2.2, SP 3, Quad 2.1, Quad 6.4, Ann 1.14, Ann 1 (alt).14, 5 HM 1, Asspt 5.3, OAsspt 6, Mich 1.4

www.ingramcontent.com/pod-product-compliance
Lightning Source LLC
Chambersburg PA
CBHW031228290426
44109CB00012B/198